15th Conference of the Association for Machine Translation in the Americas (AMTA 2022)

Volume 1: MT Research Track

Orlando, Florida, USA
12 – 16 September 2022

Editors:

Kevin Duh
Francisco Guzman
Stephen Richardson

ISBN: 978-1-7138-6757-9

Printed from e-media with permission by:

Curran Associates, Inc.
57 Morehouse Lane
Red Hook, NY 12571

Some format issues inherent in the e-media version may also appear in this print version.

Association for Computational Linguistics
209 N. Eighth Street
Stroudsburg, Pennsylvania 18360

Phone: 1-570-476-8006
Fax: 1-570-476-0860

acl@aclweb.org

Additional copies of this publication are available from:

Curran Associates, Inc.
57 Morehouse Lane
Red Hook, NY 12571 USA
Phone: 845-758-0400
Fax: 845-758-2633
Email: curran@proceedings.com
Web: www.proceedings.com

AMTA ORLANDO 2022

The 15th Conference of the Association for Machine Translation in the Americas

2022.amtaweb.org

PROCEEDINGS

Volume 1: MT Research Track

Editor:

Kevin Duh, Francisco Guzman (Research Track Co-chairs)

Stephen Richardson (General Conference Chair)

Welcome to the 15th biennial conference of the Association for Machine Translation in the Americas – AMTA 2022!

Dear MT Colleagues and Friends,

For this year's conference of the Association for Machine Translation in the Americas – AMTA 2022 – we are finally able to come together in person at the venue we had intended to enjoy two years ago, the spectacular Sheraton Orlando Lake Buena Vista Resort in Orlando, Florida! We are very grateful that the COVID pandemic is now sufficiently controlled (albeit still with us) that we can once again meet, network, and enjoy one another's company while expanding our knowledge of the ever-accelerating field of machine translation. At the same time, we will be joined by likely more than twice the number of remote attendees, as the last two years of virtual conferences and ongoing health concerns will forever more require us to adopt a hybrid conference format. While this format certainly creates complexity for organizers, and it can feel a little less personal as we interact with remote speakers and attendees, it nevertheless provides significantly greater accessibility and opportunities to learn from colleagues around the globe. We are grateful for their very positive contributions to our conference!

Since the MT Summit we hosted last year, we have continued to witness amazing progress in MT technology and tremendous growth in the adoption of this technology by individual translators, language services providers, small businesses, large enterprises, non-profits, governments, and NGOs. Indeed, a unique aspect of AMTA conferences is that it brings together users and practitioners from across the MT spectrum of academia, industry, and government so that R&D personnel can learn from those who are using the technology and vice versa.

We are pleased once again with the number of submissions to our conference. As MT has become more mainstream than ever, we have had to be more selective in the presentations included in our conference tracks. This is unfortunate on the one hand, but on the other, it demonstrates the growth of our field and the increasing quality and relevance of the work performed by so many people. Of special note this year is the emphasis on speech translation and dubbing, MT quality evaluation, and massively multilingual MT systems. These topics are reflected by the topics of our keynote speakers and panels in the conference schedule, and we trust you will find them most enlightening.

As with all our conferences, AMTA 2022 would simply not have been possible without the selfless work of so many people on the AMTA board and organizing committee, all of whom are volunteers. I express my deepest thanks, respect, and admiration to each one of them. They include:

Patti O'Neill-Brown, AMTA VP, Local Arrangements, Networking
Natalia Levitina, AMTA Secretary, Sponsorships
Jen Doyon, AMTA Treasurer, Local Arrangements
Kevin Duh, Research Track
Paco Guzman, Research Track
Janice Campbell, Users and Providers Track, Networking
Jay Marciano, Users and Providers Track, Workshops and Tutorials
Konstantin Savenkov, Users and Providers Track

Alex Yanishevsky, Users and Providers Track, Conference Online Platform
Steve La Rocca, Government Track
Kenton Murray, Student Mentoring,
Konstantin Dranch, Communications
Lara Daly, Marketing
Alon Lavie, AMTA Consultant
Elaine O'Curran, AMTA Counselor, Publications
Elliott Macklovitch, Publications
Derick Fajardo, Exhibitions

Finally, I express my gratitude to our amazing sponsors, whose tremendous financial support has enabled us to handle the added complexity and cost of the hybrid format. Once again, greatly discounted student registrations have been provided by Microsoft, our Visionary++ sponsor, as well as an included conference banquet for in-person attendees. Systran has also contributed significantly to our online platforms as a Visionary sponsor. Our Leader-level sponsors are Pangeanic, Meta, Acclaro, AppTek, and Intento, and our Patron-level sponsors are AWS, Google RWS, Star, and Welocalize. Additional exhibitors are ModelFront and Unbabel, and our Media and Marketing sponsors are Slator, Multilingual, and Akorbi. Many of these sponsors and exhibitors will provide demonstrations of their systems and software during our Technology Exhibition sessions, and we hope that all our attendees will take advantage of this great opportunity to see the very latest commercial offerings and advancements in the world of MT.

Again, welcome to AMTA 2022! I look forward to finally being with many of you in person in Orlando and to interacting with many others online.

Steve Richardson
AMTA President and AMTA 2022 General Conference Chair

Introduction

The research track at AMTA 2022 continues the tradition of bringing MT practitioners together from academia, industry and government from around the world.

This year we have a very rich program with 25 papers from a variety of topics. The most popular subject this year is low-resource machine translation (32%), spanning from pre-training and adaptation to unseen languages, to gender bias evaluation for low-resource languages. In addition, we have many works discussing pre-processing and data adaptation (e.g. analyses on subword tokenization); applications of MT (e.g. website engagements, e-commerce search); and even papers discussing sign language translation. We are also excited about our invited keynote speakers for the research track: Angela Fan (Meta AI) will talk about Massively Multilingual MT.

We hope that this conference brings many productive exchanges of ideas and sparks future collaborations.

We would like to thank the hard work of individuals that made this happen: the authors, the reviewers, the timely emergency reviewers, the AMTA organizing committee; and Akiko Eriguchi for her help in preparing the proceedings and organizing session chairs.

Sincerely,

Kevin Duh and Francisco Guzmán (Research Track Co-Chairs)

Program committee

Abraham Glasser (Rochester Institute of Technology)
Akiko Eriguchi (Microsoft)
Alina Karakanta (Fondazione Bruno Kessler)
M. Amin Farajian (Unbabel)
Asif Ekbal (IIT Patna)
Atsushi Fujita (NICT, Japan)
Beatrice Savoldi (UNINT)
Bing Zhao (SRI International)
Boxing Chen (Alibaba Group)
Chao-Hong Liu (ADAPT Centre, Dublin City University)
Chenhui Chu (Kyoto University)
Christian Federmann (Microsoft)
Claudio Russello (UNINT)
Colin Cherry (Google)
Constantin Orasan (University of Surrey)
David Chiang (University of Notre Dame)
Derek F. Wong (University of Macau)
Dimitar Shterionov (Tilburg University)
Duygu Ataman (UZH)
Elijah Rippeth (University of Maryland)
Evgeny Matusov (AppTek)
Federico Gaspari (ADAPT Centre, Dublin City University)
Flammie Pirinen (UiT–Norgga Árktalaš Universitehta)
François YVON (CNRS)
Hailong Cao (Harbin Institute of Technology)
Haitao Mi (Tencent America)
Huda Khayrallah (Johns Hopkins University)
Jampierre Rocha (Lenovo)
Jan Niehues (KIT)
Jasper Kyle Catapang (University of Birmingham)
Jeremy Gwinnup (Air Force Research Laboratory)
John McCrae (National University of Ireland Galway)
Jörg Tiedemann (University of Helsinki)
Josep Maria Crego (Systran)
Juan Pino (Meta AI)
Katharina Kann (University of Colorado Boulder)
Katsuhito Sudoh (NAIST)
Kelly Marchisio (Johns Hopkins University)

Kenji Imamura (NICT)
Kevin Duh (Johns Hopkins University)
Koichiro Watanabe (The University of Tokyo)
Loic Barrault (Meta AI)
Marco Gaido (Fondazione Bruno Kessler)
Marco Turchi (Zoom)
Maria Antonette Clariño (University of the Philippines)
Marianna Martindale (University of Maryland)
Mathias Müller (University of Zurich)
Matthias Huck (SAP SE)
Mehdi Rezagholizadeh (Huawei Noah's Ark Lab)
Nathaniel Oco (De La Salle University, Philippines)
Neha Verma (Johns Hopkins University)
Ohnmar Htun (Rakuten Asia Pte.Ltd.)
Patrick Simianer (Lilt)
Philipp Koehn (Johns Hopkins University)
Priya Rani (National University of Ireland Galway)
Raj Dabre (NICT)
Rebecca Knowles (National Research Council Canada)
Rico Sennrich (University of Zurich)
Rosalee Wolfe (ILSP / Athena RC)
Sangjie Duanzhu (Qinghai Normal University)
Santanu Pal (Saarland University)
Sara Papi (FBK)
Shankar Kumar (Google)
Shinji Watanabe (Carnegie Mellon University)
Sunit Bhattacharya (Charles University)
Takashi Ninomiya (Ehime University)
Taro Watanabe (NAIST)
Tetsuji Nakagawa (Google Japan G.K.)
Thepchai Supnithi (NECTEC, National Science and Technology Development Agency)
Tomek Korybski (University of Surrey)
Toshiaki Nakazawa (The University of Tokyo)
Tsz Kin Lam (Heidelberg University)
Valentin Malykh (Huawei Noah's Ark lab)
Vedanuj Goswami (Meta AI)
Vishrav Chaudhary (Microsoft)
Xinyi Wang (Carnegie Mellon University)
Xuan Zhang (Johns Hopkins University)

Contents

Building Machine Translation System for Software Product Descriptions Using Domain-specific Sub-corpora Extraction

Pintu Lohar pintu.lohar@adaptcentre.ie
ADAPT Centre, Dublin City University, Dublin, Ireland
Maja Popović maja.popovic@adaptcentre.ie
ADAPT Centre, Dublin City University, Dublin, Ireland

Tanya Habruseva thabruseva@linkedin.com
LinkedIn Corporation, Dublin, Ireland

Abstract

Building Machine Translation systems for a specific domain requires a sufficiently large and good quality parallel corpus in that domain. However, this is a bit challenging task due to the lack of parallel data in many domains such as economics, science and technology, sports etc. In this work, we build English-to-French translation systems for software product descriptions scraped from LinkedIn website. Moreover, we developed a first-ever test parallel data set of product descriptions. We conduct experiments by building a baseline translation system trained on general domain and then domain-adapted systems using sentence-embedding based corpus filtering and domain-specific sub-corpora extraction. All the systems are tested on our newly developed data set mentioned earlier. Our experimental evaluation reveals that the domain-adapted model based on our proposed approaches outperforms the baseline.

1 Introduction

The development of Machine Translation (MT) systems for a specific domain (e.g., science, politics, economics) is often a challenging task because of the lack of parallel corpus in these domains. It is impractical to develop large corpora in every domain as it requires a huge amount of time and cost even for a single domain. There can be following methods to build MT systems in this scenario: (i) training an MT system on the available data set from other domains while tuning the model parameters on in-domain development set, or (ii) extracting in-domain parallel texts from one or more corpora and then building an MT system on the concatenation of these extracted text pairs. The first method, although tuned on an in-domain development data, is not much useful because the training is done only on an out-of-domain data set. In contrast, the second method is better because it is aimed to extract the in-domain data which are then used for training. However, producing a sufficiently large in-domain data set is a difficult task. In this work, we mainly focus on the second method, i.e, we extract parallel texts similar to in-domain in order to build an MT system and also tune the parameters on the in-domain data set. This approach is useful for building MT system in a specific scenario, which is the domain of software product descriptions from LinkedIn[1] web pages in our case. LinkedIn is an American business and employment-oriented online service that operates via websites and mobile apps.

[1]https://linkedin.com

It is primarily used for professional networking and career development, and allows job seekers to post their curricula vitae (CVs) and employers to post jobs. It also contains product pages for brands to promote their products and grow their businesses, for product users to share their experiences and be recognised for their expertise, and for buyers to make confident decisions about products in a trusted environment. This work involves an initial analysis of domain-specific MT for public taxonomies on software product descriptions available in LinkedIn web pages using a novel approach of sub-corpora extraction. Our contributions in this work are as follows: (i) we develop a first ever parallel development and test corpus of software product descriptions which are originally written in English and then manually translated into French; we used this corpus to tune the system parameters and to test our MT systems, and (ii) we investigate methods for filtering a parallel corpus; first, we use LASER (Artetxe and Schwenk, 2019), the state-of-the-art tool for bitext mining with the help of measuring bilingual sentence similarity and then we use KeyBERT (Grootendorst, 2020) to extract key phrases from the in-domain data set developed by us, which is further used to extract relevant parallel texts from several corpora. More precisely, we exploit our development data set to extract parallel data which is similar to the domain of software production. We refer to this extracted data as sub-corpus. Afterwards, we build MT systems using these sub-corpora for training and the same development data set for tuning parameters. Finally, we evaluate all the systems on a separately held-out test data set. Our experimental results show that our approach of corpus filtering and keyphrase-based sub-corpus extraction improves the performance of the MT system even when trained on a much smaller data set.

2 Related Work

NMT has undergone huge evolution during the last few years. For example, in the shared tasks on News and biomedical translation in WMT 2019, it is found that several NMT systems perform at the same level of a human translator for some high-resource language pairs according to human judgement (Barrault et al., 2019a; Bawden et al., 2019). However, for many language pairs and for many domains, there is still no (sufficient) data available in order to build high-quality MT systems.

Domain adaptation is a well-explored research area in MT. The main objective is to facilitate adaptation of the MT system to a specific domain. For example, Hu et al. (2019) propose an approach of lexicon induction to extract an in-domain lexicon and then build a pseudo-parallel in-domain corpus with word-for-word back-translation of monolingual in-domain target sentences. Chu and Wang (2018) conduct a survey of the state-of-the-art domain adaptation techniques for neural machine translation (NMT). The work of (Poncelas et al., 2019) demonstrates the usefulness of Infrequent n-gram Recovery (INR) and Feature Decay Algorithms (FDA) for domain adaptation. Back-translation (or forward translation) is often used for domain adaptation, too (Hoang et al., 2018; Graça et al., 2019).

The vast majority of investigated MT systems covers only a limited set of domains, predominantly news (Akhbardeh et al., 2021; Barrault et al., 2020, 2019b). There is also work on biomedical domain, spoken language (Bérard et al., 2020; Duh, 2018) and some types of user-generated content (Lohar et al., 2019; Xu and Yvon, 2021). However, to the best of our knowledge, there is no previous work that involves the development of MT systems for software product descriptions. Moreover, no parallel corpus in this domain has been published so far.

3 Data Development

We develop the first ever corpus of software product descriptions in English and their manual translations into French. The corpus is suitable for development and testing of MT systems in this domain. The data set is collected from the LinkedIn webpage of software product descriptions.[2] We scrape the contents of webpages and collect $1,395$ text segments in English on the description of software products. These texts are then manually translated by native French speakers who are also proficient in English. Product descriptions are usually different from natural texts and should be translated with special considerations. Bearing this in mind, the translators used the following guidelines to perform the translation task:

- some of the texts are not full sentences, which is perfectly acceptable in product-related texts and they need to be translated without considering the whole context,
- some of the texts contain URLs which should be left untranslated,
- names of the software products which contain valid English words should remain untranslated, and
- the translators should not delete any symbols or unwanted characters during the translation process

English text	**French translation**
Kronologic is the world's first Calendar Monetization Platform.	Kronologic est la première plateforme mondiale de monétisation calendaire.
Cerebra is an Artificial Intelligence Platform powering connected operations, impacting Yield, Reliability, and Operational Excellence in a Sustainable way.	Cerebra est une plateform d'Intelligence d'Intelligence Artificielle alimentant des opérations connectées, impactant le rendement, la fiabilité et l'excellence opérationelle à travers une démarche durable.
- Multi-platform endpoint remote monitoring and management (RMM)	- Télésurveillance et télégestion de bout en bout multiplateforme
Prodoscore™ is a software solution that measures your most valuable asset: your people.	Prodoscore™ est une solution logicielle qui mesure vos actifs de plus grande valeur: votre personel.

Table 1: Some example translations

Table 1 shows some example translations done by the native French speakers. As mentioned earlier, some texts in the data set are not full sentences. For instance, example 3 in the above table can be considered as an incomplete sentence or merely a text segment. Such segments are often seen in product descriptions and so the French translation is done accordingly.

The whole translation process was a challenging task and took a significant amount of time. One of the reasons was the presence of a large number of software or technical terms, some of which are not easy or straightforward to translate into French. People often use them as is, i.e, they keep them in English instead of translating into French. For example, the phrase "stacking-plans" was found to be very difficult to translate into French as its literal translation does not make much sense and therefore it should be left untranslated. In addition, the translators have to remember which terms should be translated and which should not, as they encounter many such terms. For example, the term "Cerebra Digital Assistants" should not be translated as it is the name of a software.

[2] `https://www.linkedin.com/products`

Once the translation of $1,395$ segments is complete, 696 were held out as tuning data set and the rest 699 as test data set. Therefore, all the MT models are tuned on these 696 segment pairs and evaluated on the 699 segment pairs. We refer to this data set as *SWP* corpus[3] which is now available online for free access.

4 Corpus Filtering for Domain Adaptation

In this section we describe our proposed approaches of corpus filtering and sub-corpora extraction for domain adaptation using LASER and KeyBERT. Here we use LASER for filtering and KeyBERT is used for extracting domain-specific sub-corpora, respectively.

4.1 Corpus Filtering

LASER is a state-of-the-art tool for calculating the Euclidean distance between a pair of bilingual sentences in order to measure their semantic similarity. This means that the smaller the distance, the more similar the sentence pairs. We use this score to filter out the pairs with low similarity score. To investigate its usefulness, we filter out the low-scoring sentence pairs from Europarl corpus (Koehn, 2005) and then the filtered corpus is used to train an MT model. On the other hand, the whole Europarl corpus is used to build a separate MT model. Table 2 shows the BLEU score produced by these three MT models, when evaluated on the test data set.

Training corpus	**#Sentence pairs**	**BLEU score**
Europarl (all)	2.05 million	19.06
Europarl (LASER-filtered)	1.93 million	**19.82**

Table 2: BLEU scores with and without corpus filtering

It can be seen from the table that the model trained on the LASER-filtered corpus produces better BLEU score than without filtering. We also used LABSE (Feng et al., 2022) with their optimal settings but it produced less BLEU score than that of LASER. We therefore decided to proceed with LASER filtering for the remaining experiments.[4]

4.2 Domain-specific Sub-corpora Extraction

Our approach of domain adaptation is different from the existing works. We compile the in-domain data by extracting sub-corpora (a part of the parallel corpus) using KeyBERT along with a tuning process. KeyBERT uses BERT-embeddings (Reimers and Gurevych, 2019) and the cosine similarity to find the key phrases in a document that are the most similar to the document itself. These key phrases can also be considered as key terms of a document. Usually, KeyBERT finds top n key terms from a document. Our goal is to find such terms from our development data set and then extract only those sentence pairs (from a corpus) that contain at least one of these key terms. However, it is not a good idea to simply extract an arbitrary number of key terms. We consider it as a tuning process and started with $n = 2,000$ and increase the value gradually. In order to identify the number of key term that should be extracted, we again use the Europarl corpus in the following steps: (i) top n key terms are extracted from development data and then only those sentences that contain at lease one of these key terms are extracted from Europarl, (ii) an MT model is trained on these extracted sentence pairs and is then evaluated on the test data to calculate BLEU score, (iii) the value of n is increased and we proceed from the first step, (iv) all the above steps are repeated until we obtain the highest BLEU score.

[3] `https://github.com/loharp/SWP`

[4] However, in future it will interesting to see how the combination of LASER and LABSE performs in corpus filtering

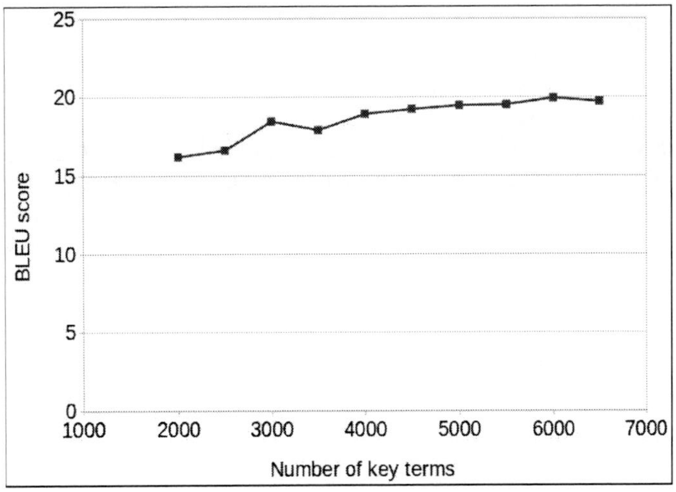

Figure 1: Tuning Europarl with different key term values

It is noticed that using a small value of n results in extraction of very small number of sentence pairs from Europarl and so the MT model built from it produces a low BLEU score. Similarly, using a very large value of n results in extraction of almost all sentence pairs from Europarl and therefore is not much helpful. Figure 1 shows the BLEU scores obtained when different values of n is considered starting from $2,000$. This is also shown in Table 3 where we also mention the number of parallel sentences extracted for each key term values. Note that

#Key terms used	#Parallel sentences extracted	BLEU score
N/A	2.05M (all)	19.06
2000	208K	16.20
2500	292K	16.62
3000	611K	18.45
3500	1.04M	17.90
4000	1.06M	18.92
4500	1.21M	19.22
5000	1.23M	19.46
5500	1.34M	19.51
6000	**1.41M**	**19.93**
6500	1.72M	19.71

Table 3: Tuning Europarl with key term values

the first row in this table shows the scenario where no key terms are used and all the sentence pairs in the corpora are used to build the MT model. It produces BLEU score of 19.06. In the second row $2,000$ key terms are used but they are capable of extracting only $208K$ sentence pairs which is insufficient for MT training and hence produces comparatively lower BLEU score of 16.20. Afterwards, we continue to increase the number of key terms and notice that the BLEU score rises with the increase of key terms. It can be seen that the highest BLEU score is achieved when $6,000$ key terms are used. Using further higher value results in bringing the number extracted sentence pairs closer to the total number of sentence pairs in the whole

Europarl corpus but it cannot increase the BLEU score. Instead, the score decreases and hence shows that using the whole corpus may not be useful. Note that the optimal BLEU score of 19.93 is obtained with 1.41 million extracted sentence pairs which is much less than that of the original corpus (30% less).

Once the tuning of Europarl with LASER and KeyBERT is done, we consider $6,000$ as the optimal value for key terms and use this optimal value for our further experiments on the larger data set.

5 Experiments

- **Data set:**

  There are a number of different parallel corpora available but not all of them are suitable for building a decent quality MT system. We explore a wide range of corpora available on the OPUS website.[5] We use Europarl corpus for tuning as mentioned earlier in Section 4. The optimal value of key terms is then applied to extract sub-corpora from a set of other corpora. Although we use several corpora in the initial stage of experiments, we consider using 12 specific corpora in our later stage of experiments and filter them using our proposed approach as discussed earlier. The statistics of the data sets used are is shown in Table 4

Corpus name	#Parallel sentences	Domain
Europarl	2.05M	Mixed domain
XLEnt	7.7M	Mixed domain
ELITR-ECA	0.4M	European Court of Auditors
TED2020	0.4M	TED talks
GNOME	0.9M	Software
QED	1.0M	Educational
PHP	45K	Software
GlobalVoices	0.2M	News
TED2013	0.2M	TED talks
Tatoeba	0.3M	Mixed domain
Ubuntu	7K	Software
KDE	0.2M	Software

Table 4: Data sets used in our experiments

  Following is a short description of the corpora we used in our experiments.

  - **Europarl**: A parallel corpus extracted from the European Parliament web site. The main intended use is to aid statistical machine translation research.
  - **XLEnt** (El-Kishky et al., 2021): This corpus was created by mining web data from Commoncrawl Snapshots and Wikipedia snapshots.
  - **ELITR-ECA** (Williams and Haddow, 2021): This is a multilingual corpus derived from documents published by the European Court of Auditors.[6]
  - **TED2020** (Reimers and Gurevych, 2020): This corpus contains a crawl of nearly $4,000$ TED and TED-X transcripts from July 2020. The transcripts have been translated by a global community of volunteers to more than 100 languages.

[5] `https://opus.nlpl.eu/`

[6] `https://www.eca.europa.eu/`

- **GNOME** (Tiedemann, 2012) : A parallel corpus of GNOME localization files.
- **QED** (Abdelali et al., 2014): The QCRI Educational Domain Corpus is an open multilingual collection of subtitles for educational videos and lectures collaboratively transcribed and translated over the AMARA web-based platform.
- **PHP** (Tiedemann, 2012): A parallel corpus originally extracted from a website containing documentation of PHP.[7] The original documents are written in English and have been partly translated into 21 languages.
- **Global Voices** (Tiedemann, 2012): A parallel corpus of news stories from the web site Global Voices compiled and provided by CASMACAT. [8]
- **TED2013** (Tiedemann, 2012): A parallel corpus of TED talk subtitles provided by CASMACAT.
- **Tatoeba** (Tiedemann, 2012): This is a collection of translated sentences from Tatoeba [9]
- **Ubuntu** (Tiedemann, 2012): A parallel corpus of Ubuntu localization files.
- **KDE** (Tiedemann, 2012): A parallel corpus of KDE4 localization files

Note that many of the above-mentioned corpora are published by Tiedemann (2012).

Although we could have used more corpora, we decided to use the above 12 corpora because of the following reasons: (i) after manually inspecting several corpora in a random manner, we found the above corpora to be good quality[10] (ii) many of them contain texts from multiple domains and thus are better to be used for domain adaptation using sub-corpora extraction, and (iii) some of them are from software domain which is useful for our experiments. We also built a separate MT model using only those corpora that belong to software domain but we obtain low BLEU score of 10.41 as they are small in size. Due to this reason, we decided to combine other corpora as well.

- **Tools and Evaluation Metrics:**

  Initially we use LASER and KeyBERT (discussed in Section 4) for corpus filtering and sub-corpus extraction, respectively. To build MT models, we use OpenNMT[11] (Klein et al., 2017) with transformer architecture (Vaswani et al., 2017). Subword NMT[12] (Sennrich et al., 2016) is used to apply Byte-pair enconding (BPE) during the preprocessing. We use sacreBLEU (Post, 2018) for automatic evaluation of MT outputs.

- **Preprocessing:**

  We perform preprocessing in the following steps:

  (i) **Filtering out long sentences:** Extremely long sentences were deleted. If either side contains too many words (100 words is set as default limit), the sentence pair is discarded.

  (ii) **Removing blank lines:** Sentence pairs with no content on either side are removed.

  (iii) **Removing sentence pairs with odd length ratio:** Sentences with marginally longer or shorter translations when compared to their original sentences were removed because of the probability of their being incorrect translations. The filtering ratio is 1 : 3 in our case.

[7] `http://se.php.net/download-docs.php.`

[8] `http://casmacat.eu/corpus/global-voices.html`

[9] `https://tatoeba.org/en/`

[10] However, we inspected only a tiny part of parallel corpus in a random manner. Inspecting whole corpora would be more useful but this is extremely impractical to achieve in a reasonable amount of time.

[11] `https://github.com/OpenNMT/OpenNMT-py`

[12] `https://github.com/rsennrich/subword-nmt`

(iv) **Removing duplicates:** All duplicate sentence pairs were discarded.

(v) **Tokenisation:** We break down the sentences into their most basic elements called tokens. Tokenisation is particularly relevant because it is the form in which MT models ingest sentences. In practice, most NMT models are fed with sub-words as tokens.

(vi) **Byte-Pair-Encoding (BPE):** In many cases, most out-of-vocabulary (OOV) words have similar morphemes to some of the words already in our vocabulary. With this in mind, the BPE technique was leveraged to resolve the OOV problem by helping the model infer the meaning of words through similarity. The BPE algorithm performs sub-word regularization by building a vocabulary using corpus statistics. Firstly it learns the most frequently occurring sequences of characters and then greedily merges them to obtain new text segments.

- **Building baseline MT systems:** In the first stage of our experiments, we explored several corpora and built different MT systems with different corpora individually and also with some combinations of them. We select one system from them that produces the best BLEU score and consider it as our baseline. Table 5 shows the BLEU scores obtained during building the baseline system.

System name	Corpus used	BLEU score
Sys-1	Europarl	19.06
Sys-2	United Nations Parallel corpus (UNPC)	12.81
Sys-3	Four different corpora: Gnome, KDE, PHP and Ubuntu (GKPU)	10.41
Sys-4 (Baseline)	12 different corpora: ELITA, Europarl, PHP, TED2020, XLEnt, Gnome, Global voice, KDE, QED, TED2013, TATOEBA and Ubuntu	**30.17**

Table 5: BLEU scores during building baseline

Table 5 shows that *Sys-1* and *Sys-2* are built from only one corpora. However, they do not produce the best BLEU score. Although the UNPC corpus is much larger than Europarl, it produces much less BLEU score because this corpus contains plenty of noise and so the MT system built from it is of low quality. We then explore some combined corpora to build *Sys-3* and *Sys-4*. These MT systems are trained from the combinations of 4 and 12 corpora, respectively. We initially consider the 4 corpora *GKPU* for MT training as it comprises of the corpora from software domain only. However, this combination still yields a small-sized corpus and therefore cannot produce a decent BLEU score. The best score is obtained by *Sys-4* which is trained from the concatenation of 12 different corpora. As explained earlier in this section we use this combination because all of them appeared to be good quality according to our random manual inspection and some of them are from software domain which is useful for us. We consider this as the baseline system for our further experiments. Note that there are numerous possible combinations of several corpora but it is impractical to try all of them. Our main focus is to select the combination that produces a decent BLEU score and proceed with the next stage of experiments on further improvement of MT systems with the same corpora combination.

- **Building domain-adapted MT system:** The domain-adapted MT system is the upgraded versions of the baseline system. The upgrade comes with our proposed approach of filtering and sub-corpus extraction. Firstly, we filter the concatenation of 12 different corpora (shown in Table 5) using LASER and then extract a sub-corpora from the filtered corpus using the optimal key term value of $6,000$ as determined in Section 4. This results in a massive reduction in corpus size. Our domain-adapted model is built from this reduced corpus. Table 6 describes the baseline and the domain-adapted systems along with the corpus description.

<table>
<tr><th>MT
system</th><th>Corpora
used</th><th>#Training
sentences</th><th>#Dev
sentences</th><th>#Test
sentences</th></tr>
<tr><td>Sys-4 (Baseline)</td><td>12 corpora
(Original)</td><td>15 million</td><td rowspan="2">696</td><td rowspan="2">699</td></tr>
<tr><td>Sys-5 (Domain-adapted)</td><td>12 corpora
(Filtered)</td><td>4.73 million</td></tr>
</table>

Table 6: Data distribution of Baseline and Domain-adapted systems

6 Results

Both the baseline and the domain-adapted systems are tuned on 696 and 699 texts from the data set of software product descriptions developed by us. The result is shown in Table 7 below.

MT system	#Sentence pairs	BLEU score
Baseline	15 million	30.17
Domain-adapted	4.73 million	**31.47**

Table 7: Baseline vs Domain-adapted system

We can notice from the table that the domain-adapted system outperforms the baseline system by 1.4 BLEU points which is 4.3% relative improvement. Another important observation is that both systems are trained on the same corpora but the domain-adapted system is the filtered version of it. Our proposed approach significantly reduces the corpus size by more than three times and at the same time produces the higher BLEU score.

7 Output Analysis

In this section we show some of the translation outputs produced by our MT system and compare them with the human translated references. Table 8 shows some examples translation outputs. In the first example of this table the output produced by our MT system is a very good translation but it misses the translation of *Instant* as compared to the reference translation. The second and the third outputs are the examples of excellent or perfect translation. The fourth example is an interesting and surprising one. Some native French speakers claimed that they would prefer this MT output than the reference translation. However, there are few cases where our MT system fails to produce good quality translations. For example, in the fifth output 'meet' and 'chat' still remain untranslated. The last example in the above table is a very good translation output except that the word 'empowers' has different ways to be translated into French. In fact, this word do not fit well in French with this context and so is difficult to translate. Moreover, although 'leurs' and 'les' are both correct but 'leurs' is better than 'les'.

8 Conclusions and Future work

In this work we proposed an approach of corpus filtering and sub-corpora extraction by using LASER and KeyBERT. In addition, we developed the first ever parallel corpus of software

English text	French translation	Reference translation
Instant analysis of millions of real-time conversations happening online.	L'analyse de millions de conversations en temps réel se déroule en ligne.	Analyse instantanée de millions de conversations en ligne en temps réel.
Find out what your customers are doing, feeling, and thinking when it comes to your brand.	Trouvez ce que vos clients font, ressentent et pensent quand il s'agit de votre marque.	Découvrez ce que vos clients font, ressentent et pensent de votre marque.
No hidden fees or long-term commitments.	Pas de frais cachés ou d'engagements à long terme.	Pas de frais cachés ni d'engagements à long terme.
Know what matters, when it matters.	Savoir ce qui compte, quand c'est important.	Sachez ce qui est important et quand c'est important.
Meet, call, chat, share files, manage tasks.	Meet, appel, chat, partager des fichiers, gérer des tâches.	Réunions, appels, discussions, partage de fichiers, gestion des tâches.
Learn more about FICO Analytics Workbench, a next-generation analytics tool that empowers companies to improve business decisions across the customer lifecycle.	Apprenez-en plus sur FICO Analytics Workbench, un outil d'analyse de nouvelle génération qui permet aux entreprises d'améliorer les décisions commerciales à travers le cycle de vie du client.	En savoir plus sur FICO Analytics Workbench, un outil d'analyse de dernière génération qui permet aux entreprises d'améliorer leurs décisions commerciales tout au long du cycle de vie du client.

Table 8: Some examples of translation outputs

product description suitable for development and testing, consisting of English product descriptions and their human translations into French. Our approach significantly reduces (more than three times) the corpus size and at the same time increases the BLEU score by 1.3 points which is more than 4% relative improvement over the baseline. This technique can easily and effectively be applied to any corpus in order to adapt or transform it into a refined corpus that is more similar to a specific domain. Moreover, the first ever corpus of software product descriptions developed by us can be beneficial for many researchers who are interested in building MT system in this domain. The data set is now freely available online. In future, our work can be extended by using the combination of multiple approaches such as LASER and LABSE together with KeyBERT. In addition, it is also possible to take the intersection of the filtered corpora obtained by applying LABSE and LASER separately. Afterwards, the intersection can be further refined by using KeyBERT. Moreover, it is to be noted that the developers of LABSE mentioned in their paper that they determine the optimal similarity threshold of 0.6 after several trials on different corpora. However, it is possible to re-optimize the threshold for a specific domain such as ours and then select the threshold that exhibits the best performance. The overall translation quality produced by our MT system appeared to be very good after manual inspection in a random manner. However, it is better to perform detailed human evaluation on the translation outputs. Although it is a time consuming task, it is better to manually evaluate at least a small part of the translation outputs which will provide the clearer picture of translation quality to some extent.

Acknowledgements

This work is funded by joint collaboration with Linkedin and the ADAPT Centre for Digital Content Technology which is funded under the Science Foundation Ireland (SFI) Research Centres Programme (Grant No. 13/RC/2106).

References

Abdelali, A., Guzman, F., Sajjad, H., and Vogel, S. (2014). The AMARA corpus: Building parallel language resources for the educational domain. In *Proceedings of the Ninth International Conference on Language Resources and Evaluation (LREC'14)*, pages 1856–1862, Reykjavik, Iceland. European Language Resources Association (ELRA).

Akhbardeh, F., Arkhangorodsky, A., Biesialska, M., Bojar, O., Chatterjee, R., Chaudhary, V., Costa-jussa, M. R., España-Bonet, C., Fan, A., Federmann, C., Freitag, M., Graham, Y., Grundkiewicz, R., Haddow, B., Harter, L., Heafield, K., Homan, C., Huck, M., Amponsah-Kaakyire, K., Kasai, J., Khashabi, D., Knight, K., Kocmi, T., Koehn, P., Lourie, N., Monz, C., Morishita, M., Nagata, M., Nagesh, A., Nakazawa, T., Negri, M., Pal, S., Tapo, A. A., Turchi, M., Vydrin, V., and Zampieri, M. (2021). Findings of the 2021 conference on machine translation (WMT21). In *Proceedings of the Sixth Conference on Machine Translation*, pages 1–88, Online.

Artetxe, M. and Schwenk, H. (2019). Massively multilingual sentence embeddings for zero-shot cross-lingual transfer and beyond. *Trans. Assoc. Comput. Linguistics*, 7:597–610.

Barrault, L., Biesialska, M., Bojar, O., Costa-jussà, M. R., Federmann, C., Graham, Y., Grundkiewicz, R., Haddow, B., Huck, M., Joanis, E., Kocmi, T., Koehn, P., Lo, C.-k., Ljubešić, N., Monz, C., Morishita, M., Nagata, M., Nakazawa, T., Pal, S., Post, M., and Zampieri, M. (2020). Findings of the 2020 conference on machine translation (WMT20). In *Proceedings of the Fifth Conference on Machine Translation*, pages 1–55, Online.

Barrault, L., Bojar, O., Costa-jussà, M. R., Federmann, C., Fishel, M., Graham, Y., Haddow, B., Huck, M., Koehn, P., Malmasi, S., Monz, C., Müller, M., Pal, S., Post, M., and Zampieri, M. (2019a). Findings of the 2019 conference on machine translation (WMT19). In *Proceedings of the Fourth Conference on Machine Translation (Volume 2: Shared Task Papers, Day 1)*, pages 1–61, Florence, Italy.

Barrault, L., Bojar, O., Costa-jussà, M. R., Federmann, C., Fishel, M., Graham, Y., Haddow, B., Huck, M., Koehn, P., Malmasi, S., Monz, C., Müller, M., Pal, S., Post, M., and Zampieri, M. (2019b). Findings of the 2019 conference on machine translation (WMT19). In *Proceedings of the Fourth Conference on Machine Translation (Volume 2: Shared Task Papers, Day 1)*, pages 1–61, Florence, Italy.

Bawden, R., Bretonnel Cohen, K., Grozea, C., Jimeno Yepes, A., Kittner, M., Krallinger, M., Mah, N., Neveol, A., Neves, M., Soares, F., Siu, A., Verspoor, K., and Vicente Navarro, M. (2019). Findings of the WMT 2019 biomedical translation shared task: Evaluation for MEDLINE abstracts and biomedical terminologies. In *Proceedings of the Fourth Conference on Machine Translation (Volume 3: Shared Task Papers, Day 2)*, pages 29–53, Florence, Italy.

Bérard, A., Kim, Z. M., Nikoulina, V., Park, E. L., and Gallé, M. (2020). A multilingual neural machine translation model for biomedical data. In *Proceedings of the 1st Workshop on NLP for COVID-19 (Part 2) at EMNLP 2020*, Online.

Chu, C. and Wang, R. (2018). A survey of domain adaptation for neural machine translation. In *Proceedings of the 27th International Conference on Computational Linguistics*, pages 1304–1319, Santa Fe, New Mexico, USA.

Duh, K. (2018). The multitarget ted talks task. `http://www.cs.jhu.edu/~kevinduh/a/multitarget-tedtalks/`.

El-Kishky, A., Renduchintala, A., Cross, J., Guzmán, F., and Koehn, P. (2021). XLEnt: Mining cross-lingual entities with lexical-semantic-phonetic word alignment. In *Preprint*, Online.

Feng, F., Yang, Y., Cer, D., Arivazhagan, N., and Wang, W. (2022). Language-agnostic BERT sentence embedding. In Muresan, S., Nakov, P., and Villavicencio, A., editors, *Proceedings of the 60th Annual Meeting of the Association for Computational Linguistics (Volume 1: Long Papers), ACL 2022, May 22-27, 2022*, pages 878–891, Dublin, Ireland.

Graça, M., Kim, Y., Schamper, J., Khadivi, S., and Ney, H. (2019). Generalizing back-translation in neural machine translation. In *Proceedings of the Fourth Conference on Machine Translation (Volume 1: Research Papers)*, pages 45–52, Florence, Italy.

Grootendorst, M. (2020). Keybert: Minimal keyword extraction with bert.

Hoang, V. C. D., Koehn, P., Haffari, G., and Cohn, T. (2018). Iterative back-translation for neural machine translation. In *Proceedings of the 2nd Workshop on Neural Machine Translation and Generation*, pages 18–24, Melbourne, Australia.

Hu, J., Xia, M., Neubig, G., and Carbonell, J. (2019). Domain adaptation of neural machine translation by lexicon induction. In *Proceedings of the 57th Annual Meeting of the Association for Computational Linguistics*, pages 2989–3001, Florence, Italy.

Klein, G., Kim, Y., Deng, Y., Senellart, J., and Rush, A. (2017). OpenNMT: Open-source toolkit for neural machine translation. In *Proceedings of ACL 2017, System Demonstrations*, pages 67–72, Vancouver, Canada. Association for Computational Linguistics.

Koehn, P. (2005). Europarl: A parallel corpus for statistical machine translation. In *Proceedings of Machine Translation Summit X: Papers*, pages 79–86, Phuket, Thailand.

Lohar, P., Popović, M., and Way, A. (2019). Building English-to-Serbian machine translation system for IMDb movie reviews. In *Proceedings of the 7th Workshop on Balto-Slavic Natural Language Processing*, pages 105–113, Florence, Italy.

Poncelas, A., de Buy Wenniger, G. M., and Way, A. (2019). Adaptation of machine translation models with back-translated data using transductive data selection methods. *CoRR*, abs/1906.07808.

Post, M. (2018). A call for clarity in reporting BLEU scores. In *Proceedings of the Third Conference on Machine Translation: Research Papers*, pages 186–191, Belgium, Brussels. Association for Computational Linguistics.

Reimers, N. and Gurevych, I. (2019). Sentence-BERT: Sentence embeddings using Siamese BERT-networks. In *Proceedings of the 2019 Conference on Empirical Methods in Natural Language Processing and the 9th International Joint Conference on Natural Language Processing (EMNLP-IJCNLP)*, pages 3982–3992, Hong Kong, China.

Reimers, N. and Gurevych, I. (2020). Making monolingual sentence embeddings multilingual using knowledge distillation. In *Proceedings of the 2020 Conference on Empirical Methods in Natural Language Processing*. Association for Computational Linguistics.

Sennrich, R., Haddow, B., and Birch, A. (2016). Neural machine translation of rare words with subword units. In *Proceedings of the 54th Annual Meeting of the Association for Computational Linguistics (Volume 1: Long Papers)*, pages 1715–1725, Berlin, Germany.

Tiedemann, J. (2012). Parallel data, tools and interfaces in opus. In Chair), N. C. C., Choukri, K., Declerck, T., Dogan, M. U., Maegaard, B., Mariani, J., Odijk, J., and Piperidis, S., editors, *Proceedings of the Eight International Conference on Language Resources and Evaluation (LREC'12)*, Istanbul, Turkey. European Language Resources Association (ELRA).

Vaswani, A., Shazeer, N., Parmar, N., Uszkoreit, J., Jones, L., Gomez, A. N., Kaiser, Ł., and Polosukhin, I. (2017). Attention is all you need. In *Advances in neural information processing systems*, pages 5998–6008, Long Beach, USA.

Williams, P. and Haddow, B. (2021). The ELITR ECA corpus. *CoRR*, abs/2109.07351.

Xu, J. and Yvon, F. (2021). Can you traducir this? machine translation for code-switched input. In *Proceedings of the Fifth Workshop on Computational Approaches to Linguistic Code-Switching*, pages 84–94, Online.

Domain-Specific Text Generation for Machine Translation

Yasmin Moslem yasmin.moslem@adaptcentre.ie
Andy Way andy.way@adaptcentre.ie
School of Computing, Dublin City University, Dublin, Ireland
Rejwanul Haque rejwanul.haque@adaptcentre.ie
School of Computing, National College of Ireland, Dublin, Ireland
John D. Kelleher john.kelleher@adaptcentre.ie
Technological University Dublin, Dublin, Ireland

Abstract

Preservation of domain knowledge from the source to target is crucial in any translation workflow. It is common in the translation industry to receive highly specialized projects, where there is hardly any parallel in-domain data. In such scenarios where there is insufficient in-domain data to fine-tune Machine Translation (MT) models, producing translations that are consistent with the relevant context is challenging. In this work, we propose a novel approach to domain adaptation leveraging state-of-the-art pretrained language models (LMs) for domain-specific data augmentation for MT, simulating the domain characteristics of either (a) a small bilingual dataset, or (b) the monolingual source text to be translated. Combining this idea with back-translation, we can generate huge amounts of synthetic bilingual in-domain data for both use cases. For our investigation, we use the state-of-the-art Transformer architecture. We employ mixed fine-tuning to train models that significantly improve translation of in-domain texts. More specifically, in both scenarios, our proposed methods achieve improvements of approximately 5-6 BLEU and 2-3 BLEU, respectively, on the Arabic-to-English and English-to-Arabic language pairs. Furthermore, the outcome of human evaluation corroborates the automatic evaluation results.

1 Introduction

Neural Machine Translation (NMT) has the ability to produce good quality translations in terms of both fluency and adequacy (Bahdanau et al., 2015). Nevertheless, NMT still faces some challenges when it comes to translation of out-of-domain texts (Koehn and Knowles, 2017). Domain adaptation of MT systems on in-domain parallel texts has been an active area of research to handle this situation. Among popular contributions to the domain adaptation research, Luong and Manning (2015) proposed to adapt an already existing NMT system to a new domain, with further training on the in-domain data only. In an effort to avoid overfitting on the in-domain data, Chu et al. (2017) employed the mixed fine-tuning approach, resuming training the baseline NMT model on a mix of in-domain and out-of-domain data. Other researchers suggested adding domain tags to either the source or target sentences of the in-domain data, to inform the NMT model about the domain during training and decoding (Britz et al., 2017; Kobus et al., 2017; Stergiadis et al., 2021).

In this sense, several research works on domain adaptation assume the availability of in-domain data. However, in-domain data scarcity is common in translation settings, due to the lack of specialized datasets and terminology, or inconsistency and inaccuracy of available in-domain translations. To tackle this problem, researchers have proposed diverse approaches, such as utilizing large monolingual datasets through selecting instances related to a given test set, then automatically translating this source-synthetic corpus, and finally fine-tuning the general NMT system on this data (Chinea-Ríos et al., 2017). Similarly, some works have investigated retrieving similar translations (fuzzy matches) from bilingual datasets, and then applying on-the-fly domain adaptation through fine-tuning the baseline model at translation time (Farajian et al., 2017), or integrating them into NMT training (Bulte and Tezcan, 2019; Xu et al., 2020).

While the aforementioned approaches prove to be helpful in certain scenarios of domain adaptation, we believe there is a need for further research in this area to address current challenges of in-domain data scarcity and synthetic data creation. Some approaches, such as on-the-fly domain adaptation, require using GPUs synchronously at translation time, which presents a challenge for some institutions due to the lack of resources. When it comes to mining monolingual or bilingual datasets for similar instances, in several domains a good similar sentence can be a mix of portions of multiple sentences. Besides, with the lack of in-house specialized translation memories, mining publicly available datasets can be an inefficient process.

In this work, we introduce a new approach to MT domain adaptation, leveraging state-of-the-art pre-trained language models (LMs) for domain-specific data augmentation. Our method can generate an unlimited number of in-domain sentences out of the box. Recently, there has been a considerable advancement in training large LMs (Radford et al., 2019; Brown et al., 2020; Black et al., 2022; Zhang et al., 2022), not only for English, but also for diverse languages (Antoun et al., 2021; Zhang et al., 2021; Müller and Laurent, 2022). More specifically, our current work exploits GPT-J (Wang and Komatsuzaki, 2021) and mGPT (Shliazhko et al., 2022) to generate texts from in-domain sentences. We investigate the feasibility of this domain-specific text generation technique when either no or limited bilingual in-domain dataset is available. Incorporating this approach in a process of bilingual in-domain synthetic data creation and then fine-tuning our baseline generic MT model on the new dataset (cf. Section 3), we report significant improvements of the translation quality of the in-domain test set (cf. Section 5).

The rest of the paper is organized as follows. In Section 2, we discuss the related work in detail. Then, we present our methods in Section 3. In Section 4, we describe the experimental setup and present the results of our experiments in Section 5. Finally, we conclude the paper and discuss future work in Section 6.

2 Related Work

In recent years, several pre-trained large LMs have been made available to the research community, covering a wide range of linguistic tasks. Among the state-of-the-art LMs are GPT-2 (Radford et al., 2019), BERT (Devlin et al., 2019), RoBERTa (Liu et al., 2019), XLNet (Yang et al., 2019), GPT-3 (Brown et al., 2020), ELECTRA (Clark et al., 2020), DeBERTa (He et al., 2020, 2021), T5 (Raffel et al., 2020), Gopher (Rae et al., 2021), GPT-J (Wang and Komatsuzaki, 2021), GPT-NeoX (Black et al., 2022), PaLM (Chowdhery et al., 2022), Chinchilla (Hoffmann et al., 2022), ELMFOREST (Li et al., 2022), MT-NLG (Smith et al., 2022), and OPT (Zhang et al., 2022). Some of these models are multilingual, such as BLOOM (BigScience, 2022), AlexaTM (FitzGerald et al., 2022) and mGPT (Shliazhko et al., 2022).

Using LMs for specialized domains has been explored by previous works for diverse tasks. Researchers explored the possibility to retrieve factual knowledge from LMs in various domains (Petroni et al., 2019; Sung et al., 2021). Similarly, Horawalavithana et al. (2022) developed large-scale models of foundational scientific knowledge that can be effectively used to perform a wide range of in-domain and out-of-domain tasks.

LMs have been used in Unsupervised NMT (Lample and Conneau, 2019; Chronopoulou et al., 2021; Wang et al., 2021). Large-scale pre-trained LMs have also been employed in a variety of MT tasks, to improve the robustness of MT models or their ability to work on domain texts (Bawden et al., 2020; Specia et al., 2020; Wenzek et al., 2021).

Recently, Chang et al. (2021) aimed at addressing the lack of training data for new application domains for data-to-text generation. They automatically augmented the data available for training by (a) generating new text samples by replacing specific values with alternative ones from the same category, (b) generating new text samples using GPT-2, and (c) proposing an automatic method for pairing the new text samples with data samples. Their approach boosted the performance of a standard seq2seq model by over 5 BLEU points. Sawai et al. (2021) investigated the use of GPT-2 for source-side data augmentation to improve the robustness of a generic pre-trained NMT model. They first fine-tuned the pre-trained model, BERT-fused (Zhu et al., 2020), on authentic bilingual data. Then, they augmented the English source with data generated by GPT-2. Thereafter, they forward-translated the source-side English monolingual data with the fine-tuned version of BERT-fused. Finally, they fine-tuned the model on a combination of the authentic and synthetic data. While the reported results showed reasonable improvement (approx. 2.0 BLEU points) for the English-to-Japanese language direction, insignificant improvement (avg. 0.3 BLEU) was achieved for both English-to-German and English-to-Chinese language directions. The authors concluded that the result could be due to the relatively small amount of the original English-to-Japanese data compared to the other two language directions. We conjecture that more factors might have led to this result, including using forward-translation (rather than back-translation) of a huge amount of data, due to the noise it introduces for the decoder (Haddow et al., 2022). In our current work, we try to be more specific about the task description, focussing on domain adaptation in the absence of enough in-domain data; utilizing back-translation as an effective data augmentation technique (Edunov et al., 2018; Caswell et al., 2019); and giving more attention to data distribution through applying approaches like mixed fine-tuning and oversampling (Chu et al., 2017).

Back-translation (Sennrich et al., 2016; Fadaee and Monz, 2018; Poncelas et al., 2019) corresponds to the scenario where target-side monolingual data is translated using an MT system to give corresponding synthetic source sentences, the idea being that it is particularly beneficial for the MT decoder to see well-formed sentences (Haddow et al., 2022). Back-translation has become a popular strategy among MT researchers, especially in low-resource scenarios (Haque et al., 2021). Burlot and Yvon (2018) performed a systematic study, which showed that forward-translation might lead to some improvements in translation quality, but not nearly as much as back-translation. Bogoychev and Sennrich (2019) concluded that forward-translation is more sensitive to the quality of the system used to produce synthetic data. Compared to back-translation, biases and errors in synthetic data are intuitively more problematic in forward-translation, since they directly affect the gold labels. The authors also reported that human evaluators favoured their back-translation systems over forward-translation systems, mostly in terms of fluency, while adequacy was largely the same across all of them, especially on the original translation direction. In their analysis, Edunov et al. (2018) showed that sampling or noisy synthetic data gives a much stronger training signal than data generated by beam or greedy search. Caswell et al. (2019) proposed a simpler alternative to noising techniques, consisting of tagging back-translated source sentences with an extra token. Hoang et al. (2018) empirically showed that the quality of the back-translation system matters for synthetic corpus creation, and that NMT performance can be improved by iterative back-translation in both high-resource and low-resource scenarios.

When it comes to fine-tuning strategies for MT domain adaptation, researchers demonstrated that applying the right data distribution can significantly mitigate catastrophic forgetting of strong baselines in domain adaptation settings. Chu et al. (2017) proposed the mixed fine-tuning method, whose training procedure is as follows: (a) train an NMT model on out-of-domain data until convergence, and (b) resume training the NMT model from the first step on a mix of in-domain and out-of-domain data (by oversampling the in-domain data) until convergence. According to the authors, mixed fine-tuning can address the overfitting problem of regular fine-tuning. In addition, mixed fine-tuning does not worsen the quality of out-of-domain translations, while regular fine-tuning does. Similarly, Hasler et al. (2021) studied the problem in an adaptation setting where the goal is to preserve the existing system quality while incorporating data for domains that were not the focus of the original MT system. They found that they could improve over the performance trade-off offered by Elastic Weight Consolidation (Kirkpatrick et al., 2017) with a relatively simple data mixing strategy.

3 Methods

In this work, we investigate two scenarios of in-domain data scarcity, and propose approaches to leverage pre-trained LMs for domain-specific data generation for MT training.

3.1 Use Case 1: Limited bilingual in-domain data available

This is a common scenario where a specialized translation project is received, and although there is a large bilingual generic dataset and a small bilingual in-domain dataset (e.g. translation memory), the in-domain data is insufficient for fine-tuning a baseline model. From now on, we will refer to this use case as "Setup 1". To handle this situation, we propose the following steps:

1. We employ text generation with a large LM in the target language to augment the in-domain data. In this process, each target sentence in the in-domain dataset is used as a prompt to generate synthetic segments using the pre-trained language model. As expected, the generated text preserves the domain characteristics of the authentic in-domain data. This step enables us to have sufficient data in the target language.
2. To obtain parallel source sentences, we back-translate the target-side synthetic sentences that were generated in the previous step.
3. We apply mixed fine-tuning proposed by Chu et al. (2017) to the baseline model. In other words, we continue training our baseline model on a mix of (a) the synthetic bilingual in-domain dataset we got from the two previous steps, and (b) a randomly sampled portion of the original generic dataset, with a data size ratio of 1:9, respectively. To apply oversampling, we employ the dataset weights feature in OpenNMT-tf[1] (Klein et al., 2020), with weights 0.9 and 0.1, respectively. Hence, the dataset weights are inversely proportional to the sizes of the two datasets.[2] As the in-domain corpus is smaller than the generic corpus, oversampling allows the model to pay equal attention to both corpora. As a result of the mixed fine-tuning process, we obtained a new model that translates in-domain data significantly better than the baseline (cf. Section 5).[3]
4. Although the new fine-tuned model can still adequately translate generic data, we noticed it can degrade performance by 1-2 BLEU points. Therefore, we experimented with checkpoint averaging (Vaswani et al., 2017) of the fine-tuned model with the baseline model to reduce variability between trainings and address rapid overfitting during fine-tuning (Tran et al., 2021). This step helps regain the higher evaluation score of the baseline model on generic data, while retaining the improved score of the fine-tuned model on in-domain data.

3.2 Use Case 2: Zero bilingual in-domain data available

In this case, we assume that there is no bilingual in-domain data at all. There is only the source text that requires translation. From now on, we will refer to this use case as "Setup 2".

The first step is to use the baseline MT model for forward-translation of the source text. The generated translation might not be perfect; however, it can still include useful information about the domain. This approach bootstraps some parallel data for a situation where there was none. Then, we follow the same four steps mentioned in the previous use case.

[1]https://github.com/OpenNMT/OpenNMT-tf

[2]This configuration creates a weighted dataset where examples are randomly sampled from the data files according to the provided weights. In simple words, it sequentially samples 9 examples from the smaller in-domain dataset, and 1 example from the larger generic dataset, and so on.

[3]Inspired by Hasler et al. (2021) who applied 20x oversampling, we experimented with a higher oversampling ratio. Increasing both the data size and weight degraded performance on the in-domain test set, compared to our applied 9x ratio, while increasing the weight only did not result in a significant improvement. We might investigate the effect of changing the oversampling ratio further in the future.

4 Experiment Setup

4.1 Datasets

For training Arabic-to-English and English-to-Arabic generic models, we collect high-quality datasets from OPUS (Tiedemann, 2012). The breakdown of segment numbers in our datasets before and after filtering is shown in Table 1. To ensure the quality of our datasets, we apply a multi-filtering process. First, we apply rule-based filtering to individual datasets, removing duplicates, source-copied segments, those with too long source/target (ratio 200% and > 200 words), and HTML tags. Then, we calculate the similarity between each source and target to semantically filter out segments with a similarity threshold lower than 0.45. Finally, we concatenate the datasets and apply global filtering. For the development and test datasets, we randomly sampled 5000 segments each from the original dataset.[4]

For in-domain NMT models, we use TICO-19 (Anastasopoulos et al., 2020), a dataset in the Public Health domain. After filtering, the dataset includes 3062 segments. Table 2 shows the dataset details. We split the TICO-19 dataset into a development dataset, with 1000 segments, and a test dataset which includes the rest, i.e. 2062 segments. The whole TICO-19 dataset is used for generating a large synthetic in-domain training dataset, as described in Section 4.5.

		Filtering	
Dataset	**Raw**	**Rule-based**	**Semantic**
Bible	62,195	47,699	43,951
ELRC_2922	15,129	14,937	14,850
GlobalVoices	63,071	55,201	51,220
GNOME	150	143	134
Infopankki	50,769	15,531	14,635
KDE4	116,239	85,003	68,180
MultiUN	9,759,125	7,807,811	7,508,443
News-Commentary	97,384	80,744	77,715
OpenSubtitles	29,823,188	23,666,245	20,176,228
Tatoeba	27,905	27,649	26,714
Ubuntu	5,978	5,617	5,340
UN	74,067	63,074	62,901
UNPC	20,044,478	15,696,210	15,441,996
Wikimedia	407,543	335,783	317,285
Wikipedia	151,136	117,859	116,940
Total	**60,698,357**	**48,019,506**	**43,926,532**
Global Filtering		**40,207,905**	

Table 1: Generic datasets

		Filtering	
Dataset	**Raw**	**Rule-based**	**Semantic**
TICO-19	3,071	3,069	3,062

Table 2: In-domain dataset (Public Health)

4.2 Vocabulary

To create our vocabulary, we first train SentencePiece unigram models (Kudo and Richardson, 2018; Kudo, 2018) for the source and target individually, to learn subword units from unto-

[4]Our MT preparation scripts are publicly available at: https://github.com/ymoslem/MT-Preparation

kenized text.[5] Then, we utilize this SentencePiece model to subword our dataset. We use a vocabulary size of 50,000. Subsequently, we convert the learned subword units into our final vocabulary in the format supported by OpenNMT-tf. Segments are automatically augmented with start and end tokens via *source_sequence_controls* option.

4.3 NMT Model Architecture

Our baseline generic NMT models use the Transformer "Big" architecture (Vaswani et al., 2017) as implemented in OpenNMT-tf, and relative position representations (Shaw et al., 2018) with a clipping distance k=20. The models consist of 6 layers with a model dimension of 1,024, split into 16 heads, and a feedforward dimension of 4,096.

4.4 Training

The training takes place on 2x NVIDIA RTX A4000 GPUs, with a batch size of 2048 tokens per GPU, for an effective batch size of 25k tokens/step. The Arabic-to-English model is trained for 240k steps, while the English-to-Arabic model is trained for 105k steps. Early stopping is used after 3 evaluations with less than 0.01 BLEU improvement on the development dataset.

4.5 Domain-Specific Data Generation with LMs

For English, we use GPT-J (Wang and Komatsuzaki, 2021), a Transformer-based language model with 6B trainable parameters.[6] For Arabic, we use mGPT (Shliazhko et al., 2022), a multilingual language model.[7]

To fit the models onto an NVIDIA RTX A4000 GPU (16 GB of GPU memory), the half-precision floating-point (float16) format is used.[8] We also use a batch size of 1.[9] For inference, we employ 50 Top-K sampling and 0.95 Top-p (nucleus) sampling (Fan et al., 2018; Holtzman et al., 2018; Radford et al., 2019; Holtzman et al., 2020). The maximum length of the generated text is set to 300 tokens, and we return 5 sequences for each segment, to get multiple independently sampled outputs. Finally, we split the generated text into sentences.[10]

As explained in Section 3, we have two use cases: (a) a small bilingual in-domain dataset is available; and (b) the source only is available, so we utilize forward-translation to generate the target side. After that, each target sentence of the in-domain dataset TICO-19 (i.e. the authentic target in the first case, or the MT-ed target in the second case) is fed to the LM as a prompt to generate synthetic in-domain segments. We use random seeds to generate multiple datasets, namely 2 for English and 3 for Arabic.[11] We filter the concatenated datasets, by removing duplicates and cleaning lines with a wrong language, and those including only dashes or filenames. Table 3 illustrates the numbers of in-domain synthetic segments generated by the LMs.

		Setup 1					Setup 2				
Language	**LM**	**1st Run**	**2nd Run**	**3rd Run**	**Total**	**Filtered**	**1st Run**	**2nd Run**	**3rd Run**	**Total**	**Filtered**
English	GPT-J	131,730	131,554	N/A	263,284	242,469	137,705	138,702	N/A	276,407	253,287
Arabic	mGPT	96,296	97,031	94,513	287,840	271,665	103,272	103,459	103,303	310,034	294,391

Table 3: Data generated by language models (LMs)

[5] In SentencePiece, we utilize the training options `--split_digits` to split all digits into separate pieces, and `--byte_fallback` to decompose unknown pieces into UTF-8 byte pieces to help avoid out-of-vocabulary tokens.

[6] https://huggingface.co/EleutherAI/gpt-j-6B

[7] https://huggingface.co/sberbank-ai/mGPT

[8] In Hugging Face Transformers, we also set the option `low_cpu_mem_usage` to `True`.

[9] It is worth mentioning though that for batch generation (i.e. >1), padding and attention masking should be used; note that left padding is required for GPT-like models.

[10] Our scripts are available at: https://github.com/ymoslem/MT-LM

[11] As two data generation runs for Arabic resulted in a less amount of data than for English, we increased the data size for Arabic by generating a third dataset (cf. Table 3).

4.6 Back-Translation

For back-translation, we use OPUS models,[12] specifically the Transformer-Big versions. For efficiency purposes, we convert the models to the CTranslate2[13] format (INT8 quantization). We use beam size 5. After back-translation, we run the same rule-based and semantic filtering on the generated dataset as we did for the original datasets. Table 4 elaborates on the numbers.

	Setup 1			Setup 2		
		Filtering			Filtering	
Language	**Translated**	**Rule-based**	**Semantic**	**Translated**	**Rule-based**	**Semantic**
English	242,469	240,329	239,931	253,287	251,357	250,317
Arabic	271,665	271,645	270,743	294,391	294,234	293,252

Table 4: Back-translated datasets

4.7 Mixed Fine-tuning

Following Chu et al. (2017), we employ the mixed fine-tuning approach. We randomly sample a portion from the generic data we used to train the baseline model, and use it during the fine-tuning step along with the in-domain dataset. Oversampling the in-domain data is a crucial step, as explained in Section 3. We first train a baseline NMT model on out-of-domain data until convergence, and then continue training the NMT baseline model on a mix of in-domain and out-of-domain data (by oversampling the in-domain data) until convergence.

In most experiments, we fine-tuned the baseline for 5000 steps. However, for Setup 2 of the English-to-Arabic language pair, we found that the best automatic evaluation scores were achieved with training for only 500 or 1000 steps. We believe that this might be due to the quality or distribution of the generated in-domain data compared to the original generic data. Although Chu et al. (2017) observed that both regular fine-tuning and mixed fine-tuning tend to converge after 1 epoch of training, it seems there is no golden rule as to how many steps or epochs the baseline model should be fine-tuned on the mixed data. Depending on the size of data, we recommend conducting less-frequent evaluations on the development dataset during the fine-tuning process for finding out the best model checkpoint.

5 Results

In this section, we elaborate on our automatic and human evaluations and discuss the results. As Table 5 shows, scores obtained from diverse automatic metics provide good correlation with the human evaluation. Moreover, the linguistic analysis (cf. Section 5.3) supports these numerical results, and demonstrates how the models fine-tuned on synthetic in-domain data produce more accurate translations of the in-domain test set compared to the baseline model.

5.1 Automatic Evaluation

For automatic evaluation, we calculated spBLEU (Papineni et al., 2002; Goyal et al., 2022) which uses a SentencePiece tokenizer with 256,000 tokens and then the BLEU score is computed on the sub-worded text. spBLEU has been recently added to sacreBLEU v2.1.0.[14] Goyal et al. (2022) showed that spBLEU exhibits a strong correlation with the tokenization-independent chrF++, yet has the advantage of keeping the familiarity of BLEU. To verify our results, we employed other evaluation metrics, namely the character-based metric chrF++ (Popović, 2017), and the word-based metric TER (Snover et al., 2006), as implemented in sacre-BLEU (Post, 2018). Furthermore, we integrated COMET[15] (Rei et al., 2020) as a semantic

[12]https://github.com/Helsinki-NLP/Tatoeba-Challenge/tree/master/models

[13]https://github.com/OpenNMT/CTranslate2

[14]https://github.com/mjpost/sacrebleu

[15]https://github.com/Unbabel/COMET

evaluation metric, with the "wmt20-comet-da" model.

We experimented with averaging parameters across multiple model checkpoints (Vaswani et al., 2017), to address bias towards recent training data (Tran et al., 2021). Sometimes, averaging multiple checkpoints of a baseline model, or averaging a baseline model with a fine-tuned model could lead to extra improvements of the automatic and/or human evaluation of our models. Table 5 shows evaluation results on the in-domain test dataset, and Figure 1 elaborates on all the automatic evaluation results, including the results for averaged models.

Language	Model	spBLEU ↑	chrF++ ↑	TER ↓	COMET ↑	Human ↑
AR-EN	Baseline	44.57	66.68	46.67	65.78	87.0
	Setup 1 Mixed Fine-Tuning	49.79	70.54	43.32	71.89	93.5
	Setup 2 Mixed Fine-Tuning	47.22	69.38	45.38	70.08	94.5
EN-AR	Baseline	36.15	58.3	58.29	57.5	87.0
	Setup 1 Mixed Fine-Tuning	42.38	62.52	53.99	67.48	90.0
	Setup 2 Mixed Fine-Tuning	37.91	59.42	55.95	59.47	88.5

Table 5: Evaluation results on the in-domain test set, TICO-19

5.2 Human Evaluation

Since translation focusses mainly on word choice, syntax, and semantics, and how people perceive it, we decided to complement our evaluation process with human evaluation.

The evaluator was an Arabic native speaker and domain expert. We conducted a bilingual evaluation, providing the evaluator with both the original source sentences and translations generated by the MT models. The human test set contained 50 sentences, randomly extracted from the original test set, and verified as accepted translations. The evaluator was asked to assess the acceptability of each translation generated by our baselines and fine-tuned MT systems, using the scale proposed by Coughlin (2003), ranging from 1 to 4, and outlined as follows:

- **4 = Ideal:** Not necessarily a perfect translation, but grammatically correct, with all information accurately transferred.
- **3 = Acceptable:** Not perfect (stylistically or grammatically odd), but definitely comprehensible, AND with accurate transfer of all important information.
- **2 = Possibly Acceptable:** Possibly comprehensible (given enough context and/or time to work it out); some information transferred accurately.
- **1 = Unacceptable:** Absolutely not comprehensible and/or little or no information is accurately transferred.

Human evaluation results on the in-domain dataset, TICO-19, are expressed in percentage points in the last column of Table 5. In addition, Table 6 elaborates on the results for all the systems, showing the mean value for each system on the 1-4 scale.[16] The models fine-tuned on the domain-specific synthetic dataset achieve improvements on the in-domain test set, while retaining the baseline's quality on the generic holdout test set.

Language	Test Set	BS	BS-Avg8	MixFT-1	MixFT-1+BS	MixFT-1+BS-Avg8	MixFT-2	MixFT-2+BS	MixFT-2+BS-Avg8
AR-EN	**Generic**	3.84	**3.90**	3.84	3.88	3.88	3.84	3.84	3.84
	TICO-19	3.48	3.62	3.74	**3.82**	3.80	3.78	3.72	3.74
EN-AR	**Generic**	**3.96**	3.90	3.82	**3.96**	3.90	3.94	**3.96**	**3.96**
	TICO-19	3.48	3.50	**3.60**	3.54	3.52	3.54	3.56	3.54

Table 6: Human evaluation of MT models for Arabic-to-English (AR-EN) and English-to-Arabic (EN-AR) language pairs, the baseline (BS), baseline averaged 8 checkpoints (BS-Avg8), mixed fine-tuning model (MixFT), averaging MixFT with BS (MixFT+BS), and averaging MixFT with BS-Avg8 (MixFT+BS-Avg8). MixFT-1 refers to Setup 1 and MixFT-2 refers to Setup 2.

[16]Sentence-level human evaluation is available at: `https://github.com/ymoslem/MT-LM`

5.3 Linguistic Analysis

We observe that in several cases, the fine-tuned (in-domain) models generate more idiomatic translations or better capture the meaning in the Public Health context. Samples from the test dataset translated by the baseline model and in-domain models reflect these improvements.

Among Arabic-to-English examples, the phrase "غير مسببة للأمراض في مضيفاتها المستودعة الطبيعية" was translated as "not pathogenic in their naturally occurring host" by the baseline, and "non-pathogenic in their natural reservoir hosts" by both in-domain models. The former translation somehow conveys the meaning; however, the latter translation is more idiomatic in the medical context. The baseline system translated "حمامات الولادة" as "maternity wards" which is an incorrect translation, while the in-domain models in Setup 1 and Setup 2 produced more relevant translations as "birthing pools" and "birth baths", respectively. The baseline model translated "مسحة بلعومية أنفية" as "a nasal laryngeal swab" which is an inaccurate translation. In contrast, both in-domain models translated the term as "a nasal nasopharyngeal swab", which uses the accurate "nasopharyngeal" medical term. It can still be edited by removing the redundant "nasal"; however, our evaluator gave it a higher score than the translation provided by the baseline. The term "اختبارات مَصليَّة" was translated as "serum tests" by the baseline, while it was translated as "serological tests" by both in-domain models, which is more idiomatic.

Examining some of the English-to-Arabic translations, the baseline model mistranslated "HCoVs" as "فيروسات نقص المناعة البشرية / متلازمة نقص المناعة المكتسب (الإيدز)" (HIV/AIDS), as opposed to the in-domain models, which correctly translated it as "فيروسات كورونا البشرية" or just "فيروسات HCoV". Interestingly, even for a simpler phrase like "five times more cases", the baseline incorrectly translated it as "خمس حالات" (five cases), whilst the in-domain models correctly conveyed the meaning as "خمسة أضعاف الحالات".

There are also examples where one of the in-domain systems generated the correct translation while the other could not. For instance, both the baseline and Setup 2 in-domain model translated "If you do wear a mask" as "إذا كنت لا ارتداء قناع", which is both syntactically and semantically incorrect. In contrast, the Setup 1 in-domain model perfectly translated it as "إذا كنت ترتدي قناعًا". The baseline model translated the phrase "passive antibody therapy" as "العلاج السلبي للأجسام المضادة", which uses the preposition "لـ" (of) instead of "بـ" (with), missing the fact that in this context "antibody" is equivalent to "antibody-based" rather than being the issue to be treated. Similarly, the Setup 2 in-domain model mistranslated it as "العلاج المضاد السلبي" while the Setup 1 in-domain model accurately translated it as "العلاج السلبي بالأجسام المضادة".

Since some phrases can be expressed in multiple ways, we notice that sometimes the evaluator equally ranked different translations. This might explain why automatic metrics evaluate Arabic-to-English Setup 1 higher than Setup 2, whereas the human evaluation shows that the translation quality of both setups is comparable.

6 Conclusion

In this paper, we propose two simple methods to utilize pre-trained language models for domain-specific data augmentation for NMT systems. We report significant improvements, supported by both automatic and human evaluation. The proposed techniques enable the generation of large amounts of data, simulating the characteristics of the specialized text to be translated, and facilitating the domain adaptation process.

For the Arabic-to-English language direction, human evaluation demonstrates that Setup 2 is on par with Setup 1 even though in the former we did not have any authentic bilingual in-domain data (cf. Section 3). Nevertheless, the English-to-Arabic model in Setup 2 has lower performance compared to the Setup 1 model, although both setups outperform the baseline on the in-domain test set. We believe this might be due to the quality of synthetic data generated for Arabic, which is an interesting aspect to explore further.

In the future, we would like to investigate utilizing terminology for domain-specific data generation, and experiment with employing the same proposed approaches for low-resource languages and multilingual settings.

Figures: Automatic Evaluation

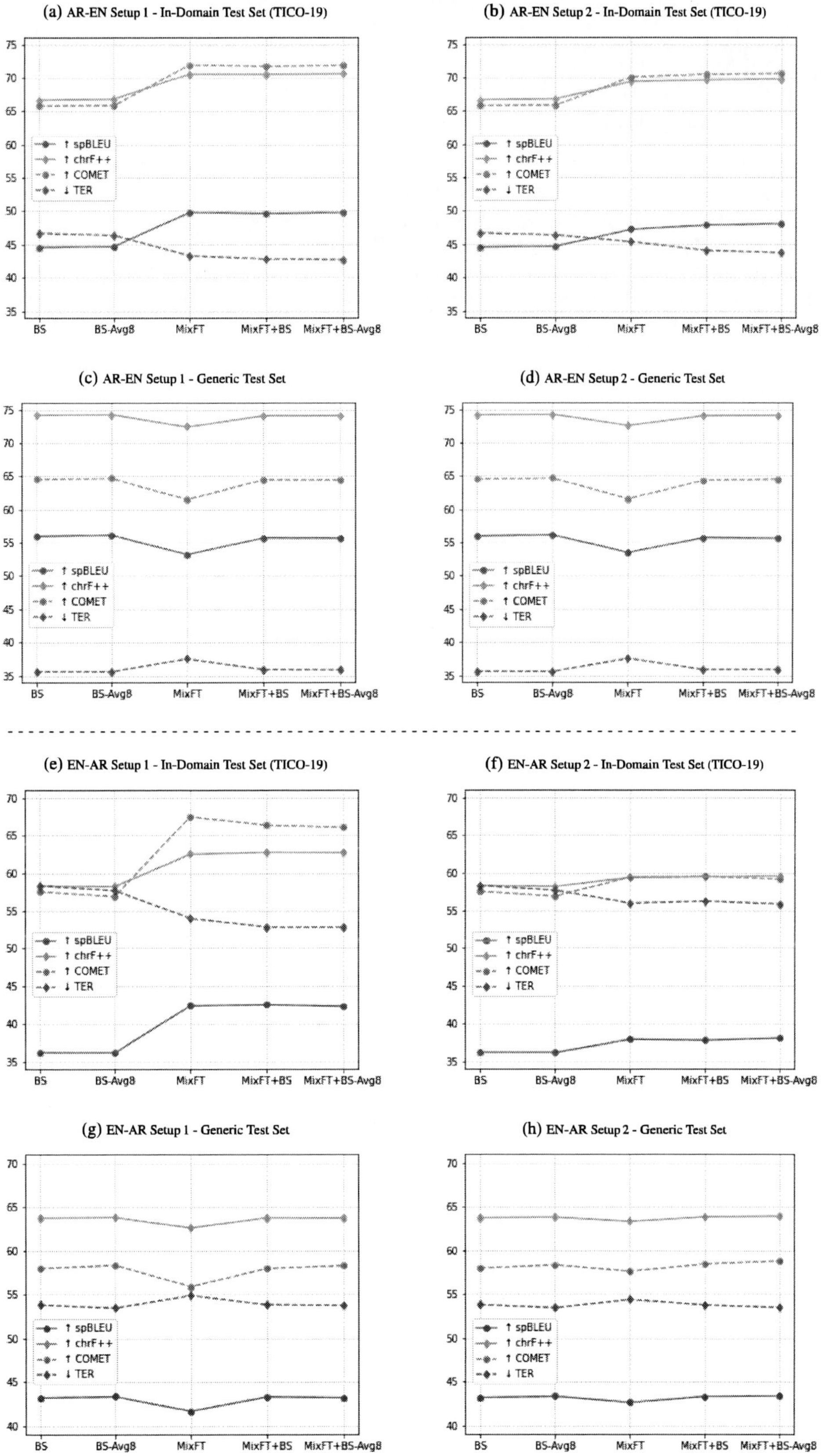

Figure 1: Performance comparison of 5 models for Arabic-to-English (AR-EN) and English-to-Arabic (EN-AR) language pairs, the baseline (BS), baseline averaged 8 checkpoints (BS-Avg8), mixed fine-tuning model (MixFT), averaging MixFT with BS (MixFT+BS), and averaging MixFT with BS-Avg8 (MixFT+BS-Avg8). The MixFT models fine-tuned on the domain-specific synthetic dataset achieve improvements on the in-domain test set (a,b & e,f), while retaining the baselines quality on the generic test set (c,d & g,h).

7 Acknowledgements

This work is supported by the Science Foundation Ireland Centre for Research Training in Digitally-Enhanced Reality (d-real) under Grant No. 18/CRT/6224, the ADAPT Centre for Digital Content Technology which is funded under the Science Foundation Ireland (SFI) Research Centres Programme (Grant No. 13/RC/2106) and is co-funded under the European Regional Development Fund, and Microsoft Research.

We would like to extend our sincere thanks to Dr Muhammed Yaman Muhaisen, Ophthalmologist at Eye Surgical Hospital (Damascus), for conducting the human evaluation of our machine translation models.

References

Anastasopoulos, A., Cattelan, A., Dou, Z.-Y., Federico, M., Federmann, C., Genzel, D., Guzmán, F., Hu, J., Hughes, M., Koehn, P., Lazar, R., Lewis, W., Neubig, G., Niu, M., Öktem, A., Paquin, E., Tang, G., and Tur, S. (2020). TICO-19: the translation initiative for COvid-19. In *Proceedings of the 1st Workshop on NLP for COVID-19 (Part 2) at EMNLP 2020*, Online. Association for Computational Linguistics.

Antoun, W., Baly, F., and Hajj, H. (2021). AraGPT2: Pre-Trained Transformer for Arabic Language Generation. In *Proceedings of the Sixth Arabic Natural Language Processing Workshop*, pages 196–207, Kyiv, Ukraine (Virtual). Association for Computational Linguistics.

Bahdanau, D., Cho, K., and Bengio, Y. (2015). Neural Machine Translation by Jointly Learning to Align and Translate. In *Proceedings of the 3rd International Conference on Learning Representations, ICLR 2015*, San Diego, CA, USA.

Bawden, R., Di Nunzio, G., Grozea, C., Unanue, I., Yepes, A., Mah, N., Martinez, D., Névéol, A., Neves, M., Oronoz, M., and Others (2020). Findings of the WMT 2020 biomedical translation shared task: Basque, Italian and Russian as new additional languages. In *5th conference on machine translation*, pages 660–687, Online. Association for Computational Linguistics.

BigScience (2022). BigScience Language Open-science Open-access Multilingual (BLOOM) Language Model. International, May 2021-May 2022.

Black, S., Biderman, S., Hallahan, E., Anthony, Q., Gao, L., Golding, L., He, H., Leahy, C., McDonell, K., Phang, J., Pieler, M., Prashanth, U. S., Purohit, S., Reynolds, L., Tow, J., Wang, B., and Weinbach, S. (2022). GPT-NeoX-20B: An Open-Source Autoregressive Language Model. In *Proceedings of BigScience Episode #5 – Workshop on Challenges & Perspectives in Creating Large Language Models*, pages 95–136, Stroudsburg, PA, USA. Association for Computational Linguistics.

Bogoychev, N. and Sennrich, R. (2019). Domain, Translationese and Noise in Synthetic Data for Neural Machine Translation. *arXiv [cs.CL]*.

Britz, D., Le, Q., and Pryzant, R. (2017). Effective Domain Mixing for Neural Machine Translation. In *Proceedings of the Second Conference on Machine Translation*, pages 118–126, Copenhagen, Denmark. Association for Computational Linguistics.

Brown, T. B., Mann, B., Ryder, N., Subbiah, M., Kaplan, J., Dhariwal, P., Neelakantan, A., Shyam, P., Sastry, G., Askell, A., Agarwal, S., Herbert-Voss, A., Krueger, G., Henighan, T., Child, R., Ramesh, A., Ziegler, D. M., Wu, J., Winter, C., Hesse, C., Chen, M., Sigler, E., Litwin, M., Gray, S., Chess, B., Clark, J., Berner, C., McCandlish, S., Radford, A., Sutskever, I., and Amodei, D. (2020). Language Models are Few-Shot Learners. In *Advances in Neural Information Processing Systems (NeurIPS 2020)*, volume 33, pages 1877–1901. Curran Associates, Inc.

Bulte, B. and Tezcan, A. (2019). Neural Fuzzy Repair: Integrating Fuzzy Matches into Neural Machine Translation. In *Proceedings of the 57th Annual Meeting of the Association for Computational Linguistics*, pages 1800–1809, Florence, Italy. Association for Computational Linguistics.

Burlot, F. and Yvon, F. (2018). Using monolingual data in neural machine translation: a systematic study. In *Proceedings of the Third Conference on Machine Translation: Research Papers*, pages 144–155, Brussels, Belgium. Association for Computational Linguistics.

Caswell, I., Chelba, C., and Grangier, D. (2019). Tagged Back-Translation. In *Proceedings of the Fourth Conference on Machine Translation (Volume 1: Research Papers)*, pages 53–63, Florence, Italy. Association for Computational Linguistics.

Chang, E., Shen, X., Zhu, D., Demberg, V., and Su, H. (2021). Neural Data-to-Text Generation with LM-based Text Augmentation. In *Proceedings of the 16th Conference of the European Chapter of the Association for Computational Linguistics: Main Volume*, pages 758–768, Online. Association for Computational Linguistics.

Chinea-Ríos, M., Peris, Á., and Casacuberta, F. (2017). Adapting Neural Machine Translation with Parallel Synthetic Data. In *Proceedings of the Second Conference on Machine Translation*, pages 138–147, Copenhagen, Denmark. Association for Computational Linguistics.

Chowdhery, A., Narang, S., Devlin, J., Bosma, M., Mishra, G., Roberts, A., Barham, P., Chung, H. W., Sutton, C., Gehrmann, S., Schuh, P., Shi, K., Tsvyashchenko, S., Maynez, J., Rao, A., Barnes, P., Tay, Y., Shazeer, N., Prabhakaran, V., Reif, E., Du, N., Hutchinson, B., Pope, R., Bradbury, J., Austin, J., Isard, M., Gur-Ari, G., Yin, P., Duke, T., Levskaya, A., Ghemawat, S., Dev, S., Michalewski, H., Garcia, X., Misra, V., Robinson, K., Fedus, L., Zhou, D., Ippolito, D., Luan, D., Lim, H., Zoph, B., Spiridonov, A., Sepassi, R., Dohan, D., Agrawal, S., Omernick, M., Dai, A. M., Pillai, T. S., Pellat, M., Lewkowycz, A., Moreira, E., Child, R., Polozov, O., Lee, K., Zhou, Z., Wang, X., Saeta, B., Diaz, M., Firat, O., Catasta, M., Wei, J., Meier-Hellstern, K., Eck, D., Dean, J., Petrov, S., and Fiedel, N. (2022). PaLM: Scaling Language Modeling with Pathways. *arXiv [cs.CL]*.

Chronopoulou, A., Stojanovski, D., and Fraser, A. (2021). Improving the Lexical Ability of Pretrained Language Models for Unsupervised Neural Machine Translation. In *Proceedings of the 2021 Conference of the North American Chapter of the Association for Computational Linguistics: Human Language Technologies*, pages 173–180, Online. Association for Computational Linguistics.

Chu, C., Dabre, R., and Kurohashi, S. (2017). An Empirical Comparison of Domain Adaptation Methods for Neural Machine Translation. In *Proceedings of the 55th Annual Meeting of the Association for Computational Linguistics (Volume 2: Short Papers)*, pages 385–391, Vancouver, Canada. Association for Computational Linguistics.

Clark, K., Luong, M.-T., Le, Q. V., and Manning, C. D. (2020). ELECTRA: Pre-training Text Encoders as Discriminators Rather Than Generators. In *Proceedings of the 8th International Conference on Learning Representations (ICLR)*, Virtual.

Coughlin, D. (2003). Correlating automated and human assessments of machine translation quality. In *Proceedings of Machine Translation Summit IX: Papers*, New Orleans, USA.

Devlin, J., Chang, M.-W., Lee, K., and Toutanova, K. (2019). BERT: Pre-training of Deep Bidirectional Transformers for Language Understanding. In *Proceedings of the 2019 Conference of the North American Chapter of the Association for Computational Linguistics: Human Language Technologies, Volume 1 (Long and Short Papers)*, pages 4171–4186, Minneapolis, Minnesota. Association for Computational Linguistics.

Edunov, S., Ott, M., Auli, M., and Grangier, D. (2018). Understanding Back-Translation at Scale. In *Proceedings of the 2018 Conference on Empirical Methods in Natural Language Processing*, pages 489–500, Brussels, Belgium. Association for Computational Linguistics.

Fadaee, M. and Monz, C. (2018). Back-Translation Sampling by Targeting Difficult Words in Neural Machine Translation. In *Proceedings of the 2018 Conference on Empirical Methods in Natural Language Processing*, pages 436–446, Brussels, Belgium. Association for Computational Linguistics.

Fan, A., Lewis, M., and Dauphin, Y. (2018). Hierarchical Neural Story Generation. In *Proceedings of the 56th Annual Meeting of the Association for Computational Linguistics (Volume 1: Long Papers)*, pages 889–898, Melbourne, Australia. Association for Computational Linguistics.

Farajian, M. A., Turchi, M., Negri, M., and Federico, M. (2017). Multi-Domain Neural Machine Translation through Unsupervised Adaptation. In *Proceedings of the Second Conference on Machine Translation*, pages 127–137, Copenhagen, Denmark. Association for Computational Linguistics.

FitzGerald, J., Ananthakrishnan, S., Arkoudas, K., Bernardi, D., Bhagia, A., Bovi, C. D., Cao, J., Chada, R., Chauhan, A., Chen, L., Dwarakanath, A., Dwivedi, S., Gojayev, T., Gopalakrishnan, K., Gueudre, T., Hakkani-Tur, D., Hamza, W., Hueser, J., Jose, K. M., Khan, H., Liu, B., Lu, J., Manzotti, A., Natarajan, P., Owczarzak, K., Oz, G., Palumbo, E., Peris, C., Prakash, C. S., Rawls, S., Rosenbaum, A., Shenoy, A., Soltan, S., Sridhar, M. H., Tan, L., Triefenbach, F., Wei, P., Yu, H., Zheng, S., Tur, G., and Natarajan, P. (2022). Alexa Teacher Model: Pretraining and Distilling Multi-Billion-Parameter Encoders for Natural Language Understanding Systems. In *The Knowledge Discovery and Data Mining Conference (KDD)*, Washington, DC.

Goyal, N., Gao, C., Chaudhary, V., Chen, P.-J., Wenzek, G., Ju, D., Krishnan, S., Ranzato, M., Guzmán, F., and Fan, A. (2022). The flores-101 evaluation benchmark for low-resource and multilingual machine translation. *Trans. Assoc. Comput. Linguist.*, 10:522–538.

Haddow, B., Bawden, R., Barone, A. V. M., Helcl, J., and Birch, A. (2022). Survey of Low-Resource Machine Translation. *Computational Linguistics*, 06:1–67.

Haque, R., Liu, C.-H., and Way, A. (2021). Recent advances of low-resource neural machine translation. *Machine Translation*, 35(4):451–474.

Hasler, E., Domhan, T., Trenous, J., Tran, K., Byrne, B., and Hieber, F. (2021). Improving the Quality Trade-Off for Neural Machine Translation Multi-Domain Adaptation. In *Proceedings of the 2021 Conference on Empirical Methods in Natural Language Processing*, pages 8470–8477, Online and Punta Cana, Dominican Republic. Association for Computational Linguistics.

He, P., Gao, J., and Chen, W. (2021). DeBERTaV3: Improving DeBERTa using ELECTRA-Style Pre-Training with Gradient-Disentangled Embedding Sharing. *arXiv [cs.CL]*.

He, P., Liu, X., Gao, J., and Chen, W. (2020). DeBERTa: Decoding-enhanced BERT with Disentangled Attention. In *Proceedings of the 9th International Conference on Learning Representations (ICLR)*, Virtual.

Hoang, V. C. D., Koehn, P., Haffari, G., and Cohn, T. (2018). Iterative Back-Translation for Neural Machine Translation. In *Proceedings of the 2nd Workshop on Neural Machine Translation and Generation*, pages 18–24, Melbourne, Australia. Association for Computational Linguistics.

Hoffmann, J., Borgeaud, S., Mensch, A., Buchatskaya, E., Cai, T., Rutherford, E., de Las Casas, D., Hendricks, L. A., Welbl, J., Clark, A., Hennigan, T., Noland, E., Millican, K., van den Driessche, G., Damoc, B., Guy, A., Osindero, S., Simonyan, K., Elsen, E., Rae, J. W., Vinyals, O., and Sifre, L. (2022). Training Compute-Optimal Large Language Models. *arXiv [cs.CL]*.

Holtzman, A., Buys, J., Du, L., Forbes, M., and Choi, Y. (2020). The Curious Case of Neural Text Degeneration. In *Proceedings of the 8th International Conference on Learning Representations (ICLR)*, Virtual.

Holtzman, A., Buys, J., Forbes, M., Bosselut, A., Golub, D., and Choi, Y. (2018). Learning to Write with Cooperative Discriminators. In *Proceedings of the 56th Annual Meeting of the Association for Computational Linguistics (Volume 1: Long Papers)*, pages 1638–1649, Melbourne, Australia. Association for Computational Linguistics.

Horawalavithana, S., Ayton, E., Sharma, S., Howland, S., Subramanian, M., Vasquez, S., Cosbey, R., Glenski, M., and Volkova, S. (2022). Foundation models of scientific knowledge for chemistry: Opportunities, challenges and lessons learned. In *Proceedings of BigScience Episode #5 – Workshop on Challenges & Perspectives in Creating Large Language Models*, pages 160–172, virtual+Dublin. Association for Computational Linguistics.

Kirkpatrick, J., Pascanu, R., Rabinowitz, N., Veness, J., Desjardins, G., Rusu, A. A., Milan, K., Quan, J., Ramalho, T., Grabska-Barwinska, A., Hassabis, D., Clopath, C., Kumaran, D., and Hadsell, R. (2017). Overcoming catastrophic forgetting in neural networks. *Proc. Natl. Acad. Sci. U. S. A.*, 114(13):3521–3526.

Klein, G., Hernandez, F., Nguyen, V., and Senellart, J. (2020). The OpenNMT Neural Machine Translation Toolkit: 2020 Edition. In *Proceedings of the 14th Conference of the Association for Machine Translation in the Americas (Volume 1: Research Track)*, pages 102–109, Virtual. Association for Machine Translation in the Americas.

Kobus, C., Crego, J., and Senellart, J. (2017). Domain Control for Neural Machine Translation. In *Proceedings of Recent Advances in Natural Language Processing*, pages 372–378, Varna, Bulgaria.

Koehn, P. and Knowles, R. (2017). Six Challenges for Neural Machine Translation. In *Proceedings of the First Workshop on Neural Machine Translation*, pages 28–39, Vancouver. Association for Computational Linguistics.

Kudo, T. (2018). Subword regularization: Improving neural network translation models with multiple subword candidates. In *Proceedings of the 56th Annual Meeting of the Association for Computational Linguistics (Volume 1: Long Papers)*, pages 66–75, Melbourne, Australia. Association for Computational Linguistics.

Kudo, T. and Richardson, J. (2018). SentencePiece: A simple and language independent subword tokenizer and detokenizer for neural text processing. In *Proceedings of the 2018 Conference on Empirical Methods in Natural Language Processing: System Demonstrations*, pages 66–71, Brussels, Belgium. Association for Computational Linguistics.

Lample, G. and Conneau, A. (2019). Cross-lingual Language Model Pretraining. In *Advances in Neural Information Processing Systems (NeurIPS 2019)*, volume 32. Curran Associates, Inc.

Li, M., Gururangan, S., Dettmers, T., Lewis, M., Althoff, T., Smith, N. A., and Zettlemoyer, L. (2022). Branch-Train-Merge: Embarrassingly Parallel Training of Expert Language Models. *arXiv [cs.CL]*.

Liu, Y., Ott, M., Goyal, N., Du, J., Joshi, M., Chen, D., Levy, O., Lewis, M., Zettlemoyer, L., and Stoyanov, V. (2019). RoBERTa: A Robustly Optimized BERT Pretraining Approach. *arXiv [cs.CL]*.

Luong, M.-T. and Manning, C. (2015). Stanford neural machine translation systems for spoken language domains. In *Proceedings of the 12th International Workshop on Spoken Language Translation: Evaluation Campaign*, pages 76–79, Da Nang, Vietnam.

Müller, M. and Laurent, F. (2022). Cedille: A Large Autoregressive French Language Model. *arXiv [cs.CL]*.

Papineni, K., Roukos, S., Ward, T., and Zhu, W.-J. (2002). Bleu: a method for automatic evaluation of machine translation. In *Proceedings of the 40th Annual Meeting of the Association for Computational Linguistics*, pages 311–318, Philadelphia, Pennsylvania, USA. Association for Computational Linguistics.

Petroni, F., Rocktäschel, T., Riedel, S., Lewis, P., Bakhtin, A., Wu, Y., and Miller, A. (2019). Language models as knowledge bases? In *Proceedings of the 2019 Conference on Empirical Methods in Natural Language Processing and the 9th International Joint Conference on Natural Language Processing (EMNLP-IJCNLP)*, pages 2463–2473, Hong Kong, China. Association for Computational Linguistics.

Poncelas, A., de Buy Wenniger, G. M., and Way, A. (2019). Adaptation of Machine Translation Models with Back-translated Data using Transductive Data Selection Methods. *Proceedings of the 20th International Conference on Computational Linguistics and Intelligent Text Processing - CICLing 2019*.

Popović, M. (2017). chrF++: words helping character n-grams. In *Proceedings of the Second Conference on Machine Translation*, pages 612–618, Copenhagen, Denmark. Association for Computational Linguistics.

Post, M. (2018). A call for clarity in reporting BLEU scores. In *Proceedings of the Third Conference on Machine Translation: Research Papers*, pages 186–191, Brussels, Belgium. Association for Computational Linguistics.

Radford, A., Wu, J., Child, R., Luan, D., Amodei, D., and Sutskever, I. (2019). Language Models are Unsupervised Multitask Learners. Technical report, OpenAi.

Rae, J. W., Borgeaud, S., Cai, T., Millican, K., Hoffmann, J., Song, F., Aslanides, J., Henderson, S., Ring, R., Young, S., Rutherford, E., Hennigan, T., Menick, J., Cassirer, A., Powell, R., van den Driessche, G., Hendricks, L. A., Rauh, M., Huang, P.-S., Glaese, A., Welbl, J., Dathathri, S., Huang, S., Uesato, J., Mellor, J., Higgins, I., Creswell, A., McAleese, N., Wu, A., Elsen, E., Jayakumar, S., Buchatskaya, E., Budden, D., Sutherland, E., Simonyan, K., Paganini, M., Sifre, L., Martens, L., Li, X. L., Kuncoro, A., Nematzadeh, A., Gribovskaya, E., Donato, D., Lazaridou, A., Mensch, A., Lespiau, J.-B., Tsimpoukelli, M., Grigorev, N., Fritz, D., Sottiaux, T., Pajarskas, M., Pohlen, T., Gong, Z., Toyama, D., de Masson d'Autume, C., Li, Y., Terzi, T., Mikulik, V., Babuschkin, I., Clark, A., de Las Casas, D., Guy, A., Jones, C., Bradbury, J., Johnson, M., Hechtman, B., Weidinger, L., Gabriel, I., Isaac, W., Lockhart, E., Osindero, S., Rimell, L., Dyer, C., Vinyals, O., Ayoub, K., Stanway, J., Bennett, L., Hassabis, D., Kavukcuoglu, K., and Irving, G. (2021). Scaling Language Models: Methods, Analysis & Insights from Training Gopher. *arXiv [cs.CL]*.

Raffel, C., Shazeer, N., Roberts, A., Lee, K., Narang, S., Matena, M., Zhou, Y., Li, W., and Liu, P. J. (2020). Exploring the Limits of Transfer Learning with a Unified Text-to-Text Transformer. *Journal of Machine Learning Research*, 21(140):1–67.

Rei, R., Stewart, C., Farinha, A. C., and Lavie, A. (2020). COMET: A neural framework for MT evaluation. In *Proceedings of the 2020 Conference on Empirical Methods in Natural Language Processing (EMNLP)*, pages 2685–2702, Online. Association for Computational Linguistics.

Sawai, R., Paik, I., and Kuwana, A. (2021). Sentence Augmentation for Language Translation Using GPT-2. *Electronics*, 10(24):3082.

Sennrich, R., Haddow, B., and Birch, A. (2016). Improving Neural Machine Translation Models with Monolingual Data. In *Proceedings of the 54th Annual Meeting of the Association for Computational Linguistics (Volume 1: Long Papers)*, pages 86–96, Berlin, Germany. Association for Computational Linguistics.

Shliazhko, O., Fenogenova, A., Tikhonova, M., Mikhailov, V., Kozlova, A., and Shavrina, T. (2022). mGPT: Few-Shot Learners Go Multilingual. *arXiv [cs.CL].*

Smith, S., Patwary, M., Norick, B., LeGresley, P., Rajbhandari, S., Casper, J., Liu, Z., Prabhumoye, S., Zerveas, G., Korthikanti, V., Zhang, E., Child, R., Aminabadi, R. Y., Bernauer, J., Song, X., Shoeybi, M., He, Y., Houston, M., Tiwary, S., and Catanzaro, B. (2022). Using DeepSpeed and Megatron to Train Megatron-Turing NLG 530B, A Large-Scale Generative Language Model. *arXiv [cs.CL].*

Snover, M., Dorr, B., Schwartz, R., Micciulla, L., and Makhoul, J. (2006). A study of translation edit rate with targeted human annotation. In *Proceedings of the 7th Conference of the Association for Machine Translation in the Americas: Technical Papers*, pages 223–231, Cambridge, Massachusetts, USA. Association for Machine Translation in the Americas.

Specia, L., Li, Z., Pino, J., Chaudhary, V., Guzmán, F., Neubig, G., Durrani, N., Belinkov, Y., Koehn, P., Sajjad, H., Michel, P., and Li, X. (2020). Findings of the WMT 2020 Shared Task on Machine Translation Robustness. In *Proceedings of the Fifth Conference on Machine Translation*, pages 76–91, Online. Association for Computational Linguistics.

Stergiadis, E., Kumar, S., Kovalev, F., and Levin, P. (2021). Multi-Domain Adaptation in Neural Machine Translation Through Multidimensional Tagging. In *Proceedings of Machine Translation Summit XVIII: Users and Providers Track*, pages 396–420, Virtual. Association for Machine Translation in the Americas.

Sung, M., Lee, J., Yi, S., Jeon, M., Kim, S., and Kang, J. (2021). Can language models be biomedical knowledge bases? In *Proceedings of the 2021 Conference on Empirical Methods in Natural Language Processing*, pages 4723–4734, Online and Punta Cana, Dominican Republic. Association for Computational Linguistics.

Tiedemann, J. (2012). Parallel data, tools and interfaces in OPUS. In *Proceedings of the Eighth International Conference on Language Resources and Evaluation (LREC'12)*, pages 2214–2218, Istanbul, Turkey. European Language Resources Association (ELRA).

Tran, C., Bhosale, S., Cross, J., Koehn, P., Edunov, S., and Fan, A. (2021). Facebook AI's WMT21 News Translation Task Submission. In *Proceedings of the Sixth Conference on Machine Translation*, pages 205–215, Online. Association for Computational Linguistics.

Vaswani, A., Shazeer, N., Parmar, N., Uszkoreit, J., Jones, L., Gomez, A. N., Kaiser, L., and Polosukhin, I. (2017). Attention Is All You Need. In *Advances in Neural Information Processing Systems (NIPS 2017)*, volume 30. Curran Associates, Inc.

Wang, B. and Komatsuzaki, A. (2021). GPT-J-6B: A 6 Billion Parameter Autoregressive Language Model. *EleutherAI.*

Wang, S., Tu, Z., Tan, Z., Wang, W., Sun, M., and Liu, Y. (2021). Language models are good translators. *ArXiv*.

Wenzek, G., Chaudhary, V., Fan, A., Gomez, S., Goyal, N., Jain, S., Kiela, D., Thrush, T., and Guzmán, F. (2021). Findings of the WMT 2021 Shared Task on Large-Scale Multilingual Machine Translation. In *Proceedings of the Sixth Conference on Machine Translation*, pages 89–99, Online. Association for Computational Linguistics.

Xu, J., Crego, J., and Senellart, J. (2020). Boosting Neural Machine Translation with Similar Translations. In *Proceedings of the 58th Annual Meeting of the Association for Computational Linguistics*, pages 1580–1590, Online. Association for Computational Linguistics.

Yang, Z., Dai, Z., Yang, Y., Carbonell, J., Salakhutdinov, R., and Le, Q. V. (2019). XLNet: Generalized Autoregressive Pretraining for Language Understanding. In *Advances in Neural Information Processing Systems (NeurIPS 2019)*, volume 32. Curran Associates, Inc.

Zhang, S., Roller, S., Goyal, N., Artetxe, M., Chen, M., Chen, S., Dewan, C., Diab, M., Li, X., Lin, X. V., Mihaylov, T., Ott, M., Shleifer, S., Shuster, K., Simig, D., Koura, P. S., Sridhar, A., Wang, T., and Zettlemoyer, L. (2022). OPT: Open Pre-trained Transformer Language Models. *arXiv [cs.CL]*.

Zhang, Z., Han, X., Zhou, H., Ke, P., Gu, Y., Ye, D., Qin, Y., Su, Y., Ji, H., Guan, J., Qi, F., Wang, X., Zheng, Y., Zeng, G., Cao, H., Chen, S., Li, D., Sun, Z., Liu, Z., Huang, M., Han, W., Tang, J., Li, J., Zhu, X., and Sun, M. (2021). CPM: A Large-scale Generative Chinese Pre-trained Language Model. *AI Open*, 2:93–99.

Zhu, J., Xia, Y., Wu, L., He, D., Qin, T., Zhou, W., Li, H., and Liu, T.-Y. (2020). Incorporating BERT into Neural Machine Translation. In *Proceedings of the 8th International Conference on Learning Representations, ICLR 2020*, Virtual.

Strategies for Adapting Multilingual Pre-training for Domain-Specific Machine Translation

Neha Verma nverma7@jhu.edu
Kenton Murray kenton@jhu.edu
Kevin Duh kevinduh@cs.jhu.edu
Johns Hopkins University, Baltimore, USA

Abstract

Pretrained multilingual sequence-to-sequence models have been successful in improving translation performance for mid- and lower-resourced languages. However, it is unclear if these models are helpful in the domain adaptation setting, and if so, how to best adapt them to both the domain *and* translation language pair. Therefore, in this work, we propose two major fine-tuning strategies: our *language-first* approach first learns the translation language pair via general bitext, followed by the domain via in-domain bitext, and our *domain-first* approach first learns the domain via multilingual in-domain bitext, followed by the language pair via language pair-specific in-domain bitext. We test our approach on 3 domains at different levels of data availability, and 5 language pairs. We find that models using an mBART initialization generally outperform those using a random Transformer initialization. This holds for languages even outside of mBART's pretraining set, and can result in improvements of over +10 BLEU. Additionally, we find that via our domain-first approach, fine-tuning across multilingual in-domain corpora can lead to stark improvements in domain adaptation without sourcing additional out-of-domain bitext. In larger domain availability settings, our domain-first approach can be competitive with our language-first approach, even when using over 50X less bitext.

1 Introduction

Recent pretrained multilingual sequence-to-sequence (seq2seq) models have provided a basis to easily create neural machine translation (MT) systems via the pretrain and fine-tune paradigm ubiquitous throughout NLP (Liu et al., 2020; Xue et al., 2021). Due to the fact that fine-tuning these models generally requires less data than is needed for from-scratch translation models, pretrained models are great candidates for MT domain adaptation tasks, where domain-specific bitext is generally less available as compared to general bitext. However, these models have seldom been studied in domain-specific settings.

For MT domain adaptation, pretrained multilingual seq2seq models must be adapted to both 1) the language pair and 2) the domain of interest. Previous work has introduced several methods for adapting general translation models to domains, including training first on general bitext to bolster the total amount of bitext available, followed by training on smaller domain-specific bitext (Luong and Manning, 2015; Freitag and Al-Onaizan, 2016). However, in the case of multilingual sequence models, the initial pretraining objective differs significantly from the task of machine translation, which suggests that alternative adaptation approaches are necessary. Additionally, approaches involving additional general bitext may not even benefit these models as they were already initially trained on large amounts of general pretraining data.

Therefore, it is currently unclear 1) if pretrained multilingual seq2seq models have useful properties for MT domain adaptation and 2) how to best adapt them to both the translation language pair *and* domain. As a result, in this work, we aim to systematically compare fine-tuning approaches for applying mBART to domain adaptation (Liu et al., 2020). We choose to focus on mBART as it has previously shown the most promising results in the MT setting among comparable models (Liu et al., 2021; Lee et al., 2022).

By framing language pair and domain as decoupled entities to learn during the fine-tuning process, we can compare two major approaches to the adaptation process. The first fine-tunes mBART on general bitext, followed by in-domain bitext. The second uses multilingual fine-tuning on in-domain bitext across several language pairs followed by bilingual fine-tuning on in-domain bitext in the language pair of interest (Tang et al., 2020). In other words, the first approach adapts to the *language pair* first, and the second approach adapts to the *domain* first, before both eventually fine-tune on the small amount of in-domain, language pair-specific bitext. We emphasize the importance of a multi-staged approach as we find that they are consistently better than naively fine-tuning mBART only on domain-specific bitext, especially when this data is limited.

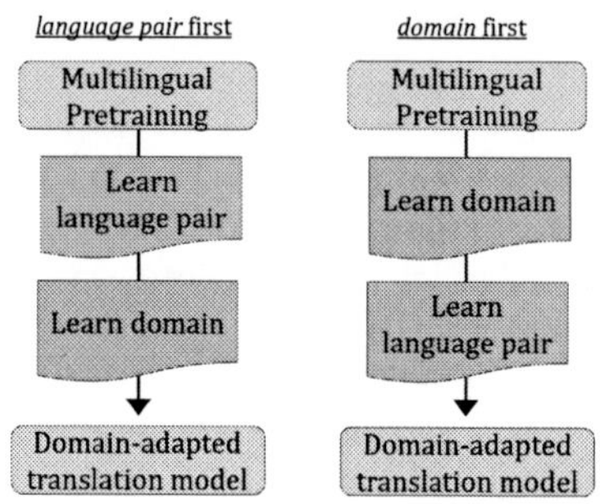

Figure 1: Summaries of our two major approaches. Our language pair first approach first fine-tunes the multilingual pretrained model on language-pair specific translation, and then on the domain. Our domain first approach first fine-tunes the multilingual pretrained model on the domain of interest, followed by the specific language pair.

We test our approach on 5 language pairs and 3 domains: TED Talks, Microblogs, and COVID-19 related information. We note that the amount of available in-domain bitext varies greatly across these domains. Because we want our method to be broadly applicable to new domains where data may be very limited and/or expensive to procure, we test our approaches on a small, fixed amount of domain data, as well as on the entirety of the domain data available. We find that in comparable approaches, those with an mBART initialization outperform those with a vanilla Transformer initialization in a majority of our language pairs and domains, and across our two domain availability settings. This holds even in the cases of higher-resourced language pairs originally unhelped by mBART's multilingual pretraining, and in language pairs outside of mBART's pretraining set. For our out-of-mBART Persian-English language pair, simply using an mBART initialization leads to +4.8 to 12.8 BLEU points across our domains. In addition, we find that our domain-first approach provides an efficient alternative to using additional general bitext by leveraging available multilingual in-domain corpora via multilingual fine-tuning. We show that in our whole domain availability setting, which is still several times smaller than the data needed for our language-first approach, our domain-first approach consistently shows improvements over baselines, and is sometimes competitive with our more data-heavy language-first approach.

This paper makes the following contributions:

- We explore various approaches for fine-tuning multilingual sequence models for specialized domains in machine translation. We demonstrate that our multi-step fine-tuning approaches can out-perform single-step and non-pretrained baselines—even for language pairs that normally do not see benefits from using multilingual models.
- We demonstrate the importance of in-domain data, showing that fine-tuning on this with multiple languages outperforms methods only using in-domain data in the target setting.
- We are able to get substantial BLEU point improvements on languages that are *not even included* during pretraining.

2 Background and Related Work

2.1 mBART

mBART is a pretrained multilingual sequence-to-sequence denoising autoencoder based on the Transformer architecture (Liu et al., 2020). Using the self-supervised BART objectives of masked language modeling and sentence permutations (Lewis et al., 2020), mBART is trained to recover noised Common Crawl texts across 25 languages. When fine-tuned on bitext for sentence-level machine translation, mBART's pretraining leads to performance gains across multiple low- and medium-resource language pairs. The shared, multilingual parameter space in the single encoder-decoder model are thought to be particularly helpful in lower-resourced language pairs. In the original release of mBART, fine-tuning on a single language pair, or bilingual fine-tuning, was the proposed method of adapting mBART to the translation task.

However, in follow up work, Tang et al. (2020) propose multilingual fine-tuning, where mBART is fine-tuned on bitext across multiple language pairs at the same time, creating a model capable of multilingual machine translation. Multilingual fine-tuning was shown to result in improvements over bilingual fine-tuning for translation, especially in the many-to-one setting where multiple languages are translated into the same target language.

2.2 Domain Adaptation

Generally, MT systems drop in performance when applied in a domain different from the training data, in a scenario known as domain mismatch (Koehn and Knowles, 2017). Additionally, while large amounts of general bitext may be available for a language pair, it is generally harder to find large amounts of data that fit a specific domain.

Continued training, or fine tuning, is a common training procedure-related approach to MT domain adaptation where a model first trains to convergence on general bitext, and then continues to train on domain-specific bitext (Luong and Manning, 2015). In this work, we expand upon the original multi-step fine-tuning ideas from continued training for domain adaptation.

Later work has focused on more complex ways to select and order data for domain adaptation. Xu et al. (2021) propose gradual fine-tuning for iteratively training a model on data that slowly approaches the distribution of the in-domain data. Xie et al. (2021) also use gradual fine-tuning to select data to adapt a multilingual MT model to in-domain data. Similar to gradual fine-tuning with respect to purposefully ordering samples for domain adaptation, curriculum learning based approaches have been proposed to sort and order samples based on their similarity to the domain of interest (Zhang et al., 2019). Dynamic data selection techniques have also been proposed to alter available training data between epochs in order to present more relevant data in later stages of training (van der Wees et al., 2017). While these methods enforce a stricter curriculum at a sample level, we draw inspiration from these methods by adhering to a coarse ordering of least-domain-relevant to most-domain-relevant (Saunders, 2021).

Recent work has introduced domain adaptation techniques for multilingual MT systems. One such work proposes methods for multilingual and multi-domain adaptation via domain-specific and language-specific adapter modules (Cooper Stickland et al., 2021). Dabre et al. (2019) exploit multi-parallel domain corpora in one-to-many multilingual MT setup to boost low-resource domain translation. Another closely related work, which specifically looks at the use of mBART for poetry translation, introduces multilingual fine-tuning for domain adaptation using mBART50 (Chakrabarty et al., 2021; Tang et al., 2020). In this domain, multilingual fine-tuning on available domain data was shown to outperform multilingual fine-tuning on general bitext, as well as bilingual fine-tuning on domain data, hinting at the use of multilingual in-domain data as an important tool in multilingual MT domain adaptation. In a comprehensive overview of the capabilities of mBART, Lee et al. (2022) find that mBART fine-tuned on smaller amounts of in-domain bitext can outperform a Transformer translation model trained on larger amounts of in-domain bitext, suggesting that mBART's pretraining may be valuable for domain adaptation in lower-resourced domains. In this work, we expand upon and formalize these initial results suggesting that mBART may be useful for domain adaptation, and provide a comparison of various techniques for pretrained model-specific domain adaptation.

3 Approach

Because mBART is a multilingual denoising autoencoder, it is trained only to reconstruct text in the source language given. We detail our two major approaches to domain adaptation using mBART, focusing on translation language pair and domain. Our approaches propose two different ways to learn these competencies. We summarize our approaches in Figures 2 and 3.

3.1 Language Pair First

In our language pair first approach, we first focus on adapting mBART to the specific language pair, and then to the domain of interest. We note that in all of our experiments, we have several source languages, and one target language. For our i^{th} source language S_i and target language T, we label general bitext as $B_{gen}(S_i, T)$, and in-domain bitext as $B_{in}(S_i, T)$. In the first stage, we fine-tune our original model, M_0 on $B_{gen}(S_i, T)$ to achieve a general-domain bilingual translation model, denoted as $M_{gen}(S_i, T)$. In the second stage, we fine-tune $M_{gen}(S_i, T)$ on $B_{in}(S_i, T)$, obtaining our final domain adapted bilingual model, $M_{in}(S_i, T)$, as desired. This approach is very similar to the conventional continued training approach for domain adaptation where a MT model is trained on out-of-domain bitext, and then subsequently fine tuned on the smaller in-domain bitext. The key difference between this approach and a general continued training approach for domain adaptation is the initialization of model parameters that mBART's pretraining provides.

Symbol	Reference
S_i	ith source language
T	target language
$B_{gen}(S_i, T)$	general bitext from S_i to T
$B_{in}(S_i, T)$	in domain bitext from S_i to T
M_0	original model, before fine-tuning
$M_{gen}(S_i, T)$	general domain translation model from S_i to T
$M_{in}(S_i, T)$	in-domain translation model from S_i to T

3.2 Domain First

In our domain-first approach, we first focus on adapting mBART to the domain of interest, and then adapt to the relevant language pair. Because at first we adapt only to the domain, and not yet language pair, we propose to perform the first stage via multilingual fine-tuning on

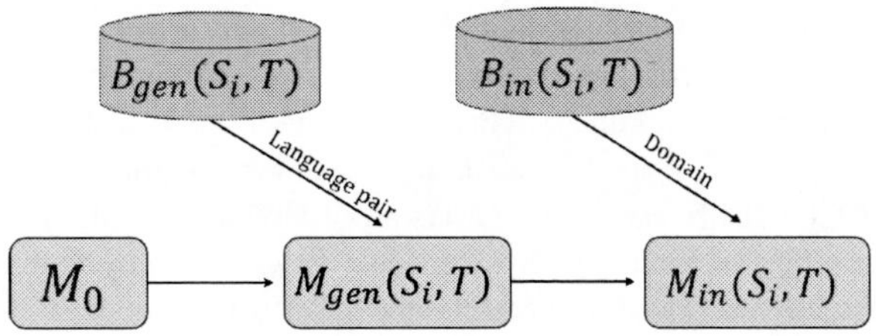

Figure 2: Our language pair first approach. We first fine-tune our original model, M_0 on general bitext, $B_{gen}(S_i, T)$, to create a language-pair adapted model, $M_{gen}(S_i, T)$. We then fine-tune our new interim model on in-domain bitext, $B_{in}(S_i, T)$, to achieve a both language pair- and domain-adapted translation model: $M_{in}(S_i, T)$.

available domain data (Tang et al., 2020). In particular, we focus on many-to-one fine-tuning. In this case, we denote a multilingual in-domain dataset as the union of all available bilingual in-domain datasets: $\bigcup_i B_{in}(S_i, T)$.

In the first stage, we multilingually fine-tune our original model, M_0 on $\bigcup_i B_{in}(S_i, T)$ to achieve a domain-specific and multilingual translation model, denoted as $M_{in}(\bigcup_i S_i, T)$. In our second step, we reintroduce $B_{in}(S_i, T)$ that matches our language pair of interest, and bilingually fine-tune $M_{in}(\bigcup_i S_i, T)$ on $B_{in}(S_i, T)$ to achieve our final domain-adapted bilingual model, $M_{in}(S_i, T)$. Because this approach only uses in-domain data and does not introduce external data, its training can use noticeably less data for domains with limited data, as compared to our language-first approach.

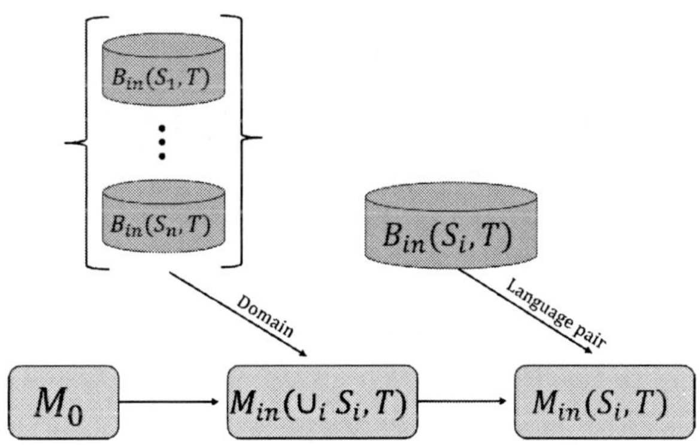

Figure 3: Our domain first approach. We first fine-tune our original model, M_0 on multilingual in-domain bitext, $\bigcup_i B_{in}(S_i, T)$, to create a domain adapted model, $M_{in}(\bigcup_i S_i, T)$. We then fine-tune our new interim model on translation pair-specific in-domain bitext, $B_{in}(S_i, T)$, to achieve a both domain- and language pair-adapted translation model: $M_{in}(S_i, T)$. We note that this approach can use far less data than our language-first approach.

3.3 Limiting the Amount of Domain Data

In comparing our approaches in adapting mBART for domain-specific MT, we also compare two scenarios in which 1) all available domain data is included, the size of which can very greatly by domain, and 2) domain data is heavily limited ($\leq$ 1000 lines). In our first scenario, where all domain data is used, we wish to provide comparisons of our domain adaptation techniques at original levels of domain availability. By keeping all data, we can make recommendations for domains that may be more available than in our limited setting. Our second scenario aims to compare our methods across each domains via a fixed amount of data, as some of our domain data is very limited ($\leq$ 1000 lines). This is the case of the Translation Initiative for COVID-19 challenge, where domain-specific translation is needed to quickly translate emergency content related to the COVID-19 pandemic (Anastasopoulos et al., 2020). Additionally, being able to create data-efficient methods helps reduce cost of dataset creation. For example, current translation services are priced around 0.06 to 0.12 US Dollars per word[1], and Germann (2001) note services costing up to 0.30 US Dollars per word. Assuming an average of 20 words per sentence, it can cost anywhere from approximately \$1,200 to \$6,000 to create a small 1000 line dataset. By including these two levels of domain availability, we hope to show the efficiency of our methods, as well as their generalizability to additional domains.

4 Experiments

4.1 Data

We translate 5 languages into English for our experiments: Arabic (ar), Persian (fa), Portuguese (pt), Russian (ru), and Chinese (zh). Arabic, Russian, and Chinese appear in mBART25's pretraining set, and Portuguese and Persian do not.

For each of our language pairs, we piece together general bitext from OPUS sources (Tiedemann, 2012). The general bitext make up part of our language-first adaptation approach. In particular, depending on availability, we sample bitext from Global Voices (GV), QCRI Educational Domain (QED), the United Nations Parallel Corpus (UN), Open Subtitles (OS), and Europarl (EP) (Nguyen and Daumé III, 2019; Abdelali et al., 2014; Ziemski et al., 2016; Lison and Tiedemann, 2016; Koehn, 2005). We first collect 1.5 million lines from these combined sources. We then remove sentences with more than 50% punctuation, deduplicate our data, remove all evaluation data from training data, and apply length ratio cleaning (Fan et al., 2021). We shuffle all lines and sample 1 million sentence pairs for a general bitext training set, and 2000 for a development set. The full composition of our general bitext is detailed in Table 1.

For domain adaptation, we choose 3 different domains with varying levels of data availability. We use translations of TED talks (Duh, 2018), Microblogs (McNamee and Duh, 2022), and documents from the Translation Initiative for COVID-19 (TICO-19) (Anastasopoulos et al., 2020). We note that originally, the TICO-19 dataset contains only 971 sentences in a development set, and 2100 in a test set. In our work, we split the original test set to create a new development and test set with 1050 lines each, and reallocate the original 971-line development set into our training set.[2] For each domain, we detail the amount available training data in Table 1. TED dev/test splits are 1958/1982 lines, and Microblog dev/test splits are 3000/3000 lines for ar-en and ru-en, and 2000/2000 lines for fa-en, pt-en, and zh-en.

For our multilingual fine-tuning experiments for our domain-first approach, we include additional languages that are available in the domain, included in mBART's pretraining set, and do not overlap with our language proxies for our out-of-mBART languages. For TED, we add Czech, German, French, Japanese, Korean, Romanian, and Vietnamese (12 languages total). For Microblogs, we add French and Korean (7 languages total). For TICO-19, we add French, Burmese, and Nepali (8 languages total).

To measure the amount of domain shift between our general bitext and our domain-specific bitext, we train a 5-gram language model with KenLM on our general bitext target-side training data, and evaluate the perplexity (including OOVs) on the target-side training data for each of our domains. We provide perplexity measures on our domain-specific bitext after applying

[1]https://gengo.com/pricing-languages/

[2]We create our own data split because the original TICO-19 data does not have a training set we could use for fine-tuning. Our TICO-19 results should not be directly compared with those from other papers.

	TED # lines	Micro. # lines	TICO # lines	Gen. # lines	GV %	QED %	UN %	OS %	EP %
ar-en	175377	18634	971	1M	3.5	33.4	31.6	31.5	0
fa-en	116525	2647	971	1M	0.7	1.1	0	98.2	0
pt-en	153357	2085	971	1M	5.8	28.8	0	32.7	32.7
ru-en	181465	36734	971	1M	11.4	37.6	25.5	25.5	0
zh-en	170341	1580	971	1M	8.5	0.9	45.3	45.3	0
add'l.	988691	35710	2991	-	-	-	-	-	-
total	1785756	97390	7976	-	-	-	-	-	-

Table 1: Sizes in # of lines for each of the domain and general corpora used in our work. We also provide the number of lines added with domain data from additional language pairs. We additionally provide a breakdown of our general bitext across 5 OPUS sources. For our limited domain experiments, we use 1K sentences per domain and language pair.

byte-pair encoding (Sennrich et al., 2016), and we measure vocabulary coverage on our data that is tokenized with the Moses tokenizer, but not byte-pair encoded (Koehn et al., 2007). We report vocabulary coverage and perplexity values in Table 2.

	TED	Micro.	TICO
vocab coverage	99.9%	95.7%	97.2%
perplexity	2.65	740.53	366.67

Table 2: Vocabulary coverage and perplexity for each of our domains. We train 5-gram language models on our general domain target data, and evaluate vocabulary coverage and perplexity on our domain target-side training data. We see that our Microblogs corpus has the largest domain shift while TED has the smallest, according to our perplexity measure.

4.2 Models

For all of our experiments using mBART, we use `mbart.cc25` which has 12 encoder and decoder layers, and covers 25 languages. We note that to begin decoding, mBART requires a language identification token. For our out-of-mBART languages, we choose a related language from the 25 mBART pretraining languages as a language identification token; we use ES as a proxy for PT, and HI for FA (Madaan et al., 2020; Cahyawijaya et al., 2021).

We train our language pair-first approach on 1M lines of general data for up to 10 epochs or 150,000 updates, whichever is first. We then fine-tune the model for up to an additional 10 epochs on domain data for the language pair, for both limited and whole domain availability. For our domain-first approach, we train on multilingual domain data for up to 200,000 updates or 60 epochs (whichever is first) in the whole domain approach, and up to 60 epochs in the limited domain approach. We then fine-tune these models for up to another 60 epochs.

We include two baseline models in our experiments. Baseline model 1 uses a Transformer with no pretraining, and trains on general bitext followed by domain bitext, much like our language first approach. This model uses the transformer_iwslt_de_en architecture as implemented by fairseq (Ott et al., 2019; Vaswani et al., 2017). This model has an embedding dimension of 512, feed-forward dimension of 1024, 4 attention heads, and 6 encoder/decoder layers each. For each language pair, we learn 16k subword operations per language on the general domain bitext, and use the subword vocabulary on our all of our Baseline 1 experiments (Sennrich et al., 2016). Baseline model 2 naively fine-tunes mBART only on in-domain bitext.

We train Baseline 1 first on our general bitext for up to 40 epochs, and then on our domain bitext for up to 10 additional epochs, keeping the best model. We train Baseline 2 for up to 40 epochs in the limited domain setting, and up to 100 epochs in the whole domain setting.

We evaluate all of our models with BLEU, as implemented by SacreBLEU[3] (Post, 2018).

5 Results

	Name	Baseline 1	Language-First	Domain-First	Baseline 2
	Initialization	Random	mBART	mBART	mBART
	Step 1	$B_{gen}(S_i, T)$	$B_{gen}(S_i, T)$	$\bigcup_i B_{in}(S_i, T)$	None
	Step 2	$B_{in}(S_i, T)$	$B_{in}(S_i, T)$	$B_{in}(S_i, T)$	$B_{in}(S_i, T)$
TED	ar-en	37.0	**37.4**	36.0	36.4
	fa-en	25.4	**30.9**	30.2	29.8
	pt-en	46.9	**48.2**	47.7	47.6
	ru-en	**30.3**	29.7	29.1	29.7
	zh-en	19.0	**22.0**	21.5	21.1
	avg	31.7	**33.6**	32.9	32.9
Microblogs	ar-en	40.0	**42.6**	40.8	40.3
	fa-en	17.6	**27.6**	20.9	10.5
	pt-en	40.0	**44.6**	39.7	33.9
	ru-en	43.2	**47.4**	46.8	45.8
	zh-en	19.7	**25.9**	25.4	22.1
	avg	32.1	**37.6**	34.7	30.5

Table 3: BLEU scores for the whole domain data experiments. In this resource setting, we have around 100K total lines in the Microblog domain, and 2M total lines in the TED domain. We find that our language pair-first approach is consistently our best system. We also note that both of our approaches outperform out baselines in a majority of language pair/domain combinations. Besides out-of-mBART languages in our Microblogs domain, our domain-first approach performs competitively, despite using 3X less data in TED, and 50X less data in the Microblogs domain.

5.1 mBART initialization improves domain adaptation

Results for our whole domain setting are summarized in Table 3, and limited domain results appear in Table 4. We recall that both Baseline 1 and our language pair-first setting are fine-tuned on 1M lines of out-of-domain data, followed by in-domain data. In this setting, their main difference is the initialization of parameters via either mBART or a random initialization. We see that in a majority of domain/language pair settings, our language-first approach is our best performing system, and in Table 5, we can see that this simple initialization can lead to drastic improvements of several BLEU points.

mBART initialization improves ru-en in TICO-19 and Microblogs, and improves zh-en in all domains. Both Chinese-English and Russian-English translation were reported to not have benefited from mBART's initialization in original fine-tuning experiments from Liu et al. (2020). We also note that this initialization improves out-of-mBART language pairs, and explain this further in Section 5.4.

5.2 The importance of in-domain data

In our limited domain setting, although our domain-first approach is not consistently competitive with our language-first approach, we do note a large BLEU difference between fine-tuning

[3]Signature: BLEU+case.mixed+numrefs.1+smooth.exp+tok.13a+version.1.5.1

	Name	Baseline 1	Language-First	Domain-First	Baseline 2
	Initialization	Random	mBART	mBART	mBART
	Step 1	$B_{gen}(S_i, T)$	$B_{gen}(S_i, T)$	$\bigcup_i B_{in}(S_i, T)$	None
	Step 2	$B_{in}(S_i, T)$	$B_{in}(S_i, T)$	$B_{in}(S_i, T)$	$B_{in}(S_i, T)$
TED	ar-en	**36.3**	33.5	25.0	17.5
	fa-en	19.9	**24.7**	9.3	2.2
	pt-en	**44.4**	44.3	32.5	22.9
	ru-en	**29.3**	27.6	22.9	17.4
	zh-en	14.6	**17.4**	14.4	9.4
	avg	28.9	**29.5**	20.8	13.9
Microblogs	ar-en	32.8	**37.4**	31.4	26.9
	fa-en	16.0	**26.3**	12.8	8.2
	pt-en	38.8	**43.6**	32.8	22.7
	ru-en	37.0	**42.6**	37.4	30.1
	zh-en	19.5	**25.0**	23.2	20.1
	avg	28.8	**35.0**	27.5	21.6
TICO-19	ar-en	29.7	**32.5**	21.4	21.2
	fa-en	10.8	**23.6**	14.5	10.6
	pt-en	42.3	**45.6**	30.7	29.3
	ru-en	26.9	**30.3**	20.5	20.7
	zh-en	18.1	**23.2**	14.1	13.9
	avg	25.6	**31.0**	20.2	19.1

Table 4: BLEU scores for the limited domain data experiments. In this setting, we limit our bilingual in-domain data to $<$1k sentence pairs. In the limited domain setting, we find that our language pair-first approach consistently outperforms our baselines and our domain-first approach, with the exception of a few language pairs in TED. Additionally, although our domain-first approach does not perform competitively in this resource setting, we see benefits of multilingual in-domain learning by noting its improvements over Baseline 2.

	Limited Domain			Whole Domain	
	TED	**Microblogs**	**TICO-19**	**TED**	**Microblogs**
ar-en	-2.8	4.6	2.8	0.4	2.6
fa-en	4.8	10.3	12.8	5.5	10.0
pt-en	-0.1	5.1	3.3	1.3	4.6
ru-en	-0.9	3.8	0.7	-0.6	4.2
zh-en	2.8	5.5	5.1	3.0	6.2
avg	0.8	5.9	4.9	1.9	5.5

Table 5: ΔBLEU between initializing domain adaptation fine-tuning with mBART vs domain adaptation fine-tuning with a random Transformer initialization. Overall, mBART's initialization improves domain adaptation over a random Transformer initialization. This holds for the fa-en and pt-en language pairs, which are outside of mBART's pretraining set, sometimes leading to improvements of over 10 BLEU points.

on multilingual domain data (domain-first) and fine-tuning on bilingual in-domain data only (Baseline 2). We report these differences in Table 6. By using multilingual in-domain data, we can see up to 10 BLEU point improvements over using in-domain data only in the target setting. We note that we see a reduced efficacy in TICO-19, which may be in part due to its

	Limited Domain			Whole Domain	
	TED	**Microblogs**	**TICO-19**	**TED**	**Microblogs**
ar-en	7.5	4.5	0.2	-0.4	0.5
fa-en	7.1	4.6	3.9	0.4	10.4
pt-en	9.6	10.1	1.4	0.1	5.8
ru-en	5.5	7.3	-0.2	-0.6	1.0
zh-en	5.0	3.1	0.2	0.4	3.3
avg	6.9	5.9	1.1	0.0	4.2

Table 6: ΔBLEU between our domain-first approach using multilingual fine-tuning and our Baseline 2 system, which uses bilingual fine-tuning on our in-domain bitext. The addition of in-domain bitext outside of our source-target pair can be very useful for domain adaptation. The use of a pretrained multilingual model allows us to utilize additional in-domain corpora for improved in-domain performance via a shared parameter space.

multi-parallel nature. This multi-parallel nature also allows any improvement in this domain to be explained purely through multilingual parameter sharing, rather than other factors like increased diversity of tokens appearing in the target setting. In our TED and Microblog domains, using multilingual corpora can lead to much better unigram vocabulary coverage of the target language. For example, only 47% of the Microblog fa-en dev set unigrams are accounted for in the corresponding in-domain training set. However, 74% of these unigrams are accounted for across the in-domain multilingual training sets, providing a possible explanation for these large improvements in our domains besides TICO-19.

In the whole domain setting, we still see strong improvements over Baseline 2 with Microblogs, but modest improvement in the TED setting. However, utilizing multilingual fine-tuning results in ≤ 1 BLEU point of difference here, but is much more efficient by sharing parameters within one model. In Table 2, we see that the TED domain and our general bitext are far more similar than the Microblog or TICO-19 domain and our general bitext. The extent of domain shift may also explain why in the whole domain setting, we see drastic improvement in the Microblogs domain using multilingual fine-tuning, but modest improvement in TED.

5.3 Language-First vs Domain-First

In the limited domain setting, our language-first approach is consistently better than our domain-first approach, and our language-first approach outperforms our baselines in a majority of settings. We believe that in this setting, our limited domain data is insufficient to properly harness the in-domain transfer across languages that we seek to gain from our domain-first approach. Therefore, we recommend the use of additional general bitext in a low resource domain setting.

In the whole domain setting, we see a similar trend, however, the difference between the two proposed approaches is less pronounced. In a majority of language pair/domain combinations, both of our proposed approaches outperform our baselines. In both of our domains in our whole domain setting, and for languages in mBART's pretraining set, the difference between our proposed approaches is within 2 BLEU points. For languages outside of mBART's pretraining set, this difference is a bit more pronounced in the Microblogs domain. This may be due to their small corpus size, where both Microblogs corpora are <3K parallel sentences for both fa-en and pt-en. However, in the TED domain, even fa-en and pt-en have similar performance across the two approaches.

While these two approaches may be comparable in terms of performance, their data and parameter efficiencies are very different. In the language pair-first setting, we use 5M total lines of bitext to create 5 different general-domain fine-tuned models. Fine-tuning these models on in-domain bitext adds additional data overhead. In the domain-first setting, we use under 2M total lines of in-domain bitext across 12 language pairs for TED, and under 100K total lines of domain bitext across 7 language pairs for our Microblogs domain. This approach is also more parameter efficient due to the shared representations across languages for one domain. This in particular holds true for adapting to new languages, as we can reuse our fine-tuned multilingual domain model, rather than bilingually fine-tune mBART on a new language pair as in our language pair-first approach.

5.4 Out-of-mBART languages

As seen in Tables 5 and 6, both of our out-of-mBART language pairs benefit from multilingual training, whether it be at the pretraining stage, or at the fine-tuning stage. In Table 5, we see clear evidence of mBART's utility for both fa-en and pt-en leading to several BLEU point improvements, even in the whole domain setting, where more in-domain bitext in these language pairs is available. We also see clear benefits of multilingual fine-tuning in these language pairs, resulting in consistent improvements in Table 6. Therefore, for languages outside of mBART25 (with a related language within mBART25), we believe that both of our proposed methods could lead to effective domain adaptation.

5.5 Examples

We choose examples from our whole domain Persian-English TED translations to examine differences in outputs generated from our approaches.

Baseline 1:	*No agricultural products will take the reformist of England.*
Baseline 2:	*Without the genetically engineered crops, hunger will take over the U.K.*
Domain-first:	*Without genetically engineered crops, Britain will be hungry.*
Reference:	*Britain will starve without genetically modified crops.*

Baseline 1:	*How are we going to apply human resources?*
Baseline 2:	*How about the resources? How do we feed not billions of people?*
Language-first:	*How about the resources? How do we want to feed nine billion people?*
Reference:	*What about resources? How are we going to feed nine billion people?*

In our first example, we see that in our domain-first approach, the addition of multilingual in-domain bitext likely improves the in-domain style of the translation. While both generated outputs are similar in their "gisting", the style of the in domain-first most closely matches the overall style of TED Talks. In our second example, we see a clear improvement of translation quality at the lexical level as a result of additional bitext in the first fine-tuning step.

6 Conclusion

In this paper, we demonstrate that multilingual pretraining can be very effective in the domain adaptation setting, and we propose two methods of adaptation that are more useful than a naive adaptation approach. We also find that between our methods, our language-first approach where models are first customized to a specific bilingual setting, is consistently our best system, especially in limited domain scenarios. However, we also find that when we first customize our models to a domain, as in our domain-first approach, we achieve considerable translation quality at a fraction of the data needed in our language-first approach. Interestingly, we are also able to show that multilingual pretraining and fine-tuning continue to be effective domain adaptation techniques even when the pretrained model has not seen the language pair before.

References

Abdelali, A., Guzman, F., Sajjad, H., and Vogel, S. (2014). The amara corpus: Building parallel language resources for the educational domain. In Chair), N. C. C., Choukri, K., Declerck, T., Loftsson, H., Maegaard, B., Mariani, J., Moreno, A., Odijk, J., and Piperidis, S., editors, *Proceedings of the Ninth International Conference on Language Resources and Evaluation (LREC'14)*, Reykjavik, Iceland. European Language Resources Association (ELRA).

Anastasopoulos, A., Cattelan, A., Dou, Z.-Y., Federico, M., Federmann, C., Genzel, D., Guzmán, F., Hu, J., Hughes, M., Koehn, P., Lazar, R., Lewis, W., Neubig, G., Niu, M., Öktem, A., Paquin, E., Tang, G., and Tur, S. (2020). TICO-19: the translation initiative for COvid-19. In *Proceedings of the 1st Workshop on NLP for COVID-19 (Part 2) at EMNLP 2020*, Online. Association for Computational Linguistics.

Cahyawijaya, S., Winata, G. I., Wilie, B., Vincentio, K., Li, X., Kuncoro, A., Ruder, S., Lim, Z. Y., Bahar, S., Khodra, M., Purwarianti, A., and Fung, P. (2021). IndoNLG: Benchmark and resources for evaluating Indonesian natural language generation. In *Proceedings of the 2021 Conference on Empirical Methods in Natural Language Processing*, pages 8875–8898, Online and Punta Cana, Dominican Republic. Association for Computational Linguistics.

Chakrabarty, T., Saakyan, A., and Muresan, S. (2021). Don't go far off: An empirical study on neural poetry translation. In *Proceedings of the 2021 Conference on Empirical Methods in Natural Language Processing*, pages 7253–7265, Online and Punta Cana, Dominican Republic. Association for Computational Linguistics.

Cooper Stickland, A., Berard, A., and Nikoulina, V. (2021). Multilingual domain adaptation for NMT: Decoupling language and domain information with adapters. In *Proceedings of the Sixth Conference on Machine Translation*, pages 578–598, Online. Association for Computational Linguistics.

Dabre, R., Fujita, A., and Chu, C. (2019). Exploiting multilingualism through multistage fine-tuning for low-resource neural machine translation. In *Proceedings of the 2019 Conference on Empirical Methods in Natural Language Processing and the 9th International Joint Conference on Natural Language Processing (EMNLP-IJCNLP)*, pages 1410–1416, Hong Kong, China. Association for Computational Linguistics.

Duh, K. (2018). The multitarget TED talks task. `http://www.cs.jhu.edu/~kevinduh/a/multitarget-tedtalks/`.

Fan, A., Bhosale, S., Schwenk, H., Ma, Z., El-Kishky, A., Goyal, S., Baines, M., Celebi, O., Wenzek, G., Chaudhary, V., Goyal, N., Birch, T., Liptchinsky, V., Edunov, S., Auli, M., and Joulin, A. (2021). Beyond english-centric multilingual machine translation. *Journal of Machine Learning Research*, 22(107):1–48.

Freitag, M. and Al-Onaizan, Y. (2016). Fast domain adaptation for neural machine translation. *arXiv preprint arXiv:1612.06897*.

Germann, U. (2001). Building a statistical machine translation system from scratch: How much bang for the buck can we expect? In *Proceedings of the ACL 2001 Workshop on Data-Driven Methods in Machine Translation*.

Koehn, P. (2005). Europarl: A parallel corpus for statistical machine translation. In *Proceedings of Machine Translation Summit X: Papers*, pages 79–86, Phuket, Thailand.

Koehn, P., Hoang, H., Birch, A., Callison-Burch, C., Federico, M., Bertoldi, N., Cowan, B., Shen, W., Moran, C., Zens, R., Dyer, C., Bojar, O., Constantin, A., and Herbst, E. (2007). Moses: Open source toolkit for statistical machine translation. In *Proceedings of the 45th Annual Meeting of the Association for Computational Linguistics Companion Volume Proceedings of the Demo and Poster Sessions*, pages 177–180, Prague, Czech Republic. Association for Computational Linguistics.

Koehn, P. and Knowles, R. (2017). Six challenges for neural machine translation. In *Proceedings of the First Workshop on Neural Machine Translation*, pages 28–39, Vancouver. Association for Computational Linguistics.

Lee, E.-S. A., Thillainathan, S., Nayak, S., Ranathunga, S., Adelani, D. I., Su, R., and McCarthy, A. D. (2022). Pre-trained multilingual sequence-to-sequence models: A hope for low-resource language translation? *arXiv preprint arXiv:2203.08850.*

Lewis, M., Liu, Y., Goyal, N., Ghazvininejad, M., Mohamed, A., Levy, O., Stoyanov, V., and Zettlemoyer, L. (2020). BART: Denoising sequence-to-sequence pre-training for natural language generation, translation, and comprehension. In *Proceedings of the 58th Annual Meeting of the Association for Computational Linguistics*, pages 7871–7880, Online. Association for Computational Linguistics.

Lison, P. and Tiedemann, J. (2016). OpenSubtitles2016: Extracting large parallel corpora from movie and TV subtitles. In *Proceedings of the Tenth International Conference on Language Resources and Evaluation (LREC'16)*, pages 923–929, Portorož, Slovenia. European Language Resources Association (ELRA).

Liu, Y., Gu, J., Goyal, N., Li, X., Edunov, S., Ghazvininejad, M., Lewis, M., and Zettlemoyer, L. (2020). Multilingual denoising pre-training for neural machine translation. *Transactions of the Association for Computational Linguistics*, 8:726–742.

Liu, Z., Winata, G. I., and Fung, P. (2021). Continual mixed-language pre-training for extremely low-resource neural machine translation. In *Findings of the Association for Computational Linguistics: ACL-IJCNLP 2021*, pages 2706–2718, Online. Association for Computational Linguistics.

Luong, M.-T. and Manning, C. (2015). Stanford neural machine translation systems for spoken language domains. In *Proceedings of the 12th International Workshop on Spoken Language Translation: Evaluation Campaign*, pages 76–79, Da Nang, Vietnam.

Madaan, L., Sharma, S., and Singla, P. (2020). Transfer learning for related languages: Submissions to the WMT20 similar language translation task. In *Proceedings of the Fifth Conference on Machine Translation*, pages 402–408, Online. Association for Computational Linguistics.

McNamee, P. and Duh, K. (2022). The multilingual microblog translation corpus: Improving and evaluating translation of user-generated text. In *Proceedings of the 13th Language Resources and Evaluation Conference*, Marseille, France. European Language Resources Association.

Nguyen, K. and Daumé III, H. (2019). Global Voices: Crossing borders in automatic news summarization. In *Proceedings of the 2nd Workshop on New Frontiers in Summarization*, pages 90–97, Hong Kong, China. Association for Computational Linguistics.

Ott, M., Edunov, S., Baevski, A., Fan, A., Gross, S., Ng, N., Grangier, D., and Auli, M. (2019). fairseq: A fast, extensible toolkit for sequence modeling. In *Proceedings of the 2019 Conference of the North American Chapter of the Association for Computational Linguistics (Demonstrations)*, pages 48–53, Minneapolis, Minnesota. Association for Computational Linguistics.

Post, M. (2018). A call for clarity in reporting BLEU scores. In *Proceedings of the Third Conference on Machine Translation: Research Papers*, pages 186–191, Brussels, Belgium. Association for Computational Linguistics.

Saunders, D. (2021). Domain adaptation and multi-domain adaptation for neural machine translation: A survey. *arXiv preprint arXiv:2104.06951*.

Sennrich, R., Haddow, B., and Birch, A. (2016). Neural machine translation of rare words with subword units. In *Proceedings of the 54th Annual Meeting of the Association for Computational Linguistics (Volume 1: Long Papers)*, pages 1715–1725, Berlin, Germany. Association for Computational Linguistics.

Tang, Y., Tran, C., Li, X., Chen, P.-J., Goyal, N., Chaudhary, V., Gu, J., and Fan, A. (2020). Multilingual translation with extensible multilingual pretraining and finetuning. *arXiv preprint arXiv:2008.00401*.

Tiedemann, J. (2012). Parallel data, tools and interfaces in opus. In Chair), N. C. C., Choukri, K., Declerck, T., Dogan, M. U., Maegaard, B., Mariani, J., Odijk, J., and Piperidis, S., editors, *Proceedings of the Eight International Conference on Language Resources and Evaluation (LREC'12)*, Istanbul, Turkey. European Language Resources Association (ELRA).

van der Wees, M., Bisazza, A., and Monz, C. (2017). Dynamic data selection for neural machine translation. In *Proceedings of the 2017 Conference on Empirical Methods in Natural Language Processing*, pages 1400–1410, Copenhagen, Denmark. Association for Computational Linguistics.

Vaswani, A., Shazeer, N., Parmar, N., Uszkoreit, J., Jones, L., Gomez, A. N., Kaiser, L., and Polosukhin, I. (2017). Attention is all you need. In Guyon, I., Luxburg, U. V., Bengio, S., Wallach, H., Fergus, R., Vishwanathan, S., and Garnett, R., editors, *Advances in Neural Information Processing Systems*, volume 30. Curran Associates, Inc.

Xie, W., Hu, B., Yang, H., Yu, D., and Ju, Q. (2021). TenTrans large-scale multilingual machine translation system for WMT21. In *Proceedings of the Sixth Conference on Machine Translation*, pages 439–445, Online. Association for Computational Linguistics.

Xu, H., Ebner, S., Yarmohammadi, M., White, A. S., Van Durme, B., and Murray, K. (2021). Gradual fine-tuning for low-resource domain adaptation. In *Proceedings of the Second Workshop on Domain Adaptation for NLP*, pages 214–221.

Xue, L., Constant, N., Roberts, A., Kale, M., Al-Rfou, R., Siddhant, A., Barua, A., and Raffel, C. (2021). mT5: A massively multilingual pre-trained text-to-text transformer. In *Proceedings of the 2021 Conference of the North American Chapter of the Association for Computational Linguistics: Human Language Technologies*, pages 483–498, Online. Association for Computational Linguistics.

Zhang, X., Shapiro, P., Kumar, G., McNamee, P., Carpuat, M., and Duh, K. (2019). Curriculum learning for domain adaptation in neural machine translation. In *Proceedings of the 2019 Conference of the North American Chapter of the Association for Computational Linguistics: Human Language Technologies, Volume 1 (Long and Short Papers)*, pages 1903–1915, Minneapolis, Minnesota. Association for Computational Linguistics.

Ziemski, M., Junczys-Dowmunt, M., and Pouliquen, B. (2016). The United Nations parallel corpus v1.0. In *Proceedings of the Tenth International Conference on Language Resources and Evaluation (LREC'16)*, pages 3530–3534, Portorož, Slovenia. European Language Resources Association (ELRA).

Prefix Embeddings for In-context Machine Translation

Suzanna Sia ssia1@jhu.edu
Kevin Duh kevinduh@cs.jhu.edu
Johns Hopkins University

Abstract

The class of large generative pretrained (GPT) language models have demonstrated the ability to translate with in-context examples, a phenomena known as few-shot prompting. However, they have not achieved state-of-art results for translating out of English. In this work, we investigate an extremely lightweight fixed-parameter method for conditioning a large language model to better translate into the target language. Our method introduces additional embeddings, refered to as prefix embeddings which do not interfere with the existing weights of the model. Using unsupervised and weakly supervised methods that train only 0.0001% of the model parameters, the simple method improves up to around 5 BLEU points over the baseline when a single prompt example is provided, and up to around 2 BLEU points when 20 prompt examples are provided across 3 domains and 3 languages. We analyze the resulting embeddings' training dynamics, where they lie in the embedding space, and show that these conditional prefixes can be used for both in-context translation and diverse generation of the monolingual target sentence.

1 Introduction

Under the paradigm of in-context learning,[1] large language models have been shown to generate translations when provided with several priming examples, each of which consists of a source sentence and the translated target sentence. These examples, also known as "prompts", are prefixed to the test source sentence, which then conditions the model to generate the test target sentence. Table 1 shows an example of this format, where `[S1]` and `[S2]` are separator tokens prefixing source and target sentence respectively.

This prompt-and-translate phenomena, or *in-context translation*, presents itself as a new paradigm for Machine Translation applications. First, the ability to adapt to different task specifications using prompts suggest that the same model can be used in multiple settings and domains. While there have been several multilingual translation models (Fan et al., 2021; Xue et al., 2021; Ma et al., 2021), the ability to perform unrelated tasks such as Question-Answering in addition to Translation is relatively new. This also presents an interesting shift from supervised Neural Machine Translation (NMT) in terms of data requirements. These models are trained on massive amounts of web text which are not explicitly parallel.[2] In contrast, modern NMT models are trained with millions of lines of parallel text. Unsuprisingly, the lack of supervision comes at a cost. Translating out of English for in-context models still lags behind state-of-art possibly due to low data quality and/or disproportionate amounts of English.

[1]This has also been termed 'few-shot prompting' (Brown et al., 2020), but the field is increasingly converging on 'in-context learning' (Bommasani et al., 2021).

[2]This does not preclude the possibility that parallel sentences may exist in various forms in the crawled web text.

`[S1]` So at this point, music diverged	`[S2]` Donc à partir de là, la musique a divergé.
`[S1]` The actual rigging on the reins on the horse are made from the same sort of thing.	`[S2]` Les attaches sur les rennes du cheval sont faites du même genre de choses.
...	
`[S1]` And that was done with a particle.	`[S2]`

Table 1: A single continuous input sequence presented to the model for decoding a single test source sentence "And that was done with a particle". Given the entire sequence as input, the model proceeds to generate the target sequence after the final `[S2]`. [· · ·] refers to several more `[S1]` en `[S2]` fr pairs.

In this work, we propose the training of **target language prefix embeddings to improve in-context translation.** Targetting specific languages has been explored in NMT models Yang et al. (2021) but much less so for the in-context setting. In contrast to fine-tuning, we do not change existing model weights. This falls into the class of 'fixed-parameter' methods where the original parameters of the model are held fixed and additional parameters are introduced which influence the activation states of the model. Our proposed method differs from the various approaches to "prefix tuning" (Li and Liang, 2021; Qin and Eisner, 2021; Asai et al., 2022; Lester et al., 2021) in that these all require explicit task supervision. Learning the weights of these prefix embeddings is technically straightforward using gradient descent optimisation machinery. We show that these embeddings can be trained unsupervised (subsection 3.2)[3] and also explore the use of a very small set of bitext sentences for weakly supervised training (subsection 3.3). Experiments were conducted across 3 en-fr domains (subsection 4.1) and from English into three languages French (fr), Portugese (pt), and German (de) (subsection 4.2). Overall, for a very small amount of engineering, data collection, and storage effort, training prefix embeddings can give up to 5 BLEU points for the 1-prompt setting, and up to around 2 BLEU points on the 20-prompt setting with a very small amount of bitext (we used 100 parallel sentences).

2 Related Work

Large language models which perform in-context translation Following GPT3 (Brown et al., 2020) which first reported the in-context translation phenomena, subsequent autoregressive Transformer decoder only architectures such as XGLM (Lin et al., 2021) and mGPT (Shliazhko et al., 2022) have explicitly trained in-context models to be multilingual. However decoding out of English still performs more poorly than decoding into English. Hence we focus on the first scenario of decoding out of English.

Prefix Tuning Unlike previous work which directly prefixes the task by prepending to the input (Li and Liang, 2021; Qin and Eisner, 2021; Asai et al., 2022; Lester et al., 2021), we substitute the trained prefixes for the delimiters throughout the prompts before the target language sequence. Our proposed method *prefixes the target sequence, not the task.* This small but significant difference allows monolingual training for the target language without explicit translation task supervision.

Embedding Tuning vs Prefix Tuning across all layers We adopt the embedding level tuning approach which was shown to be competitive with model tuning with an increasing number of parameters on SuperGLUE tasks (Lester et al., 2021). The focus on training prefix embeddings instead of training additional parameters to directly influence activations across all layers is a design choice primarily to accommodate for very large models. Li and Liang (2021) report

[3]Unsupervised in the terminology of Machine Translation means without parallel bitext sentences.

using 250K-500K of parameter training vs. a 345M Roberta model (Liu et al., 2019), which is 4-7% of the parameter space. If we had applied the same parameter ratio to our current model of 2.7B parameters, this would be equivalent to having to train 195M parameters – which is in the same order of magnitude of the Roberta model. We do acknowledge that embedding tuning is less expressive by virtue of having fewer entry points to influence the model's activations, and leave a middle ground solution such as combining with adaptor layers (Houlsby et al., 2019) to future work.

Language ID token training is a typical method in multilingual models, to condition the model for the source and target language. However these tokens are typically trained together with the rest of the model parameters and is a design choice that needs to be made upfront. In contrast, we use a generic large language model that was pretrained with minimal design choices, and then posthoc train a language specific prefix to condition the model to generate sentences in the target language, with the goal of improving in-context translation.

3 Methods

Our approach is motivated by the knowledge that for very large language models trained on web corpora, there is a weaker target language (being translated into) because English is the dominant language on the web. This trend persists even for explicitly multilingual language models (Lin et al., 2021). Our method therefore aims to condition the language model to decode the weaker target language, by learning a language-specific prefix. We first describe the in-context translation setup at test time (subsection 3.1), followed by unsupervised training (subsection 3.2) and weakly supervised training (subsection 3.3) of the target language prefix embedding. At inference time, the corresponding prefix will be used as the separator token between source and target language. Figure 1 illustrates this process.

3.1 In-context Translation

Let $(\mathbf{x}, \mathbf{y}) \in \mathcal{D}_\text{b}$ be a set of translation pairs that the model has access to at inference time, where $\mathbf{x}$ refers to the source sentence and $\mathbf{y}$ refers to the target sentence. Given the separator tokens `[Sx]`, `[Sy]` and the test source sentence $\mathbf{x}_\text{test}$, we can define a prompt layout format $u(\mathbf{x}_\text{test}, \mathcal{D}_\text{b}, \texttt{[Sx]}, \texttt{[Sy]})$ (Table 2), where `[...]` refers to several similarly formatted $\mathbf{x}, \mathbf{y}$ examples from $\mathcal{D}_b$. The default in-context learning model autoregressively generates the target sequence by greedily decoding $\hat{\mathbf{y}} = \text{argmax}_\mathbf{y} p(\mathbf{y}|u(\mathbf{x}, \mathcal{D}_\text{b}, \texttt{[Sx]}, \texttt{[Sy]}))$. Our goal is to learn a target specific prefix `[S*]` that achieves higher $p(\mathbf{y}|u(\mathbf{x}, \mathcal{D}_\text{b}, \texttt{[Sx]}, \texttt{[S*]}))$ for the correct sequence $\mathbf{y}$. We use "*" to indicate that the prefix can be of any length.[4]

`[Sx]` $\mathbf{x}_1$	`[Sy]` $\mathbf{y}_1$
`[Sx]` $\mathbf{x}_2$	`[Sy]` $\mathbf{y}_2$
...	
`[Sx]` $\mathbf{x}_\text{test}$	`[Sy]` ?

Table 2: The prompt layout format from $u(\mathbf{x}_\text{test}, \mathcal{D}_\text{b}, \texttt{[Sx]}, \texttt{[Sy]})$.

3.2 Unsupervised Training (monolingual)

The primary strategy is simple, train `[S*]` such that it conditions the model to generate sequences $\mathbf{y}$ from the target language. We expand the tokenizer and the corresponding embedding

[4]In practice, we use special tokens such as `[0]`, `[1]` $\cdots$, `[n]` for a prefix of length n and verify that these do not have a collision in the tokenizer namespace.

matrix by the number of prefix tokens, and then prepend the special token `[S⋆]` to monolingual sentences during training. A single training sequence is given by "`[S⋆]` $\mathbf{y}$", where $\mathbf{y}$ is typically a sentence or paragraph. Given m sequences from a target language training set $\mathbf{y}_1, \cdots, \mathbf{y}_m \in \mathcal{D}_y$, we train the embedding parameters $\theta = \texttt{Embed([S}\star\texttt{])}$, where `[S⋆]` indexes the additional rows in the embedding matrix. We use cross-entropy loss as is standard with language modeling, and freeze the parameters of the entire network except for θ.

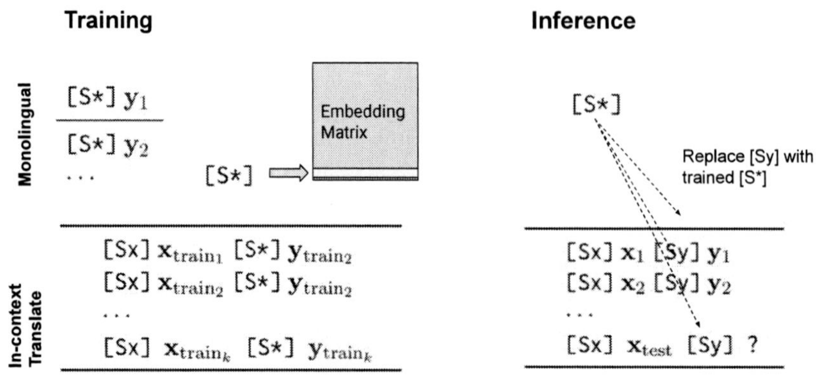

Figure 1: Prompt format for training and inference time. Training loss is computed on the sequences in blue. The token `[S⋆]` corresponds to additional row(s) of the embedding matrix which are the only parameters trained by backpropagation. At inference time, we replace `[Sy]` with the trained `[S⋆]` to conditionally generate $\mathbf{y}_{\text{test}}$. Note that `[S⋆]` can also be used to generate sequences in the target language directly (subsection 5.4).

3.3 Weakly Supervised Training (In-context Translate with Bitext)

In the previous section, training of θ uses only the target language, without any bilingual supervision for the in-context translation task. To guide θ to a better local optima, we include a very small amount of bitext, 100 parallel sentence pairs which are a subset of the training set. We adopt a weakly supervised setup where we initialise the prefix embeddings using existing tokens, and also where the prefix embeddings are initialised from the monolingual trained prefix embeddings (referred to as *mono-trained-lang* in section 4).[5] An alternative training approach is a multi-task setup where losses from the monolingual language modeling and translation tasks are minimised in alternative batches, however this was thought to be less effective due to the extreme data imbalance of the setting that we consider (30k monolingual sentences to 100 bitext pairs), which might require arbitary reweighting schemes. Since the end-goal is translation, directly tuning towards this is a more straightforward approach.

Figure 1 shows a single in-context translate training sample for the model. Note that loss is computed only for the last target sentence $\mathbf{y}_{\text{train}_k}$. In all our experiments we use $k = 6$ for training, i.e., 5 priming examples. For each datapoint, we randomly sample from the $\mathcal{D}_{\text{train}}$ to construct the prompt set, so that the parameters of `[S⋆]` do not overfit to any particular choice of prompt set. Note that for large language models, $|\mathcal{D}_{\text{train}}|$ is less than the number of parameters being trained; a single prefix token has already over 2000 dimensions. We do not

[5]Note that since monolingual data had been used to initialise the prefix, this can be interpreted as a continual semi-supervised learning set up.

expect $\mathcal{D}_{\text{train}}$ to allow the model to learn a mapping for translations, and its role is merely to weakly supervise the training of the monolingual prefix towards loss basins that are compatible with the prompt-translate paradigm.

4 Experiments

We organise our experiments investigating the effects of prefix embedding tuning 1) across three en-fr domains, medical, social media, and TED talks, 2) across three languages in TED Talks.[6] In both sets of experiments, we explore three basic initializations (described in **Prefix Embedding Initialisations**). We also use priming examples of various sizes to investigate if the effects persist across different prompt sizes. To account for prompt selection and ordering effects, all inference runs were repeated with 5 randomly sampled prompt sets from the training data, where each of the source sentences in the prompt examples are between 10 to 20 words long. Scores are reported using SacreBLEU(Post, 2018).[7]

Model We use GPTNeo2.7B (32 layers, 20 heads) (Black et al., 2021) which has been pre-trained on The Pile (Gao et al., 2020). The Pile contains Europarl which has been fed into the model at a document level and not a sentence level.[8] To our knowledge, there has not been any reports of sentence level parallel corpora in the training dataset of this model. Note that unlike most dedicated Machine Translation models which have an encoder-decoder architecture, this model is trained autoregressively and is decoder only. [9]

Data We adopt three datasets; multilingual TED talks (Duh, 2018), MED (Bawden et al., 2019), and MTNT (Michel and Neubig, 2018). We use 30,000 monolingual sentences for unsupervised training of the prefix embeddings (`mono` in results table). For TED, MED and MTNT, the monolingual sentences are obtained from their bitext training data. We use 100 bitext sentence pairs for the weakly supervised case (`bitext` in results table). These bitext sentence pairs served as a self-contained prompt set and training data instances as described in subsection 3.3. In both the unsupervised and weakly supervised scenarios, During testing, we sample sentence pairs for prompts examples from the training set. The sentence pairs in weakly supervised training, validation, and inference time prompt selection are all separate splits; there is no overlap between prompt sets seen across these phases.

Preprocessing We preprocess digits to _ as we find that this helps the prefix tuning to converge for the MED and TED domains, without compromising on the ability to copy or generate digits. We run a langid check and restrict training sentence length to 3 to 25 words to avoid trivial sequences and out-of-memory errors.

Prefix Embedding Initialisation We investigate two simple forms of initialisation

- *random* refers to the default behavior of the model when adding new parameters to the embedding. For GPTNeo model, this is drawn from $\mathcal{N}(0, 0.02)$ as the model uses GELU activation units (Hendrycks and Gimpel, 2016). We report results for *random* using the best out of 3 trained prefix embeddings based on the dev set.

- *lang* uses existing words from the vocabulary which is related to the language and the domain. For fr, pt, de, we initialise with the words "French, Portuguese, German", for

[6] Code at `https://github.com/suzyahyah/prefixes_incontext_machinetranslation`.

[7] nrefs:1 | case:lower | eff:no | tok:13a | smooth:exp | version:2.0.0

[8] `https://github.com/thoppe/The-Pile-EuroParl`

[9] We report SOTA results on the datasets although this is not directly comparable because of completely different training data setup of the base model. TED en-fr: 35.9 en-pt: 38.3 en-de: 28.1 (Renduchintala et al., 2019) MED: 39.5 (Bawden et al., 2019) MTNT: 29.7 (Michel and Neubig, 2018)

MTNT, MED and TED we use "social, medical, talks" respectively. This means that for French MED, we would initialise the first prefix with the embedding corresponding to " French" and the second prefix with the embedding corresponding to "medical". [10]

- *mono-trained-lang* are embeddings initialised from monolingual training (the previous bullet point) for further (weakly) supervised training using 100 additional parallel sentences.

Validation Loss For both monolingual training and weakly supervised bitext training, we use the prompt-translation paradigm as the validation loss. This avoids overfitting to the monolingual target sentence at the expense of being able to translate in the in-context setup. The set of translation prompts for the validation set are randomly drawn from within that set itself, removing dependency on any particular prompt set used at inference time. It may be possible to achieve better performance if practitioners were to use the same prompt set at train, validation and test time.

Training Details We apply early stopping with patience over 5 epochs and threshold 0.001 loss. We adopt 4 gradient accumulation steps with a batch size of 8 for an effective batch size of 32 for the monolingual training, and 4 gradient accumulation steps with a batch size of 2 for an effective batch size of 8 for the weakly supervised bitext training to avoid out-of-memory errors. All experiments can be run with a single NVIDIA-TITAN RTX GPUs (24GB). Monolingual training takes about 1 hour per epoch and can range from 8-20 hours for convergence.

Prompt Format (u) We tried several manual variants of `[Sx]` and `[Sy]` but did not optimise over this extensively. Our preliminary experiments showed that using untrained *lang* tokens in the separator performed slightly better, i.e., using the token "French" as `[Sy]` performed better than a separator choice such as ' `A:`'. We also experimented with prepending the entire prompt sequence with Natural Language Instructions: "Translate English to French" but found that this did not help consistently across datasets, hence we opted to exclude it to simplify design choices and isolate the effects of the trained prefix.

4.1 Results for Performance Across Domains [Table 3]

We present the results for 1-prompt and 20-prompt setting in Table 3. The 1-prompt example shows the extreme case of having no bitext data. While this is perhaps an overly restrictive assumption especially in industrial settings, the goal of this experimental setting is to illustrate the effect of the extreme monolingual scenario. The 20-prompt setting simulates a "saturated" prompt setting, which we also investigate with more prompt intervals in Figure 2.

Unsupervised (monolingual) Prefix Training helps 1-prompt setting. Across all domains, unsupervised (`mono`) prefix training tends to improve BLEU score. This improvement is much more prominent in the 1-prompt setting, with improvements of around 5 BLEU points across the three data domains of MED, TED and MTNT. Recall that the `mono` trained *lang* initialised token embedding has no knowledge of translation and only serves to condition the model to generate the target language.

Weakly supervised (bitext) Prefix Training helps the 20-prompt "saturated" setting. A very small amount of supervision with 100 examples can be used to do better than the baseline (0.3 to 1.3 BLEU point gains).[11] It is not always clear whether initialising from a *mono-trained-lang* embedding helps as the performance is the same for TED and MED, but slightly better (0.5 gains) for MTNT. Looking at the 1-prompt case for `bitext`, *mono-trained-lang* always does

[10]Note that having two words does not necessarily correspond to having two tokens.

[11]How much supervision is required? We separately find that increasing from 100 to 1000 training examples performs within 0.1 BLEU points of the `bitext` *mono-trained-lang* (last column of Table 3.

			untrained	mono (unsupervised)		bitext (supervised)	
exp	direction	nprompts	*lang*	*random*	*lang*	*lang*	*mono-trained-lang*
MED	en-fr	1	8,8 (1.6)	**13.3*(2.4)**	12.0*(4.8)	7.6 (4.8)	10.7 (4.1)
MTNT	en-fr	1	10.7 (3.5)	7.3 (4.2)	**15.5*(2.5)**	14.2 (2.6)	18.4 (1.3)
TED	en-fr	1	12.7 (4.7)	16.4*(3.8)	**17.7*(2.1)**	18.8 (1.1)	19.1 (0.9)
MED	en-fr	20	17.9 (0.7)	11.5 (1.4)	18.1 (0.8)	**18.4*(0.5)**	**18.4*(0.5)**
MTNT	en-fr	20	21.0 (0.6)	1.5 (0.9)	21.2 (0.3)	21.5*(0.4)	**22.0*(0.4)**
TED	en-fr	20	22.5 (0.2)	21.2 (0.9)	22.2 (0.2)	**22.8 (0.2)**	**22.8 (0.1)**

Table 3: BLEU points across different domains of Medical (MED), Social Media (MTNT) and TED Talks. We report the average of 5 random prompt sets with standard deviation. The best result is in bold row-wise, and (*) indicates $p < 0.01$ for a paired permutation test (1000 rounds) against the baseline (untrained). For 1-prompt case, this assumes that there is no bitext available, although we report bitext results (in lightgray) for the sake of completeness. The number of prefixes tokens for all experiments in this table is 2.

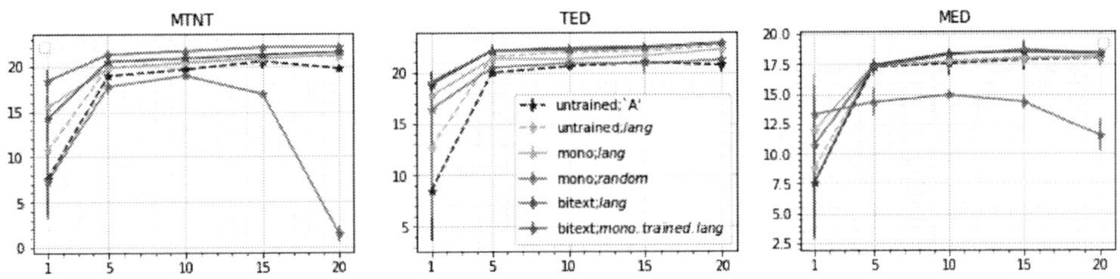

Figure 2: k-shot performance with trained prefixes on MTNT, TED and MED datasets for en-fr. Plots show $k = \{1, 5, 10, 15, 20\}$ examples on the x-axis. Baselines include lang token without further training (untrained; *lang*), an "A" token without further training (untrained; *'A'*), and the best out of 3 randomly initialised embeddings (mono; *random*).

better than *lang*, indicating that there is still an effect of having higher scores over the target language logits, but that this effect vanishes with increasing prompts.

Plateau effect across increasing number of prompt sets. We observe a plateau effect after 5 prompts which is consistent with the hypothesis that the primary role of prompts is task location rather than instruction (Reynolds and McDonell, 2021). With regards to individual prompt set selection, we find that improvements occur across all prompt sets that had been randomly selected, strongly suggesting that the improvements from training the target language prefix are orthogonal (or can be used independently) of prompt selection and ordering effects to achieve better translation results. We further analyse the improvements at a sentence level in subsection 5.3.

Random initialisation has high variance. If not correctly initialised, the prefix might not converge to a good local optima for in-context translation and can result in worse performances than baseline despite having low perplexity on the monolingual training set. Very occasionally we might observe a stronger performance, in the case of mono *random* in the 1-prompt setting). This suggests that the primary reason why a monolingual trained prefix can still have good performance when used in the in-context translation setting, is because it still retains properties from the word embedding that it is initialised from that are compliant with the activation states for in-context translation.

4.2 Performance Across Languages

In this section we presents experiments with GPTNeo2.7B on TED talks for German(de) and Portugese (pt). Overall the results are encouraging for prefix training; we observe improvements in the 1-prompt setting with `mono` *lang*, and in the 20-prompt setting with `bitext` *mono-trained-lang* with en-de and en-pt. The limited en-pt gain may be explained by the already high scores on the `untrained` *lang* at 22.0 BLEU, but it remains unclear why the improvements are limited for en-de.

exp	direction	nprompts	`untrained` *lang*	`mono` (unsupervised) *lang*	`bitext` (supervised) *lang*	`bitext` (supervised) *mono-trained-lang*
TED	en-fr	1	12.7 (4.7)	**17.7*(2.1)**	18.8 (1.1)	19.1 (0.9)
TED	en-de	1	8.5 (2.2)	**9.7*(2.2)**	13.6 (0.6)	15.1 (0.5)
TED	en-pt	1	22.0 (0.7)	**22.9*(0.8)**	24.3 (0.8)	25.0 (1.2)
TED	en-fr	20	22.5 (0.2)	22.2 (0.2)	**22.8 (0.2)**	**22.8 (0.1)**
TED	en-de	20	16.6 (0.3)	16.1 (0.6)	17.4*(0.2)	**17.6*(0.2)**
TED	en-pt	20	24.9 (0.4)	25.8*(0.9)	**27.2*(0.4)**	26.8*(0.2)

Table 4: BLEU points across different language directions translating from English (en) to French (fr), Portugese (pt), German (de). We report the average of 5 random prompt sets with standard deviation. The best result is in bold row-wise and (*) indicates $p < 0.01$ for a paired permutation test (1000 rounds) against the baseline (`untrained`). For 1-prompt case, this assumes that there is no bitext available, although we report bitext results (in lightgray) for the sake of completeness. The number of prefixes tokens for all experiments in this table is 2.

Effect across languages are not equal. Translation into de and pt for the 20-prompt setting under very weak supervision of 100 bitext examples gives around 1 to 2 point gains which is slightly more encouraging than en-fr, suggesting that the performance gains are not equal across languges. Curiously, the corresponding gains from the 1-prompt setting for en-de and en-pt are much smaller around 1 point compared to the 5 point gain for the 1-prompt setting in en-fr.

5 Analysis

5.1 Trained Prefix in Embedding Space

What is the difference between *lang* initialised and *random* initialised prefix embeddings? To get a better of understanding of the local minima, we compare them before and after training. In Table 5 we present the top 20 closest tokens by cosine distance to the prefix (before and after), and in Figure 3 we observe the 'density' of the closest 50 tokens by cosine distance in a PCA plot. A similar pattern emerged across all domains regardless of whether unsupervised or weakly supervised training.

Observations

1. For the *lang* token1, the closest 10 words are in the similar theme of country/language. However after the 10th word, this diverges to a different set of words. From the PCA plots, we can see that the red points (the closest 50 words) are largely a different set of words in a different part of the embedding space.

2. For the *lang* token2, we observe that the top 20 words do not change much unlike *lang* token1. This indicates that *lang* token1 may play a more critical role in conditioning the model. We do not plot *lang* token2 in Figure 3 as this is domain specific and different across different domains.

[Before Training]	
lang token1	French, French, France, french, Spanish, Italian, German, Dutch, Swedish, Belgian, Danish, Portuguese, Russian, Frenchman, Japanese, Paris, Turkish, Irish, Polish, Norwegian
lang token2	social, social, Social, Social, socially, societal, socio, SOC, soc, Facebook, cultural, facebook, FB, Soci, Twitter, sociop, civic, twitter, hugely, Instagram
random token1	exponent, Occ, ashi, 070, Redd, multiplication, Consumer, ost, grinning, promul, pos, crafted, apex, Import, justifying, 778, Ing, std, spit, grad
random token2	Apply, EN, round, ail, private, fruit, su, San, marks, akra, wi, atin, tar, arb, ank, ADVERTISEMENT, gi, ORN, ize
[After Training]	
lang token1	French, French, french, France, Italian, German, France, Spanish, Russian, Dutch, Paris, scrut, amazingly, showcasing, fueling, meticulously, nurturing, boosters, fiercely, British
lang token2	social, social, Social, Social, socially, societal, socio, SOC, soc, Facebook, FB, facebook, twitter, Twitter, Soci, cultural, incess, sociop, Instagram, hugely
random token1	452, 647, 339, Maurit, 467, 751, 466, 146, bustling, 338, 383, 546, 626, 340, 604, 267, 287, 649, 447
random token2	soDeliveryDate, istg, Skydragon, ÛÛ, srfN,¯¯¯¯¯¯, embedreportprint, = = , quickShipAvailable, natureconservancy, guilcon,externalToEVA, RandomRedditorWithNo, largeDownload

Table 5: Top 20 tokens by cosine similarity to the prefix token before and after training. *lang* token1, *rand* token1 and 2 are the same across MTNT, TED and MED datasets. *lang* token2 is a domain specific word, in this case "social" for the prefix trained in MTNT dataset. Note that the trained prefix token1 and token2 are concatenated as a prefix of length 2.

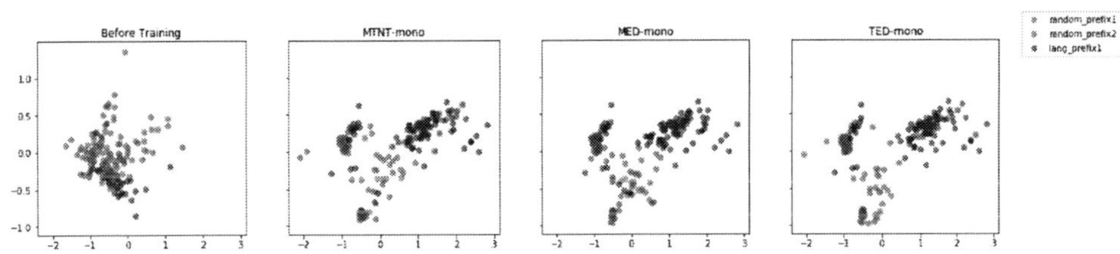

Figure 3: Each point in the plot corresponds to a token which is closest to the prefix by cosine similarity in the full embedding space dimensionality before and after training. The top 50 nearest tokens are plot in 2D as reduced by PCA. Orange and red are tokens closest to random prefix 1 and 2 respectively, while blue are tokens closest to the lang prefix 1, which corresponds to the token "French".

3. *random* token1 and token2 start out in a visually similar density spread to *lang* token1 and the similar tokens are in some generic random space. However after training, the cluster of similar words become very concentrated in the same 2D space (Figure 3). For *random* token1 this is three digit numbers and for *random* token2 this is CamelCased words.

5.2 Validation Loss Across Training Epochs

We present the validation loss under a 5-prompt setting, as training loss for unsupervised and weakly supervised are not directly comparable. We can observe that at the beginning of training, the *lang* initialised prefixes are already performant. This corresponds to the `untrained` *lang* prefix in Table 3. Validation loss increases for the `mono` although this is validation at the 5-prompt validation setting. As reported in Table 4, the trained `mono` prefix give 5 BLEU points at the 1-prompt test setting. For the weakly supervised bitext setting, the loss continues to fall very gradually and consistently under the weakly supervised bitext setting.

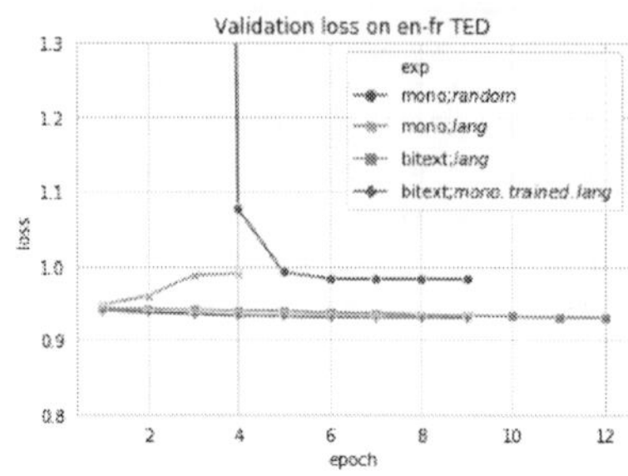

Figure 4: Validation (log) loss plots on en-fr for the TED dataset. The validation loss is the in-context translate loss using 5 prompts. The validation loss for *random* which initially starts at 17.6 is not shown in this chart.

5.3 Sentence Level Analysis for 1-prompt setting

In Table 3 and Table 4, we reported BLEU scores averaged across 5 random prompt sets. We find that when the mono trained prefix method is performant in the 1-shot setting, it does better than the baseline consistently across all 5 random prompt sets. We thus look at the scatter plot of sentence level scores to see whether improvements are coming from across all sentences or from a small group of sentences. Points in red are sentences which did not get translated into the target language in the baseline case. We show the scatterplot for a single prompt set and MTNT domain, as other plots follow a similar pattern.

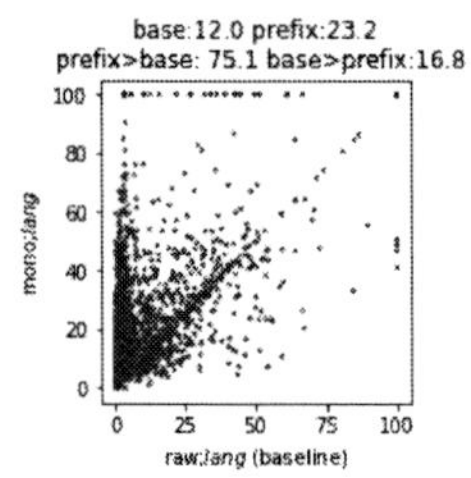

domain	prefix>base	prefix=base	prefix<base
MED	70.4%	10.4%	19.2%
MTNT	70.0%	7.7%	22.3%
TED	64.5%	12.8%	22.7%

Figure 5: Scatter plot for the 1-prompt setting, for en-fr in MTNT, where each point is a single sentence, Y-axis shows mono trained *lang* prefix versus the baseline (untrained prefix) on the X-axis. We report % of sentences where the prefix underperforms, equals to, and outperforms the baseline, averaged across 5 prompt sets, for unsupervised (monolingual) trained prefix.

Observations

1. **Prefix embedding does better "on average" rather than universally across all sentences.** We quantify the % of sentences where using prefix outperforms baseline and vice versa. Many sentences which score higher with the prefix occurs when the baseline has very low scoring sentences. This likely accounts for the higher BLEU scores. Interestingly, about 20-25% of the sentences across the three domains perform worse with the trained prefix, than without. Overall this suggests that a potential next direction might be in translation reranking methods.

2. Most points in red appear to be above the diagonal, indicating that sentences that were previously not translated into the target language are mostly scoring higher.

5.4 Sampling from Prefix

Using `[S*]` as the starting token in a sentence, we sample subsequent tokens from the LM using the vanilla softmax probability distribution without any other probability rescoring tricks. We observe that the prefix token conditions the model to generate naturally diverse outputs, indicating that it has a non-peaky distribution over the target language space. This indicates that the prefix is highly flexible in conditioning the model to generate sequences from that language and the domain. This might be potentially useful as a generic domain prefix for other tasks beyond translation, such as generating dialogue in a particular style.

MTNT	Après un peu d'attention, qu'est-ce que vous voudriez *(after a little attention, what would you like)*
	Et quelle est la façon d'interdire que ça ait lieu? Laisse moi parler le pignon, ... *(And what is the way of prohibiting that it takes place? Let me speak the gable, ...)*
MED	Une étude met en évidence une association entre ces facteurs et le degré d'état de santé chez les adolescents... *(A study highlights an association between these factors and the degree of health in adolescents ...)*
	Nous avons interrogé une grande majorité des parents ayant reçu des soins de santé pour connaître le résultat ... *(We interviewed a large majority of parents who received health care to find out the result ...)*
TED	Le taux annuel des demandeurs d'un emploi est de 2,4 %. L'enregistrement de ce taux en janvier... *(The annual rate of job seekers is 2.4 %. Recording this rate in January ...)*
	Sérieusement. Et c'était quand même pas trop. L'air mou et froide comme ça et la réalité se révéla que mes souvenirs *(Seriously. And it was not too much. The soft and cold air like that and the reality turned out that my memories)*

Table 6: Random samples from prefixes trained on monolingual data for french MTNT, MED and TED, together with their English translations (from Google Translate) in italics for readability.

6 Conclusion

In this paper, we show that priming of in-context learning models can be improved using primarily unsupervised methods. To our knowledge, this is the first work which emphasises the target side language during decoding of a large language model for in-context translation. The gains are modest but so are the number of parameters trained. In our experiments we have shown that the simple method gives up to 5 BLEU point gains for monolingual training in the 1-shot setting, and weakly supervised bitext training in the 20-shot setting gives up to around 2 BLEU point gains across 3 domains and 3 languages. Given that we leverage primarily on unsupervised (monolingual) target side training and carefully control for random prompt selection, this could be a generic approach for improving decoding into a weaker target distribution, which is complementary to the vast literature on prompt example selection and optimisation (Liu et al., 2021).

Limitations We have used one model, GPTNeo2.7B, in this set of experiments. Although this accessible off-the-shelf model is considered a replication of GPT3 in terms of architecture and is highly used (88k downloads in the month of January 2022), other factors such as different training data or scale of the model (100B parameter vs 2B parameters) may affect generalisability of the results. There are no known ethical concerns.

Acknowledgements We thank Marc Marone, Tony Ramirez, and Neha Verma for useful comments and discussion, and Benjamin Van Durme for computational resources for some portion of the experiments.

References

Asai, A., Salehi, M., Peters, M. E., and Hajishirzi, H. (2022). Attentional mixtures of soft prompt tuning for parameter-efficient multi-task knowledge sharing. *arXiv preprint arXiv:2205.11961*.

Bawden, R., Bretonnel Cohen, K., Grozea, C., Jimeno Yepes, A., Kittner, M., Krallinger, M., Mah, N., Neveol, A., Neves, M., Soares, F., Siu, A., Verspoor, K., and Vicente Navarro, M. (2019). Findings of the WMT 2019 biomedical translation shared task: Evaluation for MEDLINE abstracts and biomedical terminologies. In *Proceedings of the Fourth Conference on Machine Translation (Volume 3: Shared Task Papers, Day 2)*, pages 29–53, Florence, Italy. Association for Computational Linguistics.

Black, S., Leo, G., Wang, P., Leahy, C., and Biderman, S. (2021). GPT-Neo: Large scale autoregressive language modeling with Mesh-Tensorflow.

Bommasani, R., Hudson, D. A., Adeli, E., Altman, R., Arora, S., von Arx, S., Bernstein, M. S., Bohg, J., Bosselut, A., Brunskill, E., et al. (2021). On the opportunities and risks of foundation models. *arXiv preprint arXiv:2108.07258*.

Brown, T., Mann, B., Ryder, N., Subbiah, M., Kaplan, J. D., Dhariwal, P., Neelakantan, A., Shyam, P., Sastry, G., Askell, A., et al. (2020). Language models are few-shot learners. *Advances in neural information processing systems*, 33:1877–1901.

Duh, K. (2018). The Multitarget TED Talks Task. `http://www.cs.jhu.edu/~kevinduh/a/multitarget-tedtalks/`.

Fan, A., Bhosale, S., Schwenk, H., Ma, Z., El-Kishky, A., Goyal, S., Baines, M., Celebi, O., Wenzek, G., Chaudhary, V., et al. (2021). Beyond English-centric multilingual Machine Translation. *Journal of Machine Learning Research*, 22:1–48.

Gao, L., Biderman, S., Black, S., Golding, L., Hoppe, T., Foster, C., Phang, J., He, H., Thite, A., Nabeshima, N., et al. (2020). The Pile: An 800GB dataset of diverse text for language modeling. *arXiv preprint arXiv:2101.00027*.

Hendrycks, D. and Gimpel, K. (2016). Gaussian Error Linear Units (GELUs). *arXiv preprint arXiv:1606.08415*.

Houlsby, N., Giurgiu, A., Jastrzebski, S., Morrone, B., De Laroussilhe, Q., Gesmundo, A., Attariyan, M., and Gelly, S. (2019). Parameter-efficient Transfer Learning for NLP. In *International Conference on Machine Learning*, pages 2790–2799. PMLR.

Lester, B., Al-Rfou, R., and Constant, N. (2021). The power of scale for parameter-efficient prompt tuning. *arXiv preprint arXiv:2104.08691*.

Li, X. L. and Liang, P. (2021). Prefix-tuning: Optimizing continuous prompts for generation. *arXiv preprint arXiv:2101.00190*.

Lin, X. V., Mihaylov, T., Artetxe, M., Wang, T., Chen, S., Simig, D., Ott, M., Goyal, N., Bhosale, S., Du, J., et al. (2021). Few-shot learning with multilingual language models. *arXiv preprint arXiv:2112.10668*.

Liu, P., Yuan, W., Fu, J., Jiang, Z., Hayashi, H., and Neubig, G. (2021). Pre-train, prompt, and predict: A systematic survey of prompting methods in Natural Language Processing. *arXiv preprint arXiv:2107.13586*.

Liu, Y., Ott, M., Goyal, N., Du, J., Joshi, M., Chen, D., Levy, O., Lewis, M., Zettlemoyer, L., and Stoyanov, V. (2019). Roberta: A robustly optimized bert pretraining approach. *arXiv preprint arXiv:1907.11692*.

Ma, S., Dong, L., Huang, S., Zhang, D., Muzio, A., Singhal, S., Awadalla, H. H., Song, X., and Wei, F. (2021). Deltalm: Encoder-decoder pre-training for language generation and translation by augmenting pretrained multilingual encoders. *arXiv preprint arXiv:2106.13736*.

Michel, P. and Neubig, G. (2018). MTNT: A testbed for machine translation of noisy text. In *Proceedings of the 2018 Conference on Empirical Methods in Natural Language Processing*, pages 543–553, Brussels, Belgium. Association for Computational Linguistics.

Post, M. (2018). A call for clarity in reporting BLEU scores. In *Proceedings of the Third Conference on Machine Translation: Research Papers*, pages 186–191, Brussels, Belgium. Association for Computational Linguistics.

Qin, G. and Eisner, J. (2021). Learning how to ask: Querying LMs with mixtures of soft prompts. In *Proceedings of the 2021 Conference of the North American Chapter of the Association for Computational Linguistics: Human Language Technologies*, pages 5203–5212.

Renduchintala, A., Shapiro, P., Duh, K., and Koehn, P. (2019). Character-aware decoder for translation into morphologically rich languages. In *Proceedings of Machine Translation Summit XVII: Research Track*, pages 244–255, Dublin, Ireland. European Association for Machine Translation.

Reynolds, L. and McDonell, K. (2021). Prompt programming for large language models: Beyond the few-shot paradigm. In *Extended Abstracts of the 2021 CHI Conference on Human Factors in Computing Systems*, pages 1–7.

Shliazhko, O., Fenogenova, A., Tikhonova, M., Mikhailov, V., Kozlova, A., and Shavrina, T. (2022). mGPT: Few-shot learners go multilingual. *arXiv preprint arXiv:2204.07580*.

Xue, L., Constant, N., Roberts, A., Kale, M., Al-Rfou, R., Siddhant, A., Barua, A., and Raffel, C. (2021). mT5: A massively multilingual pre-trained text-to-text transformer. In *Proceedings of the 2021 Conference of the North American Chapter of the Association for Computational Linguistics: Human Language Technologies*, pages 483–498, Online. Association for Computational Linguistics.

Yang, Y., Eriguchi, A., Muzio, A., Tadepalli, P., Lee, S., and Hassan, H. (2021). Improving multilingual translation by representation and gradient regularization. In *Proceedings of the 2021 Conference on Empirical Methods in Natural Language Processing*, pages 7266–7279.

Fast Vocabulary Projection Method via Clustering for Multilingual Machine Translation on GPU

Hossam Amer hossamamer [at] microsoft.com
Young Jin Kim youki [at] microsoft.com
Mohamed Afify mafify [at] microsoft.com
Hitokazu Matsushita hitokazu.matsushita [at] microsoft.com
Hany Hassan Awadallah hanyh [at] microsoft.com
Microsoft

Abstract

Multilingual Neural Machine Translation has been showing great success using transformer models. Deploying these models is challenging because they usually require large vocabulary (vocab) sizes for various languages. This limits the speed of predicting the output tokens in the last vocab projection layer. To alleviate these challenges, this paper proposes a fast vocabulary projection method via clustering which can be used for multilingual transformers on GPUs. First, we offline split the vocab search space into disjoint clusters given the hidden context vector of the decoder output, which results in much smaller vocab columns for vocab projection. Second, at inference time, the proposed method predicts the clusters and candidate active tokens for hidden context vectors at the vocab projection. This paper also includes analysis of different ways of building these clusters in multilingual settings. Our results show end-to-end speed gains in float16 GPU inference up to 25% while maintaining the BLEU score and slightly increasing memory cost. The proposed method speeds up the vocab projection step itself by up to 2.6x. We also conduct an extensive human evaluation to verify the proposed method preserves the quality of the translations from the original model.

1 Introduction

Neural machine translation (NMT) has witnessed significant advances by the introduction of the transformer model (Vaswani et al., 2017) where excellent performance has been shown for bilingual translation initially, mainly to and from English. Later, the model has been extended to multiple language pairs e.g. (Johnson et al., 2017) and is referred to as multilingual neural machine translation (MNMT). The multilingual model usually comes with a significant increase in the number of parameters and the vocabulary (vocab) size to accommodate various languages.

This work focuses on implementing efficient vocab projection in transformer models. The problem becomes very important for MNMT. While bilingual NMT typically use vocab of around 32K sub-words, MNMT has significantly larger vocab size to adequately cover all the languages. For example, the recent MNMT submission from Microsoft to the WMT21 shared task that covers 100+ languages has a vocab size of 250K sub-words (Yang et al., 2021). The increased vocab makes the projection very compute-intensive and it can take up to 25% of the total computation in our internal benchmark. Hence, the need to speedup this operation becomes even more important.

Fast vocab projection is well-studied for NMT and natural language processing (NLP). In (Shi and Knight, 2017), the authors propose two methods to reduce the effective vocab for NMT.

The first formulates the problem as a nearest neighbor search and uses locality sensitive hashing (LSH) to speedup the computation while the second uses alignment information to select a subset of the vocab based on the input. It is found that the alignment-based method leads to around 2X speedup. The work (Chen et al., 2018) proposes an efficient screening model to exploit the clustering structure of context features right before vocab projection. The authors formulate a joint optimization problem to learn the clusters and their corresponding vocab subspace. In the same paper, a thorough comparison to the existing literature is done including graph-based nearest-neighbor search (Zhang et al., 2018), SVD approximation(Shim et al., 2017), a modified version of hierarchical softmax (Grave et al., 2016) and locality sensitive hashing (LSH) for maximum inner product search (MIPS) (Neyshabur and Srebro, 2014). It is shown that the clustering solution can outperform the latter techniques in terms of accuracy-speed trade-off in bilingual LSTMs on CPU.

This paper extends the clustering based approach from (Chen et al., 2018) to MNMT for both dense and sparse transformer models on GPU. To simplify integration and accessibility in the MNMT large-scale model settings, we propose to use kmeans clustering to split the vocab search space into disjoint clusters given the hidden context vector of the decoder output. The multilingual extension comprises experimenting with different ways to build the cluster maps as well as testing different configurations such as number of centroids and corresponding vocab subspace to make the method efficiently work at large scale. In (Shi et al., 2018), it is shown how to extend LSH to run efficiently within beam search on GPU but here we use and develop optimized kernels. These kernels are developed for FasterTransformer, a highly optimized transformer-based encoder and decoder implementation offered by NVIDIA[1]. Serving GPU inference is essential because GPUs give several orders of magnitude speedups relative to CPUs for large transformer models [2]. Experimental results show end-to-end speed gains in float16 GPU inference up to 25% while maintaining the BLEU score and slightly increasing memory cost. The proposed method speeds up the vocab projection step itself by up to 2.6x. We also conduct an extensive human evaluation to verify the proposed method preserves the quality of the translations from the original model.

The paper is organized as follows. Section 2 describes the proposed method focusing on the multilingual aspect and GPU implementation. This is followed by experimental results for both dense and sparse transformer models and for 6 translation directions in Section 3. Finally, Section 4 concludes the paper.

2 Method

2.1 Problem Motivation

The last layer of decoder in MNMT transformer models is typically a vocab projection layer followed by softmax activation to get the predicted probability of output tokens. Let $W \in \mathbb{R}^{d \times N}$ be a weight matrix of the trained model, $b \in \mathbb{R}^N$ be the bias of the trained model, and $h \in \mathbb{R}^{d \times M}$ be the hidden context vector before the vocab projection layer. Here, N is the vocab size of the MNMT transformer model, d is the transformer embedding dimension, and M is the product of batch and beam sizes. For a total of M tokens and current time step t, we compute the vocab projection as follows:

$$z_{(m,t)} = W^T h_{(m,t)} + b \tag{1}$$

where $z_{(m,t)}$ is the logits of the current input token, m, at the current time step t. To compute the probabilities of the predicted token $\hat{p}_{m,t}$, we compute $\hat{p}_{m,t} = softmax(z_{(m,t)})$. These

[1] https://github.com/NVIDIA/FasterTransformer

[2] https://www.nvidia.com/en-us/on-demand/session/gtcspring22-s42518/

probabilities are sorted in descending order for which they are used for the search algorithms such as beam search, greedy search, sampling, and etc. in machine translation.

In MNMT transformer models, the weights for vocab projection , W, is usually large to cover different languages. Our profiling results show that vocab projection occupies about 25% or more depending on the beam and batch size from the end-to-end inference time. To speedup the inference while keeping the accuracy under control, we propose a vocab projection method via clustering for MNMT transformer models. The proposed vocab projection consists of two major steps: 1) Offline training of clusters based on hidden context vectors which is the output of the last decoder layer; 2) Online inference using the created clusters. Both steps will be explained in the following sections.

2.2 Offline Training of Clusters

Figure 1 shows an overview of the offline training step of the proposed clustering-based vocab projection method. Using an unlabelled training set, this method first records the hidden context vectors $h_{(m,t)}$ and corresponding K candidate likely tokens from $\hat{p}_{m,t}$ given the pre-trained model. K here indicates the number of likely predicted output tokens for each input token. The use of unlabelled data is a benefit of the proposed method as data is not always available in MNMT. Next, we partition the context vectors into disjoint clusters, C, of a specific number of centroids, where similar context vectors are grouped in the same cluster. From the context vector members of each cluster, we construct an active tokens label set called A. Each active token set, $aj \in A$, of the corresponding cluster is the union of the K predicted tokens of all members of this cluster. For example at K=3, suppose that we have only 2 tokens from the training set in the same cluster has the following predicted tokens $\{2, 4, 6\}, \{2, 8, 9\}$ according to the model's predicted probabilities. Then, the a_j for this cluster will be $\{2, 4, 6, 8, 9\}$.

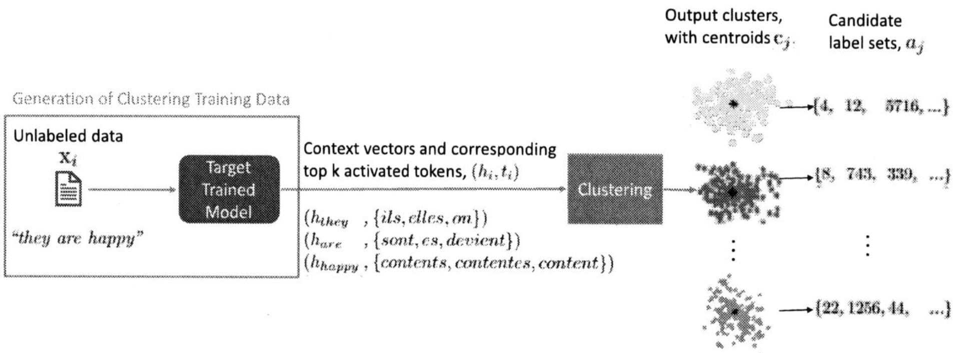

Figure 1: Overview of Vocab Projection via Clustering.

There are different ways to create the clusters and corresponding active tokens set to utilize different information such as source and target languages. Among these ways, we can create the clusters as well as the active tokens while assuming either the target language is only known or the source and target language are known. To compare these two ways, we carried out an experiment on the Italian-to-English (ItEn) language direction, where we varied the number of clusters from 100 to 500 with a step size of 100 at K=1. To construct the clusters of ItEn using source and target information, we feed ItEn training data into the model and get the corresponding clusters and active tokens. For target "en" only known, we feed ItEn, French-to-English (FrEn), and Spanish-to-English (EsEn), data to the model. Later, we run clustering with this mixture of data and construct the corresponding active tokens. In both cases, we measured the maximum percentage of active vocab columns when the number of clusters ranges from 100 to 500. For instance, Figure 2 shows that the percentage of maximum activated vocabs among whole vocabs with 400 clusters is 17.5% when the target only is known, while the percentage is 12.5% when both source and target information is used. Because we favor speed improvements, we chose to run the rest of all our experiments by constructing the models while assuming that source and target languages are known, which is typical in machine translation. This results in fewer activated vocabs for the projection and a faster matrix product at the expense of only an insignificant increase in memory costs as will be shown in the results section.

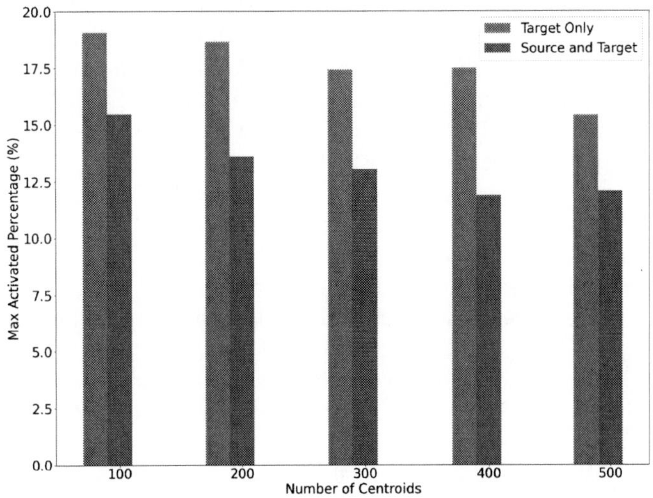

Figure 2: Comparison Between Ways to Build the Clusters and Active Tokens.

2.3 Vocab Projection via Clustering for GPU Inference

This section outlines the proposed method steps at inference time. The input of our method is the number of clusters, corresponding centroid vectors and active tokens set obtained from offline training and hidden context vectors. To compute the output logits, the first step of vocab projection via clustering at inference time is to adaptively get the predicted selected cluster indices based on the hidden context vectors. Suppose that G is the cluster indices of the hidden context vectors, and C_j is the centroid vector of cluster j, we compute the predicted centroid indices using the Euclidean distance for a token m at time step t as follows:

$$G_{(m,t)} = \arg\min_{j} \|C_j^2 - 2h_{(m,t)}^{test} C_j\| \quad (2)$$

where j is between 0 and a given number of clusters. Since the centroid vectors, C_j are constant at inference time, we pre-compute C_j^2 for all j and save C_j^2 in GPU memory.

In practice, the inference is usually done in batch mode where the batch of context vectors can be of different nature and can belong to different clusters as well as candidate label sets. A possible approach is to independently calculate vocab projection for each context vector based on its cluster and corresponding candidate label set. However, this computation will limit the speed on GPUs because they by architecture typically prefer large-scale data in a single computation to hide latency (Cheng et al., 2014). To overcome this challenge, we propose to union the candidate label sets of the context vectors motivated by the possible overlap of label candidate sets within the beam. Although the vocab projection weight matrix of this union set will be larger than the one for independent computation, a single kernel GPU launch for the batch saves inference time while maintaining accuracy.

To efficiently compute this union on GPU, we create a boolean list to indicate whether a vocab token should be active (=1), which is initialized as inactive (=0). We then launch threads to turn on particular vocab columns in this boolean list depending on the active tokens corresponding to the predicted centroids. Suppose that the predicted centroids list is $G = \{0, 1, 2\}$ and corresponding active tokens set is $\{2, 4, 6\}, \{2, 8, 9\}, \{1, 3\}$, respectively. The union of the latter token list yields a reduced vocab column set: $\{1, 2, 3, 4, 6, 8, 9\}$. To get the union, we construct a boolean list equals to [0, 1, 1, 1, 1, 0, 1, 0, 1, 1]. Using the CUB Toolkit function on GPU by Nvidea routines, we efficiently get the vocab columns where this boolean list equals 1. The final reduced weight matrix is substituted in Equation 1 using the newly released gather and scatter fusion with GEMM kernel from Nvidia CUTLASS 2.9. To put together our method steps at inference time, we list them as follows:

1. Compute the predicted centroids c by substituting the context vectors in Equation 2.
2. Get the activated weight column index of the reduced matrix from the union of active tokens for the given predicted centroids.
3. Compute the logits by substituting the reduced weight matrix in Equation 1.
4. Scatter the computed logits in their original locations while setting the non-included weight positions to -INF.
5. Compute the softmax based on this scattered logits matrix.

Theoretical speed-up Based on the steps above, the proposed method turns the theoretical complexity of the vocab projection in Equation 1 from $\mathcal{O}(dN)$ to $\mathcal{O}((r + \bar{N})d)$. The average number of activated weight columns in the reduced vocab matrix, $\bar{N}$, is much less than N. $\bar{N}$ is at most to $\approx$15% of N as shown in the results section. Also, the number of centroids, r is far less than N (typically set to 2000).

3 Experimental Results

In this section, we present the evaluation results for the proposed vocab projection method in a multi-lingual transformer setting on GPU. We first introduce the experimental setup, then assess the impact of the proposed method on vocab projection itself as well as show the speed and accuracy performance results. We conducted an extensive human evaluation to verify the translation quality is preserved. Finally, we study how different configurations such as the number of centroids and K likely tokens affect the performance of our method.

3.1 Experimental Setup

Task and Models We employ the proposed method in MNMT via two transformer models: 1) ZCode Dense; 2) ZCode M3 reviewed and presented in Kim et al. (2021). Both models are based on the transformer encoder-decoder architecture (Vaswani et al., 2017). For better inference efficiency, the architecture of these models utilizes the deeper encoders and shallower decoders architecture presented in (Kim et al., 2019) and (Kasai et al., 2020). Also, both use pre-layer normalization which is known to be more stable for the deeper transformer architecture presented in (Xiong et al., 2020). Both models are constructed from 24 encoder layers and 12 decoder layers with 1024 hidden dimension and 4096 feedforward layer hidden dimension with 16 multi-head attention heads. For ZCode Dense, the number of parameters is 0.7B and vocab size is 250,000. The ZCode M3 has 32 experts, 5B parameters, and 128,000 vocab size.

Cluster Data and Training Settings An in-house training set is used to offline train the clusters as indicated in Section 2.2. This set encompasses 6 language directions. These directions are Spanish to English (EsEn), French to English (FrEn), Italian to English (ItEn), English to Span-

ish (EnEs), English to French (EnFr), and English to Italian (EnIt). To support multilinguality, we offline create for each language direction a number of clusters based on the hidden context vector similarity. Training the clusters for each language direction used 20 million sentence examples and was done using Faiss, where we run 20 training iterations of kmeans clustering. Faiss is an open source code for clustering training offered by Facebook (Johnson et al., 2019).
Validation Data Table 1 indicates the number of sentence examples in our two in-house sets. EX means from English language pairs, while XE means to English language pairs.

Table 1: Statistics of the in-house validation sets. Set 1 is a mix of multiple domains with focus on news, while Set 2 is a mix of news, industry, government, and finance domains.

	Language Direction	Set 1 Size	Set 2 Size
EX	EnEs	5551	9639
	EnFr	20038	13725
	EnIt	9747	13747
XE	FrEn	20039	6149
	ItEn	9747	7492
	EsEn	5460	4539

Inference Hardware and Environment Inference experiments are carried out on a single NVIDIA Tesla V100 GPU. Float16 inference is enabled because it speeds up the inference while maintaining accuracy. Our inference environment is the highly optimized FasterTransformer from NVIDIA.

3.2 Impact of Clustering on Vocab Projection Matrix Multiplication

Our proposed method via clustering noticeably reduces the time to complete the vocab projection matrix multiplication. To verify this insight, we carried out an experiment to compare the proposed solution with the default inference without clustering on set 1. In ZCode Dense, the vocab projection runs in about 720 μs, while the vocab projection runs in about 600 μs for ZCode M3 as the vocab size is smaller. As shown in Table 2, the proposed method only activates up to 12.39% on average out of the original weight matrix in ZCode Dense, while running 2.4x faster than the default matrix multiplication in beam 2, batch 20, and float16 inference. For example, the default elapsed time of the vocab projection step in ZCode Dense is 720 (μs), while the elapsed time using the proposed approach is 230.09 (μs) for EnEs language direction. Along the same line, ZCode M3 activates up to 15.8% of the original vocab projection weight matrix, while improving the time of vocab projection up to 2.6x.

Table 2: Proposed Method Gains of 2.4x to 2.6x on Vocab Projection using Set 1.

Lang	ZCode Dense (720 μs default)		ZCode M3 (600 μs default)	
	Active Percentage (%)	Time (μs)	Active Percentage (%)	Time (μs)
EnEs	6.36	230.09	12.70	215.90
EnFr	6.37	228.90	12.18	218.05
EnIt	7.46	231.84	15.80	227.80
FrEn	16.50	348.49	15.70	230.50
ItEn	10.05	274.90	13.60	217.30
EsEn	12.39	299.97	12.70	213.50

3.3 End-to-end Accuracy and Speed Performance Comparison

Tables 3 and 4 compare the speed percentage and BLEU scores of the ZCode Dense and ZCode M3 before and after clustering on our validation sets. Speed percentages are done based on the number of tokens per second in the default and proposed method, where higher numbers indicate more tokens per second for the proposed method. For ZCode Dense, end-to-end inference speed percentages range from 13.0% to 25.7% across different language directions while maintaining the BLEU score and slightly increasing the memory required for the model due to the extra information needed by the clustering (see Table 5 for memory). Similarly, the proposed vocab projection method speeds up the ZCode M3 with a range between 6% to 8.8% across different language directions. It is worth noting that this performance evaluation is done in FasterTransformer, which showed noticeable speedups for encoder-decoder transformer architectures. In addition, authors in (Chen et al., 2018) have done extensive comparisons to the prior art and showed that clustering-based solutions are better than other solutions in bi-lingual settings on CPU. This paper extends (Chen et al., 2018), scales the clustering to the multilingual setting as well as large vocab sizes on GPU, and shows positive results for both dense and sparsely activated transformers.

Table 3: Performance Evaluation of the Proposed Vocab Projection Method using Set 1.

Model	Lang	beam=1, batch=1			beam=2, batch=20		
		BLEU		Speedup (%)	BLEU		Speedup (%)
		Baseline	Clus		Baseline	Clus	
ZCode Dense	EnEs	43.29	43.21	25.70	43.89	43.81	13.00
	EnFr	38.90	38.80	25.90	39.55	39.55	10.20
	EnIt	38.58	38.49	23.55	39.24	39.30	13.96
	FrEn	44.83	44.80	22.25	45.37	45.46	15.51
	ItEn	44.55	44.28	26.60	45.37	45.38	16.34
	EsEn	45.28	45.36	21.03	45.99	45.96	11.85
	EX AVG	**39.50**	**39.40**	**25.00**	**40.14**	**40.15**	**11.70**
	XE AVG	**45.03**	**44.80**	**23.30**	**45.57**	**45.60**	**14.60**
ZCode M3	EnEs	45.99	45.96	6.80	46.07	46.09	7.87
	EnFr	45.50	45.46	7.58	45.68	45.69	7.58
	EnIt	43.09	43.08	6.59	43.31	43.35	8.84
	FrEn	50.06	49.92	4.70	50.21	50.31	4.90
	ItEn	49.28	49.12	6.84	49.28	49.36	7.78
	EsEn	50.01	50.04	7.50	50.21	50.32	6.00
	EX AVG	**44.86**	**44.83**	**7.00**	**45.02**	**45.04**	**8.10**
	XE AVG	**49.78**	**49.69**	**6.30**	**49.90**	**49.90**	**6.20**

3.4 Human Evaluation

We conduct quality evaluation to examine whether the proposed method retained the same output quality as Baseline and does not introduce any quality degradation. For this investigation, we employ Direct Assessment human evaluation (DA; Bentivogli et al., 2018). In particular, we use segment-level contrastive source-based DA (contrastive DA; Akhbardeh et al., 2021).

Table 4: Performance Evaluation of the Proposed Vocab Projection Method on Set 2 at beam=2, batch=20, and float16 inference.

Lang	ZCode Dense			ZCode M3		
	BLEU		Speedup (%)	BLEU		Speedup (%)
	Baseline	Clus		Baseline	Clus	
EnEs	43.95	43.95	12.29	47.21	47.25	6.70
EnFr	41.46	41.46	11.83	46.74	46.77	5.95
EnIt	41.79	41.81	11.82	47.28	47.34	6.50
FrEn	46.31	46.24	11.49	48.64	48.75	6.00
ItEn	44.15	44.01	13.34	47.89	47.99	6.48
EsEn	45.02	44.89	12.05	47.56	47.68	7.00
EX AVG	**42.40**	**42.40**	**12.00**	**47.07**	**47.12**	**6.40**
XE AVG	**45.16**	**45.04**	**12.30**	**48.03**	**47.81**	**6.50**

Table 5: Memory cost Comparisons under Different Models at beam=2, batch=20 and float16 inference. Selected number of centroids vary a bit more for ZCode M3 than ZCode Dense.

Language Direction	ZCode Dense		ZCode M3	
	Memory Baseline (GB)	Memory Clus (GB)	Memory Baseline (GB)	Memory Clus (GB)
EnEs	4.37	4.39	10.19	10.31
EnFr	4.37	4.39	10.19	10.35
EnIt	4.37	4.39	10.19	10.29
FrEn	4.37	4.39	10.19	10.35
ItEn	4.37	4.39	10.19	10.28
EsEn	4.37	4.39	10.19	10.37

In contrastive DA, human annotators see two randomly selected output segments generated by Baseline and our method side-by-side anonymized along with the corresponding source segment. Annotators are prompted to rate each output segment on a continuous scale of 0 to 100, based on the translation adequacy. Because both system output segments are presented simultaneously in contrastive DA, humans are encouraged to highlight translation differences with scores they assign, which allows us to capture quality differences between Baseline and our method effectively. The contrastive DA score annotations were collected with the Appraise framework (Federmann, 2018). We use paid professional annotators for all the evaluation tasks.

For evaluation data, we use 200,000 monolingual segments for each language direction sampled from our in-house evaluation data pool consisting of various data sources or domains. Among these test items, we confirmed that approximately 92% of translations generated by our method and Baseline for each language direction are identical, which indicates that there was no quality degradation with these test items. Then we randomly sampled 1,700 output translation pairs among the non-identical pairs found in the remaining 8% (roughly 16,000 pairs) for the contrastive DA evaluation.

Table 6 shows the contrastive DA results. We observed no cases where Baseline scores were better than those of our method with statistical significance. Moreover, our method outperformed Baseline for English into Spanish and French ($p < 0.01$) and English into Italian

($p < 0.05$). These results clearly indicates that our method did not sacrifice any translation quality for the efficiency gains. Also, our method was better than Baseline with statistical significance for all the from-English directions. This seems promising, but it still requires a deeper insight to justify overall quality improvement for from-English directions with these small positive deltas found in a limited number of language pairs. Further investigation with a wider variety of language pairs is necessary to confirm such quality improvement exists.

Table 6: Contrastive DA Human Evaluation Results. Scores in the third and fourth columns are the mean of item scores for each language direction of each system. Positive Δ indicates that the Clustering score is larger (better) than the Baseline score. We used Wilcoxon Rank Sum Test for significance testing. Score differences are statistically significant at $p < 0.05$ ($\star$), $p < 0.01$ ($\star\star$), $p < 0.001$ ($\star\star\star$), or not at all.

Model	Language Direction	Baseline	Clustering	Δ	*P*-value
ZCode M3	EnEs	87.20	88.10	0.90	$\star\star$
	EnFr	88.10	88.90	0.80	$\star\star$
	EnIt	85.10	85.5	0.40	$\star$
	FrEn	86.70	87.1	0.40	
	ItEn	79.40	79.40	0.00	
	EsEn	86.10	86.60	0.50	

3.5 Clustering Hyperparameters Selection

To demystify the impact of the number of K likely tokens and centroids in the proposed method, we carried out two experiments on ItEn language direction on a validation set. The results of these experiments were also consistent for other language pairs.

The goal of the first experiment is to select the best number of centroids and K likely tokens for ItEn, where we varied the number of centroids from 100 to 2000 with a step size of 100 and setting the K likely tokens to either 1, 3, or 5. Figure 3 shows the outcome of this experiment for the ItEn language direction on ZCode Dense, where speed percentages are calculated to the ZCode Dense without clustering. From the figure, we can observe that the highest speed percentages usually occur at the higher centroids. In this case, 1300 centroids is the best setting in terms of speed. In addition, we can observe that K=1 leads to the highest speed percentages among K=3 and K=5. This observation goes with one's intuition as K=1 uses only the most likely predicted token to build the activated weight vocab indices for each cluster.

To confirm this intuition, we carried out another experiment for ItEn under ZCode Dense while setting the number of centroids to 1300. In this experiment, we recorded the percentage of weight active columns at each centroid index from 0 to 1299 for each of K=5, K=3, and K=1. As shown in Figure 4, K=1 has less activated weight indices for each centroid index relative to K=3 and K=5. If a hidden context vector is a member of cluster index 0 for example, K=5, K=3, and K=1 have around 6%, 5%, and 2% of weight matrix active, respectively. These percentages confirm that K=1 usually leads to the highest speed percentages among K=3 and K=5.

4 Conclusion

This paper proposes a fast vocab projection method via clustering for multilingual neural machine translation with large vocab sizes and practically applied models on GPU. The method splits the large vocab search space into smaller subspaces to run efficient GPU inference. Results reveal end-to-end speed improvements up to 25% while maintaining the BLEU, and up

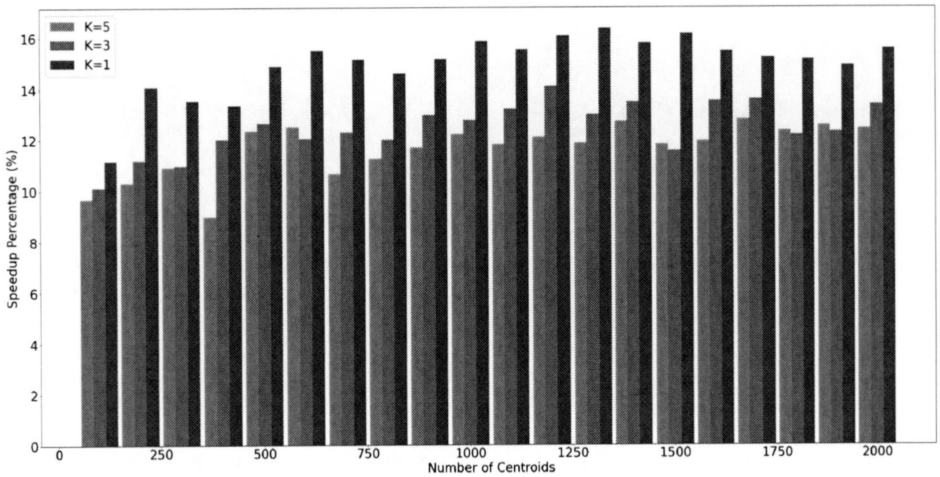

Figure 3: Impact of Varying the Number of Centroids and K likely tokens on Speed Percentage carried out on ItEn language direction from Development Set.

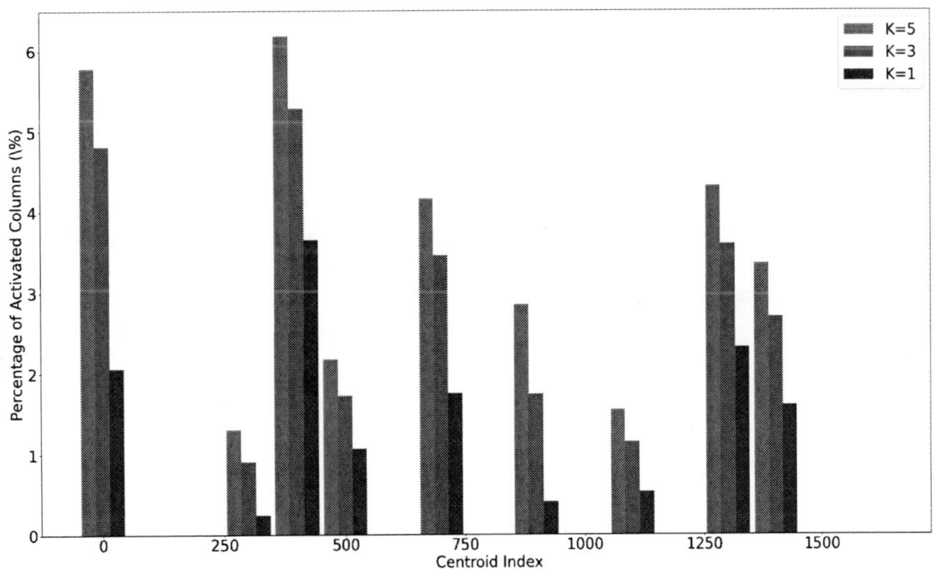

Figure 4: Comparison between K=5, K=3, and K=1 likely tokens in terms of Percentage Activated Weight Columns out of Vocab Elements When Number of Centroids = 1300 for ItEn.

to 2.6x speed improvement on the vocab projection step. We conducted human evaluations to verify the translation quality. In the future, we wish to explore our method in an X-Y machine translation scenario.

References

Akhbardeh, F., Arkhangorodsky, A., Biesialska, M., Bojar, O., Chatterjee, R., Chaudhary, V., Costa-jussà, M. R., España-Bonet, C., Fan, A., Federmann, C., et al. (2021). Findings of the 2021 conference on machine translation (WMT21). In *Proceedings of the Sixth Conference on Machine Translation*, pages 1–88.

Bentivogli, L., Cettolo, M., Federico, M., and Christian, F. (2018). Machine translation human evaluation: an investigation of evaluation based on post-editing and its relation with direct assessment. In *15th International Workshop on Spoken Language Translation 2018*, pages 62–69.

Chen, P. H., Si, S., Kumar, S., Li, Y., and Hsieh, C.-J. (2018). Learning to screen for fast softmax inference on large vocabulary neural networks. *arXiv preprint arXiv:1810.12406*.

Cheng, J., Grossman, M., and McKercher, T. (2014). *Professional CUDA c programming*. John Wiley & Sons.

Federmann, C. (2018). Appraise evaluation framework for machine translation. In *Proceedings of the 27th International Conference on Computational Linguistics: System Demonstrations*, pages 86–88.

Grave, E., Joulin, A., Cissé, M., Grangier, D., and Jégou, H. (2016). Efficient softmax approximation for gpus.

Johnson, J., Douze, M., and Jégou, H. (2019). Billion-scale similarity search with GPUs. *IEEE Transactions on Big Data*, 7(3):535–547.

Johnson, M., Schuster, M., Le, Q. V., Krikun, M., Wu, Y., Chen, Z., Thorat, N., Viégas, F., Wattenberg, M., Corrado, G., Hughes, M., and Dean, J. (2017). Google's multilingual neural machine translation system: Enabling zero-shot translation. *Transactions of the Association for Computational Linguistics*, 5:339–351.

Kasai, J., Pappas, N., Peng, H., Cross, J., and Smith, N. A. (2020). Deep encoder, shallow decoder: Reevaluating non-autoregressive machine translation. *arXiv preprint arXiv:2006.10369*.

Kim, Y. J., Awan, A. A., Muzio, A., Salinas, A. F. C., Lu, L., Hendy, A., Rajbhandari, S., He, Y., and Awadalla, H. H. (2021). Scalable and efficient moe training for multitask multilingual models. *arXiv preprint arXiv:2109.10465*.

Kim, Y. J., Junczys-Dowmunt, M., Hassan, H., Aji, A. F., Heafield, K., Grundkiewicz, R., and Bogoychev, N. (2019). From research to production and back: Ludicrously fast neural machine translation. In *Proceedings of the 3rd Workshop on Neural Generation and Translation*, pages 280–288.

Neyshabur, B. and Srebro, N. (2014). On symmetric and asymmetric lshs for inner product search.

Shi, X. and Knight, K. (2017). Speeding up neural machine translation decoding by shrinking run-time vocabulary. In *Proceedings of the 55th Annual Meeting of the Association for Computational Linguistics (Volume 2: Short Papers)*, pages 574–579, Vancouver, Canada. Association for Computational Linguistics.

Shi, X., Xu, S., and Knight, K. (2018). Fast locality sensitive hashing for beam search on gpu.

Shim, K., Lee, M., Choi, I., Boo, Y., and Sung, W. (2017). Svd-softmax: Fast softmax approximation on large vocabulary neural networks. In *NIPS*.

Vaswani, A., Shazeer, N., Parmar, N., Uszkoreit, J., Jones, L., Gomez, A. N., Kaiser, L., and Polosukhin, I. (2017). Attention is all you need.

Xiong, R., Yang, Y., He, D., Zheng, K., Zheng, S., Xing, C., Zhang, H., Lan, Y., Wang, L., and Liu, T. (2020). On layer normalization in the transformer architecture. In *International Conference on Machine Learning*, pages 10524–10533. PMLR.

Yang, J., Ma, S., Huang, H., Zhang, D., Dong, L., Huang, S., Muzio, A., Singhal, S., Awadalla, H. H., Song, X., et al. (2021). Multilingual machine translation systems from microsoft for wmt21 shared task. *arXiv preprint arXiv:2111.02086*.

Zhang, M., Liu, X., Wang, W., Gao, J., and He, Y. (2018). Navigating with graph representations for fast and scalable decoding of neural language models.

Language Tokens: A Frustratingly Simple Approach Improves Zero-Shot Performance of Multilingual Translation

Muhammad ElNokrashy muelnokr@microsoft.com
Amr Hendy amrhendy@microsoft.com
Mohamed Maher mohamedmaher@microsoft.com
Mohamed Afify mafify@microsoft.com
Microsoft ATL, Cairo

Hany Hassan Awadalla hanyh@microsoft.com
Microsoft, Redmond

Abstract

This paper proposes a simple yet effective method to improve direct (*X-to-Y*) translation for both cases: zero-shot and when direct data is available. We modify the input tokens at both the encoder and decoder to include signals for the source and target languages. We show a performance gain when training from scratch, or finetuning a pretrained model with the proposed setup. In the experiments, our method shows nearly 10.0 BLEU points gain on in-house datasets depending on the checkpoint selection criteria. In a WMT evaluation campaign, *From-English* performance improves by 4.17 and 2.87 BLEU points, in the zero-shot setting, and when direct data is available for training, respectively. While *X-to-Y* improves by 1.29 BLEU over the zero-shot baseline, and 0.44 over the many-to-many baseline. In the low-resource setting, we see a $1.5 \sim 1.7$ point improvement when finetuning on *X-to-Y* domain data.

1 Introduction

Neural machine translation (**NMT**) has witnessed significant advances since the introduction of the transformer model (Vaswani et al., 2017). This model has shown impressive performance for bilingual translation commonly from and to English (Hassan et al., 2018). It has also been shown that the proposed model could be easily extended to multiple language pairs (Aharoni, Johnson, & Firat, 2019; Fan et al., 2020; Johnson et al., 2017; X. Wang, Tsvetkov, & Neubig, 2020), to and/or from English, by simple modifications to the basic architecture. This holds promise for improved performance for low-resource pairs through transfer learning, as well as better training and deployment costs per language pair. This setting is referred to as multilingual neural machine translation (**MNMT**).

The mainstream method of training MNMT is to introduce an additional input tag at the encoder to indicate the target language, while the decoder uses the usual begin-of-sentence (`BOS`) token. This simple modification to the bilingual architecture is shown to work well up to hundreds of language pairs (Fan et al., 2020; Tran et al., 2021), given a corresponding increase in the number of parameters to handle the increased training data. Despite the emergence of modified architectures which add language-specific parameters, like language specific sub-networks (LASS) (Lin, Wu, Wang, & Li, 2021), and adapters (Bapna & Firat, 2019), the basic architecture remains the most effective choice for deploying large scale production systems.

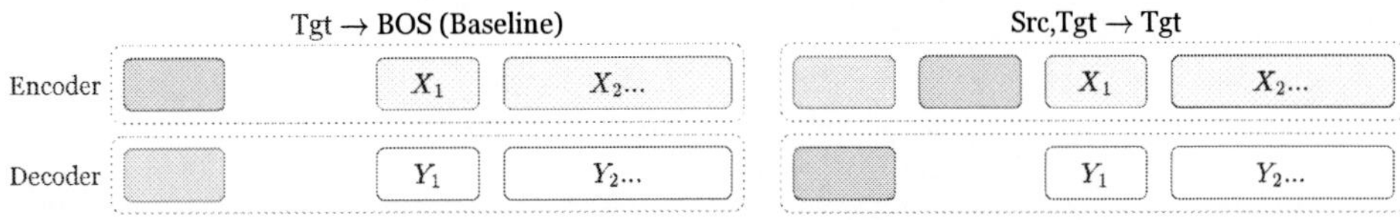

Figure 1: Comparing tokens as seen by the Encoder and the Decoder in the *(Left)* baseline (`T-B`) and in the *(Right)* top proposed method (`ST-T`).

2 Motivation

While MNMT was originally focused on English-centric translation, there is increasing interest interest in direct translation[1] rather than pivoting through a common language (ex. English). In Freitag and Firat (2020), the authors mine direct translation data by matching the English part of English-centric corpora, then use modified temperature sampling to alleviate the over-representation of English as target. Another work (Fan et al., 2020) leverages public direct translation data including CCMATRIX (Schwenk, Wenzek, Edunov, Grave, & Joulin, 2019) and CCALIGNED (El-Kishky, Chaudhary, Guzman, & Koehn, 2019) as well as improved sampling and sparse modeling to develop a 100-by-100 direct translation model.

While the availability of direct translation training data helps improve the corresponding directions, the zero-shot case remains of particular importance considering the difficulty in maintaining coverage of the set of rapidly increasing directions, and handling the corresponding increase in data size and compute time and resources. Hence the interest in techniques that improve zero-shot translation performance, benefit from parallel training data as it becomes available, and which can be easily applied to the basic architecture and pretrained models.

Related Works. Yang et al. (2021) approaches the off-target translation problem using gradient projection and no direct training data. Zhang, Williams, Titov, and Sennrich (2020) improves the zero-shot case using online back-translation and by specializing layers (ex. LayerNorm) for the target language. Rios, Müller, and Sennrich (2020) utilizes separately-trained vocabularies per language. Arivazhagan et al. (2019) proposes an alignment loss to enforce source language invariance. Ha, Niehues, and Waibel (2016) proposes tagging input tokens by the source language and indicating the target language directly to a shared decoder.

Proposal. We propose a simple yet effective method that improves the performance of direct translation: The input tokens used in MNMT are changed to `ST-T` instead of `T-B` (see Figure 1). The encoder takes tokens for both the source and target languages (`S,T`) while the decoder takes one for only the target language (`T`). It is shown that using these modified tokens significantly improves the performance on direct translation pairs without any parallel $X \Leftrightarrow Y$ translation data—training only on English-centric data ($E \Leftrightarrow X$). Remarkably, these gains are quickly obtained if we start from a model trained using the baseline tokens and continue training after adding the new tokens. In subsequent experiments, we also show that some gains are still observed if we continue training the baseline model using a mix of direct ($X \Leftrightarrow Y$) and English-centric training data—suggesting the method extends to the non zero-shot case as well.

The paper is organized as follows: We describe the proposed method in Section 3. This is followed by describing the data and the models used in our experiments in Section 4 and Section 5 respectively. Section 6 gives the experimental results (domain finetuning results in Section 6.2). Finally, Section 7 gives the conclusion.

[1] Also known as *X-Y* translation. In the rest of the paper we refer to translation between any two language pairs not involving English as *direct* or *X-Y* translation.

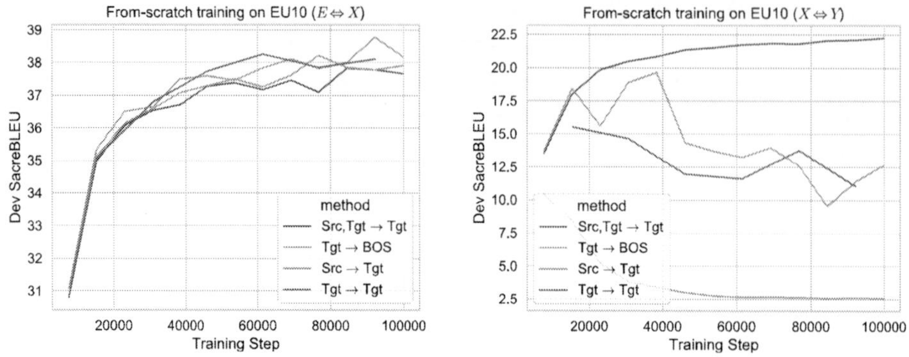

(a) SacreBLEU for $E \Leftrightarrow X$ dev.

(b) SacreBLEU for $X \Leftrightarrow Y$ dev.

Figure 2: **Validation for from-scratch training.** All training uses English-centric data and no direct ($X \Leftrightarrow Y$) data. The baseline (`T-B`) quickly loses performance on $X \Leftrightarrow Y$ dev. The `S-T` method fails on $X \Leftrightarrow Y$ dev, but matches or exceeds alternatives on $E \Leftrightarrow X$ dev. The proposed method (`ST-T`) matches the alternatives on $E \Leftrightarrow X$ dev (within 1.0 BLEU) and maintains high performance for $X \Leftrightarrow Y$ generalization.

3 Approach

In basic MNMT, the source sentence is followed by a token indicating the target language at the encoder side, and with the begin-of-sentence token at the decoder side. This setup is `T-B` in **Figure 1**. In the proposed method, we perform a simple modification by adding both the source and target tokens to the input at the encoder side[2], and the target at the decoder side. This setup is `ST-T` in Figure 1. Y. Wang, Zhang, Zhai, Xu, and Zong (2018) shows that adding the `TGT` language to the decoder input helps English-to-X translation. In a recent submission to WMT21, Tran et al. (2021) uses a `SRC` token at the encoder and a `TGT` token at the decoder, which can be observed from the public evaluation code[3]. In initial experiments we try several variants of indicating the languages to the model. We find that most are similar for the English-centric case, but the proposed method (`ST-T`) performs the best for zero-shot direct translation.

3.1 Initial Experiments

To validate the proposed method, we train a model on 10 European languages using in-house English-centric data—Once using the baseline tokens, and once using the new tokens. Details of the model and the training are given in Section 5. The graph of the dev BLEU score during training is shown for the English-centric devset and the direct devset in **Figures 2a** and **2b**. Also shown in the figure is the `S-T` setup similar to (Tran et al., 2021), and the `T-T` setup which passes the target language to both encoder and decoder.

3.2 Language Coding and Model Conditioning

While all models perform similarly for the English-centric set on which they are trained, the behavior is different for the novel direct set. The baseline and proposed models are close at the beginning of the training but the baseline quickly deteriorates *as it improves in its assigned task* on English-centric data. One explanation is that the conditioning in the `T-B` case explicitly

[2] Note that the order of source and target is not significant and that we also add the target at the decoder.

[3] Found at: `https://github.com/facebookresearch/fairseq/blob/47c58f0858b5484a18f39549845790267cffee1a/examples/wmt21/eval.sh`

Directions	T-B	ST-T
$E \Leftrightarrow X$	0.14%	0.15%
$X \Leftrightarrow Y$	29.36%	1.69%
Both	23.49%	**1.35%**

Table 1: Percentage of *off-target* samples in the $E \Leftrightarrow X$ and $X \Leftrightarrow Y$ dev sets for EU10 measured at 53k steps. Training graphs in Figure 2.

indicates only the target language, while the source language is inferred. Consider also the absence of direct $X \Leftrightarrow Y$ training data, then an *implicit, and valid, pattern* emerges: When `TGT≠en`, it is implied that `SRC=en`. Thus, in the $X \Leftrightarrow Y$ test case, the model expects the source to be in English, which may be a source of confusion. Conversely, the model with the `S-T` setup performs very poorly from the beginning for the direct set. We propose that this is in line with findings that show that encoder capacity may be of higher importance to MT than decoder capacity (Kasai, Pappas, Peng, Cross, & Smith, 2020; Kim et al., 2019). Removing the `TGT` signal from the encoder would then be a significant handicap. It may work in the English-centric case because the *implicit pattern* described above is sufficient conditioning.

Off-Target Translations. **Table** 1 shows Language ID mis-matches for `T-B` and `ST-T` using fasttext language identification on the *from-scratch* experiments on EU10 (fig. 2).

3.3 Building on Pretrained Models

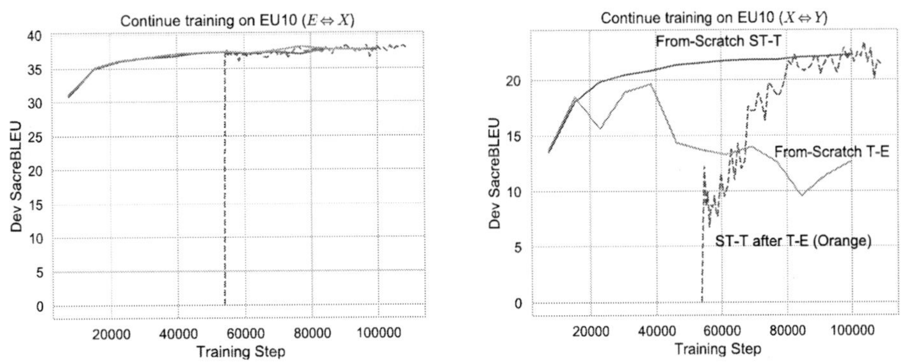

(a) SacreBLEU for $E \Leftrightarrow X$ dev. (b) SacreBLEU for $X \Leftrightarrow Y$ dev.

Figure 3: Orange is the baseline (`T-B`) setup, while blue is the proposed (`ST-T`) setup. The solid lines start from scratch. The dashed line continues training from step 53k of the baseline, using `ST-T` tokens, on English-centric ($E \Leftrightarrow X$) data. No direct $X \Leftrightarrow Y$ data is used for training. $E \Leftrightarrow X$ performance is quickly regained. $X \Leftrightarrow Y$ performance approaches that of from-scratch training within a similar *total* training budget (dashed vs. solid blue lines).

An interesting scenario is how to make use of already trained models that would be costly to retrain. We validate our top proposed method in that case by continuing training from a midway checkpoint of the baseline. The performance on both dev sets is shown in **Figure** 3. Performance (dashed blue line) on the $E \Leftrightarrow X$ set starts at zero but rapidly regains its baseline value, then remains steady as training progresses. The same happens for $X \Leftrightarrow Y$ data but at a slower pace. The weights already trained on English-centric data seem to realign to the new setup efficiently.

To summarize: Compared to the baseline, the proposed tokens perform similarly on English-centric tests and significantly outperform on direct translation tests while training using English-centric data in both cases. If we continue training the baseline model by adding the proposed tokens we quickly recover the performance of both the English-centric and direct data to levels obtained by training from scratch, as seen in the initial experiments. Therefore, in the rest of this paper we focus on continuing training a model pretrained using the baseline tokens.

4 Data

In initial experiments we build a model for 10 European languages using in-house data (Section 4.1). Follow-up experiments use WMT data (Akhbardeh et al., 2021) as well as other publicly available data covering 6 languages (Section 4.2). Most experiments use English-centric training data, some use direct training data (Section 4.3), and some use domain data (Section 4.5). Validation data is described in Section 4.4. Tables are in Appendix A.

4.1 EU10 Training Data

EU10 is an in-house web-crawled parallel dataset with a total of 3.35 billion sentence pairs covering 10 European languages: Dutch (nl), English (en), French (fr), German (de), Greek (el), Italian (it), Polish (pl), Portuguese (pt), Spanish (es), and Romanian (ro). Details in Table 8.

4.2 WMT Training Data

For WMT, we use the data for 12 English-centric language pairs provided by the news translation shared task in WMT21[4], and additionally data from the public sources CCMATRIX (Schwenk et al., 2019) and CCALIGNED (El-Kishky et al., 2019). The combined set covers the directions of English (en) to and from: Czech (cs), German (de), Icelandic (is), Japanese (ja), Russian (ru), and Chinese (zh). We apply some preprocessing steps to filter noisy data. We filter for the expected languages using fasttext (Joulin, Grave, Bojanowski, & Mikolov, 2017); normalize punctuation using moses[5]; then discard sentences longer than 250 words or with a source/target or target/source length ratio exceeding 3. The filtered data totals 2.16 billion sentence pairs. Details on filtered parallel data sizes are shown in Table 10. Note the difference in the parallel data of English-centric directions for the same non-English language is due to having different amounts of synthetic data released by the WMT21 shared task.

4.3 Direct Training Data

For experiments with direct $X \Leftrightarrow Y$ data covering the 7 languages in the WMT dataset (Section 4.2), we build a dataset of parallel training data in 42 translation directions, including the English-centric directions. We collect $X \Leftrightarrow Y$ data from publicly available sources as described in Section 4.2. The resulting size of the collected bitext $X \Leftrightarrow Y$ data is shown in Table 9. We then sample 10 million sentence pairs from the WMT English-centric dataset for each direction to avoid catastrophic forgetting on $E \Leftrightarrow X$ directions. We end up with a many-to-many dataset with a total of 525 millions sentence pairs that contains 405 millions sentence pairs in $X \Leftrightarrow Y$ directions, and 120 millions sentence pairs in English-centric directions.

4.4 Development and Test Data

We evaluate the translation performance on various devsets depending on the training dataset and the language list. For experiments using in-house training data (Section 4.1), we use in-

[4] `https://www.statmt.org/wmt21/translation-task.html` (Akhbardeh et al., 2021).

[5] `https://github.com/moses-smt/mosesdecoder` (Koehn et al., 2007).

house dev sets covering all the many-to-many 90 translation directions. For experiments using the WMT data described in Section 4.2 and 4.3, we use publicly available dev sets composed of: WMT21-provided sets to cover the 12 English-centric directions, and the FLORES-101 benchmark (Goyal et al., 2022) to cover the remaining 30 $X \Leftrightarrow Y$ directions.

4.5 Data for Domain Experiments

We utilize domain data from the OPUS project[6]. We collect the EMEA, JRC-ACQUIS and TANZIL domains in the directions German to/from Czech. The data is shuffled and split into train, test and validation sets. Any sentences that occur in the validation or test sets are removed from training. The sizes of the splits are shown in Table 7. EMEA is a parallel corpus of PDF documents from the European Medicines Agency. JRC-ACQUIS is a collection of legislative text of the European Union that comprises selected texts written between the 1950s and now. TANZIL is a collection of Quran translations compiled by the Tanzil project.

5 Models

All experiments use the same architecture and configuration. We use the Transformer encoder-decoder architecture (Vaswani et al., 2017) as the base model and opt for a deep encoder and a shallower decoder as presented in Kim et al. (2019) and Kasai et al. (2020), with 24 encoder layers and 12 decoder layers. Dimensions are 1024 for model width, 4096 for the feed-forward hidden layer, and 16 attention heads. We use pre-layer normalization which is becoming more common for similar architectures (Xiong et al., 2020). We use a vocabulary of size $128,000$ with the sentencepiece tokenizer[7]. The model size is 0.6B parameters. All models are trained by the RAdam optimizer (Liu et al., 2019). See Appendix A, Table 6 for other hyper-parameters.

6 Experimental Results

In this section, we show experimental results using the WMT model as described in Section 5. We first continue training the WMT model using the proposed tokens on English-centric data only, then we continue training using direct data[8]. In other experiments, we use $X \Leftrightarrow Y$ data from start, once with each of `T-B` and `ST-T` tokens. In all cases, we report the BLEU score for both the direct and English-centric dev sets. See Table 2. The results of continuing training the baseline tokens with direct data are shown in the fourth row (`D` *Direct FT*). Note that the third row (`P-D` *Proposed* $\hookrightarrow$ *Direct FT*) corresponds to continuing training with new tokens for 47k iterations, then adding the direct data—running for 112k steps in total.

6.1 Medium-resource MNMT

In **Table** 2, the first row shows the scores of the base WMT model on both English-centric and direct dev sets (in zero-shot setting) with the `T-B` setup. Continuing to train the model using the new tokens shows gains on both dev sets, although less than what would be expected from the initial results on EU10 (Section 3.1). Continuing to train the base model using direct data shows larger gains on the direct dev set, but a smaller gain on English-centric dev.

The third and last rows show that we still observe some gain from the new tokens after adding the direct data. The best strategy (row 3) is two phases: to train first using the English-centric data, then add the direct data. Consider Figure 4b: It may require a smaller $X \Leftrightarrow Y$ dataset (fewer steps) in the two-phase setup than when using direct data from the start.

[6] https://opus.nlpl.eu/index.php (Tiedemann, 2012).

[7] https://github.com/google/sentencepiece (Kudo & Richardson, 2018).

[8] This is a mix of $X \Leftrightarrow Y$ and $E \Leftrightarrow X$ data (Section 4.3) to avoid catastrophic forgetting of English-centric translation.

[9] SacreBLEU signature: `nrefs:1|case:mixed|eff:no|tok:13a|smooth:exp|version:2.1.0`. For targets in Chinese and Japanese, the tokenizers used are `zh` and `ja-mecab`. (Post, 2018)

#	Setup	**Direct**	English-Centric	$X \Rightarrow E$	$E \Rightarrow X$	Best At
B	Base Model	13.67	26.30	27.37	25.28	-
P	↪ Proposed	14.96	**30.27**	**31.10**	**29.45**	63k
P-D	↪ Direct FT (from 47k)	**23.59**	*28.83*	*29.52*	*28.15*	112k
D	↪ Direct FT	23.15	28.10	28.90	27.30	120k
DP	↪ Proposed & Direct FT	23.09	28.19	28.85	27.52	102k

Table 2: **SacreBLEU**[9] of the base WMT model (first row) when finetuned in various setups. A hooked arrow (↪) indicates a row that continues training from the parent model. Thus rows `P`, `D`, and `DP` show finetuning using the proposed (`ST-T`) tokens, direct data, or both; while row `P-D` continues from row `P`. *Direct FT* refers to finetuning with direct data. The ***Direct*** column uses FLORES-100 dev, while the *English-centric* column uses WMT21 dev. The *Best At* column reports the *total* training steps starting from *Base Model*.

#	Setup	**Direct**	English-Centric	$X \Rightarrow E$	$E \Rightarrow X$	Best At
B	Base Model	-16.23	36.00	32.69	39.31	-
P	↪ Proposed	6.36	**49.87**	**45.21**	**54.54**	63k
P-D	↪ Direct FT (from 47k)	**54.30**	*47.14*	*44.18*	*50.10*	112k
D	↪ Direct FT	51.74	44.71	41.73	47.69	120k
DP	↪ Proposed & Direct FT	51.57	44.47	41.82	47.12	102k

Table 3: Average **COMET**[10] ($\times 100$) of the set of WMT experiments. Same notation as Table 2.

Table 3 shows the COMET scores for the same experiments set. While both metrics agree in rankings, COMET suggests larger gains than suggested by BLEU.

See **Table** 4 for COMET-based statistical significance model comparison aggregates across language directions.

See **Figure** 4 for training performance curves for rows 1–4. Consider that row `P-D` sees only $E \Leftrightarrow X$ for the first phase (corresponding to `P`), and then sees a small amount of $X \Leftrightarrow Y$ data before improving. It may thus help in making better use of a smaller $X \Leftrightarrow Y$ dataset.

6.2 Low-resource Adaptation

For the low-resource setting, we use a domain adaptation example. We start from the WMT model with the baseline and new tokens (corresponding to the first and second rows of Table 2). We finetune a separate model for each adaptation experiment: for German to and from Czech, and for the domains EMEA, JRC and Tanzil as obtained from OPUS. Details of the data are found in Table 7. The results for CS-DE and DE-CS are shown in Table 5.

From **Table** 5, the new tokens improve both the pretrained and the finetuned models. The difference depends on the direction and the domain but is generally noticeable. This is an interesting scenario because we can start from an English-centric baseline and continue training using the new tokens to create a stronger base model that improves downstream performance for different directions and domains.

[10]COMET model `wmt20-comet-da` version `1.1.1` (Rei, Stewart, Farinha, & Lavie, 2020).

Direction	Without $X \Leftrightarrow Y$ train data		With $X \Leftrightarrow Y$ train data	
	`B` Base Model	`P` Proposed	`D` Direct FT	`P-D` Proposed $\hookrightarrow$ Direct
$X \Rightarrow E$	0	**6**	0	**4**
$E \Rightarrow X$	0	**6**	0	**3**
$X \Leftrightarrow Y$	10	**20**	0	**10**
Total/42	10	**32**	0	**17**

Table 4: To compare models to the nearest baseline, we calculate statistical significance with the Paired T-Test and bootstrap resampling at $p < 0.05$, following Koehn (2004). Each cell shows the count of *wins* for a model and direction. In the zero-shot setting, the proposed method outperforms the baseline in $32/42$ directions. With direct parallel data available, the proposed method outperforms the continued training baseline in $17/42$ directions, and is tied in the rest.

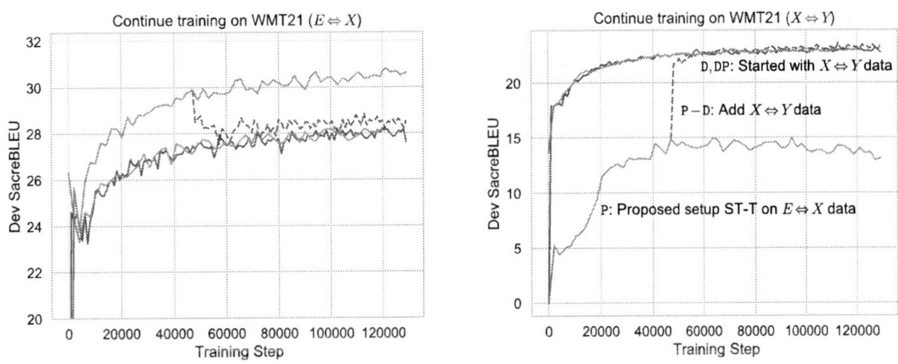

(a) SacreBLEU for $E \Leftrightarrow X$ dev.

(b) SacreBLEU for $X \Leftrightarrow Y$ dev.

Figure 4: All solid line models start from the **pretrained base model** (row `B` in Tables 2 & 3). Orange is the proposed setup trained on $E \Leftrightarrow X$ data (row `P`). Blue adds $X \Leftrightarrow Y$ data (rows `P-D` & `DP`) where: Run `P-D` (dashed line) continues training on $X \Leftrightarrow Y$ data from step 47k of run `P`, while run `DP` (solid blue) starts with that data. Note that `D` and `DP` perform similarly on both dev sets, but `P-D` improves $X \Leftrightarrow Y$ performance while lessening the loss of $E \Leftrightarrow X$ performance that is gained from run `P`. `P-D` reaches similar performance to `D` and `DP` in fewer steps with access to $X \Leftrightarrow Y$ data directly, suggesting improved data efficiency.

7 Conclusion

This paper proposes a simple and effective method to improve direct translation for both the zero-shot case and when direct data is available. The input tokens used for MNMT are changed from `T-B` (encoder $\rightarrow$ decoder) to `ST-T`. Moreover, the performance of the new tokens can be readily obtained if we continue training the baseline model with the new tokens but the same training data. For a WMT-based setting, we see around 1.3 BLEU points improvement for zero-shot direct translation and around 0.4 BLEU point improvement when using direct data for training. In both cases the English-centric performance is also improved—by as much as 3.97 in WMT21 for one setup. COMET scores see noticeable bumps as well—by 2.56 points. on $X \Leftrightarrow Y$ dev, and 15.23 points on $E \Rightarrow X$ dev. On another front, the proposed tokens are effective when finetuning a general model for direct translation using domain data.

For three tested domains and two translation directions, we see significant improvements over the baseline. Results for EU10 (Section 3.1) suggest a stronger potential given more similar language and domain sets.

Model	Domain	CS-DE			DE-CS		
		B Base	P Proposed	*Delta*	B Base	P Proposed	*Delta*
Zero-Shot	EMEA	35.2	35.3	+0.1	36.9	39.5	+2.6
	JRC	45.0	48.0	+3.0	45.1	47.6	+2.5
	Tanzil	6.6	10.5	+3.9	6.5	9.7	+3.2
Finetuned	EMEA	45.8	46.4	+0.6	46.2	48.2	+2.0
	JRC	53.7	56.0	+2.3	52.7	54.5	+1.8
	Tanzil	24.4	26.0	+1.6	26.0	27.2	+1.2
Zero-Shot	*Average*	28.9	31.3	**+2.4**	29.5	32.3	**+2.8**
Finetuned	*Average*	41.3	**42.8**	+1.5	41.6	**43.3**	+1.7

Table 5: Results of finetuning on different domains using the baseline and proposed tokens for Czech from and to German. The model is finetuned separately for each domain and direction.

A Appendix

Parameter	WMT			EU10
	Pretraining	Finetuning	Domain adaptation	
Optimizer	RAdam	RAdam	RAdam	RAdam
Learning Rate	0.001	0.008	0.00089	0.015
LR Scheduler	Inverse Sqrt	Inverse Sqrt	Inverse Sqrt	Inverse Sqrt
Warmup	4,000	5,000	800	5,000
Batch Size	0.8M	1.5M	1M	2M

Table 6: Hyper-parameters comparison between experiment sets. The LR values were not optimized for these experiments, but inherited from unrelated trials. Note that between any two *phases* of an experiment (for example in P-D, adding $X \Leftrightarrow Y$ data in the second phase), all non-parameter state is re-initialized, including LR scheduler and optimizer state.

Domain	Training Set Size	Validation Set Size	Test Set Size
EMEA	1.06M	561	582
JRC-acquis	1.15M	609	1,190
Tanzil	45k	326	302

Table 7: Sentence counts of train, development, and test sets for domain data.

Language pair (XE)	**# sentences** (M)	**Language pair** (EX)	**# sentences** (M)
Dutch → English	195	English → Dutch	233
French → English	298	English → French	251
German → English	250	English → German	219
Greek → English	166	English → Greek	117
Italian → English	237	English → Italian	170
Polish → English	175	English → Polish	161
Portuguese → English	108	English → Portuguese	64
Spanish → English	260	English → Spanish	171
Romanian → English	162	English → Romanian	112

Table 8: In-house web crawled parallel data statistics used in EU10 training. We report the list of 18 language directions and the number of sentences (Millions) per each language pair.

Language pair (XY)	**# sentences** (M)	**Language pair** (XY)	**# sentences** (M)
Czech ↔ German	33	German ↔ Chinese	19
Czech ↔ Icelandic	0.6	Icelandic ↔ Japanese	1.1
Czech ↔ Japanese	11	Icelandic ↔ Russian	2.1
Czech ↔ Russian	28	Icelandic ↔ Chinese	0.7
Czech ↔ Chinese	6.6	Japanese ↔ Russian	9.5
German ↔ Icelandic	3.4	Japanese ↔ Chinese	12.4
German ↔ Japanese	15	Russian ↔ Chinese	14
German ↔ Russian	46		

Table 9: Bitext data for 30 X→Y language directions collected from CCMatrix and CCAligned. We report the number of sentences (Millions) per each language pair.

Language pair (XE)	**# sentences** (M)		**Language pair** (EX)	**# sentences** (M)	
	Raw	**Cleaned**		**Raw**	**Cleaned**
Czech → English	206	189	English → Czech	181	165
German → English	436	411	English → German	436	411
Icelandic → English	15	13.4	English → Icelandic	15	13.4
Japanese → English	85	81	English → Japanese	85	81
Russian → English	289	273	English → Russian	292	280
Chinese → English	139	132	English → Chinese	119	113

Table 10: Bitext data includes data released by the WMT21 shared task, CCMatrix and CCAligned. We report the list of 12 language directions and the number of sentences (Millions) per each language pair.

References

Aharoni, R., Johnson, M., & Firat, O. (2019, June). Massively multilingual neural machine translation. In *Proceedings of the 2019 conference of the north American chapter of the association for computational linguistics: Human language technologies, volume 1 (long and short papers)* (pp. 3874–3884). Minneapolis, Minnesota: Association for Computational Linguistics. Retrieved from https://aclanthology.org/N19-1388 doi: 10.18653/v1/N19-1388

Akhbardeh, F., Arkhangorodsky, A., Biesialska, M., Bojar, O., Chatterjee, R., Chaudhary, V., ... Zampieri, M. (2021, November). Findings of the 2021 conference on machine translation (WMT21). In *Proceedings of the sixth conference on machine translation* (pp. 1–88). Online: Association for Computational Linguistics. Retrieved from https://aclanthology.org/2021.wmt-1.1

Arivazhagan, N., Bapna, A., Firat, O., Aharoni, R., Johnson, M., & Macherey, W. (2019). *The missing ingredient in zero-shot neural machine translation.* arXiv. Retrieved from https://arxiv.org/abs/1903.07091 doi: 10.48550/ARXIV.1903.07091

Bapna, A., & Firat, O. (2019, November). Simple, scalable adaptation for neural machine translation. In *Proceedings of the 2019 conference on empirical methods in natural language processing and the 9th international joint conference on natural language processing (emnlp-ijcnlp)* (pp. 1538–1548). Hong Kong, China: Association for Computational Linguistics. Retrieved from https://aclanthology.org/D19-1165 doi: 10.18653/v1/D19-1165

El-Kishky, A., Chaudhary, V., Guzman, F., & Koehn, P. (2019). *Ccaligned: A massive collection of cross-lingual web-document pairs.* arXiv. Retrieved from https://arxiv.org/abs/1911.06154 doi: 10.48550/ARXIV.1911.06154

Fan, A., Bhosale, S., Schwenk, H., Ma, Z., El-Kishky, A., Goyal, S., ... Joulin, A. (2020). *Beyond english-centric multilingual machine translation.* arXiv. Retrieved from https://arxiv.org/abs/2010.11125 doi: 10.48550/ARXIV.2010.11125

Freitag, M., & Firat, O. (2020). *Complete multilingual neural machine translation.* arXiv. Retrieved from https://arxiv.org/abs/2010.10239 doi: 10.48550/ARXIV.2010.10239

Goyal, N., Gao, C., Chaudhary, V., Chen, P.-J., Wenzek, G., Ju, D., ... Fan, A. (2022). The Flores-101 evaluation benchmark for low-resource and multilingual machine translation. *Transactions of the Association for Computational Linguistics*, *10*, 522–538. Retrieved from https://aclanthology.org/2022.tacl-1.30 doi: 10.1162/tacl_a_00474

Ha, T.-L., Niehues, J., & Waibel, A. (2016, December 8-9). Toward multilingual neural machine translation with universal encoder and decoder. In *Proceedings of the 13th international conference on spoken language translation.* Seattle, Washington D.C: International Workshop on Spoken Language Translation. Retrieved from https://aclanthology.org/2016.iwslt-1.6

Hassan, H., Aue, A., Chen, C., Chowdhary, V., Clark, J., Federmann, C., ... Zhou, M. (2018). *Achieving human parity on automatic chinese to english news translation.*

Johnson, M., Schuster, M., Le, Q. V., Krikun, M., Wu, Y., Chen, Z., ... Dean, J. (2017). Google's multilingual neural machine translation system: Enabling zero-shot translation. *Transactions of the Association for Computational Linguistics*, *5*, 339–351. Retrieved from https://aclanthology.org/Q17-1024 doi: 10.1162/tacl_a_00065

Joulin, A., Grave, E., Bojanowski, P., & Mikolov, T. (2017, April). Bag of tricks for efficient text classification. In *Proceedings of the 15th conference of the European chapter of the association for computational linguistics: Volume 2, short papers* (pp. 427–431).

Valencia, Spain: Association for Computational Linguistics. Retrieved from https://aclanthology.org/E17-2068

Kasai, J., Pappas, N., Peng, H., Cross, J., & Smith, N. A. (2020). Deep encoder, shallow decoder: Reevaluating non-autoregressive machine translation. *arXiv preprint arXiv:2006.10369.*

Kim, Y. J., Junczys-Dowmunt, M., Hassan, H., Aji, A. F., Heafield, K., Grundkiewicz, R., & Bogoychev, N. (2019). From research to production and back: Ludicrously fast neural machine translation. In *Proceedings of the 3rd workshop on neural generation and translation* (pp. 280–288).

Koehn, P. (2004, July). Statistical significance tests for machine translation evaluation. In *Proceedings of the 2004 conference on empirical methods in natural language processing* (pp. 388–395). Barcelona, Spain: Association for Computational Linguistics. Retrieved from https://aclanthology.org/W04-3250

Koehn, P., Hoang, H., Birch, A., Callison-Burch, C., Federico, M., Bertoldi, N., ... Herbst, E. (2007, June). Moses: Open source toolkit for statistical machine translation. In *Proceedings of the 45th annual meeting of the association for computational linguistics companion volume proceedings of the demo and poster sessions* (pp. 177–180). Prague, Czech Republic: Association for Computational Linguistics. Retrieved from https://aclanthology.org/P07-2045

Kudo, T., & Richardson, J. (2018, November). SentencePiece: A simple and language independent subword tokenizer and detokenizer for neural text processing. In *Proceedings of the 2018 conference on empirical methods in natural language processing: System demonstrations* (pp. 66–71). Brussels, Belgium: Association for Computational Linguistics. Retrieved from https://aclanthology.org/D18-2012 doi: 10.18653/v1/D18-2012

Lin, Z., Wu, L., Wang, M., & Li, L. (2021, August). Learning language specific sub-network for multilingual machine translation. In *Proceedings of the 59th annual meeting of the association for computational linguistics and the 11th international joint conference on natural language processing (volume 1: Long papers)* (pp. 293–305). Online: Association for Computational Linguistics. Retrieved from https://aclanthology.org/2021.acl-long.25 doi: 10.18653/v1/2021.acl-long.25

Liu, L., Jiang, H., He, P., Chen, W., Liu, X., Gao, J., & Han, J. (2019). *On the variance of the adaptive learning rate and beyond.* arXiv. Retrieved from https://arxiv.org/abs/1908.03265 doi: 10.48550/ARXIV.1908.03265

Post, M. (2018, October). A call for clarity in reporting BLEU scores. In *Proceedings of the third conference on machine translation: Research papers* (pp. 186–191). Belgium, Brussels: Association for Computational Linguistics. Retrieved from https://www.aclweb.org/anthology/W18-6319

Rei, R., Stewart, C., Farinha, A. C., & Lavie, A. (2020, November). COMET: A neural framework for MT evaluation. In *Proceedings of the 2020 conference on empirical methods in natural language processing (emnlp)* (pp. 2685–2702). Online: Association for Computational Linguistics. Retrieved from https://aclanthology.org/2020.emnlp-main.213 doi: 10.18653/v1/2020.emnlp-main.213

Rios, A., Müller, M., & Sennrich, R. (2020, November). Subword segmentation and a single bridge language affect zero-shot neural machine translation. In *Proceedings of the fifth conference on machine translation* (pp. 528–537). Online: Association for Computational Linguistics. Retrieved from https://aclanthology.org/2020.wmt-1.64

Schwenk, H., Wenzek, G., Edunov, S., Grave, E., & Joulin, A. (2019). *Ccmatrix: Mining billions of high-quality parallel sentences on the web.* arXiv. Retrieved from https://

arxiv.org/abs/1911.04944 doi: 10.48550/ARXIV.1911.04944
Tiedemann, J. (2012, May). Parallel data, tools and interfaces in OPUS. In *Proceedings of the eighth international conference on language resources and evaluation (LREC'12)* (pp. 2214–2218). Istanbul, Turkey: European Language Resources Association (ELRA). Retrieved from http://www.lrec-conf.org/proceedings/lrec2012/pdf/463_Paper.pdf
Tran, C., Bhosale, S., Cross, J., Koehn, P., Edunov, S., & Fan, A. (2021). *Facebook ai wmt21 news translation task submission.* arXiv. Retrieved from https://arxiv.org/abs/2108.03265 doi: 10.48550/ARXIV.2108.03265
Vaswani, A., Shazeer, N., Parmar, N., Uszkoreit, J., Jones, L., Gomez, A. N., ... Polosukhin, I. (2017). *Attention is all you need.*
Wang, X., Tsvetkov, Y., & Neubig, G. (2020, July). Balancing training for multilingual neural machine translation. In *Proceedings of the 58th annual meeting of the association for computational linguistics* (pp. 8526–8537). Online: Association for Computational Linguistics. Retrieved from https://aclanthology.org/2020.acl-main.754 doi: 10.18653/v1/2020.acl-main.754
Wang, Y., Zhang, J., Zhai, F., Xu, J., & Zong, C. (2018, October-November). Three strategies to improve one-to-many multilingual translation. In *Proceedings of the 2018 conference on empirical methods in natural language processing* (pp. 2955–2960). Brussels, Belgium: Association for Computational Linguistics. Retrieved from https://aclanthology.org/D18-1326 doi: 10.18653/v1/D18-1326
Xiong, R., Yang, Y., He, D., Zheng, K., Zheng, S., Xing, C., ... Liu, T. (2020). On layer normalization in the transformer architecture. In *International conference on machine learning* (pp. 10524–10533).
Yang, Y., Eriguchi, A., Muzio, A., Tadepalli, P., Lee, S., & Hassan, H. (2021). *Improving multilingual translation by representation and gradient regularization.* arXiv. Retrieved from https://arxiv.org/abs/2109.04778 doi: 10.48550/ARXIV.2109.04778
Zhang, B., Williams, P., Titov, I., & Sennrich, R. (2020). *Improving massively multilingual neural machine translation and zero-shot translation.* arXiv. Retrieved from https://arxiv.org/abs/2004.11867 doi: 10.48550/ARXIV.2004.11867

Low-Resource Chat Translation: A Benchmark for Hindi–English Language Pair

Baban Gain[1] gainbaban@gmail.com
Ramakrishna Appicharla[1] ramakrishnaappicharla@gmail.com
Soumya Chennabasavraj[2] soumya.cb@flipkart.com
Nikesh Garera[2] nikesh.garera@flipkart.com
Asif Ekbal[1] asif@iitp.ac.in
Muthusamy Chelliah[2] muthusamy.c@flipkart.com
[1]Department of Computer Science and Engineering, Indian Institute of Technology Patna, India
[2]Flipkart, India

Abstract

Chatbots or conversational systems are used in various sectors such as banking, healthcare, e-commerce, customer support, etc. These chatbots are mainly available for resource-rich languages like English, often limiting their widespread usage to multilingual users. Therefore, making these services or agents available in non-English languages has become essential for their broader applicability. Machine Translation (MT) could be an effective way to develop multilingual chatbots. Further, to help users be confident about a product, feedback and recommendation from the end-user community are essential. However, these question-answers (QnA) can be in a different language than the users. The use of MT systems can reduce these issues to a large extent. In this paper, we provide a benchmark setup for Chat and QnA translation for English-Hindi, a relatively low-resource language pair. We first create the English-Hindi parallel corpus comprising of synthetic and gold standard parallel sentences. Thereafter, we develop several sentence-level and context-level neural machine translation (NMT) models, and measure their effectiveness on the newly created datasets. We achieve a BLEU score of 58.7 and 62.6 on the English-Hindi and Hindi-English subset of the gold-standard version of the WMT20 Chat dataset. Further, we achieve BLEU scores of 52.9 and 76.9 on the gold-standard Multi-modal Dialogue Dataset (MMD) English-Hindi and Hindi-English datasets. For QnA, we achieve a BLEU score of 49.9. Further, we achieve BLEU scores of 50.3 and 50.4 on question and answers subsets, respectively. We also perform thorough qualitative analysis of the outputs by the real users.

1 Introduction

Chatbots or conversational systems serve a crucial role in various sectors such as banking, healthcare, e-commerce, customer support, etc. While chatbots are convenient and fast, most are available only for resource-rich languages like English, limiting their widespread usage to users from languages other than the chatbot's language. It is essential to make these services available in non-English languages for their broader applicability. Machine Translation (MT) can be an effective technology for developing multilingual chatbots to meet the need of multilingual societies. In recent years, there has been significant progress in Neural Machine Translation (NMT) with applications in a variety of domains, such as document (Yu et al., 2020), biomedical Yeganova et al. (2021), news (Hassan et al., 2018; Ng et al., 2019) etc. However, NMT requires a huge amount of data (Koehn and Knowles, 2017), and its manual creation requires significantly a lot of human effort. Chat translation poses more challenges than sentence-level translation due to the following: (i). Translation of the current utterance may depend on the contextual sentences. To translate the current sentence properly, we may need to refer to the previous sentences in the chat to grasp the meaning and generate appropriate translation; (ii). Chat often contains informal sentences, urban slang, stretched words (e.g., niceeee), code-mixed phrases, etc.

Further, communicating with chatbots or customer service may not be enough to make an informed decision regarding a product. Queries regarding a product can effectively be answered by the community of customers who use a similar product, leading to the requirement of a QnA system. Hence, it is also vital to perform QnA translation. This paper provides a benchmark setup for Chat and QnA translation for Hindi–English language pair, which has very little to no resources for such tasks. Firstly, we create a synthetic and gold-standard parallel corpus for English-Hindi chat and QnA translation. We use the existing MT systems described in section 5 to generate synthetic translation. With this model, we get a BLEU score of 47.8, indicating the translation is of good quality. Further, we create gold-standard parallel corpus by professional translators.

We employ the transfer-learning technique by initializing the transformer architecture using the model trained on similar domain data (Zoph et al., 2016). Further, we report the results on using same-speaker context to generate context-aware translation, which was useful for better translations for English–German (Gain et al., 2021). For QnA, we combine the QnA pair to generate consistent translation. We used to question and answer tags during training to help the model learn QnA-specific properties. Further, we compare the results with models trained on only question corpus or only answer corpus. We report BLEU (Papineni et al., 2002; Post, 2018) and TER (Snover et al., 2005) scores. To our knowledge, there is no publicly available dialogue dataset for the English–Hindi Chat or QnA translation. We introduce two datasets containing a total of 68.7K synthetic sentences, as well as 3,037 sentences of gold-standard data for chat translation. Further, we provide about 2.1 million QnA pairs (4.2 million sentences), their corresponding translation (synthetic), and 1,000 gold-standard sentences for each validation and test set, respectively. We make all the data and codes publicly available[1]. To summarize, our work has the following attributes: (i). introduce three English-Hindi parallel corpora for Chat Translation in Service and E-Commerce domains; (ii). use several context-aware and context-agnostic methods and observe their effectiveness on Chat Translation in (extremely) low-resource language settings, especially for the task at hand; (iii). propose a method to generate consistent translation performance in question-answer settings, where question-answers can be treated as a short chat with only two utterances; (iv). MT outputs have been quality checked by the actual users recruited by the well-known e-commerce company.

[1]https://github.com/babangain/en_hi_chat_qna_translation

2 Related Work

There are several approaches to applying Chatbots in E-commerce. Zhang et al. (2018) proposed a system that asks aspect-based questions to the user in a sequence, and recommendations are provided when the system is confident. Sun and Zhang (2018) proposed a personalized recommendation model which considers past ratings of products rated by the user and queries in the current conversation session to generate product recommendations. Chen et al. (2019) integrated the recommender system and dialog system, where the dialog system enhanced the recommendation system by introducing knowledge-grounded information about users' preferences. Further, the recommender system improved the dialog generation system by providing recommendation-aware vocabulary bias. Lai et al. (2018) showed that a simple transfer learning technique from an existing large-scale community question answering helped to generate 10% more accurate answers. Qu et al. (2019) proposed positional history answer embedding method to encode conversation history with position information. Further, they proposed a method that attends to conversational utterances with different weights based on their helpfulness in answering the current question. Deng et al. (2020) generated opinion-aware answers by jointly learning answer generation and opinion mining with a unified model. However, it is to be noted that all of the systems are monolingual.

Despite its demand, the field of dialogue translation remains mostly unexplored due to the lack of publicly available chat corpus. Farajian et al. (2020) introduced an English-German parallel conversational corpus. Berard et al. (2020) adopted several methods including replacement of rare characters with a special '<copy>' token, inline casing, tagged back-translation (BT) (Caswell et al., 2019), Byte-Pair-Encoding (BPE) (Sennrich et al., 2016), dropout (Provilkov et al., 2020), tagged synthetic noise, and ensemble of models using domain-specific adaptive layers, etc. While the largest single contributor to the improvement of translation quality was fine-tuning, the ensemble method with a domain-specific adaptor layer generated the best translation on WMT20 Chat data. Moghe et al. (2020) used the pre-trained models (Ng et al., 2019) and fine-tuned them on the pseudo-in-domain and in-domain data. Wang et al. (2020) adapted Cross-lingual Language Model Pre-training (Conneau and Lample, 2019) objectives into document-level NMT by using three previous contexts along with the current sentence. Bao et al. (2020) used the transformer architecture, modified with an additional encoder to process one previous context. Additional encoder failed to generate better overall translation in terms of BLEU score.

Gain et al. (2021) proposed a rule-based context selection technique where previous sentences by the same user are used to enhance the translation quality. Liang et al. (2021a) introduced an English-Chinese dialogue dataset named BMELD, which is an automatically translated and manually post-edited version of the MELD dataset (Poria et al., 2019). Further, they introduced a conditional variational auto-encoder (CVAE) model that captures role preference, dialogue coherence, and translation consistency. Liang et al. (2021b) proposed a multi-tasking system performing monolingual response generation, cross-lingual response generation, subsequent utterance discrimination, and speaker identification along with NMT. Here, the context-aware multi-tasking methods could generate better translation than context-agnostic models. Liang et al. (2022b) extended the same by introducing an additional objective, cross-lingual subsequent utterance discrimination, and evaluated the models with BMELD (English–Chinese) and BConTrast (English–German) datasets. Wang et al. (2021) proposed a multi-task learning-based NMT system to identify missing pronouns and typos and utilize context to translate dialogue utterances for English-Chinese language pairs. Liang et al. (2022a) observed visual features helps to generate better quality translation on multi-modal dialogue.

Our task is different from others in the following aspects: a). we focus on dialogue or chat translation in low-resource language settings and the e-commerce domain; b). the existing works primarily focus on dialogues or formal conversations. In contrast, we focus on noisy and informal conversations or chat (specifically for QnA); c). we perform experiments on the sentence-level system (transformer) with domain adaptation and transfer learning. We also report the evaluation results on a context-based system exploiting source-side context.

3 Corpus Creation

We create the English-Hindi parallel corpus from the existing English dialogue corpora. Specifically, we choose MultiModal Dialogue (MMD) corpus (Saha et al., 2018) and English part of German-English corpus from WMT20 chat translation task (Farajian et al., 2020), which is based on Taskmaster-1 corpus (Byrne et al., 2019). Further, we translate the Flipkart QnA corpus, consisting of 2.1M QnA pairs. This dataset contains the queries about a product asked by users of the website, which have been answered by either of (a). Other Customers or (b). Seller of the product. The QnA covers queries of a large range of products, including Electronics, Clothing, Appliances, etc., on the E-Commerce website, while the aspect is about the quality of the product, its features, compatibility, durability, and others.

We create two types of parallel corpora, synthetic corpus and gold standard corpus. The synthetic corpus is created through forward-translation or backward-translation (depending upon the translation direction of the task) of English corpora into Hindi with the existing NMT models. The gold standard corpus is created by manually translating English into Hindi. Table 1 shows the statistics of the prepared synthetic and gold standard corpora.

Subset	#Dialogues	Dialogue Avg. length	#Sentences	English Avg. length	Hindi Avg. length	Type
			WMT20 Chat Corpus			
Train	550	25.17	13,845	8.07	9.08	Synthetic
Validation	78	24.61	1,902	8.08	9.11	Synthetic
Test	18	27.89	502	7.29	8.20	Manual
			MMD Corpus			
Train	1,366	35.6	50,000	8.72	9.42	Synthetic
Validation	25	37.04	926	12.50	13.01	Manual
Test	46	34.97	1,609	12.78	13.61	Manual
			QnA Corpus			
Train	-	-	4,191,608	5.31	6.15	Synthetic
Validation	-	-	1,000	25	28.9	Manual
Test	-	-	1,000	25.8	28.2	Manual

Table 1: Statistics of the created English-Hindi WMT20 Chat, MMD, and QnA parallel corpora. **#Dialogues**: Total number of dialogues, **Dialogue Avg. length**: Average dialogue length, **#Sentences**: Total number of sentences, **English Avg. length**: Average English sentence length, **Hindi Avg. length**: Average Hindi sentence length, **Type**: Type of translation (synthetic/manual). The QnA corpus consists of the question and answers pairs.

3.1 Synthetic Corpus Creation

We extract all English sentences from the training and validation sets of the WMT20 chat translation task. Similarly, we extract the first 50k sentences from the MMD corpus out of 5 million sentences in the dataset (Saha et al., 2018). The synthetic corpus is prepared by translating the extracted data through google translate[2] (Wu et al., 2016). Note that the translations generated are with a sentence-level NMT model. For Flipkart QnA data, we translate all the available data with a sentence-level MT system, which is trained on Samanantar Corpus-v3 (Ramesh et al., 2021) containing general-domain sentences. Table 1 shows the statistics of the prepared synthetic corpora. To assess the quality of synthetic corpus, we randomly select 100 English-Hindi sentence pairs from the prepared WMT20 chat, MMD, and QnA corpora and evaluate the quality of generated Hindi sentences based on adequacy and fluency. Table 2 shows the average adequacy and fluency scores of the generated Hindi sentences for all three domains. Based on the scores, we observe that the prepared synthetic corpora are of good quality, specifically the WMT20 chat and MMD corpora, where sentences are usually more formal and less noisy than QnA data. However, it is to be noted that despite its excellent quality, it lacks discourse awareness. Therefore, using these translation models directly (instead of training using discourse-aware models) may not be preferred.

Corpus	Adequacy	Fluency
WMT20 Chat	4.87	4.75
MMD	4.93	4.85
QnA	4.59	4.53

Table 2: Adequacy and Fluency of the prepared synthetic corpora. The scores are averaged from randomly picked 100 sentences from each corpus.

3.2 Gold-standard Corpus Creation

We create a gold-standard corpus by manually translating English data into Hindi. We extract the first 502 sentences (18 dialogues) from the WMT20 chat translation task testset and the first 1,436 sentences (43 dialogues) from the MMD dataset. We employed two annotators who are fluent in Hindi and English. The annotators are instructed to prefer commonly used words over conventional words for translation To be consistent with the nature of the dataset. They are further instructed to translate the sentences based on the previous sentences in a particular dialogue. For QnA, we observe that a large proportion of the answers are yes/no type, which may not be indicative of the true performance of the MT systems. Therefore, we extract 1,000 QnA pairs with large sentence lengths for answers to curate test and validation sets. We divide them into validation and test sets containing 500 QnA pairs (1,000 sentences) for each set. Then the annotators are instructed to translate the questions manually based on the corresponding answers and vice-versa. Table 1 shows the statistics of prepared gold-standard corpora.

4 Description of Corpora

This section describes the WMT20 chat, MMD, and QnA corpus.

[2]Translation through google translate is done between September-November 2021

WMT20 Chat Corpus: The WMT20 chat translation dataset (Farajian et al., 2020) is initially released for German–English language pair. The dataset is derived from Taskmaster-1 (Byrne et al., 2019) corpus, which is a monolingual conversational dataset.

The dataset consists of conversations from six domains. We create a Hindi version of this corpus following the process as described in Section 3. If the customer speaks in Hindi, it is to be translated into English, and if the assistant speaks in English, then it is to be translated into Hindi. The training, validation, and test sets contain 13,845, 1,902, and 502 sentences, respectively. The dialogues contain an average of 25 sentences. Table 1 shows the detailed statistics of the prepared Hindi–English WMT20 Chat corpus. The datasets can be divided into two subsets[3]. The agent and customer subsets contain 271 and 231 utterances on the English–Hindi test set.

MMD Corpus: MultiModal Dialogue Corpus (MMD) (Saha et al., 2018) is a monolingual dialogue dataset containing an English sentence or an image as an utterance, where the conversation is between shoppers and sales agents. The dataset is created by a semi-automatic method using automata and feedback from the experts. Since we require only conversations in text, we remove all the occurrences of the images. The training, validation, and test sets contain 50,000, 926, and 1,609 sentences. Table 1 shows the detailed statistics of prepared Hindi–English MMD corpus.

QnA Corpus We introduce a parallel (synthetic target side) QnA corpus containing 2.1M QA pairs (4.2M sentences). The dataset contains questions asked by the users and their answers, which are provided by either other users or seller of the product. The dataset contains queries about a wide range of products, including Electronics, Lifestyle, Appliances, etc. We specifically choose longer sentences for validation and test sets to avoid high performance due to shorter "Yes/No" type questions. Table 1 shows the statistics of prepared Hindi–English QnA corpus.

5 Methodology and Experimental Setup

We use Samanantar (Ramesh et al., 2021) corpus as a general domain corpus that contains 10M sentence pairs for English–Hindi. We train the transformer (Vaswani et al., 2017) model on the Samanantar corpus and consider it a baseline model.

5.1 Methodology

Domain Adaptation: We fine-tune the baseline model with the prepared WMT20 chat, MMD, and QnA corpora. The models are trained at the sentence level, and no context information is utilized for training the models or generating translation.

Transfer learning: Since we have two conversational datasets (WMT20 chat and MMD), we try to use knowledge from the trained model on one corpus to generate a better translation for the model trained on the other corpus via two-stage fine-tuning. For the first stage, we fine-tune the baseline model on the MMD corpus, and in the second stage, we fine-tune the model on the WMT20 chat corpus. Finally, we evaluate on WMT20 chat testset. Similarly, in the case of MMD experiments, for the first stage, we fine-tune WMT20 chat data and then MMD data in the second stage.

Domain adaptation with user specific context: We follow context-aware domain adaptation strategy proposed by Gain et al. (2021). In this approach, the context is selected by considering the previous utterances until the occurrence of an utterance from different speakers, subject to a maximum of three previous sentences. After selecting the

[3]The structure of the dataset is described at: https://github.com/Unbabel/BConTrasT

context, we add a special '<context>' token, representing the beginning of the context. We concatenate all the contexts, followed by a special '<end>' token, representing the end of the context. Then we concatenate the current source sentence and context and use them as input to the encoder.

For the QnA corpus, since there is no context associated with the question and answer pairs, we consider *answer* as a context for *question*, and vice-versa. We concatenate the question and answer pairs by the '<sep>' token and feed them to the encoder as input. For QnA, the decoder is trained to generate the translation for both questions and answers separated by '<sep>' at the output side. Encoding and translating the question and answer simultaneously makes the model effectively encode both questions and answers.

Pre-processing and Experimental Setup: Chat utterances are often written in lowercase and do not follow usual Capitalization Rules. Therefore, for the experiments in the English-Hindi direction, we convert every source sentence to lowercase. For Hindi-English, we do not convert to lowercase as the target side is English, and the true case of the sentences should be generated. Then, we jointly learn byte-pair-encoding (Sennrich et al., 2016) by combining source and target sides with fastBPE. We use fairseq (Ott et al., 2019) to train all our models. We use six layered encoder-decoder stacks with eight attention heads. The embedding and feed-forward layer sizes are set to 512 and 2048, respectively, with a dropout of 0.2. We set the maximum tokens per training batch to 4,000 with update frequencies of 64 and 4 during pre-training and fine-tuning, respectively. Thus maximum effective token per update during pre-training is (4000 * 64 * 2 GPUs) = 768,000. During fine-tuning, we use one GPU. We set an update frequency of 4 during fine-tuning on WMT20 and MMD datasets. Thus, effective number of tokens per update is (4000 * 4 * 1 GPUs) = 16,000. For all settings mentioned above, the initial learning rate is set to 0.0005, whereas 0.1 is set for label smoothing. We train the model for 30 epochs for pre-training and a maximum of up to 5000 updates during fine-tuning. Due to a large number of data in QnA, we fine-tune QnA models for a maximum of 10,000 updates and set the update frequency to 16. We deploy early stopping with patience set to five. We select the model checkpoint with the lowest perplexity on the validation set. We train our systems on two GeForce RTX 2080 Ti GPU with half-precision (FP16) for faster training. During the inference, the beam size to set to 5.

6 Results and Analysis

6.1 Results

We report BLEU[4] and TER[5] scores of all the trained models, calculated with sacreBLEU (Post, 2018). Tables 3 and 4 shows the BLEU and TER scores of all models on prepared corpora. For the WMT20 Chat dataset, the Baseline model achieves 39.1 and 43.8 BLEU points for Agent and Customer subsets, respectively. After domain adaptation, we achieve 19.1 and 17.5 BLEU score improvements. Transfer from MMD boosted BLEU by 1.3 points for the Customer Subset test set, mostly consisting of informal utterances. However, the improvement was 0.5 BLEU for the Agent Subset, containing mostly formal utterances. Further, we report our results on Overall (En-Hi), combining both user and customer subsets, then flip the source and target for the Customer subset (where the source is English and the Target is Hindi). Similarly, for

[4]sacreBLEU Signature: nrefs:1|case:mixed|eff:no|tok:13a|smooth:exp|version:2.1.0

[5]TER signature: nrefs:1|case:lc|tok:tercom|norm:no|punct:yes|asian:no|version:2.1.0

Overall (Hi-En), we flip the source and target side of the Agent subset. Although the context-based method caused degradation in the BLEU score, it can achieve the best TER score on the Customer subset.

Model	Customer		Agent		Overall (En-to-Hi)		Overall (Hi-to-En)	
	BLEU	TER	BLEU	TER	BLEU	TER	BLEU	TER
WMT20 Chat Results								
Baseline	43.8	47.2	39.1	48.1	37.5	48.8	37.0	49.2
Domain Adaptation	61.3	29.8	58.2	30.9	57.4	31.7	61.4	25.3
Transfer Learning	**62.6**	29.6	**58.7**	**30.6**	**57.9**	**31.3**	**61.7**	**25.1**
Domain Adaptation with Context	62.0	**29.0**	57.9	31.1	-	-	-	-
MMD Results								
Baseline	30.8	47.3	38.3	47.0	38.3	46.0	29.9	51.0
Domain Adaptation	76.6	17.4	52.4	**33.0**	56.4	29.6	62.3	26.4
Transfer Learning	76.8	17.7	**52.9**	33.4	**57.1**	**29.5**	**62.4**	**26.0**
Domain Adaptation with Context	**76.9**	**17.1**	52.3	34.1	-	-	-	-

Table 3: Results on English–Hindi WMT20 Chat and MMD corpora. Transfer Learning: Fine-tuning the model trained on the MMD corpus for the WMT20 Chat model and the model trained on the WMT20 Chat corpus for the MMD model. Translation direction of Agent and Customer subsets are En-Hi and Hi-En, respectively. Note that Agent and Customer correspond to System and User Subsets of MMD Data. En: English, Hi: Hindi.

Model	Questions		Answers		Overall	
	BLEU	TER	BLEU	TER	BLEU	TER
Baseline	48.2	36.5	47.8	39.5	47.8	39.0
Domain Adaptation	49.2	36.3	49.1	37.3	49.1	37.1
Domain Adaptation with Context	50.1	35.8	49.9	36.9	**49.9**	**36.7**
Tagged Fine-tuning	**50.3**	35.9	48.7	37.2	48.9	37.0
Domain Specific NMT	50.2	**35.1**	**50.4**	**36.1**	-	-

Table 4: Results on English–Hindi QnA corpus. En: English, Hi: Hindi. Domain Adaptation with Context: Used question as the context for the answer and vice-versa; Tagged-Finetuning: Provided Question or Answer tags with sentences; Domain-Specific NMT: Models Trained on either question or answer.

For the MMD dataset, the Baseline model achieves 30.8 and 38.3 BLEU scores for user and system subsets. The model trained with the Domain Adaptation method achieves 45.8 and 14.1 BLEU improvement over the Baseline on Customer and Agent subsets, respectively. Transfer learning from the WMT20 Chat dataset yields a better signal and improves performance on all subsets regarding the BLEU score. However, it is noted that transfer learning models use more data than other models as they are fine-tuned on top of already fine-tuned models on WMT20 chat data.

Context-based model was able to improve BLEU by 0.3 for *user* subset whereas BLEU score decreased for *System* subset. The system subsets usually consist of a long description of products and sufficient information to translate the sentence. The context here acts as noise and negatively affects the translation quality.

For the QnA dataset, we achieved a 47.8 BLEU score and 39.0 TER on the baseline MT system, which is trained on general domain data. After fine-tuning on in-domain data, we achieve a BLEU score of 49.1, improving the 1.3 BLEU score over the Baseline. For fine-tuning with context, we achieve a BLEU score of 49.9, which is better by 0.8 than the previous model.

Effects of tagged fine-tune: Tagged fine-tune is a popular method to train the models on diverse datasets. (Caswell et al., 2019) used tags for back-translated (BT) sentences to train a model with a combination of bitext and BT data. We supply <question> tag for every question and <answer> tag for every answer. This is to help the model learn to question and answer specific properties. While this method improved the translation quality of Questions, the same was not reflected in Answers. This can be attributed to the fact that questions are usually ambiguous as there are missing question marks, grammatical errors framing questions as statements, etc. Tag for questions helped to disambiguate such errors, but the tags were not of much use for answers.

Domain specific NMT: We divide our data into two subsets: (i). Questions and (ii). Answers. We train two separate sentence-level MT systems on the two subsets to help the model learn question/answer property without other domain data. We achieve a 50.4 BLEU score with this method on the Answer subset, which is the best among all methods. We suggest this is due to the absence of a question subset during training. The question subsets negatively impact the learning of answer translation as they contain a more significant portion of erroneous references on the target side due to mistranslation. On the question subset, we obtain a BLEU score of 50.2, which is 0.1 less than that of the best model. It is to be noted that each of the systems is trained on only mutually exclusive 50% of the dataset[6]. Therefore, it generates a bit poor translation than the model trained on complete data.

Context	6, okay great! let me catch you the rates really quickly.
Source	The rate I found for an UberXL will be $45.66.
Translation without Context	मुझे uberxl के लिए $45.66 की दर मिलेगी। *(For an uberxl, the rate I will find is $45.66)*
Translation with Context	मुझे एक uberxl के लिए $45.66 की दर मिली। *(For an uberxl, the rate I found is $45.66)*

Table 5: Example of generated output sentences with and without context.

6.2 Analysis

In the example about ride-booking from Table 5, translations from non-context based systems are in future tense. This can be attributed to the presence of the word *will* in the source utterance. However, translation with context was able to translate it correctly to present tense.

6.3 Quality testing

The proposed model is evaluated in the well-known E-commerce industry, Flipkart[7] with the help of real-time human evaluators. The evaluators rated them with respect to the scale of 1-3, where 1-*Bad*, 2-*Can be Better* and 3- *Good.* During the evaluation, while assigning the labels to the output samples, 'tense preservation,' 'syntax of output

[6]The in-domain dataset contains 50% questions and 50% answers. However, these models are trained on either questions or answers, not both. These (questions or answers) are effectively 50% of the available in-domain dataset

[7]https://www.flipkart.com/

Model	WMT20 Chat			MMD			QnA		
	Good	Can be better	Bad	Good	Can be better	Bad	Good	Can be better	Bad
Baseline	28%	60%	12%	40%	56%	4%	29%	36%	34%
Domain-Adaptation	76%	20%	4%	68%	28%	4%	31%	35%	34%
Context-Based	76%	20%	4%	64%	32%	4%	30%	38%	32%

Table 6: Real-time quality evaluation of trained models on the prepared corpora between Baseline, Transfer Learning, and Domain Adaptation with Context models.

sentence,' 'choice of in-domain output tokens' are some important factors that are kept in mind. Table 6 shows the statistics of the real-time evaluation. A sample of 25 sentences from Baseline and Domain-Adaptation, Domain Adaptation with Context models for analysis for both MMD and WMT20 chat corpora. For the MMD corpus, 4% of the translations are rated as *Bad* from each model. While 56% and 40% are rated as *Can be better* and *Good*, respectively, for Baseline. Domain-Adaptation model achieves the best rating with 68% as *Good* and 28% as *Can be better*. Similarly for WMT20 Chat corpus, the baseline model outputs are rated as, 28% as *Good* quality, 60% & 12% as *Can be better* and *Bad* respectively. Domain Adaptation and Domain Adaptation with Context models achieves 76%, 20% and 4% as *Good*, *Can be better* and *Bad*, respectively.

For the QnA corpus, a sample of 250 sentences is taken for evaluation. 34% of the translations are rated as *Bad* from Baseline and Domain Adaptation and 32% for Domain Adaptation with Context model. While 35% and 31% are rated as *Can be better* and *Good* for Domain Adaptation model respectively. For Domain Adaptation with Context model, 38% were rated as *Can be better* and 30% were rated as *Good*. Based on the evaluation results, the Domain Adaptation method significantly improves the "Good" category from the "Can be better" category.

7 Conclusion

Dialogue translation is different from sentence translation due to several additional challenges. The particular field could not be adequately explored in Indian languages due to a lack of datasets. Multilingual chatbots are in high demand as many of the world's population are not fluent in English and other major languages. We introduce two English–Hindi parallel datasets for Dialogue Translation and one large-scale English–Hindi parallel corpus for QnA translation. The datasets contain various domains, including fashion, making reservations, ordering foods, E-commerce products, etc., and contain sentences from different roles and languages. Demands for online chatbot services involving the domains mentioned above are tremendous. The multilingual property of the datasets will be beneficial in building multilingual chatbots and QnA translators. We report a baseline result on some sentence-level and a context-level model exploiting context. In the future, we would like to introduce better ways to utilize context and use other chat-specific characteristics, including informality, code-mixing, etc. Further, we would like to extend the work into other Indian languages, including Tamil, Telugu, Malayalam, etc.

Acknowledgment

Authors gratefully acknowledge the unrestricted research grant received from the Flipkart Internet Private Limited to carry out the research. Authors thank Anubhav Tripathee for gold standard parallel corpus creation and translation quality evaluation.

References

Bao, C., Shiue, Y.-T., Song, C., Li, J., and Carpuat, M. (2020). The University of Maryland's Submissions to the WMT20 Chat Translation Task: Searching for More Data to Adapt Discourse-Aware Neural Machine Translation. In *Proceedings of the Fifth Conference on Machine Translation*, pages 456–461.

Berard, A., Calapodescu, I., Nikoulina, V., and Philip, J. (2020). Naver Labs Europe's Participation in the Robustness, Chat, and Biomedical Tasks at WMT 2020. In *Proceedings of the Fifth Conference on Machine Translation*, pages 460–470.

Byrne, B., Krishnamoorthi, K., Sankar, C., Neelakantan, A., Goodrich, B., Duckworth, D., Yavuz, S., Dubey, A., Kim, K.-Y., and Cedilnik, A. (2019). Taskmaster-1: Toward a realistic and diverse dialog dataset. In *Proceedings of the 2019 Conference on Empirical Methods in Natural Language Processing and the 9th International Joint Conference on Natural Language Processing (EMNLP-IJCNLP)*, pages 4516–4525, Hong Kong, China. Association for Computational Linguistics.

Caswell, I., Chelba, C., and Grangier, D. (2019). Tagged Back-Translation. In *Proceedings of the Fourth Conference on Machine Translation (Volume 1: Research Papers)*, pages 53–63, Florence, Italy.

Chen, Q., Lin, J., Zhang, Y., Ding, M., Cen, Y., Yang, H., and Tang, J. (2019). Towards knowledge-based recommender dialog system. In *Proceedings of the 2019 Conference on Empirical Methods in Natural Language Processing and the 9th International Joint Conference on Natural Language Processing (EMNLP-IJCNLP)*, pages 1803–1813, Hong Kong, China. Association for Computational Linguistics.

Conneau, A. and Lample, G. (2019). Cross-lingual language model pretraining. In *Advances in Neural Information Processing Systems*, volume 32, pages 7059–7069.

Deng, Y., Zhanng, W., and Lam, W. (2020). Opinion-aware answer generation for review-driven question answering in e-commerce. *Proceedings of the 29th ACM International Conference on Information & Knowledge Management.*

Farajian, M. A., Lopes, A. V., Martins, A. F. T., Maruf, S., and Haffari, G. (2020). Findings of the WMT 2020 Shared Task on Chat Translation. In *Proceedings of the Fifth Conference on Machine Translation*, pages 64–74, Online.

Gain, B., Haque, R., and Ekbal, A. (2021). Not all contexts are important: The impact of effective context in conversational neural machine translation. In *2021 International Joint Conference on Neural Networks (IJCNN)*, pages 1–8.

Hassan, H., Aue, A., Chen, C., Chowdhary, V., Clark, J., Federmann, C., Huang, X., Junczys-Dowmunt, M., Lewis, W., Li, M., Liu, S., Liu, T.-Y., Luo, R., Menezes, A., Qin, T., Seide, F., Tan, X., Tian, F., Wu, L., Wu, S., Xia, Y., Zhang, D., Zhang, Z., and Zhou, M. (2018). Achieving human parity on automatic chinese to english news translation.

Koehn, P. and Knowles, R. (2017). Six challenges for neural machine translation. In *Proceedings of the First Workshop on Neural Machine Translation*, pages 28–39, Vancouver. Association for Computational Linguistics.

Lai, T. M., Bui, T., Lipka, N., and Li, S. (2018). Supervised transfer learning for product information question answering. In *2018 17th IEEE International Conference on Machine Learning and Applications (ICMLA)*, pages 1109–1114.

Liang, Y., Meng, F., Chen, Y., Xu, J., and Zhou, J. (2021a). Modeling bilingual conversational characteristics for neural chat translation. In *Proceedings of the 59th Annual Meeting of the Association for Computational Linguistics and the 11th International Joint Conference on Natural Language Processing (Volume 1: Long Papers)*, pages 5711–5724, Online. Association for Computational Linguistics.

Liang, Y., Meng, F., Xu, J., Chen, Y., and Zhou, J. (2022a). MSCTD: A multimodal sentiment chat translation dataset. In *Proceedings of the 60th Annual Meeting of the Association for Computational Linguistics (Volume 1: Long Papers)*, pages 2601–2613, Dublin, Ireland. Association for Computational Linguistics.

Liang, Y., Meng, F., Xu, J., Chen, Y., and Zhou, J. (2022b). Scheduled multi-task learning for neural chat translation. In *Proceedings of the 60th Annual Meeting of the Association for Computational Linguistics (Volume 1: Long Papers)*, pages 4375–4388, Dublin, Ireland. Association for Computational Linguistics.

Liang, Y., Zhou, C., Meng, F., Xu, J., Chen, Y., Su, J., and Zhou, J. (2021b). Towards making the most of dialogue characteristics for neural chat translation. In *Proceedings of the 2021 Conference on Empirical Methods in Natural Language Processing*, pages 67–79, Online and Punta Cana, Dominican Republic. Association for Computational Linguistics.

Moghe, N., Hardmeier, C., and Bawden, R. (2020). The University of Edinburgh-Uppsala University's Submission to the WMT 2020 Chat Translation Task. In *Proceedings of the Fifth Conference on Machine Translation*, pages 471–476.

Ng, N., Yee, K., Baevski, A., Ott, M., Auli, M., and Edunov, S. (2019). Facebook FAIR's WMT19 News Translation Task Submission. In *Proceedings of the Fourth Conference on Machine Translation*, pages 314–319, Florence, Italy.

Ott, M., Edunov, S., Baevski, A., Fan, A., Gross, S., Ng, N., Grangier, D., and Auli, M. (2019). fairseq: A fast, extensible toolkit for sequence modeling. In *Proceedings of the 2019 Conference of the North American Chapter of the Association for Computational Linguistics (Demonstrations)*, pages 48–53, Minneapolis, MN.

Papineni, K., Roukos, S., Ward, T., and Zhu, W.-J. (2002). Bleu: a method for automatic evaluation of machine translation. In *Proceedings of the 40th Annual Meeting of the Association for Computational Linguistics*, pages 311–318, Philadelphia, Pennsylvania, USA. Association for Computational Linguistics.

Poria, S., Hazarika, D., Majumder, N., Naik, G., Cambria, E., and Mihalcea, R. (2019). MELD: A multimodal multi-party dataset for emotion recognition in conversations. In *Proceedings of the 57th Annual Meeting of the Association for Computational Linguistics*, pages 527–536, Florence, Italy. Association for Computational Linguistics.

Post, M. (2018). A call for clarity in reporting BLEU scores. In *Proceedings of the Third Conference on Machine Translation: Research Papers*, pages 186–191, Belgium, Brussels.

Provilkov, I., Emelianenko, D., and Voita, E. (2020). BPE-Dropout: Simple and Effective Subword Regularization. In *Proceedings of the 58th Annual Meeting of the Association for Computational Linguistics*, pages 1882–1892.

Qu, C., Yang, L., Qiu, M., Zhang, Y., Chen, C., Croft, W. B., and Iyyer, M. (2019). Attentive history selection for conversational question answering. In *Proceedings of the 28th ACM International Conference on Information and Knowledge Management*, CIKM '19, page 1391–1400, New York, NY, USA. Association for Computing Machinery.

Ramesh, G., Doddapaneni, S., Bheemaraj, A., Jobanputra, M., AK, R., Sharma, A., Sahoo, S., Diddee, H., J, M., Kakwani, D., Kumar, N., Pradeep, A., Nagaraj, S., Deepak, K., Raghavan, V., Kunchukuttan, A., Kumar, P., and Khapra, M. S. (2021). Samanantar: The largest publicly available parallel corpora collection for 11 indic languages.

Saha, A., Khapra, M. M., and Sankaranarayanan, K. (2018). Towards building large scale multimodal domain-aware conversation systems. In *AAAI*.

Sennrich, R., Haddow, B., and Birch, A. (2016). Neural Machine Translation of Rare Words with Subword Units. In *Proceedings of the 54th Annual Meeting of the Association for Computational Linguistics (Volume 1: Long Papers)*, pages 1715–1725, Berlin, Germany.

Snover, M. G., Dorr, B., Schwartz, R. M., Micciulla, L., and Weischedel, R. M. (2005). A study of translation error rate with targeted human annotation.

Sun, Y. and Zhang, Y. (2018). Conversational recommender system. In *The 41st International ACM SIGIR Conference on Research & Development in Information Retrieval*, SIGIR '18, page 235–244, New York, NY, USA. Association for Computing Machinery.

Vaswani, A., Shazeer, N., Parmar, N., Uszkoreit, J., Jones, L., Gomez, A. N., Kaiser, L., and Polosukhin, I. (2017). Attention is All You Need. In *Proceedings of the 31st International Conference on Neural Information Processing Systems*, page 6000–6010, Red Hook, NY, USA.

Wang, L., Tu, Z., Wang, X., Ding, L., Ding, L., and Shi, S. (2020). Tencent AI Lab Machine Translation Systems for WMT20 Chat Translation Task. In *Proceedings of the Fifth Conference on Machine Translation*, pages 483–491.

Wang, T., Zhao, C., Wang, M., Li, L., and Xiong, D. (2021). Autocorrect in the process of translation — multi-task learning improves dialogue machine translation. In *Proceedings of the 2021 Conference of the North American Chapter of the Association for Computational Linguistics: Human Language Technologies: Industry Papers*, pages 105–112, Online. Association for Computational Linguistics.

Wu, Y., Schuster, M., Chen, Z., Le, Q. V., Norouzi, M., Macherey, W., Krikun, M., Cao, Y., Gao, Q., Macherey, K., Klingner, J., Shah, A., Johnson, M., Liu, X., Kaiser, L., Gouws, S., Kato, Y., Kudo, T., Kazawa, H., Stevens, K., Kurian, G., Patil, N., Wang, W., Young, C., Smith, J., Riesa, J., Rudnick, A., Vinyals, O., Corrado, G., Hughes, M., and Dean, J. (2016). Google's neural machine translation system: Bridging the gap between human and machine translation. *CoRR*, abs/1609.08144.

Yeganova, L., Wiemann, D., Neves, M., Vezzani, F., Siu, A., Jauregi Unanue, I., Oronoz, M., Mah, N., Névéol, A., Martinez, D., Bawden, R., Di Nunzio, G. M., Roller, R., Thomas, P., Grozea, C., Perez-de Viñaspre, O., Vicente Navarro, M., and Jimeno Yepes, A. (2021). Findings of the WMT 2021 biomedical translation shared task: Summaries of animal experiments as new test set. In *Proceedings of the Sixth Conference on Machine Translation*, pages 664–683, Online. Association for Computational Linguistics.

Yu, L., Sartran, L., Huang, P.-S., Stokowiec, W., Donato, D., Srinivasan, S., Andreev, A., Ling, W., Mokra, S., Dal Lago, A., Doron, Y., Young, S., Blunsom, P., and Dyer, C. (2020). The DeepMind Chinese–English document translation system at WMT2020. In *Proceedings of the Fifth Conference on Machine Translation*, pages 326–337, Online. Association for Computational Linguistics.

Zhang, Y., Chen, X., Ai, Q., Yang, L., and Croft, W. B. (2018). Towards conversational search and recommendation: System ask, user respond. In *Proceedings of the 27th ACM International Conference on Information and Knowledge Management*, CIKM '18, page 177–186, New York, NY, USA. Association for Computing Machinery.

Zoph, B., Yuret, D., May, J., and Knight, K. (2016). Transfer learning for low-resource neural machine translation. In *Proceedings of the 2016 Conference on Empirical Methods in Natural Language Processing*, pages 1568–1575, Austin, Texas. Association for Computational Linguistics.

How Robust is Neural Machine Translation to Language Imbalance in Multilingual Tokenizer Training?

Shiyue Zhang[♠*], **Vishrav Chaudhary**[♣†], **Naman Goyal**[♡],
James Cross[♡], **Guillaume Wenzek**[♡], **Mohit Bansal**[♠], **and Francisco Guzmán**[♡]
[♠]UNC Chapel Hill [♡]Meta AI [♣]Microsoft Turing
{shiyue, mbansal}@cs.unc.edu vchaudhary@microsoft.com
{naman, jcross, guw, fguzman}@fb.com

Abstract

A multilingual tokenizer is a fundamental component of multilingual neural machine translation. It is trained from a multilingual corpus. Since a skewed data distribution is considered to be harmful, a sampling strategy is usually used to balance languages in the corpus. However, few works have systematically answered how language imbalance in tokenizer training affects downstream performance. In this work, we analyze how translation performance changes as the data ratios among languages vary in the tokenizer training corpus. We find that while relatively better performance is often observed when languages are more equally sampled, the downstream performance is more robust to language imbalance than we usually expected. Two features, *UNK rate* and *closeness to the character level*, can warn of poor downstream performance before performing the task. We also distinguish language sampling for tokenizer training from sampling for model training and show that the model is more sensitive to the latter.

1 Introduction

Tokenization is an essential pre-processing step for most natural language processing (NLP) models. Out of different tokenization methods, subword tokenization (Schuster and Nakajima, 2012; Sennrich et al., 2016; Kudo, 2018) has become *de facto*. The creation of each subword is mainly based on frequency, i.e., if two characters often appear together, they will be merged into a subword. When more than one language is involved, instead of learning independent tokenizers for each language, people usually train a joint tokenizer from a multilingual training corpus (Sennrich et al., 2016; Devlin et al., 2019). In this case, the data percentage of each language directly affects how it will be represented. If one language dominates the training corpus, its words will mostly stay intact and hardly be split into subwords. In contrast, if the language gets starved, it will be excessively tokenized into characters, thus, the sentence length will be dramatically longer, and some tokens will be considered as unknown (UNK). Moreover, Neural machine translation (NMT) is known to be bad at dealing with long sentences and UNKs (Koehn and Knowles, 2017).

Recently, there is an increasing interest in building multilingual neural models that can process multiple languages (Devlin et al., 2019; Liu et al., 2020; Xue et al., 2021b). A challenge

*Work done during an internship at Meta AI.
†Work done while at Meta AI.

that comes with this important task is to balance languages with different amounts of training data to avoid low-resource languages being under-represented, e.g., being excessively tokenized and being less seen by the neural models. Existing works usually adopt the *temperature sampling* strategy (Devlin et al., 2019; Arivazhagan et al., 2019; Conneau and Lample, 2019; Xue et al., 2021b) (see detailed descriptions in Section 2.2). However, very few investigations of how language imbalance affects downstream performance have been conducted. Additionally, whenever previous works apply a certain language balancing strategy, they apply it for both *tokenizer training* (balancing the data sizes of different languages in the tokenizer training corpus) and *model training* (balancing the frequencies of sampling training mini-batches from different languages). Until now, it is unclear how each of them separately affects the downstream performance.

In this work, we specifically investigate how robust NMT is to language imbalance in tokenizer training. We propose to vary the data ratio among languages in the tokenizer training corpus while keeping other settings (e.g., language sampling for model training, hyperparameters) fixed, and then check how translation results change (Section 3.1). However, finding the best data ratio through performing the downstream task is highly expensive. To provide an easy indication of tokenizer quality (or early prediction of downstream performance), we examine two intermediate features (Section 3.2): *UNK rate* – the average percentage of unknown words (marked with the UNK token) in each sentence, and *closeness to the character level* – the average sentence length in subwords divided by sentence length in characters.

Through comprehensive bilingual and multilingual experiments among 8 languages (English, Tagalog, Icelandic, Danish, Indonesian, Tamil, Greek, and Chinese), we make the following **five main observations**: (1) NMT performance is more robust to language imbalance than we usually expected: especially when languages share scripts, performance drops only happen when the data ratio of two languages is as disparate as $1{:}10^5$. (2) Better performance is often achieved when languages are more balanced: we observe moderate Pearson correlations between translation performance and the degree of language balance. (3) English can "never" be starved because English tokens often appear in the "monolingual" data of other languages. (4) In most cases, the two features (UNK rate and closeness to the character level) can hint at poor translation performances before performing the task. (5) NMT is more sensitive to language imbalance in model training than in tokenizer training. See more observations and discussions in Section 3 and Section 4.

Based on these observations, we provide the following **two practical suggestions**: (1) Instead of using temperature sampling, we want to keep the involved languages as balanced as possible when training a new multilingual tokenizer; (2) Before applying a pretrained tokenizer for new experiments or languages, we suggest evaluating it on a development set to make sure every language's UNK rate is low (lower than around 3.7%, according to our experiments) and every language's closeness to the character level is also low (lower than around 0.87, according to our experiments).[1]

2 Related Works

2.1 Tokenization Methods

Over the years, many tokenization methods have been proposed. Early works tokenize texts into "words", e.g., `MosesTokenizer` (Koehn et al., 2007). However, language-specific tokenizers are needed and it often ends up with many rare tokens or UNKs. *Subword tokenization* methods

[1]The exact threshold numbers (3.7% and 0.87) are based our experiments and may not always hold. But we believe that the concept of checking the two features (UNK rate and the closeness to the character level) to make sure they are low enough should generalize to other situations.

were introduced to tackle this problem: the idea is to keep frequent words intact and split rare words into frequent subwords. Subword tokenization has become *de facto*. Schuster and Nakajima (2012) introduce `WordPiece` that starts from all characters and gradually merges two units that improve language model (LM) likelihood the most. Sennrich et al. (2016) propose to learn subwords via Byte-Pair Encoding (`BPE`) that merges the most frequent pairs first. Kudo (2018) propose a `unigram LM` method. It starts with a large vocabulary and gradually prunes it down to the desired size by removing tokens that are less likely to reduce the unigram LM likelihood. Subword tokenization methods usually assume the existence of pre-tokenization (e.g., split by whitespaces), which can cause de-tokenization ambiguity. To address this, `SentencePiece` (Kudo and Richardson, 2018) treats whitespace as a special symbol, _ (U+2581), to achieve *lossless* tokenization. This toolkit supports both BPE and unigram LM tokenization. Despite the success of subword tokenization, it is no panacea, e.g., it is out-of-the-box and agnostic to the downstream tasks, it has no guarantee that subwords are meaningful, and it is vulnerable to typos (Sun et al., 2020). Thus, "tokenization-free" models that directly encode characters or bytes or visuals have been introduced (Chung et al., 2016; Lee et al., 2017; Salesky et al., 2021) and are gaining more interest recently (Clark et al., 2022; Xue et al., 2021a; Tay et al., 2021).

2.2 Multilingual Tokenization

Along with the development of multilingual models, people start to deal with multilingual tokenization. Firat et al. (2016) learn a 30K subword vocabulary for each language. Johnson et al. (2017) oversample languages to the same size and train a joint WordPiece vocabulary. Recent multilingual works adopt this joint-vocabulary method, but instead of oversampling languages to the same size, they use *temperature sampling* which was first introduced by multilingual BERT (mBERT) (Devlin et al., 2019). Given the original data distribution $\{p_i\}_{i=1}^N$, where p_i is the percentage of the ith language out of the total N languages, they exponentiate each p_i by a factor S ($0 \leq S \leq 1$), i.e., p_i^S. Then, they re-normalize them to get the new percentage of each language $\hat{p}_i = p_i^S / \sum_i p_i^S$, and they sample data according to the new percentages. Essentially, it down-samples high-resource languages and up-samples low-resource ones. Arivazhagan et al. (2019) redefine S as $\frac{1}{T}$ (T stands for temperature). S is usually set around 0.2 to 0.7, i.e., *flattening the data distribution to some degree but not to uniform distribution* (Arivazhagan et al., 2019; Conneau and Lample, 2019; Conneau et al., 2020; Xue et al., 2021b). Chung et al. (2020) challenge this joint vocabulary recipe and propose to learn separate vocabularies for each language cluster.

2.3 Analysis and Assessment of Tokenization

Since the choice of tokenization algorithm and training parameters affects downstream performances, previous works try to analyze or assess tokenization. Some works focus on the choice of vocabulary size. Gowda and May (2020) show that the near-optimal vocabulary size is when 95% of tokens appear more than 100 times in the training set. Ding et al. (2019) find that low-resource language pairs usually require fewer than 4K BPE merge-operations. Xu et al. (2021) evaluate vocabularies by Marginal Utility of Vocabularization and propose to tokenize as well as find the optimal vocabulary size via the Optimal Transport method. Some other works compare different tokenization algorithms. Domingo et al. (2018) compare 5 tokenizers and the best tokenizer varies across language pairs. Bostrom and Durrett (2020) compare BPE to unigram LM for LM pretraining and show that unigram LM learns subwords that align better with morphology and leads to better performance.

When multiple languages are involved, Gerz et al. (2018) show that language typology is correlated with LM performance. Ács (2019) find that mBERT (Devlin et al., 2019) vocabulary are dominated by subwords of European languages, and the tokenizer keeps English mostly

Language	Code	Script	En-* bitext	Mono. text
English	en	Latin	-	2B
Tagalog	tl	Latin	71K	107M
Icelandic	is	Latin	1M	37M
Danish	da	Latin	11M	343M
Indonesian	id	Latin	39M	1B
Tamil	ta	Tamil	97K	68M
Greek	el	Greek	24M	200M
Chinese	zh	Han	38M	293M

Table 1: 8 languages in our experiments. K/M/B stands for thousand/million/billion. Mono. stands for monolingual. Numbers are the number of sentences (pairs).

intact while generating different distributions for morphologically rich languages. Rust et al. (2021) observe that mBERT usually performs worse than its monolingual counterparts because language-specific tokenizers keep the language from being excessively tokenized. Some works compare different *temperature sampling* factors (S or T). Arivazhagan et al. (2019) compare multilingual translation results of using temperature T=1, 5, 100, and find that T=5 works best. Xue et al. (2021b) compare multilingual LM performances for sampling factor S=0.2-0.7 and find that $S = 0.3$ is the best. However, note that the performance difference is a joint effect of both tokenizer and model training because the sampling is applied for both. Differently, in this paper, we analyze how language imbalance specifically in multilingual tokenizer training affects the downstream translation performance.

3 Bilingual Experiments

To examine how language imbalance in tokenizer training affects downstream translation performance, we first conduct English-centric bilingual experiments in which imbalance only happens for one single pair of languages (i.e., English and anther language). This gives us a more controlled setting compared to when multiple languages are involved. Nonetheless, we conduct multilingual experiments in Section 4. Our main methodology is to keep the total tokenizer training data size fixed, gradually "starve" English, i.e., reduce English data percentage and increase the percentage of the other language, and then check the downstream translation performance. It is important to note that, to separate the influences of tokenizer and model, we use different data for tokenizer training and model training, and the model training data are always the same.

3.1 Experimental Setup

Languages. We experiment with 8 languages: English (en), Tagalog (tl), Icelandic (is), Danish (da), Indonesian (id), Tamil (ta), Greek (el), Chinese (zh). The data statistics are shown in Table 1. According to FLORES101 (Goyal et al., 2021), Icelandic, Tamil, and Tagalog are *low-resource* ($\leq$ 1M bitext), while Danish, Greek, Chinese, and Indonesian are *mid-resource* ($\leq$ 100M bitext). Tagalog, Icelandic, Danish, and Indonesian are Latin languages and thus share scripts with English; while Tamil, Greek, and Chinese are non-Latin.

Translations. We conduct English-centric bilingual translations in 14 directions: en-tl, tl-en, en-is, is-en, en-da, da-en, en-id, id-en, en-ta, ta-en, en-el, el-en, en-zh, zh-en. We train one translation model for each direction.

Variables. For each translation direction, we have the following controlled, independent, and dependent variables:
Controlled variables

- Tokenizer training data: We use the same monolingual data as FLORES101 (Goyal et al., 2021). The total monolingual data sizes of each language are listed in Table 1. We sample from these monolingual datasets to get the desired tokenizer training data size.[2] We keep the total tokenizer training data size as 2M, which contains $x\%$ English data and $1 - x\%$ data of the other language.

- Tokenizer parameters: We use SentencePiece model (SPM) with unigram LM algorithm (Kudo, 2018; Kudo and Richardson, 2018). We set vocabulary size as 5K,[3] total training data size as 2M, and character coverage as 0.99995 (or 0.995 when Chinese is involved because Chinese has a richer character set).
- Translation training data: We also use the same parallel data as FLORES101 (Goyal et al., 2021) (data sizes are in Table 1). As mentioned above, we do not change this model training data across different experiments. And following previous works (Section 2.2), we always use temperature sampling with $S = 0.2$ for model training.
- Translation evaluation data: We evaluate on FLORES101 (Goyal et al., 2021) dev sets and report results on its devtest sets.
- Translation model: Transformer (Vaswani et al., 2017) with 12-layer encoder and 12-layer decoder (Transformer 12-12).
- Model training and testing hyper-parameters: Adam optimizer (Kingma and Ba, 2015), learning rate = 0.001, and beam size = 5. See more implementation details in A.1.

Independent variable

- English data percentage in 2M tokenizer training data[4]: we experiment with 9 different percentages (0%, 0.001%, 0.1%, 10%, 50%, 90%, 99.9%, 99.999%, 100%). E.g., if we conduct en-zh/zh-en translations with English percentage=0.001%, there are 20 English sentences and 2M - 20 Chinese sentences in SPM tokenizer training data. Hence, for each translation direction, we have 9 experiments with 9 different vocabularies. See examples of how sentences are tokenized at different English percentages in Table 4 of A.5.

Dependent variable

- Translation performance: we evaluate it by sentence-piece BLEU (spBLEU) (Goyal et al., 2021)[5] and chrF (Popović, 2015). Metrics are computed by SacreBLEU (Post, 2018).[6] We report the 3-seed average for each experiment.

3.2 Intermediate Features

Previous works have shown that without training downstream models, some intermediate features can be good indicators of the tokenizer's quality (Gowda and May, 2020; Chung et al., 2020; Xu et al., 2021). In this work, as the English data percentage varies, either English or the other language will get starved – sentence lengths will become longer and unknown words (UNKs) will appear. Hence, we examine the following two features:

[2]To minimize sampling influence, we shuffle each monolingual dataset once and then always sample the first X sentences.

[3]We set vocabulary size as 5K because (1) a small vocab size makes the "competition" between languages more "fierce" and thus makes it easier to show the problem of language imbalance, and (2) it resembles a multilingual setting: FLORES101 uses a 256K vocabulary for 101 languages – 2.5K tokens per language on average.

[4]We choose to directly vary the data percentage rather than sampling temperature because it grants us the flexibility of making high-resource languages hypothetically low-resource and experimenting with extreme data ratios (100%: 0%).

[5]Computing BLEU (Papineni et al., 2002) requires a tokenizer. However, not all languages have language-specific tokenizers available. spBLEU (Goyal et al., 2021) unifies the evaluation across languages by first tokenizing languages via a 256K multilingual SPM and then computing BLEU.

[6]https://github.com/ngoyal2707/sacrebleu/tree/adding_spm_tokenized_bleu

- *Closeness to the character level*, defined as the average $\frac{sentence\ length\ in\ subwords}{sentence\ length\ in\ characters}$. Some languages may intrinsically have longer sentence lengths than others. To be comparable across languages, we normalize it by the upper bound – sentence length in characters.
- *UNK rate*, which is defined as the average $\frac{number\ of\ UNKs}{sentence\ length\ in\ subwords}$. Note that when the UNK rate increases, long unknown tokens will not get split into subwords, and thus the sentence length will be shorter and the closeness to the character level will decrease.

The first two columns of Figure 1 illustrate how the intermediate features change as the English data percentage changes. The first row (a) shows features of the 4 Latin languages, while the second row (b) is those of the 3 non-Latin languages. Note that both features are computed on FLORES101 (Goyal et al., 2021) devtest sets.

Closeness to the character level. In Figure 1 (a), as the English percentage increases, the closeness to the character level of English (gray markers) decreases while that of other languages (makers with other colors) increases. It is because when the English percentage gets larger, the other language's tokens will become rarer and be excessively tokenized into subwords. Differently, in Figure 1 (b), though the trend of English stays the same, the trend of other languages first increases close to 1.0 and then decreases because UNKs start to appear. Even when English occupies 100%, Latin languages still have sentence lengths much shorter than the sentence length in characters because they share scripts with English. In contrast, each of the 3 non-Latin languages reaches close to the character level at a certain point. English never have very long sentence lengths.

UNK rate. In Figure 1 (a), most UNK rates are trivial (close to 0), except that Icelandic (is) and Danish (da) have non-trivial UNK rates when English percentage $\geq$ 99.999%. In Figure 1 (b), all three non-Latin languages have very high UNK rates after the English percentage increases to a certain point. For example, Chinese (zh) has a 45.7% UNK rate at English=99.9%, and it is when its closeness to the character level drops dramatically. English always has trivial UNK rates.

3.3 Translation Results

The second two columns of Figure 1 shows how the translation results change as the English data percentage changes. The first row (a) shows spBLEU and chrF scores of the 4 Latin languages, while the second row (b) are those of the 3 non-Latin languages. We obtain the following takeaways.

NMT performance is quite robust to language imbalance especially when languages share scripts. It can be observed from Figure 1 (a) that the performance stays quite stable across all English percentages for Latin languages. Performance drops only happen for English to Icelandic (en-is) and English to Danish (en-da) at extremely high English percentages ($\geq$99.999%), i.e., only 20 Icelandic or Danish sentences are in the 2M tokenizer training data. And it still does not affect the translation performances of is-en and da-en. Differently, in Figure 1 (b), the performance is less stable for non-Latin languages, but drops still happen when the English percentage is $\geq$90%. English to Chinese (en-zh) drops at English=90%. English to Tamil (en-ta)[7] and English to Greek (en-el) both drop at English=99.9%. Similarly, into-English directions are more stable and get worse later (at higher English percentages). Surprisingly, in both (a) and (b), the translation performance usually stays stable or drops less significantly as the English percentage decreases to 0%.

[7] Note that at English=99.9%, Tamil's chrF scores only drop slightly while its spBLEU scores drop more significantly (en-ta drops from 1.9 to 0.4 and ta-en drops from 1.1 to 0.1).

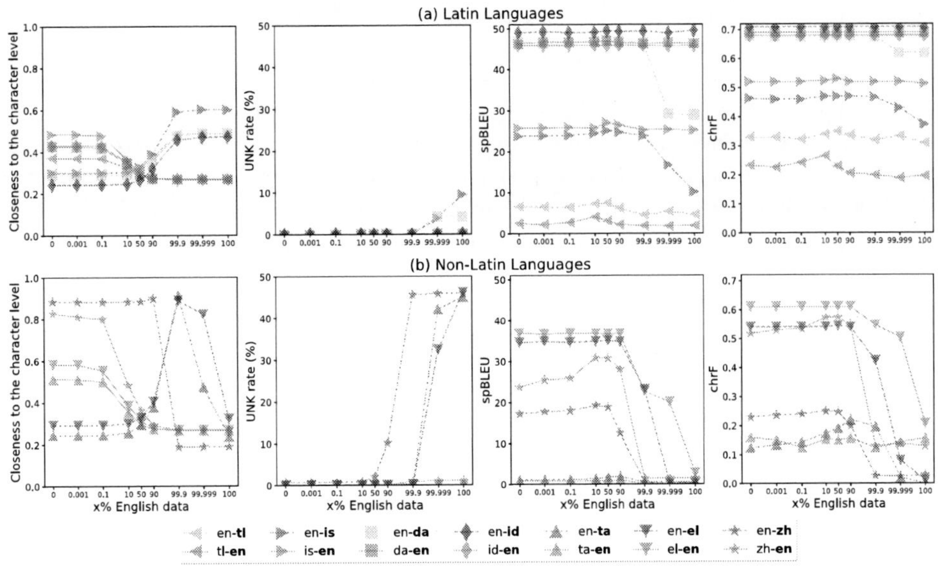

Figure 1: Results of our main bilingual experiments. Marker shapes denote the language pairs; dash or solid lines represents out-of-English or into-English directions; colors are for each target language. E.g., --▲-- (en-**ta**) denotes Tamil features (*Closeness to the character level* or *UNK rate*) or English to Tamil translation results (*spBLEU* or *chrF* scores); -▲- (ta-**en**) represents English features or Tamil to English translation results. X axes are in log10 scale.

Better performance is often achieved when languages are more balanced. Out of the 14 translation directions, 12 directions get the best spBLEU scores between English=10% to English=90%. We evaluate the Pearson correlation between spBLEU scores and *data ratios* of two languages. The data ratio is 1 when English=50%, and it is 0 when English=0% or 100%, i.e., the more balanced the two languages are, the higher the data ratio is. The average correlation across 14 directions is 0.38 (moderate correlation (Cohen, 1988)). Thus, we are more likely to get a good performance when languages are more equally sampled.

English can "never" be starved. Initially, we were expecting a symmetric trend, i.e., if the performance drops as the English percentage increases, it should also drop when the percentage decreases. However, as shown in Figure 1, for both Latin and non-Latin languages, the performance stays relatively stable as the English percentage decreases to 0%. We suspect that other languages' monolingual data contains many English words. First, we find that about 3.6% and 2.6% characters in Tamil and Chinese monolingual data are English characters (a-zA-Z) respectively. Then, we remove all English characters from Tamil or Chinese monolingual data and re-conduct the experiments of English=0.001%. English-Tamil/Tamil-English spBLEU scores reduce from 1.0/0.8 to 0.0/0.3. Similarly, English-Chinese/Chinese-English spBLEU scores drop from 17.7/25.5 to 0.2/0.1. Hence, the results support our hypothesis.

Closeness to the character level and UNK rate can warn of poor downstream performance. We find that the translation performance usually drops greatly when the two features surpass some thresholds. As shown in Figure 1 (a), both English to Icelandic (en-is) and English to Danish (en-da) get noticeably worse at English=99.999%, and it is exactly when Icelandic and Danish have non-trivial UNK rates (3.9% for is and 4.3% for da). Similarly, in Figure 1 (b), English to Chinese (en-zh) deteriorates at English=90% when Chinese UNK rate is 10.2%. English to Tamil (en-ta) and English to Greek (en-el) both drop at English=99.9% when they have trivial UNK rates but their closeness to the character level are 0.91 and 0.89 respectively. Additionally, we examine whether the same pattern can still be observed when getting the features on a different evaluation set. We get features from the dev set and a subset of our training set (5000 sentence pairs). Despite the slightly lower thresholds (3.7% UNK rate and 0.87 closeness to the character level), the same trends are observed. See details in Appendix A.2. Hence, we suggest checking these two features on an evaluation set before performing the task. Poor translation performances are likely to be obtained when any language's UNK rate is larger than around 3.7% or its closeness to the character level is larger than around 0.87.

3.4 Ablations

Here, we want to verify our takeaways under several different experimental settings.

Reducing the translation model size or using BPE does not affect the robustness to language imbalance. Model capacity can affect its robustness. Hence, we replace our default Transformer 12-12 (Vaswani et al., 2017) model with a smaller model, Transformer 6-6 (6-layer encoder and 6-layer decoder). The intermediate features are the same as Figure 1, and the translation results are illustrated in Figure 4. It has exactly the same trends as for the larger model (Figure 1). In addition, we verify if our takeaways can generalize to a different tokenization algorithm, BPE (Sennrich et al., 2016). Figure 5 shows that BPE gets very similar performances to unigram LM across all translation pairs. The same trends are also observed as Figure 1 but with slightly higher thresholds. See details in A.3.2.

Increasing the vocabulary size can improve the robustness when languages do not share scripts. Our default vocabulary size is 5K because it simulates a multilingual setting (see footnote2). However, earlier works used a larger vocabulary for bilingual experiments (Firat et al., 2016). Intuitively, a larger vocabulary can be more robust to language imbalance because it has a larger capacity to include more infrequent words. Hence, we test a 32K vocabulary, and results are shown in Figure 6. Compared to Figure 1, it has two distinctions: (1) For non-Latin languages, performance drops happen later: English to Chinese drops at 99.9% (instead of 90%) when Chinese UNK rate is 7.8%; English to Tamil and English to Greek both deteriorate greatly at 99.99% (instead of 99.9%) when Tamil and Greek UNK rates are 42.3% and 32.5% respectively; (2) Surprisingly, translations between English and Tagalog perform obviously worse when English$\geq$99.999%, despite Tagalog's trivial UNK rate and short sentence length. Overall, increasing the vocabulary size improves the robustness to language imbalance for translations between English and non-Latin languages but not for that between English and Latin languages.

Applying byte-fallback does not improve the robustness. Here, we apply the "byte-fallback" feature of `SentencePiece` (Kudo and Richardson, 2018) which uses 256 UTF-8 bytes to represent unknown characters and thus eliminates UNKs. Figure 7 illustrates the results. As expected, UNK rates are all 0, while closeness to the character level can be larger than 1 because one character can be represented by multiple bytes. For Latin languages, noticeable drops still only happen for Icelandic and Danish starting from 99.999%, but differently, they have 0 UNK rates and not high closeness to the character level (0.65 and 0.53). Moreover, performance drops are surprisingly more dramatic compared to Figure 1. The performances of all 3 non-Latin languages get worse at the same percentages as Figure 1, and the drop is more significant for Greek to English while less significant for Chinese to English. Overall, applying byte-fallback does not improve the robustness reliably.

When English=100%, adding characters of the non-Latin language to the vocabulary can improve the performance. When English occupies 100% of the tokenizer's training data, the tokenizer only "knows" English. Other Latin languages share scripts with English, so it shows surprisingly good generalizability. However, for non-Latin languages, near all tokens are UNKs, and thus translation performances are very poor. We wonder how much the performance will increase by simply adding the characters of the non-Latin language to the vocabulary. We conduct this experiment for each of the 3 non-Latin languages, and the results are shown in Table 3. Compared to the original setting (100%), adding characters (100%+char) dramatically improves the performance except for ta-en. Despite that, for Tamil or Greek, it works greatly worse than the best we can achieve when Tamil or Greek data involves in tokenizer training. But, for Chinese, it outperforms the best results probably because one Chinese character is usually one "word".

4 Multilingual Experiments

Here, we move to a more complex multilingual setting. Similarly, we want to understand how the data percentages of the involved languages affect their downstream translation performance.

4.1 Experiment Setup & Features

We still experiment with the 8 languages and the 14 translation directions, as introduced in Section 3.1. Differently, we use one model (Transformer 12-12) to conduct all the 14 translations at the same time. As a result, the model capacity for each translation direction is dramatically reduced. Most of the *controlled variables* stay the same as Section 3.1, except that we increase the vocabulary size to 20K (maintaining around 2.5K per language) and increase the total tokenizer training data size to 10M. Since here we have 8-language data to train the tokenizer, we can not use the old *independent variable*. Instead, we propose to first choose one language and then vary its percentage (0.001%, 0.1%, 1%, 12.5%, 25%, 90%) while keeping the other 7 languages equally weighted. So, if the selected language's percentage is 12.5%, all 8 languages are equally weighted. We only use 4 languages (Tamil, Chinese, Icelandic, and English) as our selected languages and change the percentage of each of them. The *dependent variable* is the same as before – translation performance (spBLEU/chrF) on FLORES101 (Goyal et al., 2021) devtest sets. We also examine the two *intermediate features*: closeness to the character level and UNK rate.

4.2 Results & Ablations

Figure 2 illustrates the translation performance evaluated by spBLEU (chrF in Figure 8 shares the same trends). Figure 9 in A.4.1 shows the features.

NMT performance is still quite robust to language imbalance especially when languages share scripts. As shown in Figure 2, for the two Latin languages (Icelandic and English), varying their percentages almost does not affect the performances. It is expectable for English because it can "never" be starved. But Icelandic's performance drops at Icelandic=0.001% (English=99.999%) in bilingual experiments. We think it is because the involvement of multiple languages makes every language relatively less frequent, so the data ratio between Icelandic and any other language is not as disparate as 0.001:99.999 ($\approx$ 1:10^5). This is also reflected by the trivial UNKs of all languages in Figure 9. For the two non-Latin languages (Tamil and Chinese), first, varying their percentages affects their own performances greatly while the performances of other languages still stay stable. And, their own performances drop quickly below 12.5% while dropping slower when percentages$\geq$12.5%.

Better performance is also often observed when languages are more balanced. In Figure 2, if we only consider the translation directions with great performance changes, i.e., Tamil and Chinese, they have relatively better performances around 12.5% when languages are balanced. We define *data ratio* as the lowest percentage of any language versus the highest percentage. So, the data ratio is 1 when the selected language's percentage is 12.5%; while the data ratio is

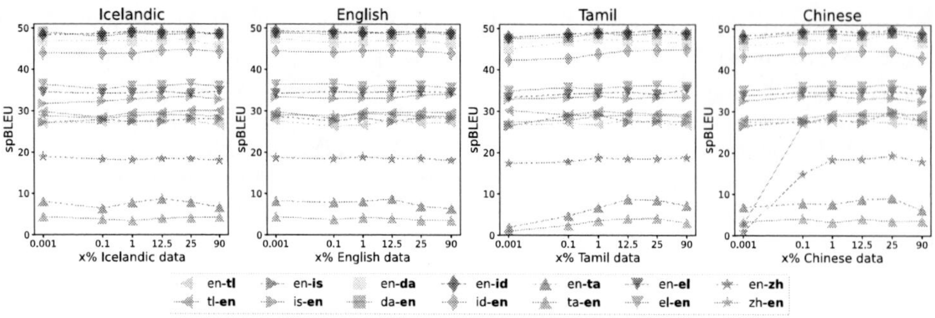

Figure 2: Translation results (spBLEU) of our main multilingual experiments. Marker shapes denote the language pairs (though all pairs share the same NMT model); dash or solid lines represents out-of-English or into-English directions; colors are for each language. E.g., --▲-- (en-**ta**) denotes English to Tamil translation results; -▲- (ta-**en**) represents Tamil to English translation results. X axes are in log10 scale.

0.07 when the selected language's percentage is 1% ($\frac{0.01}{(1-0.01)/7} = 0.07$). Then, we compute the correlation between spBLEU scores and data ratios for each of the 4 selected languages. The average correlation is 0.49 (moderate correlation (Cohen, 1988)), which is consistent with what we observe in bilingual experiments.

Performance can drop without surpassing the thresholds of the two features. For Chinese, a more obvious performance drop happens at 0.1% following the indication of two features (UNK rate=5.4% and closeness to the character level=0.97). However, for Tamil, though its performance drops at 1%, it has a trivial UNK rate and not long sentence length. This is probably due to the greatly compressed model capacity for each language pair, compared to bilingual experiments. Hence, though surpassing the thresholds can often hint at poor performances, it is neither a sufficient nor necessary condition.

Using byte-fallback still does not improve the robustness We apply *byte-fallback* under the setting of using Chinese as the selected language, and results are shown in Figure 10. Compared to Figure 2, though we observe slightly more stable performance when Chinese$\geq$1%, the translation result drops more dramatically when Chinese$\leq$0.1%.

NMT is more sensitive to language imbalance in model training. In both bilingual or multilingual settings, we find that the performance is quite robust to language imbalance and relatively better performance is often observed when languages are more balanced. In other words, we want to set sampling factor $S = 0$, following the temperature sampling paradigm (Devlin et al., 2019). However, many existing works show significantly different performances of different S, and the best S is around 0.2 to 0.7 (Arivazhagan et al., 2019; Conneau and Lample, 2019; Xue et al., 2021b). We think this inconsistency has resulted from the fact that we fix $S = 0.2$ for model training while only varying it (via changing data percentages) for tokenizer training. We conjecture that NMT is more sensitive to language imbalance in model training. To verify this, first, we fix model training sampling $S = 0.2$ and compare 3 tokenizer training sampling factors ($S = 0, 0.3, 1.0$). Results are shown in the second row (starting with "tokenizer") in Table 2. Though with small differences (0.4, 0.1 points), $S = 0$ overall works best. Second, we fix tokenizer training sampling $S = 0$ and compare 3 model training sampling factors ($S = 0, 0.2, 1.0$). As shown in Table 2, the differences are more prominent (1.4, 0.6 points), and $S = 0.2$ overall works best. Hence, for tokenizer training, we want languages to be balanced, whereas, for model training, we want to flatten the original distribution to some

	S	*-en								en-*								overall
		tl	is	da	id	ta	el	zh	avg.	tl	is	da	id	ta	el	zh	avg.	avg.
tokenizer	0	29.6	33.1	48.5	44.6	4.0	36.1	29.1	**32.1**	27.9	27.4	47.0	49.1	8.7	34.6	18.5	30.5	**31.3**
	0.3	28.6	33.6	49.0	44.0	3.4	36.6	28.5	32.0	26.6	27.5	46.2	48.7	7.6	34.2	18.4	29.9	30.9
	1	29.0	32.4	48.4	44.1	3.4	35.6	28.8	31.7	27.5	29.0	47.8	49.7	7.6	34.6	19.1	**30.8**	31.2
model	0	28.2	32.6	47.4	41.6	3.6	34.2	26.7	30.6	26.9	27.8	45.9	47.3	6.9	33.1	17.1	28.3	29.9
	0.2	29.6	33.1	48.5	44.6	4.0	36.1	29.1	32.1	27.9	27.4	47.0	49.1	8.7	34.6	18.5	**30.5**	**31.3**
	1	27.2	33.3	49.7	46.2	4.0	37.6	31.7	**32.9**	16.9	25.7	47.8	50.1	3.4	35.7	19.8	28.5	30.7

Table 2: Comparison of language sampling factors used in tokenizer or model training. All numbers are spBLEU. S is the exponential factor used in temperature sampling (see Section 2.2).

degree but not to uniform distribution. And we want to pay more attention to sampling for model training because NMT is more sensitive to it.

5 Conclusion

We systematically analyze how language imbalance in multilingual tokenizer training affects translation performances. Overall, we find that NMT performance is quite robust to language imbalance especially when languages share scripts. Better performance is often achieved when languages are more balanced. We suggest keeping the involved languages as balanced as possible in the tokenizer training corpus and evaluating pretrained tokenizers on an evaluation set to make sure no language's UNK rate $\geq$ around 3.7% and no language's closeness to the character level $\geq$ around 0.87. We hope our work can provide some guidance for future multilingual tokenizer training and usage.

6 Limitation

This work is an empirical study. It is important to be aware that our observations and conclusions are made based on our experiments, which may or may not be generalizable to other settings. We try our best to include diverse languages, but still, our experiments are English-centric and at most have 8 languages involved. We tend to believe that the five main observations we made (as listed in the second last paragraph of Section 1) are generalizable to other experimental settings. However, the exact thresholds of the two features (UNK rate and closeness to the character level) for indicating poor downstream performance may not be always hold (as mentioned in Footnote 1).

7 Ethical Consideration

The main ethical consideration of this work is that our experiments are many, so it is not very easy to finish them in a reasonable time without a decent number of computation resources. In the bilingual setting, we have 9 percentages, 14 directions, 5 ablations (including our basic setting), and 3 seeds. So we have 1890 experiments in total. Each experiment takes from less than 1 hour to about 2 days (based on the training data size) using 8 NVIDIA Tesla V100 Volta GPUs. In the multilingual setting, we only have 31 experiments in total, but each experiment takes 1.5 days using 64 GPUs.

However, we expect that our empirical results can help guide the training and usage of multilingual tokenizers, so future works do not have to re-conduct these expensive investigations. Based on our results, the downstream performance is not highly sensitive to language imbalance in tokenizer training, and keeping languages as balanced as possible is a safe choice. Additionally, the two features (closeness to the character level and UNK rate) can serve as intermediate quality evaluators of pretrained tokenizers before performing the task.

Acknowledgments

We thank the reviewers for their helpful comments and thank Angela Fan, Chau Tran, Xiang Zhou, Simeng Sun for helpful discussions. This work was done while SZ was interning at Meta AI and later supported at UNC by NSF-CAREER Award 1846185, ONR Grant N00014-18-1-2871, and a Bloomberg Data Science Ph.D. Fellowship. The views contained in this article are those of the authors and not of the funding agency.

References

Arivazhagan, N., Bapna, A., Firat, O., Lepikhin, D., Johnson, M., Krikun, M., Chen, M. X., Cao, Y., Foster, G., Cherry, C., et al. (2019). Massively multilingual neural machine translation in the wild: Findings and challenges. *arXiv preprint arXiv:1907.05019*.

Bostrom, K. and Durrett, G. (2020). Byte pair encoding is suboptimal for language model pretraining. In *Proceedings of the 2020 Conference on Empirical Methods in Natural Language Processing: Findings*, pages 4617–4624.

Chung, H. W., Garrette, D., Tan, K. C., and Riesa, J. (2020). Improving multilingual models with language-clustered vocabularies. In *Proceedings of the 2020 Conference on Empirical Methods in Natural Language Processing (EMNLP)*, pages 4536–4546.

Chung, J., Cho, K., and Bengio, Y. (2016). A character-level decoder without explicit segmentation for neural machine translation. In *Proceedings of the 54th Annual Meeting of the Association for Computational Linguistics (Volume 1: Long Papers)*, pages 1693–1703.

Clark, J. H., Garrette, D., Turc, I., and Wieting, J. (2022). Canine: Pre-training an efficient tokenization-free encoder for language representation. *Transactions of the Association for Computational Linguistics*, 10:73–91.

Cohen, J. (1988). *Statistical Power Analysis for the Behavioral Sciences*. Routledge.

Conneau, A., Khandelwal, K., Goyal, N., Chaudhary, V., Wenzek, G., Guzmán, F., Grave, É., Ott, M., Zettlemoyer, L., and Stoyanov, V. (2020). Unsupervised cross-lingual representation learning at scale. In *Proceedings of the 58th Annual Meeting of the Association for Computational Linguistics*, pages 8440–8451.

Conneau, A. and Lample, G. (2019). Cross-lingual language model pretraining. *Advances in Neural Information Processing Systems*, 32:7059–7069.

Devlin, J., Chang, M.-W., Lee, K., and Toutanova, K. (2019). Bert: Pre-training of deep bidirectional transformers for language understanding. In *Proceedings of the 2019 Conference of the North American Chapter of the Association for Computational Linguistics: Human Language Technologies, Volume 1 (Long and Short Papers)*, pages 4171–4186.

Ding, S., Renduchintala, A., and Duh, K. (2019). A call for prudent choice of subword merge operations in neural machine translation. In *Proceedings of Machine Translation Summit XVII Volume 1: Research Track*, pages 204–213, Dublin, Ireland. European Association for Machine Translation.

Domingo, M., Garcıa-Martınez, M., Helle, A., Casacuberta, F., and Herranz, M. (2018). How much does tokenization affect neural machine translation? *arXiv preprint arXiv:1812.08621*.

Firat, O., Cho, K., and Bengio, Y. (2016). Multi-way, multilingual neural machine translation with a shared attention mechanism. In *Proceedings of the 2016 Conference of the North American Chapter of the Association for Computational Linguistics: Human Language Technologies*, pages 866–875.

Gerz, D., Vulić, I., Ponti, E. M., Reichart, R., and Korhonen, A. (2018). On the relation between linguistic typology and (limitations of) multilingual language modeling. In *Proceedings of the 2018 Conference on Empirical Methods in Natural Language Processing*, pages 316–327.

Gowda, T. and May, J. (2020). Finding the optimal vocabulary size for neural machine translation. In *Findings of the Association for Computational Linguistics: EMNLP 2020*, pages 3955–3964, Online. Association for Computational Linguistics.

Goyal, N., Gao, C., Chaudhary, V., Chen, P., Wenzek, G., Ju, D., Krishnan, S., Ranzato, M., Guzmán, F., and Fan, A. (2021). The FLORES-101 evaluation benchmark for low-resource and multilingual machine translation. *CoRR*, abs/2106.03193.

Johnson, M., Schuster, M., Le, Q., Krikun, M., Wu, Y., Chen, Z., Thorat, N., Viégas, F., Wattenberg, M., Corrado, G., et al. (2017). Google's multilingual neural machine translation system: Enabling zero-shot translation. *Transactions of the Association for Computational Linguistics*, 5:339–351.

Kingma, D. P. and Ba, J. (2015). Adam: A method for stochastic optimization. In Bengio, Y. and LeCun, Y., editors, *3rd International Conference on Learning Representations, ICLR 2015, San Diego, CA, USA, May 7-9, 2015, Conference Track Proceedings.*

Koehn, P., Hoang, H., Birch, A., Callison-Burch, C., Federico, M., Bertoldi, N., Cowan, B., Shen, W., Moran, C., Zens, R., et al. (2007). Moses: Open source toolkit for statistical machine translation. In *Proceedings of the 45th annual meeting of the association for computational linguistics companion volume proceedings of the demo and poster sessions*, pages 177–180.

Koehn, P. and Knowles, R. (2017). Six challenges for neural machine translation. *ACL 2017*, page 28.

Kudo, T. (2018). Subword regularization: Improving neural network translation models with multiple subword candidates. In *Proceedings of the 56th Annual Meeting of the Association for Computational Linguistics (Volume 1: Long Papers)*, pages 66–75.

Kudo, T. and Richardson, J. (2018). Sentencepiece: A simple and language independent subword tokenizer and detokenizer for neural text processing. In *Proceedings of the 2018 Conference on Empirical Methods in Natural Language Processing: System Demonstrations*, pages 66–71.

Lee, J., Cho, K., and Hofmann, T. (2017). Fully character-level neural machine translation without explicit segmentation. *Transactions of the Association for Computational Linguistics*, 5:365–378.

Liu, Y., Gu, J., Goyal, N., Li, X., Edunov, S., Ghazvininejad, M., Lewis, M., and Zettlemoyer, L. (2020). Multilingual denoising pre-training for neural machine translation. *Transactions of the Association for Computational Linguistics*, 8:726–742.

Papineni, K., Roukos, S., Ward, T., and Zhu, W.-J. (2002). Bleu: a method for automatic evaluation of machine translation. In *Proceedings of the 40th annual meeting of the Association for Computational Linguistics*, pages 311–318.

Popović, M. (2015). chrF: character n-gram F-score for automatic MT evaluation. In *Proceedings of the Tenth Workshop on Statistical Machine Translation*, pages 392–395, Lisbon, Portugal. Association for Computational Linguistics.

Post, M. (2018). A call for clarity in reporting BLEU scores. In *Proceedings of the Third Conference on Machine Translation: Research Papers*, pages 186–191, Belgium, Brussels. Association for Computational Linguistics.

Rust, P., Pfeiffer, J., Vulić, I., Ruder, S., and Gurevych, I. (2021). How good is your tokenizer? on the monolingual performance of multilingual language models. In *Proceedings of the 59th Annual Meeting of the Association for Computational Linguistics and the 11th International Joint Conference on Natural Language Processing (Volume 1: Long Papers)*, pages 3118–3135.

Salesky, E., Etter, D., and Post, M. (2021). Robust open-vocabulary translation from visual text representations. In *Proceedings of the 2021 Conference on Empirical Methods in Natural Language Processing*, pages 7235–7252, Online and Punta Cana, Dominican Republic. Association for Computational Linguistics.

Schuster, M. and Nakajima, K. (2012). Japanese and korean voice search. In *2012 IEEE International Conference on Acoustics, Speech and Signal Processing (ICASSP)*, pages 5149–5152. IEEE.

Sennrich, R., Haddow, B., and Birch, A. (2016). Neural machine translation of rare words with subword units. In *Proceedings of the 54th Annual Meeting of the Association for Computational Linguistics (Volume 1: Long Papers)*, pages 1715–1725.

Sun, L., Hashimoto, K., Yin, W., Asai, A., Li, J., Yu, P., and Xiong, C. (2020). Adv-bert: Bert is not robust on misspellings! generating nature adversarial samples on bert. *arXiv preprint arXiv:2003.04985.*

Tay, Y., Tran, V. Q., Ruder, S., Gupta, J., Chung, H. W., Bahri, D., Qin, Z., Baumgartner, S., Yu, C., and Metzler, D. (2021). Charformer: Fast character transformers via gradient-based subword tokenization.

Vaswani, A., Shazeer, N., Parmar, N., Uszkoreit, J., Jones, L., Gomez, A. N., Kaiser, Ł., and Polosukhin, I. (2017). Attention is all you need. In *Proceedings of the 31st International Conference on Neural Information Processing Systems*, pages 6000–6010.

Xu, J., Zhou, H., Gan, C., Zheng, Z., and Li, L. (2021). Vocabulary learning via optimal transport for neural machine translation. In *Proceedings of ACL 2021.*

Xue, L., Barua, A., Constant, N., Al-Rfou, R., Narang, S., Kale, M., Roberts, A., and Raffel, C. (2021a). Byt5: Towards a token-free future with pre-trained byte-to-byte models. *arXiv preprint arXiv:2105.13626.*

Xue, L., Constant, N., Roberts, A., Kale, M., Al-Rfou, R., Siddhant, A., Barua, A., and Raffel, C. (2021b). mt5: A massively multilingual pre-trained text-to-text transformer. In *Proceedings of the 2021 Conference of the North American Chapter of the Association for Computational Linguistics: Human Language Technologies*, pages 483–498.

Ács, J. (2019). Exploring bert's vocabulary. In *Judit Ács's blog*, Online.

A Appendix

A.1 Model Implementation Details

We implement translation models using fairseq.[8] During training, we use Adam optimizer (Kingma and Ba, 2015), learning rate=0.001, and warmup for 2 epochs. We use batch size=4K tokens and gradient accumulation=4. For bilingual experiments, we use 8 NVIDIA Tesla V100 Volta GPUs for each experiment, and we run 3 seeds (2, 7, 42) for each experiment and report the average. For multilingual experiments, we use 64 GPUs and only run seed=2 for each experiment. We apply early stop with patience of 20 epochs. During testing, we use batch size=32 sentences and beam size=5.

[8]`https://github.com/pytorch/fairseq`

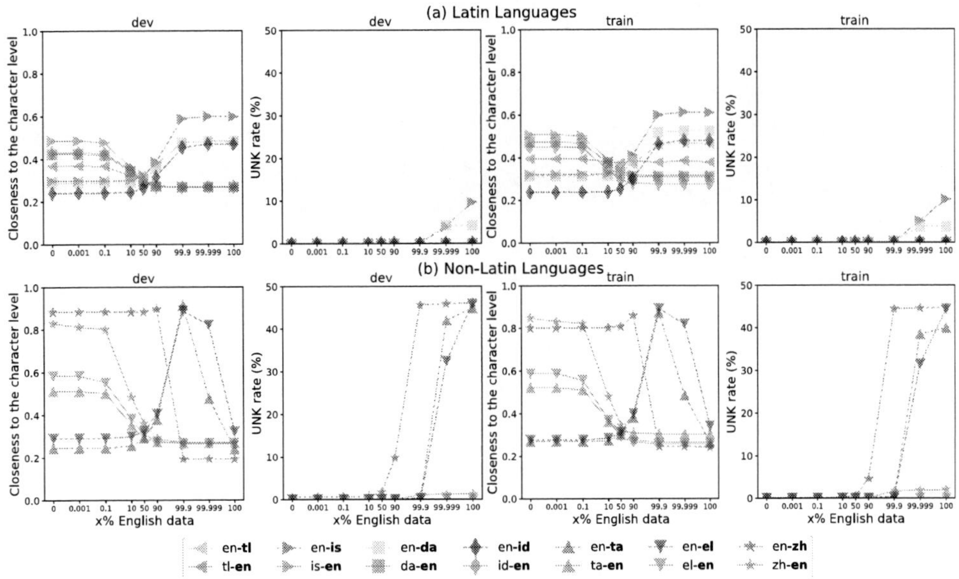

Figure 3: In each row, the first two subplots are features computed on the FLORES101 dev set; the second two subplots are features computed on a subset of our training set. Markers share the same meanings as Figure 1. X axes are in log10 scale.

A.2 Compute features on a different evaluation set

In the main paper, we compute intermediate features on FLORES101 devtest set where we also report translation performances. However, usually, we are blind to the testing sets. We want to ask whether the same pattern can still be observed when we get the features on a different evaluation set. Therefore, we get features from the dev set and a subset of the training set (with 5000 sentence pairs). The first and the second two columns of Figure 3 illustrate the features obtained from the dev and training set respectively. Compared to the features in Figure 1, very similar trends are observed, except for slightly different thresholds. When evaluating on the dev set, English to Icelandic (en-is) and English to Danish (en-da) get worse when Icelandic and Danish have 4.0% and 4.2% UNK rates respectively; English to Chinese (en-zh) drops when Chinese UNK rate is 9.8%; English to Tamil (en-ta) and English to Greek (en-el) drops when the closeness to the character level is 0.91 and 0.89 respectively. On the subset of the training set, when performances deteriorate, Icelandic, Danish, and Chinese have 5.0%, 3.7%, and 4.6% UNK rates respectively, and Tamil and Greek have 0.87 and 0.89 closeness to the character level respectively. Overall, despite the thresholds being lower (3.7% UNK rate and 0.87 closeness to the character level), the same takeaways still hold when getting features from different evaluation sets.

A.3 Bilingual Ablations

A.3.1 Smaller Model

The translation results of using a smaller model (Transformer 6-6) are shown in Figure 4. We observe that performances drop at the same English percentages as Figure 1. Meanwhile, the features are the same as Figure 1. Thus, the exact same conclusions are obtained.

A.3.2 BPE

The features and translation results of using a BPE tokenizer are shown in Figure 5. It shares the same trends with Figure 1 but with slightly higher thresholds: English to Icelandic (en-is) and English to Danish (en-da) deteriorate when Icelandic and Danish have 3.9% and 4.6% UNK rates respectively; English to

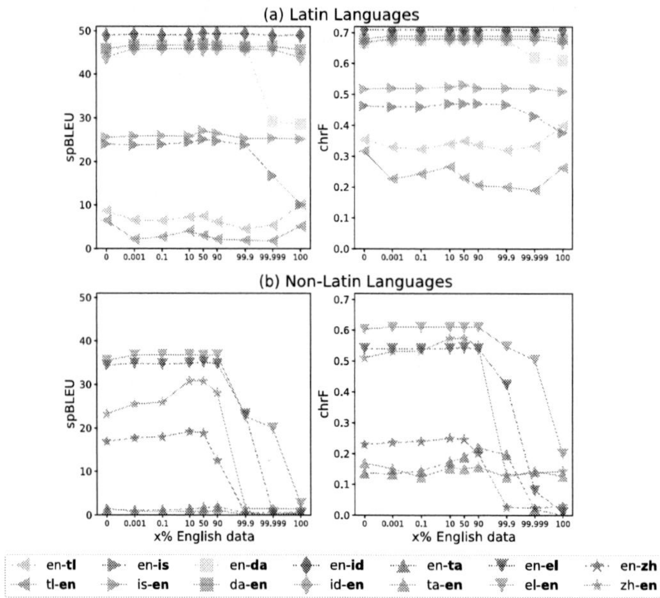

Figure 4: Translation results of bilingual experiments with a smaller model (Transformer 6-6). Markers share the same meanings as Figure 1. X axes are in log10 scale.

	100%	**100%+char**	**best**
en-ta	0.0	0.1	**1.9**
ta-en	0.2	0.1	**1.1**
en-el	0.3	18.6	**35.1**
el-en	2.7	18.5	**36.7**
en-zh	0.6	**20.0**	19.2
zh-en	1.5	**31.2**	30.9

Table 3: Translation results (spBLEU scores) of adding the non-Latin language's characters to the vocabulary at English=100% (**100%+char**). For comparison, the **100%** column shows the results before adding characters and the **best** column shows the best results out of all percentages.

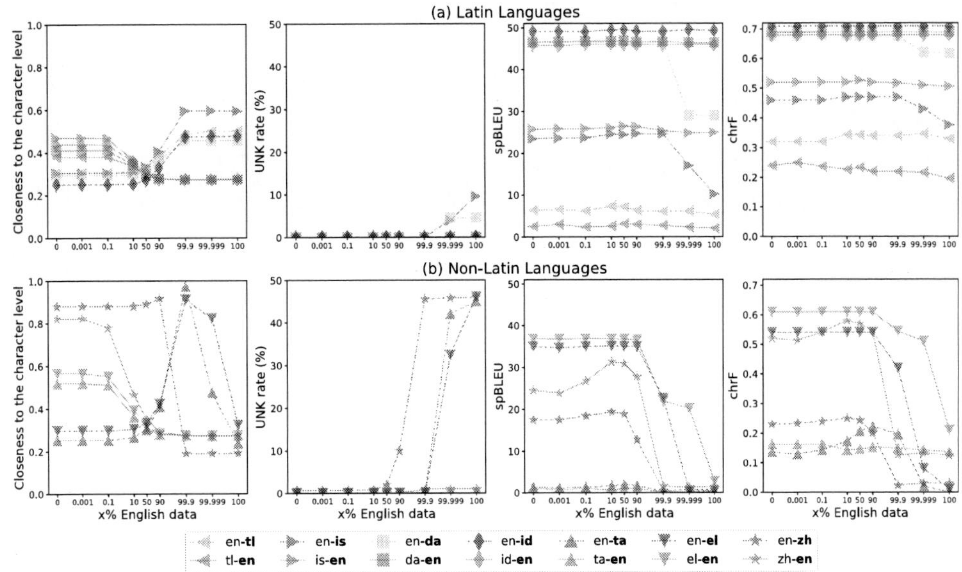

Figure 5: Intermediate features and translation results of bilingual experiments with a BPE tokenizer. Markers share the same meanings as Figure 1. X axes are in log10 scale.

Chinese (en-zh) drops when Chinese UNK rate is 10.0%; English to Tamil (en-ta) and English to Greek (en-el) get worse when the closeness to the character level is 0.97 and 0.91 respectively.

A.3.3 Larger Vocabulary

The features and translation results of using a 32K vocabulary are shown in Figure 6. It has two distinctions from Figure 1 which are discussed in Section 3.4.

A.3.4 Byte-fallback

The features and translation results of using a 32K vocabulary are shown in Figure 7. Discussions are in Section 3.4.

A.3.5 Adding characters

Table 3 shows the results of adding the non-Latin language's characters to the vocabulary when English=100%.

A.4 Multilingual Results and Ablations

A.4.1 Main Translation Results (chrF) and Features

Figure 8 shows the chrF scores of our main multilingual experiments. It shares the same trends with Figure 2. Figure 9 show the features of each of the 8 languages. Different from features in bilingual experiments, here, we do not have to distinguish language pairs because all languages are mixed together to train one joint vocabulary.

A.4.2 Byte-fallback

Figure 10 illustrates the translation results and features of the multilingual experiments with byte-fallback when only the Chinese percentage varies. Discussions are in Section 4.2.

A.5 Examples

Table 4 are examples of how sentences in English, Indonesian, and Chinese are tokenized at different English percentages under the main bilingual setting (Section 3.1).

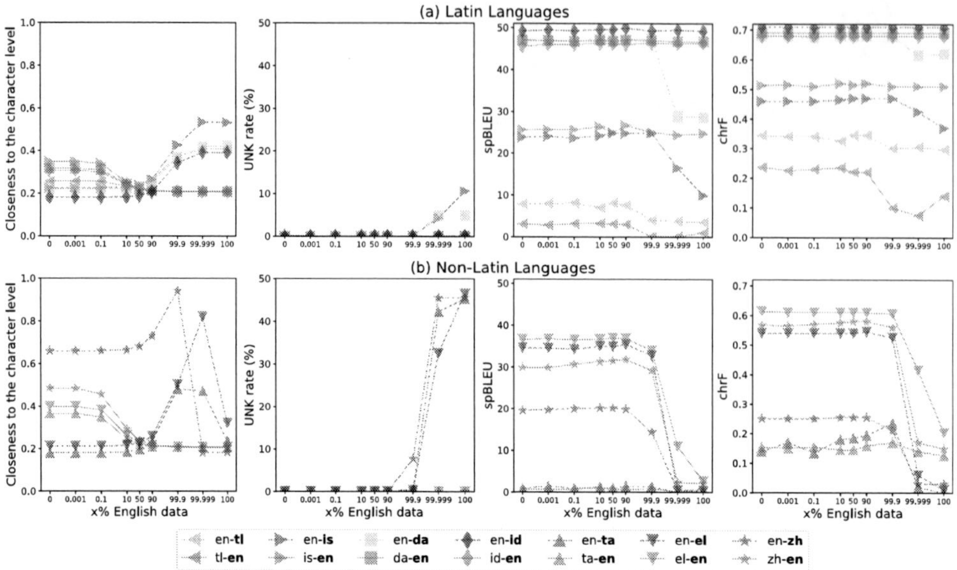

Figure 6: Intermediate features and translation results of bilingual experiments with a 32K vocabulary. Markers share the same meanings as Figure 1. X axes are in log10 scale.

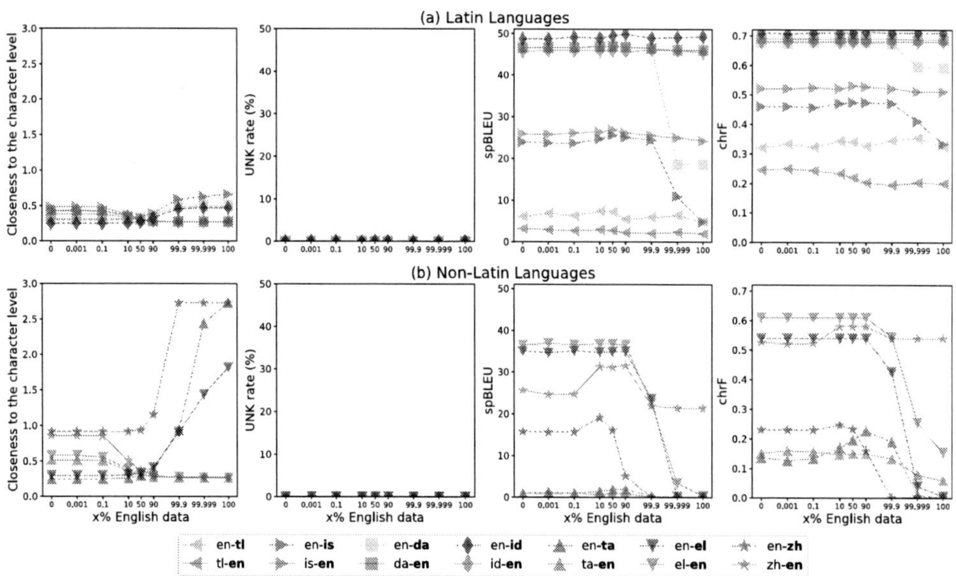

Figure 7: Intermediate features and translation results of bilingual experiments with byte-fallback. Note that here the UNK rates are all 0, and closeness to the character level can be larger than 1 because one character can be represented by multiple bytes. Markers share the same meanings as Figure 1. X axes are in log10 scale.

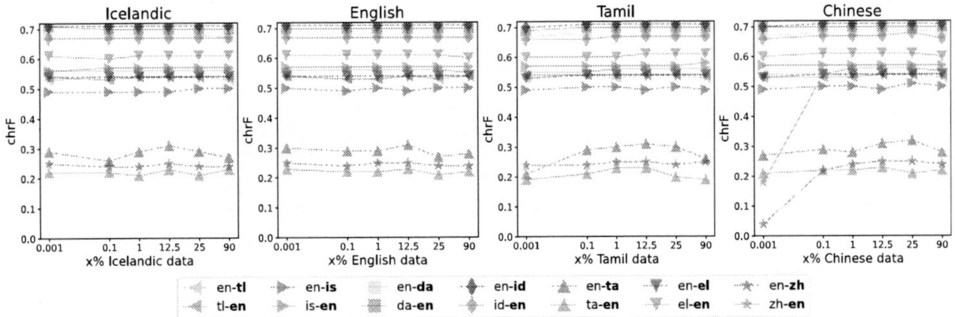

Figure 8: Translation results (chrF) of our main multilingual experiments. Markers have the same meanings as Figure 2. X axes are in log10 scale.

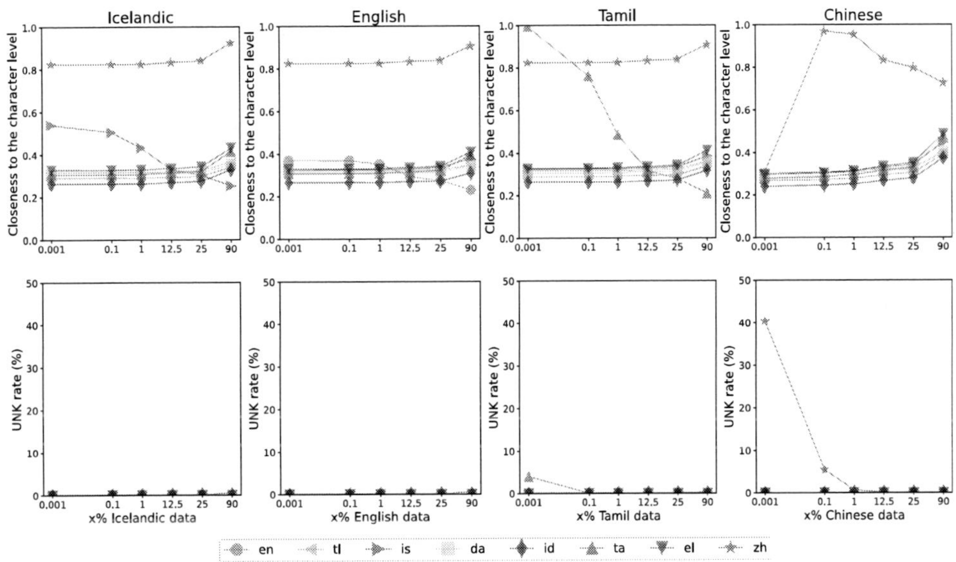

Figure 9: Intermediate features of our main multilingual experiments. Different from Figure 2, here, marker shapes and colors both denote the language. E.g., -▲- (ta) denotes Tamil features. X axes are in log10 scale.

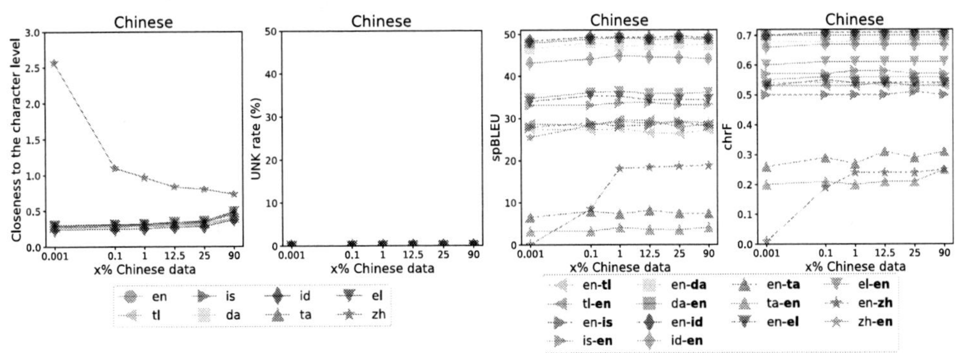

Figure 10: Intermediate features and translation results of the multilingual experiments with byte-fallback. Markers of the first two subplots have the same meanings as Figure 9, and markers of the second two subplots have the same meanings as Figure 2. X axes are in log10 scale.

x% English	English	Indonesian
0	_" W e _no w _ha ve _4 - mon th - ol d _mi ce _th at _a re _non - dia be tic _th at _ us ed _to _be _dia be tic ," _he _ad de d .	_“ S a at _ini _ada _men ci t _umur _4 _bulan _non dia bet es _yang _dulu nya _diabetes ,” _tambah nya .
0.1	_" W e _no w _ha ve _4 - mon th - ol d _mi ce _th at _a re _non - dia be tic _th at _ us ed _to _be _dia be tic ," _he _ad de d .	_“ S a at _ini _ada _men ci t _umur _4 _bulan _non dia bet es _yang _dulu nya _diabetes ,” _tambah nya .
50	_" We _now _have _4 - mon th - old _mi ce _that _are _non - dia be tic _that _used _to _be _dia be tic ," _he _added .	_“ S a at _ini _ada _men ci t _umur _4 _bulan _non dia bet es _yang _dulu nya _diabetes ,” _tambah nya .
99.9	_" We _now _have _4 - mon th - old _mi ce _that _are _non - d ia be tic _that _used _to _be _di a be tic ," _he _added .	_“ S a at _in i _a da _men ci t _ um ur _4 _bu lan _non di ab et es _ya ng _du lu nya _diabetes ,” _ta mb ah nya .
100	_" We _now _have _4 - mon th - old _mi ce _that _are _non - d ia be tic _that _used _to _be _di a be tic ," _he _added .	_“ S a at _in i _a da _men ci t _ um ur _4 _b ul an _non di ab et es _ya ng _du lu ny a _diabetes ,” _ta mb ah ny a .

x% English	English	Chinese
0	_ " W e _ n o w _ h a v e _ 4 - m on t h - o l d _ m ic e _ t h at _ ar e _ n on - d i a b et ic _ t h at _ u s e d _ t o _ b e _ d i a b et ic , " _ h e _ ad d e d .	_他 补 充 道 :“ 我们 现在 有 _4 _ 个月 大 没有 糖 尿 病 的 老 鼠 , 但 它们 曾 经 得 过 该 病 。”
0.1	_ " W e _ n o w _ h a v e _ 4 - m on th - o l d _ m ic e _ th at _ ar e _ n on - d i a b et ic _ th at _ u s ed _ t o _ b e _ d i a b et ic , " _ h e _ ad d ed .	_他 补 充 道 :“ 我们 现在 有 _4 _ 个月 大 没有 糖 尿 病 的 老 鼠 , 但 它们 曾 经 得 过 该 病 。”
50	_" We _now _have _4 - mon th - old _mi ce _that _are _no n - dia be tic _that _used _to _be _ dia be tic , " _he _add ed .	_他 补 充 道 :“ 我们 现在 有 _4 _ 个 月 大 没有 糖 尿 病 的 老 鼠 , 但 它 们 曾 经 得 过 该 病 。”
99.9	_" We _now _have _4 - mon th - old _ m ice _that _are _non - dia be tic _that _used _to _be _ dia be tic ," _he _added .	_ <unk> : “ <unk> _4 _ <unk> , <unk> ”
100	_" We _now _have _ 4 - mon th - old _ m ice _that _are _non - dia be tic _that _used _to _be _ dia be tic ," _he _added .	_ <unk> : “ <unk> _ 4 _ <unk> , <unk> ”

Table 4: Examples of how sentences in English, Indonesian, and Chinese are tokenized at different English percentages under our main bilingual setting (Section 3.1). The sentence is the first sentence of FLORES101 devtest set. Subwords are separated by whitespaces, and unknown tokens are replaced by ‘<unk>’.

How Effective is Byte Pair Encoding for Out-Of-Vocabulary Words in Neural Machine Translation?

Ali Araabi a.araabi@uva.nl
Christof Monz c.monz@uva.nl
Vlad Niculae v.niculae@uva.nl
Informatics Institute, University of Amsterdam, Amsterdam, The Netherlands

Abstract

Neural Machine Translation (NMT) is an open vocabulary problem. As a result, dealing with the words not occurring during training (a.k.a. out-of-vocabulary (OOV) words) have long been a fundamental challenge for NMT systems. The predominant method to tackle this problem is Byte Pair Encoding (BPE) which splits words, including OOV words, into sub-word segments. BPE has achieved impressive results for a wide range of translation tasks in terms of automatic evaluation metrics. While it is often assumed that by using BPE, NMT systems are capable of handling OOV words, the effectiveness of BPE in translating OOV words has not been explicitly measured. In this paper, we study to what extent BPE is successful in translating OOV words at the word-level. We analyze the translation quality of OOV words based on word type, number of segments, cross-attention weights, and the frequency of segment n-grams in the training data. Our experiments show that while careful BPE settings seem to be fairly useful in translating OOV words across datasets, a considerable percentage of OOV words are translated incorrectly. Furthermore, we highlight the slightly higher effectiveness of BPE in translating OOV words for special cases, such as named-entities and when the languages involved are linguistically close to each other.

1 Introduction

One of the key challenges of neural machine translation (NMT) (Sutskever et al., 2014; Bahdanau et al., 2015) is vocabulary sparsity; irrespective of the amount of data available for training. As a consequence, all NMT models suffer from out-of-vocabulary (OOV) words. Accordingly, a significant proportion of sentences in the test set have OOV words. Even with millions of sentence pairs in training data,[1] 15% of test sentences contain OOV words, while with limited training data,[2] OOV words appear in more than 60% of the test sentences.

Earlier approaches to tackling the OOV problem include using a very large vocabulary (Jean et al., 2015), backing off to a dictionary look-up (Luong et al., 2015), and copying OOV words from source to the target sentence (Gülçehre et al., 2016). However, most recent approaches are based on splitting the words into smaller units and can be divided into: language-specific approaches (Smit et al., 2014; Huck et al., 2017), language-agnostic approaches (Sennrich et al.,

[1] Russian-English from WMT
[2] Kazakh-English from WMT

2016; Kudo, 2018; Kudo and Richardson, 2018; Costa-jussà and Fonollosa, 2016; Cherry et al., 2018), and hybrid approaches (Huck et al., 2017; Banerjee and Bhattacharyya, 2018; Pan et al., 2020) which inject linguistic information into language-agnostic methods.

Nowadays, the mainstream approach to address the open-vocabulary challenge in the context of NMT is Byte Pair Encoding (BPE Sennrich et al., 2016), due to its simplicity, applicability to a wide range of languages, and high performance in terms of automatic evaluation metrics. BPE incrementally merges the frequent bigrams such that it keeps the most frequent words intact while splitting the rare ones into multiple segments and the granularity of these subword units is controlled by a hyperparameter. It is often assumed that by using BPE, NMT systems are capable of handling OOV words [3], since it represents them as a sequence of subword units (Sennrich et al., 2016; Wu et al., 2016) and as a result there are very few unseen tokens in the test set thereby implying that the OOV problem has been almost solved (Huck et al., 2017; Banerjee and Bhattacharyya, 2018; Liu et al., 2019; Luo et al., 2019; Hu et al., 2020).

Previous approaches only analyze and compare BPE and/or other segmentation strategies based on their effect on the overall translation performance (Huck et al., 2017; Kudo, 2018; Gallé, 2019; Provilkov et al., 2020; He et al., 2020). To the best of our knowledge, there is no study to investigate whether BPE solves the OOV problem at the word-level. In this paper, we aim to explore 1) to what extent OOV words still hurt the translation quality when using BPE, 2) how useful is BPE in translating different OOV types, and 3) three potential factors that improve the translation of BPE-segmented OOV words.

We first explore the translation quality of sentences containing OOV words, showing the negative effect of the presence of OOV words on translation quality, while all of them are segmented into subword units. We further examine the translation quality of different types of OOV words, showing the improved ability of BPE in translating named entities for linguistically close language pairs, compared to moderate to relatively poor translation quality for other types of OOV words. We also show that OOV words that received strong cross-attention weights, have high translation qualities. Next, we explore how the granularity of segments impacts the translation quality of OOV words. Finally, we show that there is no evidence to support the positive correlation between the translation quality of an OOV word and occurrences of its n-grams in the training set.

2 Experimental setup

Datasets We use German-English, Russian-English, and Romanian-English as language pairs for our experiments. The main reasons to select these languages are twofold: the data sizes are large enough to eliminate the effect of the amount of data on translation quality, especially for rare words. Also, since two common types of OOVs are inflected and compound words in general, we choose Russian, Romanian, and German with varying degrees of morphology and compound words and as a representative of Slavic, Romance, and Germanic languages, respectively. For the Russian-English direction, we use the Yandex corpus, Common Crawl, News Commentary, and Wiki Titles from WMT2020. We preprocess the data by limiting the length of the sentences to 200 tokens and removing sentence pairs with a source/target length ratio exceeding 1.5, following previous work (Ng et al., 2019). We use the concatenation of newstest2017, newstest2018, and newstest2019 for evaluation. As German-English training set we use Europarl, Common Crawl, and News Commentary from WMT2017 and for the test set we use newstest2014. Also for Romanian-English, we use all available training data from WMT2016 and newstest2016 for evaluation purposes. The data prepossessing pipeline for German-English and Russian-English is similar to Russian-English. We end up with 2.64M, 3.95M, and 612K training sentences and 1078 / 1363, 1830 / 2411, and 926 / 1385 OOV word

[3] Throughout the paper, OOV refers to an actual non-segmented out-of-vocabulary word, unless otherwise stated.

types / tokens for Russian-English, German-English, and Romanian-English, respectively. In order to obtain sub-word segmentations, we train a joint BPE model for German-English and Romanian-English and we train a BPE model separately for the Russian-English as suggested by Ng et al. (2019). The number of BPE merge operations is reported for different experiments in later sections.

Translation model We use the Fairseq [4] NMT system to train the transformer-base model. Since we are dealing with large enough training data, it is not essential to tune the hyper-parameters (Araabi and Monz, 2020) and we stick to the default set of parameters reported in the original transformer paper (Vaswani et al., 2017).

3 Data annotation

In order to analyze BPE usability for different OOV words, we randomly sample 400 unique OOV words from the set of all OOV words for each language. First, we manually label OOV types. For this annotation process, we employ a highly qualified native annotator for each language. It is worthwhile mentioning that one given OOV word may belong to more than one category. Then, we extract their corresponding translation from the reference sentence. Below, we explain how we extract the translations of OOV words from the hypothesis sentences and also how we assign quality labels to them in more details .

Translation of OOV words In order to obtain the word-level translation correspondences of NMT output, one naive approach is to use statistical word alignments (Dyer et al., 2013). However, their accuracy for OOV words is poor, due to the very low frequency of OOV words. Inspired by Garg et al. (2019) and Chen et al. (2020), we use the average wights over heads of the encoder-decoder cross-attention in the penultimate layer of the transformer to obtain the corresponding output word for a given OOV word based on the maximum attention and then manually double-check the results. Also, in order to find the ground truth translations of the OOV words, we manually inspect the reference sentences to extract the corresponding words.

Translation label In order to measure the translation quality of OOV words, we make use of adequacy and fluency (Koehn and Monz, 2006) as assessment criteria. Given an OOV word, we manually assign one of the following three labels to its translation:

- *Correct*: when the translation is the exact same word or a synonym of the ground truth, such that when replaced in the reference, it does not hurt the fluency nor adequacy. For example, "throat inflammation" is acceptable for "laryngitis".

- *Partly correct*: when the translation only hurts either adequacy or fluency of the sentence, but not both. For example, when the translation needs a small morphological change to be considered correct, e.g., "reserves" instead of "reserve". Also, a single spelling error which is most likely to happen in named entities or technical words, falls under this category. While we acknowledge that some translations labeled "partly correct" might be factually wrong in possibly harmful ways, we choose to be lenient in the annotation, as NMT systems are susceptible to make such mistakes.

- *Wrong*: this translation hurts the adequacy and fluency of the sentence such as addition, omission, or miss-translation of the word or any part of it, e.g., when the model generates "donated" instead of "imposing".

[4] https://github.com/pytorch/fairseq

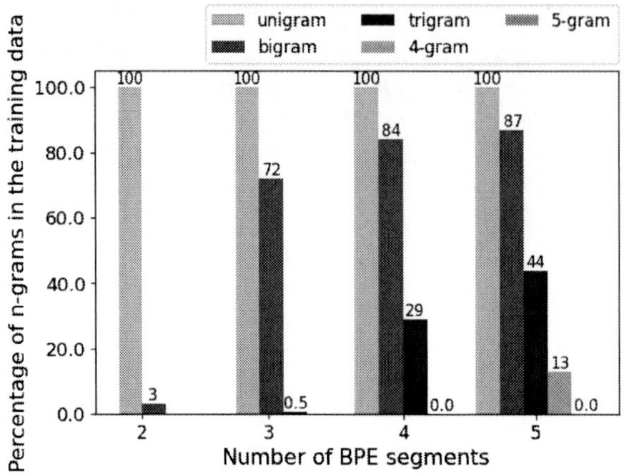

Figure 1: Presence of n-grams of BPE segmented OOV in the De-En training set for OOV words with different number of segments.

4 How does BPE segmentation benefit OOV words?

With the experimental setup described above, we now focus on answering our research questions. In this section, we first explore lack of which n-gram is responsible for OOV creation. Next, we measure to what extent the presence of OOVs impacts translation quality, while practically there is no unknown sub-word token when using BPE. Then, we see how translation quality differs for various OOV types. Finally, we investigate three potential factors responsible for different translation quality of OOV words.

4.1 OOV words in BPE segmented data

Before evaluating how OOV words affect translation quality, we explore which n-grams of the sequence of BPE segments in the training data are responsible for creation of an OOV word at inference time. In Figure 1, the horizontal axis shows German OOV words with different BPE lengths and the vertical axis shows the percentage of their n-grams present in the training set. For example, given OOV words with three segments, obviously all of the unigrams are present in the training set, only 72% of their bigrams, and interestingly 0.5% of their trigrams are present in the training set as part of words that have more BPE segments. We observe that as the number of BPE segments increases, the presence of BPE n-grams in the training data increases as well. For various lengths of BPE segmented words, unigrams and bigrams of BPE segments are very frequent in the training data, while the longer n-grams of BPE segmentes are less frequent. Therefore, we conclude that lack of presence of longer sequences of OOV n-grams in the training set are responsible for OOV occurrences, while shorter n-grams are seen in the training data with a higher rate.

4.2 The effect of OOV words on translation quality

Translation quality can be measured either by automatic evaluation metrics such as BLEU or by human assessments. While it has been shown that automatic MT evaluations usually fall short of human assessments (Callison-Burch, 2009; Graham et al., 2014), NMT system development has mainly focused on improving automatic evaluation metrics. Therefore, we use both Direct Assessment (DA Graham et al., 2013) as a strong human evaluation score as well as the BLEU score to see to what extent the translation quality is affected by OOV words when BPE is

#OOV	0	1	2	≥3
Kazakh	78	74	70	69
Russian	92	90	80	62

Table 1: Median of direct assessment scores for sentences containing various number of OOV words in Kazakh-English (low-resource) and Russian-English (high-resource). Since the scores are not normally distributed, we use the median. The higher the better.

applied. In Direct Assessment, sentences are assigned a score between zero and 100 based on how adequately they express the meaning of the corresponding reference.

We download the available DA scores of TALP-UPC's submission (Casas et al., 2019) and Facebook FAIR's submission (Ng et al., 2019) to WMT19 [5] for the Kazakh-English and Russian-English translation tasks, respectively. The choice of these language pairs is on the grounds that we require well-performing systems trained on BPE segmented data together with their available DA scores. Besides, we select Russian-English as a high-resource regime and Kazakh-English to represent a low-resource setting. Table 1 shows the median of DA scores for sentences containing various number of OOV words in Kazakh and Russian. In spite of using BPE which ensures almost no unknown tokens at inference time, translation quality still suffers from actual OOV words which existed before applying BPE segmentation. In particular, we observe that as the number of OOV words increases in a sentence, the DA score drops. This holds for both languages, where Kazakh is considered a low-resource language and Russian as a high-resource language. This implies that there is an inverse relationship between translation quality and the number of OOV words. Therefore, although there are no OOV words in the test sentences after applying BPE, the translation quality is lower for sentences that contain more OOV words in the absence of BPE.

To investigate the effect of OOV words on translation quality from the BLEU's point of view when using BPE, we take the Romanian-English dataset and add more OOV words to the test set. In particular, we remove the least frequent words occurring in the training set—that have also occurred in the test set—from the training set by replacing them with "<unk>" token. It should be noted that having high rates of OOV words (ratio of number of OOV types to the vocabulary of test set) is a realistic scenario. Given the Romanian training set with 612K sentences, newstest2016 has an OOV rate of 10% and the Romanian test set from the Flores-101 (Goyal et al., 2021) as a NMT benchmark has 42% OOV rate. Also, for the Kazakh-English training set with 100K samples, the OOV rates for newstest2019 and the Flores-101 test set are 19% and 30%, respectively. It is also plausible to have higher OOV rates for extremely low-resource language pairs with less than 100K training samples. Figure 2 indicates the decrease in Romanian-English BLEU score by increasing the rate of OOV words for both word-level and BPE-level models. Word-level is the model trained with vocabulary set of all actual words without involving any segmentation, while BPE-level models are trained on varying rates of segmentation.

It is worthwhile to mention that in order to ascertain whether additional "<unk>" tokens have not the slightest effect on BLEU score, we use the same "<unk>" rates and randomly replace them in the training set. These experiments confirm that the drop in BLEU score is not due to the added "<unk>" tokens and it is solely attributable to model failure in translating higher rates of OOV words. Based on Figure 2, the model trained with smaller numbers of BPE merge operations, which splits words into more and shorter segments, is less affected by increasing

[5] www.statmt.org/wmt19/

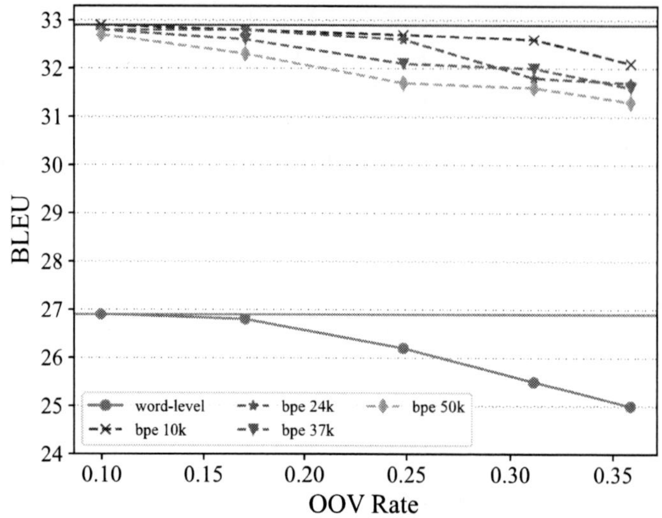

Figure 2: Comparing performance drop in word-level and BPE-level systems with different number of merge operations with increasing OOV rate in the Romanian-English test set. The horizontal lines show the performance of baselines without added OOV words.

the OOV rate. For example, with an OOV rate of 32%, comparing with the word-level model, BPE-10K line is very close to its baseline without added OOV words. With a larger number of BPE merge operations, the performance drop increases and gets closer to the performance drop of the word-level model. Thus, we can conclude that a smaller number of BPE merge operations alleviates the OOV problem. In the next section, we examine this conclusion in more detail.

4.3 Translation quality of different OOV types

In the previous section, we showed how OOV words still affect the translation quality and using a smaller number of BPE merge operations is presumably more effective to tackle OOV problem. In this section, we manually analyze the translation quality of OOV words for the systems trained on BPE segmented data with 10K and 37K BPE merge operations. Figure 3 (a) illustrates the translation quality of OOV words for three language pairs. Our manual analysis is consistent with Figure 2, confirming that a smaller number of BPE merge operations is beneficial for translating OOV words. However,there is an apparent contradiction with Figure 2 showing that a smaller number of BPE merge operations solves the OOV issue of the word-level model, while based on our manual analysis, BPE is only able to translate roughly 60% of the OOVs. This contradiction is due to the fact that BLEU tends to neglect local errors (Guillou et al., 2018) and the manual assessment is the more precise way to analyze the translation quality of OOV words.

Our preliminary analysis shows that OOV words usually fall into six categories: named entities (NE), compounds (C), morphological variants (MV), spelling errors (SE), technical words (T), and foreign words (F). In order to see how well a model trained on BPE segmented data can translate different types of OOV words, we manually label our sample of 400 OOV words as described in Section 3 for three different language directions. For each language pair, we only plot the OOV types with more than 10 OOVs in the corresponding sample of 400 OOV types. As shown in Figure 3 (b-d), for all language directions, the number of wrong translations is lower for named entities, especially for German-English and Romanian-English presumably due to their high rate of lexical similarity and the same Latin script (except for Romanian declensions).

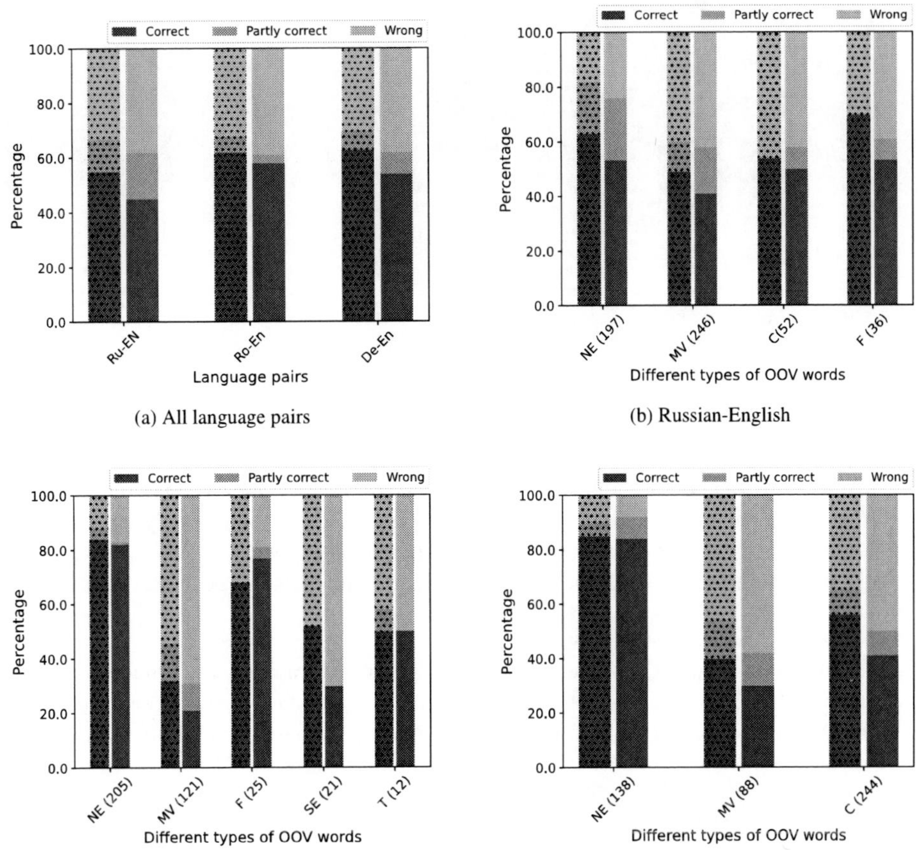

(a) All language pairs

(b) Russian-English

(c) Romanian-English

(d) German-English

Figure 3: Statistics of translation quality for systems trained with 10k (dotted bars indicate BPE-10K everywhere) and 37k BPE merge operations for named-entities (NE), morphological variants (MV), compounds (C), foreign words (F), spelling errors (SE), and technical words (T). Numbers in the parenthesis show the count of OOV type in the corresponding sample.

Morphological variants have the lowest rate of correct translations in all language pairs, which is especially problematic for Russian and Romanian as two morphologically rich languages. Also, for German as a compounding language, only 56% of compound OOVs are translated accurately. Translation quality of foreign words, spelling errors, and technical words that are very rare compared to the other three OOV types, is moderate to slightly higher for foreign words, as they are mostly English words that are translated to English. In the next sections, we explore some potential reasons for the quality differences of OOV translations.

4.4 The amount of attention received by OOV words

As mentioned earlier, in order to find the word alignments between source and target sentences, we use the average over heads of the encoder-decoder attention in the penultimate layer of Transformer. Specifically, for each BPE segment in the source language, the target token with the maximum value of attention weight is identified as the aligned token (Garg et al., 2019; Chen et al., 2020). We use this value to explore the amount of attentions received by OOV words. For

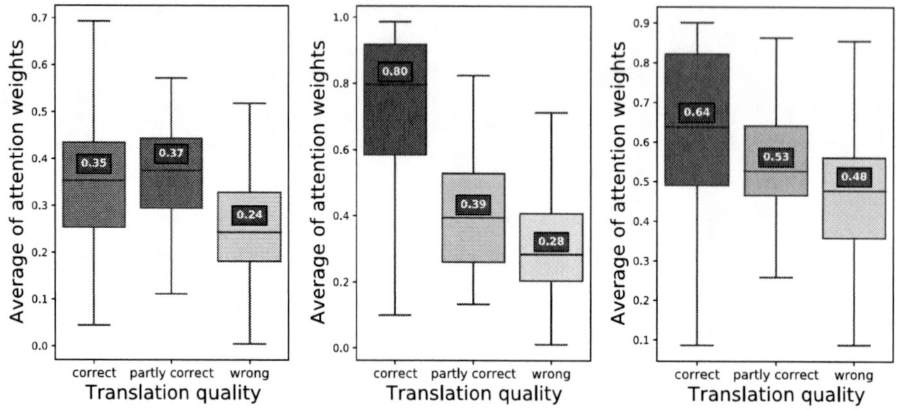

(a) Russian-English (b) Romanian-English (c) German-English

Figure 4: Average of attention weights received by OOV segments from hypothesis token for OOV words with different translation qualities. Each cross-attention weight is computed based on the average weights over heads of the penultimate decoder block. Vertical axis indicates the weight average over the OOV segments. The higher the median, the darker the color.

this purpose, for each OOV, we take the average over the amounts of attention received by its segments as the amount of attention payed by the corresponding generated segments. It should be noted that the same also holds for the maximum over segments in addition to average. Figure 4 indicates that OOV words that are translated accurately have received a significantly higher rate of attention compared to OOV words with wrong translations. Thus, we hypothesize that the ability of the model to translate segmented OOV words correlates well with the attention received by its constituents. Also, we observe that correct OOV translations in Romanian-English and German-English receive stronger attention than correct OOV translations in Russian-English. Furthermore, Figure 3 highlights the limited ability of BPE to facilitate the translation of Russian OOVs into English. Therefore, we conjecture there is an inverse relationship between the distance of languages involved in the translation and the usefulness of the BPE in translating OOV words. Another conjecture is that BPE is not a good choice for morphologically-rich languages as Russian. Although, strategies for morphologically driven segmentations fail at consistently improving overall translation quality over BPE (Huck et al., 2017; Domingo et al., 2018), no study is yet to explore the effectiveness of these morphology aware methods with the focus on OOV words.

4.5 Length of BPE segmented OOV word

BPE keeps the most frequent words intact and splits the rare and unseen words into longer sequences of segments. In order to scrutinize the relationship between the number of BPE segments for a given OOV word and its translation quality, we use 10K merge operations, as it is superior in translating BPE segmented OOV words, shown in Section 4.3. Figure 5 depicts the quality of OOV translation based on their length. First of all, we find that there is no significant correlation between the type of OOV and the length of BPE segmented OOV in each language. While the shorter lengths seem to have better translations for Russian-English, the opposite is true for Romanian-English. Also, OOV words with a length of 3 or 4 segments have a slightly higher rate of correct translations in the case of German-English. Therefore, we hypothesize splitting OOV words into longer sequences, which is the spirit of BPE, is more

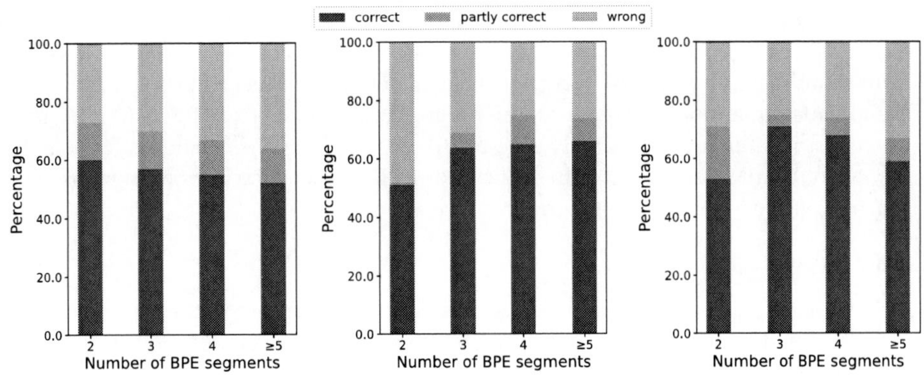

(a) Russian-English (b) Romanian-English (c) German-English

Figure 5: Translation quality for OOV words with different number of BPE segments.

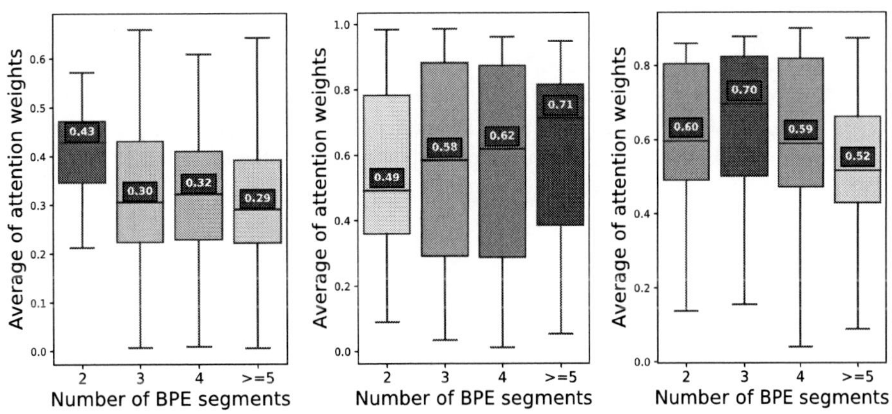

(a) Russian-English (b) Romanian-English (c) German-English

Figure 6: Average of cross-attention weights received by OOV segments from hypothesis token for OOV words with different number of segments. Each cross-attention weight is computed based on the average weights over heads of the penultimate decoder block. Vertical axis indicates the weight average over the OOV segments. The higher the median, the darker the color.

effective where there is a higher degree of similarity between language pairs such as Romanian-English and German-English, while having more BPE segments seems to be less effective for Russian-English. Accordingly we hypothesize more effectiveness of BPE for linguistically similar languages which is consistent with the results of Section 4.4. Figure 6 details the attention weights received by OOV words with different lengths which is in complete agreement with Figure 5 showing stronger attention where the length of the OOV words has resulted in higher translation quality.

4.6 Effect of frequency of BPE segments in training data

In this section, we examine if the translation quality is higher where the n-grams of the BPE segments of an OOV word are more frequent in the training data. We compare the distribution of n-gram frequencies for different quality labels using the one-sided Mann-Whitney U test (Mann and Whitney, 1947), a non-parametric test to compare the distribution of two groups of data againts each other. Specifically, for unigrams, we compare the frequency distribution of training unigrams that have occurred in correct and partly correct, correct and wrong, and partly correct and wrong translations. We repeat this for n-grams with $n \in \{1, 2, 3, 4, 5\}$. We find that no two distributions are significantly different ($\alpha = 0.1$). Thus, there is no evidence in the data to support that the distribution of frequencies of BPE segments for various n-grams are different across different translation qualities.

4.7 Target-side OOVs

So far in the paper, the OOV has always referred to the lack of a source-side word in the training vocabulary at inference time. One can also consider the target-side OOV word which is not the purpose of this paper. However, we investigate the relationship between the quality of the translation of a source-side OOV word and the presence of its corresponding reference or correct translation in the vocabulary. In particular, the question is to what extent the translation quality of a given source-side OOV word can be affected when its corresponding correct translation or its corresponding reference in the target side is also an OOV? In our exploration, we observe that for a significant number of correct translations, the reference or the correct output of the model is not present in the training set, which highlights the model ability to generate target-side OOV words. For German-English and Russian-English the number of correct source-side OOV translations with the target-side OOV words is higher than the correct translations for the target-side non-OOV words. However, Romanian-English is vice-versa. Therefore, there is not a consistent behaviour in all language pairs to support that the target-side OOV has a negative effect on the translation of the source-side OOV.

5 Conclusion

In this paper, we analyze the translation quality of OOV words in BPE segmented datasets. Our analysis shows that while BPE has brought significant improvements to NMT in terms of automatic evaluation metrics, the translation quality still suffers from OOV words. Our experiments show that splitting OOV words into subwords is more effective where there is higher degree of language similarity. Also, there is a strong correlation between the translation quality and the amount of attention received by OOV words. On the other hand, there is no evidence to support that the translation quality is dependent on the frequency of BPE segment n-grams in the training data. Moreover, we find that the translation quality is better for named entity OOV words compared to other word types, especially for language pairs with more lexical similarity. Furthermore, we showed that automatic evaluation metrics such as BLEU are not able to capture the effectiveness of a word segmentation method for translations of OOVs. Therefore, manual analysis on the translation quality of OOV words is essential to compare different approaches, although it needs annotators in each language and it is very laborious. In future work, we compare suggested approaches for morphologically-rich languages at the word level.

6 Acknowledgements

This research was funded in part by the Netherlands Organization for Scientific Research (NWO) under project number VI.C.192.080. We thank all the members of the UvA Language Technology Lab for their constant feedback on our work. Special thanks to the following people for their support, without whose help and annotation this work would never have been possible: Evgeniia Tokarchuk, Kata Naszadi, Maria Heuss, Mozhdeh Ariannezhad, and Vera Provatorova. Finally, we want to thank the anonymous reviewers for their valuable input and suggestions.

References

Araabi, A. and Monz, C. (2020). Optimizing transformer for low-resource neural machine translation. In Scott, D., Bel, N., and Zong, C., editors, *Proceedings of the 28th International Conference on Computational Linguistics, COLING 2020, Barcelona, Spain (Online), December 8-13, 2020*, pages 3429–3435. International Committee on Computational Linguistics.

Bahdanau, D., Cho, K., and Bengio, Y. (2015). Neural machine translation by jointly learning to align and translate. In Bengio, Y. and LeCun, Y., editors, *3rd International Conference on Learning Representations, ICLR 2015, San Diego, CA, USA, May 7-9, 2015, Conference Track Proceedings*.

Banerjee, T. and Bhattacharyya, P. (2018). Meaningless yet meaningful: Morphology grounded subword-level NMT. In *Proceedings of the Second Workshop on Subword/Character LEvel Models*, pages 55–60, New Orleans. Association for Computational Linguistics.

Callison-Burch, C. (2009). Fast, cheap, and creative: Evaluating translation quality using amazon's mechanical turk. In *Proceedings of the 2009 Conference on Empirical Methods in Natural Language Processing, EMNLP 2009, 6-7 August 2009, Singapore, A meeting of SIGDAT, a Special Interest Group of the ACL*, pages 286–295. ACL.

Casas, N., Fonollosa, J. A. R., Escolano, C., Basta, C., and Costa-jussà, M. R. (2019). The TALP-UPC machine translation systems for WMT19 news translation task: Pivoting techniques for low resource MT. In Bojar, O., Chatterjee, R., Federmann, C., Fishel, M., Graham, Y., Haddow, B., Huck, M., Jimeno-Yepes, A., Koehn, P., Martins, A., Monz, C., Negri, M., Névéol, A., Neves, M. L., Post, M., Turchi, M., and Verspoor, K., editors, *Proceedings of the Fourth Conference on Machine Translation, WMT 2019, Florence, Italy, August 1-2, 2019 - Volume 2: Shared Task Papers, Day 1*, pages 155–162. Association for Computational Linguistics.

Chen, Y., Liu, Y., Chen, G., Jiang, X., and Liu, Q. (2020). Accurate word alignment induction from neural machine translation. In Webber, B., Cohn, T., He, Y., and Liu, Y., editors, *Proceedings of the 2020 Conference on Empirical Methods in Natural Language Processing, EMNLP 2020, Online, November 16-20, 2020*, pages 566–576. Association for Computational Linguistics.

Cherry, C., Foster, G. F., Bapna, A., Firat, O., and Macherey, W. (2018). Revisiting character-based neural machine translation with capacity and compression. In Riloff, E., Chiang, D., Hockenmaier, J., and Tsujii, J., editors, *Proceedings of the 2018 Conference on Empirical Methods in Natural Language Processing, Brussels, Belgium, October 31 - November 4, 2018*, pages 4295–4305. Association for Computational Linguistics.

Costa-jussà, M. R. and Fonollosa, J. A. R. (2016). Character-based neural machine translation. In *Proceedings of the 54th Annual Meeting of the Association for Computational Linguistics, ACL 2016, August 7-12, 2016, Berlin, Germany, Volume 2: Short Papers*. The Association for Computer Linguistics.

Domingo, M., García-Martínez, M., Helle, A., Casacuberta, F., and Herranz, M. (2018). How much does tokenization affect neural machine translation? *CoRR*, abs/1812.08621.

Dyer, C., Chahuneau, V., and Smith, N. A. (2013). A simple, fast, and effective reparameterization of IBM model 2. In Vanderwende, L., III, H. D., and Kirchhoff, K., editors, *Human Language Technologies: Conference of the North American Chapter of the Association of Computational Linguistics, Proceedings, June 9-14, 2013, Westin Peachtree Plaza Hotel, Atlanta, Georgia, USA*, pages 644–648. The Association for Computational Linguistics.

Gallé, M. (2019). Investigating the effectiveness of BPE: the power of shorter sequences. In Inui, K., Jiang, J., Ng, V., and Wan, X., editors, *Proceedings of the 2019 Conference on Empirical Methods in Natural Language Processing and the 9th International Joint Conference on Natural Language Processing, EMNLP-IJCNLP 2019, Hong Kong, China, November 3-7, 2019*, pages 1375–1381. Association for Computational Linguistics.

Garg, S., Peitz, S., Nallasamy, U., and Paulik, M. (2019). Jointly learning to align and translate with transformer models. In Inui, K., Jiang, J., Ng, V., and Wan, X., editors, *Proceedings of the 2019 Conference on Empirical Methods in Natural Language Processing and the 9th International Joint Conference on Natural Language Processing, EMNLP-IJCNLP 2019, Hong Kong, China, November 3-7, 2019*, pages 4452–4461. Association for Computational Linguistics.

Goyal, N., Gao, C., Chaudhary, V., Chen, P., Wenzek, G., Ju, D., Krishnan, S., Ranzato, M., Guzmán, F., and Fan, A. (2021). The FLORES-101 evaluation benchmark for low-resource and multilingual machine translation. *CoRR*, abs/2106.03193.

Graham, Y., Baldwin, T., Moffat, A., and Zobel, J. (2013). Continuous measurement scales in human evaluation of machine translation. In Dipper, S., Liakata, M., and Pareja-Lora, A., editors, *Proceedings of the 7th Linguistic Annotation Workshop and Interoperability with Discourse, LAW-ID@ACL 2013, August 8-9, 2013, Sofia, Bulgaria*, pages 33–41. The Association for Computer Linguistics.

Graham, Y., Mathur, N., and Baldwin, T. (2014). Randomized significance tests in machine translation. In *Proceedings of the Ninth Workshop on Statistical Machine Translation, WMT@ACL 2014, June 26-27, 2014, Baltimore, Maryland, USA*, pages 266–274. The Association for Computer Linguistics.

Guillou, L., Hardmeier, C., Lapshinova-Koltunski, E., and Loáiciga, S. (2018). A pronoun test suite evaluation of the english-german MT systems at WMT 2018. In Bojar, O., Chatterjee, R., Federmann, C., Fishel, M., Graham, Y., Haddow, B., Huck, M., Jimeno-Yepes, A., Koehn, P., Monz, C., Negri, M., Névéol, A., Neves, M. L., Post, M., Specia, L., Turchi, M., and Verspoor, K., editors, *Proceedings of the Third Conference on Machine Translation: Shared Task Papers, WMT 2018, Belgium, Brussels, October 31 - November 1, 2018*, pages 570–577. Association for Computational Linguistics.

Gülçehre, Ç., Ahn, S., Nallapati, R., Zhou, B., and Bengio, Y. (2016). Pointing the unknown words. In *Proceedings of the 54th Annual Meeting of the Association for Computational Linguistics, ACL 2016, August 7-12, 2016, Berlin, Germany, Volume 1: Long Papers*. The Association for Computer Linguistics.

He, X., Haffari, G., and Norouzi, M. (2020). Dynamic programming encoding for subword segmentation in neural machine translation. In Jurafsky, D., Chai, J., Schluter, N., and Tetreault, J. R., editors, *Proceedings of the 58th Annual Meeting of the Association for Computational Linguistics, ACL 2020, Online, July 5-10, 2020*, pages 3042–3051. Association for Computational Linguistics.

Hu, W., Luo, Y., Meng, J., Qian, Z., and Huo, Q. (2020). A study of bpe-based language modeling for open vocabulary latin language OCR. In *17th International Conference on Frontiers in Handwriting Recognition, ICFHR 2020, Dortmund, Germany, September 8-10, 2020*, pages 133–138. IEEE.

Huck, M., Riess, S., and Fraser, A. M. (2017). Target-side word segmentation strategies for neural machine translation. In Bojar, O., Buck, C., Chatterjee, R., Federmann, C., Graham, Y., Haddow, B., Huck, M., Jimeno-Yepes, A., Koehn, P., and Kreutzer, J., editors, *Proceedings of the Second Conference on Machine Translation, WMT 2017, Copenhagen, Denmark, September 7-8, 2017*, pages 56–67. Association for Computational Linguistics.

Jean, S., Cho, K., Memisevic, R., and Bengio, Y. (2015). On using very large target vocabulary for neural machine translation. In *Proceedings of the 53rd Annual Meeting of the Association for Computational Linguistics and the 7th International Joint Conference on Natural Language Processing of the Asian Federation of Natural Language Processing, ACL 2015, July 26-31, 2015, Beijing, China, Volume 1: Long Papers*, pages 1–10. The Association for Computer Linguistics.

Koehn, P. and Monz, C. (2006). Manual and automatic evaluation of machine translation between european languages. In Koehn, P. and Monz, C., editors, *Proceedings on the Workshop on Statistical Machine Translation, WMT@HLT-NAACL 2006, New York City, NY, USA, June 8-9, 2006*, pages 102–121. Association for Computational Linguistics.

Kudo, T. (2018). Subword regularization: Improving neural network translation models with multiple subword candidates. In Gurevych, I. and Miyao, Y., editors, *Proceedings of the 56th Annual Meeting of the Association for Computational Linguistics, ACL 2018, Melbourne, Australia, July 15-20, 2018, Volume 1: Long Papers*, pages 66–75. Association for Computational Linguistics.

Kudo, T. and Richardson, J. (2018). Sentencepiece: A simple and language independent subword tokenizer and detokenizer for neural text processing. In Blanco, E. and Lu, W., editors, *Proceedings of the 2018 Conference on Empirical Methods in Natural Language Processing, EMNLP 2018: System Demonstrations, Brussels, Belgium, October 31 - November 4, 2018*, pages 66–71. Association for Computational Linguistics.

Liu, Z., Xu, Y., Winata, G. I., and Fung, P. (2019). Incorporating word and subword units in unsupervised machine translation using language model rescoring. In Bojar, O., Chatterjee, R., Federmann, C., Fishel, M., Graham, Y., Haddow, B., Huck, M., Jimeno-Yepes, A., Koehn, P., Martins, A., Monz, C., Negri, M., Névéol, A., Neves, M. L., Post, M., Turchi, M., and Verspoor, K., editors, *Proceedings of the Fourth Conference on Machine Translation, WMT 2019, Florence, Italy, August 1-2, 2019 - Volume 2: Shared Task Papers, Day 1*, pages 275–282. Association for Computational Linguistics.

Luo, G., Yang, Y., Yuan, Y., Chen, Z., and Ainiwaer, A. (2019). Hierarchical transfer learning architecture for low-resource neural machine translation. *IEEE Access*, 7:154157–154166.

Luong, T., Sutskever, I., Le, Q. V., Vinyals, O., and Zaremba, W. (2015). Addressing the rare word problem in neural machine translation. In *Proceedings of the 53rd Annual Meeting of the Association for Computational Linguistics and the 7th International Joint Conference on Natural Language Processing of the Asian Federation of Natural Language Processing, ACL 2015, July 26-31, 2015, Beijing, China, Volume 1: Long Papers*, pages 11–19. The Association for Computer Linguistics.

Mann, H. B. and Whitney, D. R. (1947). On a test of whether one of two random variables is stochastically larger than the other. *The annals of mathematical statistics*, pages 50–60.

Ng, N., Yee, K., Baevski, A., Ott, M., Auli, M., and Edunov, S. (2019). Facebook fair's WMT19 news translation task submission. In Bojar, O., Chatterjee, R., Federmann, C., Fishel,

M., Graham, Y., Haddow, B., Huck, M., Jimeno-Yepes, A., Koehn, P., Martins, A., Monz, C., Negri, M., Névéol, A., Neves, M. L., Post, M., Turchi, M., and Verspoor, K., editors, *Proceedings of the Fourth Conference on Machine Translation, WMT 2019, Florence, Italy, August 1-2, 2019 - Volume 2: Shared Task Papers, Day 1*, pages 314–319. Association for Computational Linguistics.

Pan, Y., Li, X., Yang, Y., and Dong, R. (2020). Morphological word segmentation on agglutinative languages for neural machine translation. *CoRR*, abs/2001.01589.

Provilkov, I., Emelianenko, D., and Voita, E. (2020). Bpe-dropout: Simple and effective subword regularization. In Jurafsky, D., Chai, J., Schluter, N., and Tetreault, J. R., editors, *Proceedings of the 58th Annual Meeting of the Association for Computational Linguistics, ACL 2020, Online, July 5-10, 2020*, pages 1882–1892. Association for Computational Linguistics.

Sennrich, R., Haddow, B., and Birch, A. (2016). Neural machine translation of rare words with subword units. In *Proceedings of the 54th Annual Meeting of the Association for Computational Linguistics, ACL 2016, August 7-12, 2016, Berlin, Germany, Volume 1: Long Papers*. The Association for Computer Linguistics.

Smit, P., Virpioja, S., Grönroos, S., and Kurimo, M. (2014). Morfessor 2.0: Toolkit for statistical morphological segmentation. In Bouma, G. and Parmentier, Y., editors, *Proceedings of the 14th Conference of the European Chapter of the Association for Computational Linguistics, EACL 2014, April 26-30, 2014, Gothenburg, Sweden*, pages 21–24. The Association for Computer Linguistics.

Sutskever, I., Vinyals, O., and Le, Q. V. (2014). Sequence to sequence learning with neural networks. In Ghahramani, Z., Welling, M., Cortes, C., Lawrence, N. D., and Weinberger, K. Q., editors, *Advances in Neural Information Processing Systems 27: Annual Conference on Neural Information Processing Systems 2014, December 8-13 2014, Montreal, Quebec, Canada*, pages 3104–3112.

Vaswani, A., Shazeer, N., Parmar, N., Uszkoreit, J., Jones, L., Gomez, A. N., Kaiser, L., and Polosukhin, I. (2017). Attention is all you need. In Guyon, I., von Luxburg, U., Bengio, S., Wallach, H. M., Fergus, R., Vishwanathan, S. V. N., and Garnett, R., editors, *Advances in Neural Information Processing Systems 30: Annual Conference on Neural Information Processing Systems 2017, December 4-9, 2017, Long Beach, CA, USA*, pages 5998–6008.

Wu, Y., Schuster, M., Chen, Z., Le, Q. V., Norouzi, M., Macherey, W., Krikun, M., Cao, Y., Gao, Q., Macherey, K., Klingner, J., Shah, A., Johnson, M., Liu, X., Kaiser, L., Gouws, S., Kato, Y., Kudo, T., Kazawa, H., Stevens, K., Kurian, G., Patil, N., Wang, W., Young, C., Smith, J., Riesa, J., Rudnick, A., Vinyals, O., Corrado, G., Hughes, M., and Dean, J. (2016). Google's neural machine translation system: Bridging the gap between human and machine translation. *CoRR*, abs/1609.08144.

On the Effectiveness of Quasi Character-Level Models for Machine Translation

Salvador Carrión salcarpo@prhlt.upv.es
Francisco Casacuberta fcn@prhlt.upv.es
PRHLT Research Center, Universitat Politècnica de València

Abstract

Neural Machine Translation (NMT) models often use subword-level vocabularies to deal with rare or unknown words. Although some studies have shown the effectiveness of purely character-based models, these approaches have resulted in highly expensive models in computational terms. In this work, we explore the benefits of quasi-character-level models for very low-resource languages and their ability to mitigate the effects of the catastrophic forgetting problem. First, we conduct an empirical study on the efficacy of these models, as a function of the vocabulary and training set size, for a range of languages, domains, and architectures. Next, we study the ability of these models to mitigate the effects of catastrophic forgetting in machine translation. Our work suggests that quasi-character-level models have practically the same generalization capabilities as character-based models but at lower computational costs. Furthermore, they appear to help achieve greater consistency between domains than standard subword-level models, although the catastrophic forgetting problem is not mitigated.

1 Introduction

Neural machine translation (NMT) has become the dominant paradigm in the field of machine translation due to the impressive results obtained with the encoder-decoder architectures (Sutskever et al., 2014; Cho et al., 2014; Wu et al., 2016; Vaswani et al., 2017) and the approaches proposed to tackle the open vocabulary problem such as subword-based models with byte-fallback or, more recently, token-free models.

However, despite these advances, low-resource languages are still problematic as there are many languages that are spoken but not written on the internet (e.g., Tigrinya, Sotho, Tsonga, etc.), and therefore, parallel text mining techniques are either not effective or not applicable at all. In these cases, it is common to use character-based models, since multiple authors have shown that these models usually perform better than (standard) subword- or word-based models in very low-resource settings.

Motivated by these ideas, we decided to study whether quasi-character-based vocabularies (defined as a subword-based vocabulary that is one or two orders of magnitude smaller than a standard subword-based vocabulary), had the same advantages as models with character-based vocabularies for low-resource languages, but with much lower computational costs, due to the exponential decrease in the average number of tokens per sentence when merging highly frequent character pairs.

Furthermore, given that the effects of the catastrophic forgetting problem are strongly related to the vocabulary of the model, we decided to study if these quasi-character-level vocabularies had the potential to mitigate them, since these vocabularies are closer to a universal-domain vocabulary (e.g., bytes or chars) than a word- or (standard) subword-based vocabulary.

The contributions of this paper are twofold:

- Quasi-character-level models appear to outperform character-based models in terms of performance, while offering practically the same generalization capabilities at much lower computational costs.
- Quasi-character-level models appear to achieve higher consistencies in performance between domains, but at the same time, they also seem to be more susceptible to the effects of the catastrophic forgetting problem.

2 Related work

Character-based models have been widely studied in the field of Natural Language Processing (NLP) to deal with the open vocabulary problem. Vilar et al. (2007) proposed one of the first character-based models, who treated source and target sentences as a string of letters. Similarly, Neubig et al. (2013) viewed translation as a single transduction between character strings in the source. However, these results were unsatisfactory, as their models generally performed worse than their word-based counterparts.

To overcome these problems, many authors have proposed strategies based on hybrid models (Luong and Manning, 2016), which mainly translated at the word level except when a rare or unknown word was encountered; subword-based model (Sennrich et al., 2016; Kudo, 2018; Kudo and Richardson, 2018), which allow to efficiently represent a word as a sequence of subwords; and more recently, token-free models (Xue et al., 2021; Clark et al., 2021), which operate directly on raw text.

Despite these improvements, character-based models are still interesting for low-resource languages since multiple authors have shown their benefits over other approaches. For example, Cherry et al. (2018) showed that character-level models have their greatest advantage when data sizes are small; Sennrich and Zhang (2019) showed that reducing the vocabulary size leads to improvements for low-resource NMT models. Similarly, by studying the Zipfian nature of languages in NMT, other authors have reached similar conclusions. Raunak et al. (2020) characterized the long-tailed phenomena in NMT, and Gowda and May (2020) proved that each dataset has an optimal vocabulary size. Although this optimal vocabulary size has been traditionally found by trial and error, very recently, Xu et al. (2020) has proposed a new technique to explore automatic vocabularization without trial and error. However, despite its impressive results, this method still requires a non-trivial amount of time[1]. Hence, heuristics will remain an effective solution to the vocabulary-size problem.

In this work, we focused our efforts on preserving the advantages of character-based models but at much lower computational costs. In this line, other authors have introduced new ideas, such as Lee et al. (2016), who used convolutional and max-pool layers to reduce the length of the character-level representations; Cherry et al. (2018) showed that alternative architectures for handling character input are better viewed as methods for reducing computation time than as improved ways of modeling longer sequences; Kreutzer and Sokolov (2018) proposed an approach to learning input and output segmentations for NMT, which favors character-level approaches; and more recently, Mielke et al. (2021) published a survey about tokenization and the open-vocabulary problem, where they concluded that it is likely that there will never be a silver bullet solution for all applications.

This work briefly studies the generalization capabilities of quasi-character-level models for different neural architectures. Many authors have extensively studied the limitations of existing tokenizations and neural architectures for text processing tasks. For instance, Conneau et al.

[1]30 GPU hours on the WMT-14 English-German translation dataset

(2016) showed a state-of-the-art CNN architecture for text processing that operated directly at the character level; Araabi and Monz (2020) showed that the effectiveness of Transformer under low-resource conditions is highly dependent on the hyper-parameter settings; Banar et al. (2020) presented a fast character transformer via gradient-based subword tokenization.

Finally, this work ends with a brief discussion on the ability of quasi-character-level models to mitigate the effects of the catastrophic forgetting problem in NMT. As far as we know, this is the first work to address this problem from this perspective, since most of the works that we know of are based on regularization (Li and Hoiem, 2016; Kirkpatrick et al., 2016), dynamic architectures (Rusu et al., 2016; Draelos et al., 2016) or Complementary Learning Systems (CLS) (Kemker and Kanan, 2017).

3 Neural Machine Translation

3.1 Neural architectures for Machine Translation

The goal of any translation system is to transform an input sequence in a given language into an output sequence in a target language.

Nowadays, this is usually done using neural models based on the encoder-decoder architecture, also known as Seq-to-Seq models in the machine translation community (Sutskever et al., 2014). The encoder part transforms the input sequence into an internal representation, and then the decoder transforms this internal representation into the output sequence.

Recurrent architectures (RNNs) were the first to be successfully applied in an encoder-decoder setup for machine translation. Even though there are many RNNs, most chain a series of unit cells sequentially to process temporal sequences. We decided to use LSTMs (Hochreiter and Schmidhuber, 1997) because their unit cells are explicitly designed to deal with long-term dependencies.

Convolution-based architectures (CNN) do not contain any recurrent elements. They can do this because the idea behind this architecture is that the convolutional filters can slide through the sequence of tokens from beginning to end (Gehring et al., 2017).

Lastly, Vaswani et al. (2017) introduced the Transformer architecture, which is a state-of-the-art model based entirely on the concept of *attention* (Bahdanau et al., 2015; Luong et al., 2015) to draw global dependencies between the input and output. Unlike RNNs or CNNs, this architecture processes its temporal sequences all at once through masks that encode temporal information.

This work is focused on the Transformer as it is the current state-of-the-art model for machine translation. Nonetheless, RNNs and CNNs are briefly explored for completeness (See Section 5.4.3).

3.2 The open vocabulary problem

In the written language, it is common to find alternative spellings (i.e., *color-colour*) and typos (i.e., *acknowledge-acknowlege*) that slightly modify the spelling of a word but do not prevent us, the humans, from understanding its meaning. However, suppose a model is using a word-level representation. In that case, it will stop knowing a *known word* at the very first moment that it is slightly modified (and this modification is not in its vocabulary). Similarly, it has to be taken into account that many languages use agglutination and compounding mechanisms to form new words, making word-based vocabularies a very inefficient approach.

As a result, researchers have proposed multiple approaches to deal with the open vocabulary problem, such as bytes- or character-based models, hybrid models, subword-based models, or, more recently, token-free models.

Arguably, a character-based vocabulary[2] is the most straightway to solve the open-vocabulary problem, as it contains the minimum set of characters with which to form every possible word in a given language. Because of this, these types of models have the potential to translate every possible word, even rare or even unseen words, if enough information is present in the training set. However, despite the many innovations (Jaszczur et al., 2021; Banar et al., 2020; Chung et al., 2016; Kreutzer and Sokolov, 2018), these models tend to be much slower, resource-hungry, and harder to train than standard subword-based or word-based models, as they have to deal with longer long-term dependencies.

Given that subword-level vocabularies can degenerate to character- or word-based vocabularies, we decided to use this property to build vocabularies that are one or two orders of magnitude smaller than the standard subword-level vocabularies[3], with the goal of having virtually the same benefits of character-level models for low-resources languages, but at much lower computational costs.

4 Experimental setup

4.1 Datasets

The data used for this work comes mainly from the WMT tasks (see Table 1).

Dataset	Training set
Europarl (es/de/cs/sv/da/bg/zh/ru-en)	50K/100K/1-2M
CommonCrawl (es-en)	100K/1.8M
SciELO (es-en)	120K/575K
NewsCommentary (de-en)	35K/357K
IWLST'16 (de-en)	196K
Multi30K (de-en)	29K
Tatoeba (mr-en)	53K
CCAligned (or-en)	3K

Table 1: These datasets contain parallel sentences from different languages and domains (political, economic, health, biological, talks, etc.). All the values in this Table indicate the number of sentences.

4.2 Training details

For preprocessing and training we used AutoNMT (Carrión and Casacuberta, 2022), with *Unigram/SentencePiece* (Kudo, 2018; Kudo and Richardson, 2018) as the subword model, shared vocabularies, and Fairseq as the training framework (v1.0.0a0), on 2x NVIDIA GP102 (TITAN XP) - 12GB.

Initially, we started to experiment with the standard Transformer (45-93M parameters), but then we switched to a smaller version (4-25M parameters), as both performed quite similarly in terms of performance ($\pm 1 - 3$ BLEU), while the latter was notably faster. Similarly, other seq-to-seq neural architectures were used for completeness (Transformer, LSTMs, and CNNs).

In all cases, the set training hyper-parameters were pretty standard[4]. Despite using similar settings in most models, we noticed that as we used smaller vocabularies and training sets,

[2]Plus a byte-level fallback

[3]Vocabularies of 100-500 tokens vs. vocabularies of 30K-40K tokens)

[4]Hyper-parameters:`lr=[0.5e-4, 1e-3]; weight-decay=[1e-3, 1e-4]; criterion=[ce, label-ce(0.1)]; scheduler=[fixed, inverse-sqrt]; warmup-updates=[4000]; optimizer=[adam, sgd, nag]; clip-norm=[0.0, 0.1, 1.0]; beam-width=5]`

these models became more sensitive to the given hyper-parameters. The training time for most models was between a few hours to one or two days, and all models were evaluated with Sacrebleu (Post, 2018) and BERTScore (Zhang et al., 2019).

5 Experimentation

5.1 On Quasi-Character-Level Hypothesis

Given two different vocabularies, A and B, we could say that they are grammatically equivalent if both can represent any possible word of a given language. Because of this, the smaller a vocabulary is, the greater the generalization capabilities of the model used will have to be to end up with good translations, as the amount of information per token will be diluted by the number of tokens needed to encode each string.

Based on this premise, we can infer that the representation power of a given model will depend on the degree of generalization required by its vocabulary, the amount of data required to learn it, and if the complexity of the model can handle it. Hence, given a model with enough complexity, the advantages of character-based vocabularies will decrease with respect to subword-based or word-based vocabularies as the amount of data increases.

Based on these premises, supported by empirical evidence Sennrich and Zhang (2019), we hypothesized that quasi-character-based models should provide practically the same generalization capabilities as character-level models, but more efficiently, by exploiting highly frequent n-grams to decrease the sentence length exponentially.

5.2 Effects of the vocabulary and corpus size

In order to test the basis of our hypothesis, we chose a medium-sized corpus such as Europarl-2M (de-en). Then, two other versions were created, where the training set was artificially reduced from 2M sentences to 100k and 50k sentences. Similarly, we created two vocabularies:

- A standard subword-level vocabulary with 32k entries.
- A quasi-character-level vocabulary with 350 entries.

The aim of this experiment was twofold. First, we sought to confirm that smaller vocabularies tend to help in low-resource environments (Cherry et al., 2018), in addition to proving additional data points for smaller datasets (less than 2M sentences), languages, and domains. Second, we sought to establish baselines for our quasi-character-based models so that we could later study their computational advantage over purely character-level models.

As expected, in Figure 1 we see that when there is enough training data, standard subword-level models outperform quasi-character-level models (first column). In contrast, when the amount of training data was reduced (second and third columns), the quasi-character-level models outperformed the standard subword-level models.

In total, we performed this experiment for three different language pairs (Spanish-English, German-English, and Czech-English) to account for potential language biases and domains (political, economical, health, biological, transcripted talks, etc.). The low-resource settings were emulated in this experiment because high-quality datasets contain less noise. Consequently, we could generalize the findings of previous authors to much smaller corpora more confidently, and also, test the basis of our hypothesis for quasi-character-level vocabularies (See section 5.3 for actual low-resource languages).

5.3 On the Effectiveness of Quasi-Character-Level Models

As the results from our previous experiment could be compromised towards a sub-optimal vocabulary size, we repeated the previous experiment, but this time, we gradually increased the

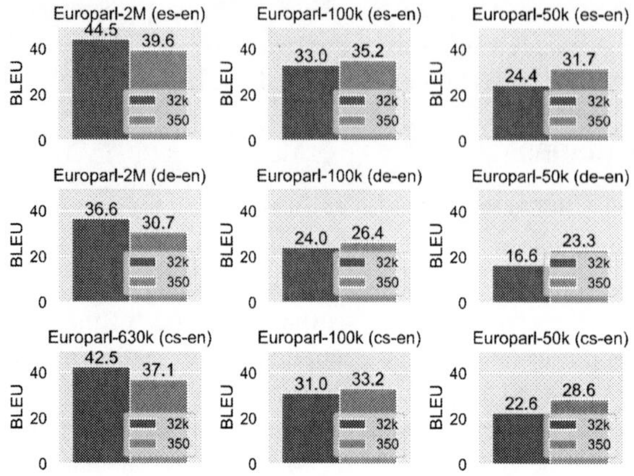

Figure 1: As we limited the training data (from left to right), quasi-character-level models perform better than standard subword-level models, regardless of language (top to bottom).

vocabulary size (at the subword-level) from 100 tokens to 16,000 tokens (plus 256 additional entries for the byte-fallback). Moreover, we added five actual low-resource languages (non-emulated) and three non-latin languages to the experiment in order to account for potential biases (See Figure 2).

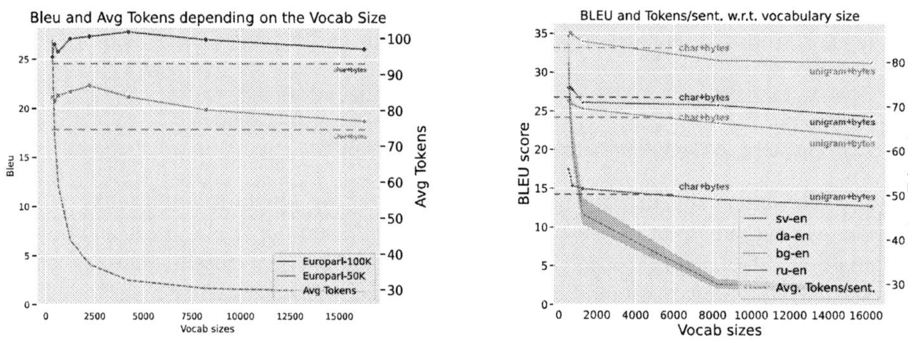

(a) (Emulated) Low-Resource languages

(b) (Actual) Low-Resource languages

Figure 2: As we decrease the size of the vocabulary, the average number of tokens per sentence increases exponentially. Hence, more complex models and more training data are needed for exploiting the generalization capabilities of these vocabularies. In contrast, by merging a few highly frequent char-pairs into a single token, we can have models that practically generalize as character-based models but at much lower computational costs.

In Figure 2a we have the BLEU scores and the average tokens per sentence as a function of the vocabulary size, for two low-resource emulations of the Europarl (de-en) dataset, one with 50k sentences (orange line) and another with 100k sentences (blue line).

Firstly, we see that for both datasets, as the number of entries in the vocabulary decreases, the performance of our models increases. However, this phenomenon is much stronger on the smaller corpus (Europarl-50k), thing that might indicate that for high-quality corpus, the advantages of character-level models could disappear much quicker than was previously thought (Cherry et al., 2018).

Secondly, we see that as vocabulary size approaches a character-level representation[5], the average number of tokens per sentence increases exponentially (dashed line). This phenomenon has a direct impact on the performance of the model due to: i) The additional complexity needed to handle the greater generalization capabilities of smaller vocabularies; ii) The problems imposed by having to deal with longer long-term dependencies; and iii) Higher computational costs at training and run-time.

Fortunately, the opposite is also true. As the vocabulary size increases, the average number of tokens per sentence decreases exponentially, and therefore, the models need less complexity. This can also be seen in Figure 2a, where the quasi-character-level models outperformed purely character-based models (dashed lines) by a significant margin without increasing the complexity of this model (or the training time).

Similarly, after repeating these experiments with actual low-resource language and non-latin languages, the results remained quite consistent for most languages (Swedish, Danish, Bulgarian, Russian) and scripts (latin and non-latin) (See Figure 2b).

However, there is no silver bullet as we noticed three language pairs where this phenomenon was not observed. The first was with Chinese-English, probably due to the large number of individual characters present. And then, with two very low-resource pairs (Marathe and Oriya), where the Bleu-Vocab curve remained flat.

5.4 On the Generalization of Quasi-Character-based approaches

In this section, we study whether the benefits of Quasi-Character-based approaches generalize to other domains, and neural architectures.

5.4.1 Domain generalization

To study whether the domain might be influencing the results from Section 5.2, we decided to repeat the same experiment but using parallel corpora from different domains, such as crawled data (CommonCrawl), political and economic news (NewsCommentary), health and biological sciences (SciELO), transcribed talks (IWLST'16) and multimodal transcriptions (Multi30k).

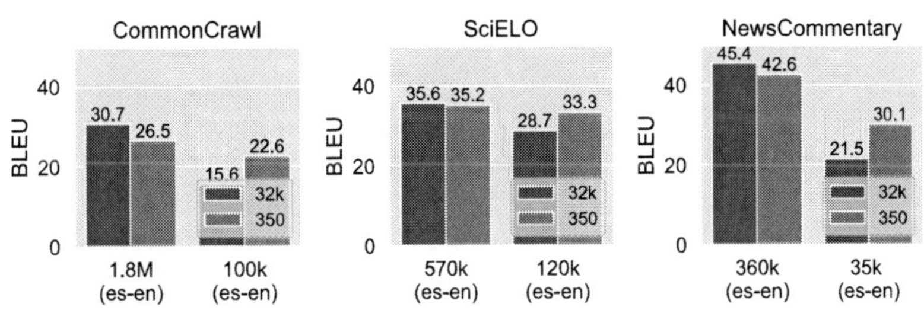

Figure 3: The benefits of quasi-character-level models for low-resource environments appear to be consistent regardless of domain.

The results from Figure 3 show the BLEU scores of the quasi-character-level and standard subword-level models trained on high- and low-resource settings[6], corresponding to different domains (Crawled data, Science and News). As in Section 5.2, the quasi-character-based models kept outperforming the standard subword-based models for the low-resource settings, re-

[5]Horizontal dashed lines indicate the character-level baselines

[6]Emulated

gardless of the training domain. These results seem to indicate that this phenomenon is not only language-agnostic, but also domain-agnostic.[7]

5.4.2 Performance comparison

In Figures 2a and 2b we see that the average amount of tokens (gray line) decreases exponentially (up to a point), when the vocabulary size is increased. As a result, our quasi-character-level models processed on average between 30% and 60% fewer tokens than the character-based models, depending on the language, the vocabulary size, and the dataset.

The exact speedup is highly dependent on the training setup, since it is not the same to limit the number of sentences per batch than to limit the number of tokens per batch. Nonetheless, in both cases, we obtained a non-negligible optimization. In the first case, the most significant improvement was in terms of memory consumption due to the quadratic complexity of the Transformer's self-attention. While in the second case, it was from reducing the number of batches needed to process a single epoch.

5.4.3 Neural architecture generalization

In this section, we study whether the above findings can be generalized to other architectures such as LSTMs or CNNs, or whether, on the contrary, the advantages of the quasi-character-level models are mainly due to the ability of Transformers to learn long-term dependencies.

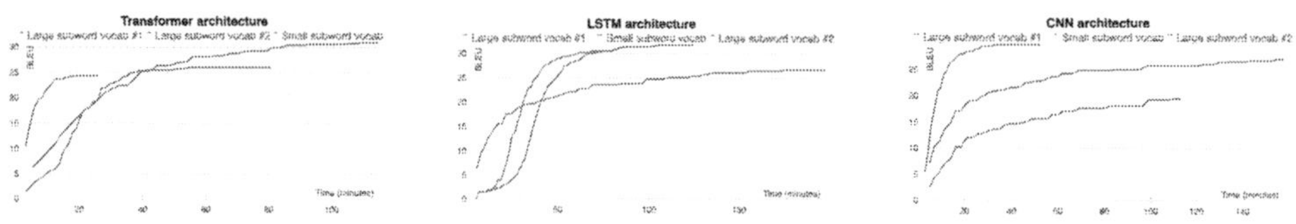

(a) Transformer architecture (b) Bi-LSTM architecture (c) CNN architecture

Figure 4: The green lines refer to the best and worst performances of the standard subword-level models, while the blue lines refer to the best performance of the quasi-character-level models.

Specifically, we focused our study on bidirectional LSTMs with attention mechanisms, and fully convolutional architectures like the one described in (Gehring et al., 2017).

Although the comparison between different neural architectures is not a trivial task, we attempted to explore this topic by only comparing models that had a similar number of parameters for a given vocabulary (i.e., 25-30M parameters for 32k subword vocabularies).

From our experimentation, we observed that when the standard subword-level models were trained with sufficient data, they outperformed all the quasi-character-level models, regardless of their architecture. However, when this experiment was repeated in the low-resource regime, the quasi-character-based models performed better than their standard subword-level counterparts, regardless of their architecture[8] (See Figure 4).

In the left figure 4a, we see that quasi-character-level Transformers consistently outperform the standard subword-level models. This phenomenon is still present for LSTMs (middle Figure 4b), but it is not as evident as with the Transformer architecture due to the problems of RNNs with modeling long-term dependencies. Finally, in the right Figure 4c we see that CNNs

[7]The experiments done with IWLST'16 and Multi30K datasets yielded similar results. In these, the improvement for the quasi-character-based models was +6.2pts (BLEU) for the IWLST'16 dataset, and +2.3pts (BLEU) for the Multi30k dataset.

[8]In Figure 4c the quasi-character-level model did not outperform the standard subword-level models. This was due to stopping the training too soon. Nonetheless, we are confident that the quasi-character-level model would have caught the standard subword-level model.

do not benefit as easily from the quasi-character-level representations as they cannot model long-term dependencies so easily.

From these results, we conclude that the ability of a neural architecture to model long-term dependencies is critical to derive benefits from either character-based or quasi-character-based representations.

5.5 On the Catastrophic Forgetting Problem

In this section, we study whether quasi-character-level models could help to mitigate the effects of the catastrophic forgetting phenomenon, whereby neural networks forget previously learned information after learning new information.

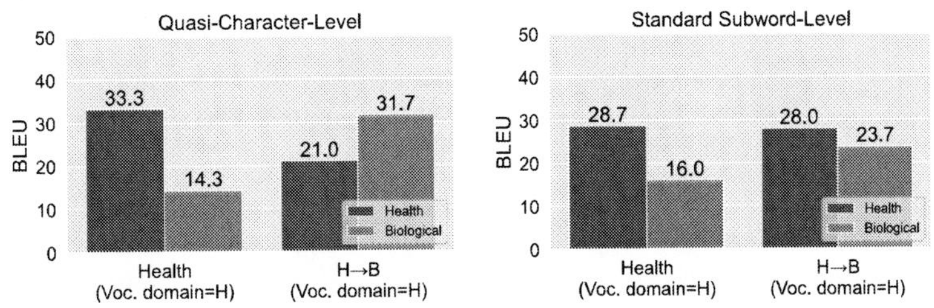

Figure 5: Vocabularies seem to have a strong impact on the catastrophic forgetting effects. While the quasi-character-level model lost 12.3pts, the large subword-level model only lost 0.7pts

To do this, we designed an experiment in which we first train a model in a domain A and it is evaluated in domains A and B to establish the baselines. Next, we fine-tuned the model trained in domain A with data from the new domain B, and then, it is evaluated it in domains A and B. In theory, the model trained in domain A should perform well in the domain A, and poorly in the unseen domain B. Similarly, after the fine-tuning on domain B, it should perform worse in A and better in domain B than the original model trained only on domain A.

In Figure 5a the quasi-character-level model trained on the health domain (SciELO) obtained a BLEU of 33.3pts on its domain (Health) and a BLEU of 14.3pts in the other domain (Biological). Then, when we fine-tuned it on the Biological domain (SciELO), the BLEU obtained on this domain increased from 14.3 to 31.7pts, while BLEU for the health domain fell from 33.3 to 21.0pts. Similarly, the standard subword-based model also suffered from the effects of the catastrophic forgetting problem. However, they were not as significant as in the quasi-character-based model, given that the BLEU score went from 28.7 to 28.0pts.

The vocabulary chosen seems to have a significant impact on the effects of catastrophic forgetting, given that the models with quasi-character vocabularies were more susceptible to the effects of catastrophic forgetting than those using standard subword-level vocabularies.

To explore this phenomenon in more detail, we repeated the previous experiment but taking into account the vocabulary domain. As a result, we found that the vocabulary domain has a more substantial impact on model performance than we thought. As shown in Figure 6, quasi-character-level models appear to be very consistent across domains, while standard subword-level models seem to be especially sensitive to their vocabulary's domain, to the point of obtaining opposite results across domains (see the right column of Figure 6).

Although the quasi-character-level models achieved better cross-domain consistencies, they also appear to suffer more severely from the effects of the catastrophic forgetting problem

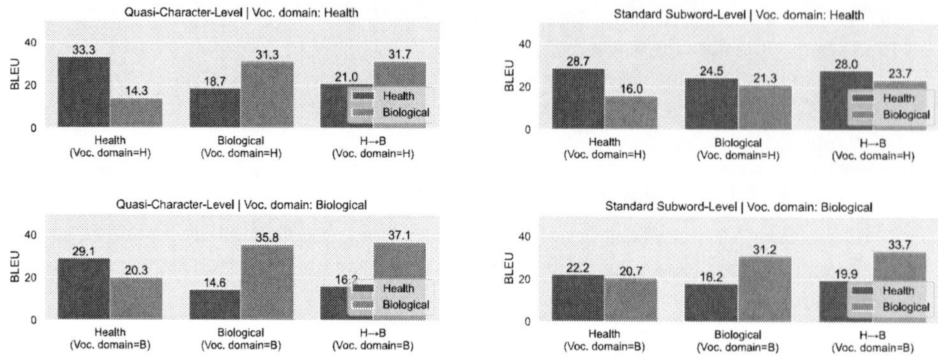

Figure 6: Quasi-character-level models (left figures) appear to be more consistent between domains than models with standard subword-level vocabularies (right figures)

than standard subword-level models. Therefore, we expect that by using regularization-based techniques such as LwF (Li and Hoiem, 2016) or EWC (Kirkpatrick et al., 2016)), these effects could be mitigated to a great extent, leading to more robust and consistent models.

6 Conclusion

In this work, we have studied the effectiveness of quasi-character-level models in terms of performance and computational efficiency relative to purely character-based models and standard subword-level models. Furthermore, we have studied the generalization of quasi-character-level vocabularies and their ability to address the problem of catastrophic forgetting.

Our studies reveal that quasi-character-level models offer practically the same generalization capabilities as character-level models, but at much lower computational costs. Furthermore, these models outperformed both the standard subword-based and character-based models in low-resource environments, regardless of language, domain, and neural architecture.

Finally, we have shown that even though quasi-character-level models do not appear to mitigate the effects of the catastrophic forgetting problem, they achieved better cross-domain consistencies, which could lead to substantial improvements if specific regularization techniques are applied to deal with the catastrophic forgetting problem.

Acknowledgment

Work supported by the Horizon 2020 - European Commission (H2020) under the SELENE project (grant agreement no 871467) and the project Deep learning for adaptive and multimodal interaction in pattern recognition (DeepPattern) (grant agreement PROMETEO/2019/121). We gratefully acknowledge the support of NVIDIA Corporation with the donation of a GPU used for part of this research.

References

Araabi, A. and Monz, C. (2020). Optimizing transformer for low-resource neural machine translation. *CoRR*, abs/2011.02266.

Bahdanau, D., Cho, K., and Bengio, Y. (2015). Neural machine translation by jointly learning to align and translate. *CoRR*, abs/1409.0473.

Banar, N., Daelemans, W., and Kestemont, M. (2020). Character-level transformer-based neural machine translation. *CoRR*, abs/2005.11239.

Carrión, S. and Casacuberta, F. (2022). Autonmt: A framework to streamline the research of seq2seq models.

Cherry, C., Foster, G. F., Bapna, A., Firat, O., and Macherey, W. (2018). Revisiting character-based neural machine translation with capacity and compression. *CoRR*, abs/1808.09943.

Cho, K., van Merriënboer, B., Bahdanau, D., and Bengio, Y. (2014). On the properties of neural machine translation: Encoder–decoder approaches. In *Proceedings of SSST-8, Eighth Workshop on Syntax, Semantics and Structure in Statistical Translation*, pages 103–111. Association for Computational Linguistics.

Chung, J., Cho, K., and Bengio, Y. (2016). A character-level decoder without explicit segmentation for neural machine translation. *CoRR*, abs/1603.06147.

Clark, J. H., Garrette, D., Turc, I., and Wieting, J. (2021). CANINE: pre-training an efficient tokenization-free encoder for language representation. *CoRR*, abs/2103.06874.

Conneau, A., Schwenk, H., Barrault, L., and LeCun, Y. (2016). Very deep convolutional networks for natural language processing. *CoRR*, abs/1606.01781.

Draelos, T. J., Miner, N. E., Lamb, C. C., Vineyard, C. M., Carlson, K. D., James, C. D., and Aimone, J. B. (2016). Neurogenesis deep learning. *CoRR*, abs/1612.03770.

Gehring, J., Auli, M., Grangier, D., Yarats, D., and Dauphin, Y. N. (2017). Convolutional sequence to sequence learning. In *Proceedings of the 34th International Conference on Machine Learning - Volume 70*, ICML'17, page 1243–1252.

Gowda, T. and May, J. (2020). Finding the optimal vocabulary size for neural machine translation. In *Findings of the ACL: EMNLP 2020*, pages 3955–3964.

Hochreiter, S. and Schmidhuber, J. (1997). Long short-term memory. *Neural computation*, 9:1735–80.

Jaszczur, S., Chowdhery, A., Mohiuddin, A., Kaiser, L., Gajewski, W., Michalewski, H., and Kanerva, J. (2021). Sparse is enough in scaling transformers. *CoRR*, abs/2111.12763.

Kemker, R. and Kanan, C. (2017). Fearnet: Brain-inspired model for incremental learning. *CoRR*, abs/1711.10563.

Kirkpatrick, J., Pascanu, R., Rabinowitz, N. C., Veness, J., Desjardins, G., Rusu, A. A., Milan, K., Quan, J., Ramalho, T., Grabska-Barwinska, A., Hassabis, D., Clopath, C., Kumaran, D., and Hadsell, R. (2016). Overcoming catastrophic forgetting in neural networks. *CoRR*, abs/1612.00796.

Kreutzer, J. and Sokolov, A. (2018). Learning to segment inputs for NMT favors character-level processing. *CoRR*, abs/1810.01480.

Kudo, T. (2018). Subword regularization: Improving neural network translation models with multiple subword candidates. In *Proceedings of the 56th Annual Meeting of the ACL (Volume 1: Long Papers)*, pages 66–75.

Kudo, T. and Richardson, J. (2018). Sentencepiece: A simple and language independent subword tokenizer and detokenizer for neural text processing. In Blanco, E. and Lu, W., editors, *Proceedings of the 2018 Conference on Empirical Methods in Natural Language Processing, EMNLP 2018: System Demonstrations, Brussels, Belgium, October 31 - November 4, 2018*, pages 66–71.

Lee, J., Cho, K., and Hofmann, T. (2016). Fully character-level neural machine translation without explicit segmentation. *CoRR*, abs/1610.03017.

Li, Z. and Hoiem, D. (2016). Learning without forgetting. *CoRR*, abs/1606.09282.

Luong, M.-T. and Manning, C. D. (2016). Achieving open vocabulary neural machine translation with hybrid word-character models. In *Proceedings of the 54th Annual Meeting of the ACL (Volume 1: Long Papers)*, pages 1054–1063.

Luong, T., Pham, H., and Manning, C. D. (2015). Effective approaches to attention-based neural machine translation. In *Proceedings of the 2015 Conference on EMNLP*, pages 1412–1421.

Mielke, S. J., Alyafeai, Z., Salesky, E., Raffel, C., Dey, M., Gallé, M., Raja, A., Si, C., Lee, W. Y., Sagot, B., and Tan, S. (2021). Between words and characters: A brief history of open-vocabulary modeling and tokenization in NLP. *CoRR*, abs/2112.10508.

Neubig, G., Watanabe, T., Mori, S., and Kawahara, T. (2013). Substring-based machine translation. *Machine Translation*, 27(2):139–166.

Post, M. (2018). A call for clarity in reporting BLEU scores. In *Proceedings of the Third Conference on Machine Translation: Research Papers*, pages 186–191.

Raunak, V., Dalmia, S., Gupta, V., and Metze, F. (2020). On long-tailed phenomena in neural machine translation. In *Findings of the Association for Computational Linguistics: EMNLP 2020*, pages 3088–3095, Online. Association for Computational Linguistics.

Rusu, A. A., Rabinowitz, N. C., Desjardins, G., Soyer, H., Kirkpatrick, J., Kavukcuoglu, K., Pascanu, R., and Hadsell, R. (2016). Progressive neural networks. *CoRR*, abs/1606.04671.

Sennrich, R., Haddow, B., and Birch, A. (2016). Neural machine translation of rare words with subword units. In *Proceedings of the 54th Annual Meeting of the ACL (Volume 1: Long Papers)*, pages 1715–1725.

Sennrich, R. and Zhang, B. (2019). Revisiting low-resource neural machine translation: A case study. In *Proceedings of the 57th Annual Meeting of the Association for Computational Linguistics*, pages 211–221, Florence, Italy. Association for Computational Linguistics.

Sutskever, I., Vinyals, O., and Le, Q. V. (2014). Sequence to sequence learning with neural networks. In Ghahramani, Z., Welling, M., Cortes, C., Lawrence, N., and Weinberger, K. Q., editors, *NIPS*, volume 27.

Vaswani, A., Shazeer, N., Parmar, N., Uszkoreit, J., Jones, L., Gomez, A. N., Kaiser, L., and Polosukhin, I. (2017). Attention is all you need. In *Proceedings of the 31st NeurIPS*, NIPS'17, page 6000–6010.

Vilar, D., Peter, J.-T., and Ney, H. (2007). Can we translate letters? In *Proceedings of the Second WMT*, StatMT '07, page 33–39.

Wu, Y., Schuster, M., Chen, Z., Le, Q. V., Norouzi, M., Macherey, W., Krikun, M., Cao, Y., Gao, Q., Macherey, K., Klingner, J., Shah, A., Johnson, M., Liu, X., Kaiser, L., Gouws, S., Kato, Y., Kudo, T., Kazawa, H., Stevens, K., Kurian, G., Patil, N., Wang, W., Young, C., Smith, J., Riesa, J., Rudnick, A., Vinyals, O., Corrado, G., Hughes, M., and Dean, J. (2016). Google's neural machine translation system: Bridging the gap between human and machine translation. *CoRR*, abs/1609.08144.

Xu, J., Zhou, H., Gan, C., Zheng, Z., and Li, L. (2020). VOLT: improving vocabularization via optimal transport for machine translation. *CoRR*, abs/2012.15671.

Xue, L., Barua, A., Constant, N., Al-Rfou, R., Narang, S., Kale, M., Roberts, A., and Raffel, C. (2021). Byt5: Towards a token-free future with pre-trained byte-to-byte models. *CoRR*, abs/2105.13626.

Zhang, T., Kishore, V., Wu, F., Weinberger, K. Q., and Artzi, Y. (2019). Bertscore: Evaluating text generation with BERT. *CoRR*, abs/1904.09675.

Improving Translation of Out Of Vocabulary Words using Bilingual Lexicon Induction in Low-Resource Machine Translation

Jonas Waldendorf jonas.waldendorf@ed.ac.uk
Alexandra Birch a.birch@ed.ac.uk
Barry Haddow bhaddow@inf.ed.ac.uk
Antonio Valerio Miceli Barone amiceli@ed.ac.uk
School of Informatics, University of Edinburgh

Abstract

Dictionary-based data augmentation techniques have been used in the field of domain adaptation to learn words that do not appear in the parallel training data of a machine translation model. These techniques strive to learn correct translations of these words by generating a synthetic corpus from in-domain monolingual data using a dictionary obtained from bilingual lexicon induction. This paper applies these techniques to low resource machine translation, where content distribution is often shifted between the parallel data and any monolingual data. English-Pashto machine translation systems are trained using a novel approach that introduces monolingual data to existing joint learning techniques for learning bilingual word embeddings, combined with word-for-word back-translation to improve the translation of words that do not or rarely appear in the parallel training data. Improvements are made in terms of BLEU, chrF and word translation accuracy for an En→Ps model, compared to a baseline and when combined with back-translation.

1 Introduction

One difficulty of low-resource neural-machine translation (NMT) is the ability of models to correctly predict words that are out of vocabulary (OOV). OOV words are of particular interest when working with low-resource language pairs as such pairs generally exhibit a more significant shift in the distribution of content between the training and test data compared to high-resource language pairs. The available training data for low-resource languages often contains a significant amount of content from specific domains such as IT and religious texts (Tiedemann, 2012) which is not the case in common down-stream tasks for NMT systems such as translating news articles. Hence, the task of improving the prediction of OOV words in low-resource NMT has significant benefits when deploying such models in realistic inference scenarios. Additionally, the overall low amount of parallel data inherent in the task means that the vocabulary covered by the training data is naturally smaller than the vocabulary covered in a more well-resourced NMT scenario. This work aims to improve the prediction of target side OOV words for an English-Pashto (En-Ps) NMT system. To improve the translation of OOV words we incorporate monolingual target-side data when training NMT models by generating synthetic source-side sentences.

Incorporating monolingual target-side data using back-translation (BT) (Sennrich et al., 2016) has been shown to improve the overall performance of low-resource NMT systems in terms of automatic sentence-level evaluation metrics such as BLEU or chrF. However, an important benefit of incorporating monolingual data is the increase in the amount of vocabulary that is observed during training, the effects of which can only be seen when evaluating NMT predictions at the level of single OOV words. Work in the field of domain adaptation has shown that word-for-word (WFW) back-translation using bilingual dictionaries extracted from bilingual word embeddings (BWE) is a suitable alternative to BT when specifically targeting improved translation of OOV words (Hu et al., 2019). Whilst the source-side sentences produced by WFW-BT have lower adequacy and fluency, the key benefit compared to BT is that they more frequently result in direct supervision of OOV words. That is to say, WFW-BT more frequently results in source-side sentences that contain a correct translation of target side OOV words and, by extension, improve the ability of the NMT model to predict those words correctly. Inspired Hu et al. (2019) we adopt the WFW-BT methodology to improve the prediction accuracy of OOV target side words for the En-Ps NMT model.

Compared to the dictionary-based techniques in domain adaptation (Hu et al., 2019; Huck et al., 2019), which aim to predict target-side words specific to the domain correctly, our goal is to correctly predict items from the more varied monolingual vocabulary which are not present in the restricted parallel vocabulary. The consequence of this is that the task is not targeted at a specific set of vocabulary, and by extension, examples of OOV words are less frequent. Additionally, OOV words are less likely to appear in similar contexts on both sides of the monolingual data because we rely on the assumption that the distribution of content is the same across languages. This assumption only holds weakly for English and Pashto, which are both linguistically and culturally distinct (Shen et al., 2021). Moreover, the morphological complexity of Pashto means that many words have considerably more surface forms than their English counterparts, all of which should all translate to the same English word.

As a result of the above observations obtaining a bilingual embedding space (BWE) that correctly maps not only frequent words but specifically OOV words is challenging. We propose a new approach to obtaining BWEs based on the findings of Søgaard et al. (2018); Ormazabal et al. (2019) that joint training (Luong et al., 2015) leads to more isomorphic BWE spaces for linguistically distinct languages. However, joint training requires parallel data to train and hence only maps the embedding spaces of words in the parallel data. Our approach trains on the parallel data using joint training to anchor an embedding space whilst simultaneously training on monolingual data. In addition, we incorporate sub-word information into the joint trai - 'v bm,ning approach as we hypothesise that sub-word information will help alleviate the data sparsity due to Pashto's morphological complexity. The main contributions of this work are as follows:

- Adapting the WFW-BT methodology to the genuine low-resource scenario of En-Ps NMT to improve the prediction of OOV target side words. This work contributes to the wider task of expanding the often more limited vocabularies of low-resource NMT systems.
- Proposing an extension to the joint training methodology of Luong et al. (2015) that simultaneously trains on monolingual data, to obtain a stronger BWE space.

2 Related Work

Hu et al. (2019); Huck et al. (2019); Peng et al. (2020) all use dictionary-based methods for data augmentation in a domain adaptation setting focusing on OOV words. Hu et al. (2019); Huck et al. (2019) both use bilingual lexicon induction (BLI), but do so in a high resource setting with artificial monolingual data, which is generated by selecting alternating sentences from a parallel corpus as monolingual data. Peng et al. (2020) make use of a high quality pre-existing dictionary to learn new translations. Our work also uses BLI and WFW-BT; however, we apply these methods to a genuine low-resource NMT problem. Rather than learning the translations of a specialised subset of vocabulary from monolingual data that contains these words on both sides, we are trying to train NMT models to correctly predict words outside the more specialised vocabularies often found in low-resource parallel data sets.

WFW translations also play an important role in unsupervised NMT (UNMT), where they are used to bootstrap NMT models (Artetxe et al., 2019; Lample et al., 2018) before applying iterative BT. However, UNMT requires careful model choices, works poorly when languages have low amounts of monolingual data (Guzmán et al., 2019) and neglects the fact that there is often a small amount of parallel data available. Additionally, it does not focus on the correct prediction of OOV words but rather on the sentence-level translation quality. This work directly uses the available parallel data to train NMT models and uses the monolingual data to improve the prediction of OOV words.

Mapping-based approaches have been the dominant methodology for BLI, reporting strong results whilst only requiring weak supervision or no supervision by using discriminator networks or identical tokens (Conneau et al., 2017; Artetxe et al., 2018). These methods are based on the assumption of isomorphism between word embedding spaces (Søgaard et al., 2018) and require sufficient monolingual data to learn semantically meaningful word embeddings (Artetxe et al., 2020). Luong et al. (2015) propose joint training of BWE spaces using automatically extracted word alignments as a parallel signal and Ormazabal et al. (2019) observe that joint training leads to increased isomorphism. Eder et al. (2020) introduce an anchor-based method to improve BLI from low-resource language pairs. This work builds on Luong et al. (2015) by incorporating monolingual data and sub-word information to learn stronger BWE spaces. Unlike other BLI tasks, which are often only evaluated on words that appear relatively frequently, we are specifically interested in the BLI performance on less frequent words.

Liu et al. (2020) proposed mBart, a masked language model (MLM) sequence-to-sequence pre-training that aligns the token level representations across many languages. Along with BT (Sennrich et al., 2016) MLM pre-training is the most common way of incorporating monolingual data. We incorporate a mBart-like[1] methodology when training our NMT models to ensure a strong baseline. Vulić et al. (2020) find that for low-resource languages static word embeddings perform better than MLM on BLI tasks which they attribute to a better lexical alignment. Based on this Chronopoulou et al. (2021) combine MLM with BWEs to initialise UNMT models. Whilst the aim of our work is different, these results demonstrate that BWEs are still a suitable tool for learning alignments between lexical items and, by extension, improving the prediction of OOV words. Finally, mRASP (Lin et al., 2020) is an alternative to MLM whereby words and phrases are brought into a similar representation space by substituting aligned words in parallel data sets using dictionaries. mRASP is more closely linked to our work than mBart as it focuses on introducing aligned words during pre-training.

3 Methodology

Our approach is split into two distinct stages. The first is obtaining a pseudo-parallel corpus, and the second is training NMT models using the corpus. Below we outline the approaches used to obtain a BWE space by combining joint training with monolingual data, extracting a dictionary from the BWEs and how the dictionary is used to translate target-side monolingual data. Together these three steps represent the WFW-BT methodology which is used to obtain the pseudo-parallel corpus. When learning the bilingual embedding spaces, sub-word information is incorporated either by using FastText (Bojanowski et al., 2017) for mapping-based approaches or by representing words as a combination of n-grams in the same manner as FastText for Bivec approaches.

[1] `https://github.com/Avmb/marian-mBART`

3.1 Mapping

In a mapping-based approach, two sets of monolingual embeddings are trained independently before the embeddings are mapped into the same vector space. Conneau et al. (2017) provide both unsupervised and supervised methods for mapping. However, due to the linguistic dissimilarities between English and Pashto, the mapping baseline focuses on the supervised approach (unsupervised training obtained no correct translations). The supervised approach uses a small seed dictionary to induce the mapping, which is extracted from automatic alignments. The embedding spaces are mapped by iteratively solving the Procrustes problem for the seed dictionary before extracting a new dictionary of nearest neighbours.

3.2 Bivec

The joint training methods are all inspired by Bivec, the approach first introduced by Luong et al. (2015). In comparison to the mapping-based approach, Bivec incorporates a bilingual signal into the loss. For languages l_1 and l_2 this can be viewed as training four skip-gram models simultaneously in the following directions $l_1 \rightarrow l_1$, $l_2 \rightarrow l_2$, $l_1 \rightarrow l_2$ and $l_2 \rightarrow l_1$. Models that train on both languages take word alignments as input, so Bivec can only train on parallel data. If a given word w_1 in l_1 is aligned with another word w_2 in l_2 then w_1 is used to predict the context of w_2 and vice versa.

$$loss = \alpha * (Mono_1 + Mono_2) + \beta * Bi_1 \tag{1}$$

During training updates occur for parallel sentence pairs according to Equation 1, where $Mono$ is the monolingual loss for a sentence, Bi is the bilingual loss for a sentence pair, where α and β are hyperparameters. Luong et al. (2015) utilise Word2Vec (Mikolov et al., 2013) in order to jointly train Skipgram models for l_1 and l_2.

3.3 Bivec with Monolingual Data

We hypothesise that we can anchor the embedding space using joint learning over the parallel data while simultaneously training on the monolingual data so that words that only appear in the monolingual data are also contained in the embedding space. We test the following methods for using monolingual data in bivec.

Bivec Para: For the baseline approach, we initialise the embedding tables with both the parallel and monolingual vocabularies whilst only training on the parallel data. As words are represented as a combination of n-grams to incorporate sub-word information, two similar words (for example perfect/imperfect marking of a verb with a suffix in Pashto) should share many of the same n-grams. Hence, there is a degree of transfer learning if one of the forms is present in the parallel corpus. The primary purpose of this baseline is to establish whether subsequent improvements are due to this inherent transfer learning or from incorporating the monolingual data more directly.

Bivec MonoPost: In this approach we train a Bivec Para model initially to anchor the embedding space. Subsequently, we train on just the monolingual data with no parallel signal to try and learn translations of the monolingual data.

Bivec MonoPre: This approach is the inverse of Bivec MonoPost, first training on just the monolingual data and then training with the Bivec approach on the parallel data. The motivation is to first learn good embedding spaces for each language independently before using Bivec to move the embeddings into the same vector space.

Bivec Combined: Combined training incorporates the monolingual data into the parallel training. In the baseline approach, each iteration updates the model in all four directions. The combined approach adds an additional update for the $l_1 \rightarrow l_1$, $l_2 \rightarrow l_2$ directions using only sentences from the monolingual data.

$$loss = \alpha * (Mono_1 + Mono_2) + \beta * Bi_1 + \gamma * JMono_1 + \delta * JMono_2 \quad (2)$$

This is formalised in Equation 2, where $JMono$ is the loss for the monolingual sentences, $Mono$ is the monolingual loss for the parallel sentences and γ and δ are hyper-parameters. The hyperparameters allow the loss to be adjusted to account for varying amounts of data in the two monolingual corpora as well as the parallel corpus.

3.4 BLI and Word-for-Word Translation

To generate a noisy pseudo-parallel corpus from the monolingual data the approach of Hu et al. (2019) is adopted. First, a bilingual lexicon is extracted from BWEs, and then target-side monolingual sentences are translated word-for-word using the dictionary. The lexicon is extracted using the CSLS (Cross Domain Similarity Scaling) distance metric first introduced by Conneau et al. (2017) to find nearest neighbours. Each word w_1 in l_1 and its nearest neighbour in l_2, w_2 are added to the lexicon if w_1 also appears in the top n nearest neighbours of the w_2 word. Lexicons are extracted separately in the $l_1 \rightarrow l_2$ and the $l_2 \rightarrow l_1$ directions. We translate monolingual target-side data word-for-word using the extracted lexicons. If a word does not appear in the lexicon the target-side token is copied into the translation. We refer to such pseudo-parallel copora as WFW-BT.

4 Experimental Design

The experimental setup is chosen to investigate a genuine low-resource language paired with English.

4.1 Training Data

The data used is adopted from Birch et al. (2021)'s data and as such the initial parallel data is the WMT 2020 data excluding Paracrawl (Barrault et al., 2020). Additional parallel data is provided by the En-Ps corpus from the ByteDance team (Koehn et al., 2020; Xu et al., 2020). The monolingual Pashto data was taken from the Pashto NewsCrawl release[2] and the English monolingual data was taken from the 2019 English NewsCrawl release[3], however only the first 5 million sentences of the English data are used as Birch et al. (2021) report no improvements when using more. The monolingual Pashto data also includes additional crawled sentences from (Birch et al., 2021).

Dataset	No. Sentences
WMT - Parallel	123,198
ByteDance - Parallel	440,000
NewsCrawl - Ps	760,379
NewsCrawl - En*	5,000,000
Crawled - Ps	589,864

Table 1: Number of sentences in corpora used to train BWE's and NMT systems. *Only the first 5,000,000 sentences were used from English NewsCrawl release.

All BWEs are trained with all the available data shown in Table 1. The initial NMT models were trained with both the WMT parallel data and the ByteDance corpus. Only mBart pretraining utilises the full English NewsCrawl corpus; any back-translations, either WFW or using NMT systems, only use the first 5 million monolingual English sentences. For both English and Pashto, the corpora are preprocessed using cleaning and punctuation normalisation scripts from the Moses[4] toolkit (Koehn et al., 2007). For the BLI task, English corpora are lower-cased, and

[2]http://data.statmt.org/news-crawl/ps/

[3]http://data.statmt.org/news-crawl/en/news.2019.en.shuffled.deduped.gz

[4]https://github.com/marian-nmt/moses-scripts

all punctuation is removed for both languages. Data for NMT is tokenised using scripts from Moses before sub-word tokenisation is performed using SentencePiece[5] (Kudo and Richardson, 2018), with a vocabulary size of 16,000. Note that all word-level evaluation metrics first perform the BLI preprocessing steps on the NMT output.

4.2 Test Data

The WMT test set as well as the BBC test set (the combined development and test sets from Birch et al. (2021)) are held out for evaluating both the BLI task and the NMT models, whilst the WMT dev set was used for early stopping when training the NMT models. The BBC test set comprises 2350 sentences from BBC news articles.

4.3 OOV and Rare Words

OOV words are defined as words that do not occur in the parallel data but are present in the BBC test set. We limit these words further by ensuring they are present in the monolingual data. Specifically, as all embeddings are learnt for words that appear ≥ 5 times in a given corpus, OOV words are taken to be words that are not in the parallel data and occur ≥ 5 times in the monolingual data. To expand the analysis we also report results on rare words. Rare words are defined as those words that are not common in the parallel data and are grouped by the frequency with which they appear in the parallel data. Table 2 shows the number of OOV and rare words appearing in the BBC test set for English and Pashto and defines the frequency-based bins for rare words. No OOV words are explicitly mined from the WMT test set.

Word Frequency	En	Ps
0 (OOV)	521	727
1-5	642	1021
6-10	389	449
11-15	295	289
16-20	199	275
21-25	205	186

Table 2: Number of OOV and rare words in the BBC test set at for each word frequency bin. The frequencies refer to the number of times a word appears in the parallel data.

4.4 Bilingual Word Embeddings

As Bivec (Luong et al., 2015) is an extension of Word2Vec, or in the sub-word unit case FastText, the standard hyperparameters are kept constant and are in line with previous work (Søgaard et al., 2018; Ormazabal et al., 2019). Embeddings are 300 dimensional and trained using skip-gram with negative sampling. The minimum word count is set to 5 occurrences across both parallel and monolingual corpora. Models are trained with a learning rate of 0.025, a window size of 10, 10 negative samples and a sampling threshold of 10^{-4}.

Mapping based approaches are trained using the MUSE[6] library (Conneau et al., 2017; Lample et al., 2017). FastAlign[7] (Dyer et al., 2013) alignments are obtained using default settings over 10 iterations on the parallel training data. The seed dictionary for MUSE is extracted using these alignments; the 5000 most frequent Pashto words and the aligned English words are used as a seed dictionary. Similarly, the Pashto words in the frequency range 5000-6500 are used as a validation dictionary when training MUSE.

All FastText embeddings for MUSE are trained for 5 epochs, whereas the combined Bivec model is trained for 20 epochs. Note that the combined Bivec model loops over the parallel datasets, whereas for the FastText embeddings the loop is over all sentences. For the combined Bivec model the learning rate hyperparameters in Equation 2 are α is 0.2, β is 2, γ is 0.5, and

[5] `https://github.com/google/sentencepiece`
[6] `https://github.com/facebookresearch/MUSE`
[7] `https://github.com/clab/fast_align`

δ is 0.2, where language one is English. These values were selected empirically based on the collected evaluation dictionary introduced below. However, this is not an exhaustive sweep of parameters. When extracting the bilingual lexicon using the CSLS metric, the nearest neighbour parameter is set to 5 for En→Ps and 10 for Ps→En. The value of n was selected empirically to provide similar coverage of the vocabulary in both directions.

4.5 Neural Machine translation

Using the Marian Toolkit (Junczys-Dowmunt et al., 2018), the NMT models were trained using the transformer-base alias. Early stopping was performed after ten epochs on the WMT validation set using the mean cross-entropy loss. Models are first trained using an mBART (Liu et al., 2020) like objective on the entire data, which pre-trains the model using the same denoising objective as mBart but only on English and Pashto data. We trained systems using only the parallel data and using pseudo-parallel corpora from BT as a comparison to the WFW-BT based methods. All pseudo-parallel corpora up-sample the parallel data so that there is an approximately equal split of genuine and pseudo-parallel data. Below is a summary of the systems trained:
Baseline: The baseline system is trained only on the parallel WMT and ByteDance data.
WFW-Bivec: Uses a pseudo-parallel corpus generated from WFW-BT using a dictionary obtained with the Bivec Combined methodology and the parallel data.
WFW-MUSE: Uses a pseudo-parallel corpus generated from WFW-BT translation using a dictionary obtained with the MUSE methodology and the parallel data.
BT: Uses a pseudo-parallel corpus generated with back-translation from the Baseline model in the opposite translation direction.
BT-from-WFW: Uses a pseudo-parallel corpus generated with back-translations from the WFW-Bivec model in the opposite translation direction.

4.6 Evaluation Metrics

As there are no freely available, machine readable dictionaries for Ps-En, a small dictionary of 1000 words was collected, which is referred to as the Parallel Dictionary. This dictionary is informed by the FastAlign alignments from the parallel training data that are outside the 6,500 most common Pashto words and are verified using online resources. A second smaller dictionary of 200 words is extracted from the BBC test set by manually aligning Pashto OOV words to their English translations using online translation tools. This dictionary is referred to as the BBC Dictionary. Both lexicons are used to evaluate the different methods of obtaining BWEs using a BLI task translating from Pashto to English.

Sentence-Level Accuracy: Complementing BLI metrics, the BBC test set is directly used to assess the performance of the extracted dictionaries for OOV and rare words. For a given target-side word, all sentences in which it appears are collected from the BBC test set. Then a positive example is defined if at least one of the corresponding source-side sentences contains the correct translation of the target-side word according to the dictionary. Accuracy is reported in both translation directions, based on whether or not a translation was found. In addition, as it is an automatic metric, it is also used to evaluate performance for rare words at each frequency.

Evaluating NMT: The NMT systems are evaluated using BLEU and chrF calculated using SacreBLEU (Post, 2018). In addition, to evaluate the performance on OOV and rare words at the word level we report the micro-averaged F1 score. Each reference translation that contains an OOV or rare word is compared to a given prediction to see if it contains the same token to calculate the F1 score.

5 Results

Table 3 gives the results for the Ps→En BLI task using the dictionaries described in Section 4.6. As expected, the introduction of joint training in the Bivec-based models improves the precision on the Parallel Dictionary, which is comprised of words predominantly present in the parallel data, compared to the precision of the MUSE baseline. Although the Bivec Combined methodology has the best precision, it only slightly improves upon the MUSE baseline on the BBC dictionary. In combination with the overall low results on the BBC dictionary, this highlights the task's difficulty. The low performance is attributed to the comparatively low amount of Pashto data and low frequency of OOV words in the monolingual data. The median number of counts for Pashto OOV words in the monolingual data is 19, which means that the distribution of the contexts in the sample is unlikely to represent the true distributions of contexts in the entire population. In addition, BLI is based on the underlying assumption that the used corpora are at least comparable; that is to say, their distributions are at least similar. This likely holds to some extent for the parallel data, but there are likely significant differences between the monolingual corpora.

Name	Precision Parallel Dictionary			Precision BBC Dictionary		
	@1	@5	@10	@1	@5	@10
Bivec MonoPost	17.56	33.56	40.44	6.63	21.43	27.04
MUSE	24.38	38.42	43.16	9.62	24.06	30.48
Bivec Para	40.62	53.53	60.59	11.22	21.94	24.49
Bivec MonoPre	40.62	55.42	60.76	8.60	15.05	18.82
Bivec Combined	**44.39**	**57.54**	**64.21**	**12.83**	**26.73**	**32.62**

Table 3: Table of the precision at 1, 5 and 10 (top nearest neighbours) for the BLI task in the Ps→En direction for the Parallel and BBC dictionaries.

Contrasting the Bivec Combined methodology to the Bivec Para baseline reveals that just training on parallel data with joint training and solely relying on sub-word information to translate unseen words achieves similar performance to incorporating monolingual data directly especially on the precision @1 metric for the BBC dictionary. This result demonstrates that the sub-word information is critical for learning OOV translations. However, for the Parallel Dictionary, Bivec Combined achieves higher precision values than Bivec Para, suggesting that while the translation of OOV words remains challenging, the introduction of the monolingual data does improve the overall quality of the BWE space.

Word Frequencies	Combined		MUSE	
	Ps	En	Ps	En
0	5.70	2.26	8.36	4.52
1-5	11.05	7.63	10.75	7.33
6-10	14.19	10.75	13.29	10.48
11-15	18.37	10.81	17.01	9.27
16-20	25.19	21.50	19.63	17.29
21-25	23.64	15.52	20.61	9.77

Table 4: Sentence-Level Accuracy metric at each frequency for MUSE and Bivec Combined. The language tag specifies the target language from which sentences are collected.

Compared to the BLI results discussed above, the sentence-level accuracy results given in Table 4 paint a slightly different picture. Although for frequencies of 5 and above Bivec Combined achieves higher accuracy, MUSE obtains a higher accuracy for OOV words. The sentence accuracy metric is noisier than BLI; for example, MUSE translates one of the Pashto OOVs to "him" instead of "regret". As the source-side sentence contains both "him" and "regret" this is still counted as a positive result. However, a qualitative evaluation of the correctly translated Pashto OOV words supports the finding that MUSE correctly translates a higher proportion of the OOV words. Finally, the translation accuracies for English OOV words are lower than those for Pashto at all frequencies, which we attribute to Pashto's higher morphological complexity.

Table 5 gives the BLEU and chrF scores for the En-Ps models for the WMT and BBC test set. Compared to the baseline, WFW-Bivec shows a slight improvement on the BBC test set. Significantly it outperforms WFW-MUSE on both test sets, and in fact, WFW-MUSE appears to decrease performance on the WMT test set compared to both the Baseline and WFW-Bivec. As expected back-translation outperforms both WFW based methods, this seems reasonable as any synthetic source-side sentences generated by back-translation are likely to be more fluent, especially as Pashto and English exhibit different sentence structures. However, the fact that the BT-from-WFW model achieves the highest BLEU and chrF scores on both test sets, albeit slightly, suggests that there is still something to be gained from training with WFW-BT data on the first run, especially considering that all the models have already seen the entire monolingual data during mBart pre-training.

Experiment	WMT Test		BBC Test	
	BLEU	chrF	BLEU	chrF
Baseline	8.3	31.2	9.0	34.2
WFW-Bivec	8.4	31.2	9.4	35.0
WFW-MUSE	8.2	30.7	9.2	34.6
BT	9.1	31.9	12.3	37.7
BT-from-WFW	**9.4**	**32.4**	**12.5**	**38.5**

Table 5: BLEU and chrF for the NMT models described in Section 4.6 in the En-Ps direction.

On the other hand, Table 6 shows the metrics for the Ps-En translation direction. In comparison to Table 5 the metrics are significantly higher across the board. This is likely an upshot of the mBart pre-training objective as the Ps-En direction uses the entire English paracrawl corpus, resulting in a stronger decoder performance. WFW-Bivec again outperforms both the Baseline and WFW-MUSE although the latter is closer in all metrics and both have a chrF of 42.7 on the BBC test set. Back-translation also leads to a significant increase in performance. However, BT-from-WFW shows small but consistent improvements for all metrics.

Experiment	WMT Test		BBC Test	
	BLEU	chrF	BLEU	chrF
Baseline	12.1	37.4	14.8	42.1
WFW-Bivec	12.2	37.7	15.0	42.7
WFW-MUSE	12.0	37.5	14.6	42.7
BT	13.6	39.7	18.8	47.9
BT-from-WFW	**13.8**	**39.9**	**19.0**	**48.1**

Table 6: BLEU and chrF for the NMT models described in Section 4.6 in the Ps-En direction.

The micro-averaged F1 scores for OOV words given in Figure 1 are on the whole low. Low recalls drive the low F1 scores at all frequencies. For all models, WFW-Bivec results in a higher F1 than the MUSE-based method in the En→Ps direction, supporting the fact that Bivec Combined results in better WFW translations. It is also evident that the F1 score is higher at all frequencies for the BT-from-WFW model that uses back-translations from the corresponding WFW-Bivec model compared to just using back-translations from the Baseline model for the En-Ps NMT models.

However, in the Ps-En direction, the situation is less clear, where BT outperforms BT-from-WFW not only at the frequencies of 15 and 25 but also for OOV words. The difference at the other frequencies, while favouring BT-from-WFW, is slight, and hence it seems likely that the improved BT-from-WFW metrics presented in Table 6 are not due to the models learning better translations of OOV or rare words.

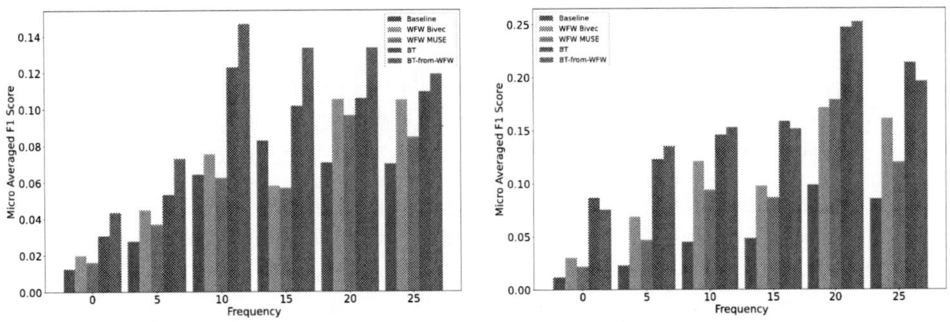

Figure 1: Micro averaged F1 scores for OOV and rare words in BBC est set at frequencies. **Left:** En-Ps **Right:** Ps-En.

Across the board, the increase in the F1 score of the WFW based corpora is significantly smaller than that of adding back-translations. This is even the case for OOV words, meaning that back-translation learns the correct translation of more OOV words. Further confirmation of this can be seen when looking at the recall of OOVs for the WFW-Bivec models, which are 0.021 for En→Ps and 0.031 for Ps→En. Such low recalls illustrate that models are learning very few OOV words from the WFW pseudo-parallel corpus.

6 Conclusion

The BWE evaluation results show that MUSE correctly translates more OOV words than the proposed Combined Bivec approach, where more weight is given to sentence-level accuracy results as they cover a higher proportion of OOV words. However, when viewed in the context of NMT, it appears that the WFW back-translations using Bivec lead to more OOV and rare words being correctly predicted. For OOV words we hypothesise that this is due to the WFW-BT model being able to leverage the higher overall quality of the Bivec Combined back-translations to predict more OOV words correctly. Specifically, this means that Bivec Combined results in a higher proportion of context words of the OOV word being translated correctly.

Regarding NMT, the results demonstrate that incorporating word-level translations benefits the model even when using back-translation when the low-resource language is on the target side. However, the results are less conclusive when the high-resource language is the target language. The low recall for all OOV words for the NMT task suggests that even when the dictionary contains accurate translations, it is difficult for these to transfer into correct model predictions. As a result, it seems that incorporating word-level translations from the monolingual data can benefit the model. It may be that for languages that exhibit a different sentence structure, WFW back-translation is not the best methodology for incorporating the OOVs and rare words. Instead, an approach of inserting them into back-translations or existing parallel data may be more appropriate to ensure a higher degree of fluency in the synthetic sentences.

Acknowledgement

This project received funding from the European Union's Horizon 2020 research and innovation programme under grant agreement 825299 (GoURMET), the European Research Council (ERC StG BroadSem 678254; ERC CoG TransModal 681760) and funding by the UK Engineering and Physical Sciences Research Council (EPSRC) fellowship grant EP/S001271/1 (MTStretch). Jonas Waldendorf is supported by the UKRI Centre for Doctoral Training in Natural Language Processing, funded by the UKRI (grant EP/S022481/1) and the University of Edinburgh.

References

Artetxe, M., Labaka, G., and Agirre, E. (2018). A robust self-learning method for fully unsupervised cross-lingual mappings of word embeddings. In *Proceedings of the 56th Annual Meeting of the Association for Computational Linguistics (Volume 1: Long Papers)*, pages 789–798, Melbourne, Australia. Association for Computational Linguistics.

Artetxe, M., Labaka, G., and Agirre, E. (2019). An effective approach to unsupervised machine translation. In *Proceedings of the 57th Annual Meeting of the Association for Computational Linguistics*, pages 194–203, Florence, Italy. Association for Computational Linguistics.

Artetxe, M., Ruder, S., Yogatama, D., Labaka, G., and Agirre, E. (2020). A call for more rigor in unsupervised cross-lingual learning. In *Proceedings of the 58th Annual Meeting of the Association for Computational Linguistics*, pages 7375–7388, Online. Association for Computational Linguistics.

Barrault, L., Biesialska, M., Bojar, O., Costa-jussà, M. R., Federmann, C., Graham, Y., Grundkiewicz, R., Haddow, B., Huck, M., Joanis, E., Kocmi, T., Koehn, P., Lo, C.-k., Ljubešić, N., Monz, C., Morishita, M., Nagata, M., Nakazawa, T., Pal, S., Post, M., and Zampieri, M. (2020). Findings of the 2020 conference on machine translation (WMT20). In *Proceedings of the Fifth Conference on Machine Translation*, pages 1–55, Online. Association for Computational Linguistics.

Birch, A., Haddow, B., Valerio Miceli Barone, A., Helcl, J., Waldendorf, J., Sánchez Martínez, F., Forcada, M., Sánchez Cartagena, V., Pérez-Ortiz, J. A., Esplà-Gomis, M., Aziz, W., Murady, L., Sariisik, S., van der Kreeft, P., and Macquarrie, K. (2021). Surprise language challenge: Developing a neural machine translation system between Pashto and English in two months. In *Proceedings of the 18th Biennial Machine Translation Summit (Volume 1: Research Track)*, pages 92–102, Virtual. Association for Machine Translation in the Americas.

Bojanowski, P., Grave, E., Joulin, A., and Mikolov, T. (2017). Enriching word vectors with subword information. *Transactions of the Association for Computational Linguistics*, 5:135–146.

Chronopoulou, A., Stojanovski, D., and Fraser, A. (2021). Improving the lexical ability of pretrained language models for unsupervised neural machine translation. In *Proceedings of the 2021 Conference of the North American Chapter of the Association for Computational Linguistics: Human Language Technologies*, pages 173–180, Online. Association for Computational Linguistics.

Conneau, A., Lample, G., Ranzato, M., Denoyer, L., and Jégou, H. (2017). Word translation without parallel data. *arXiv preprint arXiv:1710.04087*.

Dyer, C., Chahuneau, V., and Smith, N. A. (2013). A simple, fast, and effective reparameterization of IBM model 2. In *Proceedings of the 2013 Conference of the North American Chapter of the Association for Computational Linguistics: Human Language Technologies*, pages 644–648, Atlanta, Georgia. Association for Computational Linguistics.

Eder, T., Hangya, V., and Fraser, A. (2020). Anchor-based Bilingual Word Embeddings for Low-Resource Languages. *arXiv:2010.12627 [cs]*. arXiv: 2010.12627.

Guzmán, F., Chen, P.-J., Ott, M., Pino, J., Lample, G., Koehn, P., Chaudhary, V., and Ranzato, M. (2019). The FLORES evaluation datasets for low-resource machine translation: Nepali–English and Sinhala–English. In *Proceedings of the 2019 Conference on Empirical Methods in Natural Language Processing and the 9th International Joint Conference on Natural Language Processing (EMNLP-IJCNLP)*, pages 6098–6111, Hong Kong, China. Association for Computational Linguistics.

Hu, J., Xia, M., Neubig, G., and Carbonell, J. (2019). Domain Adaptation of Neural Machine Translation by Lexicon Induction. In *Proceedings of the 57th Annual Meeting of the Association for Computational Linguistics*, pages 2989–3001, Florence, Italy. Association for Computational Linguistics.

Huck, M., Hangya, V., and Fraser, A. (2019). Better OOV Translation with Bilingual Terminology Mining. In *Proceedings of the 57th Annual Meeting of the Association for Computational Linguistics*, pages 5809–5815, Florence, Italy. Association for Computational Linguistics.

Junczys-Dowmunt, M., Heafield, K., Hoang, H., Grundkiewicz, R., and Aue, A. (2018). Marian: Cost-effective high-quality neural machine translation in C++. In *Proceedings of the 2nd Workshop on Neural Machine Translation and Generation*, pages 129–135.

Koehn, P., Chaudhary, V., El-Kishky, A., Goyal, N., Chen, P.-J., and Guzmán, F. (2020). Findings of the WMT 2020 Shared Task on Parallel Corpus Filtering and Alignment. In *Proceedings of the Fifth Conference on Machine Translation*, pages 726–742, Online. Association for Computational Linguistics.

Koehn, P., Hoang, H., Birch, A., Callison-Burch, C., Federico, M., Bertoldi, N., Cowan, B., Shen, W., Moran, C., Zens, R., Dyer, C., Bojar, O., Constantin, A., and Herbst, E. (2007). Moses: Open source toolkit for statistical machine translation. In *Proceedings of the 45th Annual Meeting of the Association for Computational Linguistics Companion Volume Proceedings of the Demo and Poster Sessions*, pages 177–180, Prague, Czech Republic. Association for Computational Linguistics.

Kudo, T. and Richardson, J. (2018). SentencePiece: A simple and language independent subword tokenizer and detokenizer for neural text processing. In *Proceedings of the 2018 Conference on Empirical Methods in Natural Language Processing: System Demonstrations*, pages 66–71, Brussels, Belgium. Association for Computational Linguistics.

Lample, G., Conneau, A., Denoyer, L., and Ranzato, M. (2017). Unsupervised machine translation using monolingual corpora only. *arXiv preprint arXiv:1711.00043*.

Lample, G., Ott, M., Conneau, A., Denoyer, L., and Ranzato, M. (2018). Phrase-based & neural unsupervised machine translation. In *Proceedings of the 2018 Conference on Empirical Methods in Natural Language Processing*, pages 5039–5049, Brussels, Belgium. Association for Computational Linguistics.

Lin, Z., Pan, X., Wang, M., Qiu, X., Feng, J., Zhou, H., and Li, L. (2020). Pre-training multilingual neural machine translation by leveraging alignment information. In *Proceedings of the 2020 Conference on Empirical Methods in Natural Language Processing (EMNLP)*, pages 2649–2663, Online. Association for Computational Linguistics.

Liu, Y., Gu, J., Goyal, N., Li, X., Edunov, S., Ghazvininejad, M., Lewis, M., and Zettlemoyer, L. (2020). Multilingual denoising pre-training for neural machine translation. *Transactions of the Association for Computational Linguistics*, 8:726–742.

Luong, T., Pham, H., and Manning, C. D. (2015). Bilingual Word Representations with Monolingual Quality in Mind. In *Proceedings of the 1st Workshop on Vector Space Modeling for Natural Language Processing*, pages 151–159, Denver, Colorado. Association for Computational Linguistics.

Mikolov, T., Le, Q. V., and Sutskever, I. (2013). Exploiting Similarities among Languages for Machine Translation. *arXiv:1309.4168 [cs]*. arXiv: 1309.4168.

Ormazabal, A., Artetxe, M., Labaka, G., Soroa, A., and Agirre, E. (2019). Analyzing the Limitations of Cross-lingual Word Embedding Mappings. *arXiv:1906.05407 [cs]*. arXiv: 1906.05407.

Peng, W., Huang, C., Li, T., Chen, Y., and Liu, Q. (2020). Dictionary-based Data Augmentation for Cross-Domain Neural Machine Translation. *arXiv:2004.02577 [cs]*. arXiv: 2004.02577.

Post, M. (2018). A call for clarity in reporting BLEU scores. In *Proceedings of the Third Conference on Machine Translation: Research Papers*, pages 186–191, Belgium, Brussels. Association for Computational Linguistics.

Sennrich, R., Haddow, B., and Birch, A. (2016). Improving neural machine translation models with monolingual data. In *Proceedings of the 54th Annual Meeting of the Association for Computational Linguistics (Volume 1: Long Papers)*, pages 86–96, Berlin, Germany. Association for Computational Linguistics.

Shen, J., Chen, P.-J., Le, M., He, J., Gu, J., Ott, M., Auli, M., and Ranzato, M. (2021). The source-target domain mismatch problem in machine translation. In *Proceedings of the 16th Conference of the European Chapter of the Association for Computational Linguistics: Main Volume*, pages 1519–1533, Online. Association for Computational Linguistics.

Søgaard, A., Ruder, S., and Vulić, I. (2018). On the Limitations of Unsupervised Bilingual Dictionary Induction. In *Proceedings of the 56th Annual Meeting of the Association for Computational Linguistics (Volume 1: Long Papers)*, pages 778–788, Melbourne, Australia. Association for Computational Linguistics.

Tiedemann, J. (2012). Parallel data, tools and interfaces in opus. In Chair), N. C. C., Choukri, K., Declerck, T., Dogan, M. U., Maegaard, B., Mariani, J., Odijk, J., and Piperidis, S., editors, *Proceedings of the Eight International Conference on Language Resources and Evaluation (LREC'12)*, Istanbul, Turkey. European Language Resources Association (ELRA).

Vulić, I., Ponti, E. M., Litschko, R., Glavaš, G., and Korhonen, A. (2020). Probing pretrained language models for lexical semantics. In *Proceedings of the 2020 Conference on Empirical Methods in Natural Language Processing (EMNLP)*, pages 7222–7240, Online. Association for Computational Linguistics.

Xu, R., Zhi, Z., Cao, J., Wang, M., and Li, L. (2020). Volctrans parallel corpus filtering system for WMT 2020. In *Proceedings of the Fifth Conference on Machine Translation*, pages 985–990, Online. Association for Computational Linguistics.

Doubly-Trained Adversarial Data Augmentation for Neural Machine Translation

Weiting Tan wtan12@jhu.edu
Center for Language and Speech Processing, Johns Hopkins University

Shuoyang Ding[‡] dings@amazon.com
AWS AI Labs

Huda Khayrallah[‡] hkhayrallah@microsoft.com
Microsoft

Philipp Koehn phi@jhu.edu
Center for Language and Speech Processing, Johns Hopkins University

Abstract

Neural Machine Translation (NMT) models are known to suffer from noisy inputs. To make models robust, we generate adversarial augmentation samples that attack the model and preserve the source-side meaning at the same time. To generate such samples, we propose a doubly-trained architecture that pairs two NMT models of opposite translation directions with a joint loss function, which combines the target-side attack and the source-side semantic similarity constraint. The results from our experiments across three different language pairs and two evaluation metrics show that these adversarial samples improve model robustness.

1 Introduction

When NMT models are trained on clean parallel data, they are not exposed to much noise, resulting in poor robustness when translating noisy input texts. Various adversarial attack methods have been explored for computer vision (Yuan et al., 2018) including Fast Gradient Sign Methods (Goodfellow et al., 2015) and generative adversarial networks (GAN; Goodfellow et al., 2014), among others. Most of these methods are white-box attacks where model parameters are accessible during the attack so that the attack is much more effective. Good adversarial samples could also enhance model robustness by introducing perturbation as data augmentation (Goodfellow et al., 2014; Chen et al., 2020).

Due to the discrete nature of natural languages, most of the early-stage adversarial attacks on NMT focused on black-box attacks (attacks without access to model parameters) and use

[‡]Work done while at Johns Hopkins University.

techniques such as string modification based on edit distance (Karpukhin et al., 2019) or random changes of words in input sentence (Ebrahimi et al., 2018)). Such black-box methods can improve model robustness. However, simple modifications based on random deletion, insertion, or swapping might not provide good adversarial examples. To better generate adversarial samples for black-box models, Zhang et al. (2021) used a Masked Language Model to help find good substitution at important positions of the input sequence. On the other hand, white-box based methods like virtual training algorithm (Miyato et al., 2017) and adversarial regularization (Sato et al., 2019) incorporate gradient-based adversarial techniques into natural languages processing. Cheng et al. (2019, 2020) further constrained the direction of perturbation with source-side semantic similarity and observed better performance.

Our work improves the gradient-based generation mechanism with a doubly-trained system, inspired by dual learning (Xia et al., 2016). The doubly-trained system consists of a forward (translate from source language to target language) and a backward (translate target language to source language) model. After pretraining both forward and backward models, our augmentation process has three steps:

1. *Attack Step*: Train forward and backward models at the same time to update the shared embedding of source language (embedding of the forward model's encoder and the backward model's decoder).
2. *Perturbation Step*: Generate adversarial sequences by modifying source input sentences with random deletion and nearest neighbor search.
3. *Augmentation Training Step*: Train the forward model on the adversarial data.

We applied our method on test data with synthetic noise and compared it against different baseline models. Experiments across three languages showed consistent improvement of model robustness using our algorithm.[1]

2 Related Work

Natural and synthetic noise affects translation performance (Belinkov and Bisk, 2018) and adversarial perturbation is commonly used to evaluate and improve model robustness in such cases. Various adversarial methods are researched for robustness, some use adversarial samples as regularization (Sato et al., 2019), some incorporate it with reinforcement learning (Zou et al., 2020), and some use it for data augmentation. When used for augmentation, black-box adversarial methods tend to augment data by introducing noise into training data. For most of the time, simple operations such as random deletion/replacement/insertion are used for black-box attack (Karpukhin et al., 2019), though such operations can be used as white-box attack with gradients as well (Ebrahimi et al., 2018). It's also possible to guide adversarial samples' search with pretrained models in black-box attack (Zhang et al., 2021).

Most white-box adversarial methods use different architecture to attack and update model (Michel et al., 2019; Cheng et al., 2020, 2019), and from which, generate augmented data. White-box adversarial methods gives more flexible modification for the token but at the same

[1] code released at: `https://github.com/steventan0110/NMTModelAttack`

time become time consuming, making it infeasible for some cases when speed matters. Though it is commonly believed that white-box adversarial methods have higher capacity, there is study that shows simple replacement can be used as an effective and fast alternative to white-box methods where it achieves comparable (or even better) results for some synthetic noise (Takase and Kiyono, 2021). This finding correlates with our research to some degree because we also find replacement useful to improve model robustness, though we perform replacement by most similar token instead of sampling a random token.

3 Background

Minimum Risk Training (MRT) Shen et al. (2016) introduces evaluation metric into loss function and assume that the optimal set of model parameters will minimize the expected loss on the training data. The loss function is defined as $\Delta(\mathbf{y}, \mathbf{y}^{(s)})$ to measure the discrepancy between model output y and gold standard translation $\mathbf{y}^{(s)}$. It can be any negative sentence-level evaluation metric such as BLEU, METEOR, COMET, BERTScore, (Papineni et al., 2002; Banerjee and Lavie, 2005; Rei et al., 2020; Zhang et al., 2020) etc. The risk (training objective) for the system is:

$$\begin{aligned} \mathcal{L}_{\text{MRT}} &= \sum_{s=1}^{S} {}_{\mathbf{y}|\mathbf{x}^{(s)};\theta} \left[\Delta(\mathbf{y}, \mathbf{y}^{(s)})\right] \\ &= \sum_{s=1}^{S} \sum_{\mathbf{y}\in C(\mathbf{x})} P(\mathbf{y}|\mathbf{x}^{(s)};\theta)\Delta(\mathbf{y}, \mathbf{y}^{(s)}) \\ \hat{\theta}_{\text{MRT}} &= \underset{\theta}{\text{argmin}}\{\mathcal{L}_{\text{MRT}}(\theta)\} \end{aligned} \tag{1}$$

where $C(\mathbf{x}^{(s)})$ is the set of all possible candidate translation by the system. Shen et al. (2016) shows that partial of risk $\mathcal{L}_{MRT}(\theta)$ with respect to a model parameter θ_i does not need to differentiate $\Delta(\mathbf{y}, \mathbf{y}^{(s)})$:

$$\frac{\partial \mathcal{L}_{\text{MRT}}(\theta)}{\partial \theta_i} = \sum_{s=1}^{S} {}_{\mathbf{y}|\mathbf{x}^{(s)};\theta} \left[\Delta(\mathbf{y}, \mathbf{y}^{(s)}) \times \sum_{n=1}^{N^{(s)}} \frac{\partial P(\mathbf{y}_n^{(s)}|\mathbf{x}^{(s)}, \mathbf{y}_{<n}^{(s)};\theta)/\partial\theta_i}{P(\mathbf{y}_n^{(s)}|\mathbf{x}^{(s)}, \mathbf{y}_{<n}^{(s)};\theta)}\right] \tag{2}$$

Hence MRT allows an arbitrary scoring function Δ to be used, whether it is differentiable or not. In our experiments, we use MRT with two metrics, BLEU (Papineni et al., 2002)—the standard in machine translation and COMET (Rei et al., 2020)—a newly proposed neural-based evaluation metric that correlates better with human judgement.

Adversarial Attack Adversarial attacks generate samples that closely match input while dramatically distorting the model output. The samples can be generated by either a white-box or a black-box model. Black-box methods do not have access to the model while white-box methods have such access. A set of adversarial samples are generated by:

$$\{\mathbf{x}'|\mathcal{R}(\mathbf{x}', \mathbf{x}) \leq \epsilon, \underset{\mathbf{x}'}{\text{argmax}} J(\mathbf{x}', \mathbf{y};\theta)\} \tag{3}$$

where $J(\cdot)$ is the probability of a sample being adversarial and $\mathcal{R}(\mathbf{x}', \mathbf{x})$ computes the degree of imperceptibility of perturbation $\mathbf{x}'$ compared to original input $\mathbf{x}$. The smaller the ϵ, the less noticeable the perturbation is. In our system, $J(\cdot)$ not only focuses on attacking the forward model, but also uses the backward model to constrain the direction of gradient update and maintain source-side semantic similarity.

4 Approach: Doubly Trained NMT for Adversarial Sample Generation

We aim to generate adversarial samples that both preserve input's semantic meaning and decrease the performance of an NMT model. We propose a doubly-trained system that involves two models of opposite translation direction (denote the forward model as θ_{st} and the backward model as θ_{ts}). Our algorithm will train and update θ_{st}, θ_{ts} simultaneously. Note that both models are pretrained before they are used for adversarial augmentation so that they can already produce good translations. Our algorithm has three steps as shown in Figure 1.

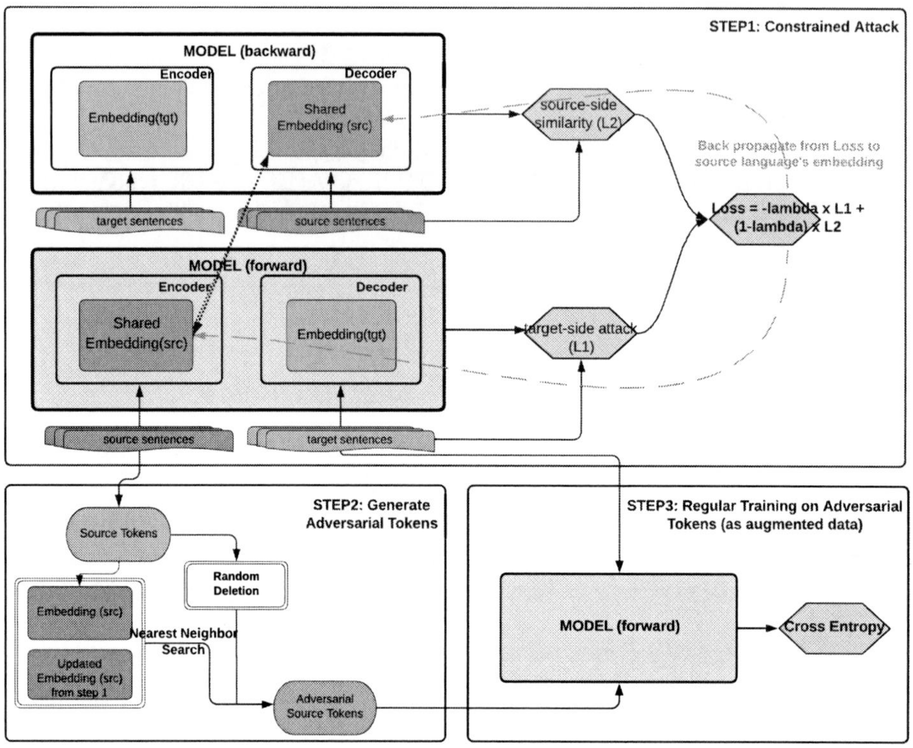

Figure 1: Visual explanation of our adversarial augmentation algorithm. Step 1: Forward and backward models are trained simultaneously and attacked by the combined objective function. (The shared embedding is modified). Step 2: input source tokens are randomly deleted or replaced by nearest neighbor search to generate adversarial samples. Step 3: forward model is trained on adversarial samples.

Step 1 – Perform constrained attack to update embedding The first step is to attack the system and update the source embedding. We train the models with Negative Log-Likelihood (NLL) or MRT and combine the loss from two models as our final loss function to update the shared embedding. We denote the loss for θ_{st} as $\mathcal{L}_1$ and loss for θ_{ts} as $\mathcal{L}_2$. Because we want to attack the forward model and preserve translation quality for the backward model, we make our final loss

$$\mathcal{L} = -\lambda\mathcal{L}_1 + (1-\lambda)\mathcal{L}_2 \tag{4}$$

where $\lambda \in [0,1]$ and is used as the weight to decide whether we focus on punishing the forward model (large λ) or preserving the backward model (small λ). When we use NLL as training objective, we have $\mathcal{L}_1 = \mathbf{NLL}(\mathbf{x}^{(s)}, \mathbf{y}^{(s)}, \theta_{st})$ where $\mathbf{x}^{(s)}$ is the input sentences, $\mathbf{y}^{(s)}$ is the gold standard translation and $\mathbf{NLL}(\cdot)$ is the Negative Log-Likelihood function that computes a loss based on training data $\mathbf{x}^{(s)}, \mathbf{y}^{(s)}$ and model parameter θ_{st}. Similarly we have $\mathcal{L}_2 = \mathbf{NLL}(\mathbf{y}^{(s)}, \mathbf{x}^{(s)}, \theta_{ts})$

We also experimented with MRT in our doubly-trained system to investigate if using sentence-level scoring functions like BLEU or COMET would help improve adversarial samples' quality. For model θ_{st}, we feed in source sentences $\mathbf{x}^{(s)}$ and we infer a set of possible translation $S(\mathbf{x}^{(s)})$ as the subset of full sample space. The loss (risk) of our prediction is therefore calculated as:

$$\begin{aligned}\mathcal{L}_1 &= \sum_{s=1}^{S} \mathbb{E}_{\mathbf{y}|\mathbf{x}^{(s)};\theta_{st}} \left[\Delta(\mathbf{y}, \mathbf{y}^{(s)})\right] \\ &= \sum_{s=1}^{S} \sum_{\mathbf{y}\in S(\mathbf{x}^{(s)})} Q(\mathbf{y}|\mathbf{x}^{(s)}; \theta_{st}, \alpha)\Delta(\mathbf{y}, \mathbf{y}^{(s)})\end{aligned} \tag{5}$$

where

$$Q(\mathbf{y}|\mathbf{x}^{(s)}; \theta_{st}, \alpha) = \frac{P(\mathbf{y}|\mathbf{x}^{(s)}; \theta_{st})^{\alpha}}{\sum_{\mathbf{y}'\in S(\mathbf{x}^{(s)})} P(\mathbf{y}'|\mathbf{x}^{(s)}; \theta_{st})^{\alpha}} \tag{6}$$

The value α here controls the sharpness of the formula and we follow Shen et al. (2016) to use $\alpha = 5e^{-3}$ throughout our experiments. To sample the subset of full inference space $S(\mathbf{x}^{(s)})$, we use Sampling Algorithm (Shen et al., 2016) to generate k translation candidates for each input sentence (During inference time, the model outputs a probabilistic distribution over the vocabulary for each token and we sample a token based on this distribution). It is denoted as **Sample**$(\mathbf{x}^{(s)}, \theta, k)$ in our Algorithm 1. Similarly, for model θ_{ts}, we feed in the reference sentences of our parallel data and generate a set of possible translation $S(\mathbf{y}^{(s)})$ in source language. We compute the loss (risk) of source-side similarity as:

$$\begin{aligned}\mathcal{L}_2 &= \sum_{s=1}^{S} \mathbb{E}_{\mathbf{x}|\mathbf{y}^{(s)};\theta_{ts}} \left[\Delta(\mathbf{x}, \mathbf{x}^{(s)})\right] \\ &= \sum_{s=1}^{S} \sum_{\mathbf{x}\in S(\mathbf{y}^{(s)})} Q(\mathbf{x}|\mathbf{y}^{(s)}; \theta_{ts}, \alpha)\Delta(\mathbf{x}, \mathbf{x}^{(s)})\end{aligned} \tag{7}$$

After computing loss using MRT or NLL, we have

$$\mathcal{L}(\theta_{st}, \theta_{ts}) = -\lambda\mathcal{L}_1 + (1-\lambda)\mathcal{L}_2, \lambda \in [0,1] \tag{8}$$

(negative sign for $\mathcal{L}_1$ since we want to attack θ_{st}) and we train the system to find

$$\hat{\theta}_{st}, \hat{\theta}_{ts} = \underset{\theta_{st},\theta_{ts}}{\text{argmin}}\{\mathcal{L}(\theta_{st}, \theta_{ts})\} \tag{9}$$

To be updated from both risks, two models need to share some parameters since $\mathcal{L}_1$ only affects θ_{st} and $\mathcal{L}_2$ only updates θ_{ts}. Because a word embedding is a representation of input tokens, we make it such that the source-side embeddings of θ_{st} and the target-side embeddings of θ_{ts} are shared. We do so because they are both representations of source language in our translation and we can use it to generate adversarial tokens for source sentences in step 2. We also freeze all other layers in two models. Thus, when we update the model parameter θ_{st}, θ_{ts}, we only update the shared embedding of source language. The process described above is summarized in Algorithm 1.

Algorithm 1 Update model embedding

Input: Pretrained Models θ_{st} and θ_{ts}, Max Number of Epochs E, Sample Size K, Sentence-Level Scoring Metric M
Output: Updated Models θ_{st} and θ_{ts} (only the shared embedding is updated)
while θ_{st}, θ_{ts} not Converged **and** $e \leq E$ **do**
  for $(\mathbf{x}^{(i)}, \mathbf{y}^{(i)}), 1 < i \leq S$ **do**
    if using MRT as objective **then**
      /* sample and compute the risk */
      $S(\mathbf{x}^{(i)}) = \textbf{Sample}(\mathbf{x}^{(i)}, \theta_{st}, K)$
      $\mathcal{L}_1 \leftarrow \textbf{MRT}(S(\mathbf{x}^{(i)}), M, \mathbf{y}^{(i)})$
      /* Repeat for another direction */
      $S(\mathbf{y}^{(i)}) = \textbf{Sample}(\mathbf{y}^{(i)}, \theta_{ts}, K)$
      $\mathcal{L}_2 \leftarrow \textbf{MRT}(S(\mathbf{y}^{(i)}), M, \mathbf{x}^{(i)})$
    else if using NLL as objective **then**
      $\mathcal{L}_1 \leftarrow \textbf{NLL}(\mathbf{x}^{(i)}, \mathbf{y}^{(i)}, \theta_{st})$
      $\mathcal{L}_2 \leftarrow \textbf{NLL}(\mathbf{x}^{(i)}, \mathbf{y}^{(i)}, \theta_{ts})$
    end if
    $\mathcal{L}(\theta_{st}, \theta_{ts}) = -\lambda \mathcal{L}_1 + (1 - \lambda)\mathcal{L}_2$
    $\theta_{st}, \theta_{ts} \leftarrow \nabla_{Emb}\mathcal{L}(\theta_{st}, \theta_{ts})$
  end for
end while

Step 2 – Perturb input sentences to generate adversarial tokens After updating the shared embedding, we can use the updated embedding to generate adversarial tokens. We introduce two kinds of noise into input sentences to generate adversarial samples: random deletion and simple replacement. To generate adversarial tokens (due to the discrete nature of natural languages), we use cosine similarity. Let model embedding be E before the embedding update, and E' after the update from Algorithm 1. Let the vocab be V and let input sentence be $S = \{s_1, s_2, \cdots s_n\}$ For each token $s_i \in S, s_i \notin \{\text{EOS, BOS, PAD}\}$, three actions are possible:

1. no perturbation, with probability P_{np}
2. perturb the token:
   (a) perturbed into most similar token by updated embedding with probability P_{rp}
   (b) perturbed to be empty token (deleted at this position) with probability $P_{rd} = 1 - P_{rp}$

Throughout our experiments, we set the hyper-parameters as $P_{np} = 0.7, P_{rp} = 0.8, P_{rd} = 0.2$. That means each token has 30 percent chance to be perturbed, and if that's the case, it has 80 percent chance to be replaced by a similar token and 20 percent chance to be deleted. For no-perturbation or deletion case, it's straightforward to implement. For replacement, we compute s_i' (the adversarial token of s_i) by cosine similarity: $s_i' = \underset{v \in V, v \neq s_i}{argmax}(\frac{E'[s_i]}{|E'[s_i]|} \cdot \frac{E[v]}{|E[v]|})$. For the credibility of this hyper-parameter setup, we perform a grid search over 9 possible combinations:

$$\underset{P_{np}}{(0.6, 0.7, 0.8)} \times \underset{P_{rp}}{(0.6, 0.7, 0.8)}$$

We found that the difference in performance is mostly due to model type instead of probability setup. Details of grid search can be found in Appendix (Table 7).

Step 3 – Train on adversarial samples After generating adversarial tokens from step 2, we directly train the forward model on them with the NLL loss function.

5 Experiment

5.1 Pretrained Model Setup

We pretrain the standard Transformer (Vaswani et al., 2017) base model implemented in fairseq (Ott et al., 2019). The hyper-parameters follow the `transformer-en-de` setup from fairseq and our script is shown in Appendix, Figure 2. We experimented on three different language pairs: Chinese-English (zh-en), German-English (de-en), and French-English (fr-en). For each language pair, two models are pretrained on the same training data using the same hyper-parameters and they share the embedding of source language. For example, for Chinese-English, we first train the forward model (zh-en) from scratch. Then we freeze the source language (zh)'s embedding from forward model and use it to pretrain our backward model (en-zh). The training data used for three languages pairs are:

1. zh-en: WMT17 (Bojar et al., 2017) parallel corpus (except UN) for training, WMT2017 and 2018 `newstest` data for validation, and WMT2020 `newstest` for evaluation.
2. de-en: WMT17 parallel corpus for training, WMT2017 and 2018 `newstest` data for validation, and WMT2014 `newstest` for evaluation.
3. fr-en: WMT14 (Bojar et al., 2014) parallel corpus (except UN) for training, WMT2015 `newdicussdev` and `newsdiscusstest` for validation, and WMT2014 `newstest` for evaluation.

For Chinese-English parallel corpus, we used a sentencepiece model of size 20k to perform BPE. For German-English and French-English data, we followed preprocessing scripts [2] on fairseq and used subword-nmt of size 40k to perform BPE. We need two validation sets because in our experiment, we fine-tune the model with our adversarial augmentation algorithm on one of the validation set and use the other for model selection. After pretraining stage, the transformer models' performances on test sets are shown in Table 1. The evaluation of BLEU score is computed by SacreBLEU[3] (Post, 2018).

[2] github.com/pytorch/fairseq/tree/master/examples/translation

[3] Signature included in Appendix, Appendix C

lang	BLEU	lang	BLEU	lang	BLEU
zh-en	22.8	de-en	30.2	fr-en	34.5
en-zh	36.0	en-de	24.9	en-fr	35.3

Table 1: Pretrained baseline models' BLEU score

5.2 Doubly Trained System for Adversarial Attack

Our adversarial augmentation algorithm has three steps: the first step is performing a constrained adversarial attack while the remaining steps generate and train models on augmentation data. In this section, we experiment with only the first step and test if Algorithm 1 can generate meaning-preserving update on the embedding. Our objective function $\mathcal{L}(\theta_{st}, \theta_{ts}) = -\lambda\mathcal{L}_1 + (1-\lambda)\mathcal{L}_2$ is a combination of two rewards from forward and backward models. The expectation is that after the perturbation on the embedding, the forward model's performance would drastically decrease (because it's attacked) and the backward model should still translate reasonably well (because the objective function preserves the source-side semantic meaning). We perform the experiment on Chinese-English and results are shown in Table 4 in appendix. We find that models corroborate to our expectation: After 15 epochs, the forward (zh-en) model's performance drops significantly while the backward (en-zh) model's performance barely decreases. After 20 epochs, the forward model is producing garbage translation while the backward model is still performing well.

5.3 Doubly Trained System for Data Augmentation

From Section 5.2, we have verified that the first step of our adversarial augmentation training is effective at generating meaning-preserving perturbation on the word embedding. We then perform all three steps of our algorithm to investigate whether it is robust as an augmentation technique, which is the focus of this work. In order to evaluate the robustness of doubly-trained model, we prepare synthetic noisy test data of different languages mentioned in Section 5.1. We follow the practice from Niu et al. (2020) and perturb the test data to varying degree, ranging from 10% to 30%. We focus on two kinds of noise: random deletion and simple replacement. The procedure we introduce synthetic noise into clean test data is the same as the procedure described in Step 2. The only difference is in the case of simple replacement: We only have the embedding E from the pretrained model and there is no attacking step to update it into E'. The perturbed token s' is therefore found by $s'_i = \underset{v \in V, v \neq s_i}{argmax}(\frac{E[s_i]}{|E[s_i]|} \cdot \frac{E[v]}{|E[v]|})$.

5.3.1 Result Analysis

We show our results in Table 2 and Table 3. For each language pair, there are 6 types of models in each plot:

1. **baseline model**: pretrained forward (src-tgt) model
2. **fine-tuned model**: baseline model fine-tuned on validation set using NLL loss
3. **simple replacement model**: baseline model fine-tuned on adversarial tokens. This model is fine-tuned using procedure described in Figure 1 without the first step. Adversarial samples

are generated the same way we introduce noise into clean test data ($s'_i = \underset{v \in V, v \neq s_i}{argmax}(\frac{E[s_i]}{|E[s_i]|} \cdot \frac{E[v]}{|E[v]|})$). Since it sees the type of noise we introduce into clean data, it's a strong baseline and resistant to perturbation in clean data.

4. **dual-nll model**: baseline model fine-tuned on adversarial tokens generated by doubly-trained system with NLL as training objective.
5. **dual-bleu model**: baseline model fine-tuned on adversarial tokens generated by doubly-trained system with MRT as training objective. It uses BLEU as the metric to compute MRT risk.
6. **dual-comet model**: same as dual-bleu model above except that it uses COMET as the metric for MRT risk.

We show the percentage of change evaluated by BLEU and COMET on Table 2 and Table 3, computed by

$$\Delta\text{Metric}(x) = 1 - \frac{\text{Metric}(x)}{\text{Metric(clean)}} \tag{10}$$

where the metric can be BLEU or COMET, and x represents the test data used, as explained in Table 2. As the ratio of noise increases, Metric(x) decreases, which increases ΔMetric(x). Therefore, robust models resist to the increase of noise ratio and have lower ΔMetric(x). From both tables, we find that doubly-trained models (dual-nll, dual-bleu, and dual-comet) are more robust than the other models regardless of test data, evaluation metrics, or language pairs used.

For any NMT model tested on the same task evaluated by two metrics (any corresponding row in Table 2 and Table 3), BLEU and COMET give similar results though COMET have a larger difference among models because its percentage change is more drastic. We performed tests using COMET in addition to BLEU because we use MRT with BLEU and COMET in attack step and we want to see if performances of dual-comet and dual-bleu model differ under either evaluation metric. From our results, there is no noticeable difference. This might happen because we used a small learning rate for embedding update in attack step or simply because BLEU and COMET give similar evaluation.

Comparing the results in Table 2 and Table 3, we see margins of models' performance are bigger when evaluated on noisy test data generated with replacement. This is expected because random deletion introduces more noise than replacement and it's hard for models to defend against it. Therefore, doubly trained systems have more improvement against other models when noise type is simple replacement.

Lastly, when we compare across doubly-trained systems (dual-nll, dual-bleu, and dual-comet), we see that they are comparable to each other within a margin of 3 percent. This implies that incorporating a sentence-level scoring metric with MRT does not greatly improve word-level adversarial augmentation. This is possible because we perturb on token level instead of sentence level while MRT objective focus on sentence-level information.

Model (ZH-EN)	RD10	RD15	RD20	RD25	RD30	RP10	RP15	RP20	RP25	RP30
Baseline	25%	36%	46%	55%	63%	8%	14%	19%	22%	25%
Finetune	23%	33%	42%	52%	60%	8%	11%	14%	17%	21%
Simple Replacement	23%	33%	41%	51%	59%	6%	8%	10%	12%	15%
Dual NLL	**21%**	**31%**	**40%**	**49%**	**56%**	4%	6%	8%	**10%**	**12%**
Dual BLEU	23%	33%	42%	51%	58%	4%	6%	9%	11%	13%
Dual COMET	22%	32%	41%	50%	58%	**4%**	**6%**	**8%**	10%	13%
Model (DE-EN)	**RD10**	**RD15**	**RD20**	**RD25**	**RD30**	**RP10**	**RP15**	**RP20**	**RP25**	**RP30**
Baseline	43%	51%	60%	68%	74%	31%	34%	37%	40%	44%
Finetune	42%	50%	58%	67%	73%	31%	34%	37%	40%	44%
Simple Replacement	42%	50%	59%	66%	72%	30%	32%	35%	37%	40%
Dual NLL	42%	49%	**56%**	**63%**	**69%**	29%	31%	33%	35%	37%
Dual BLEU	**41%**	49%	57%	64%	71%	**28%**	**30%**	**33%**	**35%**	**37%**
Dual COMET	42%	**48%**	57%	64%	70%	29%	31%	33%	35%	38%
Model (FR-EN)	**RD10**	**RD15**	**RD20**	**RD25**	**RD30**	**RP10**	**RP15**	**RP20**	**RP25**	**RP30**
Baseline	47%	54%	61%	67%	74%	38%	40%	44%	47%	50%
Finetune	47%	54%	60%	67%	73%	37%	40%	44%	48%	49%
Simple Replacement	45%	53%	60%	66%	73%	35%	37%	40%	43%	46%
Dual NLL	**45%**	**52%**	59%	65%	71%	35%	37%	40%	43%	45%
Dual BLEU	45%	52%	59%	66%	72%	35%	**36%**	**39%**	**41%**	**44%**
Dual COMET	45%	52%	**58%**	**65%**	**71%**	**34%**	37%	39%	42%	44%

Table 2: Models' performance on noisy synthetic data generated from random deletion (RD) and simple replacement (RP). Number after RD/RP is the percentage of noise introduced in clean data (e.g RD15 is the test set generated by randomly deleting 15% of clean test data). Generated translation are measured by ΔBLEU. We define BLEU(x) as the BLEU score evaluated on test dataset x (e.g. RD10), $\Delta\text{BLEU}(x) = 1 - \frac{\text{BLEU}(x)}{\text{BLEU(clean)}}$,where BLEU(clean) is BLEU score of the model evaluated on the clean dataset. The higher the ΔBLEU, the worse the model on noisy data. The details of the six models and analysis are included in Section 5.3.1.

Model (ZH-EN)	RD10	RD15	RD20	RD25	RD30	RP10	RP15	RP20	RP25	RP30
Baseline	99%	158%	210%	278%	342%	48%	68%	95%	116%	137%
Finetune	66%	105%	143%	189%	236%	30%	41%	56%	67%	80%
Simple Replacement	63%	105%	139%	184%	230%	19%	27%	36%	48%	62%
Dual NLL	64%	103%	**135%**	**176%**	225%	20%	29%	37%	47%	56%
Dual BLEU	64%	102%	138%	181%	**224%**	**18%**	**26%**	**35%**	**46%**	**56%**
Dual COMET	**63%**	**102%**	136%	180%	227%	18%	27%	38%	47%	57%
Model (DE-EN)	**RD10**	**RD15**	**RD20**	**RD25**	**RD30**	**RP10**	**RP15**	**RP20**	**RP25**	**RP30**
Baseline	124%	159%	196%	230%	265%	76%	88%	99%	113%	127%
Finetune	116%	150%	186%	220%	255%	72%	83%	95%	108%	122%
Simple Replacement	113%	145%	179%	212%	245%	**68%**	78%	88%	98%	109%
Dual NLL	114%	146%	177%	208%	241%	71%	80%	88%	97%	108%
Dual BLEU	**113%**	**144%**	**176%**	**208%**	**240%**	69%	**78%**	**86%**	**95%**	**106%**
Dual COMET	114%	144%	177%	209%	242%	70%	79%	87%	96%	107%
Model (FR-EN)	**RD10**	**RD15**	**RD20**	**RD25**	**RD30**	**RP10**	**RP15**	**RP20**	**RP25**	**RP30**
Baseline	132%	156%	178%	204%	228%	104%	113%	122%	132%	142%
Finetune	122%	147%	171%	197%	221%	91%	100%	109%	119%	128%
Simple Replacement	121%	144%	167%	193%	217%	89%	96%	104%	113%	120%
Dual NLL	120%	143%	165%	**190%**	**213%**	89%	97%	105%	112%	121%
Dual BLEU	121%	144%	167%	192%	216%	89%	96%	104%	110%	**117%**
Dual COMET	**120%**	**143%**	**165%**	191%	214%	**88%**	**95%**	**102%**	**110%**	118%

Table 3: Models' performance on noisy synthetic data generated from random deletion (RD) and simple replacement (RP). Set-up is the same as Table 2 except that evaluation metric is COMET instead of BLEU, so we show ΔCOMET here. Note that ΔCOMET can go over 100% because COMET score can be negative.

6 Conclusion

We proposed a white-box adversarial augmentation algorithm to improve model robustness. We use a doubly-trained system to perform constrained attack and then train the model on adversarial samples generated with random deletion and gradient-based replacement. Experiments across different languages and evaluation metrics have shown consistent improvement for model robustness.

References

Banerjee, S. and Lavie, A. (2005). METEOR: An automatic metric for MT evaluation with improved correlation with human judgments. In *Proceedings of the ACL Workshop on Intrinsic and Extrinsic Evaluation Measures for Machine Translation and/or Summarization*, pages 65–72, Ann Arbor, Michigan. Association for Computational Linguistics.

Belinkov, Y. and Bisk, Y. (2018). Synthetic and natural noise both break neural machine translation.

Bojar, O., Buck, C., Federmann, C., Haddow, B., Koehn, P., Leveling, J., Monz, C., Pecina, P., Post, M., Saint-Amand, H., Soricut, R., Specia, L., and Tamchyna, A. (2014). Findings of the 2014 workshop on statistical machine translation. In *Proceedings of the Ninth Workshop on Statistical Machine Translation*, pages 12–58, Baltimore, Maryland, USA. Association for Computational Linguistics.

Bojar, O., Chatterjee, R., Federmann, C., Graham, Y., Haddow, B., Huang, S., Huck, M., Koehn, P., Liu, Q., Logacheva, V., Monz, C., Negri, M., Post, M., Rubino, R., Specia, L., and Turchi, M. (2017). Findings of the 2017 conference on machine translation (WMT17). In *Proceedings of the Second Conference on Machine Translation*, pages 169–214, Copenhagen, Denmark. Association for Computational Linguistics.

Chen, C., Qin, C., Qiu, H., Ouyang, C., Wang, S., Chen, L., Tarroni, G., Bai, W., and Rueckert, D. (2020). Realistic adversarial data augmentation for mr image segmentation.

Cheng, Y., Jiang, L., and Macherey, W. (2019). Robust neural machine translation with doubly adversarial inputs.

Cheng, Y., Jiang, L., Macherey, W., and Eisenstein, J. (2020). Advaug: Robust adversarial augmentation for neural machine translation.

Ebrahimi, J., Lowd, D., and Dou, D. (2018). On adversarial examples for character-level neural machine translation.

Goodfellow, I. J., Pouget-Abadie, J., Mirza, M., Xu, B., Warde-Farley, D., Ozair, S., Courville, A., and Bengio, Y. (2014). Generative adversarial networks.

Goodfellow, I. J., Shlens, J., and Szegedy, C. (2015). Explaining and harnessing adversarial examples.

Karpukhin, V., Levy, O., Eisenstein, J., and Ghazvininejad, M. (2019). Training on synthetic noise improves robustness to natural noise in machine translation.

Michel, P., Li, X., Neubig, G., and Pino, J. M. (2019). On evaluation of adversarial perturbations for sequence-to-sequence models.

Miyato, T., Dai, A. M., and Goodfellow, I. (2017). Adversarial training methods for semi-supervised text classification.

Niu, X., Mathur, P., Dinu, G., and Al-Onaizan, Y. (2020). Evaluating robustness to input perturbations for neural machine translation. In *Proceedings of the 58th Annual Meeting of the Association for Computational Linguistics*, pages 8538–8544, Online. Association for Computational Linguistics.

Ott, M., Edunov, S., Baevski, A., Fan, A., Gross, S., Ng, N., Grangier, D., and Auli, M. (2019). fairseq: A fast, extensible toolkit for sequence modeling.

Papineni, K., Roukos, S., Ward, T., and Zhu, W.-J. (2002). Bleu: a method for automatic evaluation of machine translation. In *Proceedings of the 40th Annual Meeting of the Association for Computational Linguistics*, pages 311–318, Philadelphia, Pennsylvania, USA. Association for Computational Linguistics.

Post, M. (2018). A call for clarity in reporting BLEU scores. In *Proceedings of the Third Conference on Machine Translation: Research Papers*, pages 186–191, Belgium, Brussels. Association for Computational Linguistics.

Rei, R., Stewart, C., Farinha, A. C., and Lavie, A. (2020). COMET: A neural framework for MT evaluation. In *Proceedings of the 2020 Conference on Empirical Methods in Natural Language Processing (EMNLP)*, pages 2685–2702, Online. Association for Computational Linguistics.

Sato, M., Suzuki, J., and Kiyono, S. (2019). Effective adversarial regularization for neural machine translation. In *Proceedings of the 57th Annual Meeting of the Association for Computational Linguistics*, pages 204–210, Florence, Italy. Association for Computational Linguistics.

Shen, S., Cheng, Y., He, Z., He, W., Wu, H., Sun, M., and Liu, Y. (2016). Minimum risk training for neural machine translation. In *Proceedings of the 54th Annual Meeting of the Association for Computational Linguistics (Volume 1: Long Papers)*, pages 1683–1692, Berlin, Germany. Association for Computational Linguistics.

Takase, S. and Kiyono, S. (2021). Rethinking perturbations in encoder-decoders for fast training.

Vaswani, A., Shazeer, N., Parmar, N., Uszkoreit, J., Jones, L., Gomez, A. N., Kaiser, L., and Polosukhin, I. (2017). Attention is all you need.

Xia, Y., He, D., Qin, T., Wang, L., Yu, N., Liu, T.-Y., and Ma, W.-Y. (2016). Dual learning for machine translation.

Yuan, X., He, P., Zhu, Q., and Li, X. (2018). Adversarial examples: Attacks and defenses for deep learning.

Zhang, T., Kishore, V., Wu, F., Weinberger, K. Q., and Artzi, Y. (2020). Bertscore: Evaluating text generation with bert.

Zhang, X., Zhang, J., Chen, Z., and He, K. (2021). Crafting adversarial examples for neural machine translation. In *Proceedings of the 59th Annual Meeting of the Association for Computational Linguistics and the 11th International Joint Conference on Natural Language Processing (Volume 1: Long Papers)*, pages 1967–1977, Online. Association for Computational Linguistics.

Zou, W., Huang, S., Xie, J., Dai, X., and Chen, J. (2020). A reinforced generation of adversarial examples for neural machine translation.

Appendix

A Pretrained model

Hyper-parameter for Pretraining the transformers (same for three language pairs) is shown in Figure 2. Note that for the fine-tune model, we use the same hyper-parameter as in pretraining, and we simply change the data directory into validation set to tune the pretrained model.

```
fairseq-train $DATADIR \
    --source-lang src \
    --target-lang tgt \
    --save-dir $SAVEDIR \
    --share-decoder-input-output-embed \
    --arch transformer_wmt_en_de \
    --optimizer adam --adam-betas '(0.9, 0.98)' --clip-norm 0.0 \
    --lr-scheduler inverse_sqrt \
    --warmup-init-lr 1e-07 --warmup-updates 4000 \
    --lr 0.0005 --min-lr 1e-09 \
    --dropout 0.3 --weight-decay 0.0001 \
    --criterion label_smoothed_cross_entropy --label-smoothing 0.1 \
    --max-tokens 2048 --update-freq 16 \
    --seed 2 \
```

Figure 2: This setup is used for all pretrained models, regardless of the language pair

B Adversarial Attack on Chinese-English Model

Adversarail Attacks are performed with hyper-parameters shown in Figure 3 and the attack result is shown in Table 4

#Epochs	BLEU (zh-en)	BLEU (en-zh)
10	20.1	34.0
15	10.9	32.4
20	0.3	33.5
30	0.0	32.1

Table 4: Forward and backward models' performance (of Chinese and English) after adversarial attack using MRT as training objective, described in Algorithm 1.

```
fairseq-train $DATADIR \
    --source-lang src \
    --target-lang tgt \
    --save-dir $SAVEDIR \
    --share-decoder-input-output-embed \
    --train-subset valid \
    --arch transformer_wmt_en_de \
    --optimizer adam --adam-betas '(0.9, 0.98)' --clip-norm 0.0 \
    --lr-scheduler inverse_sqrt \
    --warmup-init-lr 1e-07 --warmup-updates 4000 \
    --lr 0.0005 --min-lr 1e-09 \
    --dropout 0.3 --weight-decay 0.0001 \
    --criterion dual_bleu --mrt-k 16 \
    --batch-size 2 --update-freq 64 \
    --seed 2 \
    --restore-file $PREETRAIN_MODEL \
    --reset-optimizer \
    --reset-dataloader \
```

Figure 3: Note that criterion is called "dual bleu" and this is our customized criterion based on fairseq. It implements the doubly trained adversarial attack algorithm discussed in this paper with sample size 16 (mrt-k = 16).

C SacreBleu Signature:

The signature generated by SacreBleu is *"nrefs:1—case:mixed—tok:13a—smooth:exp—version:1.5.1"*. When evaluated with Chinese test data, we manually tokenize the predictions from our en-zh model with **tok=sacrebleu.tokenizers.TokenizerZh()** before computing corpus bleu with SacreBleu. The implementation can be found in our code.[4]

D Data Augmentation

Hyper-parameter for fine-tuning the base model with proposed doubly-trained algorithm on validation set is shown in Figure 4

Note that the criterion is either "dual mrt" (using BLEU as metric for MRT), "dual comet" (using COMET as metric for MRT) or "dual nll" (using NLL as training objective). These are customized criterion that we wrote to implement our algorithm.

BLEU score for doubly-trained model's performance on noisy test data is shown in Table 2 and COMET score is shown in Table 3. Note that sometimes the ΔCOMET can be larger than 100% because COMET score can go from positive to negative.

[4]https://github.com/steventan0110/NMTModelAttack

```
fairseq-train $DATADIR \
    -s $src -t $tgt \
    --train-subset valid \
    --valid-subset valid1 \
    --left-pad-source False \
    --share-decoder-input-output-embed \
    --encoder-embed-dim 512 \
    --arch transformer_wmt_en_de \
    --dual-training \
    --auxillary-model-path $AUX_MODEL \
    --auxillary-model-save-dir $AUX_MODEL_SAVE \
    --optimizer adam --adam-betas '(0.9, 0.98)' --clip-norm 0.0 \
    --lr-scheduler inverse_sqrt \
    --warmup-init-lr 0.000001 --warmup-updates 1000 \
    --lr 0.00001 --min-lr 1e-09 \
    --dropout 0.3 --weight-decay 0.0001 \
    --criterion dual_comet/dual_mrt/dual_nll --mrt-k 8 \
    --comet-route $COMET_PATH \
    --batch-size 4 \
    --skip-invalid-size-inputs-valid-test \
    --update-freq 1 \
    --on-the-fly-train --adv-percent 30 \
    --seed 2 \
    --restore-file $PRETRAIN_MODEL \
    --reset-optimizer \
    --reset-dataloader \
    --save-dir $CHECKPOINT_FOLDER \
```

Figure 4: Script for using doubly trained system for data augmentation

E Choosing Hyper-parameter: Grid Search

E.1 Grid Search for λ

lambda is the hyper-parameter used to balance the weight for the two risks in our doubly trained system. Recall the formula of our objective function: $\mathcal{L}(\theta_{st}, \theta_{ts}) = \lambda\mathcal{R}_1 - (1-\lambda)\mathcal{R}_2$. We perform grid search over $\underset{\lambda}{(0.2, 0.5, 0.8)}$ using dual-bleu and dual-comet model. It can be shown in Table 5 and Table 6 that λ value does not have a large impact on evaluation results and we pick $\lambda = 0.8$ throughout the experiments.

E.2 Grid Search for P_{np}, P_{rp}

We perform grid search for P_{np}, the probability of not perturbing a token, and P_{rp}, the probability of replacing the token if decided to modify it. Our search space is $\underset{P_{np}}{(0.6, 0.7, 0.8)} \times \underset{P_{rp}}{(0.6, 0.7, 0.8)}$ and the results are shown in Table 7. Since there is no noticeable difference across various

λ	BLEU(zh-en)	BLEU(de-en)	BLEU(fr-en)
0.2	28.6	46.9	40.0
0.5	28.5	47.1	39.9
0.8	28.4	47.0	39.8

Table 5: dual-bleu model's performance on varying λ values

λ	BLEU(zh-en)	BLEU(de-en)	BLEU(fr-en)
0.2	28.6	47.1	39.8
0.5	28.7	46.9	39.9
0.8	28.5	46.8	39.8

Table 6: dual-comet model's performance on varying λ values

P_{np}, P_{rp} values, we pick $P_{np} = 0.7, P_{rp} = 0.8$ throughout our experiments.

model (zh-en)		$P_{rp} = 60$	$P_{rp} = 70$	$P_{rp} = 80$
simple replacement	$P_{np} = 60$	26.8	26.8	26.8
	$P_{np} = 70$	26.8	26.9	26.8
	$P_{np} = 80$	27.0	27.1	27.0
dual-bleu	$P_{np} = 60$	28.1	28.2	28.2
	$P_{np} = 70$	28.4	28.4	28.4
	$P_{np} = 80$	28.4	28.5	28.6
dual-comet	$P_{np} = 60$	28.4	28.5	28.4
	$P_{np} = 70$	28.4	28.4	28.4
	$P_{np} = 80$	28.6	28.7	28.7
model (de-en)		$P_{rp} = 60$	$P_{rp} = 70$	$P_{rp} = 80$
simple replacement	$P_{np} = 60$	43.8	43.9	43.9
	$P_{np} = 70$	44.0	44.0	44.0
	$P_{np} = 80$	44.3	44.3	44.3
dual-bleu	$P_{np} = 60$	46.4	46.6	46.5
	$P_{np} = 70$	46.7	46.7	47.0
	$P_{np} = 80$	47.2	47.1	47.3
dual-comet	$P_{np} = 60$	46.5	46.6	46.7
	$P_{np} = 70$	46.7	46.7	46.8
	$P_{np} = 80$	47.2	47.3	47.3
model (fr-en)		$P_{rp} = 60$	$P_{rp} = 70$	$P_{rp} = 80$
simple replacement	$P_{np} = 60$	37.6	37.6	37.6
	$P_{np} = 70$	37.8	37.7	37.6
	$P_{np} = 80$	37.8	37.8	37.7
dual-bleu	$P_{np} = 60$	39.5	39.8	39.6
	$P_{np} = 70$	39.6	39.9	39.9
	$P_{np} = 80$	40.0	40.1	40.1
dual-comet	$P_{np} = 60$	39.9	39.7	39.8
	$P_{np} = 70$	39.9	39.7	39.7
	$P_{np} = 80$	40.0	40.1	40.0

Table 7: Evaluation performance based on varying probability of modification and replacement. P_{rp} : Probability of replacing the token, P_{np} : Probability of not perturbing a token. $P_{np} = 60$ means we only perturb 40 percent of the input tokens

Limitations and Challenges of Unsupervised Cross-lingual Pre-training

Martín Quesada Zaragoza mquesadazaragoza@gmail.com
Francisco Casacuberta fcn@prhlt.upv.es
Research Center of Pattern Recognition and Human Language Technology, Universitat Politècnica de València, Valencia, 46022, Spain

Abstract

Cross-lingual alignment methods for monolingual language representations have received notable attention in recent years. However, their use in machine translation pre-training remains scarce. This work tries to shed light on the effects of some of the factors that play a role in cross-lingual pre-training, both for cross-lingual mappings and their integration in supervised neural models. The results show that unsupervised cross-lingual methods are effective at inducing alignment even for distant languages and they benefit noticeably from subword information. However, we find that their effectiveness as pre-training models in machine translation is severely limited due to their cross-lingual signal being easily distorted by the principal network during training. Moreover, the learned bilingual projection is too restrictive to allow said network to learn properly when the embedding weights are frozen.

1 Introduction

Unsupervised cross-lingual embeddings (CLE) concern a group of methods that exploit latent similarities between word embeddings in different languages to generate their own bilingual dictionary or parallel corpus. Fully unsupervised cross-lingual mappings have received notable attention due to being solely reliant on the distributional similarities of language continuous vector representations.

However, semi-supervised cross-lingual pre-training methods, which require very small amounts of parallel corpora – and in some cases only a simple bilingual dictionary for initialization – tend to outperform their unsupervised counterparts (Vulic et al., 2019; Doval et al., 2019; Patra et al., 2019). It is only in situations where no bilingual data exists that unsupervised techniques are preferable. In the case of languages with extensive written records where resources are plentiful, there is little reason to use a fully unsupervised method rather than one that takes advantage of a small bilingual dataset (Artetxe et al., 2020). Even for low-resource languages for which a reduced number of corpora exist, it is exceedingly probable that some sort of translation dictionary that associates them with a more widely studied language is available. This leads us to the question: are unsupervised cross-lingual models useful at all?

While they might not be the best performing tools in a realistic use case, drawing a hard line between unsupervised and semi-supervised cross-lingual mappings does not make much sense, because they are extremely similar processes. Semi-supervised cross-lingual methods are just forfeiting the generation of a seed bilingual dictionary in favor of one provided by the user or other strategies based on back-translation. But their remaining steps are analogous to that of unsupervised cross-lingual projection methods: they both use the seed translation dictionary to align and project the monolingual subspaces in a hypothetical cross-lingual space. In the case of many unsupervised models, seed generation is actually an adaptation of these previous steps, where some assumption on the structures of the matrices is made in order to obtain an initial set of translation pairs. Given that unsupervised and semi-supervised cross-lingual strategies share so many traits, most improvements over unsupervised methods can be transferred to semi-supervised ones.

This work aims to uncover some of the limitations of pre-training strategies based on unsupervised cross-lingual embeddings. These methods are fully dependent on intrinsic language similarities to operate, and therefore constitute a great vehicle to explore how different continuous representations may capture distinct linguistic and structural features. Previous research has already taken advantage of this property to analyze the behavior of language representation spaces (Nakashole and Flauger, 2018). In this work, we consider three different approaches to unsupervised cross-lingual embedding projection, and explore their interaction with different linguistic characteristics and model features, such as subword encoding and vector space structure. The resulting evaluations are put into context to propose potential improvements to language representation strategies as a whole.

2 Related Work

Modern mapping-based cross-lingual embeddings, which are sometimes also called projection-based embeddings, have become very popular by outperforming earlier mapping methods and many supervised cross-lingual methods that are dependent on segment-level alignment. As many initial mapping-based approaches (Mikolov et al., 2013b; Faruqui and Dyer, 2014), they require monolingual embeddings, but often also a small parallel corpus or a bilingual seed translation dictionary to perform the initial alignment. However, some do not need any parallel signal at all, as they can also perform the original alignment relying only in estimations based on structural similarities between the monolingual vector spaces (Artetxe et al., 2018; Lample et al., 2017). Another family of cross-lingual word embeddings are the so-called pseudo-bilingual word embeddings (Ruder, 2017). These approaches use a concatenation of large monolingual corpora and integrate it with some amount explicit bilingual information – such as replacing translation pairs in the dataset Gouws and Søgaard (2015) or substituting tokens based on their semantic cluster (Ammar et al., 2016) – . Both mapping-based and pseudo-bilingual word embeddings are especially useful for prototyping in extremely low-resource language models when no parallel data is available.

However, cross-lingual embeddings have not been particularly effective in deep neural network pre-training, and often do not seem to represent a significant improvement over using off-the-shelf monolingual embeddings (Qi et al., 2018). In contrast, cross-lingual language models such as BERT (Devlin et al., 2019) have fared better. Some approaches try to create a universal neural language model for all the languages included in a final multilingual system (Ji et al., 2020; Lin et al., 2020). A very successful alternative to these strategies has also been proposed by Lample and Conneau (2019), who create a cross-lingual neural language model by training a masked language model (Devlin et al., 2019) using a shared vocabulary between languages and subsampling frequent outputs as per Mikolov et al. (2013c). Ren et al. (2019) refine this masked language model (MLM) by introducing an explicit cross-language training objective, creating a cross-lingual masked language model (CMLM). Recent research in Wang and Zhao (2021) has obtained top-of-the-line results by using a large-scale CMLM and training the final supervised model using a joint optimization objective (Sun et al., 2019) that aims to maintain the original distribution of the CMLM while maximizing translation performance.

3 Unsupervised Cross-lingual Pre-training

3.1 Unsupervised cross-lingual embeddings

This work explores cross-lingual pre-training through three particular unsupervised cross-lingual embedding methods: VecMap (Artetxe et al., 2018), MUSE (Lample et al., 2017) and embeddings trained over multilingual corpora.

Both VecMap and MUSE are projection-based cross-lingual embeddings. Projection-based CLE generate an alignment between monolingual word embeddings, subsequently projecting them into a common representation space that facilitates a direct mapping between the distribution of both embeddings. The initial alignment is commonly produced using a seed dictionary of translation pairs. However, in some cases these translation pairs are estimated by the cross-lingual method itself. This capacity to generate a common vector space of aligned embeddings with no bilingual signal defines fully unsupervised cross-lingual embeddings.

The specifics behind alignment and projection are also dependent on the general topology of the embeddings that are to be mapped. In this work, all experiments are performed over Word2Vec embeddings, which offers two possible topologies: continuous bag-of-words (CBOW) and skip-gram. The former trains a shallow network to predict a word given an input context, while the latter learns to predict a context window from an input word. In this work, only skip-gram is used for all experiments, particularly skip-gram with negative sampling (SGNS) (Mikolov et al., 2013c).

For VecMap, Artetxe et al. (2018) assume that word translations have approximately identical vectors of monolingual similarity distribution. The proposed method operates on top of this idea, adding empirically motivated enhancements that make the procedure more robust.

In contrast, MUSE (Lample et al., 2017) uses adversarial training to create a generator network able to project word vectors from each monolingual embedding in a way such that it is very difficult to distinguish the space to which they originally belonged, thus achieving a common mapping between both embeddings.

Another approach to cross-lingual embeddings explored in this work are embeddings trained over multilingual corpora. The model proposed in this section is trained on corpora with no alignment or contextual proximity. The procedure is remarkably simple: two monolingual corpora in different languages are concatenated, and a word embedding is trained over the resulting multilingual text. Just as in the previous two methods, the result is a bilingual vector space that tends to group translation candidates close to each other. Therefore, it can also be used as bilingual pre-training for a translation model in the task studied in this work. This approach serves as a baseline to determine how much of the alignment achieved from cross-lingual embeddings is innate to the distribution of both languages and can be extracted with no mapping procedures.

3.2 Cross-lingual Pre-training

The aforementioned cross-lingual embeddings are integrated as pre-training in the input and output embedding layers of a machine translation neural network, in substitution of the embedding transformation that would otherwise be initialized randomly. The model used follows the Transformer architecture proposed by Vaswani et al. (2017), with some slight modifications that are described in detail in section 4.3.4. Although Qi et al. (2018) report that orthogonal alignment was not helpful when pre-training embeddings for an attention-based neural machine translation model, in this work we aim to evaluate new strategies that may influence pre-training performance. Namely, by trying out other state-of-the-art cross-mapping strategies based on orthogonal mapping Lample et al. (2017); Artetxe et al. (2018) and considering techniques that help better transfer and maintain cross-lingual alignment during training, such as using a joint BPE vocabulary or freezing the embedding layers of the translation model.

4 Experimental framework

4.1 Corpora

The corpora used in this work were selected from the data collection provided in the WMT14 Machine Translation shared task[1] (Macháček and Bojar, 2014). This collection of corpora allows to study language similarity as a variable, since all of the language pairs available feature English data aligned with languages with which it presents varying degrees of phylogenetic relatedness and typological similarity. The language pairs chosen are French–English, German–English, Russian–English and Hindi–English. This selection was also motivated by the interesting properties of the relationship triangle formed by English, German and French. English and German are the closest genetic relatives, and both are included in the West Germanic family. While German and English are similarly phylogenetically distant to French according to their classification, French and English share many more typological features. Notably, an estimated 25% of English loanwords come from French (Cannon, 1989). This three-way relationship is interesting because it juxtaposes genetic and typological features, both of which can have different effects over cross-lingual mappings. Additionally, Russian and Hindi provide increasingly more distant languages that help study projection methods for cases with low cross-lingual similarity and different alphabets.

Language	Corpora	Sentences	Tokens
English	News Crawl 2011-2013	51M	1,167M
French	News Crawl 2007-2013	30M	696M
German	News Crawl 2012-2013	55M	970M
Russian	News Crawl 2007-2013	32M	576M
Hindi	News Crawl 2007-2013 + HindMonoCorp 0.5	43M	932M

Table 1: Breakdown of training monolingual corpora sources, number of sentences and total number of tokens by source.

Language pair	Corpora	Sentences	Tokens	
			Source	English
French–English	Europarlv7 + Common Crawl corpus	5M	117M	129M
German–English	Europarlv7 + Common Crawl corpus	4.1M	99M	94M
Russian–English	Common Crawl corpus + Yandex 1M corpus v1.3	1.8M	41M	39.5M
Hindi–English	HindiEnCorp 0.5	0.26M	2.6M	4.1M

Table 2: Breakdown of training parallel corpora sources, number of sentences and total number of tokens by source.

The monolingual training set, which is described in Table 1, also includes a corpus outside the WMT14 set, HindMonoCorp (Bojar et al., 2014) collections. This dataset was added in order to keep a roughly similar volume of training data between all monolingual corpora, which is especially important for embedding cross-mapping procedures. Similarly, parallel corpora have been built by combining different corpora in such a way that the volume of data is comparable across all languages, as shown in Table 2

For all datasets, the following pre-processing steps have been applied: 1. Normalization of unicode punctuation encoding; 2. Tokenization; 3. Clean and eliminate empty sentences, those containing more than 60 words, and sentences with a source-target ratio greater than 1-9.

[1] `https://www.statmt.org/wmt14/translation-task.html`

4.2 Evaluation Metrics

4.2.1 Bilingual Lexicon Induction

The quality of the different cross-lingual representations generated is evaluated according to their bilingual lexicon induction (BLI) performance. As in Artetxe et al. (2018), this is calculated as the average accuracy of the induced cross-lingual vector space in a word translation task for a ground-truth bilingual dictionary, which in this work will be referred to as word translation accuracy. The evaluation only considers the source language words from this bilingual ground-truth dictionary that are also included in the vocabulary of the source language embedding. For each of these source language words, the closest word vector in the target embedding is found and taken as the most likely translation. The procedure then compares the translations obtained with this method and those provided by the bilingual dictionary, taking as correct the translation induced from the cross-lingual space if the target language closest vector is included in the list of possible translations that appears in the bilingual dictionary. The distance between word vectors is calculated using cross-domain similarity local scaling (CSLS), proposed by Lample et al. (2017). The ground-truth bilingual dictionaries used are provided by the MUSE toolkit[2], specifically those belonging to the "full" set. The purpose of this evaluation is not to obtain a state-of-the-art unsupervised BLI system. Instead, it is to assess the interactions of the different cross-mapping methodologies studied in this work with the different degrees of language similarities present in each of the language pairs.

4.2.2 Machine Translation

As mentioned previously, the generated cross-lingual embeddings are also assessed on their utility as pre-training embeddings. To this end, they are integrated in a Transformer-based machine translation model, which then receives limited training and is evaluated using multi-BLEU as provided by the Moses toolkit (Koehn et al., 2007).

4.3 Model Configuration

4.3.1 BPE

In some experiments, Byte Pair Encoding (BPE), particularly the subword-level adaptation of this method proposed by Sennrich et al. (2015), is applied to the corpora in order to study its effect in the performance of cross-lingual embedding mappings. BPE encodings build a shared subword-level vocabulary for the source and target language corpora, which reduces the total size of the vocabulary. Moreover, it allows the model to represent words not seen during training by combining subword units. As a result, some lexical information is transferred more effectively between languages, particularly in the case of certain word classes such as proper nouns, compounds, cognates and loanwords (Sennrich et al., 2015). The number of merge operations used in BPE is its single determining hyperparameter, which governs vocabulary size. Gowda and May (2020) show that large vocabulary sizes only maximize BLEU performance when using vast datasets with 4.5M sentences. However, since our monolingual datasets are all far bigger, and given that for Transformer-based neural machine translation it is recommended the largest possible BPE vocabulary (Gowda and May, 2020), we opt to guarantee a large vocabulary by using 48,000 merge operations.

4.3.2 Embeddings

All skip-gram word embeddings used in the experiments proposed in this work are trained during 5 epochs with a learning rate of 0.05. Changes in epoch size have not had any significant effect, as the corpora used to train the embeddings is sufficiently large and does not require of more training cycles. The main parameter to study when training the embeddings has been

[2]https://github.com/facebookresearch/MUSE

their dimension. A range of values between 100 and 1000, with steps of size 100, is used to examine the effect of embedding dimension in unsupervised cross-lingual methods. The results are displayed in Figure 1 as an evolution of the BLI performance of the model relative to the dimensionality of the embeddings.

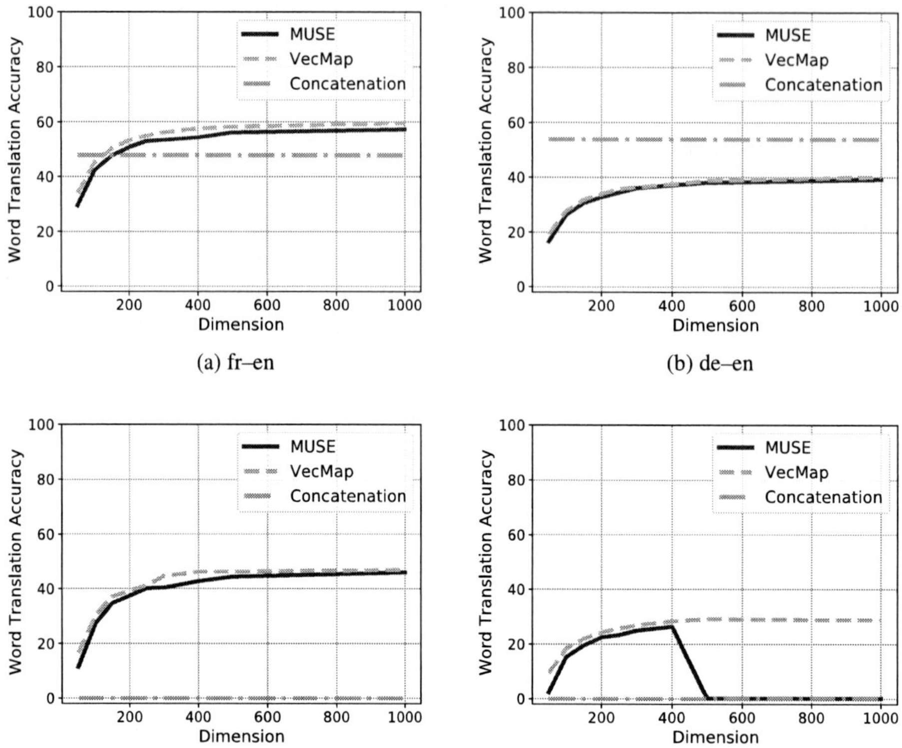

(a) fr–en

(b) de–en

(c) ru–en

(d) hi–en

Figure 1: BLI performance evolution for each language pair and cross-mapping method according to the dimension of the monolingual embeddings. Each plot corresponds to a language pair, and the different series to one of the cross-mapping approaches considered.

In the case of the cross-mapping strategies of VecMap and MUSE, BLI increases rapidly with dimension up to close to 300 dimensions. From here on to 500 dimensions, performance still seems to be correlated to dimension, and it only sees very marginal growth from this point. This behavior is in line with the directives originally given for Word2Vec embeddings (Mikolov et al., 2013a). However, as seen in the section (d) of figure 1, relative to the hi–en language pair, it seems that increasing the dimension of the embeddings past a certain point may affect the viability of learning an effective cross-lingual projection for the adversarial approach in MUSE. In the absence of additional experiments with a larger number of distant languages, it is hypothesized that using too many dimensions while dealing with a complicated projection between very different languages that do not even share a common alphabet can lead to a failure in learning a reasonable projection matrix. VecMap is not affected by this phenomenon for the showcased experiments, which may be due to the use of ZCA whitening (Bell and Sejnowski, 1997), which encourages exploring dimensions that may not fit the current solution to help escape poor local optima.

Lastly, in the case of embeddings trained over concatenation of monolingual corpora, dimension does not affect significantly their BLI score as a cross-lingual model. This can be attributed to the fact that the implicit bilingual alignment in which this method relies is not influenced by any transformations or projections of the vector space, so long as the distance between points is measured with a dimension-invariant metric. This work uses CSLS to measure word translation accuracy between embeddings, which relies only on cosine similarity between the embedding vectors, a metric that remains unaffected by dimension scaling.

Since the embeddings used in this work will be integrated is a Transformer neural network in charge of machine translation, a dimension value of 512 has been chosen for them. This is in the range where cross-lingual performance is stabilized, while being a common encoder-decoder dimension value for Transformer-derived machine translation models (Vaswani et al., 2017; Lample and Conneau, 2019).

4.3.3 Cross-lingual mappings

Both the MUSE and Vecmap cross-mapping techniques have a number of parameters that dictate some of the characteristics of the alignment procedure. For VecMap we use the standard unsupervised configuration, which is equivalent to that of the models presented in VecMap, Artetxe et al. (2018). The maximum vocabulary is set to 20,000 words, the vocabulary used to generate the initial unsupervised translation table is limited to 4,000 words, the CSLS neighborhood used for vector distance calculations is of size 10 and the embeddings are normalized before the cross-mapping is initiated. In contrast, all MUSE cross-mappings are performed using the default unsupervised parameters. The only explicit adjustments made are the maximum size of vocabulary considered, which is set to 20,000, and the number of word vectors used for discrimination, which is set to the 7,500 more frequent words. Distance between vectors is calculated using a CSLS neighborhood of size 10, and the embeddings are normalized before the cross-mapping process begins. Memory limitations for the available setup meant that reproducing the VecMap benchmark was far easier than that of MUSE, and these changes were made to keep VecMap and MUSE running over with as similar of a set of parameters as possible.

4.3.4 Neural Machine Translation Pre-training

For the neural machine translation model that integrates cross-lingual embeddings for pre-training, we rely on an OpenNMT-py (Klein et al., 2017) model that mimics the original Transformer architecture proposed by Vaswani et al. (2017). It contains a stack of 6 encoder and 6 decoder layers . Each encoder layer includes positional encoding, 8 attention heads and a dense feed-forward network. The decoders use instead an initial masked multi-head attention layers that receives the shifted outputs, followed by another multi-head attention layer that is fed by the output of the encoder stack, and have a final feed-forward layer. All feed-forward layers and attention heads use a dropout probability of 0.1, and rely on the Adam optimization criterion (Kingma and Ba, 2015). The feed-forward layers have been changed to have a dimension of 1,024 units from the original 2,048 present in Vaswani et al. (2017). This accelerates model training and does not massively impact performance for models that are not trained extensively (Lample and Conneau, 2019). Similarly, the number of training steps is reduced from 200,000 to 20,000 maintaining a batch size of 4,096 tokens, as a compromise between training cost and minimum performance of the model to allow for pre-training integration.

5 Results and Discussion

5.1 Cross-lingual models

5.1.1 BPE

In the past, Lample et al. (2017) have shown that BPE (Sennrich et al., 2015) improves considerably the alignment of monolingual language spaces, particularly for cases where the languages share the same alphabet or anchor tokens (Smith et al., 2017). Anchor tokens are words with equivalent meaning that are written identically across languages and are therefore common vocabulary to both languages, such as proper nouns of places, organizations or people, acronyms, loanwords and digits.

Model	Dimension	BPE	Word Translation Accuracy			
			fr–en	de–en	ru–en	hi–en
MUSE	512	No	56.2	38.1	44.3	0.1
MUSE	512	Yes	62.2	41.4	0.1	42.3
VecMap	512	No	58.2	38.8	46.2	29.2
VecMap	512	Yes	**65.0**	46.2	**60.0**	**44.8**
Concatenation	512	No	47.7	**53.8**	0	0
Concatenation	512	Yes	46.6	45.3	0	0

Table 3: Results obtained for the best cross-lingual embeddings selected for neural model pretraining. Accuracy is measured comparing pairs from ground-truth bilingual dictionaries and employing CSLS as distance metric.

Table 3 illustrates the effect of BPE on the BLI performance of the generated cross-lingual embeddings. BPE usage seems to generally improve the score of the projection-based mappings, while having a slightly negative or non-existent influence on embeddings trained over concatenation of monolingual corpora. While the former result is expected (Lample et al., 2017), the latter phenomenon is more interesting, and can be explained by the fact that these embeddings are jointly learning both languages, but no cross-mapping is performed, so the relative position of words in the representation space should remain similar whether subword information is captured or not. In many cases there may be a certain loss of semantic information when creating a shared byte-paired encoding between languages (Ren et al., 2019). Since they will not will be compensated by the subword features that are retrieved – as the approach does not take advantage of them – , the overall effect of BPE tends to be negative.

The impact of BPE is especially significant for the MUSE mapping in language pairs ru–en and hi–en. In the case of ru–en, the use of this tokenization approach apparently does not allow for any sensible alignment, unlike the projection that uses non-BPE embeddings, which performs fine. A likely explanation for this is that Russian and English do not use the same alphabet or share many common words and anchor tokens. Therefore, almost no joint subword information is learned, while some semantic features may be diluted (Ren et al., 2019). However, the hi–en pair in Table 3 shows the opposite phenomenon, where the application of BPE has made possible a previously unavailable alignment. This case is especially puzzling, since Hindi also uses a completely different alphabet from that of English there should be very little transfer of information between the subword vocabularies. Upon closer inspection, both BPE vocabularies for ru–en and hi–en have a very similar size, which indicates that this behavior is not a function of semantic diversity. Moreover, the size of the common lexicon found in the training corpus between English and Hindi is an order of magnitude lower than that of English and Russian[3], which puts into question really how relevant anchor tokens are when it comes to generating a joint BPE vocabulary. A possible explanation for this phenomenon could be that the generated vector spaces simply have a slightly different distribution when using BPE, which can affect the chances of finding a good projection into a common bilingual space for the embeddings. The VecMap projection does not seem to be affected in the same way, which could be due to it having a more robust initialization and being able to escape local optima better than MUSE, as shown in (Vulic et al., 2019; Glavaš et al., 2019).

5.1.2 Language similarity

Table 3 showcases the performance of the considered cross-lingual models for all language pairs. Language similarity does seem to be somewhat indicative of BLI performance, although a weak signal at that.

The fr–en language pair is the best performing one across the board, especially for the projection-based alignments. This is expected, since these methods are reliant on semantic similarities. They also make great use of anchor tokens in their initial unsupervised dictionary induction (Lample et al., 2017), of which there are plenty in the English–French pair.

Although English and German are phylogenetically closer to each other, the performance for this pair is inferior to that of English and French for MUSE and VecMap. In contrast, embeddings trained over a concatenation of monolingual corpora surpass projection-based cross-maping methods, and their own BLI score for the fr–en pair. French and English share many anchor tokens, whereas German and English have a noticeably smaller common vocabulary, but show a greater degree of similarity in other typological features common in languages from the same family tree, such as word ordering or verbal categorization. Since for the concatenation strategy the pair de–en is actually performing better than fr–en, it can be hypothesized that the natural alignment resulting of training embedding over multilingual text is more sensible to other typological categories. This is especially likely for word ordering, since the skip-gram architecture is learning to predict contexts in a reduced local window (Mikolov et al., 2013a,c), which is sensible to large discrepancies in sentence structure.

For the ru–en and hi–en pairs, training embeddings over a multilingual corpus seems to produce no alignment whatsoever, as the selected languages do not share a common alphabet. However, both of the projection-based cross-lingual techniques, ru–en and hi–en are shown to be competitive with de–en. This casts some doubts on which are actually the typological features that govern explicit cross-linguality, since by all accounts German should be more semantically and grammatically similar to English than Russian or Hindi (Georgi et al., 2010). Further research that isolates typological features for cross-lingual evaluation is needed in order to produce meaningful guidelines on the adaptation of cross-lingual models according to language similarity, though the experiments show that semantic relatedness is not the only factor at play.

Overall, VecMap has been shown to be the best performing cross-lingual method and also the most robust one when dealing with distant languages, which is consistent with previous research (Vulic et al., 2019; Glavaš et al., 2019). MUSE appears to be generally weaker for cases where inducing an initial translation table is more difficult due to low language similarity, though seems to perform fine when this phase is completed successfully, which is a common trend in projection-based cross-lingual methods. Remarkably, training word embeddings over a concatenation of monolingual corpora outperforms projection-based methods for the de–en pair, although is not effective for distantly related languages. From this it can be inferred that some features learned by skip-gram word embeddings during training are valuable when it

[3]For 1M sentences considered, where numeric tokens have been discarded, there are around 11,800 common tokens for the ru–en pair, but only 1,670 for hi–en.

comes to producing an alignment and, like many other typological characteristics, are not being considered by current explicit cross-mapping methods but could prove to be valuable.

5.2 Neural machine translation pre-training

Pre-trained embeddings			Frozen embeddings	BLEU			
Cross-mapping	Dimension	BPE		fr–en	de–en	ru–en	hi–en
(None)	512	Yes	No	**34.1**	25.4	28.7	6.1
(None)	512	Yes	Yes	32.1	23.6	26.8	5.8
MUSE	512	Yes	No	33.9	26.0	29.4	6.7
MUSE	512	Yes	Yes	32.2	24.3	27.9	6.1
VecMap	512	Yes	No	33.4	**26.3**	30.0	**9.2**
VecMap	512	Yes	Yes	32.4	24.1	28.9	8.4
Concatenation	512	Yes	No	33.5	25.5	**30.2**	6.6
Concatenation	512	Yes	Yes	33.1	24.9	29.6	6.2

Table 4: Results obtained for the best Transformer translation models that use pre-trained vectors. Cross-mapping is indicated as (None) when no explicit cross-lingual technique is applied to the pre-trained word embeddings.

5.2.1 Freezing embeddings

As indicated in Sun et al. (2019) and Wang and Zhao (2021), embeddings used as the encoder-decoder pieces of an attention-based neural network tend to degenerate as the global model is fine-tuned for a particular task, which for this work corresponds to machine translation. For this reason, it has been decided to assess the impact of freezing the encoder and decoder embeddings during training. The results are shown in Table 4. Freezing the pre-trained embeddings does not improve BLEU performance in comparison with models that do modify the weights of their encoder and decoder during supervised training, which score slightly better. This effect is in line with prior work (Sun et al., 2019; Wang and Zhao, 2021), which shows that the integrated model needs to modify the pre-trained components during fine tuning to maximize its performance, but this behavior tends to break the cross-lingual alignment created previously. As a result, they propose to optimize supervised training based on two different objectives: maintaining the structural correspondence of the initial pre-trained components and maximizing the translation objective. Though the implementation of this strategy is not readily available for general use – which is the reason why they have not been considered for these experiments – , they have been shown to be the best current approach to transfer cross-lingual knowledge in pre-training.

5.2.2 Cross-linguality

The effect of cross-linguality in the pre-trained embeddings is relatively low across the board. We think that this could be attributed to two main factors. First, as shown by Qi et al. (2018), most of the increase in performance provided by pre-trained embeddings can usually be attributed to a better encoding of the source sentence. Since the cross-lingual alignment contained in the embeddings does not aid significantly in this task, the overall performance may not increase much. The second is the degeneration phenomenon (Sun et al., 2019), which distorts the structure of the embeddings during training, and therefore their cross-lingual alignment.

Still, the cross-ling projection-based cross-lingual methods showcase some amount of improvement, that seems to increase the more distant the languages are. This result can seem counter-intuitive at first, since BLI performance is generally a strong indicator of performance for a pre-training method in translation models. Such a behavior is shown in Lample and Conneau (2019), where cross-lingual language models outperform unsupervised cross-lingual embeddings both in terms of BLI performance and effectiveness as pre-training strategy. However, we should keep in mind that the scenarios involving distant language pairs correspond to the cases where cross-lingual alignments have the biggest impact on the global structure on the embeddings. For similar source and target languages, the projection learned by the neural network is of higher quality, and therefore initialization is less relevant. In contrast, translation of distant language pairs requires that the model learns a more complex projection, and therefore in this case it benefits more from a stronger initialization. This is in line with previous claims on the importance of initialization in attention-based encoder-decoder translation models (Devlin et al., 2019; Liu et al., 2020), and the results derived from cross-lingual language models such as that of Lample and Conneau (2019). It most importantly also suggests that initialization is a factor that can limit the quality of a translation model even when de facto unlimited training data and time is available. Recent advances on cross-lingual language models appear to follow this trend by consistently improving substantially on translation models for distant language pairs (Wang and Zhao, 2021).

6 Conclusions

This work makes use of fully unsupervised cross-lingual models to explore some of the factors that affect the performance of cross-lingual methods. The experimental results showcase agreement with prior publications regarding the usefulness of subword information in cross-linguality, and suggest that character-level encoding might be especially relevant for language pairs of low similarity. Moreover, reveal that phylogenetic relatedness should not be directly taken to dictate cross-lingual performance, and that purely semantic similarity is not the only typological feature captured by projection-based mappings.

Cross-lingual transfer remains ineffective even if the structure of the pre-trained encoder and decoder is fixed during fine-tuning, which is indicative of the degeneration of cross-lingual projections in supervised training, and the limited scope of pre-trained embeddings. Current pre-training approaches that rely on joint optimization appears to be the most promising approach going forward.

Future research may benefit from designing strategies that adapt cross-mapping methods to different language pairs according to their features, and that are able to capture typological information that is currently lost. Model initialization seems to be a fundamental factor that is able to limit machine translation ceiling, especially for long distance pairs.

Acknowledgements

This work received funds from the Generalitat Valenciana under project DeepPattern (PROMETEO 2019/121).

References

Ammar, W., Mulcaire, G., Ballesteros, M., Dyer, C., and Smith, N. A. (2016). Many languages, one parser. *Transactions of the Association for Computational Linguistics*, 4:431–444.

Artetxe, M., Labaka, G., and Agirre, E. (2018). A robust self-learning method for fully unsupervised cross-lingual mappings of word embeddings. In *Proceedings of the 56th Annual Meeting of the Association for Computational Linguistics (Volume 1: Long Papers)*, pages 789–798.

Artetxe, M., Ruder, S., Yogatama, D., Labaka, G., and Agirre, E. (2020). A call for more rigor in unsupervised cross-lingual learning. *CoRR*, abs/2004.14958.

Bell, A. J. and Sejnowski, T. J. (1997). The 'independent components' of natural scenes are edge filters. *Vision Research*, 37(23):3327–38.

Bojar, O., Diatka, V., Rychlý, P., Straňák, P., Suchomel, V., Tamchyna, A., and Zeman, D. (2014). HindMonoCorp 0.5. LINDAT/CLARIAH-CZ digital library at the Institute of Formal and Applied Linguistics, Faculty of Mathematics and Physics, Charles University.

Cannon, G. (1989). Historical change and english word-formation : recent vocabulary. *Language*, 65:880.

Devlin, J., Chang, M.-W., Lee, K., and Toutanova, K. (2019). BERT: Pre-training of deep bidirectional transformers for language understanding. In *Proceedings of the 2019 Conference of the North American Chapter of the Association for Computational Linguistics: Human Language Technologies, Volume 1 (Long and Short Papers)*, pages 4171–4186.

Doval, Y., Camacho-Collados, J., Anke, L. E., and Schockaert, S. (2019). On the robustness of unsupervised and semi-supervised cross-lingual word embedding learning. *CoRR*, abs/1908.07742.

Faruqui, M. and Dyer, C. (2014). Improving vector space word representations using multilingual correlation. In *Proceedings of the 14th Conference of the European Chapter of the Association for Computational Linguistics*, pages 462–471.

Georgi, R., Xia, F., and Lewis, W. (2010). Comparing language similarity across genetic and typologically-based groupings. In *Proceedings of the 23rd International Conference on Computational Linguistics*, pages 385–393.

Glavaš, G., Litschko, R., Ruder, S., and Vulić, I. (2019). How to (properly) evaluate cross-lingual word embeddings: On strong baselines, comparative analyses, and some misconceptions. In *Proceedings of the 57th Annual Meeting of the Association for Computational Linguistics*, pages 710–721.

Gouws, S. and Søgaard, A. (2015). Simple task-specific bilingual word embeddings. In *Proceedings of the 2015 Conference of the North American Chapter of the Association for Computational Linguistics: Human Language Technologies*, pages 1386–1390. Association for Computational Linguistics.

Gowda, T. and May, J. (2020). Finding the optimal vocabulary size for neural machine translation. In *Findings of the Association for Computational Linguistics: EMNLP 2020*, pages 3955–3964, Online. Association for Computational Linguistics.

Ji, B., Zhang, Z., Duan, X., Zhang, M., Chen, B., and Luo, W. (2020). Cross-lingual pre-training based transfer for zero-shot neural machine translation. *Proceedings of the AAAI Conference on Artificial Intelligence*, 34(01):115–122.

Kingma, D. P. and Ba, J. (2015). Adam: A method for stochastic optimization. *CoRR*, abs/1412.6980.

Klein, G., Kim, Y., Deng, Y., Senellart, J., and Rush, A. (2017). OpenNMT: Open-source toolkit for neural machine translation. In *Proceedings of the 55th Annual Meeting of the Association for Computational Linguistics*, pages 67–72.

Koehn, P., Hoang, H., Birch, A., Callison-Burch, C., Federico, M., Bertoldi, N., Cowan, B., Shen, W., Moran, C., Zens, R., Dyer, C., Bojar, O., Constantin, A., and Herbst, E. (2007). Moses: Open source toolkit for statistical machine translation. In *Proceedings of the 45th Annual Meeting of the Association for Computational Linguistics Companion Volume Proceedings of the Demo and Poster Sessions*, pages 177–180.

Lample, G. and Conneau, A. (2019). Cross-lingual language model pretraining. *CoRR*, abs/1901.07291.

Lample, G., Denoyer, L., and Ranzato, M. (2017). Unsupervised machine translation using monolingual corpora only. *CoRR*, abs/1711.00043.

Lin, Z., Pan, X., Wang, M., Qiu, X., Feng, J., Zhou, H., and Li, L. (2020). Pre-training multilingual neural machine translation by leveraging alignment information. In *Proceedings of the 2020 Conference on Empirical Methods in Natural Language Processing*, pages 2649–2663.

Liu, Y., Gu, J., Goyal, N., Li, X., Edunov, S., Ghazvininejad, M., Lewis, M., and Zettlemoyer, L. (2020). Multilingual denoising pre-training for neural machine translation. *CoRR*, abs/2001.08210.

Macháček, M. and Bojar, O. (2014). Results of the WMT14 metrics shared task. In *Proceedings of the Ninth Workshop on Statistical Machine Translation*, pages 293–301.

Mikolov, T., Chen, K., Corrado, G., and Dean, J. (2013a). Efficient estimation of word representations in vector space. *1st International Conference on Learning Representations, Workshop Track Proceedings. CoRR*, abs/1301.3781.

Mikolov, T., Le, Q. V., and Sutskever, I. (2013b). Exploiting Similarities among Languages for Machine Translation. *CoRR*, abs/1309.4168.

Mikolov, T., Sutskever, I., Chen, K., Corrado, G., and Dean, J. (2013c). Distributed representations of words and phrases and their compositionality. *CoRR*, abs/1310.4546.

Nakashole, N. and Flauger, R. (2018). Characterizing departures from linearity in word translation. In *Proceedings of the 56th Annual Meeting of the Association for Computational Linguistics (Volume 2: Short Papers)*, pages 221–227.

Patra, B., Moniz, J. R. A., Garg, S., Gormley, M. R., and Neubig, G. (2019). Bilingual lexicon induction with semi-supervision in non-isometric embedding spaces. In *Proceedings of the 57th Annual Meeting of the Association for Computational Linguistics*, pages 184–193.

Qi, Y., Sachan, D. S., Felix, M., Padmanabhan, S. J., and Neubig, G. (2018). When and why are pre-trained word embeddings useful for neural machine translation? *CoRR*, abs/1804.06323.

Ren, S., Wu, Y., Liu, S., Zhou, M., and Ma, S. (2019). Explicit cross-lingual pre-training for unsupervised machine translation. *CoRR*, abs/1909.00180.

Ruder, S. (2017). A survey of cross-lingual embedding models. *CoRR*, abs/1706.04902.

Sennrich, R., Haddow, B., and Birch, A. (2015). Neural machine translation of rare words with subword units. *CoRR*, abs/1508.07909.

Smith, S. L., Turban, D. H. P., Hamblin, S., and Hammerla, N. Y. (2017). Offline bilingual word vectors, orthogonal transformations and the inverted softmax. *CoRR*, abs/1702.03859.

Sun, H., Wang, R., Chen, K., Utiyama, M., Sumita, E., and Zhao, T. (2019). Unsupervised bilingual word embedding agreement for unsupervised neural machine translation. In *Proceedings of the 57th Annual Meeting of the Association for Computational Linguistics*, pages 1235–1245.

Vaswani, A., Shazeer, N., Parmar, N., Uszkoreit, J., Jones, L., Gomez, A. N., Kaiser, L., and Polosukhin, I. (2017). Attention is all you need. *CoRR*, abs/1706.03762.

Vulic, I., Glavas, G., Reichart, R., and Korhonen, A. (2019). Do we really need fully unsupervised cross-lingual embeddings? *CoRR*, abs/1909.01638.

Wang, R. and Zhao, H. (2021). Advances and challenges in unsupervised neural machine translation. In *Proceedings of the 16th Conference of the European Chapter of the Association for Computational Linguistics: Tutorial Abstracts*, pages 17–21.

Few-Shot Regularization to Tackle Catastrophic Forgetting in Multilingual Machine Translation

Salvador Carrión salcarpo@prhlt.upv.es
Francisco Casacuberta fcn@prhlt.upv.es
PRHLT Research Center, Universitat Politècnica de València

Abstract

Increasing the number of tasks supported by a machine learning model without forgetting previously learned tasks is the goal of any lifelong learning system. In this work, we study how to mitigate the effects of the catastrophic forgetting problem to sequentially train a multilingual neural machine translation model using minimal past information. First, we describe the catastrophic forgetting phenomenon as a function of the number of tasks learned (language pairs) and the ratios of past data used during the learning of the new task. Next, we explore the importance of applying oversampling strategies for scenarios where only minimal amounts of past data are available. Finally, we derive a new loss function that minimizes the forgetting of previously learned tasks by actively re-weighting past samples and penalizing weights that deviate too much from the original model. Our work suggests that by using minimal amounts of past data and a simple regularization function, we can significantly mitigate the effects of the catastrophic forgetting phenomenon without increasing the computational costs.

1 Introduction

The catastrophic forgetting is the phenomenon whereby a neural network forgets previously learned information after learning new one (McCloskey and Cohen, 1989).

Given the ubiquity nature of machine learning models in our lives, tackling the catastrophic forgetting phenomenon is a problem of particular interest for the industry as machine learning models tend to lose performance over time due to the changing nature of our world. To counteract this problem, researchers and engineers must periodically re-train these models. However, despite the inefficiency of re-training a large model from scratch and the carbon footprint that this practice entails in the long run, previous training data is not always available due to privacy issues, licensing, data losses, or simply, because the training data is not available.

This problem is incredibly challenging since any learning system with a limited amount of memory will, at some point, have to forget past information in order to keep learning new information (Carpenter and Grossberg, 1987). Fortunately, we can develop mechanisms so that our machine learning models can selectively forget as little information as possible by penalizing changes in weights that deviate too much from a reference model (Li and Hoiem, 2016; Kirkpatrick et al., 2016), designing dynamic architectures that grow linearly with the number of tasks (Rusu et al., 2016; Draelos et al., 2016), or using Complementary Learning Systems (CLS) that, inspired by how the human brain work, generate synthetic data to control the forgetting (Kemker and Kanan, 2017).

From a practical point of view, these approaches tend to be quite hard to implement and often are very computationally intensive. In addition, most of these strategies are not specifically designed for natural language tasks, making their implementation even more difficult. Therefore, we decided to tackle the catastrophic forgetting problem in machine translation, framed as a sequential learning problem for a multilingual machine translation system, where each new task is a different language pair (English-Spanish, English-French, English-German, and English-Czech).

The contributions of this work are the following:

- First, we describe the catastrophic forgetting phenomenon in machine translation as a function of the tasks learned (language pairs) and the ratios of past data used during the learning of the new task, and show that even with minimal amounts of past data we can significantly mitigate these effects.
- Next, we explore the effectiveness of oversampling strategies, where we show that they are particularly useful for scenarios where only minimal amounts of past data are available.
- Finally, we derive a new loss function that minimizes the forgetting of past tasks using a few-shot strategy based on actively re-weighting past tasks and penalizing weights that deviate too much from the original model.

2 Related Work

The *Catastrophic Forgetting* (CF) phenomenon has been widely studied since it was introduced for the first time by McCloskey and Cohen (1989). However, despite the numerous works that have delved into the root causes that produce it (Carpenter and Grossberg, 1987), these findings could be reduced to the stability-plasticity dilemma, whereby there is a trade-off between the ability of a model to preserve past knowledge (stability) and the ability to learn new information effectively (plasticity).

Given this dilemma, most approaches are based on adjusting the network weights during training to control the forgetting of the model, expanding the model's capacity to support new tasks, or using some refreshing mechanism to remember past tasks.

For example, Li and Hoiem (2016) presented a model with shared parameters across tasks and task-specific parameters; Kirkpatrick et al. (2016) identified which weights were important for the past tasks so that they could penalize the updates on those weights; Jung et al. (2016) penalized changes in the final hidden layer; Zenke et al. (2017) introduced the concept of intelligent synapses that accumulate task-relevant information; Hu et al. (2019) trained a model with a set of parameters that was shared by all tasks and the second set of parameters that were dynamically generated to adapt the model to each new task. However, despite the number of works, these strategies are constrained by the model's capacity (Kaplan et al., 2020).

To deal with this issue, many researchers decided to focus their efforts on linearly expanding the model's capacity as the number of tasks grows. Accordingly, (Rusu et al., 2016) retained a pool of pre-trained models throughout training to learn lateral connections for the new task; (Draelos et al., 2016), which was inspired by the neurogenesis in the hippocampus of the brain decided to add new neurons to deep layers so that novel information could be acquired more efficiently; and (Lee et al., 2017a) introduced an architecture that dynamically controls the network capacity.

Similarly, other researchers have addressed this problem by using data from past tasks during the training of new tasks, such as Lopez-Paz and Ranzato (2017), who proposed a model that alleviates the catastrophic forgetting problem by storing a subset of the observed examples from an old task (episodic memory), and Shin et al. (2017), who instead of storing actual training data from past tasks, trained a deep generative model that replayed past data (synthetically) during training to prevent forgetting.

In addition to these works, there are others worth to mention due to their results and original approaches, such as iCaRL (Rebuffi et al., 2016), PathNet (Fernando et al., 2017), FearNet (Kemker and Kanan, 2017), IMM (Lee et al., 2017b) or MAS (Aljundi et al., 2017).

Nonetheless, despite the progress made on lifelong learning strategies and the recent breakthroughs in the natural language field (Sutskever et al., 2014; Sennrich et al., 2016; Vaswani et al., 2017; Zhang et al., 2019), the catastrophic forgetting problem has not been so widely studied in the field of machine translation. Along these lines, Xu et al. (2018) proposed a meta-learning method that exploits knowledge from past domains to generate improved embeddings for a new domain; Qi et al. (2018) showed that pre-trained embeddings could be effective in low-resource scenarios; Liu et al. (2019) learned corpus-dependent features by sequentially updating sentence encoders (previously initialized with the help of corpus-independent features) using Boolean operations of conceptor matrices; Sato et al. (2020) presented a method to adapt the embeddings between domains by projecting the target embeddings into the source space, and then fine-tuning them on the target domain; Garcia et al. (2021) introduced a vocabulary adaptation scheme to extend the language capacity of multilingual machine translation models; and more recently, Thompson et al. (2019) adapted the Elastic Weight Consolidation method (Kirkpatrick et al., 2016) to mitigate the drop in general-domain performance of NMT models.

3 Models

3.1 Transformer architecture

Neural encoder-decoder architectures such as the Transformer (Vaswani et al., 2017) are the current standard in Machine Translation (Barrault et al., 2020), and most Natural Language Tasks (Devlin et al., 2018).

This state-of-the-art architecture is based entirely on the concept of *attention* (Bahdanau et al., 2015; Luong et al., 2015) to draw global dependencies between the input and output. Because of this, it can process all its sequences in parallel and achieve significant performance improvements compared to previous architectures (Sutskever et al., 2014; Cho et al., 2014; Wu et al., 2016). Furthermore, this architecture does not use any recurrent layer to deal with temporal sequences. Instead, it uses a mask-based approach along with positional embeddings to encode the temporal information of its sequences.

4 Experimental setup

4.1 Datasets

The data used for this work comes from the Europarl dataset (See Table 1), which contain parallel sentences extracted from the European Parliament website[1].

Dataset	Languages	Train size	Val/Test size
Europarl	en-es	100K	1000
Europarl	en-fr	100K	1000
Europarl	en-de	100K	1000
Europarl	en-cz	100K	1000

Table 1: Datasets partitions. In order to avoid potential biases during the experimentation, each dataset was forced to contain 100,000 sentences.

[1]Europarl dataset: `https://www.statmt.org/europarl/`

4.2 Training details

First, all language pairs were concatenated to train a multilingual vocabulary based on Unigrams (Kudo, 2018), with a size of 16,000 tokens plus another 256 for byte-fallback, using SentencePiece (Kudo and Richardson, 2018). Moreover, to avoid language biases, all language pairs had the same number of sentences (and a similar amount of tokens).

To train our models, we used AutoNMT (Carrión and Casacuberta, 2022), a tool to streamline the research of seq2seq models, by automating the preprocessing, training, and evaluation of NMT models. Specifically, we used a simplified version of the standard Transformer with around 4.1M to 25M parameters depending on the vocabulary size. This small Transformer consisted of 3 layers, 8 heads, 256 for the embedding dimension, and 512 for the feedforward layer. Similarly, the training hyper-parameters were quite standard for all models: CrossEntropy (without label smoothing), Adam as the optimizer, 4096 tokens/batch or a batch of 128 sentences, max token length of 150, clip-norm of 1.0, a maximum epoch of 50 epochs with early stopping (patience=10).

The training order was always the same: 1) English-Spanish; 2) English-French; 3) English-German; and 4) English-Czech. Similarly, all models were evaluated for each language pair plus an additional one, where all pairs were merged.

All training was done using two NVIDIA GeForce RTX 2080, with 8GB each.

4.3 Evaluation metrics

Automatic metrics compute the quality of a model by comparing its output with a reference translation written by a human.

Given that BLEU (Papineni et al., 2002) is the most popular metric for machine translation, but it is pretty sensitive to chosen parameters and implementation, we used SacreBLEU (Post, 2018), the reference BLEU implementation for the WMT conference. Additionally, we contrasted our results using BERTScore (Zhang et al., 2019).

- **BiLingual Evaluation Understudy (BLEU)**: Computes a similarity score between the machine translation and one or several reference translations, based on the n-gram precision and a penalty for short translations.

5 Experimentation

5.1 Characterizing the catastrophic forgetting in Machine Translation

In this experiment, we trained a multilingual machine translation (MNMT) model sequentially to study the effects of the catastrophic forgetting phenomenon, as a function of the number of tasks learned (language pairs) and the ratios of past data used during the learning of the new task.

To do so, we began by training a base model for the English-Spanish pair alone (Task #1). Then, we re-trained it using the English-French pair (Task #2) and the English-German pair (Task #3). Later, we added the English-Czech pair (Task #4) for completeness. For each of these tasks, we trained several models for which we varied the ratio of past data that those models could see during the learning of the new task (interleaved data). Finally, we trained another multilingual model using all language pairs (en-es/fr/de) at once to serve as a comparison against the multilingual NMT model trained sequentially.

In Figure 1 we have the results of this experiment. The rows indicate the task being learned, and the columns show the performance of each model for each of the past tasks during the learning of the new task. Moreover, the values annotated at the end of each line indicate the ratio of past data used per batch during the learning of the new task. By looking at Figure 1, we can see that after training for the English-Spanish task, the model achieved a performance

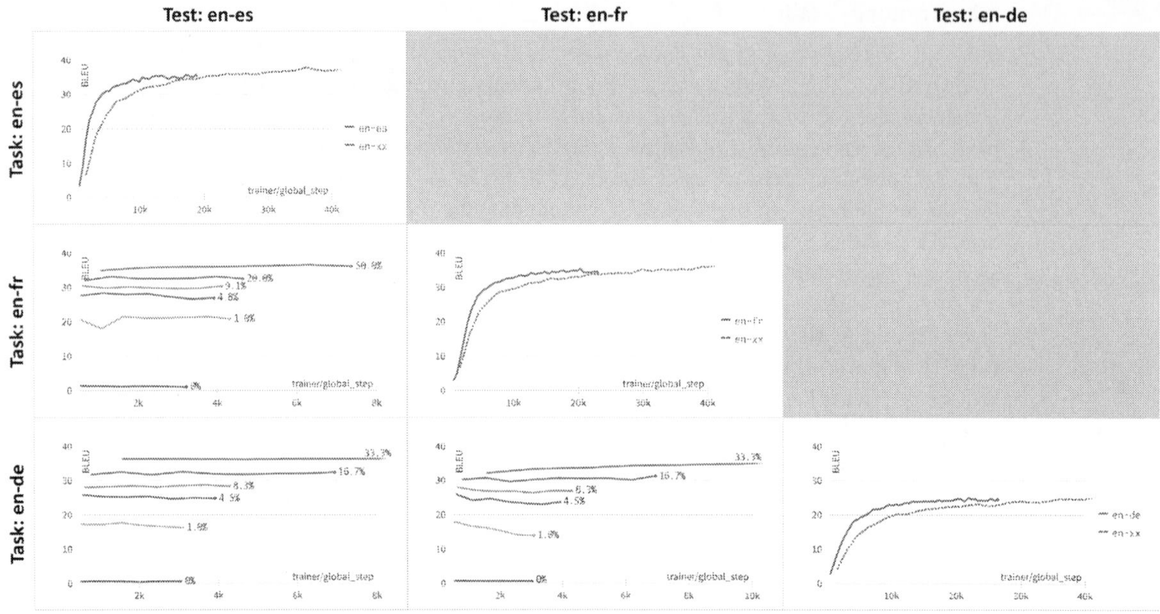

Figure 1: **Using past data to naïvely tackle the CF problem**: When no past data (0%) is used during the learning of a new task, the model forgets everything about the past tasks (flat red lines). However, when a minimal amount of past data is added as a reminder (>1%) during the learning of the new task, the forgetting of these past tasks is significantly reduced.

of 35pts of BLEU. However, when that same model was re-trained for the English-French task, the performance for the past task (English-Spanish) was significantly affected depending on the ratio of past data used during the re-training. For example, when no past data was used during the learning of the new task (English-French), the model's performance on the past task (English-Spanish) dropped to zero (flat red lines). In contrast, as soon as we increased the ratio of past data per batch from 0.0% to 1.0%, the model retained around 60% of its previous performance for that task and 95% of it when 20% of past data was used per batch. Similarly, this very same effect was observed after re-training that trained model (*en-es* $\rightarrow$ *en-fr*) for the English-German task. When no past data was used, the model forgot both the English-Spanish and the English-French tasks. However, as soon as the ratio of past data was slightly increased, the model could retain most of its past knowledge for these tasks.

Interestingly, another thing to point out from these results is that, as the model learns the new task, the performance on the previous tasks remained fairly stable overall. This was quite unexpected for us since it is expected to observe a constant decline in the performance of all tasks as the new task was being learned. However, we did not see this effect until at least two tasks had been learned, and only when we used minimal ratios of past data (i.e., 1%).

Consequently, we explored this phenomenon more closely and added a fourth task to the experiment, the English-Czech pair. As a result, we can see in Figure 3 that with the addition of this new task (en-cz), the effects of the catastrophic forgetting problem became more significant when compared to the previous experiment (see red lines for the en-es/fr/de tasks) since now, the performance in past tasks was steadily declining while the new task was being learned. Hence, this confirmed our previous assumption, given that as the model reaches its learning capacity, that is, its saturation point, it has to forget more and more information despite the refreshments of past data to keep learning new information.

Next, we decided to compare these results with the very same model architecture but trained from scratch, for which all language pairs were available at the training time. Interestingly, no significant differences were found between this model and its sequential version (See dashed (en-xx) and solid (en-es/fr/de) red lines in Figure 1). Therefore, this confirms that as long as a model has sufficient capacity, its performance should not vary significantly regardless of whether it has been trained for all tasks simultaneously or has been trained sequentially using a continual learning approach, such as the one from this experiment using minimal amounts of past data to retain past knowledge. Furthermore, training a model sequentially, using this approach or any other, has the advantage that the training is much more efficient since it only has to re-train the model for the new task rather than for all tasks again.

Finally, these results appear to indicate that by following a strategy as simple as adding tiny fractions of past data during the training of the new task, it is possible to significantly mitigate the effects of catastrophic forgetting problem, enabling sequential training when training data are very scarce. For example, a typical scenario for this could be to extend the number of tasks or classes supported by a pre-trained model for which we do not have the original training data but have access to other similar despite minimal datasets, or even when we do not have more data, but we can afford to annotate a few extra samples semi-automatically.

Furthermore, with this experiment we demonstrate that contrary to popular belief, to maintain the performance of a model on past tasks, one does not need to use all the previous data, but a minimal amount of past data during the learning of the new task.

5.2 Oversampling past data

Given that our base model had sufficient capacity to cope with these tasks, either sequentially or jointly (obtaining very similar performances), we decided to focus our efforts on maximizing the performance in past tasks but minimizing the amount of past data needed to control the forgetting. The reason for adopting this approach was to improve the learning efficiency of new tasks since it is not the same to learn a new single task using minimal past data refreshments than to use large amounts of past data. Besides, in a data loss scenario, it will always be more accessible to label a few past samples manually to control the catastrophic forgetting than to label a whole new dataset from scratch.

Consequently, we first tried to control the catastrophic forgetting by oversampling these sets of past data so that they would have the same weight as the new data. That is, if the new task had 10,000 samples and the previous tasks had 1,000 and 2,000 samples, we would assign a weighting coefficient of 1.0 for the first task, and 10.0 and 5.0 for the second and third tasks. We then used these weighting coefficients to oversample these task samples.

This experiment can be seen in Figure 2, where the non-oversampled models are characterized by dashed lines and the oversampled models by solid lines. This oversampling approach proved to be quite beneficial when the ratios of oversampled data were minimal (around 1%), achieving up to +4pts of BLEU with respect to the non-oversampled models. However, when we increased the ratio of past data from 1% to 4.5% or more, this strategy did not provide significant results and made the models more prone to overfitting on past tasks compared to the non-oversampled models. In addition to this, the non-oversampled models performed slightly better on the new task than the oversampled ones due to the use of higher ratios of new data per batch (i.e., 1% English-Spanish + 99% English-French vs. 50% English-Spanish (oversampled) + 50% English-French).

This oversampling experiment was initially conducted *physically*, that is, by repeating sentences, due to the simplicity of this approach. However, in order to reduce the performance gap between the oversampled and non-oversampled models that was observed during the learning

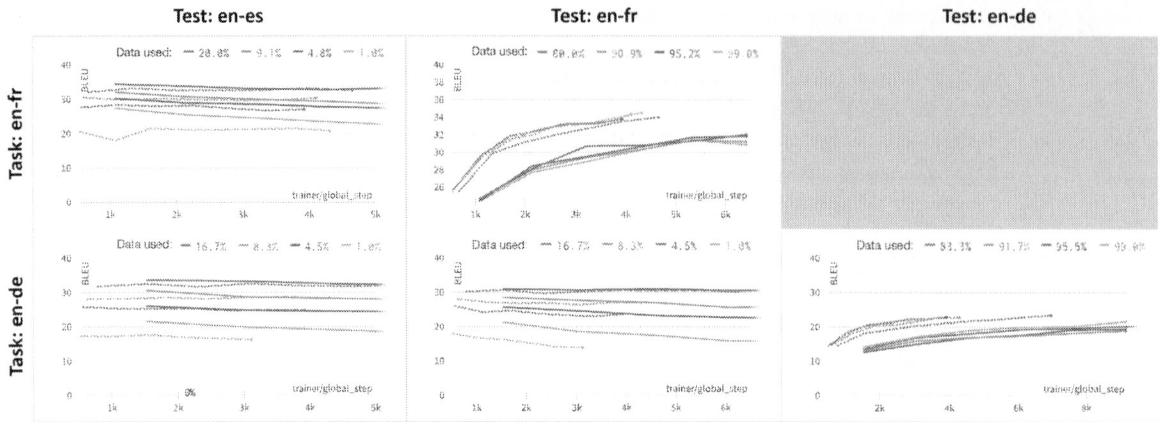

Figure 2: **Oversampling of past data** was effective, especially in scenarios where only minimal amounts of past data were available (<1%). Furthermore, in the case where all tasks had the same weighting (this figure), the oversampled models (solid lines) needed more time than the non-oversampled models (dashed lines) to achieve similar performance levels. Hence, we later reduced the weight of these past tasks.

of the new task, we decided to repeat the previous experiment but this time, performing a *virtual* oversampling so that we could actively rescale the task-weights to perform minor adjustments to better control for these convergence issues.

This idea is described in Equation 1, where x is the input, y is the target, t is the task and w_t is the weight of the task t.

$$\mathcal{L}_w(x, y, t) = \{l_1, l_2, ...l_n\}, \quad l_i = -w_t \log \frac{exp(x_i)}{\sum_{j=1}^{K} exp(x_j))} \cdot 1 \{y_i \neq ignore\_index\} \quad (1)$$

These weights were determined both manually and automatically (learned). However, we obtained better results by determining them manually than automatically, since the automatic approach tended to overweight the easiest task in detriment of the others. Nevertheless, we were able to compensate part of the performance mismatches mentioned before, although we found that when weights were determined manually, it was much easier to overfit for a specific task. Besides, due to the *pareto frontier*, we could not improve performance on all tasks simultaneously by simply performing an active task re-weighting because when we improved performance on one or more tasks, we always ended up compromising performance improvements on another task.

Even though this task re-weighting strategy was primarily beneficial for low-resource scenarios of past data, we found it to be quite helpful in finding better balance compromises between the performances of the different tasks, and avoiding greedy behaviors during learning of the new task.

5.3 Few-Shot Regularization

As discussed in Section 5.1, if we increase the number of tasks learned and do not increase the capacity of the model, sooner or later, the model will reach a saturation point. Therefore, the performance on past tasks will start to worsen instead of remaining stable as before. Furthermore, we have shown that the presence of this phenomenon is accelerated in scenarios where the amount of past data is minimal (<1%), but at the same time, we know that not much past data is needed to mitigate the effects of the catastrophic forgetting. Accordingly, we learned a fourth task (English-Czech) where the model could only see a few samples (1% of past data per batch) in order to make this forgetting phenomenon more noticeable during our experimentation (See Figure 3, red lines). Therefore, our goal here was to show that with a minimal amount of past samples and a simple regularization mechanism, we could be able to mitigate the effects of the catastrophic forgetting phenomenon, and even, improve the performance on some past tasks.

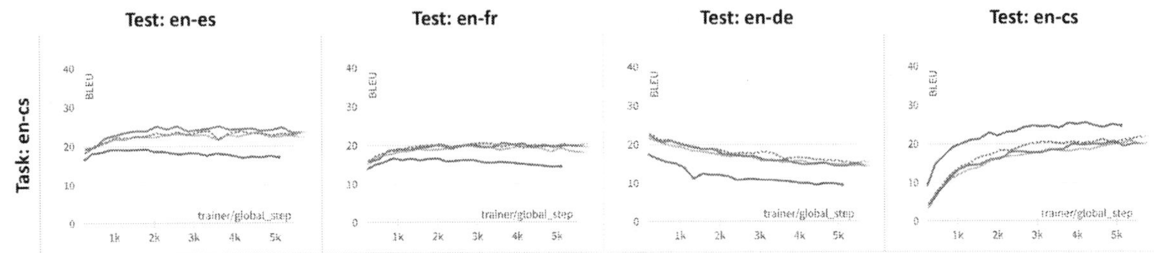

Figure 3: **Few-shot regularization**: The effects of the catastrophic forgetting problem become more noticeable as the model reaches its saturation point after learning more tasks than it can handle, so it starts to degrade its performance of past tasks (see red lines). In contrast, when using the loss function proposed in this section, we can appreciate how the effects of catastrophic forgetting are significantly reduced (see blue lines), albeit at the cost of obtaining slower convergence on the new task.

Consequently, we derived a loss function that minimizes the forgetting of previously learned tasks by actively re-weighting past samples and penalizing weights that deviate too much from the original model. That is, initially, all tasks should contribute equally to the loss regardless of the amount of past data available (oversampling), but then, these weights were slightly modified to ease the convergence of the new task (re-weighting). Additionally, errors should be penalized more severely on past tasks than on the new ones so that we could have more control over the forgetting effects. Furthermore, we wanted to penalize changes in weights that are assumed to be relevant for the past tasks but are not for the new task. To do so, we added a regularization term, based on the knowledge distillation loss derived by Hinton et al. (2015), that allowed us to control for these deviations in past tasks with respect to the previous version of the same model, which is presumed to be better in past tasks due to the effects of catastrophic forgetting phenomenon. Finally, we added the well-known L2 regularization.

This loss function is described in Equation 2, where $\mathcal{L}_w$ is the weighted loss from Section 5.2, $\mathcal{L}_m$ is the weight penalization function described above, t is the task from which the pair (x, y) belongs, y_{ref} is the output of the reference model (i.e., epoch 0), α and β are hyperparameters to define the importance of the current loss, and the weight deviation w.r.t the past model, and δ is a vector to control the importance of past tasks with an exponential penalization. These (hyper-)parameters can be either set manually or learned during training (see below).

$$\mathcal{L}(x, y, t) = (\alpha \cdot \mathcal{L}_w(x, y, t) + \beta \cdot \mathcal{L}_m^{(t \neq T)}(y, y_{ref}))^{\delta_i} + \gamma \cdot \|\theta\|_2^2, \quad \delta_T = 1 \qquad (2)$$

This equation has four components. The first component is the weighted loss $\mathcal{L}_w$, whose purpose is to ensure that each task is equally important regardless of the number of samples. The second term is the distillation loss, which acts as a regularizer to penalize the changes in the past task between the current model (output y) and the reference model (output y_{ref}), that is, the version that was used as a starting point for this new task. The third component is the vector δ, which penalizes pasts tasks exponentially for a faster response to the effects of the catastrophic forgetting problem (during our experimentation, we set $\delta_T = 1.0$, although it could have had other values). The fourth component is the L2 regularization to help with overfitting. Finally, the hyperparameters α and β were determined both manually and (semi-)automatically. First, we tried to learn these hyperparameters (along with δ) automatically during the training of the new task. However, we obtained worse results than when we adjusted them manually due to the problems mentioned in Section 5.2 related to the *Pareto frontier* and because we were considering which tasks were more challenging to learn. Then, we tried to learn them semi-automatically. That is, we learned them automatically while clamping them into a predefined range.

As a result, in Figure 3 we find the comparison between a model trained previously on the English-German task (red line), which only adds a minimal amount of past data (1%) to alleviate the forgetting, and the very same model (blue lines), which in addition to using minimal past data during training (1%) to tackle the forgetting problem, it uses the loss function proposed in this section. Also, we have included a few runs (not cherry-picked) of this proposed model instead of just one to better represent its behavior and support our conclusions more robustly. Accordingly, it can be seen in Figure 3 that the proposed model (blue lines) significantly mitigates the effects of catastrophic forgetting with regard to the other model. For example, on the first two tasks (en-es, en-fr), it even improves the base performance; and on the third task, despite losing some performance concerning its initial result, the loss is significantly smaller than the one from the reference model (red line). However, although our model tends to converge a bit slower due to the additional control terms, both models end up converging to similar performances [2].

Therefore, this loss function, in addition to a minimal amount of past data to exploit past knowledge information, presents itself as an extremely simple mechanism to tackle the catastrophic problem with no additional computational costs.

6 Conclusions

This work has studied the catastrophic forgetting problem in machine translation framed as a sequential learning problem for a multilingual machine translation system, where each new language pair is considered a new task.

From studying the effects of the catastrophic forgetting problem as a function of the number of learned tasks and the ratios of past data used during the learning of the new task, we discovered that even with minimal amounts of past data, we could retain up a 95% of the performance in past tasks. Then, we tried to boost the performance in past tasks through an oversampling strategy. However, this approach was primarily beneficial for scenarios where only minimal amounts of past data were available (<1%).

Finally, we derived a new loss function based on actively re-weighting past tasks and penalizing weights that deviate too much from the original model to minimize forgetting past tasks while learning the new one. This approach has practically no extra cost and shines by simplicity when compared to other popular but more complex and resource-hungry approaches.

This work suggests that to easily mitigate the effects of the catastrophic forgetting in machine translation with no extra cost, we only need a minimal amount of past data and a simple regularization function that exploits past knowledge information.

[2] With a smaller learning rate and bit more training both reached the same performance.

Acknowledgment

Work supported by the European Commission (H2020) under the SELENE project (grant agreement no 871467) and the project Deep learning for adaptive and multimodal interaction in pattern recognition (DeepPattern) (grant agreement PROMETEO/2019/121). We gratefully acknowledge the support of NVIDIA Corporation with the donation of a GPU used for part of this research.

References

Aljundi, R., Babiloni, F., Elhoseiny, M., Rohrbach, M., and Tuytelaars, T. (2017). Memory aware synapses: Learning what (not) to forget. *CoRR*, abs/1711.09601.

Bahdanau, D., Cho, K., and Bengio, Y. (2015). Neural machine translation by jointly learning to align and translate. *CoRR*, abs/1409.0473.

Barrault, L., Biesialska, M., Bojar, O., Costa-jussà, M. R., Federmann, C., Graham, Y., Grundkiewicz, R., Haddow, B., Huck, M., Joanis, E., Kocmi, T., Koehn, P., Lo, C.-k., Ljubešić, N., Monz, C., Morishita, M., Nagata, M., Nakazawa, T., Pal, S., Post, M., and Zampieri, M. (2020). Findings of the 2020 conference on machine translation (WMT20). In *Proceedings of the Fifth Conference on Machine Translation*, pages 1–55.

Carpenter, G. A. and Grossberg, S. (1987). A massively parallel architecture for a self-organizing neural pattern recognition machine. *Computer Vision, Graphics, and Image Processing*, 37(1):54–115.

Carrión, S. and Casacuberta, F. (2022). Autonmt: A framework to streamline the research of seq2seq models.

Cho, K., van Merriënboer, B., Gulcehre, C., Bahdanau, D., Bougares, F., Schwenk, H., and Bengio, Y. (2014). Learning phrase representations using RNN encoder–decoder for statistical machine translation. In *Proceedings of the 2014 Conference on EMNLP*, pages 1724–1734.

Devlin, J., Chang, M., Lee, K., and Toutanova, K. (2018). BERT: pre-training of deep bidirectional transformers for language understanding. *CoRR*, abs/1810.04805.

Draelos, T. J., Miner, N. E., Lamb, C. C., Vineyard, C. M., Carlson, K. D., James, C. D., and Aimone, J. B. (2016). Neurogenesis deep learning. *CoRR*, abs/1612.03770.

Fernando, C., Banarse, D., Blundell, C., Zwols, Y., Ha, D., Rusu, A. A., Pritzel, A., and Wierstra, D. (2017). Pathnet: Evolution channels gradient descent in super neural networks. *CoRR*, abs/1701.08734.

Garcia, X., Constant, N., Parikh, A., and Firat, O. (2021). Towards continual learning for multilingual machine translation via vocabulary substitution. In *Proceedings of the 2021 Conference of the North American Chapter of the Association for Computational Linguistics: Human Language Technologies*, pages 1184–1192, Online. Association for Computational Linguistics.

Hinton, G., Vinyals, O., and Dean, J. (2015). Distilling the knowledge in a neural network.

Hu, W., Lin, Z., Liu, B., Tao, C., Tao, Z., Ma, J., Zhao, D., and Yan, R. (2019). Overcoming catastrophic forgetting for continual learning via model adaptation. In *ICLR*.

Jung, H., Ju, J., Jung, M., and Kim, J. (2016). Less-forgetting learning in deep neural networks. *CoRR*, abs/1607.00122.

Kaplan, J., McCandlish, S., Henighan, T., Brown, T. B., Chess, B., Child, R., Gray, S., Radford, A., Wu, J., and Amodei, D. (2020). Scaling laws for neural language models. *CoRR*, abs/2001.08361.

Kemker, R. and Kanan, C. (2017). Fearnet: Brain-inspired model for incremental learning. *CoRR*, abs/1711.10563.

Kirkpatrick, J., Pascanu, R., Rabinowitz, N. C., Veness, J., Desjardins, G., Rusu, A. A., Milan, K., Quan, J., Ramalho, T., Grabska-Barwinska, A., Hassabis, D., Clopath, C., Kumaran, D., and Hadsell, R. (2016). Overcoming catastrophic forgetting in neural networks. *CoRR*, abs/1612.00796.

Kudo, T. (2018). Subword regularization: Improving neural network translation models with multiple subword candidates. In *Proceedings of the 56th Annual Meeting of the ACL (Volume 1: Long Papers)*, pages 66–75.

Kudo, T. and Richardson, J. (2018). Sentencepiece: A simple and language independent subword tokenizer and detokenizer for neural text processing. In Blanco, E. and Lu, W., editors, *Proceedings of the 2018 Conference on Empirical Methods in Natural Language Processing, EMNLP 2018: System Demonstrations, Brussels, Belgium, October 31 - November 4, 2018*, pages 66–71.

Lee, J., Yoon, J., Yang, E., and Hwang, S. J. (2017a). Lifelong learning with dynamically expandable networks. *CoRR*, abs/1708.01547.

Lee, S., Kim, J., Ha, J., and Zhang, B. (2017b). Overcoming catastrophic forgetting by incremental moment matching. *CoRR*, abs/1703.08475.

Li, Z. and Hoiem, D. (2016). Learning without forgetting. *CoRR*, abs/1606.09282.

Liu, T., Ungar, L., and Sedoc, J. (2019). Continual learning for sentence representations using conceptors. *ArXiv*, abs/1904.09187.

Lopez-Paz, D. and Ranzato, M. (2017). Gradient episodic memory for continuum learning. *CoRR*, abs/1706.08840.

Luong, T., Pham, H., and Manning, C. D. (2015). Effective approaches to attention-based neural machine translation. In *Proceedings of the 2015 Conference on EMNLP*, pages 1412–1421.

McCloskey, M. and Cohen, N. J. (1989). Catastrophic interference in connectionist networks: The sequential learning problem. volume 24 of *Psychology of Learning and Motivation*, pages 109–165. Academic Press.

Papineni, K., Roukos, S., Ward, T., and Zhu, W.-J. (2002). Bleu: A method for automatic evaluation of machine translation. In *Proceedings of the 40th Annual Meeting on ACL*, ACL '02, page 311–318.

Post, M. (2018). A call for clarity in reporting BLEU scores. In *Proceedings of the Third Conference on Machine Translation: Research Papers*, pages 186–191.

Qi, Y., Sachan, D., Felix, M., Padmanabhan, S., and Neubig, G. (2018). When and why are pre-trained word embeddings useful for neural machine translation? In *Proceedings of the 2018 Conference of the North American Chapter of the Association for Computational Linguistics: Human Language Technologies, Volume 2 (Short Papers)*.

Rebuffi, S., Kolesnikov, A., and Lampert, C. H. (2016). icarl: Incremental classifier and representation learning. *CoRR*, abs/1611.07725.

Rusu, A. A., Rabinowitz, N. C., Desjardins, G., Soyer, H., Kirkpatrick, J., Kavukcuoglu, K., Pascanu, R., and Hadsell, R. (2016). Progressive neural networks. *CoRR*, abs/1606.04671.

Sato, S., Sakuma, J., Yoshinaga, N., Toyoda, M., and Kitsuregawa, M. (2020). Vocabulary adaptation for domain adaptation in neural machine translation. In *Findings of the Association for Computational Linguistics: EMNLP 2020*, pages 4269–4279, Online. Association for Computational Linguistics.

Sennrich, R., Haddow, B., and Birch, A. (2016). Neural machine translation of rare words with subword units. In *Proceedings of the 54th Annual Meeting of the ACL (Volume 1: Long Papers)*, pages 1715–1725.

Shin, H., Lee, J. K., Kim, J., and Kim, J. (2017). Continual learning with deep generative replay. *CoRR*, abs/1705.08690.

Sutskever, I., Vinyals, O., and Le, Q. V. (2014). Sequence to sequence learning with neural networks. In Ghahramani, Z., Welling, M., Cortes, C., Lawrence, N., and Weinberger, K. Q., editors, *NIPS*, volume 27.

Thompson, B., Gwinnup, J., Khayrallah, H., Duh, K., and Koehn, P. (2019). Overcoming catastrophic forgetting during domain adaptation of neural machine translation. In *Proceedings of the 2019 Conference of the North American Chapter of the Association for Computational Linguistics: Human Language Technologies, Volume 1 (Long and Short Papers)*, pages 2062–2068, Minneapolis, Minnesota. Association for Computational Linguistics.

Vaswani, A., Shazeer, N., Parmar, N., Uszkoreit, J., Jones, L., Gomez, A. N., Kaiser, L., and Polosukhin, I. (2017). Attention is all you need. In *Proceedings of the 31st NeurIPS*, NIPS'17, page 6000–6010.

Wu, Y., Schuster, M., Chen, Z., Le, Q. V., Norouzi, M., Macherey, W., Krikun, M., Cao, Y., Gao, Q., Macherey, K., Klingner, J., Shah, A., Johnson, M., Liu, X., Kaiser, L., Gouws, S., Kato, Y., Kudo, T., Kazawa, H., Stevens, K., Kurian, G., Patil, N., Wang, W., Young, C., Smith, J., Riesa, J., Rudnick, A., Vinyals, O., Corrado, G., Hughes, M., and Dean, J. (2016). Google's neural machine translation system: Bridging the gap between human and machine translation. *CoRR*, abs/1609.08144.

Xu, H., Liu, B., Shu, L., and Yu, P. S. (2018). Lifelong domain word embedding via meta-learning. In *Proceedings of the Twenty-Seventh International Joint Conference on Artificial Intelligence, IJCAI-18*, pages 4510–4516.

Zenke, F., Poole, B., and Ganguli, S. (2017). Continual learning through synaptic intelligence. In Precup, D. and Teh, Y. W., editors, *Proceedings of the 34th International Conference on Machine Learning*, volume 70 of *Proceedings of Machine Learning Research*, pages 3987–3995. PMLR.

Zhang, T., Kishore, V., Wu, F., Weinberger, K. Q., and Artzi, Y. (2019). Bertscore: Evaluating text generation with BERT. *CoRR*, abs/1904.09675.

Quantized Wasserstein Procrustes Alignment of Word Embedding Spaces

Prince Osei Aboagye[1]*, Yan Zheng[2], Chin-Chia Michael Yeh[2], Junpeng Wang[2], Zhongfang Zhuang[2], Huiyuan Chen[2], Liang Wang[2], Wei Zhang[2], Jeff M. Phillips[1]
[1]University of Utah, [2]Visa Research
[1]{prince,jeffp}@cs.utah.edu
[2]{yazheng,miyeh,junpenwa,zzhuang,hchen,liawang,wzhan}@visa.com

Abstract

Optimal Transport (OT) provides a useful geometric framework to estimate the permutation matrix under unsupervised cross-lingual word embedding (CLWE) models that pose the alignment task as a Wasserstein-Procrustes problem. However, linear programming algorithms and approximate OT solvers via Sinkhorn for computing the permutation matrix come with a significant computational burden since they scale cubically and quadratically, respectively, in the input size. This makes it slow and infeasible to compute OT distances exactly for a larger input size, resulting in a poor approximation quality of the permutation matrix and subsequently a less robust learned transfer function or mapper. This paper proposes an unsupervised projection-based CLWE model called quantized Wasserstein Procrustes (qWP). qWP relies on a quantization step of both the source and target monolingual embedding space to estimate the permutation matrix given a cheap sampling procedure. This approach substantially improves the approximation quality of empirical OT solvers given fixed computational cost. We demonstrate that qWP achieves state-of-the-art results on the Bilingual lexicon Induction (BLI) task.

1 Introduction

In natural language processing (NLP), the problem of aligning monolingual embedding spaces to induce a shared cross-lingual vector space has been shown not only to be useful in a variety of tasks such as bilingual lexicon induction (BLI) (Mikolov et al., 2013; Barone, 2016; Artetxe et al., 2017; Aboagye et al., 2022), machine translation (Artetxe et al., 2018b), cross-lingual information retrieval (Vulić & Moens, 2015), but it plays a crucial role in facilitating the cross-lingual transfer of language technologies from high resource languages to low resource languages.

Cross-lingual word embeddings (CLWEs) represent words from two or more languages in a shared cross-lingual vector space in which words with similar meanings obtain similar vectors regardless of their language. There has been a flurry of work dominated by the so-called *projection-based* CLWE models (Mikolov et al., 2013; Artetxe et al., 2016, 2017, 2018a; Smith et al., 2017; Ruder et al., 2019), which aim to improve CLWE model performance significantly. *Projection-based* CLWE models learn a transfer function or mapper between two independently trained monolingual word vector spaces with limited or no cross-lingual supervision.

Famous among *projection-based* CLWE models are the unsupervised *projection-based* CLWE models (Artetxe et al., 2017; Lample et al., 2018; Alvarez-Melis & Jaakkola, 2018;

*work done while interning at Visa Research

Grave et al., 2019): they eliminate the initial seed bilingual lexicon and rely on the topological similarities between monolingual spaces, known as the isometry assumption, to extract seed bilingual lexicons. This makes them attractive since they require no cross-lingual supervision. One of the ways of framing unsupervised CLWE models is to pose the alignment task as a Wasserstein-Procrustes problem aiming to jointly estimate a permutation matrix and an orthogonal matrix (Grave et al., 2019; Ramírez et al., 2020). Most existing unsupervised CLWE models that solve the Wasserstein-Procrustes problem resort to Optimal Transport (OT) based methods to estimate the permutation matrix.

Optimal Transport (OT) (Monge, 1781; Kantorovich, 1942) provides a natural geometric and probabilistic toolbox to compare probability distributions or measures. OT is concerned about determining an optimal transport plan for moving probability mass between two probability distributions with the cheapest cost. In theory, optimal transport is beautiful and well defined and has been well studied under continuous distribution. However, in practice or specifically in machine learning, we only have access to samples given an underlying distribution, so we turn to observe discrete distributions. This resonates with how empirical OT solvers have been built; they accept samples as inputs from input probability distributions or measures.

When the discrete distributions are composed of a large number of point cloud in higher dimensions, it becomes slow, impractical, and infeasible to compute OT distances exactly given the empirical OT solvers. A common scalable approach adopted by Grave et al. (2019) in their stochastic optimization framework to approximate the exact OT distance in order to extract the permutation matrix was to randomly draw k monolingual embeddings from the source and target spaces, respectively. However, this approximation approach poses two main challenges:

1) Sampling Efficiency Does the OT distance computed between the k sampled embeddings provide a useful or quality OT distance approximation of the true underlying distributions of the source and target spaces? Theoritical bounds and results have shown that the quality of this approximation has a convergence rate of $k^{-\frac{1}{d}}$ to the true OT distance, where d is the ambient dimension (Dudley, 1969; Weed & Bach, 2019). Therefore, an effective approximation of the true OT distance requires large k samples since we are constrained by the curse of dimensionality from the power $-\frac{1}{d}$. Thus, we need more samples to approximate the true OT distance in higher dimensions.

2) Computational Efficiency Empirical OT solvers such as linear programming algorithms (Burkard et al., 2012) and approximate solvers via Sinkhorn (Cuturi, 2013) for computing the permutation matrix have a computational cost of $\mathcal{O}\left(k^3 \log k\right)$ and $\mathcal{O}\left(k^2\epsilon^{-2}\right)$, respectively, in the input size, k, and regularization term ϵ defined later in Equation 7. It becomes slow and infeasible in higher dimensions to compute OT distances exactly for a larger input size. We are therefore restricted by the maximum k samples to draw for an effective approximation of the true OT distance. The constraint here is not the availability of data but computational cost.

Given these two challenges, Beugnot et al. (2021) proposed two efficient OT estimators. The empirical OT solvers remain the same, either the linear programming solver or the entropic-regularized OT via Sinkhorn. However, instead of drawing only k samples as input to the OT solver, they rely on a cheap quantization step like k-means ++ (Arthur & Vassilvitskii, 2007) that is consistent with the computational complexity of the OT solver. Since sampling is cheap, they draw more than k samples and then use k-means++ to quantize the oversampled points from the source and target spaces, respectively, by partitioning them into k clusters and then select the k weighted anchor points as input to the OT solver. This quantization step improves the approximation quality to the true OT distance. Aside from the theoretical guarantees of the benefits of this quantization step, they showed that the new variant of the unregularized OT estimator yield an improvement in the convergence rate by $k^{-2\alpha}$ in the best case or $k^{-\alpha}$ in the worst case, which is on par with the computational complexity existing empirical OT estimators, where $\alpha = \frac{1}{d}$.

Inspired by the work of Beugnot et al. (2021), our paper proposes a new unsupervised CLWE model called quantized Wasserstein Procrustes (qWP). We follow the stochastic algorithm framework by Grave et al. (2019) and the refinement procedure from Lample et al. (2018).

Our contribution. This work proposes a new unsupervised CLWE model: **quantized Wasserstein Procrustes (qWP)** that relies on a quantization step of the source and target distributions to estimate the alignment and linear transformation jointly. Firstly, we use the stochastic optimization framework in Grave et al. (2019). However, instead of randomly drawing k samples at each iteration, we use a quantization step to preprocess the source and target distributions to find the optimal k point compression or summary needed to estimate the permutation matrix. It leads to a much-refined sample as opposed to a random sampling of the k points. This approach substantially improves the approximation quality of the true OT distance and bias of empirical OT solvers given fixed computational cost (Beugnot et al., 2021). The main idea behind qWP is to oversample the k samples and then reduce them to k-weighted samples through quantization such as k-means++. After this, a linear program solver or regularized Sinkhorn algorithm can be used on the resulting quantized distribution. The translation pairs obtained from the permutation matrix are then used to learn the linear transformation. Finally, we use the refinement approach from Lample et al. (2018) to improve the orthogonal mapping. We demonstrate that qWP achieves state-of-the-art results on the BLI task.

2 Related Work

At the heart of Cross-lingual NLP are CLWE models. It has quickly evolved into a large subarea with a wide variety of approaches and perspectives, so we provide context by overviewing this work first.

Projection-based CLWE models can be categorized into (Ruder et al., 2019): **1)** fully supervised projection-based CLWE models, **2)** weakly supervised projection-based CLWE models, and **3)** fully unsupervised projection-based CLWE models. The main idea governing all CLWE models is to independently train monolingual embeddings on large monolingual corpora in different languages or use pre-trained monolingual embeddings and then learn a transfer function to map them into a shared cross-lingual word vector space.

The first fully supervised projection-based CLWE model to learn a shared cross-lingual word vector space from monolingually-trained word embedding was proposed by Mikolov et al. (2013). They learned a linear transform from the source embedding space to the target language by minimizing the sum of squared Euclidean distance between the translation pairs of a seed dictionary based on the assumption that two embedding spaces exhibit similar geometric structures (i.e., approximately isomorphic). Their model requires word-level supervision from several thousand seed translation dictionaries (Dict). Subsequent works by Xing et al. (2015); Artetxe et al. (2016); Smith et al. (2017) argued and proved that the quality of the learned CLWEs could be improved by modifying the objective function in Mikolov et al. (2013).

A more recent line of research has shown that the shared cross-lingual word vector space can be induced with weaker supervision from a small initial seed dictionary (Vulic & Korhonen, 2016; Glavaš et al., 2019; Vulić et al., 2019). Weakly supervised projection-based CLWE models start with a small initial seed dictionary; however, the initial seed dictionary is iteratively expanded through a self-learning procedure. For example, Bootstrap Procrustes (PROC-B) (Glavaš et al., 2019) is semi-supervised in that it starts with a small pairwise correspondence (of 500-1000 words), aligns those to infer a larger correspondence, and repeats applying Procrustes alignment. The quest to eliminate cross-lingual supervision has led to the development of fully unsupervised projection-based CLWE models.

Fully unsupervised projection-based CLWE models use the topological similarities between monolingual embedding spaces to induce the shared cross-lingual vector space (Lample et al., 2018; Artetxe et al., 2018a; Mohiuddin & Joty, 2019). The translation dictionaries are produced from scratch based on monolingual data only.

3 Background

In this section, we describe the mathematical formulation of supervised *projection-based* CLWE models and unsupervised *projection-based* CLWE models. We also defined what the 2-Wasserstein distance is and looked in detail at how the Wasserstein-Procrustes problem under the unsupervised CLWE model is solved in practice.

We define two monolingual embedding spaces as $X, Y \in \mathbb{R}^{n \times d}$, where n is the number of words, and d is the dimension of the monolingual word embeddings.

Supervised *Projection-Based* CLWE Models require word-level supervision from seed translation dictionaries such that word x_i in X is the translation of word y_i in Y. The linear transformation, W^*, from the source monolingual embedding space to the target monolingual embedding space is learned by solving the least square problem (Mikolov et al., 2013):

$$W^* = \underset{W \in \mathbb{R}^{d \times d}}{\arg\min} \|XW - Y\|_F^2 \tag{1}$$

Xing et al. (2015), modified the objective function in Eq. (1) to improve the quality of the learned CLWEs by unit length normalizing the word embeddings and imposing an orthogonality constraint on the linear transformation (W) during training:

$$W^* = \underset{W \in \mathcal{O}_d}{\arg\min} \|XW - Y\|_F^2, \tag{2}$$

where $\mathcal{O}_d$ is the set of orthogonal matrices. The orthogonality constraint preserves the original monolingual embedding space's similarities and geometric structure. These assumptions and constraints imposed on the linear transform make the problem of learning a transfer function an orthogonal **Procrustes** problem (Eq. 2), which has a closed-form solution: $W^* = UV^\top$, where $U \Sigma V^\top$ is the singular value decomposition of $X^\top Y$ (Schönemann, 1966).

2-Wasserstein distance is a distance function used to compute the OT-distance given two set of points X and Y:

$$W_2^2(X, Y) = \min_{P \in \mathcal{P}_n} \sum_{i,j=1}^{n} \|x_i - y_j\|_2^2 P_{ij} \tag{3}$$

where $\mathcal{P}_n$ is the set of permutation matrices, $\mathcal{P}_n = \left\{P \in \{0,1\}^{n \times n}, P1_n = 1_n, P^\top 1_n = 1_n\right\}$.

Unsupervised *Projection-Based* CLWE Models Without any initial seed bilingual lexicon some unsupervised CLWE models solves the **Wasserstein-Procrustes** problem (Eq. 4) to jointly estimate the permutation matrix or alignment (P) and linear transformation (W) (Grave et al., 2019; Ramírez et al., 2020):

$$W^*, P^* = \underset{W \in \mathcal{O}_d, P \in \mathcal{P}_n}{\arg\min} \|XW - PY\|_F^2 \tag{4}$$

The permutation matrix P^* provides a one-to-one mapping or correspondence between the source and target samples.

Under unsupervised CLWE models that solve the Wasserstein-Procrustes problem, we aim to estimate the two unknown variables W and P. One way to solve Eq. (4) is by alternating the minimization of W and P. Given P, we use the translation pairs obtained between the source and target spaces to learn the linear transformation, W^* from Eq. (2). Similarly, given the linear transformation W^*, Eq. (4) is equivalent to minimizing the 2-Wasserstein distance between XW and Y to solve for the permutation matrix, P:

$$W_2^2(XW, Y) = \min_{P \in \mathcal{P}_n} \sum_{i,j=1}^{n} \|x_i W - y_j\|_2^2 P_{ij} \tag{5}$$

Equation (5) is the standard OT problem, and it can be solved using a linear programming solver, which has a computational cost of $\mathcal{O}\left(n^3 \log n\right)$. For a large n, a linear programming solver is impractical. Another variant and approximation of the optimal transport problem were proposed by (Cuturi, 2013). This variant adds an entropic regularization term leading to the Sinkhorn algorithm with a computational cost of $\mathcal{O}\left(n^2 \epsilon^{-2}\right)$:

$$W_2^2(XW, Y) = \min_{P \in \mathcal{P}_n} \sum_{i,j=1}^{n} \|x_i W - y_j\|_2^2 P_{ij} + \epsilon \sum_{i,j=1}^{n} \log P_{ij} \tag{6}$$

Grave et al. (2019) proposed a stochastic optimization scheme to jointly estimate W and P by randomly sampling $\hat{X}, \hat{Y} \in \mathbb{R}^{k \times d}$ from X and Y, where $k < n$. Due to how slow and infeasible a linear programming solver for a larger input size can be, Grave et al. (2019) used the Sinkhorn algorithm to compute the permutation matrix, P by minimizing:

$$W_2^2\left(\hat{X}W, \hat{Y}\right) = \min_{P \in \mathcal{P}_k} \sum_{i,j=1}^{k} \|x_i W - y_j\|_2^2 P_{ij} + \epsilon \sum_{i,j=1}^{k} \log P_{ij} \tag{7}$$

4 Proposed Method

This section introduces our new unsupervised CLWE model: quantized Wasserstein Procrustes (qWP). We use the previous stochastic algorithm framework and refinement procedure from Grave et al. (2019) and Lample et al. (2018) respectively in our model, but we rely on a quantization step to estimate the permutation matrix.

4.1 quantized Wasserstein Procrustes (qWP)

We consider two languages with vocabularies V_x and V_y, represented by word embeddings $\mathrm{X} = \{x_i\}_{i=1}^n, \mathrm{Y} = \{y_i\}_{i=1}^n$, respectively. We assume two empirical distributions over the embedding spaces, X and Y: $\mu = \sum_{i=1}^{n} p_i \delta_{x^{(i)}}$ and $\nu = \sum_{j=1}^{n} q_j \delta_{y^{(j)}}$, where p_i and q_i are the probability weights associated with each word vector, δ_x and δ_y is the Dirac function supported on point x and y respectively.

The main crux of our proposed unsupervised CLWE model: quantized Wasserstein Procrustes (qWP) is that we rely on a quantization step like k-means++ (Arthur & Vassilvitskii, 2007) instead of random sampling to estimate the permutation matrix and then use gradient descent and Procrustes to extract the orthogonal matrix. We take Eq. (4) as our loss function. However, Eq. (4) is not jointly convex in W and P, but as we saw in Section 3 we can fix one variable and then solve for the other variable. Alternating the minimization in each variable W and P is therefore employed to find a solution (Alaux et al., 2018; Grave et al., 2019).

First, we have to induce the translation dictionary by solving for the permutation matrix, P^* in Eq. (5) and then find the orthogonal projection matrix from Eq. (2). Naively doing an

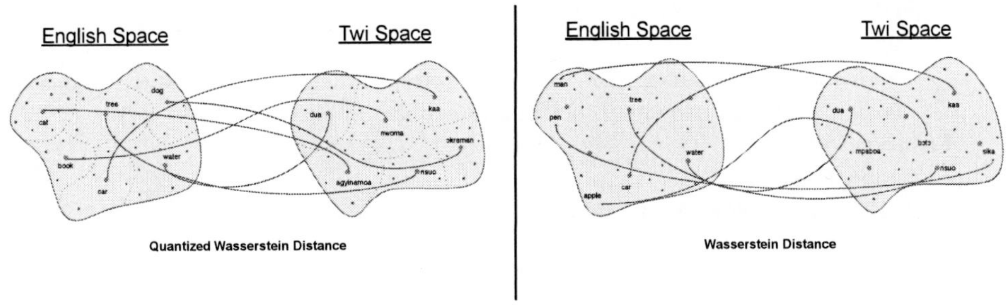

Figure 1: Illustration on toy $2d$ data showing the potential advantage of Quantized Wasserstein Distance (qWD) over Wasserstein Distance (WD). We want to align or translate words in the English Space to words in the Twi Space without knowing aforehand the translation pairs or the linear transformation. Twi is a language spoken in Ghana, West Africa. First, we must induce the translation pairs by estimating the permutation matrix, P, either through qWD or WD. Each dot represents a word in that space; specifically, the red points are the k centers from k-means++. The edge connecting two red points means the two words are accurate translation pairs, whereas the edge between two black points is the wrong translation pair. Here we want to induce six translation pairs through P.

alternating full minimization in each variable W and P of Eq. (4) does not scale, and even on smaller problems, empirical results show that it quickly converges to a bad local minima (Zhang et al., 2017). A scalable stochastic approach adopted by Grave et al. (2019) was to instead, at each iteration, t, randomly sample a minibatch $\mathrm{X}_k = \{x_i\}_{i=1}^{k}$, and $\mathrm{Y}_k = \{y_i\}_{i=1}^{k}$ of size k from X and Y. The optimal coupling or permutation matrix, P^*, was then computed from Eq. (7) using the Sinkhorn algorithm. The translation pairs obtained from P^* between the source and target spaces are then used to learn the orthogonal matrix, W^*, that maps the source to the target spaces from Eq. (2) by using Procrustes and gradient descent to update W. The procedure for updating W is detailed in Grave et al. (2019).

The stochastic optimization scheme adopted by Grave et al. (2019) to make the alternating minimization process scale and achieve a better convergence to a good local minimum when computing the permutation matrix suffers from the sampling efficiency and computational efficiency challenges discussed in Section 1.

To address these two challenges following Beugnot et al. (2021), we will quantize the source and target word embedding space by finding the optimal k point compression or summary as input to the 2-Wasserstein distance (Pollard, 1982; Canas & Rosasco, 2012) through the use of k-means++. The resulting convergence rate of $k^{-2\alpha}$ in the best case or $k^{-\alpha}$ in the worst case from using this quantization step makes the OT solver yields a better approximation quality of the permutation matrix and subsequently a more robust learned transfer function, where $\alpha = \frac{1}{d}$.

4.1.1 New Alignment Algorithm

The goal of our proposed new CLWE algorithm is to quantize the source and target embedding spaces X and Y to be aligned to obtain a much-refined coreset [1] that is less noisy compared to just randomly sampling from X and Y. Our proposed new method is summarized in Algorithms 1 and 2. For each iteration t (Algorithm 1), we compute the permutation matrix P^* from Algorithm 2. The main idea of Algorithm 2 is to draw more than k samples using the coreset size $m > k$ and then reduce them to k-weighted samples through quantization such as k-means++. Here the computational cost of k-means++ is $\mathcal{O}\,(mk)$. To satisfy the computational complexity of the OT

[1] A coreset is a summary or an approximation of the shape of a larger point cloud with a smaller point cloud.

Algorithm 1 Quantized Wasserstein Procrustes

Require:
Word embedding matrix, $X, Y \in \mathbb{R}^{n\times d}$ of the source language and target language respectively, entropy regularization coefficient ϵ, number of anchor point k

Ensure:
Orthogonal matrix, W

for $e = 1, \ldots, E$ **do**
  for $t = 1, \ldots, T$ **do**
    $P \leftarrow qW\left(X, Y, \epsilon, k\right)$
    $W \leftarrow$Update W by gradient descent and Procrutes
  end for
end for
return W

solver, we must ensure that the quantization step used to preprocess the source and target space takes $\mathcal{O}\left(k^3 \log k\right)$ time. In view of this, we set $m = k^2 \log k$ so that we are consistent with the computational complexity $\mathcal{O}\left(k^3 \log k\right)$ of the OT solver. We then sample $\mathrm{X}_m = (x_1, \ldots x_m)$ i.i.d from X and $\mathrm{Y}_m = (y_1, \ldots y_m)$ i.i.d from Y. Using k-means++ we find the k weighted centers. Following each Voronoi cell, we weight each center proportionally to the number of samples to obtain the weights a and b. We then can use either the linear program solver or the regularized Sinkhorn algorithm (Cuturi, 2013) to estimate the permutation matrix, P, between the two quantized point clouds. In our case, we used the entropic-regularized OT solver via Sinkhorn, which we call ApproxOT(C, a, b, ϵ).

Algorithm 2 Quantized 2-Wasserstein Distance ($qW\left(X, Y, \epsilon, k\right)$)

Require:
$\mathrm{X} = \{x_i\}_{i=1}^n, \mathrm{Y} = \{y_i\}_{i=1}^n$, entropy regularization coefficient ϵ, number of anchor points k

Ensure:
Permutation Matrix, P

Sample m points:
  Set $m = k^2 \log k$
  Sample $\mathrm{X}_m = (x_1, \ldots x_m)$ i.i.d from X and $\mathrm{Y}_m = (y_1, \ldots y_m)$ i.i.d from Y
Subsample k anchor points:
  Compute $(c_1, \ldots c_k)$ with $k-$means++
  Compute $(d_1, \ldots d_k)$ with $k-$means++
Compute weights:
  Set $a_i = \sum_{j=1}^{n} \mathbf{1}_{i=\arg\min_{l} \|x_j - c_l\|_2^2} \forall i \in \{1, \ldots, k\}$
  Set $b_i = \sum_{j=1}^{n} \mathbf{1}_{i=\arg\min_{l} \|x_j - d_l\|_2^2} \forall i \in \{1, \ldots, k\}$
Cost matrix:
  Set $C_{ij} = \|c_i - d_j\|_2^2 \; \forall i, j \in \{1, \ldots, n\}$
Regularized transport solver:
return $P \leftarrow$ ApproxOT(C, a, b, ϵ)

See the example in Figure 1 where the translation pairs obtained under qWD yield perfect matches compared to WD, which gave some wrong translation pairs. Under qWD we use k-means++ to quantize the English and Twi Space to select the k weighted centers as input to the OT solver instead of randomly drawing k points under WD, which could be noisy.

As a quick review of k-means++ (Arthur & Vassilvitskii, 2007), it initializes a set of cluster centers for the k-means objective. Each step iteratively increases the set of cluster centers by choosing a new center from the dataset proportional to the squared distance to the closest already chosen center. In one variant we explore, we run one step of the standard Lloyd's algorithm after initializing, moving each center found to the average of data points closest to it.

5 Experimental Analysis

We provide an evaluation of our proposed methods using English (EN) and five languages embeddings pre-trained on Wikipedia (Bojanowski et al., 2017): Spanish (ES), French (FR), German (DE), Russian (RU), and Italian (IT). We use the 300-dimensional fastText (Bojanowski et al., 2017) embeddings, and all vocabularies are trimmed to the 200K most frequent words.

Alignment evaluation tasks: BLI We evaluate and compare our proposed CLWE method mainly on the Bilingual Lexicon Induction (BLI) task, a word translation task. BLI is more direct and has become the de facto evaluation task for CLWE models. For words in the source language, this task retrieves the nearest neighbors in the target language after alignment to check if it contains the translation. We report two different translation accuracies: precision at 1 (P@1) and mean average precision (MAP) (Glavaš et al., 2019) translation accuracy, which is equivalent to the mean reciprocal rank (MRR) of the translation.

Implementation Details The monolingual word embeddings are unit length normalized and centered before entering the model. The first 2.5k words are used to determine Q_0 given P^* obtained from the Frank-Wolfe algorithm (Frank & Wolfe, 1956). We trained qWp on the first 20k most frequent words and evaluated them on separate 1.5k source test queries. We used the MUSE publicly available translation dictionary (Lample et al., 2018). We used the regularized Sinkhorn algorithm (Cuturi, 2013) and always set the entropy regularization term (ϵ) to $\epsilon = 0.05$.

We use the *Refinement* approach from (Lample et al., 2018) and run it for five epochs. This approach iteratively improves the orthogonal mapping Q. After learning Q^* from Eq. (4), we build another (slightly larger) dictionary of translation pairs by translating each word to its nearest neighbor under the transformation Q. The newly learned dictionary of translation pairs is then used to learn a new mapping Q from Eq. (2), and then we repeat the process, each time building an incrementally larger dictionary.

We consider both balanced and unbalanced OT. The unbalanced OT does not require strict mass preservation (Chizat et al., 2018), contrary to the standard or balanced OT problem, Eq. (5). Under the unbalanced OT, Eq. (5) is relaxed by adding two KL-divergence terms to ensure a more relaxed mass preservation. This helps to solve the polysemy problem.

Baselines: BLI We evaluated and compared the published result of qWP to several supervised and unsupervised CLWE models on the BLI task. The baselines include Procrustes (PROC) (Artetxe et al., 2016), Ranking-Based Optimization (RCSLS) (Joulin et al., 2018), Gromov Wasserstein (GW) (Alvarez-Melis & Jaakkola, 2018), Adversarial Training (Adv + Refine) (Lample et al., 2018) and the density matching method (Dema + Refine) (Wang et al., 2019). We used the baseline results

Main Results Tables 1, 2 and 3 summarize the effect of the coreset size within the qWP algorithm. We proceed with four experiments. In tables 1 and 3 we report the mean average precision (MAP) (Glavaš et al., 2019) translation accuracy, which is equivalent to the mean reciprocal rank (MRR) of the translation, whereas, Tables 2 and 4, the translation accuracy reported is the precision at 1 (P@1).

Table 1: Bilingual lexicon Induction (BLI) task, (MAP) - Without Refinement

Trans. Pairs	Sampling	Coreset Size 200	500	1000	2000	3000
EN-ES	Random	36.40	47.22	48.90	49.66	50.08
	KMeans ++	45.21	48.69	49.64	49.71	50.09
ES-EN	Random	43.74	50.36	52.04	53.84	54.67
	KMeans ++	47.24	52.21	52.55	54.10	54.90
EN-FR	Random	37.22	47.94	49.31	50.59	50.88
	KMeans ++	46.54	49.45	50.12	50.54	51.07
FR-EN	Random	38.87	53.36	54.91	55.47	55.85
	KMeans ++	52.67	54.43	55.54	56.11	56.70
EN-DE	Random	27.18	36.10	38.00	38.49	39.29
	KMeans++	32.80	37.44	38.58	38.77	39.72
DE-EN	Random	30.97	41.26	40.44	41.87	41.78
	KMeans ++	39.03	41.90	40.21	43.93	42.42
EN-RU	Random	18.68	27.91	30.91	31.75	32.43
	KMeans ++	26.97	27.12	29.90	32.25	31.41
RU-EN	Random	27.26	39.93	41.50	43.56	43.81
	KMeans ++	16.13	37.07	42.69	42.82	44.54
EN-IT	Random	34.04	46.10	47.99	49.28	50.79
	KMeans ++	44.83	47.31	49.00	50.29	51.12
IT-EN	Random	38.50	52.44	52.92	54.70	57.04
	KMeans ++	47.80	51.77	54.60	57.03	57.49
Avg	Random	33.28	44.26	45.69	46.92	47.66
	KMeans ++	**39.92**	**44.74**	**46.28**	**47.55**	**47.94**

Table 2: Bilingual lexicon Induction (BLI) task, (P@1) Without Refinement

Translation Pairs	Sampling	Coreset Size 500	1000	2000	3000
EN-ES	Random	73.53	75.20	76.73	80.40
	KMeans ++	77.80	79.47	78.20	81.53
EN-FR	Random	77.07	79.40	80.00	81.00
	KMeans ++	78.27	79.60	80.20	81.13
EN-DE	Random	62.73	67.60	70.40	70.60
	KMeans++	65.60	68.87	71.40	71.40
EN-RU	Random	33.13	35.53	35.47	36.87
	KMeans ++	34.53	36.07	36.53	36.60
EN-IT	Random	70.67	72.47	75.13	75.73
	KMeans ++	73.20	74.87	76.73	76.93
Avg	Random	63.43	66.04	67.55	68.92
	KMeans ++	**65.88**	**67.78**	**68.61**	**69.52**

The first experiments in Table 1 show the MRR scores without refinement, and the following Table 3 shows the same MRR scores with refinement. In each table, we increase the coreset size from 200 to 3000, and this is either chosen as in prior work as a random sample or in our proposed approach via k-means++. As expected, on all language pairs, the performance increases as the coreset size increases. Also, notice that the improvement by increasing the coreset size plateaus and is not as significant from 2000 to 3000, indicating that probably 2000 coreset points are usually sufficient.

We also observe that in almost all cases, the performance is improved when using the k-means++ coreset instead of the random sample coreset. The few exceptions are mostly in the comparison with Russian (RU) with refinement, but this gap narrows as the coreset size increases. Notably, by coreset size of 2000, the k-means++ coresets have a clear advantage with an average improvement of from 46.92 to 47.55 without refinement and from 53.05 to 53.76 with refinement. This follows the general trend of better scores when the refinement phase is used.

Table 2 shows a similar experiment on the BLI tasks but reports the precision at 1 (P@1) score. The results show a strong average improvement while using k-means++, with the exception being EN-RU with a small advantage of random sampling at 3000 coreset size; however, with MAP, the results for k-means++ are already basically as good with 2000 points.

Table 3: Bilingual lexicon Induction (BLI) task, (MAP) With Refinement

		Coreset Size				
Trans. Pairs	Sampling	200	500	1000	2000	3000
EN-ES	Random	54.45	54.35	54.54	54.56	54.61
	KMeans ++	54.41	54.48	54.55	54.67	54.72
ES-EN	Random	60.96	58.24	58.56	58.88	59.69
	KMeans ++	58.01	58.26	59.22	59.11	59.55
EN-FR	Random	54.93	55.26	55.31	55.31	55.24
	KMeans ++	55.05	55.41	55.44	55.38	55.30
FR-EN	Random	56.00	61.36	61.44	61.46	61.51
	KMeans ++	61.81	61.68	61.54	61.60	61.64
EN-DE	Random	43.42	43.28	43.42	43.46	43.37
	KMeans++	43.12	43.32	43.56	43.59	43.52
DE-EN	Random	48.45	48.70	45.74	46.03	46.72
	KMeans ++	45.91	49.05	46.69	48.78	48.54
EN-RU	Random	40.34	41.56	42.92	42.50	42.76
	KMeans ++	41.57	40.08	41.41	43.07	41.39
RU-EN	Random	48.01	49.28	48.64	50.09	50.48
	KMeans ++	38.69	46.24	50.16	49.05	50.43
EN-IT	Random	55.93	56.82	57.36	57.48	57.54
	KMeans ++	56.23	56.55	57.32	57.75	57.41
IT-EN	Random	59.71	61.44	60.22	60.70	65.10
	KMeans ++	60.13	59.55	60.61	64.62	64.71
Avg	Random	**52.22**	**53.02**	52.82	53.05	53.70
	KMeans ++	51.49	52.46	**53.05**	**53.76**	**53.72**

The final experiment in Table 4 shows the results of our proposed methods against state-of-the-art techniques. We used a fixed coreset size of 2000. Each entry shows the P@1 scores on the BLI task. The first two lines show PROC and RCSLS, which are supervised methods, so they know the alignment between 5000 pairs of works across embeddings and use this knowledge to determine the alignment. Notice our techniques (which are unsupervised) improve upon the standard Procrustes alignment (PROC) and are almost competitive with the RCSLS method, which optimizes for the BLI task specifically.

Our method also outperforms Gromov-Wasserstein (GW) alignment, as well as Adv + Refine, Dema + Refine, and a random sample coreset when using refinement.

In this table, we also show experiments with two other enhancements. The first is to improve the cluster centers and the quantization found with k-means++ with a run of Lloyd's algorithm (the standard k-means optimization procedure) for 1 step. This moves the quantization point to the center of the points it represents, making it more representative on average. This provides a small improvement. The second extension is to use unbalanced optimal transport instead of balanced OT. Surprisingly, this offers no advantage on average.

Table 4: Bilingual lexicon Induction (BLI) task, Comparison with other Methods

Method		EN-ES		EN-FR		EN-DE		EN-RU		EN-IT		Avg
	Dict	→	←	→	←	→	←	→	←	→	←	
PROC	5K	81.9	83.4	82.1	82.4	74.2	72.7	51.7	63.7	77.4	77.9	74.7
RCSLS	5K	84.1	86.3	83.3	84.1	79.1	76.3	57.9	67.2			77.3
GW	None	81.7	80.4	81.3	78.9	71.9	78.2	45.1	43.7	78.9	75.2	71.5
Adv + Refine	None	81.7	83.3	82.3	82.1	74.0	72.2	44.0	59.1	77.9	77.5	73.4
Dema + Refine	None	82.8	84.9	82.6	82.4	75.3	74.9	46.9	62.4			74.0
Random WP + Refine	None	82.8	84.1	82.6	82.9	75.4	73.3	43.7	59.1			73.0
Unbalanced OT												
(Ours) KMeans++ qWP + Refine	None	83.9	84.5	83.6	83.1	77.0	74.9	48.0	60.1	80.5	80.7	**75.6**
(Ours) LloydRefine qWP + Refine	None	83.8	84.9	84.3	83.4	77.0	75.2	48.2	61.3	80.5	80.9	**75.9**
Balanced OT												
(Ours) KMeans++ qWP + Refine	None	83.5	84.3	84.0	83.1	76.9	74.9	46.6	59.8	80.6	80.3	**75.4**
(Ours) LloydRefine qWP + Refine	None	83.6	84.4	84.0	83.1	77.1	74.8	47.3	60.4	80.1	80.4	**75.5**

6 Conclusion

This paper presents an approach to aligning embeddings in high-dimensional space. While the overall problem is non-convex and computationally expensive, we present an efficient stochastic algorithm to solve the problem based on a refined sample set. This paper focuses on the matching procedure of the BLI task. Our key insight is that our quantization algorithm can outperform the current state-of-art unsupervised algorithm on both balanced and unbalanced settings of the loss function.

References

Prince Osei Aboagye, Jeff Phillips, Yan Zheng, Junpeng Wang, Chin-Chia Michael Yeh, Wei Zhang, Liang Wang, and Hao Yang. Normalization of language embeddings for cross-lingual alignment. In *International Conference on Learning Representations*, 2022. URL https://openreview.net/forum?id=Nh7CtbyoqV5.

Jean Alaux, Edouard Grave, Marco Cuturi, and Armand Joulin. Unsupervised hyper-alignment for multilingual word embeddings. In *International Conference on Learning Representations*, 2018.

David Alvarez-Melis and Tommi S. Jaakkola. Gromov-wasserstein alignment of word embedding spaces. In *Proceedings of the 2018 Conference on Empirical Methods in Natural Language Processing*, pp. 1881–1890, 2018.

Mikel Artetxe, Gorka Labaka, and Eneko Agirre. Learning principled bilingual mappings of word embeddings while preserving monolingual invariance. In *Proceedings of the 2016 Conference on Empirical Methods in Natural Language Processing*, pp. 2289–2294, Austin, Texas, November 2016. Association for Computational Linguistics. doi: 10.18653/v1/D16-1250. URL https://aclanthology.org/D16-1250.

Mikel Artetxe, Gorka Labaka, and Eneko Agirre. Learning bilingual word embeddings with (almost) no bilingual data. In *Proceedings of the 55th Annual Meeting of the Association for Computational Linguistics (Volume 1: Long Papers)*, pp. 451–462, Vancouver, Canada, July 2017. Association for Computational Linguistics. doi: 10.18653/v1/P17-1042. URL https://aclanthology.org/P17-1042.

Mikel Artetxe, Gorka Labaka, and Eneko Agirre. A robust self-learning method for fully unsupervised cross-lingual mappings of word embeddings. In *Proceedings of the 56th Annual Meeting of the Association for Computational Linguistics (Volume 1: Long Papers)*, pp. 789–798, Melbourne, Australia, July 2018a. Association for Computational Linguistics. doi: 10.18653/v1/P18-1073. https://github.com/artetxem/vecmap.

Mikel Artetxe, Gorka Labaka, Eneko Agirre, and Kyunghyun Cho. Unsupervised neural machine translation. In *Proceedings of the Sixth International Conference on Learning Representations*, April 2018b.

David Arthur and Sergei Vassilvitskii. k-means++: The advantages of careful seeding. In *ACM Symposium on Discrete Algorithms*, 2007.

Antonio Valerio Miceli Barone. Towards cross-lingual distributed representations without parallel text trained with adversarial autoencoders. In *Proceedings of the 1st Workshop on Representation Learning for NLP*, pp. 121–126, 2016.

Gaspard Beugnot, Aude Genevay, Justin M Solomon, and Kristjan Greenewald. Improving approximate optimal transport distances using quantization. In *UAI 2021: Uncertainty in Artificial Intelligence*, 2021.

Piotr Bojanowski, Edouard Grave, Armand Joulin, and Tomas Mikolov. Enriching word vectors with subword information. *Transactions of the Association for Computational Linguistics*, 5:135–146, 2017. doi: 10.1162/tacl_a_00051. URL https://www.aclweb.org/anthology/Q17-1010.

Rainer Burkard, Mauro Dell'Amico, and Silvano Martello. *Assignment Problems. Revised reprint.* SIAM - Society of Industrial and Applied Mathematics, 2012. ISBN 978-1-611972-22-1. 393 Seiten.

Guillermo Canas and Lorenzo Rosasco. Learning probability measures with respect to optimal transport metrics. In F. Pereira, C.J. Burges, L. Bottou, and K.Q. Weinberger (eds.), *Advances in Neural Information Processing Systems*, volume 25. Curran Associates, Inc., 2012. URL `https://proceedings.neurips.cc/paper/2012/file/c54e7837e0cd0ced286cb5995327d1ab-Paper.pdf`.

Lenaic Chizat, Gabriel Peyré, Bernhard Schmitzer, and François-Xavier Vialard. An interpolating distance between optimal transport and fisher–rao metrics. *Foundations of Computational Mathematics*, 18(1):1–44, 2018.

Marco Cuturi. Sinkhorn distances: Lightspeed computation of optimal transport. In C. J. C. Burges, L. Bottou, M. Welling, Z. Ghahramani, and K. Q. Weinberger (eds.), *Advances in Neural Information Processing Systems*, volume 26. Curran Associates, Inc., 2013. URL `https://proceedings.neurips.cc/paper/2013/file/af21d0c97db2e27e13572cbf59eb343d-Paper.pdf`.

R. M. Dudley. The speed of mean glivenko-cantelli convergence. *Annals of Mathematical Statistics*, 40(1):40–50, 1969.

Marguerite Frank and Philip Wolfe. An algorithm for quadratic programming. *Naval Research Logistics Quarterly*, 3(1-2):95–110, 1956. doi: https://doi.org/10.1002/nav.3800030109. URL `https://onlinelibrary.wiley.com/doi/abs/10.1002/nav.3800030109`.

Goran Glavaš, Robert Litschko, Sebastian Ruder, and Ivan Vulić. How to (properly) evaluate cross-lingual word embeddings: On strong baselines, comparative analyses, and some misconceptions. In *Proceedings of the 57th Annual Meeting of the Association for Computational Linguistics*, pp. 710–721, Florence, Italy, July 2019. Association for Computational Linguistics. doi: 10.18653/v1/P19-1070. URL `https://aclanthology.org/P19-1070`.

Edouard Grave, Armand Joulin, and Quentin Berthet. Unsupervised alignment of embeddings with wasserstein procrustes. In Kamalika Chaudhuri and Masashi Sugiyama (eds.), *Proceedings of the Twenty-Second International Conference on Artificial Intelligence and Statistics*, volume 89 of *Proceedings of Machine Learning Research*, pp. 1880–1890. PMLR, 16–18 Apr 2019. URL `https://proceedings.mlr.press/v89/grave19a.html`.

Armand Joulin, Piotr Bojanowski, Tomas Mikolov, Hervé Jégou, and Edouard Grave. Loss in translation: Learning bilingual word mapping with a retrieval criterion. In *Proceedings of the 2018 Conference on Empirical Methods in Natural Language Processing*, pp. 2979–2984, Brussels, Belgium, October-November 2018. Association for Computational Linguistics. doi: 10.18653/v1/D18-1330. `https://github.com/facebookresearch/fastText/tree/master/alignment`.

Leonid V Kantorovich. On the translocation of masses. In *Dokl. Akad. Nauk. USSR (NS)*, volume 37, pp. 199–201, 1942.

Guillaume Lample, Alexis Conneau, Marc'Aurelio Ranzato, Ludovic Denoyer, and Hervé Jégou. Word translation without parallel data. In *International Conference on Learning Representations*, 2018.

Tomas Mikolov, Quoc V Le, and Ilya Sutskever. Exploiting similarities among languages for machine translation. *arXiv preprint arXiv:1309.4168*, 2013.

Tasnim Mohiuddin and Shafiq Joty. Revisiting adversarial autoencoder for unsupervised word translation with cycle consistency and improved training. In *Proceedings of the 2019 Conference of the North American Chapter of the Association for Computational Linguistics: Human Language Technologies, Volume 1 (Long and Short Papers)*, pp. 3857–3867, Minneapolis, Minnesota, June 2019. Association for Computational Linguistics. doi: 10.18653/v1/N19-1386. URL https://aclanthology.org/N19-1386.

Gaspard Monge. Mémoire sur la théorie des déblais et des remblais. *Mem. Math. Phys. Acad. Royale Sci.*, pp. 666–704, 1781.

D. Pollard. Quantization and the method ofk-means. *IEEE Transactions on Information Theory*, 28(2):199–205, 1982. doi: 10.1109/TIT.1982.1056481.

Guillem Ramírez, Rumen Dangovski, Preslav Nakov, and Marin Soljačić. On a novel application of wasserstein-procrustes for unsupervised cross-lingual learning. *arXiv preprint arXiv:2007.09456*, 2020.

Sebastian Ruder, Ivan Vulić, and Anders Søgaard. A survey of cross-lingual word embedding models. *J. Artif. Int. Res.*, 65(1):569–630, may 2019. ISSN 1076-9757. doi: 10.1613/jair.1.11640. URL https://doi.org/10.1613/jair.1.11640.

Peter H Schönemann. A generalized solution of the orthogonal procrustes problem. *Psychometrika*, 31(1):1–10, 1966.

Samuel L. Smith, David H. P. Turban, Steven Hamblin, and Nils Y. Hammerla. Offline bilingual word vectors, orthogonal transformations and the inverted softmax. *CoRR*, abs/1702.03859, 2017. URL http://arxiv.org/abs/1702.03859.

Samuel L. Smith, David H. P. Turban, Steven Hamblin, and Nils Y. Hammerla. Offline bilingual word vectors, orthogonal transformations and the inverted softmax. In *ICLR (Poster)*, 2017.

Ivan Vulic and Anna Korhonen. On the role of seed lexicons in learning bilingual word embeddings. In *ACL*, 2016.

Ivan Vulić and Marie-Francine Moens. Monolingual and cross-lingual information retrieval models based on (bilingual) word embeddings. In *Proceedings of the 38th international ACM SIGIR conference on research and development in information retrieval*, pp. 363–372, 2015.

Ivan Vulić, Goran Glavaš, Roi Reichart, and Anna Korhonen. Do We Really Need Fully Unsupervised Cross-Lingual Embeddings? *arXiv e-prints*, art. arXiv:1909.01638, September 2019.

Zihao Wang, Datong P. Zhou, Yong Zhang, Hao Wu, and Chenglong Bao. Wasserstein-fisher-rao document distance. *ArXiv*, abs/1904.10294, 2019.

Jonathan Weed and Francis Bach. Sharp asymptotic and finite-sample rates of convergence of empirical measures in wasserstein distance. *Bernoulli*, 25:2620–2648, 2019.

Chao Xing, Dong Wang, Chao Liu, and Yiye Lin. Normalized word embedding and orthogonal transform for bilingual word translation. In *Proceedings of the 2015 Conference of the North American Chapter of the Association for Computational Linguistics: Human Language Technologies*, pp. 1006–1011, 2015.

Meng Zhang, Yang Liu, Huanbo Luan, and Maosong Sun. Earth mover's distance minimization for unsupervised bilingual lexicon induction. In *Proceedings of the 2017 Conference on Empirical Methods in Natural Language Processing*, pp. 1934–1945, Copenhagen, Denmark, September 2017. Association for Computational Linguistics. doi: 10.18653/v1/D17-1207. URL https://aclanthology.org/D17-1207.

Refining an Almost Clean Translation Memory Helps Machine Translation

Shivendra Bhardwaj shivendra.bhardwaj@umontreal.ca
David Alfonso-Hermelo david.alfonso.hermelo@gmail.com
Philippe Langlais felipe@iro.umontreal.ca
RALI/DIRO, Université de Montréal, Montréal, QC H3C 3J7, Canada

Gabriel Bernier-Colborne Gabriel.Bernier-Colborne@nrc-cnrc.gc.ca
Cyril Goutte Cyril.Goutte@nrc-cnrc.gc.ca
Michel Simard Michel.Simard@nrc-cnrc.gc.ca
Multilingual Text Processing, National Research Council, Ottawa, ON K1A 0R6, Canada

Abstract

While recent studies have been dedicated to cleaning very noisy parallel corpora to improve Machine Translation training, in this work we focus on filtering a large and mostly clean Translation Memory. This problem of practical interest has not received much consideration from the community, in contrast with, for example, filtering large web-mined parallel corpora. We experiment with an extensive, multi-domain proprietary Translation Memory and compare five approaches involving deep-, feature-, and heuristic-based solutions. We propose two ways of evaluating this task, manual annotation and resulting Machine Translation quality. We report significant gains over a state-of-the-art, off-the-shelf cleaning system, using two MT engines.

1 Introduction

Major language service providers that handle huge numbers of translation requests in various domains typically call upon a large pool of translators (internal and freelance) whose translations are fed into one or several internal *Translation Memories* (TM). Translators access these TMs through a dedicated interface to match requested translations with previously completed ones, speeding up the translation process. Given their provenance and purpose, it is normally assumed that TMs are mostly exempt of incorrect translations (henceforth "*noise*"). Unfortunately, because of the high number of translators involved, with varying levels of expertise, tight deadlines, and other technological issues, noise inevitably accumulates over the years.

TM noise falls under two broad categories. First, *mechanical noise*, which occurs because of the pipeline used to populate the TM, whereby text is extracted from source and target documents, segmented into sentences and then aligned — all three processes producing occasional errors. Second, *human-induced noise*, which can arise for a variety of reasons, including spelling or morphosyntax that do not meet established norms, missing translation units on the target side, as well as typical translation errors such as calques, the use of false friends, etc. These errors reduce the usefulness of a TM, and motivate our investigation into whether *Parallel Corpus Filtering* methods may be useful to increase the quality of a large TM. This contrasts with the typical use of these methods, which are more commonly applied to large, very noisy bilingual corpora automatically extracted from the Web (or other uncontrolled sources).

In the following section (Sec. 2), we discuss related work in more details. We then describe the large TM on which our experiments are based in Section 3, and the corpus filtering methods we implemented in Section 4. We evaluate the performance of these methods by measuring their impact on Neural Machine Translation (NMT) in Section 5, and report our results and analysis in Section 6. We show that, surprisingly, significant translation quality gains can be obtained by cleaning an "already clean" Translation Memory.

2 Related Work

2.1 Identifying Translation

Munteanu and Marcu (2005) presented an early successful method to identify translated sentence pairs (SPs) in a comparable corpus, using a feature-based classifier trained in a supervised way. Features included source-to-target length ratio, bilingual lexicon matches, and a set of features based on IBM word translation models (Brown et al., 1993). The authors showed that the parallel material mined from news extracted over the web improved a downstream statistical translation engine. Progress in deep learning methods recently led to a number of classifiers trained without feature engineering. Notably, Grégoire and Langlais (2018) describe a siamese recurrent neural network that encodes source and target sentences into vectors that are then fed through a non-linear transformation in order to classify a sentence pair as parallel or not. The authors show that training such a model yields better performance than the aforementioned approach, and that adding parallel material extracted from Wikipedia using this model leads to systematic (although modest) gains in both statistical and neural machine translation performance. While these studies convincingly show that parallel sentences can be mined from comparable corpora, it remains unclear whether these methods are also useful for filtering out noise from a relatively clean translation memory.

2.2 Filtering Out Noise

In an early attempt to tackle this issue, Macklovitch (1994) used simple heuristics to detect specific problems observed in real (professional) translations, such as errors in numerical entities, calques, or abnormal translation sizes. Barbu (2015) extended this line of work, proposing 17 features, some based on formal clues (e.g., presence/absence of XML tags, emails, URLs, numbers, capital letters or punctuation), or using external resources (Bing translation API and the language detector Cybozu). Using these features, classifiers were trained to recognize bad translations, using a very small training set (1243 sentence pairs). The best model achieved 81% F-score on 309 test sentence pairs. The author concluded that applying it on MyMemory (Trombetti, 2009) would filter out too many good sentence pairs.

Jalili Sabet et al. (2016) introduced a fully unsupervised Translation Memory cleaning tool called TMOP. It uses 25 different features, some adapted from Barbu (2015), others based on the work of de Souza et al. (2014) and focus on estimating the quality of the translation. They also use multilingual word embeddings, following Søgaard et al. (2015). Each feature acts as a filter for which a score is returned, then TMOP transforms these scores into a final decision (Section 4.3 provides more details). Tested on a subset of the English-Italian MyMemory, their system produced results comparable to Barbu (2015) while being unsupervised.

Recently, there has been increased interest in filtering very noisy, usually web-mined parallel corpora using unsupervised deep learning. Chaudhary et al. (2019) trained multilingual sentence embeddings using LASER (Artetxe and Schwenk, 2018), scoring sentence pairs using an ensemble of evaluation methods like Zipporah (Xu and Koehn, 2017), Bicleaner (Sánchez-Cartagena et al., 2018), and dual conditional cross-entropy filtering (Junczys-Dowmunt, 2018). We tried this approach in our work, but found LASER alone to be significantly more efficient: In the evaluation reported in Table 2 (Section 6), the ensemble approach reached an accuracy of 0.54 vs. 0.84 for LASER alone. Wang et al. (2018) proposed another state-of-the-art online data

Corpus	TM-XL	META-H	BALANCED	MT-TRAIN	MT-TEST	TEST2021
#SPs	139.5M	18.9M	7M	14M	10k	2021
#Types (fr)	1.1M	571k	463k	388k	10.7k	3.48k
#Types (en)	1.4M	681k	444k	466k	12.9k	4.30k

Table 1: Corpora statistics. "#SPs" is the number of sentence pairs. "#Types" are the number of space-separated strings of 15 characters or less containing only alphabetical symbols.

`ori`	If you feel like sleeping , stand up and move to back .
`cor`	If you feels **just napp**ing, **S**tand up and move**s** to **ab**ck .
`ori`	The government of Canada will match your contribution dollar for dollar .
`cor`	The gover**n**nment of **Quebec** will match your **C**ontribution dol**l**lar for dollar.

Figure 1: Examples of original (`ori`) and corrupted (`cor`) sentences.

selection method for de-noising training material and adapting to a specific domain, but this is less suited for large TMs with many domains (200 in our corpus, see below).

3 Datasets

For our experiments, we obtained access to a large English-French corporate TM from a major language service provider (LSP). From this, we extracted various datasets (see also Tab. 1):

TM-XL: From over 1.8M TMX files across more than 200 broad domains (e.g. health, environment), we extracted a total 139 454 913 sentence pairs (SPs). In the TM system used by the LSP, translators may flag a problem with a sentence pair, which marks the entire TMX file containing it as problematic. Flagged material represents 7.7% of all SPs, but we don't know which SP from a flagged TMX was the cause of the problem.

MT-TRAIN: For training the translation engines used for evaluation (Sec. 5), we sampled 14M sentence pairs from TM-XL using stratified sampling to get comparable amounts of SPs in each domain. Of these, 4.3M sentence pairs were sampled from the flagged part of the corpus, so that we could monitor if this material impacts translation.

MT-TEST: We also sampled a test set of 10 000 sentence pairs from TM-XL. To minimize the noise in the test set, our sampling excluded sentences from flagged files as well as SPs labeled as noise by heuristics (see Section 4.1).

META-H: To obtain a training set for our supervised classifiers, we applied the two meta-heuristics described in Sec. 4.1 on TM-XL and identified 17.7M sentence pairs labelled as good and 1.2M labelled as bad, for a total corpus of 18.9M annotated SPs.

BALANCED: Due to the heuristics deployed, most bad SPs in META-H feature obvious errors (gibberish, typos, non-translations, etc.), but lack simple misalignment or subtle translation errors. We extend META-H automatically by: a) 1.15M English sentences paired with a random French sentence (misalignments), and b) 1.15M SPs where each token of 4 or more characters is replaced with one of its top five nearest neighbours in a space of `fastText` word embeddings (Bojanowski et al., 2016) (see corrupted SPs in Fig. 1). Joining those 2.3M artificially generated pairs, the 1.2M bad pairs from META-H, and 3.5M SPs sampled from the 17.7M good pairs in META-H, yields a BALANCED corpus of 7M SPs.

en	Section 34 verification and certification
fr	Fiches de spécimen de signature.
en	Native Women's Association of Canada.
fr	Anaya, Doc. NU A/HRC/9/9, 11 août 2008. Native Women's Association of Canada.
en	Since 2005, we have received some \$1.4 billion to purchase 17 vessels.
fr	Conflicting sovereignty claims to the Arctic are resulting in a race to the North.
en	`OPnj#ϕ'L O- nSk`
fr	`i@n [u05ce \x9b}`

Figure 2: Example noise in TM-XL. Top to bottom: poorly aligned section heads; segmentation problem leading to partial alignment; complete misalignment; character encoding issue.

TEST2021: We conducted targeted manual evaluations on a reduced but representative sample of 2021 SPs, used for evaluation purposes (cf. Sec. 4.1). TEST2021 contains 1182 (58.5%) good and 839 (41.5%) bad SPs.

4 Noisy Sentence Pair Detection

We compare five approaches to identify and filter out noisy sentence pairs.

4.1 Heuristics

A visual inspection[1] of TM-XL led us to identify specific problems that could be detected by rules (see Fig. 2 for examples). We developed 13 heuristics, most of which similar to those implemented in other systems described in Section 2. All heuristics take as input a sentence pair (SP) and produce a score between 0 (noisy SP) and 1 (good SP).

Some heuristics reward matching numerical expressions (NUM), cognates (COG), punctuation (PUNC), or URLs (URL) across pairs of sentences. Two heuristics exploit lists of matching tokens between French and English: one for stop words, based on a lexicon of 93 entries (e.g. *the / la, le, les*) (STOP), one for general vocabulary (LEX) based on a 60k-word bilingual lexicon. One heuristic (ION) matches words ending with suffix *-ion* in French with an identical suffix in English (e.g., *félicitations / congratulations*). Other heuristics aim at detecting common problems: LEN checks the source-to-target length ratio (in words); GIBB detects character encoding problems (last example in Fig. 2); MONO flags pairs where the target segment contains source-language words, suggesting untranslated material; FRIEND penalizes SPs containing false friends, based on a lexicon of 175 entries (e.g. *fabric/fabrique*). We also noticed that segmentation issues within tables of contents led to alignment errors: heuristic TOC aims at filtering these out. Finally, a rudimentary proxy to spell checking (SPELL) counts the number of correctly spelled tokens, using a list of words seen at least 1000 times in Wikipedia.

We evaluate the performance of each heuristic using a set of 1721 sentences pairs: 1321 randomly sampled from TM-XL, plus 400 picked for specific problems. We annotated these 1721 sentence pairs and used them to adjust the thresholds of our heuristics and to select the optimal combination of heuristics to discriminate good SPs from bad. For detecting good SPs, the solution that worked best is a weighted combination of 4 heuristics: NUM, LEX, ION, and PUNC, while the meta-heuristic that worked best to predict problematic SPs is a mix of 9 heuristics. To further evaluate these two "meta-heuristics", we manually inspected a random sample of 150 SPs selected by each (i.e. identified as good or bad respectively) and found 115 good SPs in the former sample (76.7%), and 121 bad SPs in the latter (80.7%).

[1] Separate from the Manual evaluation.

4.2 Feature-based Classifiers

We trained support vector machines (SVM) and random forest classifiers on the BALANCED corpus to detect noisy pairs of segments. The features for each SP are the scores (between 0 and 1) of each of the 13 heuristics in Sec. 4.1, plus some intermediate values produced while computing the heuristics, for a total of 60 features. We added two features: the percentage of heuristics that label the pair as *good* (resp. *bad*). We trained the classifiers with `scikit-learn`[2] on standard desktop CPUs, which took approximately 10 hours per classifier.

4.3 TMOP

TMOP (Jalili Sabet et al., 2016) uses 25 binary functions meant to capture misalignments, poor translation quality or large semantic distance between source and target. Three ready-made configurations control how these functions combine into a final decision. The configuration we use classifies an SP as noise if at least five functions signal a problem. In our experiments, this configuration was by far the most useful: the "one reject" configuration produced far too many false negatives, while the "majority vote" hardly detected any *bad* sentence pair. Similarly to Munteanu and Marcu (2005), TMOP relies (among other things) on IBM Model features computed with MGIZA.[3] Running MGIZA on the 14M SPs in MT-TRAIN on a 16-core cluster equipped with 70Gb of memory took 13 days. After alignment, TMOP ran on a dedicated cluster of 32 CPUs with 300Gb of RAM, and took 5 more days, including 6 hours to compute embeddings. Therefore, applying TMOP on the full TM-XL corpus would be rather challenging.

4.4 Deep-Learning Classifier

We reimplemented the model of Grégoire and Langlais (2018) in Keras (Chollet et al., 2015), introducing a few variants we found useful. The model architecture consists of two bidirectional LSTMs (Hochreiter and Schmidhuber, 1997), each with 300 hidden units encoding sentences into two continuous vector representations. In their original paper, Grégoire and Langlais (2018) use 512-dimensional word embeddings and 512-dimensional recurrent states and learn the word embeddings from scratch. For easier and faster training, we adapt pre-trained 300-dimensional `fastText` embbedings. Also, we do not tie the parameters of the two encoders, contrary to Grégoire and Langlais (2018). Source and target representations are then fed into a Feed-Forward Neural Network with two hidden layers of 150 and 75 units (respectively), followed by a sigmoid activation function, which outputs the probability that the input SP is well aligned. We trained the model using the Adadelta optimizer (Zeiler, 2012) with gradient clipping (clipped at 5) to avoid exploding gradient and a batch of size 300, which took about 2.5 hours using 4 Tesla V100-SXM2 for 10 epochs.

4.5 LASER

We also use the LASER toolkit[4] (Artetxe and Schwenk, 2018) to detect noisy pairs. LASER is a bi-LSTM encoder trained on data from 93 different languages, written in 23 alphabets, such that semantically similar sentences in different languages are close in the embedding space. For each source-language sentence s_i in MT-TRAIN, we use the multilingual-similarity search (MSS) method from the toolkit to find the closest target-language sentence t_j in the embedding space. If $i = j$, the sentence pair is considered *good*, otherwise it is *bad* and filtered out. Obviously, we could investigate a less stringent scenario, which we leave for future work. This is entirely unsupervised, using the model *as is*, out of the box. Running this method on one

[2]`https://scikit-learn.org/stable/`.

[3]`http://www.cs.cmu.edu/~qing/giza/`.

[4]`https://github.com/facebookresearch/LASER`.

Tesla V100-SXM2 took approximately 14 hours, despite the quadratic number of comparisons involved.

5 Neural Machine Translation Models

We evaluate the quality of a TM using the performance of a translation engine trained on it as a task-based proxy. To reach conclusions that are independent of a specific system, we experiment with two very different neural translation models: XLM, a deep transformer model, and ConvS2S, a convolutional seq2seq model. Typical training time on 4 Tesla V100-SXM2 was 22-30 hours for XLM and 72-96 hours for ConvS2S, depending on the dataset.

5.1 Cross-lingual Language Model

Lample and Conneau (2019) proposed a supervised model, the Translation Language Modeling (TLM), tackling cross-lingual pre-training in a way similar to BERT (Devlin et al., 2018), with notable differences. First, XLM is based on a shared source-target sub-word vocabulary, computed using byte pair encoding (BPE) (Sennrich et al., 2016). We used the 60k BPE vocabulary from the pre-trained language model.[5] Second, XLM is trained to predict both source and target masked words, leveraging surrounding words and context on both sides and encouraging the model to align source and target representations. Third, XLM embeds the tokens *and* their position, building a relationship between the related tokens in both languages. XLM is implemented in PyTorch and supports distributed training on multiple GPUs.[6] We modified the original pre-processing code so that XLM accepts a parallel corpus for training TLM. The translation is produced using a beam search of width 6 and unity length penalty.

5.2 Convolutional Sequence to Sequence

The predominant method for sequence to sequence (seq2seq) learning is to map an input sequence to an output sequence of variable length via a recurrent neural network such as an LSTM (Hochreiter and Schmidhuber, 1997). Gehring et al. (2017) showed that convolutional neural networks (CNN) could also be used for seq2seq. The ConvS2S model uses CNNs with Gated Linear Units (Dauphin et al., 2016) for both the encoder and decoder, and includes a multi-step attention layer. We used the fairseq toolkit (Ott et al., 2019), with a source and target vocabulary of 60k BPE types. The translation is generated by a beam-search decoder with log-likelihood scores normalized by sentence length.

6 Experimental Results

We now report results on noisy SP detection and its impact on machine translation.

6.1 Sentence Pair Detection

Table 2 reports the tested methods' accuracy on the manually annotated TEST2021. The meta-heuristics alone perform worst. Training RF and SVM classifiers on top of heuristics features clearly helps, with the SVM showing a slight advantage. TMOP delivers comparable results, suggesting that combining heuristics, word-based translation and embeddings makes a good detector. The bi-LSTM model, without any feature engineering, yields much better results overall, confirming observations by Grégoire and Langlais (2018) on artificial data. Surprisingly, the best results are obtained by the fully unsupervised LASER. Of course, TEST2021 is a rather small test set, and results here should be taken with a grain of salt.

[5]Training TLM without pre-training proved unstable. Back translation gave better results, at a high training cost.

[6]`https://github.com/facebookresearch/XLM.git.`

Method	TMOP*	meta-h*	RF	SVM	bi-LSTM	LASER*
Accuracy	0.60	0.42	0.60	0.63	0.79	0.84

Table 2: Accuracy on TEST2021. See text for method details (* are unsupervised). 95% error bars on estimates are $\approx \pm 2\%$.

Train set	MT-TRAIN	−flagged	TMOP	meta-h	SVM	bi-LSTM	LASER	∩ALL
#SP (M)	14	9.67	13.38	8.15	7.50	6.13	9.65	5.80
XLM	36.25	36.29	36.49	36.80	36.53	‡37.52	‡37.23	‡37.57
ConvS2S	33.04	33.33	33.51	†33.78	†33.91	‡33.96	33.58	†33.93

Table 3: BLEU scores of the XLM and ConvS2S translation engines. −flagged is MT-TRAIN without the flagged documents (Sec. 3). ‡ (resp. †) means improvement over MT-TRAIN is significant at the 99% (resp. 95%) confidence level using `multeval` (Clark et al., 2011).

6.2 Machine Translation Evaluation

Machine translation is used as an extrinsic evaluation of our corpus cleaning methods. Note that the goal is not to optimize the use of a TM on a single MT engine as in (Cao and Xiong, 2018, for example), but to evaluate systematic differences in MT performance before and after cleaning, using two very different state-of-the-art neural translation engines. Similarly, we acknowledge that neither of the MT systems used here is optimized to reach current state-of-the-art (although in separate experiments, we observed that XLM came close). We are mainly interested in observing relative performance differences for different filtering, and as we will see below, these trends are consistent, despite significant differences in absolute performance.

Table 3 shows BLEU scores obtained by XLM and ConvS2S on portions of MT-TRAIN produced by different filtering approaches. ConvS2S is consistently about 3 BLEU points worse than XLM, but reflects the same trends overall. Removing the flagged material (-flagged) from MT-TRAIN hardly impacts BLEU, which supports our observations that the flagged material was generally of good quality. Out of the box, TMOP filters out very few SPs (less than 5%), without producing any significant gain in BLEU. Some adaptation to the Translation Memory may be needed to deploy it efficiently. Table 3 also shows that all methods described in Section 4 filter a significant portion of MT-TRAIN (31% to 56%), resulting in BLEU gains that are sometimes highly significant. This is already a surprising outcome, for a corpus sampled from a TM, which is supposed to be already clean. The largest gains come from the supervised bi-LSTM approach, which also filters out more material, with the unsupervised LASER not far behind. Using the intersection of all our filters (last column in Tab. 3) filters a few more SPs, and further improves performance. The final BLEU gain is +1.22 for XLM (+0.89 for ConvS2S) with only 42% of MT-TRAIN remaining. It is interesting to note that -flagged and LASER yield very similar amounts of training material, but the latter results in significantly higher BLEU. This suggests that 1) as mentioned previously, the flagged material contains clean material that is useful to the MT engine, while 2) the non-flagged portion of the TM contains noisy material that has not been flagged by translators, but can be filtered out to improve MT performance.

Fig. 3 plots the BLEU scores on the test set (versus epochs) for XLM translation engines trained on the different portions of MT-TRAIN. We observe similar training curves, including a sharp increase in performance at epoch 10, for all systems, and systematic gains at each epoch.

6.3 Analysis

We now investigate various aspects of the cleaning process.

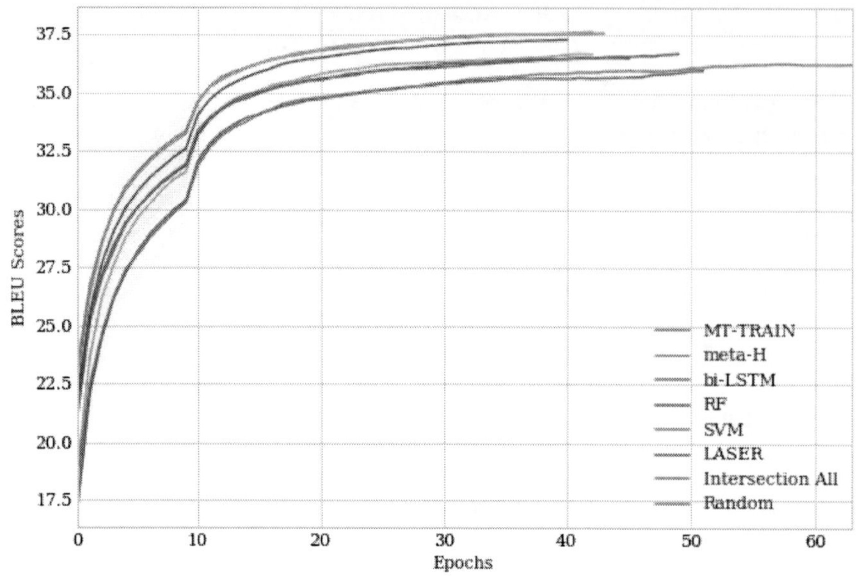

Figure 3: BLEU scores of XLM versus epochs for the different training sets we considered.

Domain Specificity. One possible concern is that the filtering is essentially performing some kind of adaptation to the test set. We first note that MT-TRAIN and MT-TEST are both sampled from TM-XL and are similarly balanced according to domain information recorded in the TM. We also compare the domain distribution in the original TM to that in MT-TRAIN and its various filtered versions, using the Kullback-Leibler (KL) divergence: All filtered subsets yield a divergence close to that computed between MT-TRAIN and the original TM (KL $= 0.0110$). This suggest that the domain distribution is not affected by any filtering method.

Combining Methods. Different filtering methods remove different amounts and portions of MT-TRAIN (Tab. 3). We checked agreement between the meta-H, bi-LSTM and LASER filters and observe that 93.4% of SPs identified as noise by LASER were also labeled as such by bi-LSTM, while the agreement on noise between LASER and either meta-H or SVM is approximately 65%. Removing SPs labeled as noise by any of meta-H, bi-LSTM or LASER (named $\cap$ALL in Tab. 3) results in a corpus of 5.8M sentence pairs, which yields BLEU scores similar to bi-LSTM. This suggests that the deep learning methods do not benefit from the other techniques, although they allow to further clean the corpus with no performance loss. As a sanity check, we randomly select a subset of 5.8M SPs from MT-TRAIN, and observe a drop in translation performance of -1.26 and -0.93 BLEU for XLM and ConvS2S respectively (not shown in Table 3). This further supports the claim that our methods do perform a useful cleaning of the translation memory.

Unknown Words. Both translation engines use a fixed set of 60k BPE subword units. Some target words in the training material can not be reproduced using that limited vocabulary. For the XLM translation engine on MT-TRAIN, we count 76k such token types. Manual inspection shows that the vast majority are gibberish words, e.g. *t0DÉlmsäoyCœ*, likely document conversion problems. Filtering the training material with SVM, bi-LSTM and LASER, reduces the number of unrepresentable token types to around 3k, 450 and 17k, respectively. This indicates that our cleaning approaches (especially bi-LSTM) efficiently reduce the number of unknown, gibberish words.

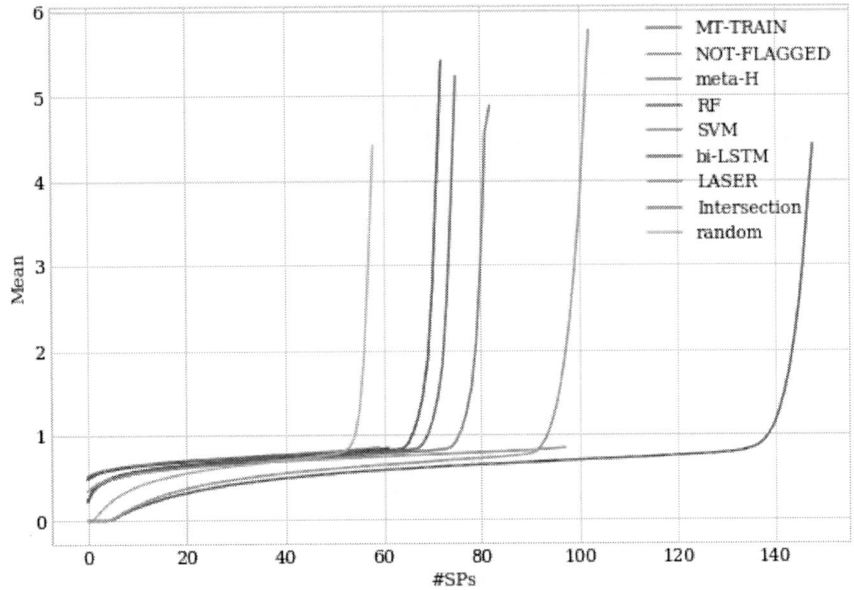

Figure 4: Average length-ratio of sentence pairs of the different sub-corpora of MT-TRAIN as a function of the number of slices of 100k SPs considered.

Length-ratio. Figure 4 shows the length ratio (|en|/|fr|) of sentence pairs in portions of MT-TRAIN filtered in different ways, in blocks of 100k SPs sorted by increasing length ratio. The curve for MT-TRAIN starts near zero (much longer French sentence) flattens slightly below 1 as expected, and peeks around 4 (longer English sentences). Both extremes very likely indicate alignment problems. Applying meta-heuristics or feature-based classifiers reduces near-zero and high ratios to some extent. Noticeably, bi-LSTM and LASER remove most of the SPs with extreme length ratios, leading to an average around 0.8 (French is about 20% longer than English, on average). This suggests that cleaning is indeed being performed, removing extreme misalignments.

Other Evidence of Cleaning. MT-TRAIN contains 25 203 sentence pairs with a *www* token in English, but not on the French side, versus 57 925 with matching *www* token, a ratio of 43.5%. SVM, bi-LSTM and LASER lower that ratio to 10.5%, 3.1% and 4.9% respectively, after filtering. We also manually annotated 100 sentence pairs from ∩ALL, i.e. classified as good by all approaches, and 100 sentence pairs classified as noise by bi-LSTM and LASER. We found 16 false positives in the former and 33 false negatives in the latter. This suggests that deep learning methods are excessively strict noise detectors. This, however, does not seem to impact MT performance adversely.

Reproducibility. While we had the opportunity to work on a large, high quality professional TM, we realize that our results can not be replicated exactly. By nature, large professional TMs are proprietary and not easily shared. We argue however that one can easily *reproduce* (Drummond, 2009) our experiments on another corpus or TM, using the information from Sections 4 to 5. In addition, the main building blocks for the better-performing filtering and translation pipelines are publicly available.

Generalizability to other languages. For the same reason (access to a large professional TM), we only performed experiments on a single language pair comprising similar languages with, e.g., many cognates. We acknowledge that it is an interesting and important issue to establish whether a similar approach applies to languages with different characteristics, e.g. complex morphology, or differing word order or sentence structure. The availability of deep learning models such as LASER on a (relatively) large number of languages should make it straightforward to experiment on many other language pairs to check whether the results presented in this paper generalize.

7 Conclusions

We explored several ways to filter a mostly clean Translation Memory, used daily by professional translators. We showed that (pre-trained) LASER and (trained in-house) bi-LSTM are able to discriminate noisy sentence pairs from clean ones with high accuracy. The former is unsupervised, delivering the best results on our small scale manual evaluation. Both methods outperform heuristics devised specifically for this task, feature-based classifiers trained with supervision, as well as the TMOP system which turned out to be very challenging to deploy. We also showed that filtering the noisy SPs results in machine translation gains. Deep learning methods allow significant gains in BLEU: the bi-LSTM classifier filters out over half the training material, and yields a gain of over one BLEU point. Future work includes better characterizing, modeling and generating subtle noise in misaligned segments, in order to build better detectors.

Acknowledgements

We wish to thank the anonymous reviewers for their insightful and helpful comments.

References

Artetxe, M. and Schwenk, H. (2018). Massively multilingual sentence embeddings for zero-shot cross-lingual transfer and beyond. *arXiv:1812.10464*.

Barbu, E. (2015). Spotting false translation segments in translation memories. In *Proc. Workshop on Natural Language Processing for Translation Memories*, pages 9–16.

Bojanowski, P., Grave, E., Joulin, A., and Mikolov, T. (2016). Enriching word vectors with subword information. *arXiv:1607.04606*.

Brown, P. F., Della Pietra, S. A., Della Pietra, V. J., and Mercer, R. L. (1993). The mathematics of statistical machine translation: Parameter estimation. *Comput. Ling.*, 19(2):263–311.

Cao, Q. and Xiong, D. (2018). Encoding gated translation memory into neural machine translation. In *Proc. Empirical Methods in Natural Language Processing*, pages 3042–3047.

Chaudhary, V., Tang, Y., Guzmán, F., Schwenk, H., and Koehn, P. (2019). Low-resource corpus filtering using multilingual sentence embeddings. *arXiv:1906.08885*.

Chollet, F. et al. (2015). Keras. `https://keras.io`.

Clark, J. H., Dyer, C., Lavie, A., and Smith, N. A. (2011). Better hypothesis testing for statistical machine translation: Controlling for optimizer instability. In *Proc. 49th Annual Meeting of the ACL: Human Language Technologies*, pages 176–181, Portland, OR.

Dauphin, Y. N., Fan, A., Auli, M., and Grangier, D. (2016). Language modeling with gated convolutional networks. *arXiv:1612.08083*.

de Souza, J. G., Turchi, M., and Negri, M. (2014). Machine translation quality estimation across domains. In *Proc. 25th Intl. Conf. on Computational Linguistics (COLING)*, pages 409–420.

Devlin, J., Chang, M.-W., Lee, K., and Toutanova, K. (2018). Bert: Pre-training of deep bidirectional transformers for language understanding. *arXiv:1810.04805*.

Drummond, C. (2009). Replicability is not reproducibility: nor is it good science. In *Proceedings of the Evaluation Methods for Machine Learning Workshop at the 26th ICML*.

Gehring, J., Auli, M., Grangier, D., Yarats, D., and Dauphin, Y. N. (2017). Convolutional sequence to sequence learning. *arXiv:1705.03122*.

Grégoire, F. and Langlais, P. (2018). Extracting parallel sentences with bidirectional recurrent neural networks to improve machine translation. In *Proc. 27th Intl Conf. on Computational Linguistics (COLING)*, pages 1442–1453, Santa Fe, NM.

Hochreiter, S. and Schmidhuber, J. (1997). Long short-term memory. *Neural Computation*, 9(8):1735–1780.

Jalili Sabet, M., Negri, M., Turchi, M., de Souza, J. G., and Federico, M. (2016). TMop: a tool for unsupervised translation memory cleaning. In *Proc. of the ACL, System Demonstrations*.

Junczys-Dowmunt, M. (2018). Dual conditional cross-entropy filtering of noisy parallel corpora. In *Proc. 3rd Conf. on Machine Translation*, pages 888–895, Belgium, Brussels.

Lample, G. and Conneau, A. (2019). Cross-lingual Language Model Pretraining. *arXiv:1901.07291*.

Macklovitch, E. (1994). Using bi-textual alignment for translation validation: the TransCheck system. In *1st Conf. Association for Machine Translation in the Americas*, Columbia, USA.

Munteanu, D. S. and Marcu, D. (2005). Improving machine translation performance by exploiting non-parallel corpora. *Computational Linguistics*, 31(4):477–504.

Ott, M., Edunov, S., Baevski, A., Fan, A., Gross, S., Ng, N., Grangier, D., and Auli, M. (2019). fairseq: A fast, extensible toolkit for sequence modeling. In *Proc. 2019 Conf. North American Chapter of the ACL (Demonstrations)*, pages 48–53, Minneapolis, MN.

Sánchez-Cartagena, V. M., Bañón, M., Ortiz-Rojas, S., and Ramírez, G. (2018). Prompsit's submission to WMT 2018 parallel corpus filtering shared task. In *Proc. 3rd Conf. on Machine Translation*, pages 955–962, Belgium, Brussels.

Sennrich, R., Haddow, B., and Birch, A. (2016). Neural machine translation of rare words with subword units. In *Proc. 54th Annual Meeting of the ACL*, pages 1715–1725.

Søgaard, A., Agić, Ž., Alonso, H. M., Plank, B., Bohnet, B., and Johannsen, A. (2015). Inverted indexing for cross-lingual NLP. In *Proc. 53rd Meeting of the ACL (ACL-IJCNLP)*.

Trombetti, M. (2009). Creating the world's largest translation memory. In *MT Summit XII*.

Wang, W., Watanabe, T., Hughes, M., Nakagawa, T., and Chelba, C. (2018). Denoising neural machine translation training with trusted data and online data selection. In *Proc. 3rd Conf. on Machine Translation*, pages 133–143, Brussels, Belgium.

Xu, H. and Koehn, P. (2017). Zipporah: a fast and scalable data cleaning system for noisy web-crawled parallel corpora. In *Proc. Empirical Methods in Natural Language Processing*, pages 2945–2950, Copenhagen, Denmark.

Zeiler, M. D. (2012). Adadelta: An adaptive learning rate method. *arXiv:1212.5701*.

Practical Attacks on Machine Translation Using Paraphrase

Elizabeth M. Merkhofer emerkhofer@mitre.org
John C. Henderson jhndrsn@mitre.org
Abigail S. Gertner gertner@mitre.org
Michael D. Doyle mdoyle@mitre.org
Lily Wong lwong@mitre.org
MITRE, McLean, Virginia, 22102, USA

Abstract

Studies show machine translation systems are vulnerable to adversarial attacks, where a small change to the input produces an undesirable change in system behavior. This work considers whether this vulnerability exists for attacks crafted with limited information about the target: without access to ground truth references or the particular MT system under attack. It also applies a higher threshold of success, taking into account both source language meaning preservation and target language meaning degradation. We propose an attack that generates edits to an input using a finite state transducer over lexical and phrasal paraphrases and selects one perturbation for meaning preservation and expected degradation of a target system. Attacks against eight state-of-the-art translation systems covering English-German, English-Czech and English-Chinese are evaluated under black-box and transfer scenarios, including cross-language and cross-system transfer. Results suggest that successful single-system attacks seldom transfer across models, especially when crafted without ground truth, but ensembles show promise for generalizing attacks.

1 Introduction

Recent studies show that natural language processing (NLP) applications are vulnerable to *adversarial perturbations*, where a small change to the input produces an undesirable change in system behavior, such as a lower-quality translation in a machine translation (MT) system (Ebrahimi et al., 2018; Cheng et al., 2019; Wallace et al., 2019; Cheng et al., 2020; Zhao et al., 2018; Zhang et al., 2021). These adversarial inputs offer insight into model robustness. They also can constitute vulnerabilities that expose everyday technology to malicious actors who would seek to deny and deceive artificial intelligence systems.

Practical concerns must be addressed to determine if these vulnerabilities persist outside of simplified scenarios. Most previous work uses the same ground truth to craft and evaluate an attack and relies on access to the model being attacked, such as model gradients (white-box) or the output of the model (black-box). We ask whether this vulnerability extends to attacks crafted with limited information about the target: without access to ground truth references, model weights or even the outputs of the particular MT system they are attacking. We examine transfer of adversarial examples among eight different MT systems with three target languages. For evaluation, we use a high threshold of success that takes into account both effect on translation quality and loss of meaning in the original text.

We introduce a novel text editing system (perturber) that rapidly generates hundreds or thousands of candidate edits using a compendium of vetted paraphrases scored to match human quality judgments. Adversarial edits are selected according to a configurable optimization trading off preservation of source-side meaning and degradation of target output. To simulate a scenario where a human reference is not available, the selector estimates degradation in translation quality using the change in translation output from a proxy MT system. These attacks meet the threshold for success when the MT system used for selection is matched to the victim model or when an ensemble of MT systems is used to do the targeting. However, we find that examples selected using a single translation model as proxy and ensembles crafted without sensitivity to source-side meaning changes do not often transfer to another victim model above the success threshold.

2 Practical Considerations

Overwhelmingly, previous work assumes high-information scenarios, using the same ground truth and model to craft and evaluate the attacks, and evaluates adversarial effect separately from the effect on the semantics of the input (Ebrahimi et al., 2018; Cheng et al., 2019; Wallace et al., 2019; Cheng et al., 2020; Zhao et al., 2018; Zhang et al., 2021). We address four considerations in evaluation of machine translation attacks with the purpose of understanding whether these attacks can be crafted in lower-information scenarios and whether the effect on system performance outweighs the degradation of the input text. First, we define our success criterion in a metric-independent way, drawing from Michel et al. (2019), to combine adversarial effect and degradation of the source in a single metric. Second, we calibrate similarity metrics so that one unit of meaning preservation in the source language side is as close as possible to one unit of translation quality in the target language side. Third, we consider whether attacks require access to ground truth to successfully degrade performance. Finally, we address whether attacks crafted using one system can be deployed against another to which it does not have access.

2.1 Successful MT Attacks

Effective adversaries do not simply change a system's behavior; they reliably degrade its performance. To attack MT, perturbations aim to maximally decrease translation quality with respect to the ground truth reference. The translations of a set of perturbed source segments should score lower than the originals under some MT metric, such as BLEU or CHRF. However, to ensure that the perturbations haven't trivially reduced translation quality by changing the meaning on the source side, we must also account for the effect of the perturbations on the meaning of the source.

We directly adopt several terms and metrics from Michel et al. (2019). We follow the convention that x and y refer to source and target language sentences, y_M is the translation produced by model M, and $\hat{x}$ and $\hat{y}_M$ are the perturbed version of the source sentence and its translation. We measure the translation quality of an attack by the *target similarity*, $s_{tgt}(y, \hat{y}_M)$, where y is a gold source reference translation and $\hat{y}_M$ is the MT system output on the perturbed input. The effect of a perturbation on the input text is measured by the *source similarity*, $s_{src}(x, \hat{x})$.

An attack degrades the target similarity by d_{tgt} in Equation 1. This is also referred to as *target relative score decrease*. It is similar to the version found in Michel et al. (2019) except we allow negative values of d_{tgt} if an attack inadvertently makes the translation *better*. We do this because we do not presume oracular access to a reference translation y at targeting time to decide when to avoid using a particular $\hat{x}$ for attack. A higher value of d_{tgt} means the output of the MT was more degraded. A value of zero means no degradation. Similarly, an attack degrades the source similarity by d_{src} in Equation 2. Using relative rather than absolute score decreases makes it possible to compare attack effectiveness across models with different original performance.

$$d_{tgt}(y, y_M, \hat{y}_M) = \frac{s_{tgt}(y, y_M) - s_{tgt}(y, \hat{y}_M)}{s_{tgt}(y, y_M)} \quad (1)$$

$$d_{src}(x, \hat{x}) = (1 - s_{src}(x, \hat{x}))/1 \quad (2)$$

A successful attack reduces the target side translation similarity more than it reduces the similarity of the perturbed $\hat{x}$ to x. This is reflected in Equation 3, also following Michel et al. (2019) aside from the difference in d_{tgt}. When success, S, is greater than one, the attack achieved that goal. S values below 1 indicate the source side texts were degraded more than the effect on the translation.

$$\begin{aligned} S &= 1 + d_{tgt}(y, y_M, \hat{y}_M) - d_{src}(x, \hat{x}) \\ &= \frac{s_{tgt}(y, y_M) - s_{tgt}(y, \hat{y}_M)}{s_{tgt}(y, y_M)} + s_{src}(x, \hat{x}) \end{aligned} \quad (3)$$

We estimate both source- and target-side similarity using CHRF (Popović, 2015). This metric has been found to be well-correlated to human perception of meaning preservation for varied machine edits (Michel et al., 2019; Merkhofer et al., 2021), and it best matches human perception of machine translation quality at a segment level for the language pairs studied (Mathur et al., 2020).

2.2 Calibrating Meaning Preservation Metrics in Multiple Languages

Most semantic similarity metrics are designed and tested to match human judgments in one language, but they generally aren't calibrated to line up with each other *across languages*. The success criterion in Equation 3 directly compares similarity in source and target languages, but a similarity reduction in the source language needs to be commensurate with the similarity reduction in the target language. Otherwise, perturbations may game the difference between the two scales rather than truly exploiting an MT weakness. A set of examples motivating the differences in CHRF values in different languages can be see in Table 1. This can be replicated for other languages and other metrics, as MT metrics are typically not calibrated across languages, especially not at sentence-level granularity.

Calibration of metrics in different languages relies on common sources of strings with the same distribution of meanings in the two languages. We collect a distribution of $s(x_i, x_j)$ values from random strings following the same sampling pattern in each of the languages. We convert those empirical distributions into complementary cumulative distribution functions (CCDF) to work well with log scale. Figure 1 shows the empirical distribution of CHRF scores accumulated using random strings sourced form WMT20 parallel data (Barrault et al., 2020). The samples were synchronized across the languages so the same underlying distributions were reflected in each curve. Using sampled $i, j \in 1 \ldots N$ from the N sentences available, strings used are $i_{\lfloor x\texttt{len}(i)\rfloor:\lfloor y\texttt{len}(i)\rfloor}$ and $j_{\lfloor z\texttt{len}(j)\rfloor:\lfloor w\texttt{len}(j)\rfloor}$, where $x < y, z < w \in [0, 1)$.

Conversion of the calibrated scores from the CCDFs to a common language and range is done by linear interpolation. Each curve is approximated with 1000 points as shown in Figure 1. To calculate an associated English CHRF$_{EN}$ for an input Chinese CHRF value, x, we find the closest two surrounding x-axis pairs of the *zh* CCDF curve and interpolate between them to get y', the estimated CCDF value for that input x. Then the process is performed again using the *en* curve. We find the two closest y-values on the *en* curve and interpolate using y' to find an x' on the x-axis of the *en* curve. The resulting converted metrics, all calibrated to English, are shown in Figure 2.

σ	CHRF	segment pair
0.21	0.61	Afghanistan boosts security for presidential election A massive security operation is in place across Afghanistan for the country's presidential election on Saturday.
	0.65	Afghanistan verstärkt die Sicherheit für die Präsidentschaftswahlen Für die Präsidentschaftswahlen am Samstag ist in ganz Afghanistan eine umfangreiche Sicherheitsoperati on im Gange.
	0.58	Afghánistán zvyšuje bezpečnostní opatření provázející prezidentské volby V Afghánistánu probíhají masivní bezpečnostní opatření pro zajištění bezpečnosti při sobotních prezide ntských volbách.
	0.13	阿富汗加强安保应对总统选举 阿富汗在全国范围内开展了大规模的安保行动，为星期六的国家总统大选做好准备。
0.29	0.89	Men undergoing surgery for prostate cancer fare as well without radiotherapy Men undergoing surgery for prostate cancer fare just as well without radiotherapy, a major study has found.
	0.48	Männern geht es nach einer Operation wegen Prostatakrebs mit und ohne Strahlentherapie gleich gut Laut einer Studie gibt es keinen Unterschied, ob sich Männer, die wegen Prostatakrebs operiert wurden, einer Strahlentherapie unterziehen oder nicht.
	0.96	Muži, kteří trpí rakovinou prostaty a jdou na operaci, nemusejí podstoupit radioterapii Muži, kteří trpí rakovinou prostaty a jdou na operaci, nemusejí podstoupit radioterapii, zjistila studie.
	0.24	前列腺癌手术后跳过放疗，效果良好 一项重大研究发现，接受前列腺癌手术的男性在不接受放射治疗的情况下状态良好。

Table 1: Examples of high CHRF variance from the WMT20 dataset. σ is the standard deviation of the set of four CHRF scores. Each pair in a set would ideally exhibit the same meaning preservation score.

2.3 Crafting Attacks without Reference Translations

Black-box adversarial examples are crafted by probing the victim system for translations, with the goal of finding a perturbed input that minimizes similarity between the system translation and the reference. In the literature, this is typically the same ground truth reference used for evaluation, but in a practical attack, acquiring a human translation for each segment would be prohibitively slow and expensive. We craft perturbations using the system translation of the original source segment in place of a targeted reference translation to simulate a more realistic, low-information scenario where an adversary doesn't have access to a ground truth. In this case, the probes reveal how system behavior changes but not how translation quality with respect to a human reference translation is affected. This allows us to examine whether simply probing the system can effectively predict perturbations to reduce system performance.

2.4 Transfer: Using one MT System as Proxy Target for Another

We examine *transfer attacks* by measuring the effect of each set of black-box perturbations on the other MT systems. Without direct white-box access to the model gradient or black-box access to repeated probes, transfer attacks rely on the nature of language or implicit similarity between systems. When perturbations succeed against another model, the first system can serve as a proxy to craft attacks on the victim system. Intuitions suggest that transfer attacks are less

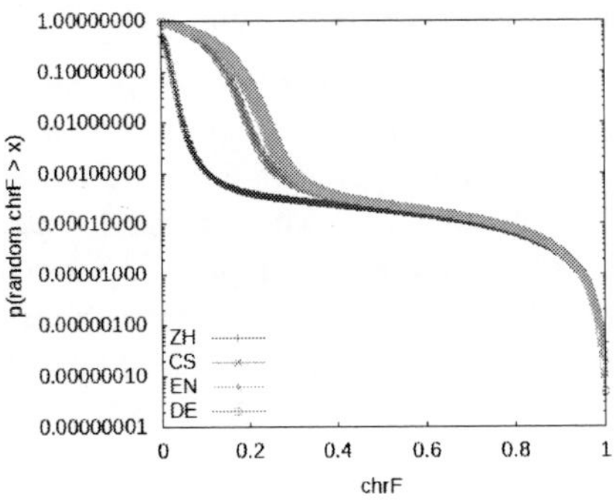

Figure 1: Complementary cumulative distribution functions for CHRF in different languages.

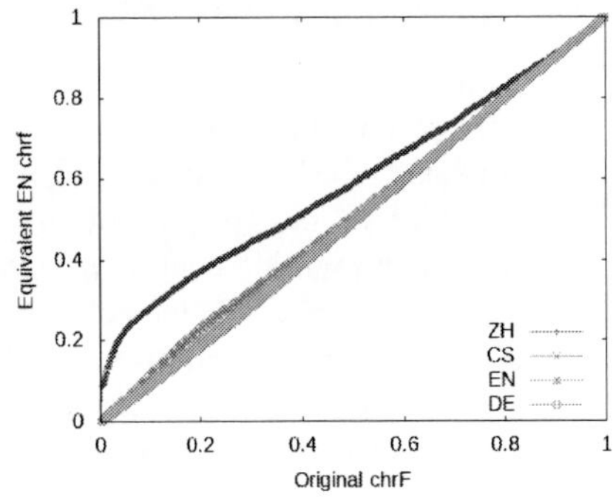

Figure 2: English-equivalent CHRF calibrations.

likely to be effective than black-box attacks, but we want to measure that effect. We also investigate ensemble perturbers, which select edits based on expected performance against multiple MT systems, as an instance of transfer.

3 Experiments

We present a novel attack mechanism that uses a finite state transducer-based paraphraser to generate paraphrases and then selects the best candidate as the attack. We test two targeting conditions, **reference**, where the attack is crafted using ground truth translations from the dataset, and **MT**, where only the system translation of the original source is used. Each set of perturbations is evaluated against the MT system used to craft it (**black box**) and each of the other MT systems (**transfer**). Much of the prior work uses reference translations for attack crafting and presents primarily black-box evaluations, but crafting perturbations using only MT outputs and testing transfer to inaccessible systems is a more realistic, low-information scenario. We compare our adversarial FST to the black-box SEQ2SICK approach from (Cheng et al., 2020) under the same conditions. The evaluation metrics are calibrated CHRF, converted into English-equivalent CHRF_{EN}, and Success using calibrated CHRF.

3.1 Data

Our experiments use the WMT 2020 test sets for EN-DE, EN-CS and EN-ZH (Barrault et al., 2020). The source for each target language test set consists of the same 1418 English-language segments from the news domain.

3.2 MT Systems

Our experiments probe eight trained machine translation systems acquired from the Transformers model zoo (HuggingFace, 2020). **mBART** English-to-Many is a transformer with multilingual pretraining that is fine tuned to translate from English into many other languages including DE, CS and ZH (Tang et al., 2020). We use separate bilingual EN-DE, EN-CS and EN-ZH models from **OPUS-MT** (Tiedemann and Thottingal, 2020). We use EN-DE bilingual models from Kasai et al. (2020) (**Allen**) and Ng et al. (2019) (**Facebook**). For every system, we use a beam size of five.

3.3 Attack: Finite State Transducer-based Paraphraser With Rescoring

We produce adversarial examples by first generating a large portfolio of paraphrases $\hat{X} = \{\hat{x}_{1...n}\}$ for the input x, then selecting the best candidate under a configurable mix of source similarity and attack effectiveness. For these experiments, we weight these two factors equally.

To preserve the semantics of an input, our method begins with high-quality paraphrases. We compile 2.3 million *equivalence* paraphrases from the Penn Paraphrase Database (PPDB) (Ganitkevitch et al., 2013) into a finite state transducer (FST) rewriting input strings. We use a log transform of the PPDB2 score, the estimate of human acceptance included with each PPDB entry, as the weight for the transduction and follow the methods of Stahlberg et al. (2019) to generate a lattice of alternatives for input strings. We minimize the lattice FST resulting from the composition of the input string with the transducer, remove epsilons and determinize, then use the shortest path search. We keep the n-best list of alternatives to use as our candidate edit pool, with $n = 1000$. It takes an average of 0.085 seconds on one CPU to obtain 1000 alternatives for the input sentences studied in this paper using the `pynini` toolkit (Gorman, 2016) built on top of OpenFST (Allauzen et al., 2007).

We select one perturbation $\hat{x}$ per segment per system that balances attack effectiveness and meaning preservation. We estimate both in terms of similarities as measured by CHRF. Meaning preservation is measured by comparing the original source and the candidate paraphrase, $s_{src}(x, \hat{x})$. For every translation system M, we obtain translations y_M for x, the original source, and $\hat{y}_M$ for each $\hat{x}$. Attack effectiveness is estimated by measuring how much the system output differs from the output on the original text, that is $s_{tgt}(y_M, \hat{y}_M)$, for the MT condition, or by measuring degradation in translation quality $s_{tgt}(y, \hat{y}_M)$ for the reference condition. For MT system M, we select the candidate $\hat{x}$ that maximizes $f(\hat{x}, M) = s_{src}(x, \hat{x}) - s_{tgt}(y_M, \hat{y}_M)$, equally weighting source attack effectiveness and meaning preservation.

Meaning preservation $s_{src}(x, \hat{x})$ and attack scores $s_{tgt}(y_M, \hat{y}_M)$ are scaled prior to selection with a simple Gaussian transform to get them into a comparable range. Without the score transform, the source language similarity scores would tend to be very high compared to the MT similarity scores. This rescaling makes the aggregate optimization more well-balanced.

3.4 Ensemble attacks

Ensemble attacks were crafted by evaluating attack candidates using multiple MT systems and averaging the resulting target similarity values, $s_{tgt}(y_M, \hat{y}_M)$, when performing the attack selection. **Mean** refers to attacks using all eight systems, $f_{mean}(\hat{x}) = \sum_i f(\hat{x}, M_i)$. Leave-one-out (denoted **loo**) refers to averaging all but the victim system's similarity estimate, $f_{loo}(\hat{x}, M_j) = \sum_{i \neq j} f(\hat{x}, M_i)$ where the victim system is M_j. The leave-one-out condition simulates attacking an otherwise unknown, inaccessible MT system. Both ensemble techniques realized gains in transfer success count as more systems were included in the ensemble.

3.5 Baseline Attack: SEQ2SICK

We use the black-box implementation of SEQ2SICK (Cheng et al., 2020) in the TextAttack python library (Morris et al., 2020b) as a baseline attack on machine translation. This targeted attack generates candidate edits by swapping words for other words that are close in word embedding space. It obtains translations for each candidate from the model and greedily applies one-word changes that minimize the number of words that are present in both the reference and the translation. For the MT condition, we treat the translation of the original source as the reference.

Using a GPU, one attack takes an average of 32 seconds and 285 probes when targeting the reference or 35 seconds and 313 probes when targeting the system translation of the original source.

		Uncal.		Calibrated	
	N	Ref	MT	Ref	MT
FST+Rerank black box	8	8	8	8	8
FST+Rerank transfer	56	31	9	16	2
FST+Rerank mean ensemble	8	8	8	8	7
FST+Rerank loo ensemble	8	8	6	7	4
S2S black box	8	2	2	1	1
S2S transfer	56	16	20	3	8

Table 2: Effects of calibration and reference access at crafting time on black box and transfer success counts. Uncalibrated and reference-crafted configurations overestimate success.

	Ref S			MT S		
	>1	=1	<1	>1	=1	<1
FST+Rerank black box	65	35	0	66	1	33
FST+Rerank transfer	26	35	39	35	1	64
FST+Rerank mean ensemble	21	68	11	51	1	48
FST+Rerank loo ensemble	16	66	18	42	1	67
S2S black box	30	0	70	34	0	66
S2S transfer	28	0	72	31	0	69

Table 3: Percent of sentences for which S was > 1 (successful), $= 1$ (no viable attack found), < 1 (unsuccessful). Crafted with access to reference (Ref) and without (MT), calibrated conditions only.

4 Results

Success Every set of perturbations degrades the translation quality of every model. All sets of black-box perturbations using the FST-based perturber meet the criterion of success under both targeting conditions. However, many transferred FST-based attacks and many SEQ2SICK attacks under both conditions do not achieve success. Table 2 counts the number of successes over both perturbers under different conditions. Table 4 presents more details for attacks using the FST-based perturber, which is more often successful. Each system's performance on the unperturbed WMT20 dataset, as measured for this study, is reported as original CHRF.

Effects of Calibration Table 2 shows the effect calibration has on success rates. Tuning and measuring performance with calibrated metrics reveals that uncalibrated metrics overestimate success. The systems in the uncalibrated conditions exploited mismatches in the CHRF scales for different languages rather than vulnerabilities of the MT systems.

Referenceless attacks Attacks crafted against the reference achieve a higher margin of success under black-box scenarios and are much more likely to transfer than attacks crafted against the original system output. This suggests that the changes made under the MT condition are more tailored to the errors in the system with which they were crafted, perhaps by further changing parts of the system translation that already do not match the ground truth. Since transfer tends to reduce adversarial effect, the effect of these weaker attacks less frequently outweighs the degradation of the source.

Attack transfer These results don't suggest trends in transfer that correspond to system/language similarity or relative performance. While Allen and Opus-DE were relatively vulnerable to reference-targeted attacks from other systems, this vulnerability doesn't extend to MT-targeted attacks. Adversaries crafted using the multilingual model, mBART, do not transfer better between its different target languages, even though they share model weights.

Ensemble attacks often transfer: The mean ensembles are successful against nearly all individual models and the leave-one-out ensemble attacks successfully transfer in eleven of the sixteen settings. Continuing to add more MT systems to a leave-one-out targeting system would likely increase its effectiveness. Favoring attacks that succeed against more targeting systems leads to better transfer to previously unseen systems.

Example 1: Changing translated day of week
(mBART MT, $s_{src} = 0.94, d_{tgt} = 0.32$)

original	Sacramento police also announced Thursday their internal investigation did not find any policy or training violations.
attack	Sacramento police also announced Today (thursday) their internal investigation did not find any policy or training violations.
reference	Die Polizei von Sacramento gab am Donnerstag ebenfalls bekannt, dass ihre innere Ermittlung keine Verletzung der Regeln oder des Trainings erkennen ließ.
original output	Sacramento Polizei gab auch am Donnerstag [Thursday] bekannt, dass ihre interne Untersuchung keine Verstöße gegen die Richtlinien oder Ausbildung gefunden hat.
attack output	Sacramento Polizei auch angekündigt Heute (Samstag) [Saturday] ihre interne Untersuchung fand keine Politik oder Ausbildung Verletzungen.

Example 2: Omitting the object in perturbed translation
(Facebook MT, $s_{src} = 0.91, d_{tgt} = 0.32$)

original	Prince Harry detonated a recently detected mine in Angola.
attack	Prince Harry detonated most recently detected mine in Angola.
reference	Prinz Harry detonierte eine kürzlich entdeckte Mine in Angola.
original output	Prinz Harry hat eine kürzlich entdeckte Mine in Angola gesprengt.
attack output	Prinz Harry detonierte zuletzt in Angola. [Prince Harry last detonated in Angola.]

Example 3: Unrelated translation
(Allen MT, $s_{src} = 0.99, d_{tgt} = 0.89$)

original	Many readers, including some who work in national security and intelligence, have criticized The Times's decision to publish the details, saying it potentially put the person's life in danger and may have a chilling effect on would-be whistle-blowers.
attack	Many readers, including some who work in national security and intelligence, have criticized The Times's decision to publish the details, 's saying it potentially put the person's life in danger and may have a chilling effect on would-be whistle-blowers.
reference	Vieler Leser, darunter auch einige, die für die nationalen Sicherheits- und Nachrichtendienste arbeiten, haben die Entscheidung von The Times, Details zu veröffentlichen, kritisiert und geäußert, dass dadurch wahrscheinlich das Leben der Person in Gefahr gebracht wurde und es einen abschreckenden Effekt auf potenzielle Whistleblower haben könnte.
original output	Viele Leser, darunter einige, die in national Sicherheit und Intelligenz arbeiten, haben die Entscheidung der Times kritisiert, die Details zu veröffentlichen, sagte, dass sie potenziell das Leben der Person in danger und könnte eine abschreckende Wirkung auf würde -@ be whistle -@ be whistle -@ blowers.
attack output	Die Times ist eine US-amerikanische Schauspielerin. [The Times is an American actress.]

Figure 3: Examples with perturbations in orange and back translations in blue.

	selector	$\mathcal{L}_{src}$	$s_{src}\uparrow$	English-Czech mbart	English-Czech opus	English-German allen	English-German fb	English-German mbart	English-German opus	English-Chinese mbart	English-Chinese opus
	original s_{tgt}, CHRF			53.9	54.8	46.7	63.9	58.2	60.0	27.9	26.1
	calibrated s_{tgt}, CHRF$_{en}$			54.5	55.3	45.7	63.3	57.5	59.3	42.6	41.1
				Success, $S\uparrow$							
Crafted with Reference	CS mbart	1.23	97.1	**1.12**	**1.02**	**1.00**	0.99	1.00	1.00	0.98	0.99
Crafted with Reference	CS opus	1.33	96.8	**1.01**	**1.14**	**1.01**	0.99	1.00	**1.00**	0.98	0.99
Crafted with Reference	DE allen	1.53	96.1	0.99	0.99	**1.27**	0.99	1.00	**1.01**	0.97	0.98
Crafted with Reference	DE fb	1.44	96.3	1.00	1.00	**1.02**	**1.13**	**1.01**	**1.02**	0.98	0.99
Crafted with Reference	DE mbart	1.29	96.9	1.00	1.00	**1.02**	1.00	**1.12**	**1.02**	0.98	0.99
Crafted with Reference	DE opus	1.36	96.6	1.00	**1.00**	**1.02**	**1.00**	**1.02**	**1.13**	0.98	0.99
Crafted with Reference	ZH mbart	0.84	98.3	1.00	1.00	1.00	1.00	1.00	1.00	**1.10**	**1.00**
Crafted with Reference	ZH opus	1.01	97.7	0.99	1.00	1.00	1.00	1.00	1.00	1.00	**1.14**
Crafted with Reference	mean	0.51	99.2	**1.02**	**1.02**	**1.07**	**1.02**	**1.02**	**1.02**	**1.01**	**1.02**
Crafted with Reference	loo	0.47	~ 99.1	**1.01**	**1.01**	**1.01**	**1.01**	**1.01**	**1.01**	1.00	**1.00**
Crafted with MT	CS mbart	2.61	92.8	**1.06**	**1.00**	0.99	0.98	0.99	0.99	0.96	0.97
Crafted with MT	CS opus	2.61	92.7	0.99	**1.08**	0.99	0.97	0.98	0.99	0.95	0.97
Crafted with MT	DE allen	2.66	92.2	0.97	0.98	**1.20**	0.97	0.98	0.99	0.95	0.96
Crafted with MT	DE fb	2.61	92.6	0.98	0.99	1.00	**1.07**	0.99	1.00	0.96	0.97
Crafted with MT	DE mbart	2.52	93.0	0.99	0.99	1.00	0.98	**1.07**	**1.00**	0.96	0.97
Crafted with MT	DE opus	2.56	93.0	0.98	0.99	1.00	0.97	0.99	**1.08**	0.96	0.97
Crafted with MT	ZH mbart	2.49	93.1	0.98	0.98	0.99	0.97	0.98	0.99	**1.04**	0.98
Crafted with MT	ZH opus	2.52	93.2	0.98	0.99	0.98	0.97	0.98	0.99	0.97	**1.08**
Crafted with MT	mean	2.67	93.7	**1.01**	**1.03**	**1.08**	**1.01**	**1.02**	**1.03**	0.99	**1.02**
Crafted with MT	loo	2.67	~ 93.6	1.00	**1.01**	**1.02**	0.99	**1.00**	**1.01**	0.97	0.99

Table 4: Full FST+Rerank targeted attack results using calibrated metrics. Successful attacks in bold. **mean** and **loo** represent targeting with the mean and leave-one-out ensembles. s_{src} measures meaning preservation on the source side using CHRF. s_{tgt} is the MT score of the output sentence, measured with CHRF calibrated to English. $\mathcal{L}_{src}$ is the mean edit distance between attacks and originals. Note reference-informed attacks exhibit more conservative edits.

Examples The examples in Figure 3 illustrate some of the range of translation errors given perturbed inputs. They are drawn from black-box FST-based perturbations against the four EN-DE translation systems.

5 Related Work

The performance of machine translation systems is vulnerable to adversarial examples of several types. Naturalistic and untargeted changes degrade system performance, while remaining largely intelligible to humans (Belinkov and Bisk, 2018). Using word- or character-level permutations, untargeted attacks simply degrade translation quality, while targeted attacks introduce particular errors such as removing or inserting selected words. White-box attacks perturb an input with access to the model's gradients (Ebrahimi et al., 2018; Cheng et al., 2019; Wallace et al., 2019; Cheng et al., 2020) while a black-box paradigm only probes the model's output, typically for salience of portions of the input and scoring of substitutions proposed via heuristics (Zhao et al., 2018; Zhang et al., 2021). Other work crafts attacks based on generally exploitable features of language that are discoverable in training data, such as polysemous words, without probing expected attack success (Emelin et al., 2020).

Adversarial examples are crafted with respect to particular models and challenge datasets and they achieve limited success when applied (transferred) to others. A range of text classification adversaries have been shown to reduce the accuracy of models that have different architectures or were trained on different datasets (Song et al., 2021; Ren et al., 2019; Song et al., 2020; Emmery et al., 2021). While transfer effectiveness varies by attack method, it does not reach the level of the matched condition. Several authors show that their adversarial examples, created using white-box attacks on known systems, transfer to some extent to publicly available APIs hosted by Google, Baidu and Bing (Zhao et al., 2018; Zhang et al., 2021; Gil et al., 2019). Emelin et al. (2020) find that their attacks based on dataset co-occurrence reduce the accuracy of several models, but there's little overlap in which examples succeed, with slightly more similarity in sets of examples that are successful on models with the same architecture. White-box, gradient-based attacks can be crafted on models "stolen" via knowledge distillation, despite mismatches in data domain and model architecture (Wallace et al., 2020).

Adversarial perturbations typically must conform to perceptual features of an original text. Most NLP attack methods apply one-off perceptual constraints or preferences (e.g. lower number of swaps or similarity among vector representations) but the tradeoff between attack effectiveness and human perception is often unaccounted for, making it difficult to discern when an adversarial effect is the result of perturbations that are easily detected by a human observer (Morris et al., 2020a). Michel et al. (2019) propose a metric for success that balances adversarial effect with the level of meaning preservation of the original.

Paraphrases have recently been used for improving evaluation of MT (Bawden et al., 2020; Thompson and Post, 2020a), for improving MT training (Khayrallah et al., 2020) and multitask MT models have been run in a clever way to generate paraphrases (Thompson and Post, 2020b). The adversarial inputs of Iyyer et al. (2018) are generated using a neural end-to-end paraphrase system.

6 Conclusion

In this paper, we considered the practicality of adversarial examples for NLP by crafting MT attacks without access to the victim system or ground truth and by measuring those attacks in a way that accounts for both attack effectiveness and source meaning preservation. We find that many attacks that reduce translation quality still fall short of a strict threshold of *success*. We investigated the ability to transfer attacks across systems and across MT target languages. Attacks that do not have access to ground truth rarely transfer between systems. When they are crafted using ground truth, they transfer more often but we did not observe patterns, like language or system similarity, that allow us to predict when transfer will occur.

Our FST perturbation process is able to select edits under configurable constraints that preserve source-side meaning while causing large changes in system output. This is due in part to a high-quality paraphrase generation process relying on millions of paraphrases with scores calibrated to human quality judgments. This selection process is sufficient to degrade translation quality with respect to ground truth. The construction of candidates and attack selection processes do not require a GPU. Ensembles performed the highest rate of successful attacks.

One direction for future work could investigate methods for improving system robustness to attacks of this type. The leave-one-out ensemble was the most reliable attack method we found with at least 50% success rate in all conditions, including transferring attacks to systems it had no previous access to. Building on that success, cultivating it to a robust attack mechanism spanning languages and systems could be another valuable contribution in the future.

Ethical Considerations

There is a risk that adversarial techniques will be used by malicious actors to attack real world NLP systems. We believe that sharing this knowledge allows people who deploy models to account for risk and create safer systems; in particular, we examine how effectiveness measures and techniques reported in recent literature might look under more practical, low-information scenarios outside of academic test harnesses.

Our work is part of a thread in AI assurance that uncovers vulnerabilities and feeds research into mitigation methods, such as model robustness and detection of deceptive inputs.

Acknowledgements

Portions of this technical data were produced for the U. S. Government under Contract No. FA8702-19-C-0001 and W56KGU-18-D-0004, and is subject to the Rights in Technical Data-Noncommercial Items Clause DFARS 252.227-7013 (FEB 2014).

References

Allauzen, C., Riley, M., Schalkwyk, J., Skut, W., and Mohri, M. (2007). Openfst: A general and efficient weighted finite-state transducer library. In *International Conference on Implementation and Application of Automata*, pages 11–23. Springer.

Barrault, L., Biesialska, M., Bojar, O., Costa-jussà, M. R., Federmann, C., Graham, Y., Grundkiewicz, R., Haddow, B., Huck, M., Joanis, E., Kocmi, T., Koehn, P., Lo, C.-k., Ljubešić, N., Monz, C., Morishita, M., Nagata, M., Nakazawa, T., Pal, S., Post, M., and Zampieri, M. (2020). Findings of the 2020 conference on machine translation (WMT20). In *Proceedings of the Fifth Conference on Machine Translation*, pages 1–55, Online. Association for Computational Linguistics.

Bawden, R., Zhang, B., Tättar, A., and Post, M. (2020). ParBLEU: Augmenting metrics with automatic paraphrases for the WMT'20 metrics shared task. In *Proceedings of the Fifth Conference on Machine Translation*, pages 887–894, Online. Association for Computational Linguistics.

Belinkov, Y. and Bisk, Y. (2018). Synthetic and natural noise both break neural machine translation. In *International Conference on Learning Representations*.

Cheng, M., Yi, J., Chen, P.-Y., Zhang, H., and Hsieh, C.-J. (2020). Seq2sick: Evaluating the robustness of sequence-to-sequence models with adversarial examples. *Proceedings of the AAAI Conference on Artificial Intelligence*, 34(04):3601–3608.

Cheng, Y., Jiang, L., and Macherey, W. (2019). Robust neural machine translation with doubly adversarial inputs. In *Proceedings of the 57th Annual Meeting of the Association for Computational Linguistics*, pages 4324–4333, Florence, Italy. Association for Computational Linguistics.

Ebrahimi, J., Lowd, D., and Dou, D. (2018). On adversarial examples for character-level neural machine translation. In *Proceedings of the 27th International Conference on Computational Linguistics*, pages 653–663, Santa Fe, New Mexico, USA. Association for Computational Linguistics.

Emelin, D., Titov, I., and Sennrich, R. (2020). Detecting word sense disambiguation biases in machine translation for model-agnostic adversarial attacks. In *Proceedings of the 2020 Conference on Empirical Methods in Natural Language Processing (EMNLP)*, pages 7635–7653, Online. Association for Computational Linguistics.

Emmery, C., Kádár, Á., and Chrupała, G. (2021). Adversarial stylometry in the wild: Transferable lexical substitution attacks on author profiling. In *Proceedings of the 16th Conference of the European Chapter of the Association for Computational Linguistics: Main Volume*, pages 2388–2402, Online. Association for Computational Linguistics.

Ganitkevitch, J., Van Durme, B., and Callison-Burch, C. (2013). PPDB: The paraphrase database. In *Proceedings of the 2013 Conference of the North American Chapter of the Association for Computational Linguistics: Human Language Technologies*, pages 758–764, Atlanta, Georgia. Association for Computational Linguistics.

Gil, Y., Chai, Y., Gorodissky, O., and Berant, J. (2019). White-to-black: Efficient distillation of black-box adversarial attacks. In *Proceedings of the 2019 Conference of the North American Chapter of the Association for Computational Linguistics: Human Language Technologies, Volume 1 (Long and Short Papers)*, pages 1373–1379, Minneapolis, Minnesota. Association for Computational Linguistics.

Gorman, K. (2016). Pynini: A python library for weighted finite-state grammar compilation. In *Proceedings of the SIGFSM Workshop on Statistical NLP and Weighted Automata*, pages 75–80.

HuggingFace (2020). Hugging face model zoo. Accessed: 2021-03.

Iyyer, M., Wieting, J., Gimpel, K., and Zettlemoyer, L. (2018). Adversarial example generation with syntactically controlled paraphrase networks. In *Proceedings of NAACL*.

Kasai, J., Pappas, N., Peng, H., Cross, J., and Smith, N. (2020). Deep encoder, shallow decoder: Reevaluating non-autoregressive machine translation. In *International Conference on Learning Representations*.

Khayrallah, H., Thompson, B., Post, M., and Koehn, P. (2020). Simulated multiple reference training improves low-resource machine translation. In *Proceedings of the 2020 Conference on Empirical Methods in Natural Language Processing (EMNLP)*, pages 82–89, Online. Association for Computational Linguistics.

Mathur, N., Wei, J., Freitag, M., Ma, Q., and Bojar, O. (2020). Results of the WMT20 metrics shared task. In *Proceedings of the Fifth Conference on Machine Translation*, pages 688–725, Online. Association for Computational Linguistics.

Merkhofer, E., Mendoza, M.-A., Marvin, R., and Henderson, J. (2021). Perceptual models of machine-edited text. In *Findings of the Association for Computational Linguistics: ACL-IJCNLP 2021*, pages 3909–3920, Online. Association for Computational Linguistics.

Michel, P., Li, X., Neubig, G., and Pino, J. (2019). On evaluation of adversarial perturbations for sequence-to-sequence models. In *Proceedings of the 2019 Conference of the North American Chapter of the Association for Computational Linguistics: Human Language Technologies, Volume 1 (Long and Short Papers)*, pages 3103–3114, Minneapolis, Minnesota. Association for Computational Linguistics.

Morris, J., Lifland, E., Lanchantin, J., Ji, Y., and Qi, Y. (2020a). Reevaluating adversarial examples in natural language. In *Findings of the Association for Computational Linguistics: EMNLP 2020*, pages 3829–3839, Online. Association for Computational Linguistics.

Morris, J., Lifland, E., Yoo, J. Y., Grigsby, J., Jin, D., and Qi, Y. (2020b). TextAttack: A framework for adversarial attacks, data augmentation, and adversarial training in NLP. In *Proceedings of the 2020 Conference on Empirical Methods in Natural Language Processing: System Demonstrations*, pages 119–126.

Ng, N., Yee, K., Baevski, A., Ott, M., Auli, M., and Edunov, S. (2019). Facebook FAIR's WMT19 news translation task submission. In *Proceedings of the Fourth Conference on Machine Translation (Volume 2: Shared Task Papers, Day 1)*, pages 314–319, Florence, Italy. Association for Computational Linguistics.

Popović, M. (2015). chrF: character n-gram F-score for automatic MT evaluation. In *Proceedings of the Tenth Workshop on Statistical Machine Translation*, pages 392–395, Lisbon, Portugal. Association for Computational Linguistics.

Ren, S., Deng, Y., He, K., and Che, W. (2019). Generating natural language adversarial examples through probability weighted word saliency. In *Proceedings of the 57th Annual Meeting of the Association for Computational Linguistics*, pages 1085–1097, Florence, Italy. Association for Computational Linguistics.

Song, C., Rush, A., and Shmatikov, V. (2020). Adversarial semantic collisions. In *Proceedings of the 2020 Conference on Empirical Methods in Natural Language Processing (EMNLP)*, pages 4198–4210, Online. Association for Computational Linguistics.

Song, L., Yu, X., Peng, H.-T., and Narasimhan, K. (2021). Universal adversarial attacks with natural triggers for text classification. In *Proceedings of the 2021 Conference of the North American Chapter of the Association for Computational Linguistics: Human Language Technologies*, pages 3724–3733, Online. Association for Computational Linguistics.

Stahlberg, F., Bryant, C., and Byrne, B. (2019). Neural grammatical error correction with finite state transducers. In *Proceedings of the 2019 Conference of the North American Chapter of the Association for Computational Linguistics: Human Language Technologies, Volume 1 (Long and Short Papers)*, pages 4033–4039, Minneapolis, Minnesota. Association for Computational Linguistics.

Tang, Y., Tran, C., Li, X., Chen, P.-J., Goyal, N., Chaudhary, V., Gu, J., and Fan, A. (2020). Multilingual translation with extensible multilingual pretraining and finetuning.

Thompson, B. and Post, M. (2020a). Automatic machine translation evaluation in many languages via zero-shot paraphrasing. In *Proceedings of the 2020 Conference on Empirical Methods in Natural Language Processing (EMNLP)*, pages 90–121, Online. Association for Computational Linguistics.

Thompson, B. and Post, M. (2020b). Paraphrase generation as zero-shot multilingual translation: Disentangling semantic similarity from lexical and syntactic diversity. In *Proceedings of the Fifth Conference on Machine Translation*, pages 561–570, Online. Association for Computational Linguistics.

Tiedemann, J. and Thottingal, S. (2020). OPUS-MT – building open translation services for the world. In *Proceedings of the 22nd Annual Conference of the European Association for Machine Translation*, pages 479–480, Lisboa, Portugal. European Association for Machine Translation.

Wallace, E., Feng, S., Kandpal, N., Gardner, M., and Singh, S. (2019). Universal adversarial triggers for attacking and analyzing NLP. In *Proceedings of the 2019 Conference on Empirical Methods in Natural Language Processing and the 9th International Joint Conference on Natural Language Processing (EMNLP-IJCNLP)*, pages 2153–2162, Hong Kong, China. Association for Computational Linguistics.

Wallace, E., Stern, M., and Song, D. (2020). Imitation attacks and defenses for black-box machine translation systems. In *Proceedings of the 2020 Conference on Empirical Methods in Natural Language Processing (EMNLP)*, pages 5531–5546, Online. Association for Computational Linguistics.

Zhang, X., Zhang, J., Chen, Z., and He, K. (2021). Crafting adversarial examples for neural machine translation. In *Proceedings of the 59th Annual Meeting of the Association for Computational Linguistics and the 11th International Joint Conference on Natural Language Processing (Volume 1: Long Papers)*, pages 1967–1977, Online. Association for Computational Linguistics.

Zhao, Z., Dua, D., and Singh, S. (2018). Generating natural adversarial examples. In *International Conference on Learning Representations*.

Sign Language Machine Translation and the Sign Language Lexicon: A Linguistically Informed Approach

Irene Murtagh irene.murtagh@adaptcentre.ie
Department of Informatics, TU Dublin, Ireland
Víctor Ubieto Nogales victoremilio.ubieto@upf.edu
Josep Blat josep.blat@upf.edu
Departament de Tecnologies de la Informació i les Comunicacions Human-Computer Interaction, graphics and Educational Technologies.

Abstract

Natural language processing and the machine translation of spoken language (speech/text) has benefitted from significant scientific research and development in recent times, rapidly advancing the field. On the other hand, computational processing and modelling of signed language has unfortunately not garnered nearly as much interest, with sign languages generally being excluded from modern language technologies. Many deaf and hard-of-hearing individuals use sign language on a daily basis as their first language. For the estimated 72 million deaf people in the world, the exclusion of sign languages from modern natural language processing and machine translation technology, aggravates further the communication barrier that already exists for deaf and hard-of-hearing individuals. This research leverages a linguistically informed approach to the processing and modelling of signed language. We outline current challenges for sign language machine translation from both a linguistic and a technical prespective. We provide an account of our work in progress in the development of sign language lexicon entries and sign language lexeme repository entries for SLMT. We leverage Role and Reference Grammar together with the Sign_A computational framework within this development. We provide an XML description for Sign_A, which is utilised to document SL lexicon entries together with SL lexeme repository entries. This XML description is also leveraged in the development of an extension to Bahavioural Markup Language, which will be used within this development to link the divide between the sign language lexicon and the avatar animation interface.

1. Introduction

Sign Languages (SLs) are visual gestural languages articulated within a three-dimensional signing space and have no written form (Murtagh, 2019a). Many deaf and hard-of-hearing individuals use SL on a daily basis as their first language. For the estimated 72 million deaf people in the world, the exclusion of sign languages from modern natural language processing and machine translation technology, further

aggravates the communication barrier that already exists for deaf and hard-of-hearing individuals (Allen, 2013). We outline our research work in progress in the development of a SL lexicon architecture, including SL lexicon entries and SL lexeme repository entries for a sign language machine translation (SLMT) system. We provide some background information on the Role and Reference Grammar (RRG) and the Sign_A framework, which are leveraged within this development. We discuss the XML specification for the Sign_A computational framework, which we leverage to define SL lexicon entires and SL lexeme repository entries. We also discuss the extension to the specification for Behavioural Markup Language in the development of a planner for SL translation.

2. SignON Project

We draw here on work we are engaged in for the Horizon 2020 funded SignON project, which seeks to create a service that translates between sign and verbal languages, facilitating new resource generation over time, which in turn will further improve the service[1] (Shterionov et al., 202; Saggion et al., 2021). SignON – Sign Language Translation Mobile Application and Open Communications Framework – seeks to reduce the communication gap that exists between deaf sign language users, hard-of-hearing and hearing people. SignON targets Irish, British, Dutch, Flemish and Spanish Sign Language, together with English, Irish, Dutch and Spanish spoken language. The overarching project goal is to increase inclusiveness through accessible translation services powered by state-of-the-art artificial intelligence (AI). The co-creation process lies at the core of this project, with tight collaboration from European deaf and hard-of-hearing communities. This collaboration informs the co-design and co-development of the SignON service and application, while also enabling continuous assessment of quality.

3. Sign Language

Sign languages are linguistically complete, very rich and complex languages (Murtagh 2019). Communication across sign languages encompasses manual features (MFs) and non-manual features (NMFs). MFs include hand shapes, hand locations, hand movements and orientation of the palm of the hands. NMFs include the use of eye gaze, facial expression, mouthing, head and upper body movements. The visual gestural realisation of a word in SL involves the simultaneous and parallel expression of a varied number of MFs and NMFs, each with their own duration, orientation and relative configuration and movement.
The SignOn project targets Irish Sign Language (ISL) Flemish Sign Language (VGT), British Sign Language (BSL), Spanish Sign Language (LSE) and Dutch Sign Language (NGT). We take Irish Sign Language (ISL) as our sign language of focus within this research paper, as this is our initial language under linguistic investigation within the SignON project.

3.1. Sign language machine translation challenges

Challenges for sign language machine translation (SLMT) exist within two separate realms. On one hand, we must consider the linguistic challenges and on the other hand, the technical challenges. While spoken language communication occurs within auditory-oral modality, sign language communication occurs within visual gestural language that is articulated within three-dimensional (3D) space (Leeson and Saeed, 2012). The modality difference for human-to-human communication together with the fact that there is no written or aural form for sign language introduces many interesting challenges for SLMT. With regard to challenges facing SLMT, (Murtagh et al., 2021), outline linguistic and technical challenges and report on the critical importance of: close engagement and co-construction of MT agendas with Deaf communities; the inclusion of deaf experts on MT project teams; the need for interdisciplinary approaches to MT work on sign languages; the need for robust data sets; and the need to manage expectations around what can be achieved to a high level as we progress with work in this domain.

[1] https://signon-project.eu

Linguistic challenges (Murtagh et al., 2021) report on the linguistic phenomena that must be addressed, but which have not been documented sufficiently to date as a result of under-resourcing. Irish Sign Language (ISL) was used as the SL of focus, but the point regarding the under-documentation of ISL 'holds equally for most sign languages of the world'. For ISL, these under-described areas include: description of the non-discrete lexicalised elements in Irish Sign Language including simultaneous constructions, body partitioning, motivations underpinning use of signing space; the absence of an ISL SignBank; the need for more research on the syntax, semantics and pragmatics of ISL; and the need for a broader base of data from which to generate linguistic rules and train MT ISL receptive models.

Technical challenges There are also many technical challenges involved in machine translation (MT) between spoken and signed language and vice-versa. Research shows that when SLs and spoken languages are compared, it is speech plus co-speech gesture rather than speech alone that should be considered as an equivalent to signing (Leeson and Vermeerbergen, 2022).

The reliance of SL on the use of space for linguistic purposes together with the (more) simultaneous organisation of SL compared to the (more) sequential organisation of spoken language are two important linguistic phenomena that pose a challenge for SLMT from a technical perspective (Leeson and Vermeerbergen, 2022). Further challenges are posed by the sign language lexicon. The SL lexicon refers to both an established lexicon and a productive lexicon. The established lexicon accounts for established signs, which are highly conventionalised in both form and meaning, whereas signs encompassed within the productive lexicon are constructed using conventional strategies to fit contextual needs (Leeson and Saeed, 2012). These strategies form the productive lexicon. The productive lexicon is composed of sets of language-specific handshapes that can combine with a wide range of movements, orientations of the palm of the hand, and locations of articulation within in the signing space/gestural space to articulate meaning. We refer to these as manual features (MFs) in SLs.These may also be accompanied by non manual features (NMFs) (e.g mouth gestures, eye-gaze, brow-raises/brow-furrows, ...) to represent clauses or sentences encoding a particular character perspective.This is particularly challenging for verbal language to SLMT and vice versa.

4. The sign language lexicon

We implement our lexicon leveraging RRG (Van Valin and La Polla, 1997; Van Valin, 2005), together with the Sign_A framework (Murtagh, 2019) to create lexicon entries that will sufficiently accommodate SL. RRG views language as a system of communicative social action. RRG defines grammatical structures in relation to both semantic and communicative functions. Syntax is viewed as being relatively motivated by semantic and pragmatic factors. RRG is sufficiently flexible and robust to accommodate SL at a semantic, syntactic and pragmatic level. It allows us to address certain characteristics that have proven problematic for head driven phrase structure grammar (HPSG), which was utilised in the development of a computational lexicon for British Sign Language (BSL) (Sáfár and Glauert, 2012). Many of the rules found in the HPSG literature do not apply to SLs, and therefore, to adequately represent SLs, we leverage the use of RRG and extend its capability using the Sign_A framework, allowing us to develop a lexicon architecture that is sufficiently robust in nature to cater for the linguistic phenomena pertinent to SLs.

4.1. Role and Reference Grammar

Role and Reference Grammar, henceforth termed RRG, is a model of grammar, which incorporates many of the points of view of current functional theories of grammar (Van Valin, 2005). In RRG, the description of a sentence in a particular language is formulated in terms of its logical structure and communicative functions, and the grammatical procedures that are available in the language for the expression of these meanings. Semantic decomposition of predicates and their semantic argument structures are represented as logical structures. The lexicon in RRG takes the position that lexical entries for verbs should contain unique information only, with as much information as possible derived from general lexical rules.

Figure 1 from Van Valin (2005) provides an illustration of the organisation of the RRG architecture including constructional schemata. Van Valin (2005) takes the position that constructions within RRG are utilised to capture language specific idiosyncratic linguistic behavior.

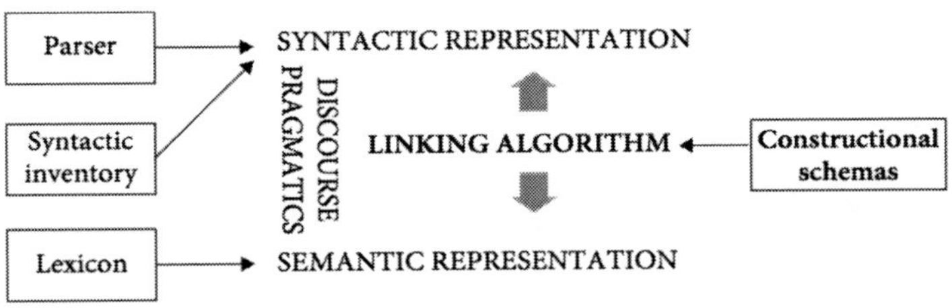

Figure 1. The organisation of the RRG architecture, Van Valin (2005)

4.2. Sign_A computational framework

The Sign_A framework, was developed by Murtagh (2019) with the "A" within this term representing 'Articulatory Structure Level'. As there is no current agreed standard with regard to the documentation of SLs, the Sign_A framework was developed with a view to accommodating the representation of sign languages within the SL lexicon. 'Articulatory Structure Level' extends the theory of the generative lexicon (GL) (Pustejovsky 1991), introducing a fifth level of lexical representation, which accounts for the essential (computational) phonological parameters of an object as defined by the lexical item.

4.3. SignON sign language lexicon architecture

With regard to our SL lexicon architecture, Figure 2 provides a high level view of the RRG + Sign_A framework architecture. It is important to note that each SL added into the architecture will have a separate lexicon, lexeme repository etc. for each respective SL. We include a lexeme repository, which maintains the NMF and MF lexemes for each SL. We also include a morpheme store, which maintains those grammatical units that demonstrate no conceptual meaning. We propose a morpheme store and a lexeme repository to cater for SL morphemes and SL lexemes respectively. We use the context of an utterance to decipher whether an item should be placed within the morpheme store or within the lexeme repository of the SL lexicon architecture. An item may exist within the morpheme store and also exist within the lexeme repository depending on its context within any given sentence. SL morphemes, which demonstrate grammatical function, but lack any conceptual meaning will be placed within a morpheme store, while SL lexemes or those morphemes that function in grammatical terms, while also exhibiting conceptual meaning will reside within a lexeme repository. The lexicon within this figure maintains the RRG + Sign_A rich logical structures for each SL. The grammar component is responsible for maintaining and assembling the clause, ensuring that word order, agreement features, tense etc. are aligned and assembled correctly.

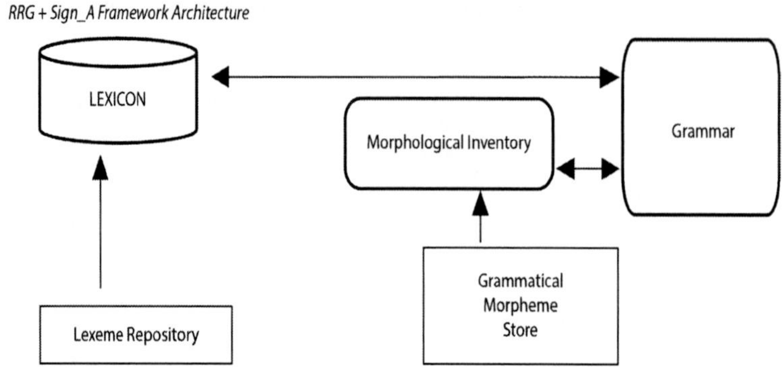

Figure 2. RRG + Sign_A Lexicon Architecture (Murtagh, 2019: 248)

4.4. Sign language lexicon and lexeme repository entries

Categories currently included in the SL lexicon are nouns, classifiers and verbs. As an example, we refer to SL verbs with regard to lexicon and lexeme repository entries. In order to provide some context, we provide a brief discussion of RRG, the theoretical model of grammar that we use in the development of this lexicon architecture. RRG semantic representation is based on a system of lexical representation and semantic roles. RRG employs the system of lexical decomposition proposed by Vendler (1967). Saeed (2016) defines the task of a semanticist as showing "how the inherent semantic distinctions carried by verbs, and verb phrases, map into a system of situation types". Saeed (ibid.: 119) identifies Vendler's influential approach to doing this (Vendler, 1967: 97-121).

Within RRG, verbs are represented in the lexicon according to their Aktionsart classification. Verbs can be divided into four distinct classes: states, activities, achievements and accomplishments. These four classes can be further defined by three features: [±static], [±punctual], and [±telic] (Binns-Dray, 2004). Static indicates if a verb represents something happening. If one can answer the question, "What happened?" or "What is happening?" then the verb is seen to be static. Telic represents whether a verb describes a state of affairs that has a terminal end point. Achievements and accomplishments are telic, or bounded, as in "The clothes are drying on the line", while states and activities are atelic, or unbounded, as in "John is running in the park". Punctual represents whether a telic verb (achievements and accomplishments) has internal duration or not (Binns-Dray, 2004). There are two additional classes; active accomplishments, which describe telic uses of activity verbs (e.g. devour) and also semelfactives (punctual events; Smith, 2009).

SL verbs will be represented in the SL lexicon according to their Aktionsart classification (Vendler, 1967). A single verb can have more than one Aktionsart interpretation. For example the verb 'march' would be listed in the lexicon as an activity verb, and lexical rules would derive the other uses from the basic activity use. The lexical representation of a verb or other predicate is termed its LOGICAL STRUCTURE [LS]. State predicates are represented simply as predicate′, while all activity predicates contain do′. Accomplishments, which are durative, are distinguished from achievements, which are punctual. Accomplishment LSs contain BECOME, while achievement LSs contain INGR, which is short for 'ingressive'. Semelfactives contain SEML. In addition, causation is treated as an independent parameter that crosscuts the six Aktionsart classes. It is represented by CAUSE in LSs. The lexical representations for each type of spoken language verb shown above are provided in Table 1.

Aktionsart Class	**Logical Structure**
State	**predicate'** (x) or (x, y)
Activity	**do'** (x, [**predicate'** (x) or (x, y)]}
Achievement	INGR **predicate'** (x) or (x, y), or INGR do' (x, [**predicate'** (x) or (x, y)]}
Accomplishment	BECOME **predicate'** (x) or (x, y), or BECOME **do'** (x, [**predicate'** (x) or (x, y)]}
Active accomplishment	**do'** (x, [**predicate**$_1$,' (x, (y))]) & BECOME **predicate**$_2$; (z, x) or (y)
Causative	α CAUSE β where α, β are representations of any type

Table 1. Lexical representation for Aktionsart classes, Van Valin and La Polla (1997: 109)

Table 2 provides a sample sentence in ISL from Murtagh (2019: 142), where the Aktionsart class or event type is provided, together with the tripartite verb class (Padden, 1988).

Gloss and English Translation	**ISL Verb**	**ISL Verb Class**	**Transi-tivity**	**Event Type**	**Reference**
REAL LOVE MY JOB 'I really love my job'	LOVE	plain	transitive	State	SOI Corpus Noeleen (03) Personal Stories (Dublin)

Table 2. ISL sentence with event type and tripartite verb type, Murtagh (2019b)

Murtagh (2019) provides a broad analysis of ISL verbs covering all event types, however, in this case, for purpose of illustration, we will focus on an ISL plain verb, according to the traditional tripartite verb class. We use the information in Table 2 to produce an RRG + Sign_A logical structure (LS) lexicon entry, capable of representing SL within our SL lexicon. An illustration of the sentence in Table 2, taken from the SOI corpus (Leeson et al., 2006), is provided in Example 1 below.

Example 1

REAL LOVE MY JOB
'I really love my job'
SOI Corpus Noeleen (03) Personal Stories (Dublin)

Plain verbs are typically not marked for person or location (McDonnell 1996: 116). The participant is referring to the fact that 'she loves her job', with job being introduced and established earlier in the discourse. The situation type for the ISL plain verb 'LOVE' within this sentence is state. Table 3 provides the Sign_A + RRG logical structure, which will be used as the lexicon entry for the sentence "I really love my job". This table also provides the lexeme repository XML description, based on the Sign_A computational framework. Section 5 provides an overview of the Sign_A framework XML description.

Gloss	REAL LOVE MY JOB
English Translation	'I really love my job'
RRG+Sign_A Logical Structure	**LOVE´** <TEMPORAL><MF><NMF> (1sg, JOB)
ISL Lexicon XML SL Verb Entry	
<ISLGlossTranslate="LOVE" IPA="/lʌv/" LogicalStructure= "LOVE´<TEMPORAL> <LOCATION><MF><NMF> (1sg, JOB);" NumberVerb="sg" P.O.S="PlainVerb" personVerb="3rd" tenseVerb="PRES" love/>	
Lexeme Repository Sign_A XML description for Manual Features <MF> of SL verb LOVE	
<HAND><dh>"right"</dh><ndh>"left"</ndh></HAND>	
<HS><HSMode>unique</HSMode><HSID><value>24</value></HSID>	
<AM><Spatial><SOURCE>"[a]locus"</SOURCE><GOAL>"[b]locus"</GOAL>EDti></EDti><EDtn></EDtn> <TLti></TLti><TLtn></TLtn> </SPATIAL><AM>	
<PO><p2><p2_i><EDti></EDti><EDtn></EDtn></p2_i><p1_n><EDti></EDti><EDtn></EDtn></p2_n><TLti></TLti><TLtn></TLtn></p1></PO>	
Lexeme Repository Sign_A XML description for Non Manual Features <NMF> of SL verb LOVE	
<MOUTHING><VERB_ONE_TO_ONE><VERBIPA>"/lʌv/"</VERBIPA></VERB_ONE_TO_ONE></MOUTHING	

Table 3. ISL plain verb lexicon and lexeme repository XML description

5. Sign_A framework XML description

The Sign_A framework XML specification was developed with a view to documenting and accommodating SL lexicon entries in computational terms[2]. We report on MF specifications, NMF specifications, and finally TEMPORAL specifications.

5.1. Manual feature specifications

With regard to SL MFs, William Stokoe (1960) originally identified the various parameters, which are relevant for the analysis of SL. He suggested that the articulation of a sign encompassed three different parameters. A designator, which was used to refer to the specific combination of hand configuration, abbreviated to *dez*. A tabulation, used to refer to the location of the hands and abbreviated to *tab*, and a *signation* used to refer to the movement of the hands and abbreviated to *sig*. Dez, tab and sig were examples of what he called *cheremes*, the signed equivalent of phonemes (Murtagh. 2019b).

Later research refers to these parameters of SL as *handshape*, *location* and *movement.* (Sutton-Spence & Woll (1999) : Valli & Lucas (1995)). Battison (1978) claimed that a fourth parameter is necessary in order to be able to fully transcribe signs. This fourth parameter is called *orientation*, and denotes the orientation of the hands and fingers during the articulation of the sign. The abbreviation of orientation is *ori.*

The Sign_A MF XML specification includes a specification for <HAND>, handshape <HS>, hand movement <HM>, palm orientation <PO>, arm movement <AM>, forearm <FA> and upperarm <UA>. For illustrative purposes we will include the <HAND> MF here. Example 2 illustrates n XML computational description for the hands, where the 'dominant hand' is defined as <dh> and the non dominant hand as <ndh>. This example provides an illustration of initialising the right hand as the dominant hand.

Example 2

```
<MF>
        <HAND>
                <dh>"right"</dh>
                <ndh>"left"</ndh>
        </HAND>
...
</MF>
```

5.2. Non-Manual feature definitions

(Murtagh, 2019b) reports that the existence of NMFs within signed languages has been well documented by researchers, including Liddell (1980), Nolan (1993), Coerts (1990), Bellugi and Klima (1990), Baker and Padden (1978b). NMFs consist of various facial expressions such as eyebrow movement, movement of the eyes, mouth patterns, blowing of the cheeks head tilting and shoulder movement. NMFs areused to convey additional information to the meaning being expressed by manual handshapes. While NMFs are normally accompanied by a signed lexical item, they can be used to communicate meaning independent to manual accompaniment (Leeson and Saeed, 2012).

---

[2] https://signon-project.eu/wp-content/uploads/2022/01/SignON_D5.4_First-Sign-Language-Specific-Lexicon-and-Structure_v1.0.pdf

Sign_A NMF XML specifications include specifications for describing articulations relating to the head <HEAD>, eyebrow <EB>, Eyelid <EL>, eye gaze <EG>, cheek <CHEEK>, mouth <MOUTH>, tongue <TNG>, nose <NOSE>, Shoulder <SHOULDER>, mouthing <MOUTHING> and mouth gesture <MOUTHGESTURE>. Example 3 provides an XML computational description of <MOUTHING>. We include an International Phonetic Alphabet (IPA) description of the respective nouns and verbs within the lexicon to cater for the one-to-one mapping between the sign and the respective noun or verb being mouthed.

Example 3

```
<MOUTHING>
  <NOUN_ONE_TO_ONE><NOUNIPA> </NOUNIPA></NOUN_ONE_TO_ONE>
  <VERB_ONE_TO_ONE><VERBIPA></VERBIPA></VERB_ONE_TO_ONE>
  <EDti></EDti><EDtn></EDtn>
  <TLti></TLti><TLtn></TLtn>
</MOUTHING>
```

5.3. Temporal feature specifications

Temporal feature specifications refer to timing information associated with both the MFs and NMFs. The *event duration* parameter <ED> is used as an attribute together with each distinct phonological parameter, for both MF and NMF. It functions linguistically at the morphological-phonological interface, defining the duration or time taken for any given MF or NMF phonological parameter to be realised. The visual gestural realisation of an ISL MF and NMF phonological parameter is considered to be an *event* within the Sign_A computational framework. The realisation of each event has a specific duration bound to it. This can be referred to as an *event duration* <EDtn>. The event duration parameter is used to allow us to synchronise the timing information relating to when each distinct MF or NMF phonological parameter, providing information on when an event may execute along a larger timeline parameter. Due to the visual gestural nature of sign language and the fact that parameters for MFs and NMFs may be articulated simultaneously along a timeline to articulate an utterance, the event duration parameter plays an essential role within the Sign_A framework. The eventDuration <EDtn> parameter of each MF and NMF phonological parameter will be executed in relation to the timing information of the entire utterance or the timeline parameter <TL>.

The following example provides an XML description for the event duration timeline parameter, where the initial eventDuration <EDti> element is responsible for storing the event start time in relation to the timeline parameter <TLtn> and end event duration element <EDtn> is responsible for storing the actual duration that a phonological parameter will play out for.

Example 4

```
<EDti></EDti> <!--initial time relative to the timeline -->
<EDtn></EDtn> <!--end time relative to the timeline -->
```

The *timeline* parameter <TL> refers to a linear timeline representing the overall time taken from the moment an ISL utterance begins until the moment an entire utterance or articulation is completed or terminates. An utterance refers in this case to an ISL lexeme, phrase or sentence that communicates something meaningful. The timeline parameter will play a central role within our computational framework as it is responsible for synchronisation and keeping track of the sequence in which each phonological parameter event will be realised.

The example below provides an XML description for the timeline parameter <TLtn>, where the initial timeline <TLti> element is responsible for providing the event duration start time <EDti>. This value is used as input to the initial event duration <EDti> and is used to allow for synchronisation. The end timeline element <TLtn> is responsible for storing the overall duration that an entire utterance will take.

Example 5
<TLti></TLti> <!—initial time relative to the sign language utterance -->
<TLtn></TLtn> <!—end time relative to the sign language utterance -->

6. Linking the divide between the lexicon and animation interface

We extend the specification for Behavioural Markup Language in the development of a planner for SL translation. This planner will be responsible for the translation from the Sign_A XML specification within the lexicon architecture, to a BML-based script for driving a SL embodied conversational agent. We extend the BML specification with a view to accommodating the Sign_A XML definitions. Table 4 below provides an example of the specification for BML, which has been extended to cater for Sign_A XML hand MF <HAND>. We refer to example 2, illustrated previously. Other Sign_A XML definitions which have been extended with regard to the BML specification include handshape <HS>, hand movement <HM>, palm orientation <PO>, arm movement <AM>, upper arm <UA>, head <HEAD>, eyebrow <EB>, eyelid <EL>, eyegaze <EG>, cheek <> CHEEK, mouth <MOUTH>, mouthing <MOUTHING>, tongue <TNG>, shoulder <SHOULDER>, body anchored locations <BA>, signing space locations <SPATIAL>, event duration <ED> and timeline <TL>.
Table 4

Feature	Defined in Sign_A	Defined in BML extension
Hand	XML element inside <MF>. <HAND> <dh>"right"</dh> <ndh>"left"</ndh> </HAND>	DomHand attribute of the BML block. <bml id="bml1" characterID="Eva" domHand="RIGHT" end="5"> [behavior blocks should go here] </bml>

7. Conclusion

We have outlined of work in progress in the development of sign language lexicon entries and sign language lexeme repository entries for SLMT. We have also outlined an XML description for Sign_A, which is leveraged within the SL lexicon entries together with SL lexeme repository entries of this development. We provide an overview of the SL lexicon architecture used within this development. We also outline current work in progress in the development of a planner for translation of our XML description with a view to synthesizing SL. Future work will focus on further developing the lexicon architecture and indeed the SL lexicon, to take into account linguistic phenomena associated with Flemish Sign Language (VGT), British Sign Language (BSL), Spanish Sign Language (LSE) and Dutch Sign Language (NGT). Future work also includes further development of routines to automatically compute these SL LSs, while also working on further developing the the BML planner and realiser in this cutting edge development.

Acknowledgements

This work is supported by the SignON project, which is funded by the European Union's Horizon 2020 Research and Innovation program, under grant number 10107255.

References

Allen, C. (2013): Equality for Deaf People: How Do We Get There? Paper presented at the Centre for Deaf Studies Occasional Lecture Series, Trinity Long Room Hub, Trinity College Dublin.

Baker C. and Padden, C. (1978). Focusing on the Non-Manual Components of American Sign Language. In: P. Siple, ed., *Understanding Language Through Sign Language Research.* London: Academic Press.

Battison, R. (1978). "Lexical Borrowing in American Sign Language", Silver Spring, MD: Linstok Press.

Bellugi, U. and Klima, E. (1990). Properties of Visual Spatial Languages. In: S. Prillwitz and T. Vollhaber eds., *Sign Language Research and Application, International studies in sign language and the communication of the deaf,* Hamburg: Signum-Press, pp. 115-143.

Binns-Dray, K. R. (2004). *Content Questions in American Sign Language: An RRG Analysis.* Unpublished PhD dissertation. State University of New York at Buffalo.

Coerts, J. (1990). The Analysis of Interrogatives and Negations in Sign Language of the Netherlands. In S. Prillwitz and T. Vollhaber eds., *Current Trends in European Sign Language Research, International studies in sign language and the communication of the deaf,* Hamburg: Signum-Press. 9, pp. 265-277.

Leeson, L., Saeed, J., Byrne-Dunne, D., Macduff, A. and Leonard C. (2006). *Developing a Digital Corpus of Irish Sign Language. The 'Signs of Ireland' Corpus Development Project. Information Technology and Telecommunications Conference.* Carlow: Carlow Institute of Technology, Ireland.

Leeson, L. and Saeed J. (2012). *Irish Sign Language* . Edinburgh, UK: Edinburgh University Press.

Leeson, L. and Vermeerbergen M. (2022). Introducing Sign Languages. Simultaneity, Multimodality and other Characteristics. Talk presented at the SignON Internal Seminar 4.

Liddell, S. (1978). Non-manual signals in ASL: A many layered system. In: W. C. Stokoe ed., *Proceedings of the First National Symposium on Sign Language Research and Training,* 1977, Chicago: National Association of the Deaf, pp. 193-228.

Nolan, E. (1993). *Non-manual features in Irish Sign Language.* Unpublished essay. Horizon deaf studies project, Centre for Language and Communication Studies (CLCS), University of Dublin, Trinity College, Dublin, Ireland.

Murtagh, I. (2019a). Motivating the Computational Phonological Parameters of an Irish Sign Language Avatar. In: B. Nolan and E. Diedrichsen (eds.), *Linguistic Perspectives on the Construction of Meaning and Knowledge Representation.* Cambridge Scholars Publishing, pp.323-339.

Murtagh, I. (2019b) *A Linguistically Motivated Computational Framework for Irish Sign Language*. PhD Dissertation. Dublin: Trinity College Dublin.

Murtagh, I., Leeson, L., and Moiselle, R. (2021). Sign Languages and Language Technology: Linguistic and Technical Challenges. In *Proceedings of the the 2021 Annual Irish Association of Applied Linguistics Conference: Applied Linguistics in the 21st Century*, Online, University College Dublin, Ireland.

Pustejovsky, J. (1991a). The Generative Lexicon. *Computational Linguistics*, 17(4), pp. 209–441.

Saeed, J. (2016). *Semantics*. Fourth ed. Malden: Wiley-Blackwell.

Sáfár, E.and Glauert J. (2012). Computer Modelling. In: R. Pfau, M. Steinbach, B.Woll eds., *Sign Language: An International Handbook*, Berlin: Mouton de Gruyter.

Saggion, H., Shterionov, D., Labaka, G., Van de Cruys, T., Vandeghinste V. and Blat J. (2021). SignON: Bridging the gap between Sign and Spoken Languages. In *Proceedings of the XXXVII Spanish Society for Natural Language Processing conference.*

Shterionov D., Vandeghinste V., Saggion H., Blat J., De Coster M., Dambre J., van den Heuvel H., Murtagh I., Leeson L., and Schuurman I. *(2021)* The SignON project: A Sign Language Translation Framework. Meeting of Computational Linguistics in the Netherlands #CLIN31

Van Valin, R. and La Polla, R. (1997). Syntax: Structure, Meaning and Function. Cambridge: Cambridge University Press.

Van Valin, R. (2005). *Exploring the Syntax-Semantics Interface*. Cambridge: Cambridge University Press.

Vendler , Z. ([1957] 1967). *Linguistics in Philosophy*. Ithaca: Cornell University Press.

Smith, C. (2009). *Linguistics of American Sign Language, 2nd Edition*. Washington: Gallaudet University Press.

Stokoe, W. (1960). Sign Language Structure: An Outline of the Visual Communication System of the American Deaf. In: Studies in Linguistics Occasional Papers, number 8. Buffalo, New York: University at Buffalo.

Sutton-Spence R and Woll B. (1999). The Linguistics of British Sign Language; an introduction. Cambridge:Cambridge University Press.

Valli, C. and Lucas, C. (1995). Linguistics of American Sign Language, 2nd Edition. I Washington.

A Neural Machine Translation Approach to Translate Text to Pictographs in a Medical Speech Translation System - The BabelDr Use Case

Jonathan Mutal[1] Jonathan.Mutal@unige.ch
Pierrette Bouillon[1] Pierrette.Bouillon@unige.ch
Johanna Gerlach[1] Johanna.Gerlach@unige.ch
Magali Norré[1,2] Magali.Norre@uclouvain.be
Lucía Ormaechea Grijalba[1] Lucia.OrmaecheaGrijalba@unige.ch

[1]TIM, FTI, University of Geneva, Geneva, 1205, Switzerland
[2]CENTAL, ILC, Catholic University of Louvain, Louvain-la-Neuve, 1348, Belgium

Abstract

The use of images has been shown to positively affect patient comprehension in medical settings, in particular to deliver specific medical instructions. However, tools that automatically translate sentences into pictographs are still scarce due to the lack of resources. Previous studies have focused on the translation of sentences into pictographs by using WordNet combined with rule-based approaches and deep learning methods. In this work, we showed how we leveraged the BabelDr system, a speech to speech translator for medical triage, to build a speech to pictograph translator using Unified Medical Language System (UMLS) and neural machine translation approaches. We showed that the translation from French sentences to a UMLS gloss can be viewed as a machine translation task and that a Multilingual Neural Machine Translation system achieved the best results.

1 Introduction

Patients, especially those with limited health literacy skills, often have trouble understanding health information. One of the ways in which medical communication can be facilitated is through the use of pictographs. In particular, pictographs have been used extensively to deliver specific medical instructions. The use of images has been shown to positively affect patient comprehension by improving attention, recall, satisfaction, and adherence (Houts et al., 2006; Katz et al., 2006).

Although the potential of pictographs has often been recognised, tools that automatically translate sentences into pictographs are still very scarce due to the lack of resources, which also impedes evaluation in this domain. Glyph is an automatic healthcare data processing system that automatically converts texts into sets of illustrations using natural language processing and computer graphics techniques (Bui et al., 2012). The system is based on 600 pictographs that are linked to Unified Medical Language System (UMLS, (Bodenreider, 2004)) and has been shown to have a positive impact on information recall, satisfaction, and the understandability of instructions (Hill et al., 2016). Some online medical translators also include pictographs, for example, "My Symptoms Translator" (Alvarez, 2014) and "Medipicto AP-HP", but they remain very limited in coverage and can only translate predefined sentences. There are generic MT systems that can produce pictographs (for example, Text2Picto and, more recently, PictoBERT), but they are not specialized in the medical domain. Both Text2Picto (Sevens, 2018; Vandeghinste et al., 2015) and PictoBERT (Pereira et al., 2022) are based on WordNet (Miller, 1995), which does not contain specialized medical terminology and mainly provides word-based mapping into pictographs. For example, "prise de sang" (blood draw) and "prendre le sang" (take blood), which both correspond to the same medical UMLS term (Collection of blood specimen for laboratory procedure), will each be represented by two WordNet concepts (blood + draw and take + blood) and therefore mapped to three different pictographs (Norré et al., 2022), even though the meaning is the same.

BabelDr (Bouillon et al., 2021) is a medical speech translation system specifically designed to allow French-speaking doctors to interview foreign patients in emergency settings when interpreters are not available. It can be characterised as a speech-enabled fixed-phrase medical translator and maps oral doctor interactions (questions and instructions) to a fixed set of sentences that have been pre-translated by humans, using neural machine translation methods and synthetic data. The synthetic data used to train the system are generated with a synchronous grammar that links possible source variations to the closest pre-translated sentence (called "core sentences" here). The system translates in two main phases: first, speech recognition is followed by back translation of the speech recognition result into a core sentence using neural approaches. Secondly, if this back-translated sentence is accepted by the doctor, the target sentence is produced for the patient. The system has been used since 2018 at the Geneva University Hospitals (HUG), in the context of medical dialogue with the migrant population (Janakiram et al, 2021). Translating sentences into pictographs can be another way of improving the communication between the doctor and the patient. Pictographs can also facilitate the translation process, since doctors may be able to validate a back translation into pictographs more intuitively than a core sentence that may be lexically and syntactically very different. For example, the source sentence "avez-vous envie de vomir" (do you feel like vomiting) will be back translated into "avez-vous des nausées ?" (do you have nausea) (Spechbach et al., 2017). Another advantage is the compositionality of pictographs, which enables the coverage of the system to be easily extended.

The aim of this paper is to show how we leveraged the BabelDr architecture and, in particular, the synchronous grammar to build a flexible translator from speech to pictographs for the medical domain, using synthetic data and neural MT architecture. We want to see if it is possible to build a MT system that translates doctor interactions into a semantic gloss based on UMLS concepts. This gloss defines the pictographic language, namely the concepts that are to be produced in pictographs and their syntax. Our hypotheses are that 1) the UMLS gloss is an effective way of characterizing pictographic language, 2) the mapping to UMLS gloss can be viewed as a machine translation task (see also, Mujjiga et al., 2019), and 3) a Multilingual Neural Machine Translation (Johnson et al., 2017) system that exploits both the core sentences and UMLS glosses achieves the best performance. Our contribution is twofold: on the one hand, our study allows us to compare different architectures that can translate BabelDr content into UMLS gloss and, on the other hand, it produces resources that can be shared with the community[1].

This paper is structured as follows: section 2 presents the background. This is followed by Section 3 which describes the synthetic data used to train the systems and Section 4 which outlines the translation systems. Section 5 describes the evaluation methodology, followed by results in Section 6 and conclusions in Section 7.

[1]The synthetic data used for training the systems to translate into UMLS gloss are available upon request.

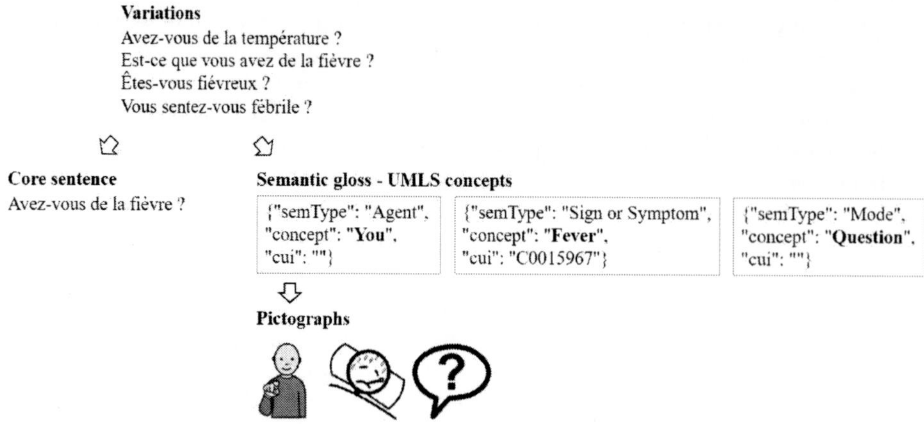

Figure 1: Overview of the steps from source variations through the semantic gloss to a sequence of Arasaac pictographs

2 Automatic translation into pictographic forms: architectures

Due to the lack of resources, translations into pictographic form are traditionally carried out using rule-based methods in three main steps. The sentence is first pre-processed and potentially simplified. Multi-word expressions are identified and lexical items are mapped to a set of disambiguated concepts. Finally, these concepts are linked to the corresponding pictographs using pictographic databases and possibly exploiting the lexical network, for example, synonyms or hyperonyms if a word has no equivalent pictograph. Existing open source databases are all based on WordNet senses (or WOLF, a WordNet equivalent for French) and link word senses to Arasaac[2] pictographs (Norré et al., 2021). In the medical Glyph system (Bui et al., 2012), the process is slightly different. Medical terminology is first identified using the UMLS ontology and images are then composed in a second step based on the semantic type and syntactic pattern.

Recently, neural methods have also been used to generate the pictographs. In particular, PictoBERT (Pereira et al., 2022) is a word-sense language representation model that predicts pictographs, also using WordNet and the Arasaac database.

In this study, we propose to translate French sentences into pictographs using NMT methods, but instead of generating the pictographs based on the WordNet word-senses, we will translate the source sentence into a semantic gloss that defines the pictographic language, namely the medical concepts to be produced in pictographs and their syntax. Like with Glyph, the gloss is based on the medical ontology and contains UMLS concepts and other linguistic elements, such as question marks and entities that are presented in a standard order based on semantic patterns (for example, <you/patient> <Sign or symptom> <time> <question>). Glossing has been used in many NLP applications, for example, in sign language MT, in which it also defines manual signs and their syntax (Ebling, 2016) and in MT of low-resourced languages (Zhou et al., 2019). For our purposes, this approach has many advantages, particularly when it comes to dealing with paraphrases of the same medical questions/instructions. For example, "je vais prendre du sang" (I will take blood), "je vais analyser le sang" (I will analyse your blood) and "je vais faire une prise de sang" (I will do a blood draw) will all be mapped to the

[2]The pictographs are the property of the Aragon Government and were created by Sergio Palao for Arasaac (`https://arasaac.org`). The Aragon Government distributes them under the Creative Commons License.

```
{
   "variations": ["de la fièvre",
    "(fiévreux | fiévreuse|fébrile)",
    "$savez_vous si vous avez de la fièvre ?(en ce moment|maintenant)",
    "$êtes_vous (fiévreux | fiévreuse|fébrile) ?(en ce moment|maintenant)",
    "$sentez_vous (fiévreux | fiévreuse|fébrile) ?(en ce moment|maintenant)",
    "$avez_vous de la (fièvre | température) ?(en ce moment|maintenant)"],
   "target": {
    "frenchCoreSent": "avez-vous de la fièvre ?",
    "umlsGloss": [{"semType": "Entity","concept": "You","cui": ""},
                  {"semType": "Sign or Symptom","concept": "Fever","cui": "C0015967"},
                  {"semType": "Mode","concept": "Question","cui": "" }]
   }
}
```

Figure 2: Example of the grammar mapping source variations to core sentence and UMLS gloss

same gloss and represented by the same pictographs. This pivot representation also makes it possible to easily generate different pictographic languages, depending on the target language of the patient. The use of UMLS instead of WordNet allows us to work with medical terms instead of words. Figure 1 provides an overview of the proposed approach.

3 Grammars and data

Due to confidentiality issues, training data for spoken French medical dialogues is scarce. As previously mentioned, all BabelDr training data are generated from a manually defined Synchronous Context Free Grammar (SCFG, Aho and Ullman, 1969) that maps source variation to core sentences, using variables that are described in a formalism similar to regular expressions. This grammar was defined in close collaboration with doctors who helped collect core sentences and their possible variations. For the current project, we extended this synchronous grammar to also generate semantic glosses. Concretely, all grammar rules were manually linked to a UMLS gloss with the help of the UMLS API. Figure 2 provides an example of a rule with the different surface variations and their corresponding core sentence and UMLS gloss.

The current version of the grammar includes 2629 utterance rules that are organised by medical domain, such as abdomen, traumatology, etc., which expand into 10'991 core sentences and UMLS glosses once variables are replaced by values. These core sentences and UMLS glosses are mapped to hundreds of millions of surface variations.

4 System Settings

In this study, we experiment with two different systems trained on the synthetic data with UMLS glosses. We compare them to a baseline trained on the variations - core sentences data. In this baseline, the system translates French sentences into a core sentence and uses the grammar to generate the UMLS gloss, as in the current BabelDr architecture (see more, Mutal et al., 2019).

In this section, we explain the settings for the systems.

4.1 Data

To produce the training data, we filtered the data generated from the grammar (see Section 3) based on source language N-grams, as described in (Mutal et al., 2020). We then built two aligned corpora: one that contains source variations and the corresponding core sentences and another one with the variations and the UMLS gloss. The former is used to train a system that maps the variations to a core sentence as in Mutal et al. (2019), and the latter is used to train a system that translates into the UMLS gloss.

Variation (Source)	le mal à la tête irradie-t-il vers le haut
Core Sentence (Target)	la douleur irradie-t-elle vers le haut de la tête ?
UMLS gloss (concept names)	Pain Radiating_to Towards Upper Head Question
UMLS gloss (CUI) (Target)	C0030193 C0332301 C3875150 C1282910 C0018670 Question

Table 1: Example of data used for the training corpora. The target is created using CUI (UMLS Concept Unique Identifier) and entities (if there is no CUI).

	#Words	#Vocabulary
Variations	7.2M	5,105
Core Sentences	6M	2,652
UMLS Glosses	3.8M	1,667

Table 2: The number of words and vocabulary for variations, core sentences and UMLS glosses for the 746,462 sentences in the training data.

Table 1 provides an example of the data used in the training corpora. The number of words and unique words (vocabulary) of the 746,462 sentences included in the filtered set are presented in Table 2.

4.2 Systems

As we wanted to compare different systems that can translate into a UMLS gloss, we trained the models using the same settings and architecture. They were trained using the open-source implementation from OpenNMT-py (Klein et al., 2018) of Transformer architecture (Vaswani et al., 2017). Since a lot of resources are required to search the optimized hyper-parameters, we re-used the same hyper-parameters for all the models.

Baseline: Baseline system that translates variations into core sentences. This system is trained with the variations to core sentences corpus. The core sentences are then mapped to the corresponding UMLS gloss using the synchronous grammar. When the system produces output that does not match a core sentence, no UMLS gloss is produced.

UMLS NMT: System that directly translates variations into a UMLS gloss. This system is trained with the aligned corpus containing the variations and the corresponding UMLS gloss. This system produces UMLS glosses for all sentences.

Multilingual NMT: System that translates variations into both UMLS gloss and core sentence. Training a multilingual system can be beneficial to produce both UMLS and core sentences using only one model. It also helps with the training step since it shares the representation space from UMLS and core sentences (Firat et al., 2016; Kudugunta et al., 2019; Zhou et al., 2019). We trained the multilingual system using both variations to French and variations to UMLS gloss. We added a special tag at the beginning of the sentence, as shown in Table 3, to identify the target language (as suggested by, Johnson et al., 2017; Wu et al., 2021).

We extracted around 5% of the data for the development set. We verified that the variations are not in the core sentences nor variations of the training set.

5 Evaluation methodology

The aim of the system is to produce a gloss that has the same meaning as the sentence and the right syntax, so that it can produce the expected pictographic form. We carried out an automatic and human evaluation to assess the systems' performance on real medical dialogue

Source	Target
<FR>les maux migrent dans la partie basse ventre	la douleur se déplace vers la partie basse du ventre ?
<UMLS>les maux migrent dans la partie basse ventre	C0030193 C1299988 C3875150 C0230166 Question

Table 3: Training example for the MNMT system

data collected at HUG with doctors using the BabelDr system. The automatic evaluation aims at giving an overview of the systems' precision and recall at the level of concepts. The human evaluation is intended to measure whether or not the gloss expresses the same meaning as the original sentence and can therefore be used as the pivot for pictographs.

In the following sections, we present the test data, followed by the automatic and human evaluation designs.

5.1 Test Data

To estimate the quality of the systems, we used the speech data collected in real settings during a cohort study at the outpatient emergency unit of the HUG (Janakiram et al., 2020). The data were collected using the BabelDr system, which was used by doctors when interviewing real patients. The doctors were familiar with system coverage and the types of utterances to use. The data were then transcribed and manually associated with the closest core sentence. Each core sentence was then linked to its corresponding UMLS gloss using the grammar. The data consist of 883 segments, which corresponds to 5,672 words in the transcriptions (average length of 6.4 words per sentence). The following example contains an extract of a sequence of doctor utterances:

avez-vous mal à la tête maintenant ? (does your head hurt now?)

pouvez-vous me montrer avec le doigt où est la douleur ? (can you show me with your finger where the pain is located?)

depuis combien de jours avez-vous mal à la tête ? (for how many days has your head hurt?)

avez-vous déjà eu ce type de douleur ? (have you ever had this kind of pain in the past?)

avez-vous la tête qui tourne ? (is your head spinning?)

The sentences were tagged as "In Domain" if a core sentence with a similar meaning was found in the BabelDr grammars and "Out Of Domain" if not. Based on this, 92% of the sentences were "In Domain". Additionally, sentences were tagged as "In Coverage" if the variation was found in the training data (18%).

	Definition
Hypothesis	UMLS gloss generated by the system
Reference	UMLS gloss generated by the grammar for the reference core sentence
True Positives	Number of correct UMLS concepts in the hypothesis
False Positives	Number of additional UMLS concepts in the hypothesis
False Negatives	Number of missing UMLS concepts in the hypothesis

Table 4: Definition of True Positive, False Negative and False Positive.

5.2 Automatic Evaluation

To evaluate the systems, we assessed the output using Precision, Recall and F_β (Powers, 2011) on UMLS concepts, as described in Table 4. We chose $\beta = 0.5$ to give more weight to precision. As the test data is not balanced in terms of distribution of core sentences, we computed the performance for each core sentence, and then averaged it over the number of core sentences, i.e. by macro-averaging (Jurafsky and Martin, 2014). The macro-average better reflects the statistics of the less frequent core sentences and is therefore more suitable for situations in which all core sentences are equally important but are not represented equally in the test data.

5.3 Human Evaluation

We carried out a human evaluation to measure the fidelity of the UMLS glosses produced by the system. For this evaluation, we only used results from the best MT system, namely Multilingual NMT. The evaluations were carried out at the segment level by two participants.

We presented the sentences (transcriptions of doctor utterances) side by side with the system output (the UMLS gloss), in the order of dialogue. For each pair, the participants were asked to rate the UMLS gloss using one of the following categories: Same meaning, Different meaning, Related meaning or I don't know. This "Related meaning" category was to be used for cases in which the gloss only partially represented the meaning of the sentence, but could be considered to be usable in the context of the medical dialogue, for example, when one of the gloss concepts was a hyperonym or hyponym, or when the gloss contained additional information or omissions (for instance, the tense marker). We then calculated the percentage for each category. We also calculated Cohen's kappa score to measure the level of agreement between the participants.

6 Results

6.1 Automatic Evaluation

Table 5 presents the results of the automatic evaluation. The results show that the systems trained with variations to UMLS outperformed the model trained with variations to core sentences in all the metrics. For In Domain segments, Multilingual NMT outperformed all the models, but for In Coverage UMLS NMT slightly outperformed the multilingual model (0.882 vs. 0.880 on $F_{0.5}$). A closer look at the In Coverage segments revealed that the multilingual NMT sometimes added adverbs that were not present in the reference, in particular when the training includes core sentences with and without these adverbs. For example, for 'est-ce que vous toussez ?" (are you coughing?), the system UMLS NMT correctly produces "You Coughing Question", while the Multilingual NMT generates "You Coughing Very_Much Question". The reference is "You Coughing Question". In context, the adverb does not considerably affect the meaning and so both glosses may be considered to be equivalent by the doctors since they allow them to collect the same medical information, as measured through human evaluation.

	In Domain			In Coverage			Out of Coverage		
	Precision	**Recall**	**F0.5**	**Precision**	**Recall**	**F0.5**	**Precision**	**Recall**	**F0.5**
Baseline	0.788	0.80	0.78	0.844	0.857	0.844	0.77	0.785	0.77
UMLS NMT	0.814	0.828	0.814	0.883	0.886	0.882	0.793	0.811	0.796
Multilingual NMT	0.819	0.83	0.819	0.882	0.883	0.880	0.802	0.815	0.802

Table 5: Results of Automatic Evaluation.

	Same Meaning	Different Meaning	Related Meaning	I don't know	Total
All	62.47% / 65.99%	20.86% / 19.27%	14.17% / 14.74%	2.49% / 0%	882
Out Of Domain	8.45% / 14.08%	67.61% / 64.79%	21.13% / 21.13%	2.82% / 0%	71
In Domain	67.20% / 70.53%	16.77% / 15.29%	13.56% / 14.18%	2.47% / 0%	811
In Coverage	82.43% / 89.86%	6.08% / 6.08%	10.81% / 4.05%	0.68% / 0%	148
Out of Coverage	58.45% / 61.17%	23.84% / 21.93%	14.85% / 16.89%	2.86% / 0%	734

Table 6: Results of Human Evaluation for the two evaluators (eval. 1/eval. 2).

Figure 3: Examples extracted from the test data. The system translated the human transcriptions (sentences in bold) to UMLS gloss (terms below each picture). The result was then mapped to Arasaac pictographs.

6.2 Human Evaluation

Human evaluation (see Table 6) shows that the system produces an incorrect gloss for 20.1% (average for the two evaluators) of interactions, which means that four speech interactions out of five may potentially provide a correct translation into pictographs. These incorrect glosses correspond to 67.61% of Out of Domain sentences but only 16.77% of the In domain sentences. For Out of Domain sentences, there is no corresponding core sentence in the training data, but in 11.3% (Same meaning) + 21.1% of cases (Related meaning), the system was able to generalize and produce a potentially useful gloss. The agreement between the participants is 0.71 (p-value=0), which suggests that there was substantial degree of consistency in the evaluation (Landis and Koch, 1977). Some examples translated by the Multilingual system using the test data are given in Figure 3.

7 Conclusion

The aim of this paper was to propose an architecture to automatically translate doctor's interactions into pictographs. Different generic systems exist, but they are not specialised for the medical domain. The proposed method contains two steps: first, sentences are translated into a UMLS gloss based on synthetic data and secondly, concepts are mapped to pictographs. The aim of the UMLS gloss is to characterise the pictographic language, i.e. both the medical concepts and the syntax. This paper focused on the first step.

Our contributions are twofold. On one hand, we confirmed our hypotheses and showed that mapping to the UMLS gloss can be seen as a MT task and that NMT models directly trained with UMLS glosses achieved higher F-scores. The resulting system is still limited in coverage, but results are encouraging, since 30% of Out of Domain utterances are translated into a potentially useful UMLS gloss. The human evaluation has also shown that the proposed UMLS gloss is readable by humans and can characterise pictographic language. On the other hand, this work is the first of its kind and constitutes an initial step in constituting resources (corpus and UMLS to pictographs database) and testing the impact of pictographs on medical communication. The synthetic data used for training the systems to translate into UMLS gloss are available upon request.

In the future, we plan to build upon this work in different directions. First, we plan to build a pictographic database that links UMLS concepts to pictographs, based on existing open source pictograph databases, such as Arasaac and SantéBD and other resources for the illustration of concepts (e.g. BabelNet). A preliminary study shows that only 69.7% of the BabelDr UMLS concepts can be linked to at least one Arasaac pictograph. For medical dialogues, the main problems include the representation of generic words (disease, infection, inflammation), the name of diseases (diabetes, syphilis, etc.) and temporal elements. This step will allow us to build a speech-to-pictographs baseline system for medical dialogues and will allow experiments to be carried out on the medical dialogue task itself.

More NMT architectures will be tested. Medical dialogues contain a lot of incomplete sentences (ellipsis), as explained in (Mutal et al., 2020). In the current version of BabelDr, the translation is performed in context (with the previous sentence of the dialogue) when an ellipsis is identified. Contextual NMT can also be used when translating into the UMLS gloss. UMLS semantic type and BabelDr human translations in other languages can also be added as another language in the multilingual system. The UMLS can also be used in the current architecture as an interlingua to improve translation into low-resource languages (Johnson et al., 2017).

One of our objectives is to produce more training data with more core sentences. We can easily change the synthetic data to include new core sentences. In the current version, each new grammar rule has to be translated into the 9 BabelDr target languages (Gerlach et al., 2018). The grammar therefore often groups together quasi-paraphrases, as shown in Figure 2 to reduce human translation effort (for example, "avez-vous de la fièvre" (do you have fever) and "avez-vous de la fièvre maintenant" (do you have fever now) are mapped to the same core sentence, based on the assumption that they allow doctors to collect the same anamnestic information. These rules may be split in order to only include exact paraphrases. Other resources will also be added, based on existing HUG terminological resources.

Finally, the selection of training data from the data generated by the grammar is based on N-grams in the source language (Mutal et al., 2020). We can try to select the training data based on UMLS N-grams. Our test corpus also contains a high number of In Coverage sentences, since it was collected with the BabelDr tool. We are in the process of collecting more data.

8 Acknowledgements

This work is part of the PROPICTO project, funded by the Fonds National Suisse (N°197864) and the Agence Nationale de la Recherche (ANR-20-CE93-0005).

References

Aho, A. and Ullman, J. (1969). Syntax directed translations and the pushdown assembler. *Journal of Computer and System Sciences*, 3(1):37–56.

Alvarez, J. (2014). Visual design. A step towards multicultural health care. *Arch Argent Pediatr*, 112(1):33–40.

Bodenreider, O. (2004). The unified medical language system (umls): integrating biomedical terminology. *Nucleic Acids Research*, 32(90001):267D – 270.

Bouillon, P., Gerlach, J., Mutal, J., Tsourakis, N., and Spechbach, H. (2021). A speech-enabled fixed-phrase translator for healthcare accessibility. In *Proceedings of the 1st Workshop on NLP for Positive Impact*, page 135–142, Online. Association for Computational Linguistics.

Bui, D. D. A., Nakamura, C., Bray, B. E., and Zeng-Treitler, Q. (2012). Automated illustration of patients instructions. In *AMIA Annual Symposium Proceedings*, volume 2012, page 1158. American Medical Informatics Association.

Ebling, S. (2016). *Automatic Translation from German to Synthesized Swiss German Sign Language*. Thesis for the degree of Doctor in Philosophy, University of Zurich.

Firat, O., Cho, K., and Bengio, Y. (2016). Multi-way, multilingual neural machine translation with a shared attention mechanism. In *Proceedings of the 2016 Conference of the North American Chapter of the Association for Computational Linguistics: Human Language Technologies*, pages 866–875, San Diego, California. Association for Computational Linguistics.

Gerlach, J., Spechbach, H., and Bouillon, P. (2018). Creating an online translation platform to build target language resources for a medical phraselator. In *Proceedings of the 40th edition of Translating and the Computer Conference (TC40)*, pages 60–65. AsLing, The International Association for Advancement in Language Technology.

Hill, B., Perri-Moore, S., Kuang, J., Bray, B. E., Ngo, L., Doig, A., and Zeng-Treitler, Q. (2016). Automated pictographic illustration of discharge instructions with Glyph: impact on patient recall and satisfaction. *Journal of the American Medical Informatics Association*, 23(6):1136–1142.

Houts, P. S., Doak, C. C., Doak, L. G., and Loscalzo, M. J. (2006). The role of pictures in improving health communication: A review of research on attention, comprehension, recall, and adherence. *Patient Education and Counseling*, 61(2):173–190.

Janakiram, A. A., Gerlach, J., Vuadens-Lehmann, A., Bouillon, P., and Spechbach, H. (2020). *User Satisfaction with a Speech-Enabled Translator in Emergency Settings*, pages 1421–1422. Digital Personalized Health and Medicine. IOS. ID: unige:139233.

Johnson, M., Schuster, M., Le, Q. V., Krikun, M., Wu, Y., Chen, Z., Thorat, N., Viégas, F., Wattenberg, M., Corrado, G., Hughes, M., and Dean, J. (2017). Google's multilingual neural machine translation system: Enabling zero-shot translation. *Transactions of the Association for Computational Linguistics*, 5:339–351.

Jurafsky, D. and Martin, J. H. (2014). *Speech and language processing*. Always learning. Pearson Education, 2. ed., pearson new internat. ed edition.

Katz, M. G., Kripalani, S., and Weiss, B. D. (2006). Use of pictorial aids in medication instructions: A review of the literature. *American journal of health-system pharmacy*, 63(23):2391–2397.

Klein, G., Kim, Y., Deng, Y., Nguyen, V., Senellart, J., and Rush, A. (2018). OpenNMT: Neural machine translation toolkit. In *Proceedings of the 13th Conference of the Association for Machine Translation in the Americas (Volume 1: Research Track)*, pages 177–184, Boston, MA. Association for Machine Translation in the Americas.

Kudugunta, S., Bapna, A., Caswell, I., and Firat, O. (2019). Investigating multilingual NMT representations at scale. In *Proceedings of the 2019 Conference on Empirical Methods in Natural Language Processing and the 9th International Joint Conference on Natural Language Processing (EMNLP-IJCNLP)*, pages 1565–1575, Hong Kong, China. Association for Computational Linguistics.

Landis, J. R. and Koch, G. G. (1977). The measurement of observer agreement for categorical data. *Biometrics*, 33(1).

Miller, G. A. (1995). WordNet: A lexical database for English. *Communications of the ACM*, 38(11):39–41.

Mujjiga, S., Krishna, V., Chakravarthi, K., and J, V. (2019). Identifying semantics in clinical reports using neural machine translation. *Proceedings of the AAAI Conference on Artificial Intelligence*, 33:9552–9557.

Mutal, J., Bouillon, P., Gerlach, J., Estrella, P., and Spechbach, H. (2019). Monolingual back-translation in a medical speech translation system for diagnostic interviews - a NMT approach. In *Proceedings of Machine Translation Summit XVII: Translator, Project and User Tracks*, pages 196–203, Dublin, Ireland. European Association for Machine Translation.

Mutal, J., Gerlach, J., Bouillon, P., and Spechbach, H. (2020). Ellipsis translation for a medical speech to speech translation system. In *Proceedings of the 22nd Annual Conference of the European Association for Machine Translation*, pages 281–290, Lisboa, Portugal. European Association for Machine Translation.

Norré, M., Vandeghinste, V., Bouillon, P., and François, T. (2021). Extending a Text-to-Pictograph System to French and to Arasaac. In *Proceedings of the International Conference on Recent Advances in Natural Language Processing (RANLP 2021)*, pages 1050–1059.

Norré, M., Vandeghinste, V., Bouillon, P., and François, T. (2022). Investigating the Medical Coverage of a Translation System into Pictographs for Patients with an Intellectual Disability. In *Ninth Workshop on Speech and Language Processing for Assistive Technologies (SLPAT-2022)*, pages 44–49. Association for Computational Linguistics.

Pereira, J. A., Macêdo, D., Zanchettin, C., Oliveira, A. L. I. d., and Fidalgo, R. d. N. (2022). Pictobert: Transformers for next pictogram prediction. *Expert Systems with Applications*, 202:117231.

Powers, D. M. W. (2011). Evaluation: From precision, recall and f-measure to roc., informedness, markedness & correlation. *Journal of Machine Learning Technologies*, 2(1):37–63.

Sevens, L. (2018). *Words Divide, Pictographs Unite: Pictograph Communication Technologies for People with an Intellectual Disability*. LOT, JK Utrecht, The Netherlands.

Vandeghinste, V., Schuurman, I., Sevens, L., and Eynde, F. V. (2015). Translating text into pictographs. *Natural Language Engineering*, 23(2):217–244.

Vaswani, A., Shazeer, N., Parmar, N., Uszkoreit, J., Jones, L., Gomez, A. N., Kaiser, L., and Polosukhin, I. (2017). Attention is all you need. In Guyon, I., Luxburg, U. V., Bengio, S., Wallach, H., Fergus, R., Vishwanathan, S., and Garnett, R., editors, *Advances in Neural Information Processing Systems*, volume 30. Curran Associates, Inc.

Wu, L., Cheng, S., Wang, M., and Li, L. (2021). Language tags matter for zero-shot neural machine translation. In *Findings of the Association for Computational Linguistics: ACL-IJCNLP 2021*, pages 3001–3007, Online. Association for Computational Linguistics.

Zhou, Z., Levin, L. S., Mortensen, D. R., and Waibel, A. H. (2019). Using interlinear glosses as pivot in low-resource multilingual machine translation. *arXiv: Computation and Language*.

Embedding-Enhanced GIZA++: Improving Word Alignment Using Embeddings

Kelly Marchisio kmarc@jhu.edu
Department of Computer Science, Johns Hopkins University, Baltimore, MD, 21211, USA

Conghao Xiong* chxiong21@cse.cuhk.edu.hk
Department of Computer Science and Engineering, The Chinese University of Hong Kong, New Territory, HKSAR

Philipp Koehn phi@jhu.edu
Department of Computer Science, Johns Hopkins University, Baltimore, MD, 21211, USA

Abstract

A popular natural language processing task decades ago, word alignment has been dominated until recently by GIZA++, a statistical method based on the 30-year-old IBM models. New methods that outperform GIZA++ primarily rely on large machine translation models, massively multilingual language models, or supervision from GIZA++ alignments itself. We introduce Embedding-Enhanced GIZA++, and outperform GIZA++ without any of the aforementioned factors. Taking advantage of monolingual embedding spaces of source and target language only, we exceed GIZA++'s performance in every tested scenario for three languages pairs. In the lowest-resource setting, we outperform GIZA++ by 8.5, 10.9, and 12 AER for Ro-En, De-En, and En-Fr, respectively. We release our code at `https://github.com/kellymarchisio/ee-giza`.

1 Introduction

Word alignment techniques were once ubiquitous in the machine translation (MT) literature, as they formed a critical part of statistical machine translation (SMT) systems. Since the advent of neural machine translation (NMT), word alignment is no longer a step in typical NMT training, but is still important for other tasks such as annotation transfer (e.g. Yarowsky and Ngai, 2001; Rasooli et al., 2018), as a post-processing step of MT to reinsert markup (e.g. Müller, 2017), and for some mapping-based unsupervised MT methods such as Artetxe et al. (2019).

GIZA++ (Och, 2003), a statistical alignment model, has been the most commonly used tool for word alignment quality for 20 years and is based the IBM translation models that are yet a decade older (Brown et al., 1993). Though a handful of neural systems have outperformed GIZA++, these rely on large MT models (e.g. Stengel-Eskin et al., 2019; Chen et al., 2020; Zenkel et al., 2020), massively multilingual language models (e.g. Garg et al., 2019b; Jalili Sabet et al., 2020; Dou and Neubig, 2021), supervision from human-annotated alignments (Nagata et al., 2020), or combinations of the above.

We introduce Embedding-Enhanced GIZA++ (EE-GIZA++), an improvement to GIZA++ without any of the aforementioned factors. EE-GIZA++ biases GIZA++ to align semantically similar words from a shared embedding space. We outperform GIZA++ in all tested settings

* Work completed at Johns Hopkins University.

on three language pairs. EE-GIZA++ is particularly strong in comparison with GIZA++ when parallel training data is scarce: using only $\sim$500 lines of bitext, it outperforms GIZA++ by 10.9 AER[1] and 12.0 AER for De-En and Fr-En, respectively.

2 Related Work

Fast-align is a statistical aligner similar to GIZA++. It is a reparameterization of IBM Model 2 (Dyer et al., 2013). eflomal is another highly-performant non-neural aligner (Östling and Tiedemann, 2016). We use GIZA++ as our base system because it commonly-used and trusted for generating high-quality alignments. Numerous improvements to GIZA++ have been proposed (e.g. Vaswani et al., 2012).

Recent work involves using neural translation models to guide or extract alignments, viewing attention as a proxy for alignment (e.g. Peter et al., 2017; Li et al., 2018; Garg et al., 2019b; Zenkel et al., 2019, 2020; Chen et al., 2020). Other aligners use massive multilingual language models with contextualized embeddings such as mBERT (Devlin et al., 2019). Like us, Jalili Sabet et al. (2020) experiment with mapped monolingual embedding spaces, but exceed the GIZA++ baseline only when using spaces such as mBERT and XLM-R (Conneau et al., 2020). Dou and Neubig (2021)'s approach is similar to the aforementioned authors, but they improve results by finetuning mBERT on auxiliary tasks. Nagata et al. (2020) use mBERT and require supervision with human-annotated alignments.

Pourdamghani et al. (2018) use word embedding similarity to augment parallel data seen by GIZA++, improving alignment and downstream low-resource MT. Jalili Sabet et al. (2016) also use nearest-neighbors in a word embedding space to alter IBM Model 1, but their performance does not match ours. Perhaps most similar to our work, Songyot and Chiang (2014) incorporate word similarity into GIZA++ using a feedforward neural network trained to model word similarity, with a hyperparameter to control the influence of the neural model.

3 Background

Let S be a source-language sentence of tokens $(s_1, s_2, ..., s_m)$ and T be a target-language sentence $(t_1, t_2, ..., t_l)$. Alignments are defined as $A \subseteq \{(s,t) \in S \times T\}$ where each s, t are meaningfully related—usually, translations of one another. Performance is typically measured with Alignment Error Rate (AER; Och and Ney, 2000a).

3.1 GIZA++

GIZA++ is a popular statistical alignment and MT toolkit (Och and Ney, 2000b, 2003) which implements IBM Models 1-5 (Brown et al., 1993) and the HMM Model (Vogel et al., 1996), trained using expectation-maximization (EM). The default training setup is to run five iterations each of IBM Model 1, HMM, Model 3, and Model 4. GIZA++ is highly effective at aligning frequent words in a corpus, but error-prone for infrequent words.

IBM Models The IBM models developed more than 30 years ago for MT are useful for alignment. IBM Model 1 relies on lexical translation probabilities $p(f|e)$ for source word e and target word f. Model 2 adds an alignment model $p(j \mid i, l, m)$, predicting source position j from target position i of sentences with lengths m and l, respectively. Model 3 adds a fertility model. Model 4 and the HMM Model replace the alignment with a relative reordering model. After training, the most likely alignment can be computed for a sentence pair.

[1] Alignment Error Rate (Och and Ney, 2000a).

3.2 Monolingual Embedding Space Mapping

Non-contextual vector representations of words ("word embeddings", "word vectors") are common in NLP (e.g. Mikolov et al., 2013; Bojanowski et al., 2017). Word vectors trained on monolingual data *embed* the word into an N-dimensional space where distance and angle have meaning. Mapping monolingual embedding spaces to a shared crosslingual space is common, particularly for bilingual lexicon induction and cross-lingual information retrieval.

Procrustes Problem Techniques that map monolingual embedding spaces to a crosslingual space often solve a variation of the generalized Procrustes problem (e.g., Artetxe et al., 2018b; Conneau et al., 2018; Patra et al., 2019; Ramírez et al., 2020). Given word embedding matrices $X, Y \in \mathbb{R}^{n \times d}$ where $x \in X$, $y \in Y$ are word vectors in source and target languages, one finds the map $W \in \mathbb{R}^{d \times d}$ that minimizes distances for each pair (x, y) known to be translations:

$$\arg\min_{W} \|XW - Y\|_F$$

When restricting W to be orthogonal ($WW^T = I$), Schönemann (1966) showed that the closed-form solution is $W = VU^T$, where $U\Sigma V$ is the singular value decomposition of $Y^T X$.

After mapping X and Y to a shared space with W, translations are extracted via nearest-neighbor search. A popular distance metric is cross-domain similarity local scaling (CSLS) to mitigate the "hubness problem" (Conneau et al., 2018).

4 Method

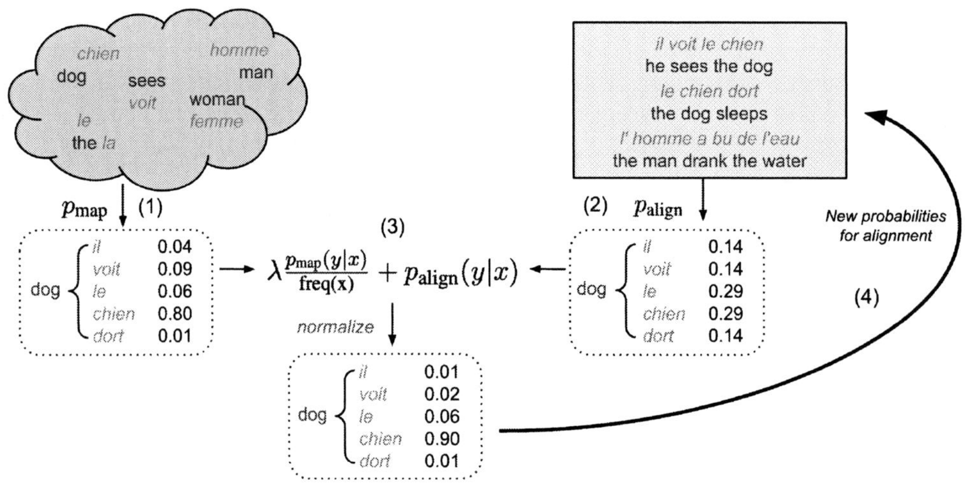

Figure 1: Proposed Method: Embedding-Enhanced GIZA++. 1) Map monolingual embeddings to crosslingual space. Calculate CSLS for cooccurring words and take softmax to calculate a probability distribution (*p_map*). 2) Use statistical aligner to calculate separate probability distribution over cooccuring words (*p_align*). 3) Interpolate distributions with weight proportional to source word's frequency. Normalize. 4) Replace the statistical model's translation probability table with updated probability distribution. 5) Repeat Steps 2-4 for each iteration of EM.

GIZA++ is highly effective at inducing the correct alignment for frequent words when parallel resources are abundant, but is error-prone for rare words. Because word embeddings can be trained on large amounts of monolingual data, rare words from a parallel corpus may be well-enough represented in a large monolingual corpus that reasonable word embeddings can be trained. Our key insight is that for infrequent words, finding a translation via nearest-neighbors in a shared embedding space may be more reliable than using a statistical aligner. We thus incorporate embedding space mapping into GIZA++ training, giving more or less influence to the statistical aligner depending on word frequency. Figure 1 shows the method.

1. Map embedding spaces. Word embedding spaces X and Y for source and target language, respectively, are mapped to a crosslingual space using VecMap[2] (Artetxe et al., 2018a).

2. Calculate translation probability distribution from mapped spaces. Let $\text{Co}_Y(x)$ be the words from the target language that cooccur with source word x in the corpus. For each x, we calculate a probability distribution over possible alignments from $\text{Co}_Y(x)$ with a softmax over the CSLS scores (We use $\tau = 0.1$.) We use the mapped embedding spaces for source and target languages to calculate CSLS.

$$p_{map}(y|x) = \frac{\exp\left(\text{CSLS}(x,y)/\tau\right)}{\sum\limits_{y' \in \text{Co}_Y(x)} \exp\left(\text{CSLS}(x,y')\right)/\tau)}$$

3. Integrate with GIZA++. Recall that IBM Models 1, 3, 4, and HMM maintain a lexical translation table of $p_{\text{align}}(y|x)$ for every cooccurring source-target word pair. During training of IBM Model 1 and the HMM, we interpolate the lexical translation table with embedding-based translation probabilities after each iteration of EM. For each cooccurring pair (x, y), calculate:

$$score(x,y) = \lambda \frac{p_{\text{map}}(y|x)}{\text{freq(x)}} + p_{\text{align}}(y|x)$$

where freq(x) is the raw frequency of x in the source-side of the corpus and λ is a hyperparameter. The effect is that p_{map} is given more weight for infrequent words, in accordance with our goal to trust the embedding space mapper for infrequent words and the statistical aligner for frequent words. Then normalize over cooccuring words:

$$p(y|x) = \frac{score(x,y)}{\sum\limits_{y_i \in \text{Co}_Y(x)} score(x,y_i)} \tag{1}$$

We update GIZA++'s lexical translation table with the new value from Equation 1 for all cooccurring pairs, then begin the next iteration of EM.[3] This process is repeated for all iterations of IBM Model 1 and HMM model training. IBM Model 3 and 4 are trained as usual. Integrating probabilites from p_{map} into IBM Models 3 and 4 is for future work.

Steps 1-3 are done in source→target and target→source directions. Alignments are symmetrized with grow-diag-final (Koehn et al., 2003).

5 Experimental Setup

We use the same training setup as previous work[4] (Garg et al., 2019b; Zenkel et al., 2019, 2020; Chen et al., 2020; Dou and Neubig, 2021). Training corpora for German-English (De-En), English-French (En-Fr), and Romanian-English (Ro-En) are 1.9M, 1.1M, and 448K lines, and test sets are 508, 447, and 248 lines, respectively. Validation sets do not exist, so we tune λ on

[2]`github.com/artetxem/vecmap`

[3]If a word from the bitext is not present in the word embedding space, its translation probability is not updated.

[4]`https://github.com/lilt/alignment-scripts`. Data: (Mihalcea and Pedersen, 2003; Koehn, 2005; Vilar et al., 2006)

1 million lines of De-En.[5] λ is set to 10,000. We use the VecMap implementation of CSLS and SciPy for some utility functions and softmax calculation (Virtanen et al., 2020; Harris et al., 2020). For pretrained word embedding spaces, we use the publicly-available Wikipedia word vectors trained using fastText from Bojanowski et al. (2017).[6] We limit vocabulary size to 200,000 and perform embedding mapping with VecMap in unsupervised mode.

	De-En		Ro-En		En-Fr	
Corpus Size	GIZA++	Ours	GIZA++	Ours	GIZA++	Ours
Test Set Only	44.2	**33.3** *(-10.9)*	42.8	**34.3** *(-8.5)*	26.9	**14.9** *(-12.0)*
1000	41.0	**31.1** *(-9.9)*	41.5	**33.6** *(-7.9)*	20.0	**11.4** *(-8.6)*
2000	37.7	**29.1** *(-8.6)*	39.6	**32.9** *(-6.7)*	17.2	**10.1** *(-7.1)*
5000	34.5	**26.9** *(-7.6)*	38.2	**32.0** *(-6.2)*	14.0	**8.5** *(-5.5)*
10,000	31.9	**25.5** *(-6.4)*	36.1	**30.4** *(-5.7)*	11.7	**7.5** *(-4.2)*
20,000	29.3	**24.2** *(-5.1)*	35.2	**30.3** *(-4.9)*	10.0	**7.1** *(-2.9)*
50,000	26.6	**22.6** *(-4.0)*	34.2	**29.7** *(-4.5)*	8.6	**6.3** *(-2.3)*
100,000	25.4	**21.9** *(-3.5)*	33.4	**29.3** *(-4.1)*	7.8	**6.1** *(-1.7)*
200,000	24.0	**21.2** *(-2.8)*	32.7	**29.4** *(-3.3)*	7.0	**5.8** *(-1.2)*
500,000	21.6	**20.3** *(-1.3)*	26.5	**25.5** *(-1.0)*	6.1	**5.7** *(-0.4)*
1,000,000	20.7	**20.1** *(-0.6)*	*n/a*	*n/a*	6.1	**5.5** *(-0.6)*
1,900,000	20.6	**19.9** *(-0.7)*	*n/a*	*n/a*	*n/a*	*n/a*

Table 1: Main Results. Alignment Error Rate (AER) of EE-GIZA++ vs. GIZA++ baseline (lower is better). Test set is included in corpus size. Ro-En 500K is the full 448K training set. Bidirectional, symmetrized (grow-diag-final).

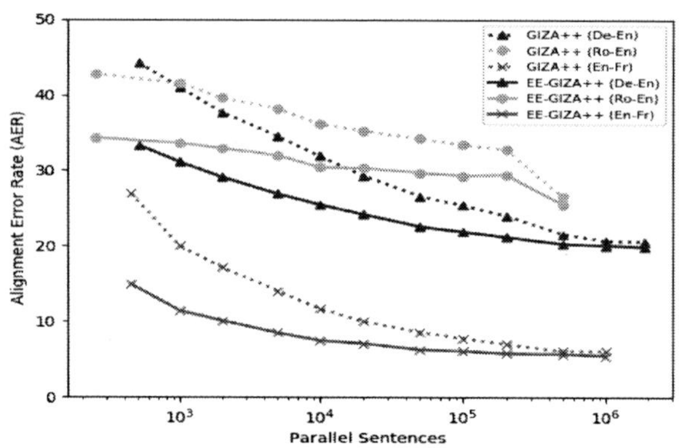

Figure 2: Visualization of Main Results. Alignment Error Rate (AER) of EE-GIZA++ vs. GIZA++ baseline for increasing amounts of training data. Lower is better.

[5]This was the approximate average size of training data for all languages.

[6]`https://fasttext.cc/docs/en/pretrained-vectors.html`

6 Results

The main results are presented in Table 1 and visualized in Figure 2. We observe that EE-GIZA++ consistently outperforms GIZA++ by a large margin in every tested scenario. When aligning the test set alone with no additional bitext, EE-GIZA++ dramatically outperforms GIZA++: by 8.5 AER for Ro-En, 10.9 AER for De-En, and 12 AER for En-Fr. This represents improvements of approximately 20%, 25%, and 45% for Ro-En, De-En, and En-Fr, respectively. The error-rate improvement is especially notable when we consider that each test set has only approximately 250-500 lines. When expanding the training set to include a total of 10,000 lines, we continue to observe strong gains with our method: with absolute improvements of 5.7, 6.4, and 4.2 AER for Ro-En, De-En, and En-Fr. These represent improvements of approximately 15.8%, 20.1%, and 35.9%, respectively.

Statistical Baselines	**De-En**	**Ro-En**	**En-Fr**
GIZA++	20.6	26.5	6.2
eflomal*	22.6	25.1	8.2
fast-align*	27.0	32.1	10.5
Massively-Multilingual			
Jalili Sabet et al. (2020)	19.†	27.2*[7]	6.†
Dou and Neubig (2021)	15.6	23.0	4.4
no fine-tuning	17.4	27.9	5.6
Bilingual NMT-Based			
Zenkel et al. (2019)	21.2	27.6	10.0
Garg et al. (2019b)	20.2	26.0	7.7
using GIZA++ output	16.0	23.1	4.6
Zenkel et al. (2020)	16.3	23.4	5.0
Chen et al. (2020)	15.4	21.2	4.7
Ours	19.9	25.5	5.3

Table 2: Supplemental results in high-resource settings compared to models that use additional resources. "Massively multilingual" models use mBERT. NMT models likely fail in low-bitext scenarios (our focus). Bidirectional. *reported in Dou and Neubig (2021). †Jalili Sabet et al. (2020) report one less significant digit.

Supplemental Results: High-Resource We use the full data sets for De-En, Ro-En, and En-Fr and compare to existing work in Table 2.[8] We outperform the three statistical baselines, except eflomal on Ro-En. EE-GIZA++ outperforms Jalili Sabet et al. (2020) on Ro-En and En-Fr, which utilizes a massively-multilingual language model. Dou and Neubig (2021) with fine-tuning outperforms our model, though they use mBERT which is trained on 104 languages. Notably, Garg et al. (2019a) use GIZA++ output as supervision. EE-GIZA++ performs better than GIZA++, so AER might improve if supervised with our alignments.

[7] As Jalili Sabet et al. (2020) use the 2005 Ro-En test set from `https://web.eecs.umich.edu/~mihalcea/wpt05`, we report Dou and Neubig (2021)'s Ro-En results here for consistency with the others, which use the 2003 test set (`https://web.eecs.umich.edu/~mihalcea/wpt`.

[8] Many of these use the grow-diag symmetrization heuristic, but we use grow-diag-final.

7 Conclusion and Future Work

We introduce EE-GIZA++, an unsupervised enhancement to GIZA++ that uses word embeddings for improved word alignment in low-bitext settings, without the use of NMT or massively-multilingual language models that to-date have been the strongest competitors to GIZA++. EE-GIZA++ outperforms GIZA++ by 8.5, 10.9, and 12 AER in lowest-bitext scenarios for Ro-En, De-En, and En-Fr, respectively. Future work should examine performance of EE-GIZA++ on a diverse set of languages with varying scripts and amounts of data available.

Acknowledgements

The authors would like to thank Elias Stengel-Eskin, Mahsa Yarmohammadi, and Marc Marone for fruitful discussion on alignment. The first author would like to thank Martin St. Denis for his ideas about the graphic used in this work.

References

Artetxe, M., Labaka, G., and Agirre, E. (2018a). Generalizing and improving bilingual word embedding mappings with a multi-step framework of linear transformations. In *Proceedings of the AAAI Conference on Artificial Intelligence*.

Artetxe, M., Labaka, G., and Agirre, E. (2018b). A robust self-learning method for fully unsupervised cross-lingual mappings of word embeddings. In *Proceedings of the 56th Annual Meeting of the Association for Computational Linguistics (Volume 1: Long Papers)*, pages 789–798, Melbourne, Australia. Association for Computational Linguistics.

Artetxe, M., Labaka, G., and Agirre, E. (2019). An effective approach to unsupervised machine translation. In *Proceedings of the 57th Annual Meeting of the Association for Computational Linguistics*, pages 194–203, Florence, Italy. Association for Computational Linguistics.

Bojanowski, P., Grave, E., Joulin, A., and Mikolov, T. (2017). Enriching word vectors with subword information. *Transactions of the Association for Computational Linguistics*, 5:135–146.

Brown, P. F., Della Pietra, S. A., Della Pietra, V. J., and Mercer, R. L. (1993). The mathematics of statistical machine translation: Parameter estimation. *Computational Linguistics*, 19(2):263–311.

Chen, Y., Liu, Y., Chen, G., Jiang, X., and Liu, Q. (2020). Accurate word alignment induction from neural machine translation. In *Proceedings of the 2020 Conference on Empirical Methods in Natural Language Processing (EMNLP)*, pages 566–576, Online. Association for Computational Linguistics.

Conneau, A., Khandelwal, K., Goyal, N., Chaudhary, V., Wenzek, G., Guzmán, F., Grave, E., Ott, M., Zettlemoyer, L., and Stoyanov, V. (2020). Unsupervised cross-lingual representation learning at scale. In *Proceedings of the 58th Annual Meeting of the Association for Computational Linguistics*, pages 8440–8451, Online. Association for Computational Linguistics.

Conneau, A., Lample, G., Ranzato, M., Denoyer, L., and Jégou, H. (2018). Word translation without parallel data. In *6th International Conference on Learning Representations, ICLR 2018, Vancouver, BC, Canada, April 30 - May 3, 2018, Conference Track Proceedings*. OpenReview.net.

Devlin, J., Chang, M.-W., Lee, K., and Toutanova, K. (2019). BERT: Pre-training of deep bidirectional transformers for language understanding. In *Proceedings of the 2019 Conference of the North American Chapter of the Association for Computational Linguistics: Human Language Technologies, Volume 1 (Long and Short Papers)*, pages 4171–4186, Minneapolis, Minnesota. Association for Computational Linguistics.

Dou, Z.-Y. and Neubig, G. (2021). Word alignment by fine-tuning embeddings on parallel corpora. In *Proceedings of the 16th Conference of the European Chapter of the Association for Computational Linguistics: Main Volume*, pages 2112–2128, Online. Association for Computational Linguistics.

Dyer, C., Chahuneau, V., and Smith, N. A. (2013). A simple, fast, and effective reparameterization of IBM model 2. In *Proceedings of the 2013 Conference of the North American Chapter of the Association for Computational Linguistics: Human Language Technologies*, pages 644–648, Atlanta, Georgia. Association for Computational Linguistics.

Garg, S., Moniz, J. R. A., Aviral, A., and Bollimpalli, P. (2019a). Learning to relate from captions and bounding boxes. In *Proceedings of the 57th Annual Meeting of the Association for Computational Linguistics*, pages 6597–6603, Florence, Italy. Association for Computational Linguistics.

Garg, S., Peitz, S., Nallasamy, U., and Paulik, M. (2019b). Jointly learning to align and translate with transformer models. In *Proceedings of the 2019 Conference on Empirical Methods in Natural Language Processing and the 9th International Joint Conference on Natural Language Processing (EMNLP-IJCNLP)*, pages 4453–4462, Hong Kong, China. Association for Computational Linguistics.

Harris, C. R., Millman, K. J., van der Walt, S. J., Gommers, R., Virtanen, P., Cournapeau, D., Wieser, E., Taylor, J., Berg, S., Smith, N. J., Kern, R., Picus, M., Hoyer, S., van Kerkwijk, M. H., Brett, M., Haldane, A., Fernández del Río, J., Wiebe, M., Peterson, P., Gérard-Marchant, P., Sheppard, K., Reddy, T., Weckesser, W., Abbasi, H., Gohlke, C., and Oliphant, T. E. (2020). Array programming with NumPy. *Nature*, 585:357–362.

Jalili Sabet, M., Dufter, P., Yvon, F., and Schütze, H. (2020). SimAlign: High quality word alignments without parallel training data using static and contextualized embeddings. In *Findings of the Association for Computational Linguistics: EMNLP 2020*, pages 1627–1643, Online. Association for Computational Linguistics.

Jalili Sabet, M., Faili, H., and Haffari, G. (2016). Improving word alignment of rare words with word embeddings. In *Proceedings of COLING 2016, the 26th International Conference on Computational Linguistics: Technical Papers*, pages 3209–3215, Osaka, Japan. The COLING 2016 Organizing Committee.

Koehn, P. (2005). Europarl: A parallel corpus for statistical machine translation. In *MT summit*, volume 5, pages 79–86. Citeseer.

Koehn, P., Och, F. J., and Marcu, D. (2003). Statistical phrase-based translation. In *Proceedings of the 2003 Human Language Technology Conference of the North American Chapter of the Association for Computational Linguistics*, pages 127–133.

Li, X., Liu, L., Tu, Z., Shi, S., and Meng, M. (2018). Target foresight based attention for neural machine translation. In *Proceedings of the 2018 Conference of the North American Chapter of the Association for Computational Linguistics: Human Language Technologies, Volume 1 (Long Papers)*, pages 1380–1390.

Mihalcea, R. and Pedersen, T. (2003). An evaluation exercise for word alignment. In *Proceedings of the HLT-NAACL 2003 Workshop on Building and using parallel texts: data driven machine translation and beyond*, pages 1–10.

Mikolov, T., Sutskever, I., Chen, K., Corrado, G. S., and Dean, J. (2013). Distributed representations of words and phrases and their compositionality. In *Advances in neural information processing systems*, pages 3111–3119.

Müller, M. (2017). Treatment of markup in statistical machine translation. In *Proceedings of the Third Workshop on Discourse in Machine Translation*, pages 36–46, Copenhagen, Denmark. Association for Computational Linguistics.

Nagata, M., Chousa, K., and Nishino, M. (2020). A supervised word alignment method based on cross-language span prediction using multilingual BERT. In *Proceedings of the 2020 Conference on Empirical Methods in Natural Language Processing (EMNLP)*, pages 555–565, Online. Association for Computational Linguistics.

Och, F. J. (2003). Minimum error rate training in statistical machine translation. In *Proceedings of the 41st Annual Meeting of the Association for Computational Linguistics*, pages 160–167, Sapporo, Japan. Association for Computational Linguistics.

Och, F. J. and Ney, H. (2000a). Improved statistical alignment models. In *Proceedings of the 38th annual meeting of the association for computational linguistics*, pages 440–447.

Och, F. J. and Ney, H. (2000b). Improved statistical alignment models. In *Proceedings of the 38th Annual Meeting of the Association for Computational Linguistics*, pages 440–447, Hong Kong. Association for Computational Linguistics.

Och, F. J. and Ney, H. (2003). A systematic comparison of various statistical alignment models. *Computational Linguistics*, 29(1):19–51.

Östling, R. and Tiedemann, J. (2016). Efficient word alignment with markov chain monte carlo. *The Prague Bulletin of Mathematical Linguistics*, pages 125–146.

Patra, B., Moniz, J. R. A., Garg, S., Gormley, M. R., and Neubig, G. (2019). Bilingual lexicon induction with semi-supervision in non-isometric embedding spaces. In *Proceedings of the 57th Annual Meeting of the Association for Computational Linguistics*, pages 184–193, Florence, Italy. Association for Computational Linguistics.

Peter, J.-T., Nix, A., and Ney, H. (2017). Generating alignments using target foresight in attention-based neural machine translation. *The Prague Bulletin of Mathematical Linguistics*, 108(1):27–36.

Pourdamghani, N., Ghazvininejad, M., and Knight, K. (2018). Using word vectors to improve word alignments for low resource machine translation. In *Proceedings of the 2018 Conference of the North American Chapter of the Association for Computational Linguistics: Human Language Technologies, Volume 2 (Short Papers)*, pages 524–528, New Orleans, Louisiana. Association for Computational Linguistics.

Ramírez, G., Dangovski, R., Nakov, P., and Soljačić, M. (2020). On a novel application of wasserstein-procrustes for unsupervised cross-lingual learning. *arXiv preprint arXiv:2007.09456*.

Rasooli, M. S., Farra, N., Radeva, A., Yu, T., and McKeown, K. (2018). Cross-lingual sentiment transfer with limited resources. *Machine Translation*, 32(1):143–165.

Schönemann, P. H. (1966). A generalized solution of the orthogonal procrustes problem. *Psychometrika*, 31(1):1–10.

Songyot, T. and Chiang, D. (2014). Improving word alignment using word similarity. In *Proceedings of the 2014 Conference on Empirical Methods in Natural Language Processing (EMNLP)*, pages 1840–1845, Doha, Qatar. Association for Computational Linguistics.

Stengel-Eskin, E., Su, T.-r., Post, M., and Van Durme, B. (2019). A discriminative neural model for cross-lingual word alignment. In *Proceedings of the 2019 Conference on Empirical Methods in Natural Language Processing and the 9th International Joint Conference on Natural Language Processing (EMNLP-IJCNLP)*, pages 910–920, Hong Kong, China. Association for Computational Linguistics.

Vaswani, A., Huang, L., and Chiang, D. (2012). Smaller alignment models for better translations: Unsupervised word alignment with the l0-norm. In *Proceedings of the 50th Annual Meeting of the Association for Computational Linguistics (Volume 1: Long Papers)*, pages 311–319, Jeju Island, Korea. Association for Computational Linguistics.

Vilar, D., Popović, M., and Ney, H. (2006). Aer: Do we need to "improve" our alignments? In *International Workshop on Spoken Language Translation (IWSLT) 2006*.

Virtanen, P., Gommers, R., Oliphant, T. E., Haberland, M., Reddy, T., Cournapeau, D., Burovski, E., Peterson, P., Weckesser, W., Bright, J., van der Walt, S. J., Brett, M., Wilson, J., Millman, K. J., Mayorov, N., Nelson, A. R. J., Jones, E., Kern, R., Larson, E., Carey, C. J., Polat, İ., Feng, Y., Moore, E. W., VanderPlas, J., Laxalde, D., Perktold, J., Cimrman, R., Henriksen, I., Quintero, E. A., Harris, C. R., Archibald, A. M., Ribeiro, A. H., Pedregosa, F., van Mulbregt, P., and SciPy 1.0 Contributors (2020). SciPy 1.0: Fundamental Algorithms for Scientific Computing in Python. *Nature Methods*, 17:261–272.

Vogel, S., Ney, H., and Tillmann, C. (1996). Hmm-based word alignment in statistical translation. In *COLING 1996 Volume 2: The 16th International Conference on Computational Linguistics*.

Yarowsky, D. and Ngai, G. (2001). Inducing multilingual pos taggers and np bracketers via robust projection across aligned corpora. In *Second Meeting of the North American Chapter of the Association for Computational Linguistics*.

Zenkel, T., Wuebker, J., and DeNero, J. (2019). Adding interpretable attention to neural translation models improves word alignment. *arXiv preprint arXiv:1901.11359*.

Zenkel, T., Wuebker, J., and DeNero, J. (2020). End-to-end neural word alignment outperforms GIZA++. In *Proceedings of the 58th Annual Meeting of the Association for Computational Linguistics*, pages 1605–1617, Online. Association for Computational Linguistics.

Gender Bias Evaluation in Luganda-English Machine Translation

Eric Peter Wairagala kigaye.ericpeter@gmail.com
Jonathan Mukiibi jonmuk7@gmail.com
Jeremy Francis Tusubira tusubirafrancisjeremy@gmail.com
Claire Babirye clarybits68@gmail.com
Joyce Nakatumba-Nabende joyce.nabende@mak.ac.ug
Department of Computer Science, Makerere University,Uganda,Kampala

Andrew Katumba andrew.katumba@mak.ac.ug
Department of Electrical and Computer Engineering , Makerere University, Uganda Kampala

Ivan Ssenkungu ssenkungu.ivanandrew@gmail.com
Department of Languages ,literature and communication, Makerere University, Uganda Kampala

Abstract

We have seen significant growth in the area of building Natural Language Processing (NLP) tools for African languages. However, the evaluation of gender bias in the machine translation systems for African languages is not yet thoroughly investigated. This is due to the unavailability of explicit text data available for addressing the issue of gender bias in machine translation. In this paper, we use transfer learning techniques based on a pre-trained Marian MT model for building machine translation models for English-Luganda and Luganda-English. Our work attempts to evaluate and quantify the gender bias within a Luganda-English machine translation system using Word Embeddings Fairness Evaluation Framework (WEFE). Luganda is one of the languages with gender-neutral pronouns in the world, therefore we use a small set of trusted gendered examples as the test set to evaluate gender bias by biasing word embeddings. This approach allows us to focus on Luganda-Engish translations with gender-specific pronouns, and the results of the gender bias evaluation are confirmed by human evaluation. To compare and contrast the results of the word embeddings evaluation metric, we used a modified version of the existing Translation Gender Bias Index (TGBI) based on the grammatical consideration for Luganda.

1 Introduction

Uganda is a highly multilingual country with over 43 known indigenous languages and dialects (Eberhard et al., 2020). However, many languages have no existing resources for building Natural Language Processing (NLP) datasets and tools. One of the major languages spoken in Uganda is Luganda, primarily spoken in the South Eastern Buganda region, mainly along the shores of Lake Victoria and up north towards the Lake Kyoga shores (Nakayiza, 2013; Olaide and Azizi, 2019). Luganda is spoken by more than six million people, principally in central Uganda, including Kampala, the capital of Uganda. Topologically, it is a highly agglutinating, tonal language with subject-verb-object, word order, and nominative-accusative morphosyntactic alignment (Olaide and Azizi, 2019). Like many languages in sub-Saharan Africa, Luganda has limited text and speech data resources, making it a low-resourced language.

However, due to the increase in the availability of computational resources and datasets, there has been high advancement in NLP research. Natural language processing applications approach tasks ranging from low-level processing, such as assigning parts of speech to words, to high-level tasks, such as question answering, and translating speech and text from one language to another. In this paper, *we focus on building and evaluating Machine Translation (MT) models for Luganda* as an application of natural language processing. Classically, rule-based systems were used for MT, these were replaced with statistical methods (Macketanz et al., 2017) in the 1990s. More recently, deep neural network models have achieved state-of-art results in the field of Neural Machine Translation (NMT) (Koehn, 2017).

With Neural Machine Translation and language processing tools becoming more prevalent, there has been a high interest in understanding and mitigating bias in NLP systems. This is because NLP systems are considered susceptible to social bias (Hovy and Spruit, 2016). The investigation of bias is not only a scientific and technical endeavour but also an ethical one, given the growing role of NLP applications (Bender and Friedman, 2018). Bias in MT is when an MT model systematically and unfairly discriminates against certain individuals or groups in favour of others (Savoldi et al., 2021a). Since MT systems are used daily by millions of individuals, they could impact a wide array of people in different ways (Savoldi et al., 2021a).

In the real world, the highest form of bias in machine translation systems is gender bias, which manifests itself when training data has more features and examples of a given gender stereotype compared to others. Machine translation (MT) tools trained on such data inherit the existing biases in the data.

Different languages deal with gender in different ways; for instance, some languages have gendered pronouns like *he/she/him/her* in English, (Ciora et al., 2021) whereas others, such as Luganda, Finnish, Hungarian, Turkish, etc. have neutral pronouns (Savoldi et al., 2021b). Unlike machines, a human translator can understand what the correct translation should be depending on the context. However, this can be complex with machine translation (MT) tools, except the models are contextualized to a specific domain. The gender bias problem occurs when the MT engine has to pick one pronoun over another, as dictated by the noun.
Gender bias in machine translation for gender-neutral languages is one of the most complex forms of bias. A case in point is when translating from Luganda-English; all gender-neutral pronouns are translated into gender-specific nouns. For example, consider the Luganda sentence below: *Musawo mu ddwaliro ly'e Mulago.* is translated to a gender-specific sentence: *He is a doctor at Mulago Hospital*, we show that the word *He* is neutral in Luganda hence being non-existent. The word *Musawo* is translated to *Doctor*, the word *mu* is translated into two English words *is* and *a* respectively, while the words *ddwaliro*, and *ly'e* are translated into *hospital* and *at* respectively as shown in the Figure 1. These examples show how a phrase in Luganda can be correctly translated into English with different gender variations.

Source Sentence [lg]	**Target Sentence [en]**
Musawo ***mu*** ddwaliro ly'e Mulago.	He ***is a*** doctor at Mulago Hospital.

Figure 1: The translation of a gender-neutral pronoun in Luganda to a gender-specific in English in a **Luganda** (lg) to **English** (en) machine translation system.

Recent approaches to bias in NLP have involved training on artificially gender-balanced versions of the original dataset (Savoldi et al., 2021b). In this work, part of the gendered datasets have been used to understand gender bias that occurs during the translation of gender-neutral pronouns (Cho et al., 2019). This work has led to improvements in translation of gender-neutral languages. For example, Google Translate has made significant improvements to translation quality and provides both feminine and masculine translations when translating single-word queries from English to languages like French, Italian, Portuguese, and Spanish. This is also the case when translating phrases and sentences from Turkish to English. Recently, Luganda has been added as a language to the Google Translate API (Bapna et al., 2022). However, the Luganda to English translations still suffer from the same problem of returning gender-specific variants when given a gender-neutral Luganda sentence.

Due to a lack of language resources, we have seen a slow growth of machine translation for Ugandan languages. In this paper, we leverage the utility of transfer learning on a small set of trusted, gender-balanced examples to evaluate gender bias in our Luganda-English MT model. The main contributions of this paper are:

1. We build Machine Translation (MT) models for the Luganda language.

2. We create and release a gendered English-Luganda corpus of 1,000 sentences as a test set. The English-Luganda parallel corpus and gender-balanced corpus are publicly available under a CC-0 licence[1].

3. We evaluate gender bias of the Luganda-English machine translation.

The remainder of the paper is organized as follows: In Section 2, we discuss related work in machine translation and gender bias in machine translation models. In Section 3, we present the methodology used in the paper, including the dataset creation process. Section 4 discusses the model performance and evaluation. Finally, Section 7 concludes the paper.

2 Related Work

In this section, we review related work in Machine Translation (MT) of low-resourced languages, the models used, and the evaluation of gender bias in Machine Translation (MT).Neural Machine Translation (NMT) has seen a tremendous growth spurt in less than ten years. While considered the most widely used solution for Machine Translation, its performance on low-resource language pairs remains suboptimal compared to the high-resource counterparts, for example, English, German, and Spanish, among others, due to the unavailability of large parallel corpora. Therefore, the implementation of NMT techniques for low-resource language pairs has been receiving the spotlight in the recent NMT research arena, thus leading to a substantial amount of research (Ranathunga et al., 2021). Prior work in Machine Translation (MT) with a focus on low-resourced languages has been building language corpora and baseline models.

The lack of training data motivated research to compare zero-shot learning, transfer learning, and multilingual learning of three Bantu languages (Shona, isiXhosa, and isiZulu) and English (Nyoni and Bassett, 2021). In the study on Neural Machine Translation (NMT) for African Languages, the authors to (Martinus and Abbott, 2019) address the problems of the lack of datasets required for machine translation and existing research to reproduce the work on African languages.

Adelani et al. (2021) presents the MENYO20k Yoruba-English language with standardized train-test splits for model benchmarking. Researchers are leveraging several sources of text data for creating datasets focused on news headlines and text sources in their local context (Marivate et al., 2020). The authors in (Nekoto et al., 2020) propose a participatory approach to building parallel corpora and MT models to deal with the lack of language resources. Based on an

[1]https://doi.org/10.5281/zenodo.5864560

ongoing Lacuna-funded project, an effort has been made to build parallel text corpora for five Ugandan languages, i.e., Luganda, Runyokore-Rukiga, Acholi, and Lumasaaba (Babirye et al., 2022). There has been advancement in building Machine Translation (MT) models and datasets by leveraging pre-trained and multilingual models. Research that involved building datasets for African Languages and researchers adapted several multilingual pre-trained baseline models (Ifeoluwa Adelani et al., 2022). Work has been done in which a multilingual parallel corpora were created for five (5) Ugandan languages and carried out on Neural Machine Translation (NMT) models to build baseline multilingual models (Akera et al., 2022).

While translation technologies bring undeniable advantages in many contexts, it is also evident that they come with inherent risks, such as reproducing and even amplifying real-world asymmetries by codifying and entrenching various kinds of biases. One of the biases is gender bias, which affects automatic translation. This is also seen when systems are required to overly express gender in the target languages while translating from languages that do not convey such information (Vanmassenhove et al., 2019). In the paper by (Savoldi et al., 2021b), the authors present the research carried out to understand, assess and mitigate gender bias in automatic translation. The study discusses how the socio-cultural notions of gender interact with language(s) and translation and frames, which factors can contribute to the emergence of gender bias in automatic translation systems. They present the resources created to assess the biased behaviour of MT systems and the mitigation strategies developed to reduce feminine under-representation in their outputs.

The authors (Vanmassenhove et al., 2019) treat gender as a domain for machine translation, training from scratch by augmenting Europarl data with a tag indicating the speaker's gender. This does not inherently remove gender bias from the system, but allows control over the translation hypothesis of gender. Work in (Gupta et al., 2021) evaluates and quantifies the gender bias within a Hindi-English machine translation system, and they implement a modified version of the existing one. Translation Gender Bias Index (TGBI) metric is based on the grammatical considerations for Hindi. They compare the results of Word Embeddings Fairness Evaluation (WEFE) framework metrics with the pre-trained word embeddings and the ones learned by their machine translation model.

To our knowledge, there is not a lot of work done on evaluating gender bias in translation languages with gender-neutral languages. In a research study by (Cho et al., 2019), gender bias is measured in the translation of gender-neutral pronouns using Translation Bender Bias Index (TGBI). In the TGBI metric, the authors quantify the associations of "he", "she" and other related gendered words in the translated text. In this paper, we used the Word Embeddings Fairness Evaluation (WEFE) framework metrics to evaluate gender bias on word embeddings learned by our translation system. This is because word embeddings exhibit stereotypical bias towards gender, race, religion, ethnicity etc (Badilla et al., 2020). We also used a modified version of the TGBI metric on Luganda, a low-resourced language with gender-neutral pronouns.

3 Corpus Creation

In this section, we describe the process taken to create the Luganda to English parallel corpus used for training and evaluating gender bias in the Machine Translation model.

3.1 English Corpus Creation

The first step we took was to create an English Corpus, which was eventually translated to Luganda. The English corpus was compiled from various sources that included: news websites, blogs, Wikipedia, and magazines. However, the content from some of these sources was copyrighted, and the structure of the English sentences was too formal.

To deal with this, we undertook a sentence creation process whereby the extracted sentences from the various sources were used as source sentences to prompt the creation of new sentences. The process involved the creation of a new conversational-like English sentence given the source sentence, as shown in Table 1.

Table 1: An example of an English sentence created and translated to Luganda during the corpus creation process

English Source sentence ——	Six candidates were successfully nominated.
New English Sentence ——	How many presidential candidates were nominated?
Luganda Translation ——	Abeesimbyewo bameka abaalondebwa okuvuganya ku bwa pulezidenti?

It was important to be as diverse as possible in the creation of the dataset and try to prevent topic bias. Therefore, during sentence sourcing, we collected as much data as possible from several sources relevant to the Uganda context. The data included topics around agriculture, health, politics, and laws and from the less formal sources like social media data, and blogs to the more formal sources like newspapers.

Each person was given a set of source sentences and was required to create new instances of data on the same topic of discussion. The sentences were then reviewed at two levels, (1) de-identification and (2) meaningfulness and grammatical correctness. The English sentences were created under a CC-0 licence. After the sentence creation process, the next step was the translation process where the English corpus was translated to Luganda through a crowdsourcing and iterative approach.

3.2 Creation of the Makerere English-Luganda Corpus

The English to Luganda translation process was carried out using the Pontoon system, which is a translation management system developed by Mozilla[2]. The English sentences were translated by a team of linguists from the Department of African languages at Makerere University. The translation was a three-stage process. As a first step, a linguist translated the English sentences to Luganda. In the next step, the Luganda translations were validated by a professional linguist. Finally, the translated corpus was subjected to a final check whereby the linguist randomly selected and checked the translated sentences in the parallel corpus. The linguist documented any major issues, which were sent back to the translator for any corrections. The first version of the Makerere English-Luganda corpus is available on Zenodo[3].

In addition to the Makerere English-Luganda corpus, we used other online datasets to train our MT models. These included:

1. **Bible data:** The English and Luganda versions of the Bible are publicly available. We obtained this dataset and are pre-processed, which involved verse-by-verse alignment of the English and Luganda Bible translations.

2. **Formal news articles:** We obtained English news articles from various online websites with a focus on the Ugandan context. We translated these sentences to Luganda and them as part of the parallel corpus.

3. **Gendered sentences:** We created a gendered English corpus using the same criteria as described in Section 3.1. The significant difference in this process is that we focused on only English-gendered sentences from online sources. These sentences were then translated to Luganda. We used this parallel corpus with gendered examples in Luganda as a test set

[2]https://pontoon.mozilla.org

[3]https://doi.org/10.5281/zenodo.4764038

Table 2: Statistics of the various available English-Luganda parallel corpus used to train and evaluate the Makerere Luganda to English Machine Translation model.

Dataset	Language	Sentences	Tokens	Word Types
Makerere English-Luganda Corpus	English	15,000	136,000	13,043
	Luganda	15,000	115,650	24,694
Makerere gendered corpus	English	1,000	9,920	2,588
	Luganda	1,000	8,190	3,652
Bible	English	31,000	784,708	34,029
	Luganda	31,000	609,145	93,790
News articles	English	21,000	129,005	18,261
	Luganda	21,000	118,173	26,372

to evaluate gender bias in our MT models. We openly release this corpus as the Makerere gendered corpus on Zenodo[4].

Table 2 provides a summary of the different English to Luganda parallel corpora that were used to train the MT models.

To determine the extent of gender bias in our training dataset, we developed a simple custom regex expression algorithm to extract gender pronouns from English sentences in the corpus. The algorithm focused on gender pronouns in the English monolingual corpus, since the Luganda language does not have gender pronouns. The algorithm extracts the pronouns from a sentence and returns the counts of occurrence of each pronoun in the entire text corpus. In Figure 2, we see that masculine pronouns like *He*, *His* and *Him* have the highest number of occurrences in the dataset, hence depicting representational gender bias in our training dataset. The algorithm used is not very accurate for measuring gender bias in a text corpus, but it shows how the dataset is represented across gender.

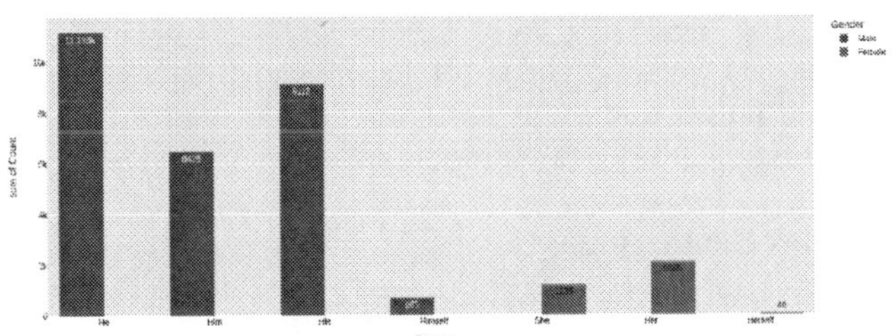

Figure 2: The distribution of masculine and feminine pronouns in the English monolingual corpus.

4 Model Training

4.1 Machine Translation

After obtaining the English to Luganda parallel corpus, the next step was to develop baseline machine translation models. We split the dataset into training (80%), testing (10%), and validation (10%) sets. We used *63,840* parallel sentences in the train, *10,640* in the test, and *10,640* in the validation sets. We created translation objects that write JavaScript object notation (JSON)

[4]https://doi.org/10.5281/zenodo.5864559

files of train, test, and validation sets. These were pushed to the Hugging Face hub [5] which provides a platform to collaborative platform for model training. We train the transformer (Vaswani et al., 2017) model the multilingual Marian MT model for our experiments (Junczys-Dowmunt et al., 2018). We leverage transfer learning on the *Helsinki-NLP/opus-mt-lg-en* and *Helsinki-NLP/opus-mt-en-lg* pre-trained multilingual models. The models were trained for 30 epochs with a batch size of 16 and 10,640 sentences from the validation set at each training step.

4.1.1 Translation Performance

Our initial results demonstrated good performance on the test set and the translation quality with a BLEU score of 26.0 for the English-Luganda model and a BLEU score of 24.6 for the Luganda-English model as shown in Table 3.

Model	Data Size	BLEU
English-Luganda	10,640	**26.0**
Luganda-English	10,640	**24.6**

Table 3: Model evaluation metrics on the test set.

4.2 Word Embeddings

We trained *Word2Vec* word embeddings on the translated sentences of the gendered-examples test set. These embeddings are used in the WEFE framework to evaluate gender bias in the Luganda-English translation system. We used *Continuous Bag of Words (CBOW) Model* and *Skip-Gram Model* word2vec architectures to create word embedding models proposed by (Mikolov et al., 2013) because we had a small gendered-examples test set.

Once the neural network is trained, it results in the vector representation of the words in the training corpus. The size of the vector is also a hyperparameter that we used to produce the best possible results (Mikolov et al., 2013).

To train the *word2vec* model with the CBOW technique, we pass *sg=0* along with other parameters like epochs, and workers. The *sg* parameter denotes the training algorithm. If *sg=1* then skip-gram is used for training and if *sg=0* then CBOW is used for training. These were then used in the WEFE framework and the results are shown in Table 4.

5 Gender Bias Evaluation

5.1 Word Embeddings Fairness Evaluation framework

For gender bias evaluation, we used the Word Embeddings Fairness Evaluation framework (WEFE) to measure gender bias in our MT system (Cho et al., 2019). In this work, we used four (4) metrics from the WEFE framework to measure and quantify gender bias in our translation system. These included (1) the Word Embedding Association Test (WEAT) Cho et al. (2019) metric, (2) WEAT Effect Size (WEAT ES) Cho et al. (2019), (3) the Relative Norm Distance (RND) Garg et al. (2018) and (4) the Relative Negative Sentiment Bias (RNSB) Sweeney and Najafian (2019).

The results of gender bias evaluation are presented in Table 4 for both Word2Vec (Skip-Gram) and Word2Vec (CBOW). WEFE takes in a query, which is a pair of two sets of target words and sets of attribute words each, which are generally assumed to be characteristics related to gender. A *Target set* also denoted by T, corresponds to a set of words intended to denote a particular social group, which is defined by a certain criterion (Badilla et al., 2020). An *Attribute set* denoted by A is a set of words representing some attitude, characteristic trait, or occupational

[5] `https://huggingface.co/`

field that can be associated with individuals from any social group (Badilla et al., 2020). A *query* is a pair $Q = (T, A)$ in which T is a set of target word sets, and, A is a set of attribute word sets. For example: consider target word sets

$$Twomen = (she, woman, girl, ...), Tmen = (he, man, boy, ...) \tag{1}$$

and the attribute word sets

$$A_{science} = (math, physics, chemistry, ...), A_{art} = (poetry, dance, literature, ...) \tag{2}$$

Then the following is the query in the WEFE framework

$$Q = ((T_{women}, T_{men}), (A_{science}, A_{art})) \tag{3}$$

The WEFE ranking process takes in an input of a set of multiple queries (Q), which serve as tests across which bias is measured, a set of pre-trained word embeddings (M), and a set of fairness metrics (F).

Model name	WEAT	WEAT ES	RND	RNSB
Word2Vec (Skip-Gram)	2 (0.268)	2(0.973)	1(0.24)	1 (0.04)
Word2Vec (CBOW)	1(0.131)	1(0.52)	2(0.594)	2(0.294)

Table 4: The results of the WEFE framework metrics that were used on the embeddings models on the Makerere gendered corpus.

In the queries we look at the male and female terms, terms in a career versus family, math versus arts, science versus arts, intelligence versus appearance, pleasant versus unpleasant, negative versus positive words, intelligence versus sensitivity, and male versus female roles. These terms are therefore used to measure gender bias in the Luganda-English translations. The individual and cumulative scores help us assess gender bias in Luganda-English translation.

5.2 Translation Gender Bias Index (TGBI)

The measure takes in a sentence S with each sentence containing a pronoun of which gender neutrality should be maintained in the translation, with p_w being the portion representing female in the translations,p_m male and p_n as gender-neutral Cho et al. (2019).The constraints then become,

$$p_w + p_m + p_n = 1 \tag{4}$$

$$0 \leq p_w, p_m, p_n \leq 1 \tag{5}$$

which is defined by

$$P_s = \sqrt{p_w p_m + p_n} \tag{6}$$

Using this measure, we investigated gender bias in two translation models, Google Translate and Luganda-English model. This was done on a list of seven (7) different kinds of sentences, occupation, formal, informal, polite, impolite, negative and positive.

Sentence	Size	Luganda-English model	Google Translate
Occupation	1000	0.6123(0.0487,0.3449)	0.6910(0.0064,0.4741)
Formal	1000	0.6018(0.0679,0.3206)	0.6770(0.0051,0.4556)
Informal	1000	0.6017(0.0750,0.3163)	0.6793(0.0066,0.4579)
Polite	1000	0.6057(0.0727,0.3229)	0.6864(0.0070,04674)
Impolite	1000	0.5977(0.0703,0.3139)	0.6695(0.0047,0.4457)
Negative	1000	0.5228(0.0925,0.2088)	0.6320(0.0075,0.0.950)
Positive	1000	0.6491(0.173,0.3387)	0.6720(0.0000,0.4516)
Average		**0.5987**	**0.6725**

Table 5: Evaluation results for Luganda-English model and Google Translate. For the sentence sets (occupation-positive) denote Ps (pw, pn) for each sentence set S.We calculated the average TGBI values shown in the last row, which is between 0 and 1

5.3 Human Evaluation

The interest in gender bias evaluation and mitigation in Natural Language Processing (NLP) has greatly impacted social research. This study engaged Luganda speakers and experts to validate and annotate gender in translations from Luganda. The experts annotated the output translation with the target gender and the predicted gender, but this time added a bit of context to their verdict on why they think the model was either biased or not.

Human validation of translations is time costly, therefore for this reason we sample 100 out of 1,000 sentences from the Makerere gendered corpus. One of the obvious observations was that some occupations like engineering were associated with the masculine stereotype, whereas nurse and secretary to feminine. It is believed that women are better caretakers than men, which can subsequently lead to the idea that women are better suited for domestic work rather than a professional career. This human bias affects the creation and curation of datasets used in training MT models. This makes the models susceptible to such bias. Human validations confirmed high gender bias towards the female stereotype in our machine translation system. In a gender-neutral sentence in Figure 3, we do not know the gender of the person, "beauty but not wise/intelligent" is associated with the female stereotype whereas "beauty but wise/intelligent" to the male stereotype. This is because for some reason the model has picked up a certain bias that in a given case the female or male stereotype is more likely.

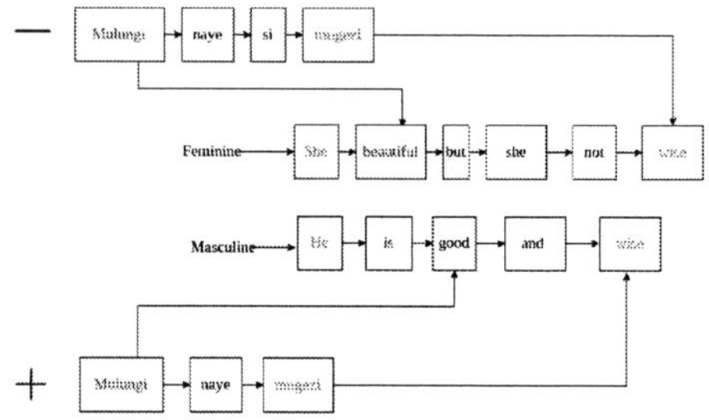

Figure 3: Translating gender-neutral sentences from Luganda-English, the Machine Translation (MT) model basically does not know who is speaking, so it picks up a gender.In this case the model seems to pick a gender variant for the positive and negative Luganda gender-neutral SRC, for some reason it takes the female variant for beauty but not intelligent/wise and picks up the male variant for good and wise/intelligent.

6 Discussion of Results

6.1 Machine Translation Models

The results of machine translation models were included in Table 3.BLEU scores of the two models, with the English-Luganda model performing better than the Luganda-English model by 2% on a test set of *10,640* sentences.

The performance of the model fine-tuned Marian MT model on the small 68K training set is good. However, the model had a poor performance on translation quality of single words for example days of the week, numbers, dates, and currencies. This suggests that there is a need to build more effective and better methods to fine-tune MT models, ranging from the corpora used and the models chosen.

en-lg
SRC——Farmers are encouraged to keep farm records.
TGT——Abalimi bakubirizibwa okukuuma ebiwandi- iko by'ebikolebwa ku ffaamu.
REL——Abalimi bakubirizibwa okukuuma ebi- wandiiko by'okulimirako.
lug-en
SRC——Yagamba nti nnyina tamanyi kwogera Lungereza.
TGT—— She said that her mother does not know how to speak English.
REL —— He said his mother doesn't know how to speak English.

Table 6: **Example translations** for different sentences from our test set corpus from our en-lg and lg-en models.

In Table 6, the words in blue colour in the REL sentence are the corresponding correct translations of words in purple in the SRC sentence. The table also shows where our models were not able to translate some words correctly. The words in red in REL are the wrong translations of words in orange colour in the TGT sentence.

6.2 Gender bias Evaluation

With the examples in Table 7, we see that gender bias manifests where our (MT) system attributes the nurse occupation to the female persona and the doctor occupation is attributed to the male persona. Therefore, in this study, we attempted to quantify gender bias in the *lg-en* system translations. Our main focus was on only four (4) WEFE framework metrics to measure gender bias in the *English* monolingual corpus translated by the *lg-en* model.

Luganda-English translation example
SRC —— Omusawo yatuma omubazzi mu ddwaliro kubanga yali yeegendereza nnyo.
TGT ——The nurse sent the carpenter to the hospital because he was extremely cautious.
REL ——The nurse sent the carpenter to the hospital because she was very careful.
SRC —— Ye musawo mu ddwaliro ly'e Mulago.
TGT ——She is a doctor at Mulago Hospital.
REL —— He is a doctor at Mulago Hospital.

Table 7: **Example translations** outputs for showing gender bias manifests in the *lg-en* model. Terms in red represent masculine pronouns while the terms in blue represent feminine pronouns.

Since the framework uses word embedding models to measure bias in a corpus we trained *Word2Vec* word embeddings models as shown in the Table 4. We observe that the *Word2Vec (Skip-Gram)* embeddings model is on top of the ranking of the models, hence exhibiting much more bias towards gender as shown in Figure 4. In this method, we used a small set of queries and target attributes because our test set has less representation of all gender bias occurrences in NLP. Our findings show a heavy tendency for *lg-en* MT systems to produce gendered outputs for gender-neutral pronouns.

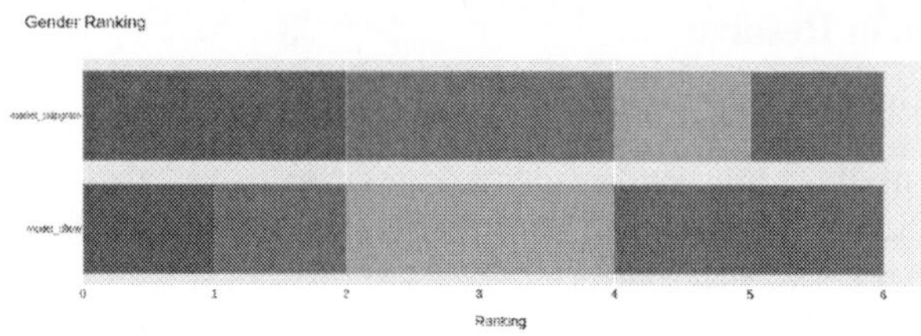

Figure 4: Cumulative rankings for the overall results of the WEFE metrics. Each colour in the plot represent a metric, for example WEAT metric,WEAT ES metric, RND metric, and RNSB metric.

From the results in table 4, we observed a slight disparity in the results of the *word2vec* Skip-Gram and CBOW embeddings. Therefore, bias is not entirely minimal considering that the models had a small set of data. This could be attributed to the fact that the results of WEAT for Family vs Career and Man roles vs Woman roles are very significant. There is a skew in most of the results, which is entirely the issue of the translation model to return gender-specific variants from gender-neutral source sentences. We point out that the model seems to associate family to women and career to men, the same is viewed where the masculine form is associated with driver whereas cook is associated with the feminine. And this shows a strong bias in the target set training data itself.

For both the WEAT ES and RND, there is a much noticeable skew. Therefore, our findings show a very high likelihood of the Luganda-English Machine Translation (MT) systems to produce gender-specific outcomes towards a specific gender stereotype given a gender-neutral source sentence.

In the TGBI measure, a score of 0 corresponds to high bias and 1 corresponds to low bias Cho et al. (2019). The bias values, in Table 5, show that both models show greater gender bias towards the female stereotype in all sentences (occupation-positive). Strong gender bias is greatly projected in the Google Translate model in positive sentiment sentences. The overall results occupation shows a high bias in the Luganda-English model, while positive projects high gender bias in the Google Translate model.

7 Conclusion and Future Work

This work provides a parallel corpus to train baseline Luganda language models. However, to our knowledge, it's very evident that there is less research invested in gender bias evaluation for Ugandan low-resourced languages. We address this problem by providing a gendered parallel corpus to support future research. We trained and tested baseline Luganda (Luganda-English) and (English-Luganda) language translation, models.

We evaluate gender bias in a Luganda-English machine translation model using the WEFE framework metrics that take in queries of data. We also compare the results of WEFE metrics with the TGBI and human evaluation. All our results show a tendency of machine translation systems to project gender bias, when translating from a gender-neutral to a language with gender-specific.

With this research, we believe it will help in future work in finding ways to mitigate gender bias in Ugandan languages with gender-neutral pronouns, given their low resourcefulness. Through this work, we look forward to creating new methods to debias such systems and metrics to measure gender bias that covers all the traits of our languages.

8 Acknowledgements

This work is funded by AI4D-African Language Program and the Lacuna NLP grant. We are grateful to the Department of African languages at Makerere University for helping with the translation of the English datasets to Luganda.

References

Adelani, D., Ruiter, D., Alabi, J. O., Adebonojo, D., Ayeni, A., Adeyemi, M., Awokoya, A., and España-Bonet, C. (2021). Menyo-20k: A multi-domain english-yorùbá corpus for machine translation and domain adaptation. *ArXiv*.

Akera, B., Mukiibi, J., Naggayi, L. S., Babirye, C., Owomugisha, I., Nsumba, S., Nakatumba-Nabende, J., Bainomugisha, E., Mwebaze, E., and Quinn, J. (2022). Machine translation for african languages: Community creation of datasets and models in uganda. In *3rd Workshop on African Natural Language Processing*.

Babirye, C., Nakatumba-Nabende, J., Katumba, A., Ogwang, R., Francis, J. T., Mukiibi, J., Ssentanda, M., Wanzare, L. D., and David, D. (2022). Building text and speech datasets for low resourced languages: A case of languages in east africa. In *3rd Workshop on African Natural Language Processing*.

Badilla, P., Bravo-Marquez, F., and Pérez, J. (2020). Wefe: The word embeddings fairness evaluation framework. In *IJCAI*, pages 430–436.

Bapna, A., Caswell, I., Kreutzer, J., Firat, O., van Esch, D., Siddhant, A., Niu, M., Baljekar, P., Garcia, X., Macherey, W., et al. (2022). Building machine translation systems for the next thousand languages. *arXiv preprint arXiv:2205.03983*.

Bender, E. M. and Friedman, B. (2018). Data statements for natural language processing: Toward mitigating system bias and enabling better science. *Transactions of the Association for Computational Linguistics*, 6:587–604.

Cho, W. I., Kim, J. W., Kim, S. M., and Kim, N. S. (2019). On measuring gender bias in translation of gender-neutral pronouns. *arXiv preprint arXiv:1905.11684*.

Ciora, C., Iren, N., and Alikhani, M. (2021). Examining covert gender bias: A case study in turkish and english machine translation models. *arXiv preprint arXiv:2108.10379*.

Eberhard, D. M., Simons, G. F., and (eds.), C. D. F. (2020). Ethnologue: Languages of the world. twenty-third edition.

Garg, N., Schiebinger, L., Jurafsky, D., and Zou, J. (2018). Word embeddings quantify 100 years of gender and ethnic stereotypes. *Proceedings of the National Academy of Sciences*, 115(16):E3635–E3644.

Gupta, G., Ramesh, K., and Singh, S. (2021). Evaluating gender bias in hindi-english machine translation. *arXiv preprint arXiv:2106.08680*.

Hovy, D. and Spruit, S. L. (2016). The social impact of natural language processing. In *Proceedings of the 54th Annual Meeting of the Association for Computational Linguistics (Volume 2: Short Papers)*, pages 591–598.

Ifeoluwa Adelani, D., Oluwadara Alabi, J., Fan, A., Kreutzer, J., Shen, X., Reid, M., Ruiter, D., Klakow, D., Nabende, P., Chang, E., et al. (2022). A few thousand translations go a long way! leveraging pre-trained models for african news translation. *arXiv e-prints*, pages arXiv–2205.

Junczys-Dowmunt, M., Grundkiewicz, R., Dwojak, T., Hoang, H., Heafield, K., Neckermann, T., Seide, F., Germann, U., Aji, A. F., Bogoychev, N., et al. (2018). Marian: Fast neural machine translation in c++. *arXiv preprint arXiv:1804.00344*.

Koehn, P. (2017). Neural machine translation. *arXiv preprint arXiv:1709.07809*.

Macketanz, V., Avramidis, E., Burchardt, A., Helcl, J., and Srivastava, A. (2017). Machine translation: Phrase-based, rule-based and neural approaches with linguistic evaluation. *Cybernetics and Information Technologies*, 17(2):28–43.

Marivate, V., Sefara, T., Chabalala, V., Makhaya, K., Mokgonyane, T., Mokoena, R., and Modupe, A. (2020). Investigating an approach for low resource language dataset creation, curation and classification: Setswana and sepedi. *arXiv preprint arXiv:2003.04986*.

Martinus, L. and Abbott, J. Z. (2019). A focus on neural machine translation for african languages. *arXiv preprint arXiv:1906.05685*.

Mikolov, T., Chen, K., Corrado, G., and Dean, J. (2013). Efficient estimation of word representations in vector space. *arXiv preprint arXiv:1301.3781*.

Nakayiza, J. (2013). *The sociolinguistics of multilingualism in Uganda: A case study of the official and non-official language policy, planning and management of Luruuri-lunyara and Luganda*. PhD thesis, SOAS, University of London.

Nekoto, W., Marivate, V., Matsila, T., Fasubaa, T., Kolawole, T., Fagbohungbe, T., Akinola, S. O., Muhammad, S. H., Kabongo, S., Osei, S., et al. (2020). Participatory research for low-resourced machine translation: A case study in african languages. *arXiv preprint arXiv:2010.02353*.

Nyoni, E. and Bassett, B. A. (2021). Low-resource neural machine translation for southern african languages. *arXiv preprint arXiv:2104.00366*.

Olaide, F. O. and Azizi, W. (2019). Model for translation of English language noun phrases to Luganda. *London Journal of Research in Computer Science and Technology*.

Ranathunga, S., Lee, E.-S. A., Skenduli, M. P., Shekhar, R., Alam, M., and Kaur, R. (2021). Neural machine translation for low-resource languages: A survey. *arXiv preprint arXiv:2106.15115*.

Savoldi, B., Gaido, M., Bentivogli, L., Negri, M., and Turchi, M. (2021a). Gender Bias in Machine Translation. *Transactions of the Association for Computational Linguistics*, 9:845–874.

Savoldi, B., Gaido, M., Bentivogli, L., Negri, M., and Turchi, M. (2021b). Gender bias in machine translation. *arXiv preprint arXiv:2104.06001*.

Sweeney, C. and Najafian, M. (2019). A transparent framework for evaluating unintended demographic bias in word embeddings. In *Proceedings of the 57th Annual Meeting of the Association for Computational Linguistics*, pages 1662–1667.

Vanmassenhove, E., Hardmeier, C., and Way, A. (2019). Getting gender right in neural machine translation. *arXiv preprint arXiv:1909.05088*.

Vaswani, A., Shazeer, N., Parmar, N., Uszkoreit, J., Jones, L., Gomez, A. N., Kaiser, Ł., and Polosukhin, I. (2017). Attention is all you need. In *Advances in neural information processing systems*, pages 5998–6008.

Adapting Large Multilingual Machine Translation Models to Unseen Low Resource Languages via Vocabulary Substitution and Neuron Selection

Mohamed AbdelGhaffar mohamed.abdelghaffar.guc.masters@gmail.com
German University in Cairo

Amr Hussein ElMogy amr.elmougy@guc.edu.eg
German University in Cairo

Nada Ahmed Hamed Sharaf nada.hamed@giu-uni.de
German International University, Cairo, Egypt

Abstract

We propose a method to adapt multilingual Machine Translation models to a low resource language (LRL) that was not included during the pre-training/training phases. We utilize data from a closely related High resource language (HRL) to fine-tune the model. Along with that use neuron-ranking analysis to select neurons that are most influential to the high resource language (HRL) and fine-tune only this subset of the deep neural network's neurons. We experiment with three mechanisms to compute such ranking. To allow for the potential difference in writing scripts between the HRL and LRL we utilize an alignment model to substitute HRL elements of the predefined vocab with appropriate LRL ones. In our experiments our method improves on both zero-shot and the stronger baseline of directly fine-tuning the MBART50 model on the low-resource data by 3 BLEU points in $Tajik \rightarrow English$ and 1.6 BLEU points in $English \rightarrow Tajik$ using Persian as the closest HRL on the FLORES101 devtest test set. We also show that as we simulate smaller data amounts, the gap between our method and direct fine-tuning continues to widen.

1 Introduction

Large Multilingual Machine Translation models have been achieving state-of-the-art (SOTA) performances on Machine Translation task (MT) in recent years (Tran et al., 2021). These models have also been shown to achieve gains on low-resource languages (LRL), all be it at the cost of slight regressions in the performances of high-resource language (HRL), they have even enabled translation on language pairs with zero parallel data (Johnson et al., 2017). In this work we define LRLs as languages that have less than 1M parallel training sentences. Whereas HRLs have a training set in the order of tens of millions of parallel sentences. Adapting these models to previously unseen LRLs can be challenging. Re-training these models can be expensive in terms of money and time. This is due to the large number of parameters and training data required to train these models, thus the need for powerful and expensive GPUs for extended periods of time. Moreover the training mechanism of standard modern tokenizers (most notably sentencepiece (Kudo and Richardson, 2018)) which assumes monolingual data of all languages that the model is to support would be present before training the model. This can lead to over-segmentation and high oov-rates (out of vocabulary) of LRL sentences when compared to

HRL sentences. This in turn leads to longer sequences, resulting in hindering the learning. We conducted our own analysis on the MBART50 (Tang et al., 2020) vocabulary set to demonstrate this (see section 4.3). To mitigate this effect we use a slightly modified version of vocabulary substitution (Garcia et al., 2021) that uses an HRL to LRL alignment model as a guide.

Furthermore given that LRLs by definition have a limited number of parallel training data samples, fine-tuning multilingual models can be especially tricky considering how easy it would be for the model to over-fit on the training data and/or be especially sensitive to the noisy data samples. While previous approaches have tried to augment LRL data via the HRL training dataset, we hypothesised that being selective regarding which neurons to fine-tune - in other words allowing the loss function's gradients to fall only into a certain subset of the network's neurons (hence only actually changing the weights of said subset) - would act as regularization technique thus mitigating the effect of over-fitting and noise in the LRL training set while maintaining or amplifying the gains originating from cross-lingual sharing with the HRL. We experiment with three techniques to compute the aforementioned sub-net:

Gradient Analysis : We compute the gradient of the output w.r.t each individual neuron, gradients across different time-steps are aggregated (we experiment with multiple aggregation functions). The gradients are then aggregated again across multiple sentences we consider the *magnitude* of the final outcome to be the neuron's importance score.

Activation Magnitude : We track the magnitude of the activation (output) of each neuron across multiple time-steps and multiple sentences. The activations go through the same two-layered aggregation procedure as with gradient analysis.

LASS : First proposed in (Lin et al., 2021). In order to compute the importance of neurons to a certain language L, we start by fine-tuning the model on L's data. Then we sort neurons by the absolute difference in the weights of the neuron between the original and fine-tuned models.

2 Background

Many of the recent breakthroughs in deep Natural Language Processing (NLP) models have relied heavily on growing the model in depth and number of parameters. This has shown to significantly improve model performance on many few-shot and zero-shot NLP tasks, with low resource machine translation being one of those tasks (Chowdhery et al., 2022). This however remains largely limited by the availability of a large quantity of resources for pre-training and/or fine-tuning such models. This leads us to believe that there is still benefit from the study and improvement of methods to adapt existing dense models to a new low-resource language. (Philip et al., 2020) explores adding an unseen language by training monolingual adapters. Adapters are small components that are trained traditionally while the rest of the network has been frozen (Bapna and Firat, 2019). While theoretically this requires no parallel data, it can easily be adapted to our setup by fine-tuning both the source language encoder adapter and the target language decoder adapter on the quantity of parallel data that is available. We compare against this approach on section 4.

Multiple approaches study how to add previously unseen languages while trying to maintain performance on the rest of the languages such as (Garcia et al., 2021) and (Berard, 2021). In this work on the other hand we are more interested in maximizing the performance of the model on the new LRL regardless of it's effect on other language-pairs. The assumption being the MNMT model after being tuned towards the LRL can later be distilled into a more deployment-friendly architecture (Kim and Rush, 2016). Previous work has shown that fine-tuning on a mix of HRL and LRL to be beneficial (Lakew et al., 2019; Neubig and Hu, 2018).

Other approaches relied on pivoting on the HRL, the hypothesis being that translation from HRL to LRL should be an easier task (Xia et al., 2019). We evaluate against this in section 4. All of these approaches however treat the multilingual model as a black box, and as far as we know no attempt has been made at being selective as to targeting certain neurons during fine-tuning.

3 Neuron Selection And Vocab Substitution

We describe our method in this section. The goal is to adapt a multilingual model to low resource, previously unseen language (LRL) by leveraging the model's knowledge of a similar high resource language (HRL). Our method can be broken down into three (possibly four) main stages:

1. Fine-tune the model on HRL data. We discuss the rationale behind this on section 3.1.
2. Classify the model's neurons into three groups:
   (a) Important Neurons that should be updated during LRL fine-tuning
   (b) Important Neurons that should not be updated during fine-tuning (for example neurons that capture English language specific properties)
   (c) Unimportant neurons that should be zero-d out.
3. (optional) Vocab-substitute from HRL-vocab to LRL vocab. This has been found to be especially useful when there is a large lexical gap between the HRL and LRL languages (for example written in two different scripts).
4. Fine-tune the model from (1), specifically the set of weights from (2.a), on the LRL data available.

In the reminder of this section we explain in some detail each phase.

3.1 Fine-tune on HRL data

Given that the HRL is by definition closely related to LRL, it stands to reason that biasing the model towards the HRL might make for a better base model for the LRL than the vanilla multilingual model. We show in 4 that this has in fact been useful.

Another important reason to fine-tune the model on HRL is that it is a prerequisite for multiple neuron sorting techniques detailed in 3.2.

3.2 Neurons Selection

The amount of *change* that the multilingual model exhibits during the fine-tuning stage is affected by a multitude of factors (for example how different are training samples from the ones the model has seen, the difficulty/complexity of the new training samples, the size of the fine-tuning dataset, etc). In our scenario the LRL has relatively few training samples. This means that directly fine-tuning all of the parameters models could potentially lead to the model exhibiting some of the following undesirable phenomena :

- **Over-fitting on noise patterns in the training data.** Due to the fact the model's extra capacity (that is model parameters were specific to other languages/language pairs than the ones we are interested in) is larger than the amount of useful information within the LRL data. Thus the risk of the fine-tuned model *forgetting* important linguistic information/properties from the HRL (that are potentailly shared with the LRL) and *memorizing* the new training data is high, and could lead to hallucinations. Bounding the fine-tuning process to the most "important" neurons can help mitigate this by limiting the model's degrees of freedom thus acting as a regularizer.

- **Missing out on potential quality of translation gains.** As we show in 4, neuron selection leads to better end-to-end quality of translation compared to fine-tuning all of the neurons directly. We hypothesized that since the fine-tuning process is limited to the most important HRL-related neurons, cross-lingual sharing would be maximized. This is also inline with the fact that with limited training samples, assuming we do not increase the learning rate value which would be dangerous, the amount of change that the model exhibits is limited. This lead us to hypothesize that steering the gradients towards the most important neurons would lead to better performance.

- **Longer training time.** This is a direct result of having to re-learn some of the patterns shared between the HRL and LRL. As stated above we hypothesize that in the case of fine-tuning all of the neurons, cross-lingual sharing could potentially be sub-optimal.

We experiment with various methods to determine the 'importance' of each neurons. We also test the importance of the neurons within two different environments.

1. Importance of neurons for language pair of interest $HRL \leftrightarrow EN$.
2. Importance of neurons for other high resourced language pairs for calibration (e.g $EN \leftrightarrow DE$ and $EN \leftrightarrow FR$.)

Neurons that are found to be important under both 1 and 2 are considered to be English-language-specific. The values of it's respective weights are not changed during fine-tuning. Whereas neurons that are found to be unimportant under 1 are zero-d out during inference and fine-tuning. Lastly neurons that are found to be important under 1 only are fine-tuned and used during inference.

We mention in more details the neuron ranking methods we considered during this work and briefly describe the rationale behind them.

3.2.1 Gradient Analysis

It is a simple importance measure where we compute the gradient of the network output w.r.t to the input features (Lei et al., 2016).

$$E_{gradient}(X, c) = \nabla f(X)_c \tag{1}$$

where f(X) is the model logits.

We adapt this method to our needs by capturing the gradient of the output w.r.t to a neuron's output instead of the actual input features. Given that the gradient is computed per-timestep we use the *average of absolute* (see eq. 2) of the value of the gradient per-timestep and that value is averaged across different input sentences. We also experiment with *max of absolute* (eq. 3).

$$Importance(X, n) = \frac{\sum_{t=0}^{t=|X|-1} |\nabla f(X)_{c_{ti}}|}{|X|} \tag{2}$$

$$Importance(X, n) = \frac{\max_{t=0}^{t=|X|-1} |\nabla f(X)_{c_{ti}}|}{|X|} \tag{3}$$

where: c_{ti} is the selected output token at timestep t_i, $|X|$ is the length of input sequence X and n is the neuron we are interested in.

In practice we found it better, empirically, to use intrinsic functions (perplexity) to compute neuron importance than to use the cross-entropy loss (see table 3) .

3.2.2 Activation Magnitude

In this method we track the magnitude of the output of the neuron of interest across different time steps of the deep neural network's execution. We use similar strategies to aggregate these values per input sequence to what was used in 3.2.1.

3.2.3 LASS

Proposed in (Lin et al., 2021), this method ranks the *weights* of the model by computing the change that weight exhibits after fine-tuning a multilingual model on a certain language pair. The rationale here being that weights that exhibit change the most during fine-tuning are language-dependent since fine-tuning on the language-pair had the most impact on their values. Formally, given the parameters of a multilingual model θ_0, a language pair $s_i \rightarrow t_i$:

1. Finetune θ_0 on $D_{s_i \rightarrow t_i}$ (i.e the dataset of the language pair of intereset), it is assumed that the resulting set of parameters (referred to as $\theta_{s_i \rightarrow t_i}$ would have amplified the set of language-dependent weights).

2. The *importance* of each weight is computed as:

$$importance(\theta_j) = \theta_{s_i \rightarrow d_i j} - \theta_{0j} \tag{4}$$

where θ_j denotes the jth weight of the set of the deep neural network's weights.

The importance of the *neuron* is computed as the average of the importance scores of it's weights.

3.3 Vocab Substitution

Depending on the relation between the HRL and LRL, vocab substitution can provide a boost to both convergence speed and quality of translation. Specifically when the HRL and the LRL are written in two different scripts. This hinders learning since the *textual representation* of the two languages is different despite being phonetically potentially similar, and in some cases mutually intelligible. We adapt the vocab substitution algorithm from (Garcia et al., 2021).

Our method assumes the existence of a small $HRL \leftrightarrow LRL$ training corpus. We also assume the existence of sufficiently large LRL and HRL monolingual corpora.

1. Given the original multilingual vocab (V_m), we use the HRL monolingual corpus to find the subset that represent the HRL (V_{hrl}). We remove elements that do not occur in the corpus more than a certain threshold. This is to help mitigate the noise in the corpus.

2. We use the LRL monolingual corpus to train a new vocab set (V_{lrl}). We experiment with different vocab sizes, the only constraint being $|V_{lrl}| <= |V_{hrl}|$.

3. Next we try to learn an appropriate mapping f, between the elements of ($V_{LRL} \rightarrow V_{lrl}$). To do so we train an alignment model using the parallel corpus.

4. Finally we apply the vocab substitution as follows:

    (a) Elements of V_{lrl} that belong to V_m are kept as is.

    (b) We sort the alignments extracted from the parallel corpus discerningly by the number of occurrences. We refer to the extracted alignments as a set of (e_{hrl}, e_{lrl}), where e_{hrl} is vocabulary element that belongs to the HRL and e_{lrl} is a vocabulary element that belongs to the LRL.

    (c) for each pair (e_{hrl}, e_{lrl}):

i. if e_{lrl} has already been placed in V_m, we skip this pair, since we definitely encountered a better alignment pair.

ii. else we replace e_{hrl} by e_{lrl} in V_m. i.e:

$$V_m = (V_m - \{e_{hrl}\}) \cup \{e_{lrl}\} \tag{5}$$

(d) Elements of V_{lrl} that are still un-assigned replace random elements of V_{hrl}.

3.4 Fine-tune On LRL data

Starting from HRL-fine-tuned model:

- We zero-out the weights of neurons that have been considered to be unimportant in order to nullify the output of that specific neuron.
- We Freeze the weights of neurons that have been considered to be English-specific. The rationale is that these weights are well-trained, so keeping their output while freezing the weights is sensible. We also experiment with jointly training them.
- The remaining neurons (important neurons that are HRL-specific). Are actively modified during fine-tuning to adapt to differences between the HRL and LRL.

4 Performance Evaluation

We chose to adapt MBART50 (Tang et al., 2020) to Tajik language (LRL) with Persian being its closest HRL language. We collect the training data for both languages from OPUS [1]. Tajik and Persian pose an especially interesting challenge since they are mutually intelligible, but written in different scripts (Cyrillic and Perso-Arabic respectively). For either language pair we use FLORES-dev as validation and FLORES-devtest for evaluation (Goyal et al., 2022). All of the computations were performed on a single Tesla T4 GPU with 16 GB of RAM.

To compare our results to (Xia et al., 2019) we train a $Persian \leftrightarrow Tajok$ MT model. We collect the training data from OPUS and use FLORES "dev" and "devtest" as validation and test sets respectively.

4.1 Data Quality

We apply some basic rule-based filtering on the data.

1. Punctuation Ratio: We remove sentence-pairs where either side has a punctuation ratio > 0.5. We adapt this filter from (Fan et al., 2020) [2].
2. Length Ratio Filtering: We only keep the sentence-pairs where the longer sentence is less than three-times the shorter one. With sentence length being determined via number of characters. This method has also been used in literature (Pinnis, 2018).
3. Script Verification: This step verifies that each sentnece is *mostly* written in its respective language's script (Latin for English, Perso-Arabic for Persian..etc). We use unicodedata2 [3] to determine the script of each character (we exclude Numeric/Punctuation characters since they are mostly script-agnostic).

See Table 1 for a detailed recount of the effect of each of the filters on the amounts of data of both language pairs.

[1] https://opus.nlpl.eu/

[2] https://github.com/facebookresearch/fairseq/blob/main/examples/m2m_100/process_data/remove_too_much_punc.py

[3] https://gist.githubusercontent.com/anonymous/2204527/raw/e940a6862de340cf23d7653969e181427176fc9b/unicodedata2.py

Filter Step	FA - EN (M)	TG - EN (M)
Original	12.8	0.268
+Punctuation Ratio	10.5	0.2
+ Length Ratio	9.36	0.194
+ Script Verification	9.35	0.19

Table 1: Number of sentences per language-pair after each filtering step.

Experiment	FA - EN	EN-FA	TG - EN	EN-TG
MBART50-Large	20.6	12.9	0.18	0.01
Full data Finetune	28.6	15.1	15.3	**9.3**
Filtered Data Finetune	**31.4**	**15.8**	**16.01**	9.1

Table 2: BLEU scores of MBART model pre-fine-tuning and post-fine-tuning.

4.2 HRL Fine-tuning

To verify that applied data filtering techniques did not harm the performance we examine its effect by fine-tuning pre and post data filtering (see table 2). We use a learning rate of 0.00003 with Polynomial decay learning rate scheduler. We set the patience window to 15 validation-runs while setting the validation interval to 500 updates. We set the batch size to 1000 tokens.

4.3 Vocab Substitution

We start by building a sentencepiece model for Tajik(TG) only. We set the vocab size to 4k although this might be a hyper-parameter that would require tuning in other scenarios/language-pairs. As stated above we collect the $FA \leftrightarrow TG$ training corpus from OPUS. We segment the Persian (FA) side using the MBART sentencepiece model while the TG side is segmented using the newly trained sentencepiece model. The parallel corpus is then used to train an alignment model and then extract piece-wise alignments. We use Fastalign to train the alignment model.

To quantify the effect of vocab substitution on Tajik sentences, we compute the average number of setnencepiece tokens per sentence of the Tajik side of the validation set using both the new sentencepiece model and the original MBART setnencepiece model. We find that on average the sequence length of a Tajik sentence using the original MBART model is approximately 64.7 tokens/sentence whereas using the new model this value drops to 45.6 . This means that Tajik sentences on average were 30% shorter when using the new model. This in addition to

[3]https://github.com/clab/fast_align

Experiment	TG - EN	EN - TG
Direct Fine-tuning (No selection)	16.01	9.1
+ Vocab Substitution	16.9	9.5
Mixed Fine-tuning (FA/TG - EN)	16.21	7.6
Pivot on HRL (FA)	7.3	3.49
Mono Adapters + Fine-tune	15.7	9.2
Neuron Activation + vocab sub	17.3	9.4
LASS + vocab sub	18.75	9.2
Loss Gradient Analysis + vocab sub	18.9	10.2
Perplexity Gradient Analysis + vocab sub	**19.03**	**10.7**

Table 3: Evaluating our method against multiple baselines on $TG \leftrightarrow EN$ BLEU score.

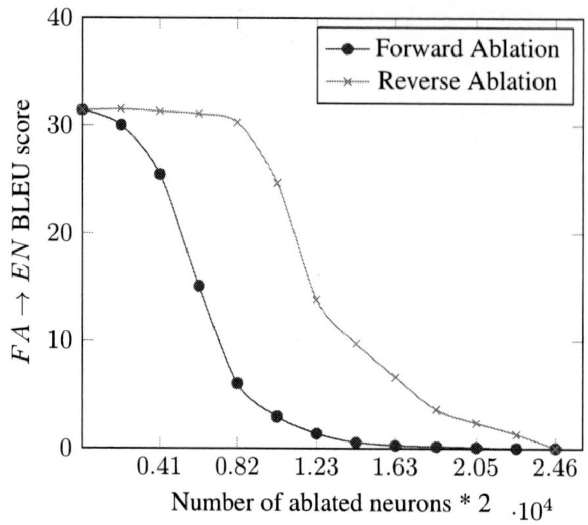

Figure 1: Forward vs Backward ablation on Encoder-Decoder attention Neurons, X-axis represents the number of zero-d out neurons and the Y-axis is the BLEU score.In Forward Ablation curve we remove-according to our ranking- the most important neurons first, while reverse ablation means we start with the most unimportant

quality of translation gains described in table 3 has also sped up training by approximately 15% in terms of time. We also observe that the oov-rate (Number of $< UNK >$ Tokens divided by the Total Number of Tokens) drops from 1.3% using the original MBART sentencepiece model to just 0.035% using the new sentencepiece model. These statistics were also collected by tokenizing the Tajik side of the validation set.

4.4 Neuron Selection

As detailed in section 3.2, we experiment with multiple methods of neuron ranking. We conduct a neuron-ablation study on the Gradient Analysis ranking, specifically for $FA \rightarrow EN$ fine-tuned model and examine the effect on BLEU score (see figure below) to verify our implementation. We limit the ablation study to the output neurons of the encoder-decoder attention module of all 12 layers (a total of 12288 neurons). The gradient analysis was performed on the validation set, and we observe that computing the gradient of the *perplexity* of the output sentence achieves better performance compared to the cross-entropy loss function.

This was not conducted for LASS nor Activation magnitude since their implementations have already been verified, we instead run end-to-end comparisons and determine which is best using BLEU score. Table 3 shows a comparison between the three aforementioned ranking methods. We observe that gradient analysis slightly outperforms LASS, while both of them show significant gains when compared to tracking the magnitude of each neuron's output. We also find that when selecting the top 20% most important neurons the intersection between using the cross-entropy loss and perplexity functions is around 96% of the selected neurons, and that is why it is to be expected that difference in BLEU score between the two methods is mostly less than 1 point. We did however find it consistently better to use perplexity as opposed to cross-entropy loss.

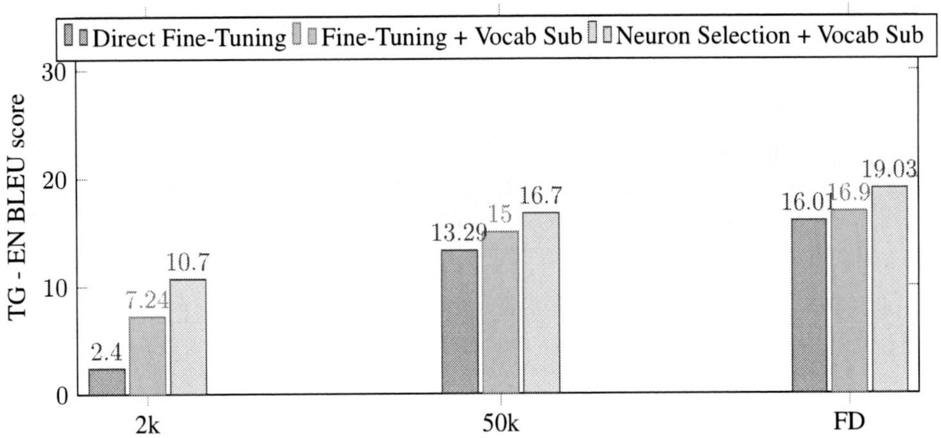

Figure 2: Effect of varying data-set size on BLEU scores. FT denotes direct Fine-tuning, VS is vocab substitution, NS is neuron selection and FD denotes full data-set size.

4.5 LRL Fine-Tuning

Using the neuron ranking methods described above, we fine-tune the top 20% most important neurons. It's also worth noting that for $Tajik \rightarrow English$ we freeze the decoder (other than the encoder-decoder attention module which is subject of neuron selection), while for $English \rightarrow Tajik$ we freeze the encoder. The idea here is that the model has been trained on a lot of English data, hence we limit the training to the encoder for $Tajik \rightarrow English$ and the decoder for $English \rightarrow Tajik$. This stems from the fact that when generating $Tajik$ we need not modify the encoder since it has already been well trained to consume English sentences we only need to train the decoder to consume the encoder representations and generate Tajik sentences and vice versa . The results are described in table 3.

We also conduct another series of experiments to examine the effect of reducing the training dataset size on the performance of our method and compare it to directly fine-tuning all of the neurons of the model. We randomly select two subsets from $TG \leftrightarrow EN$ training set of sizes 2k and 50k.

In figure 2 below we show the effect of varying the training set data size across different fine-tuning techniques.

5 Conclusion And Future Work

In this section we discuss the results detailed in the previous section and propose possible extension to the analysis described throughout the paper.

As detailed in table 3 we find that our method achieves better performance compared to earlier approaches. We also find that as we *emulate* smaller training dataset sizes the relative improvement in performance between our method and simply fine-tuning the whole model on the LRL continues to grow as hypothesized. Namely the gap between our method and direct fine-tuning grows from roughly 3 BLEU points at full data to 8.2 points when we limit the data to 2k samples.

For future work we propose extending this analysis horizontally by experimenting with more than one HRL-LRL, and vertically by applying the analysis on other available MNMT. We find that M2M might be a good candidate for this, and is especially interesting since it already has language-dependant parameters. Another interesting area of research would be how to integrate self-supervised learning into this setup. Specifically how will our method fair given zero parallel data but assuming the abundance of monolingual data.

References

Bapna, A. and Firat, O. (2019). Simple, scalable adaptation for neural machine translation. In *Proceedings of the 2019 Conference on Empirical Methods in Natural Language Processing and the 9th International Joint Conference on Natural Language Processing (EMNLP-IJCNLP)*, pages 1538–1548, Hong Kong, China. Association for Computational Linguistics.

Berard, A. (2021). Continual learning in multilingual NMT via language-specific embeddings. *CoRR*, abs/2110.10478.

Chowdhery, A., Narang, S., Devlin, J., Bosma, M., Mishra, G., Roberts, A., Barham, P., Chung, H. W., Sutton, C., Gehrmann, S., Schuh, P., Shi, K., Tsvyashchenko, S., Maynez, J., Rao, A., Barnes, P., Tay, Y., Shazeer, N., Prabhakaran, V., Reif, E., Du, N., Hutchinson, B., Pope, R., Bradbury, J., Austin, J., Isard, M., Gur-Ari, G., Yin, P., Duke, T., Levskaya, A., Ghemawat, S., Dev, S., Michalewski, H., Garcia, X., Misra, V., Robinson, K., Fedus, L., Zhou, D., Ippolito, D., Luan, D., Lim, H., Zoph, B., Spiridonov, A., Sepassi, R., Dohan, D., Agrawal, S., Omernick, M., Dai, A. M., Pillai, T. S., Pellat, M., Lewkowycz, A., Moreira, E., Child, R., Polozov, O., Lee, K., Zhou, Z., Wang, X., Saeta, B., Diaz, M., Firat, O., Catasta, M., Wei, J., Meier-Hellstern, K., Eck, D., Dean, J., Petrov, S., and Fiedel, N. (2022). Palm: Scaling language modeling with pathways.

Fan, A., Bhosale, S., Schwenk, H., Ma, Z., El-Kishky, A., Goyal, S., Baines, M., Celebi, O., Wenzek, G., Chaudhary, V., Goyal, N., Birch, T., Liptchinsky, V., Edunov, S., Grave, E., Auli, M., and Joulin, A. (2020). Beyond english-centric multilingual machine translation. *arXiv preprint*.

Garcia, X., Constant, N., Parikh, A. P., and Firat, O. (2021). Towards continual learning for multilingual machine translation via vocabulary substitution. *CoRR*, abs/2103.06799.

Goyal, N., Gao, C., Chaudhary, V., Chen, P.-J., Wenzek, G., Ju, D., Krishnan, S., Ranzato, M., Guzmán, F., and Fan, A. (2022). The Flores-101 Evaluation Benchmark for Low-Resource and Multilingual Machine Translation. *Transactions of the Association for Computational Linguistics*, 10:522–538.

Johnson, M., Schuster, M., Le, Q. V., Krikun, M., Wu, Y., Chen, Z., Thorat, N., Viégas, F., Wattenberg, M., Corrado, G., Hughes, M., and Dean, J. (2017). Google's Multilingual Neural Machine Translation System: Enabling Zero-Shot Translation. *Transactions of the Association for Computational Linguistics*, 5:339–351.

Kim, Y. and Rush, A. M. (2016). Sequence-level knowledge distillation. *CoRR*, abs/1606.07947.

Kudo, T. and Richardson, J. (2018). Sentencepiece: A simple and language independent subword tokenizer and detokenizer for neural text processing. *CoRR*, abs/1808.06226.

Lakew, S. M., Karakanta, A., Federico, M., Negri, M., and Turchi, M. (2019). Adapting multilingual neural machine translation to unseen languages. *CoRR*, abs/1910.13998.

Lei, T., Barzilay, R., and Jaakkola, T. S. (2016). Rationalizing neural predictions. *CoRR*, abs/1606.04155.

Lin, Z., Wu, L., Wang, M., and Li, L. (2021). Learning language specific sub-network for multilingual machine translation. *CoRR*, abs/2105.09259.

Neubig, G. and Hu, J. (2018). Rapid adaptation of neural machine translation to new languages. *CoRR*, abs/1808.04189.

Philip, J., Berard, A., Gallé, M., and Besacier, L. (2020). Monolingual adapters for zero-shot neural machine translation. In *Proceedings of the 2020 Conference on Empirical Methods in Natural Language Processing (EMNLP)*, pages 4465–4470, Online. Association for Computational Linguistics.

Pinnis, M. (2018). Tilde's parallel corpus filtering methods for WMT 2018. In *Proceedings of the Third Conference on Machine Translation: Shared Task Papers*, pages 939–945, Belgium, Brussels. Association for Computational Linguistics.

Tang, Y., Tran, C., Li, X., Chen, P., Goyal, N., Chaudhary, V., Gu, J., and Fan, A. (2020). Multilingual translation with extensible multilingual pretraining and finetuning. *CoRR*, abs/2008.00401.

Tran, C., Bhosale, S., Cross, J., Koehn, P., Edunov, S., and Fan, A. (2021). Facebook AI WMT21 news translation task submission. *CoRR*, abs/2108.03265.

Xia, M., Kong, X., Anastasopoulos, A., and Neubig, G. (2019). Generalized data augmentation for low-resource translation. *CoRR*, abs/1906.03785.

Measuring the Effects of Human and Machine Translation on Website Engagement

Geza Kovacs geza@alumni.stanford.edu
John DeNero john@lilt.com
Lilt Inc, San Francisco, CA, USA

Abstract

With the internet growing increasingly multilingual, it is important to consider translating websites. However, professional translators are much more expensive than machines, and machine translation quality is continually increasing, so we must justify the cost of professional translation by measuring the effects of translation on website engagement, and how users interact with translations. This paper presents an in-the-wild study run on 2 websites fully translated into 15 and 11 languages respectively, where visitors with non-English preferred languages were randomized into being shown text translated by a professional translator, machine translated text, or untranslated English text. We find that both human and machine translations improve engagement, users rarely switch the page language manually, and that in-browser machine translation is often used when English is shown, particularly by users from countries with low English proficiency. We also release a dataset of interaction data collected during our studies, including 3,332,669 sessions from 190 countries across 2 websites.

1 Introduction

The userbase of the internet is becoming increasingly linguistically diverse (Group, 2020). As a result, publishers increasingly need to translate websites to make content available to global audiences. Professional translators can be expensive, so localization decisions involve many tradeoffs. Should we show translations generated by professional translators, or is machine translation quality sufficiently high that showing machine translations will not negatively impact user engagement? If a human translation is not available in the user's preferred language, is it preferable to show English or a machine translation? Does the website need to be translated at all, given that browsers have built-in machine translation functionality? To make informed decisions, we need to know the effects of each form of translation on website engagement.

This paper quantifies the effects of translation on engagement metrics and how users interact with translations, by running large-scale (over 3 million sessions), in-the-wild A/B tests on the homepages of two different open-source software projects. Our contributions in this paper are a set of studies quantifying how users interact with website-provided translations and in-browser machine translations, interface recommendations on how to incorporate translations into websites based on these findings, and a public dataset of interactions and code that can be used to reproduce our results and conduct follow-up research.

2 Related Work

Previously published work has not evaluated the effects of machine translation, human translation, and non-translation on in-the-wild website user engagement in a randomized, A/B test fashion.

While machine translation quality has historically been negatively perceived (Läubli and Orrego-Carmona, 2017), some machine translation systems claim to have reached parity in translation quality with professional translators in certain settings (Hassan et al., 2018; Barrault et al., 2019; Popel et al., 2020). Other work has questioned these claims of human parity (Läubli et al., 2018; Toral et al., 2018; Toral, 2020). Website translation has been found to benefit search engine optimization by attracting users who search in their native language (Cappelli, 2007). Machine translation of product listings has been found to help increase purchases on eBay (Brynjolfsson et al., 2019). This work seeks to measure the effects of human and machine translation on user engagement in the context of software-centric websites.

3 Research Questions

The studies in this paper aim to answer the following research questions:

- Does showing a human translation result in better website engagement than showing a machine translation or an untranslated page?
- Should we automatically show machine translations based on browser language preferences, or show English by default and let users view a translation by clicking a button?
- When users are shown untranslated English pages, do they end up using their browser's built-in machine translation system?

4 Methodology

We ran A/B tests on two sites, both of which are open-source software projects with a single-page design, shown in Figure 1. Both sites had been translated from English to several languages[1] by professional translators two years before we began running this experiment. We will call these *supported languages* for each site. We refer to the preferred language in the user's browser settings as the *preferred language*. Site 1 had 3,298,635 sessions total, of which 1,233,841 (37.4%) had a supported non-English preferred language. Site 2 had 34,034 sessions total, of which 9,316 (27.4%) had a supported non-English preferred language. Data was gathered from Nov 25, 2020 to Jan 14, 2022 (415 days). We obtained machine translated text from Google Translate in Nov 2020. See the Appendix for the demographics of visitors to the websites.

4.1 Experiment Conditions

Each session with a non-English preferred language for which translations are available are randomized into one of five conditions:

- *UE (Untranslated English)*: Shows the page in English only; user cannot switch languages.
- *HTT (Human Translation, show Translation by default)*: Shows a human translation to the user's preferred language by default. Users can switch to English or to a human translation in any supported language via the language switcher. See right side of Figure 1.
- *HTE (Human Translation, show English by default)*: Shows English by default. Users can switch to a human translation in their preferred language or any supported language via the language switcher. See left side of Figure 1.
- *MTT (Machine Translation, show Translation by default)*: Shows a machine translation to the user's preferred language by default. Users can switch to English or any supported language via the language switcher.
- *MTE (Machine Translation, show English by default)*: Shows English by default. Users can

[1]Site 1 is translated into 15 languages: Chinese (Simplified), Chinese (Traditional), Danish, Dutch, English, French, German, Greek, Hebrew, Hungarian, Italian, Malaysian, Portuguese, Spanish, and Turkish. Site 2 is translated into 11 languages: Chinese (Simplified), Chinese (Traditional), Czech, Dutch, English, French, German, Greek, Portuguese, Spanish, and Turkish.

Figure 1: Sites we ran our study on; left is Site 1 (`https://unetbootin.github.io`), right is Site 2 (`https://habitlab.github.io`). On the bottom-left of each screenshot is the language-selection widget from the Transifex Live localization toolkit; it shows the current language by default (left); if clicked it allows the user to select a language from a list (right). The switcher in the middle includes a button to switch between English and the user's preferred language with a single click; the preferred language is Simplified Chinese in these screenshots.

Site 1 Engagement Metrics	HTT vs UE	HTT vs MTT	MTT vs UE
Download link clicked	$\chi^2 = 14.25, p = 0.0002$	$\chi^2 = 4.190, p = 0.041$	$\chi^2 = 2.968, p = 0.085$
Non-download link clicked	$\chi^2 = 191.9, p < 0.0001$	$\chi^2 = 13.60, p = 0.0002$	$\chi^2 = 103.2, p < 0.0001$
User scrolled	$\chi^2 = 190.6, p < 0.0001$	$\chi^2 = 10.43, p = 0.001$	$\chi^2 = 111.7, p < 0.0001$
Visit duration $\geq$ 17 seconds	$\chi^2 = 321.0, p < 0.0001$	$\chi^2 = 1.595, p = 0.207$	$\chi^2 = 277.0, p < 0.0001$
Site 2 Engagement Metrics	**HTT vs UE**	**HTT vs MTT**	**MTT vs UE**
Download link clicked	$\chi^2 = 2.477, p = 0.116$	$\chi^2 = 0.010, p = 0.921$	$\chi^2 = 2.963, p = 0.085$
Non-download link clicked	$\chi^2 = 0.025, p = 0.874$	$\chi^2 = 0.042, p = 0.838$	$\chi^2 = 0.216, p = 0.642$
User scrolled	$\chi^2 = 0.341, p = 0.560$	$\chi^2 = 1.196, p = 0.274$	$\chi^2 = 2.933, p = 0.087$
Visit duration $\geq$ 17 seconds	$\chi^2 = 7.373, p = 0.007$	$\chi^2 = 0.025, p = 0.874$	$\chi^2 = 8.479, p = 0.004$

Table 1: χ^2 tests for engagement metrics on Sites 1+2, comparing the HTT (Human Translation, show Translation by default), MTT (Machine Translation, show Translation by default), and UE (Untranslated English) conditions. See Figure 2 and Figure 3 for mean values.

switch to a machine translation in their preferred language or any supported language via the language switcher.

5 Study 1: Effects of human and machine translation availability on engagement

We study the effect of showing a human translation, machine translation, or no translation on the following engagement metrics:

- Percent of sessions where the user clicks on a download link.
- Percent of sessions where the user clicks on a non-download link.
- Percent of sessions where the user scrolls.
- Percent of sessions where the visit duration is in the top quartile of visit durations. (This is 17 or more seconds, for both Site A and B).

We chose these metrics as they are conversion events and proxies for reading. Clicking the download button is the "conversion event" for these sites, or what the site's most salient call to action is attempting to get the user to do. Clicking a non-download link suggests that the user is reading the text, as the non-download links are text-only, so users would presumably only click them if they read the associated link text and understood what the link points to. Scrolling likewise suggests that the user is reading, as both websites are long, single-page documents that

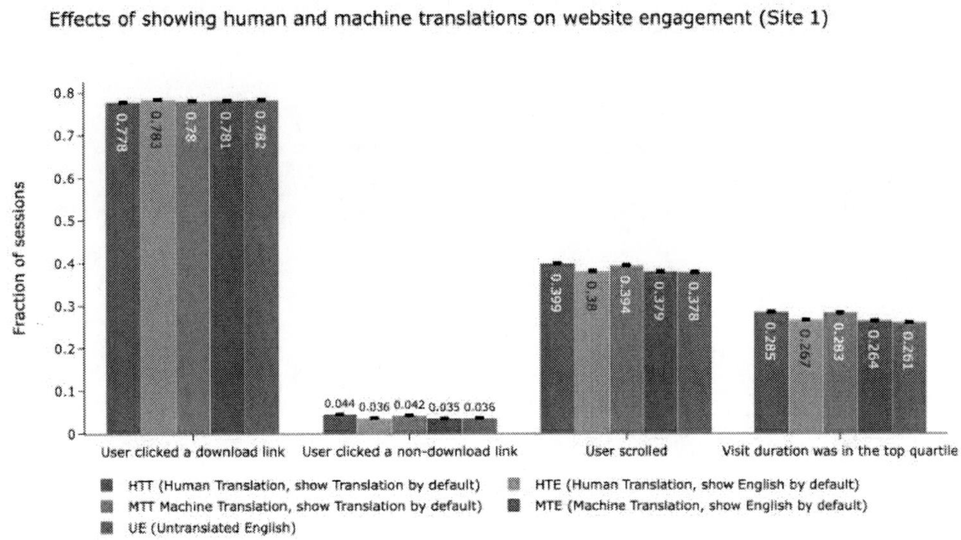

Figure 2: Engagement metrics for Site 1, for users whose preferred language is supported and not English. Error bars indicate 95% confidence intervals. Study 1 analyzes only the HTT, MTT, and UE conditions; the HTE and MTE conditions are analyzed in Study 2.

have the majority of textual content describing the software below the fold when viewed on a standard monitor. A visit duration in the top quartile (17 seconds or more) suggests the user is likely reading the page, as there are only images and no videos on the sites, so the non-textual portions of the websites can likely be skimmed in less than 17 seconds.

Results showing engagement metrics for Site 1 are in Figure 2. For Site 1, which had 1.23 million sessions from users with a supported non-English preferred language, χ^2 tests indicate there are significant differences for all 4 measured engagement metrics between the HTT, MTT, and UE conditions. These conditions have a significant effect on the proportion of sessions where the user clicks a download link (χ^2 omnibus test: $\chi^2 = 24.95, p < 0.0001$), the proportion of sessions where the user clicks a non-download link ($\chi^2 = 376.0, p < 0.0001$), the proportion of sessions where the user scrolls ($\chi^2 = 326.4, p < 0.0001$), and the proportion of sessions where the visit duration is in the top quartile—17 seconds or more ($\chi^2 = 562.3, p < 0.0001$). Post-hoc χ^2 analysis results are shown in Table 1. Users are significantly more likely to click a non-download link, scroll, or have a visit duration in the top quartile when shown a translation (HTT, MTT) than when shown untranslated English (UE). Scrolling and clicking on non-download links increases with human translations (HTT) over machine translations (MTT), but other engagement metrics do not significantly differ. Surprisingly, users are significantly more likely to click the download link if shown an untranslated English page (UE), than if shown a translation (HTT, MTT); perhaps this is due to the graphically salient nature of the download button.

Results for Site 2 are shown in Figure 3. For Site 2, which had only 9,316 sessions from users with a non-English preferred language, χ^2 tests indicate that between the HTT, MTT, and UE conditions, there are no significant differences in clicking on download links (χ^2 omnibus test: $\chi^2 = 9.285, p = 0.054$), clicking on non-download links ($\chi^2 = 0.392, p = 0.983$), or scrolling ($\chi^2 = 3.704, p = 0.447$). The only engagement metric with significant differences between conditions is whether the visit duration was in the top quartile – 17 seconds or more (χ^2 omnibus test: $\chi^2 = 13, 37, p = 0.0096$). Post-hoc χ^2 analysis results are shown in Table 1. Users are significantly more likely to stay on-page for at least 17 seconds if shown translations

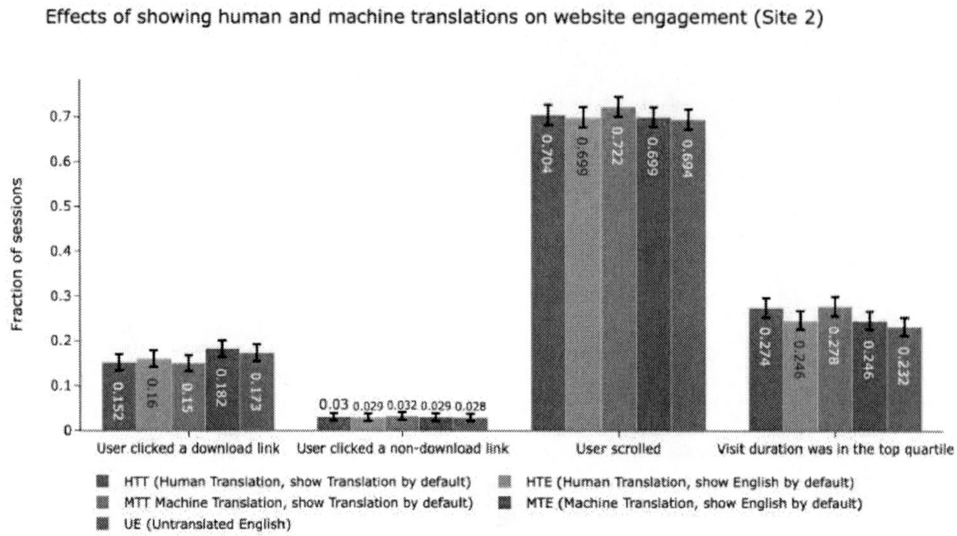

Figure 3: Engagement metrics for Site 2, for users whose preferred language is supported and not English. Error bars indicate 95% confidence intervals. Study 1 analyzes only the HTT, MTT, and UE conditions; the HTE and MTE conditions are analyzed in Study 2.

Site 1 Engagement Metrics	HTT vs HTE	MTT vs MTE	HTE vs UE	MTE vs UE
Download link clicked	$\chi^2 = 21.13, p < 0.0001$	$\chi^2 = 0.285, p = 0.594$	$\chi^2 = 0.679, p = 0.410$	$\chi^2 = 1.409, p = 0.235$
Non-download link clicked	$\chi^2 = 180.3, p < 0.0001$	$\chi^2 = 118.8, p < 0.0001$	$\chi^2 = 0.155, p = 0.694$	$\chi^2 = 0.539, p = 0.463$
User scrolled	$\chi^2 = 152.8, p < 0.0001$	$\chi^2 = 94.31, p < 0.0001$	$\chi^2 = 2.028, p = 0.154$	$\chi^2 = 0.737, p = 0.391$
Visit duration $\geq$ 17 seconds	$\chi^2 = 185.2, p < 0.0001$	$\chi^2 = 198.6, p < 0.0001$	$\chi^2 = 18.33, p < 0.0001$	$\chi^2 = 6.548, p = 0.010$
Site 2 Engagement Metrics	**HTT vs HTE**	**MTT vs MTE**	**HTE vs UE**	**MTE vs UE**
Download link clicked	$\chi^2 = 0.347, p = 0.556$	$\chi^2 = 5.970, p = 0.015$	$\chi^2 = 0.858, p = 0.354$	$\chi^2 = 0.428, p = 0.513$
Non-download link clicked	$\chi^2 = 0.005, p = 0.943$	$\chi^2 = 0.094, p = 0.759$	$\chi^2 = 0.000, p = 1.000$	$\chi^2 = 0.004, p = 0.950$
User scrolled	$\chi^2 = 0.083, p = 0.773$	$\chi^2 = 2.024, p = 0.155$	$\chi^2 = 0.064, p = 0.801$	$\chi^2 = 0.075, p = 0.785$
Visit duration $\geq$ 17 seconds	$\chi^2 = 3.222, p = 0.073$	$\chi^2 = 4.160, p = 0.041$	$\chi^2 = 0.749, p = 0.387$	$\chi^2 = 0.757, p = 0.384$

Table 2: χ^2 tests for engagement metrics on Sites 1+2, comparing the HTT (Human Translation, show Translation by default), MTT (Machine Translation, show Translation by default), HTE (Human Translation, show English by default), MTE (Machine Translation, show English by default), and UE (Untranslated English) conditions. See Figure 2 and Figure 3 for mean values.

(HTT, MTT) than if shown untranslated pages (UE).

Thus, we observe that while the availability of a translation increases the proportion of users who are retained for at least 17 seconds on both sites, the improvements in non-download link click rates and scrolling were observed only on Site 1 and not Site 2. Contrary to our expectations, we did not observe an increase in download rates due to translations being shown on either site. One explanation is that users may have read about the software in their native language elsewhere (referral logs indicated many visitors were coming from non-English sites), so they have no need to read the site's contents before downloading. Another explanation is that the download button is visually prominent, so perhaps some users just download and try the software to learn how it works, instead of reading about it first.

6 Study 2: Effects of default language choice and language switcher use

Websites commonly display translations in two ways: one is to determine users' preferred language via browser settings or their geographic region, and automatically show pages translated

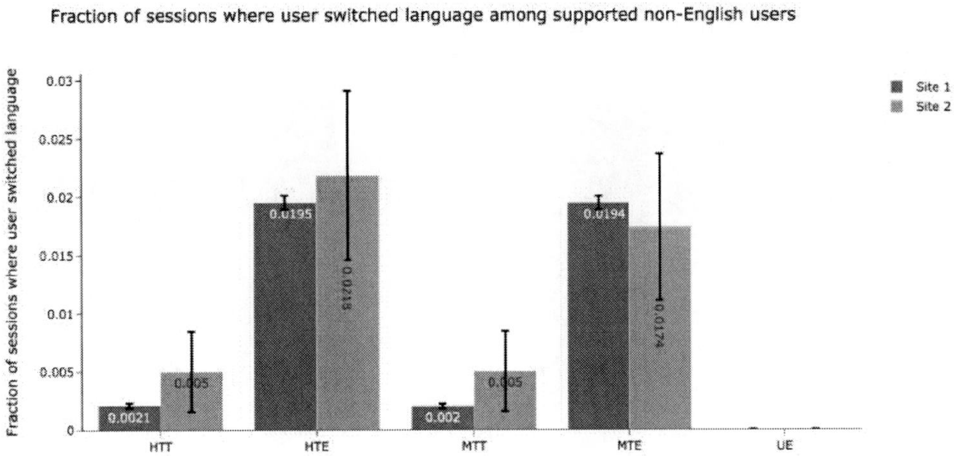

Figure 4: Use of the language switcher on Sites 1+2 in each condition, for users whose preferred language is supported and not English. Error bars indicate 95% confidence intervals.

to that language. Another approach is to show untranslated pages by default, and ask the user to use a language selector or click a link in order to see the translation. We wished to see how often users would use a language selector, and the effects of requiring language selection on user engagement. The language selector interface used in this experiment is shown in Figure 1.

Figure 4 shows the fraction of users who used the language selector in each condition on Sites 1 and 2. On both sites, there is a significant increase in usage of the language selector when English is shown by default (HTE, MTE) vs when a translation is shown by default (HTT, MTT). On Site 1, the language switcher is used in 1.95% of sessions in HTE vs 0.21% of sessions in HTT ($\chi^2 = 3095, p < 0.0001$). On Site 1, the language switcher is used in 1.94% of sessions in MTE vs 0.20% of sessions in MTT ($\chi^2 = 3123, p < 0.0001$). On Site 2, the language switcher is used in 2.18% of sessions in HTE vs 0.50% of sessions in HTT ($\chi^2 = 15.81, p < 0.0001$). On Site 2, the language switcher is used in 1.74% of sessions in MTE vs 0.50% of sessions in MTT ($\chi^2 = 10.14, p < 0.005$). Users hardly engage with language switchers on either site—even though it takes only a single button click to see the page in the user's preferred language, only 2% of users click it when English is shown by default. Switching away from the preferred language is even less frequent. Thus, automatically detecting the user's preferred language and showing translations accordingly is important—otherwise users will not see translations.

Showing English by default and requiring the user to use a language selector to view the page in their preferred language is detrimental to engagement. As we can see in Figure 2, the improvement in engagement metrics from translation we had previously observed for Site 1 are lost in the HTE and MTE conditions. χ^2 tests are shown in Table 2; there is a significant decrease in engagement (clicking non-download links, scrolling, and visit durations in the top quartile) when users need to click to switch to their preferred language. For most metrics, the HTE and MTE conditions do not display significantly higher engagement than the UE condition (Table 2). The same χ^2 tests were not significant on Site 2 (Table 2).

There are no significant differences in language switcher use between HTE vs MTE (Site 1: $\chi^2 = 0.021, p = 0.886$; Site 2: $\chi^2 = 0.616, p = 0.432$) or between HTT vs MTT (Site 1: $\chi^2 = 0.342, p = 0.559$; Site 2: $\chi^2 = 0, p = 1$). The fact that on both sites less than 0.6% in the MTT condition switch to English, and this is not significantly higher than the HTT condition, suggests that the machine translation was sufficiently usable that users did not switch to English.

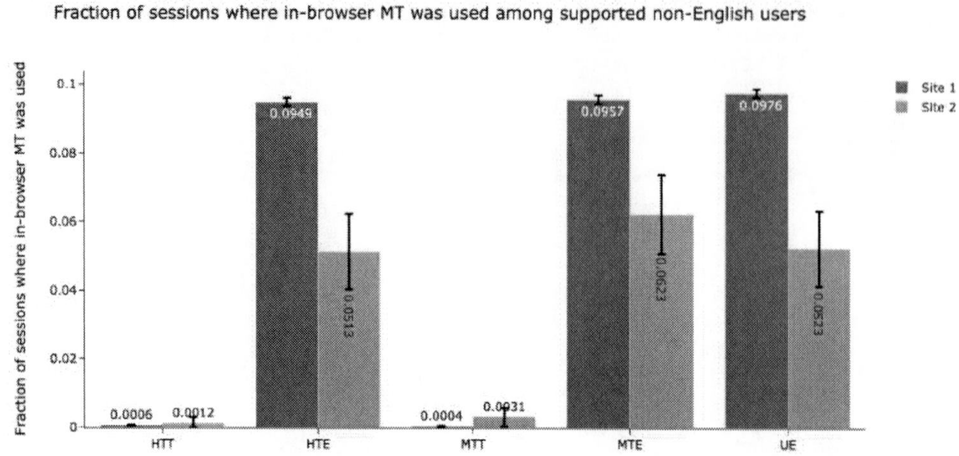

Figure 5: Use of in-browser machine translation on Sites 1+2 in each condition, for users whose preferred language is supported and not English. Error bars indicate 95% confidence intervals.

7 Study 3: In-browser machine translation use

We were surprised by our results from Study 1 that there was high engagement with untranslated English pages, even though the user's browser language preference was a non-English language that the site had been translated to, and our result from Study 2 that users rarely switch the page to their preferred language. We suspected that users may be viewing pages through the machine translation functionality that is built into browsers, so we measured the use of in-browser machine translation. Results are shown in Figure 5 for Sites 1 and 2. When a page is only available in English, 9.76% of users use in-browser machine translation on Site 1, and this number is 5.23% on Site 2. When a human translation is available in the user's preferred language, but the page is shown in English by default, 9.49% of users will use in-browser machine translation on Site 1, and this number is 5.13% on Site 2. This is higher than the 2% of users who used the language switcher from Study 2, meaning that if users are required to click a button to see a translation, users will be more likely to end up seeing their browser's machine translation than clicking the button to see a human translation.

We were curious whether the user's language and country has an influence on their use of in-browser machine translation. Is in-browser machine translation used at roughly equal levels everywhere, or is it used much more in some countries than others? Perhaps users whose preferred language is a language where the quality of machine translation from English is high will be more likely to use machine translation? Perhaps users whose preferred language has high lexical overlap with English, or uses the same Latin alphabet as English, will need to rely on machine translation less? Perhaps users from countries with a high level of English proficiency will be less likely to use machine translation? We display the in-browser machine translation usage broken down by the target language from Site 1 in Figure 6. Site 2 results are in Figure 8 of the Appendix.

Interestingly, it does not appear to be the case that machine translation use is highest for languages where the machine translation quality is better. For example, observe that Vietnamese (vi) has the highest proportion of users using the browser's built-in machine translation on Site 1 (14.8%) and is the fourth highest on Site 2 (11.3%), despite it being a low-resource language for which parallel data for training machine translation systems is scarce (Ngo et al., 2020). We can also observe the contrast in machine translation use between Spanish (es, 11.80% on Site 1

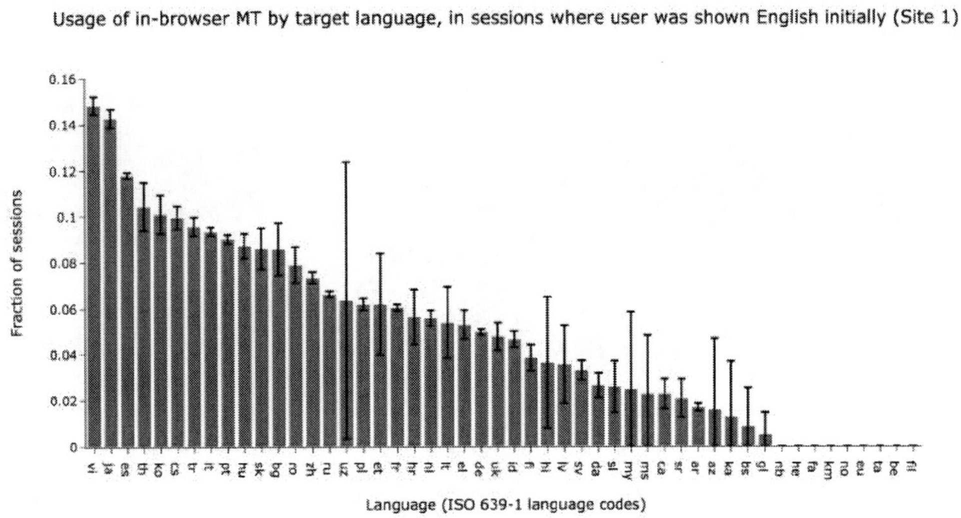

Figure 6: Use of in-browser machine translation on Site 1 by language, for users whose preferred language is not English. Error bars indicate 95% confidence intervals.

and 6.41% on Site 2) vs French (fr, 6.05% on Site 1 and 2.90% on Site 2)—despite both being high-resource Romance languages with high machine translation quality from English, and high lexical overlap with English for technical vocabulary. The type of script the language is written in does not seem to be the main influence on machine translation use either—the top 4 languages with the most machine translation use in Site 1 and Site 2 include both those written in non-Latin (Japanese, Thai, Bulgarian) and Latin scripts (Vietnamese, Spanish, Romanian).

Perhaps we should consider countries rather than the properties of the languages themselves? We show the in-browser machine translation usage broken down by country from Site 1 in Figure 7. Site 2 results are in Figure 8 of the Appendix. Since we suspected that English proficiency may influence machine translation usage, we group countries by their English proficiency ranking on the EF English Proficiency Index 2020 (Index, 2020). We find that among users with non-English preferred languages, those from countries with lower English proficiency tend to use machine translation more. On Site 1, 9.84% of sessions with non-English preferred languages from countries with "moderate" or lower English proficiency use in-browser machine translation, whereas only 6.10% of such sessions from counties with "high" or "very high" English proficiency used in-browser machine translation; this difference was statistically significant ($\chi^2 = 3797, p < 0.0001$). On Site 2, 6.33% of sessions with non-English preferred languages from countries with "moderate" or lower English proficiency use in-browser machine translation, whereas only 4.05% of such sessions from counties with "high" or "very high" English proficiency used in-browser machine translation; this difference was statistically significant ($\chi^2 = 18.67, p < 0.0001$).

8 Dataset and Code

To help replicate this study and enable researchers to run further analyses, we publicly release the datasets for both websites and the notebooks to reproduce our results at `https://transabtest.github.io/` under the Creative Commons Attribution license. The dataset represents the full 3,298,635 sessions from Site 1, and the full 34,034 sessions from Site 2, and the site content and translations.

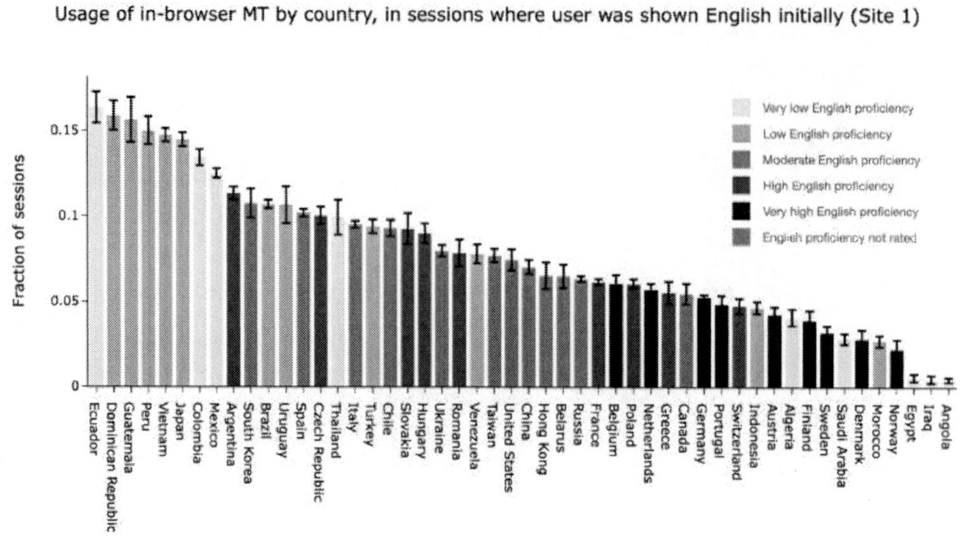

Figure 7: Use of in-browser machine translation on Site 1 by country, for users whose preferred language is not English. Colors indicate English proficiency ratings by the EF English Proficiency Index 2020. Error bars indicate 95% confidence intervals.

9 Conclusion

As the population of internet users grows increasingly linguistically diverse, it is increasingly important for websites to consider whether they should translate their websites, and how to present translations. Machine translation quality has considerably increased over the years, and in-browser machine translation has likewise become integrated into major browsers, which leads us to ask how much benefit websites can expect from translating their website with human translators, as opposed to showing machine translations or leaving pages untranslated.

Through an A/B test we run on the homepages of two open-source software projects, we find that both human and machine translations improve engagement metrics that are indicative of reading the page, though download rates remain high regardless of whether a translation is shown or not. Compared to machine translations, human translations increase two engagement metrics (scrolling and clicking on non-download links), but had no effect on others. If we require users to click a button to switch to their preferred language, they rarely do so, and the gains in engagement metrics we observed from translation are negated. A significant minority of users with non-English preferred languages use machine translation systems integrated into browsers, especially from countries with low English proficiency. This, along with our finding that only a small fraction of users switch to English if shown a machine translation to their preferred language, suggests that machine translations are often of acceptable quality to some users.

While showing machine translations performed well on the software-centric sites we studied, our findings may not generalize to other types of content; perhaps human translations will have more visible benefits on more text-centric content such as news. The effects of translation on engagement will also change over time, as machine translation quality improves, the web's userbase becomes increasingly multilingual, and as foreign language reading abilities change. Localization decision makers choosing between human and machine translations should also consider website demographics such as their visitors' countries and preferred languages, and the quality of machine translation for the languages they are considering supporting.

References

Barrault, L., Bojar, O., Costa-Jussa, M. R., Federmann, C., Fishel, M., Graham, Y., Haddow, B., Huck, M., Koehn, P., Malmasi, S., et al. (2019). Findings of the 2019 conference on machine translation (wmt19). In *Proceedings of the Fourth Conference on Machine Translation (Volume 2: Shared Task Papers, Day 1)*, pages 1–61.

Brynjolfsson, E., Hui, X., and Liu, M. (2019). Does machine translation affect international trade? evidence from a large digital platform. *Management Science*, 65(12):5449–5460.

Cappelli, G. (2007). The translation of tourism-related websites and localization: problems and perspectives. *Rassegna italiana di linguistica applicata*, 39(1/2):97.

Group, M. M. (2020). Interet world stats usage and population statistics. *Retrieved April*, 27:2021.

Hassan, H., Aue, A., Chen, C., Chowdhary, V., Clark, J., Federmann, C., Huang, X., Junczys-Dowmunt, M., Lewis, W., Li, M., et al. (2018). Achieving human parity on automatic chinese to english news translation. *arXiv preprint arXiv:1803.05567*.

Index, E. E. P. (2020). Ef english proficiency index a ranking of 100 countries and regions by english skills. *Retrieved April*, 27:2021.

Läubli, S. and Orrego-Carmona, D. (2017). When google translate is better than some human colleagues, those people are no longer colleagues.

Läubli, S., Sennrich, R., and Volk, M. (2018). Has machine translation achieved human parity? a case for document-level evaluation. *arXiv preprint arXiv:1808.07048*.

Ngo, T.-V., Nguyen, P.-T., Ha, T.-L., Dinh, K.-Q., and Nguyen, L.-M. (2020). Improving multilingual neural machine translation for low-resource languages: French-, english-vietnamese. *arXiv preprint arXiv:2012.08743*.

Popel, M., Tomkova, M., Tomek, J., Kaiser, Ł., Uszkoreit, J., Bojar, O., and Žabokrtskỳ, Z. (2020). Transforming machine translation: a deep learning system reaches news translation quality comparable to human professionals. *Nature communications*, 11(1):1–15.

Toral, A. (2020). Reassessing claims of human parity and super-human performance in machine translation at wmt 2019. *arXiv preprint arXiv:2005.05738*.

Toral, A., Castilho, S., Hu, K., and Way, A. (2018). Attaining the unattainable? reassessing claims of human parity in neural machine translation. *arXiv preprint arXiv:1808.10432*.

A Appendix: Demographics and Supplementary Figures

Country from IP geolocation: *Site 1*: Top 20 countries are USA (12.411%), Germany (6.397%), Russia (5.501%), India (5.48%), Italy (5.044%), France (4.579%), Brazil (4.041%), Spain (3.736%), Mexico (3.293%), United Kingdom (2.829%), Vietnam (2.314%), Indonesia (2.219%), Poland (2.105%), Canada (2.018%), Ukraine (1.675%), Japan (1.618%), Argentina (1.557%), Turkey (1.462%), Netherlands (1.412%), Colombia (1.165%). *Site 2*: Top 20 countries are USA (19.047%), Germany (8.65%), France (5.109%), Italy (4.91%), India (4.719%), Russia (4.633%), Spain (3.514%), United Kingdom (3.179%), Brazil (2.917%), Canada (2.574%), Poland (2.248%), Mexico (2.212%), Netherlands (1.669%), Ukraine (1.654%), Australia (1.595%), Vietnam (1.325%), Argentina (1.257%), Japan (1.257%), China (1.143%), Turkey (1.134%).
Preferred Language: *Site 1*: Top 20 are English (46.115%), Spanish (11.831%), Russian (6.567%), French (6.021%), German (5.932%), Italian (4.624%), Portuguese (4.088%), Chinese (2.032%), Polish (1.732%), Vietnamese (1.646%), Japanese (1.407%), Arabic (1.305%), Turkish (1.03%), Dutch (0.873%), Indonesian (0.688%), Czech (0.688%), Hungarian (0.542%), Swedish (0.356%), Korean (0.253%), Ukrainian (0.25%). *Site 2*: Top 20 are English (53.679%), Spanish (8.259%), German (6.529%), Russian (5.809%), French (5.248%), Italian (4.51%), Portuguese (2.738%), Chinese (2.271%), Polish (1.828%), Arabic (1.275%), Japanese (0.97%), Vietnamese (0.92%), Dutch (0.855%), Turkish (0.77%), Czech (0.526%), Hungarian (0.461%), Korean (0.42%), Swedish (0.373%), Indonesian (0.291%), Ukrainian (0.253%).
Gender from Google Analytics: *Site 1*: 24.6% female, 75.4% male. *Site 2*: 29.2% female, 70.8% male.
Age from Google Analytics: *Site 1*: 30.14% of users are 18-24 years old, 30.44% are 25-34, 15.68% are 35-44, 11.78% are 45-54, 6.57% are 55-64, 5.40% are over 65. *Site 2*: 20.9% of users are 18-24 years old, 28.7% are 25-34 years old, 19.1% are 33-44, 13.9% are 45-54, 8.70% are 55-65, 8.70% are over 65.

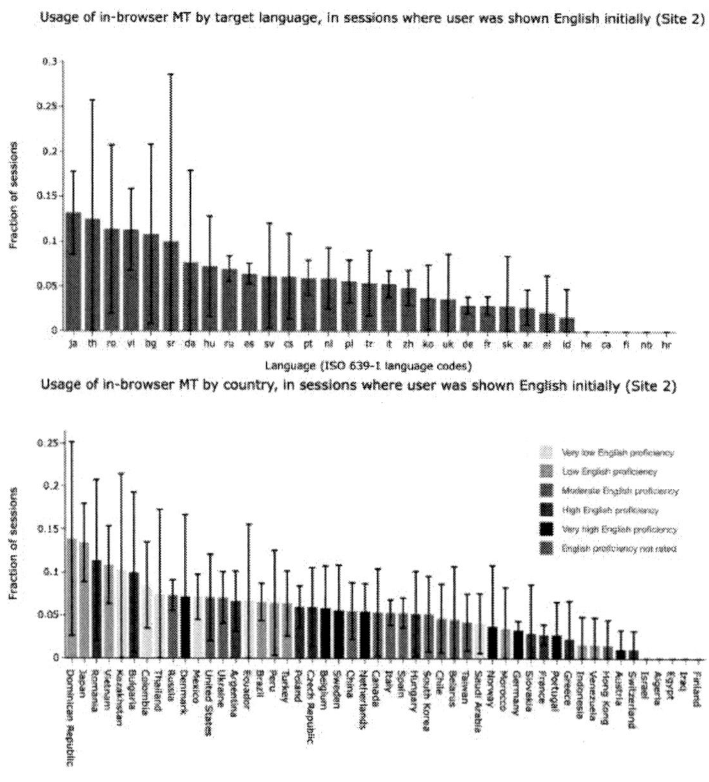

Figure 8: Use of in-browser machine translation on Site 2 for users whose preferred language is not English. Error bars show 95% confidence intervals. Top: by language. Bottom: by country.

Consistent Human Evaluation of Machine Translation across Language Pairs

Daniel Licht META AI dlicht@fb.com
Cynthia Gao META AI cynthiagao@fb.com
Janice Lam META AI janilam@fb.com
Francisco Guzmán META AI fguzman@fb.com
Mona Diab* META AI mdiab@fb.com
Philipp Koehn* META AI / Johns Hopkins University phi@jhu.edu

Abstract

Obtaining meaningful quality scores for machine translation systems through human evaluation remains a challenge given the high variability between human evaluators, partly due to subjective expectations for translation quality for different language pairs. We propose a new metric, XSTS, that is more focused on semantic equivalence. Moreover, we introduce a cross-lingual calibration method that enables more consistent assessment. We demonstrate the effectiveness of these novel contributions in large scale evaluation studies across up to 14 language pairs, with translation both into and out of English.

1 Introduction

While machine translation systems are typically evaluated with automatic metrics like BLEU (Papineni et al., 2001), the gold standard for quality assessment is evaluation of machine translation output by human evaluators. In fact, the validity of automatic metrics is justified by correlation to human evaluations.

However, in practice individual human evaluators apply very different standards when assessing machine translation output, depending on their expectation of translation quality, their exposure to machine translation output, their language abilities, the presentation of source or reference translation, and vague category descriptions like "mostly correct". This is especially a problem when the goal is to obtain meaningful scores across language pairs, to assess, for instance, if a machine translation system for any given language pair is of sufficiently high quality to be put to use.

We address this problem of high variability and cross-lingual consistency by two novel contributions: (1) a new scoring metric XSTS that is focused on meaning; and, (2) an evaluation protocol that allows for calibration of scores across evaluators and across language pairs. Our studies show that the XSTS score yields higher inter-annotator agreement compared against a 5-Point Raw Scale. We also show that our calibration leads to improved correlation of system scores to our subjective expectations of quality based on linguistic and resource aspects as well as improved correlation with automatic scores.

* Equal contribution as senior authors.

2 Related Work

The DARPA evaluation of the 1990s tasked human evaluators to assign scores from 1 to 5 to judge the fluency and adequacy of translations (White and O'Connell, 1996), with vague definitions like *much meaning* for an adequacy score of 3 or the slightly offensive *non-native English* for a fluency score of 3. This scale was also used in the first human evaluation of the Workshop on Statistical Machine Translation (WMT) (Koehn and Monz, 2006).

Note that these evaluations aim at a different goal than the one we are concerned with here: their main purpose is to rank the output of different machine translation systems against one another — without the need to report a meaningful score that is an absolute measure of their translation quality. Hence, it should come as no surprise that the WMT evaluation then moved towards pairwise comparisons of different system outputs (Callison-Burch et al., 2007). For many years, evaluators were asked to rank up to 5 system outputs against each other.

Due to the problem that for n systems, $O(n^2)$ pairwise comparisons need to be done (Bojar et al., 2016), recent WMT evaluations switched to Direct Assessment (Graham et al., 2013). Evaluators are required to indicate absolute quality of a machine translated sentence using a slider which is converted into a score on a 100 point scale. Such finer grained scores allow for easier normalization of scores between annotators. Direct Assessment is also used by Microsoft for shipping decisions (Kocmi et al., 2021). Google uses a 5-point scale to evaluate their machine translation systems but specifics have not been published.

Recently, Mariana et al. (2015) proposed the Multidimensional Quality Metrics (MQM) Framework, rooted in the need for quality assurance for professional translators, that aims at generating meaningful scores. In MQM, fine-grained error categories like *omission, register* and *capitalization* are assessed and the error counts per category are combined into a single score. Such fine-grained errors can typically only be detected in relatively high-quality translations (Freitag et al., 2021). This metric is predominantly used for quality assurance in the translation industry to evaluate translations from professional translations.

3 A New Metric: XSTS

We propose a new metric that is inspired by the Semantic Text Similarity metric (STS) used in research on paraphrase detection and textual entailment (Agirre et al., 2012). The metric emphasises adequacy rather than fluency. We do this for several reasons but mainly because we deal with many low resource language pairs where preservation of meaning during translation is a pressing challenge. Arguably, assessing fluency is also much more subjective and thus leads to higher variance. Another reason is that we are interested in evaluating the translation of social media text where the source and reference translation may be disfluent, so lack of fluency should not be counted against machine translation.

As in many previously proposed scoring rubrics, we use a 5-point scale. For a detailed definition of the meaning of each score, see Figure 1. There are various ways this metric could be used. The examples in the figure show two English sentences, such as machine translation output and a human reference translation, but our core evaluation protocol presents the source sentence and corresponding machine translation to a bilingual evaluator. Different from previous evaluation protocols, XSTS asks explicitly about meaning (semantic) correspondence, all the more while obfuscating which sentence is the source and which is the translation.

Note that the score has a fairly high bar for a score of 4: semantic equivalence, only allowing for differences in style, emphasis, and connotation. This allows us to detect differences in quality at the very high end. We experimented with both this 5 point scale and a reduced scale where the categories 4 and 5 were collapsed.

1 **The two sentences are not equivalent, share very little details, and may be about different topics. If the two sentences are about similar topics, but less than half of the core concepts mentioned are the same, then 1 is still the appropriate score.**

Example A (different topics):
Text 1: *John went horseback riding at dawn with a whole group of friends.*
Text 2: *Sunrise at dawn is a magnificent view to take in if you wake up early enough for it.*

Example B (similar/related topics):
Text 1: *The woman is playing the violin.*
Text 2: *The young lady enjoys listening to the guitar.*

2 **The two sentences share some details, but are not equivalent. Some important information related to the primary subject/verb/object differs or is missing, which alters the intent or meaning of the sentence.**

Example A (opposite polarity):
Text 1: *They flew out of the nest in groups.*
Text 2: *They flew into the nest together.*

Example B (word order changes meaning)
Text 1: *James voted for Biden.*
Text 2: *Biden voted for James.*

Example C (missing salient information):
Text 1: *"He is not a suspect anymore." John said.*
Text 2: *John said he is considered a witness but not a suspect.*

Example D (substitution/change in named entity)
Text 1: *I bought the book at Amazon.*
Text 2: *The book was purchased at Barnes and Noble by me.*

3 **The two sentences are mostly equivalent, but some unimportant details can differ. There cannot be any significant conflicts in intent or meaning between the sentences, no matter how long the sentences are.**

Example A (minor details that are not salient to the meaning):
Text 1: *In May 2010, US troops invaded Kabul.*
Text 2: *The US army invaded Kabul on May 7th last year, 2010.*

Example B (minor verb tense and/or unit of measurement differences):
Text 1: *He bought 2 LBs of rice at Whole Foods.*
Text 2: *He buy 1 KG. of rice at WholeFoods.*

Example C (small, non-conflicting differences in meaning):
Text1: *She loves eating ripe apples in the fall.*
Text2: *She usually eats ripened apple in autumn.*

Example D (omitted non-critical information, but no contradictory info introduced):
Text1: *Several of the sailors set out on a rainy Tuesday morning.*
Text2: *Several of the sailors set out on a Tuesday morning.*

4 **The two sentences are paraphrases of each other. Their meanings are near-equivalent, with no major differences or information missing. There can only be minor differences in meaning due to differences in expression (e.g., formality level, style, emphasis, potential implication, idioms, common metaphors).**

Example A (different level of formality):
Text 1: *This is Europe the so-called human rights country*
Text 2: *This is Europe, the country of alleged human rights*

Example B (added sense of urgency, advertising style):
Text1: *Special bike for more info call 0925279927*
Text2: *Special bike for more information call now 0925279927*

5 **The two sentences are exactly and completely equivalent in meaning and usage expression (e.g., formality level, style, emphasis, potential implication, idioms, common metaphors).**

Example A (same style and level of formality):
Text 1: *What's up yu'all?*
Text 2: *Howdy guys!*

Example B (disfluency is not penalized):
Text 1: *One two three apples oranges green*
Text 2: *One two three apples oranges green*

Figure 1: Part of the instruction given to evaluators to explain the XSTS scoring rubric. We also used a variant of this scale where 4 and 5 are collapsed into a single category.

Metric Study	Calibration Study	
Arabic	Amharic	Romanian
Estonian	Arabic	Sindhi
Indonesian	Azerbaijani	Slovenian
Mongolian	Bosnian	Swahili
Spanish	Georgian	Urdu
Tamil	Hindi	Zulu
	Brazilian Portuguese	

Table 1: Languages used. Both translation directions into and out of English were evaluated.

4 Cross-Lingual Consistency via Calibration Sets

Even after providing evaluators with instruction and training, they still show a large degree of variance in how they apply scores to actual examples of machine translation output. This is especially the case when different language pairs are evaluated, which necessarily requires different evaluators assessing different output.

We address this problem with a calibration set. Note that we are either evaluating X–English or English–X machine translation systems. In either case, this requires evaluators who are fluent in English. Hence, we construct a calibration set by pairing machine translation output from various X–English systems with human reference translations — so that the evaluators compare two English sentences. The sentence pairs are carefully chosen to cover the whole range of scores, based on consistent judgments from prior evaluation rounds.

Evaluators assess this fixed calibration set in addition to their actual task of assessing translations for their assigned language pair. We then compute the average score each evaluator gives to the calibration set. If this evaluator-specific calibration score is too high, then we conclude that the evaluator is generally too lenient and their scores for the actual task need to be adjusted downward, and vice versa.

There are various ways how scores for each evaluator could be adjusted. After exploring various options, we settled on a simple linear shift (with an option for moderating large calibration shifts or shifts near the edges of the scale if desired). To give an example, if the consensus score for the calibration set is 3.0 but an evaluator assigned it a score of 3.2, then we deduct 0.2 from all their scores for the actual evaluation task.

5 Study Design

We report on two large-scale human evaluation studies to assess the two novel contributions of this work. The first study compares XSTS and its variants against other evaluation methods like a raw 5-Point scale modelled (RAW) after Direct Assessment. The second study assesses the effectiveness of our calibration method.

Language Pairs We selected languages with the goal to cover both high-resource languages with good machine translation quality and low-resource languages with weaker machine translation quality. The languages also differ in writing system, morphological complexity, and other linguistic dimensions. See the Table 1 for the list of languages in our studies.

Selection of Evaluators Evaluators were selected for each language pair and they evaluated both language directions (English–X and X–English). The evaluators were professional translators who were recruited by a translation agency. They had to have at least three years of translation experience, be native speakers of the language X, high level of English proficiency, and pass through a training process (detailed documentation of the task and training examples).

We speculate, but have not yet tested, that the XSTS protocol may be employable by evaluators with less rigorous translation training than traditional DA; so long as they still have high levels of fluency in both languages being evaluated. This could potentially facilitate the evaluation of low-resource languages where qualified annotators may be difficult to source.

User Interface and Training Since we are working with language service providers who subcontract the work to professional translators who differ in their technical setup, we do not always have full control over the way text is presented to them and how they register their evaluations. Throughout our studies, the employed tools vary from simple spreadsheets to a customized annotation tool similar to the one used in WMT evaluations.

Machine Translation Systems Most of the machine translation systems used in this studies were trained in-house with fairseq (Ott et al., 2019) on public data sets at different times in 2020 and 2021, each designed to optimized translation quality given available data and technology. The most recent system, used in the calibration study, is a 100-language multilingual system, similar to the one developed for the WMT 2021 Shared Task (Tran et al., 2021).

Test Set The translated sentences to be evaluated are selected from social media messages and Wikipedia — the later being part of the FLORES test set which comprises close to 200 languages at the time of writing (Guzmán et al., 2019). Note that social media messages have the additional challenge of disfluency and creative language variation in the source sentence.

5.1 Study on Evaluation Metrics

We compare the newly proposed XSTS to RAW and variants of XSTS. We report here on an experiment that used a 4-point XSTS scale but a subsequent study with a 5-point scale confirmed the findings. In all evaluations, the identity of the translation system was hidden and sentence translations of the different systems are randomly shuffled.

Raw 5-Point Scale (RAW) In this protocol, the evaluators are required to judge translation output with respect to a source sentence on a 5-point qualitative rating scale. The evaluators render these ratings for machine translations (MT1 , MT2, MT3) and a human translation (HT0), while shown the source sentence. This method is based on source-based direct assessment (Graham et al., 2013) — however there are important differences: direct assessment uses a continuous slider scale which internally gets converted into a 100-point scale, while we adapted it to a quantized 5-point scale.

Cross Lingual Semantic Textual Similarity (XSTS) XSTS is the cross-lingual variant of STS. Evaluators indicate the level of correspondence between source and target directly. This protocol does not rely on reference translations. We apply XSTS to all directions for all translations (MT* and HT0).

Monolingual Semantic Textual Similarity (MSTS) MSTS is a protocol where the evaluators indicate the level of correspondence between two English strings, a machine translation (MT*) or human translation (HT0) and an additional human reference translation (HT1), using the XSTS scale. This evaluation was only carried out for translations into English since we have two reference translations for English (HT0, HT1) but not for other languages.

Back-translated Monolingual Semantic Textual Similarity (BT+MSTS) BT+MSTS is an attempt to make MSTS work for English-X translation when two reference translations are only available in English. Each translation from the English–X MT systems is manually back-translated into English, which allows us to compare it against the English reference

Language	Morphological complexity	Resource presence	Writing system	Inherent variants	Language family
Arabic (AR)	xxxx	High	Arabic	Yes	Semitic
Estonian (ET)	xxx	Medium	Latin	No	Uralic
Indonesian (ID)	x	Medium	Latin	Yes	Austronesian
Mongolian (MN)	xxx	Low	Cyrillic	No	Mongolic
Tamil (TA)	xxx	Low	Tamil	No	Dravidian
Spanish (ES)	xx	High	Latin	Yes	Indo-European

Table 2: Details on Languages used in the Metrics Study

translations HT1 while also allowing for scoring the back-translation of HT0. Note that the manual back-translation will unlikely have fluency problems but any failures to preserve adequacy of the machine translation system will not be recovered by the professional translator.

Post Editing with critical errors (PE) In this protocol, evaluators are required to provide the minimal necessary edits for the translations to render them correspondent to the source. Crucially however, evaluators are required to indicate the number of critical errors rendered in the post editing. The impetus behind this level of annotation is to transcend the traditional count of the number of edits needed to fix a translation. This protocol does not rely on a reference translation. Given the corrections, we computed three scores: critical edit counts, Levenshtein distance, and ChrF.

As test sets we used 250 sentences of social media messages (collected from public Facebook posts). We primarily report on results on this social media test set but an additional study on the Wikipedia test set (FLORES) confirms these findings. We evaluated two internal machine translation systems (MT0 and MT1) and translations obtained from Google Translate (MT2). See Figure 2 for details on the languages involved.

5.2 Study on Calibration

In a second study, we examined the introduction of a calibration set to create meaningful scores that can be compared across language pairs. This enables better absolute inter-direction comparison; for instance the decision if a machine translation system for a language pair is good enough to be put into production.

Evaluators judge 1012 sentence pairs for a single language pair in both language directions. In this study, we only use the XSTS score. Translations are judged against the source sentence. Machine translations are generated with a state-of-the-art multilingual machine translation system. Evaluators also judge the human reference translation similar to Fan et al. (2021). The crucial addition to the sentence pairs to be judged is a calibration set of sentence pairs that is common across all languages. It consists of 1000 pairs of a machine translation into English and a corresponding English reference translation. These sentence pairs are carefully selected to span a wide quality range, based on human-scored translations from previous evaluations where multiple evaluators agreed on the score (200 sentence pairs from each quality score).

A fair objection to using such a calibration set is that we are asking evaluators to perform two different tasks — comparing machine translation against a source sentence (English and non-English), and comparing machine translation against a reference (English and English) — but posit that they will use the same standards when making quality assessments.

Because the calibration set is fixed, its quality is fixed, and the average score each evaluator assigns to the sentence pairs in the set should be the same. Hence, we can use the actual score assigned by each evaluator and the official fixed score as the basis to make adjustments to each evaluator's score. For instance, if an evaluator gives the calibration too high score, then we detect that they are too lenient and their scores need to be corrected downward. For simplicity and robustness, we applied calibration corrections after taking majority scores across annotators for an evaluation item; correcting for the overall bias of the group rather than a single individual.

Note that there is also a second fixed point that could be used for score adjustment: the average score each evaluator gives to the reference translation. These professionally translated and vetted translations should receive high scores, and we could adjust each evaluator's scores so that the average adjusted score for reference translations is a fixed value. The underlying assumption here is that reference translations are of identical quality across all language pairs. We opted against utilizing this point, in favor of the monolingual calibration set, because knowing how harsh or generous our annotators are on a set of only high quality translations does not as well inform us as to how they will behave on the intermediate or low quality translations which will likely be in the machine translations they are evaluating. This was backed up by lower correlations between automatic metrics and XSTS when using these human reference translations than when using our calibration set. Additionally such reference translations can be expensive and time consuming if applied to a new use case.

The calibration study generates a set of data points for each assigned score that contain the following information: (1) language pair, (2) machine translation system, reference translation, or calibration set, (3) evaluator, (4) sentence pair, and (5) raw XSTS score.

So far, we discussed calibration to adjust the scores for each evaluator. Our real goal, however, is to adjust scores for each language pair. Hence, we aggregate the individual data points into the following statistics: (1) language pair, (2) machine translation system, reference translation, or calibration set, and (3) average of median raw XSTS scores. We first take judgments of different evaluators for the same translation and determine the median value. Then, we average these scores for each combination of language pair and translation source (machine translation, reference translation, calibration set).

Based on this, we determine an adjustment function

$$f_{\text{language-pair}} : \text{raw-score} \rightarrow \text{adjusted-score} \quad (1)$$

The simplest form of this function is a linear shift $f(x) = x + \alpha$ where α is the adjustment parameter. To ensure that adjusted scores agree on the consensus set, we compute α for each language pair as

$$\alpha_{\text{language-pair}} = \text{consensus-score} - \text{avg-median-score(language-pair,calibration-set)} \quad (2)$$

With two fix points (score on calibration set and score on human reference translations), we use an adjustment formula $f(x) = \beta x + \alpha$ and determine the parameters α and β in a similar fashion.

5.3 Proposed Robustness Improvements

As we look towards applying the calibration methodology described above in a variety of circumstances, there are a few undesirable edge cases which we may wish to better handle.

The first of these are large calibration shifts. Our analysis has suggested that when annotators rate a calibration set especially low or high, this is increasingly an indication that their behavior or bias on the calibration set is less indicative of their behavior or bias on the primary translation task, and that the calibration factor may be too large or in error. Large calibration scores ($\alpha > 0.5$) tend to over-correct. Internal experiments limiting the magnitude of the calibration score found an increase in correlation between XSTS scores and automatic metrics (ChrF++, spmBLEU) when applying a calibration shift cap between 0.5 and 1.0 (smaller than

0.5 and we begin to chip way the benefits of calibration and the correlation decreases). To reduce this affect we propose to introduce a moderating term into the calibration calculation.

The second case of concern occurs near the boundaries of the scale. Imagine a simple case where annotators give a mean score of 4.8 to a translation model. But the same annotators are somewhat harsh on the calibration set, giving it a score of 2.7, resulting in a calibration correction term $\alpha = +0.3$. Applying calibration in this case yields $4.8 + 0.3 = 5.1$, overshooting the end of our 5-point quality scale. An analogous problem can occur at the bottom of the scale. Moreover, small differences in scores near the top of the XSTS quality scale are arguable more meaningful than such differences in the middle (a translation model moving from 4.6 to 4.8 may be of more practical significance than a model moving from 2.4 to 2.6 if the scores are accurate). We would like to be more cautious of overstating model quality near the top of the scale, in particular. To eliminate the possibility of scores being calibrated off the evaluation scale, and to moderate calibrations towards the top end we propose introducing another moderating term to the calibration formula; this one multiplicative the previously moderated score.

- **Simple Calibration**: $f(x) = x + \alpha$
- **Moderated Calibration**: $f(x) = x + EA$

where

$$A = \tanh(\alpha)$$

$$E = \begin{cases} -\tanh(x - s_{\text{top}}) = +\tanh(s_{\text{top}} - x) & \text{if } \alpha > 0 \\ 0 & \text{if } \alpha = 0 \\ +\tanh(x - s_{\text{bottom}}) & \text{if } \alpha < 0 \end{cases}$$

For our 5 point implementation of the XSTS protocol, $s_{top} = 5$ and $s_{bottom} = 1$.

We selected hyperbolic tangent as our moderating factor because it has the behavior of approaching $f(x) = x$ for small x, especially $x < 0.5$, and asymptotically approaching 1 for larger values. This behavior allows it to both moderate large calibration shifts as well as to act as the moderation function as points approach the end of our scale. Additionally we had the requirement that the function be monotonic between s_{top} and s_{bottom}, and never push calibrated scores outside of that same range. Other moderating terms may also be possible.

We are currently piloting this more robust form of calibration and will share results with its application in the upcoming No Language Left Behind paper (NLLB Team et al., 2022).

6 Results

6.1 Evaluation Metrics

While automatic metrics are typically evaluated against gold standard human evaluation, we do not have such a gold standard when assessing different human evaluation protocols. Instead, we appeal to desirable aspects of human evaluation and assess these. Different evaluators should give the same translation the same score (inter-evaluator reliability). Evaluations should properly detect the quality difference between machine translation and gold standard human translation (meaningfulness). The amount of human effort for evaluations is also a significant factor (cost).

Inter-Evaluator Reliability Reliability measures the reproducibility of the measurements obtained during evaluation. Variability in ratings is an indication of complexity of the evaluation, lack of clarity in the guidelines rendering it highly subjective. It should be noted that evaluating translations is inherently subjective, yet protocols that are able to transcend the inherent subjectivity should yield more reproducible measures leading to more reliable protocols.

	AR	ES	ET	ID	MN	TA	AVG	Rank
X–English								
RAW	0.36	0.39	0.26	0.50	0.16	0.40	0.34	3
PE	0.32	0.63	0.54	0.09	0.11	0.15	0.31	4
XSTS	0.64	0.29	0.50	0.12	0.19	0.81	0.43	2
MSTS	0.57	0.48	0.46	0.56	0.52	0.62	0.54	1
English–X								
RAW	0.50	0.63	0.67	0.35	0.23	0.74	0.52	3
PE	0.54	0.56	0.56	0.45	0.37	0.68	0.53	2
XSTS	0.85	0.60	0.49	0.99	0.57	0.50	0.67	1
BT+MSTS	0.46	0.43	0.47	0.43	0.48	0.46	0.46	4

Table 3: **Fleiss Kappa Inter-Evaluator Reliability** averaged across HT0, MT0, MT1, and MT2 per protocol. AVG indicates average Kappa across all language directions per protocol. Rank is based on AVG, the highest rank (1) is a reflection of the protocol that yielded the inter-annotator agreement.

We use Fleiss Kappa to measure three-way inter-evaluator reliability scores. Kappa numbers above 0.4 typically indicate moderate to excellent agreement (the higher the better). Table 3 shows the average Kappa across all evaluators for all translations HT0, MT0, MT1, MT2 for each of the protocols.

In Table 6, we also note the overall average Kappa per protocol across all languages (AVG). MSTS is the highest scoring protocol as it exhibits the highest average Kappa across languages per protocol. BT+MSTS also performs well. For the protocols that apply to both language directions XSTS (0.43 and 0.67, average 0.55) ranks above RAW (0.34 and 0.52, average 0.43) and PE (0.31 and 0.53, average 0.42).

Score difference between human reference translation and machine translation A simple test of the meaningfulness of each protocol is whether we can clearly see a distinction between Human level translation quality (manually yielded by humans) and our Machine Translation quality. If a protocol cannot meaningfully distinguish between HT and MT then it will not be very useful as a quality measure. This measure makes two crucial assumptions: (1) human translation is indeed excellent and (2) the data selected for annotation evaluation is reflective of various levels of quality for the machine translation. Accordingly, both within each language, and overall between languages, we expect to see a clear progression of: *human translation (HT0) > better machine translation (MT1) > worse machine translation (MT2).*

RAW, XSTS, and PE passed this test and were reasonably good at separating the three types of translation. But, at least with our sample sizes MSTS and BT-MSTS had a very difficult time distinguishing between HT0 and MT1 or MT1 and MT2, even in cases where the other protocols did not have that difficulty.

6.2 Calibration

The goal of calibration is the adjust raw human evaluation scores so that they reflect meaningful assessment the quality of the machine translation system for a given language pair. When comparing different adjustment methods, we are faced with the problem, that there is no real ground truth. However, we do have some intuitions under which circumstances our machine translation systems will likely do well. More training data, the more related languages are to English in terms of proximity in the language family tree, low degree of syntactic and semantic divergence, or the same writing system should be correlated with better machine translation

Language	Language family	Writing system	Linguistic properties		Training size
Amharic	Semitic	Ethiopian	SOV	fusional	2,011,822
Arabic	Semitic	Arabic	VSO	fusional	51,979,453
Bosnian	Balto-Slavic	Latin	SVO	fusional	14,325,281
Bulgarian	Balto-Slavic	Cyrillic	SVO	fusional	51,044,962
Georgian	Georgian-Zan	Georgian	SOV	agglutinative	950,086
Hindi	Indo-Iranian	Devanagari	SOV	fusional	8,607,078
North Azerbaijani	Southern Turkic	Latin	SOV	agglutinative	869,224
Portuguese (Brazil)	Italic	Latin	SVO	fusional	57,210,510
Romanian	Italic	Latin	SVO	fusional	63,737,708
Sindhi	Indo-Iranian	Arabic	SOV	fusional	420,354
Slovenian	Balto-Slavic	Latin	SVO	fusional	30,300,765
Swahili	Volta-Congo	Latin	SVO	agglutinative	5,529,619
Urdu	Indo-Iranian	Arabic	SOV	fusional	4,767,174
Zulu	Volta-Congo	Latin	SVO	agglutinative	4,117,686

Table 4: Languages used in the calibration study and their properties. Training corpus size is number of sentence pairs of the publicly available parallel data used for training. Note that sometimes a large part of the training corpus is of low quality.

quality, in both English–X and X–English translation systems (Birch et al., 2008). See Table 4 for such details for the languages used in the study. Note that the training data comes of sources of varying quality. For instance, the bulk of the Romanian data comes from Open Subtitles — a notoriously noisy corpus.

Additionally, we can also compute the correlation to automatic scores such as the BLEU score. Of course, BLEU scores are notoriously meaningless, for instance they are highly dependent on the literalness of the human reference translation and typically lower when translating into morphologically richer targeted languages. But note that we are using a test set that is shared across all languages. Thus, BLEU scores for translation systems from any language into English are scored against exactly the same English reference translation.

Table 5 shows how the scores for the language pairs were adjusted from the raw baseline scores by (1) the consensus calibration score, (2) fixing the human translation score to 4.687 (determined by averaging scores given to human translations across all language pairs), and (3) both. Intuitively, one of the easiest language is Portuguese due large amounts of data and closeness to English. After adjusting with the calibration score Portuguese-English ranks above Hindi–English and Arabic–English.

The second method to assess the effectiveness of our calibration methods is by computing correlation. We measure correlation with 3 different statistical methods: Pearson's R, r^2, and LinReg[1]. Results are shown in Table 6 and an illustration in Figure 2. Independent of the correlation method, or if we compute correlation into English, out of English, or both, the calibration method of adjusting the score based on the calibration set yields the highest correlation, clearly outperforming the baseline of unadjusted scores.

7 Conclusion

We introduced two novel contribution to the human evaluation of machine translation for multiple language pairs and validated their effectiveness in industrial-scale user studies: We proposed

[1]The "LinReg" score was calculated as the mean r2 goodness of fit metric for training a simple sklearn linear regression model on spmBLEU scores and the calibrated XSTS scores using k-fold Cross-Validation with a 1:1 Train/test split, with the cross-validation split randomly bootstraped 5000 times.

X–English				English-X			
RAW	CS	HT	CS+HT	RAW	CS	HT	CS+HT
4.94 Hindi	4.73 Bosnian	4.64 Hindi	4.64 Hindi	4.95 Hindi	4.88 Bosnian	4.68 Bosnian	4.68 Bosnian
4.88 Slovenian	4.65 Portuguese	4.57 Slovenian	4.56 Slovenian	4.93 Slovenian	4.82 Portuguese	4.67 Hindi	4.67 Hindi
4.75 Bosnian	4.64 Hindi	4.51 Portuguese	4.53 Portuguese	4.90 Bosnian	4.74 Arabic	4.65 Portuguese	4.65 Portuguese
4.62 Arabic	4.58 Arabic	4.49 Bosnian	4.52 Bosnian	4.79 Arabic	4.66 Hindi	4.63 Slovenian	4.62 Slovenian
4.61 Portuguese	4.47 Slovenian	4.40 Arabic	4.43 Arabic	4.78 Portuguese	4.56 Bulgarian	4.58 Bulgarian	4.58 Bulgarian
4.56 Sindhi	4.34 Sindhi	4.30 Sindhi	4.31 Sindhi	4.41 Swahili	4.52 Slovenian	4.56 Arabic	4.58 Arabic
3.98 Swahili	4.19 Bulgarian	4.19 Bulgarian	4.19 Bulgarian	4.12 Romanian	4.41 Swahili	4.38 Swahili	4.38 Swahili
3.96 Urdu	3.98 Swahili	4.14 Urdu	4.03 Urdu	4.07 Bulgarian	4.27 Romanian	4.26 Romanian	4.26 Romanian
3.74 Romanian	3.89 Romanian	3.98 Swahili	3.98 Swahili	3.97 Urdu	3.86 Urdu	4.14 Urdu	4.03 Urdu
3.70 Bulgarian	3.86 Urdu	3.83 Romanian	3.86 Romanian	3.62 Zulu	3.73 Zulu	3.76 Zulu	3.75 Zulu
2.90 Amharic	2.98 Amharic	3.12 Azerbaijani	2.98 Amharic	3.15 Amharic	3.23 Amharic	3.12 Amharic	3.21 Amharic
2.80 Zulu	2.91 Zulu	3.00 Zulu	2.91 Zulu	2.99 Georgian	2.96 Georgian	3.07 Georgian	2.96 Georgian
2.66 Azerbaijani	2.91 Azerbaijani	2.92 Amharic	2.91 Azerbaijani	2.24 Azerbaijani	2.50 Azerbaijani	2.63 Azerbaijani	2.46 Azerbaijani
1.04 Georgian	1.02 Georgian	1.12 Georgian	0.90 Georgian	2.16 Sindhi	1.94 Sindhi	1.89 Sindhi	1.97 Sindhi

Table 5: Adjustment of average XSTS scores based on fixing the score on the calibration set (CS), the human reference translation (HS) or both (CS+HS), compared to unadjusted scores. The languages Hindi, Portuguese, Arabic, Bulgarian, and Swahili are highlighted. CS adjustment ranks them more closely to our expectations based on corpus size and language similarity.

Method	**Pearson's R**			r^2			**LinReg**		
	X-EN	EN-X	both	X-EN	EN-X	both	X-EN	EN-X	both
baseline	.897	.711	.797	.804	.506	.635	.715	.288	.566
CS	**.946**	**.772**	**.854**	**.895**	**.595**	**.730**	**.833**	**.342**	**.650**
HT	.926	.749	.834	.858	.561	.696	.767	.276	.604
CS+HT	.934	.757	.839	.874	.573	.704	.803	.283	.612

Table 6: Correlation of XSTS scores with spmBLEU scores fixing the score on the calibration set (CS), the human reference translation (HS) or both (CS+HS), compared to raw scores.

the scoring metric XSTS which is focused on meaning and introduced a calibration method that allows us to achieve meaningful scores that rank the quality of machine translation systems for different language pairs so that they match more closely with our intuition (plausibility) and automatic scores.

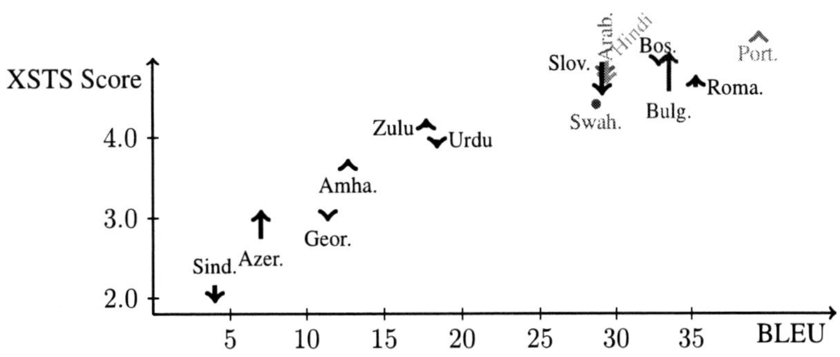

Figure 2: Adjusted X–English scores using calibration set increases correlation with BLEU.

References

Agirre, E., Cer, D., Diab, M., and Gonzalez-Agirre, A. (2012). SemEval-2012 task 6: A pilot on semantic textual similarity. In **SEM 2012: The First Joint Conference on Lexical and Computational Semantics – Volume 1: Proceedings of the main conference and the shared task, and Volume 2: Proceedings of the Sixth International Workshop on Semantic Evaluation (SemEval 2012)*, pages 385–393, Montréal, Canada. Association for Computational Linguistics.

Birch, A., Osborne, M., and Koehn, P. (2008). Predicting success in machine translation. In *Proceedings of the 2008 Conference on Empirical Methods in Natural Language Processing*, pages 745–754, Honolulu, Hawaii. Association for Computational Linguistics.

Bojar, O., Chatterjee, R., Federmann, C., Graham, Y., Haddow, B., Huck, M., Jimeno Yepes, A., Koehn, P., Logacheva, V., Monz, C., Negri, M., Névéol, A., Neves, M., Popel, M., Post, M., Rubino, R., Scarton, C., Specia, L., Turchi, M., Verspoor, K., and Zampieri, M. (2016). Findings of the 2016 conference on machine translation. In *Proceedings of the First Conference on Machine Translation: Volume 2, Shared Task Papers*, pages 131–198, Berlin, Germany. Association for Computational Linguistics.

Callison-Burch, C., Fordyce, C., Koehn, P., Monz, C., and Schroeder, J. (2007). (meta-) evaluation of machine translation. In *Proceedings of the Second Workshop on Statistical Machine Translation*, pages 136–158, Prague, Czech Republic. Association for Computational Linguistics.

Fan, A., Bhosale, S., Schwenk, H., Ma, Z., El-Kishky, A., Goyal, S., Baines, M., Celebi, O., Wenzek, G., Chaudhary, V., Goyal, N., Birch, T., Liptchinsky, V., Edunov, S., Auli, M., and Joulin, A. (2021). Beyond english-centric multilingual machine translation. *Journal of Machine Learning Research*, 22(107):1–48.

Freitag, M., Foster, G., Grangier, D., Ratnakar, V., Tan, Q., and Macherey, W. (2021). Experts, Errors, and Context: A Large-Scale Study of Human Evaluation for Machine Translation. *Transactions of the Association for Computational Linguistics*, 9:1460–1474.

Graham, Y., Baldwin, T., Moffat, A., and Zobel, J. (2013). Continuous measurement scales in human evaluation of machine translation. In *Proceedings of the 7th Linguistic Annotation Workshop and Interoperability with Discourse*, pages 33–41, Sofia, Bulgaria. Association for Computational Linguistics.

Guzmán, F., Chen, P.-J., Ott, M., Pino, J., Lample, G., Koehn, P., Chaudhary, V., and Ranzato, M. (2019). The FLORES evaluation datasets for low-resource machine translation: Nepali–English and Sinhala–English. In *Proceedings of the 2019 Conference on Empirical Methods in Natural Language Processing and the 9th International Joint Conference on Natural Language Processing (EMNLP-IJCNLP)*, pages 6098–6111, Hong Kong, China. Association for Computational Linguistics.

Kocmi, T., Federmann, C., Grundkiewicz, R., Junczys-Dowmunt, M., Matsushita, H., and Menezes, A. (2021). To ship or not to ship: An extensive evaluation of automatic metrics for machine translation. In *Proceedings of the Sixth Conference on Machine Translation*, pages 478–494, Online. Association for Computational Linguistics.

Koehn, P. and Monz, C. (2006). Manual and automatic evaluation of machine translation between European languages. In *Proceedings on the Workshop on Statistical Machine Translation*, pages 102–121, New York City. Association for Computational Linguistics.

Mariana, V., Cox, T., and Melby, A. (2015). The Multidimensional Quality Metrics (MQM) framework: a new framework for translation quality assessment. *The Journal of Specialised Translation*, pages 137–161.

NLLB Team, Costa-jussà, M. R., Cross, J., Çelebi, O., Elbayad, M., Heafield, K., Heffernan, K., Kalbassi, E., Lam, J., Licht, D., Maillard, J., Sun, A., Wang, S., Wenzek, G., Youngblood, A., Akula, B., Barrault, L., Gonzalez, G. M., Hansanti, P., Hoffman, J., Jarrett, S., Sadagopan, K. R., Rowe, D., Spruit, S., Tran, C., Andrews, P., Ayan, N. F., Bhosale, S., Edunov, S., Fan, A., Gao, C., Goswami, V., Guzmán, F., Koehn, P., Mourachko, A., Ropers, C., Saleem, S., Schwenk, H., and Wang, J. (2022). No language left behind: Scaling human-centered machine translation.

Ott, M., Edunov, S., Baevski, A., Fan, A., Gross, S., Ng, N., Grangier, D., and Auli, M. (2019). fairseq: A fast, extensible toolkit for sequence modeling. In *Proceedings of the 2019 Conference of the North American Chapter of the Association for Computational Linguistics (Demonstrations)*, pages 48–53, Minneapolis, Minnesota. Association for Computational Linguistics.

Papineni, K., Roukos, S., Ward, T., and Zhu, W.-J. (2001). BLEU: a method for automatic evaluation of machine translation. Technical Report RC22176(W0109-022), IBM Research Report.

Tran, C., Bhosale, S., Cross, J., Koehn, P., Edunov, S., and Fan, A. (2021). Facebook AI's WMT21 news translation task submission. In *Proceedings of the Sixth Conference on Machine Translation*, pages 205–215, Online. Association for Computational Linguistics.

White, J. S. and O'Connell, T. A. (1996). Adaptation of the DARPA machine translation evlauation paradigm to end-to-end systems. In *Conference of the Association for Machine Translation in the Americas*, Montreal, Canada.

Evaluating Machine Translation in Cross-lingual E-Commerce Search

Bryan Zhang bryzhang@amazon.com
Liling Tan lilingt@amazon.com
Amita Misra misrami@amazon.com
Amazon.com

Abstract

Multilingual query localization is integral to modern e-commerce. While machine translation is widely used to translate e-commerce queries, evaluation of query translation in the context of the down-stream search task is overlooked. This study proposes a search ranking-based evaluation framework with an edit-distance based search metric to evaluate machine translation impact on cross-lingual information retrieval for e-commerce search query translation, The framework demonstrate evaluation of machine translation for e-commerce search at scale and the proposed metric is strongly associated with traditional machine translation and traditional search relevance-based metrics.

1 Introduction

Multilingual search capability is essential for modern e-commerce product discovery (Lowndes and Vasudevan, 2021). Localization of e-commerce sites have led users to expect search engines to handle multilingual queries. Recent proposals of cross-lingual information retrieval handles multilingual queries and language-agnostic cross-borders product indexing have gained traction with neural search engines (Hui et al., 2017; McDonald et al., 2018; Nigam et al., 2019a; Lu et al., 2021; Li et al., 2021), but legacy e-commerce search indices are still built on monolingual product information and support for multilingual search is bridged using machine translation (Nie, 2010; Rücklé et al., 2019; Saleh and Pecina, 2020; Bi et al., 2020; Jiang et al., 2020).

Machine translation (MT) is notoriously hard to evaluate manually; *human evaluation is slow, expensive and inconsistent* (Pierce and Carroll, 1966; Callison-Burch et al., 2007; Graham et al., 2013; Tan et al., 2015; Scarton and Specia, 2016; Freitag et al., 2021). Automated machine translation evaluation metrics have evolved from simple word error rates (Levenshtein et al., 1966; Tillmann et al., 1997) to modern string based metrics that usually ignores the source inputs and uses a single reference (Papineni et al., 2002; Doddington, 2002; Banerjee and Lavie, 2005; Popović, 2015). Neural evaluation metrics (Vela and Tan, 2015; Sellam et al., 2020; Thompson and Post, 2020; Rei et al., 2020) have gain recent popularity as they attempt to incorporate human annotations and multi-references through supervised learning. Although neural metrics have shown to agree more with human evaluation, they are built off language models that introduces new biases (Amrhein and Sennrich, 2022).

Despite the usefulness of evaluation metrics, machine translation is often used as interim application and objectives of the downstream tasks could have varying levels of tolerance of the inherent translation quality. Keeping the actual utility of machine translation in mind, extrinsic task-based evaluations were developed for spoken-language systems (Thomas, 1999; Akiba et al., 2004; Schneider et al., 2010; Anastasopoulos et al., 2021; Roy et al., 2021), information extraction (Sudo et al., 2004; Laoudi et al., 2006), automatic post-editing (Chatterjee et al., 2015, 2017) and domain-specific translation that requires different fidelity requirements (Cuong et al., 2016; Song et al., 2019; Li et al., 2020).

Information retrieval evaluation usually involves human-annotated relevance labels of search results candidates. Industrially, the scale of annotating a representative sample is impractical and can only serve as anecdotal evidence of search quality. As a proxy for human annotations, it is common to use behavioral signals from clicks and purchases (Wu et al., 2018). However, these behavioral signals pose a cold-start problem where such information is unavailable for newly established marketplaces.

In this paper, we examine the evaluation of machine translation of search query in the context of cross-lingual e-commerce search. We propose:

1. a **rank-based evaluation framework** to evaluate MT in Cross-lingual information retrieval (CLIR) through ranking-based search metrics using behavioral signals (from the marketplace of the target language) as a proxy to relevance information without any human annotation; this framework can be used to create for e-commerce CLIR test sets at scale.

2. a novel **edit-distance based metric** using Levenshtein edit distance to measure the divergence between the search results from machine translated queries and the search results from the human translated queries, this metric does not need any relevance information.

The rest of the paper is structured as follows. Section 2 gives an overview of the proposed ranking-based evaluation framework and edit-distance based evaluation framework for e-commerce Cross-lingual Information Retrieval (CLIR). Section 3 describes the experiment setup on the test set used to evaluate Machine Translation (MT) models tuned on search data and the edit-distance metric hyper-parameters. Section 4 presents our experiment results and analysis of the association between MT metric, traditional nDCG and the Levenshtein edit-distance based metric proposed in this paper. Section 5 presents related work and Section 6 concludes the paper.

2 Cross-Lingual Information Retrieval (CLIR) Evaluation Framework for E-commerce Search

Different from static test sets in academia, industrial search applications are dynamic as user queries and behavioral signals change with world trends. Moreover, product inventory is dynamic, changes often and quickly.

Previous study Sloto et al. (2018) proposes the traditional Normalized Discounted Cumulative Gain (nDCG) for CLIR using all search results from the reference translation as relevance ground truth to compute nDCG for MT translation (aka nDCG-MT). However, their approach imposes a strong assumption that the top-k search results from reference translation are all relevant to the query and relevance is inversely scaled by the ranking of the results.

Although behavioral signals from users' clicks and purchases are useful proxy (Wu et al., 2018) to expensive human relevance annotations, these are dynamic and change according to product life cycle and seasonal business trends. These behavioral signals need to be updated at regular cadence to accurately represent relevance information needed to compute search metrics.

We introduce a ranking-based evaluation framework through search ranking metrics using behavioral signals as a proxy to relevance information without any human annotation; and a novel edit-distance based framework to measure the difference in search candidate ranks between the human and machine translated queries without the need for relevance information.

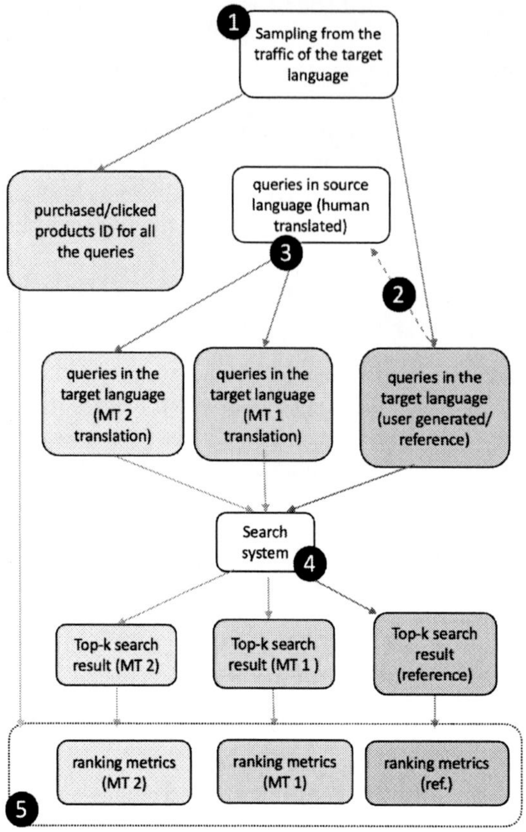

Figure 1: Ranking-based Evaluation Framework to Evaluate MT in E-commerce CLIR

To our best knowledge, there is no systematic study on cross-lingual information retrieval study for e-commerce search that neither requires ground-truth click/purchase information nor human annotated relevance data.

2.1 Ranking-based Evaluation Framework

Figure 1 illustrates the ranking-based evaluation framework to evaluate machine translation in the context of cross-lingual information retrieval for e-commerce.

1. Create a sample of query data from the historical search traffic in the target language (the language that the search index is built on).[1] *We refer to these queries as Q_{ref}.*

    (a) To allow computation of traditional relevance metrics, record the clicks and/or purchase product IDs associated with the queries, if they are available. *We refer to the products IDs associated with the query and their click/purchase frequency as P_{id} and P_{freq}.*

[1]We recommend to sample that queries from the top 30%, bottom 30% and the middle 40% in frequency bins to better simulate the user traffic.

2. Create human reference translation of the search queries sample in the source language (the language that users will be searching in). *We refer to these human translated queries as* Q_{src}.

3. Translate the Q_{src} with the different MT models in consideration, e.g. MT1 and MT2 systems. *We refer to these machine translated queries as* Q_{mt1} *and* Q_{mt2}.

4. Search for the respective candidate products using the machine translated queries Q_{mt1}, Q_{mt2} and original Q_{ref}; retrieving top-k search results respectively, R_{mt1}, R_{mt2} and R_{ref}.

5. Use R_{mt1}, R_{mt2} and R_{ref} to directly compute edit-distance based evaluation metric (refer to section 2.2). If available, additionally use P_{id} and P_{freq} (as ground truth) with R_{mt1}, R_{mt2} and R_{ref} to compute traditional relevance based metrics such as nDCG.

We propose the above framework to evaluate machine translation in the context of Cross-lingual Information Retrieval (CLIR) for e-commerce queries. Using clicks and purchase relevance information P_{id} and P_{freq} as ground truth, we can compute an upper-bound for traditional search metrics from R_{ref}.

We provide an example of how an evaluation data can be created using the proposed ranking-based framework to evaluate a Spanish to English translation model:

Step 1: Given a sample query in the target language that the search index is built on, e.g. "*turn signal bulb*", Q_{ref}, we first extract the clicks and purchase product IDs associated with the query (P_{id} and P_{freq}).

Step 2: Next, we collect the human reference translation for the query "*foco para luz direccional*" and use that as (Q_{src})

Step 3: Then, we translate Q_{src} with MT1 and MT2 translation models, e.g. "*turn signal light bulb*" as Q_{mt1} and "*bulb for directional light*" as Q_{mt2}

Step 4: We put the translated queries, Q_{mt1} and Q_{mt2}, and the original English query, Q_{ref}, through the e-commerce search engine to retrieve the product search results R_{mt1}, R_{mt2} and R_{ref}

Step 5: Finally, we can compute the traditional search metrics, e.g. nDCG, with the R_{mt1}, R_{mt2} and R_{ref} using P_{id} and P_{freq} as relevance ground truth.

Using the search results from Step 4, the next section introduces the edit-distance based CLIR metric in additional to the traditional search metrics in Step 5.

2.2 Edit-distance based Evaluation metric without Relevance Information

In cold-start situations, clicks and purchases behavioral data is not available making it impossible to compute relevance based metric for machine translation in CLIR setting. Hence, we propose a novel edit-distance based evaluation framework using edit-distance based metric to approximate search performance without the need of relevance information.

Using the search results from the reference translation R_{ref} as a silver standard, we formulate the problem of measuring difference between the product candidates R_{ref} and R_{mt}. Edit-distance based similarity between R_{ref} and R_{mt} is computed by treating each product candidate like a character in a string. In short, we expect the search results of a good MT system not to diverge much from the search results produced by the reference translation.

We propose to use Levenshtein distance (Levenshtein et al. (1966)) to model this divergence. Levenshtein distance (Levenshtein et al., 1966) is widely used to measure string sequence difference, e.g. for string correction (Navarro, 2001). Any distance algorithm in effect

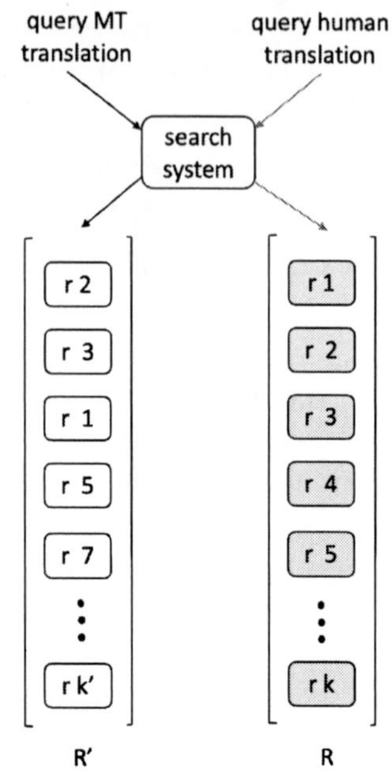

Figure 2: Edit-distance based Metric

would work but Levenshtein distance has more advantages over some of other distance metrics: we observe that it is common that some products are not shared by the two search results returned from different query translations of the same source query. Similarity metrics such as Spearman's rank correlation coefficient (Daniel (1990)) and Kendall Tau (Kendall (1938)) measure the ranking / ordering similarity of products only shared by two search results, Jaccard similarity coefficient (Jaccard (1912)) is a set-based similarity measure without consideration of the ranking/ ordering of the products in the search results. The Levenshtein distance (Levenshtein et al. (1966)) has the edit operations of insertions, deletions or substitutions, those edit operations can reflect both the products discrepancy between two search results, and also the ranking/ordering difference of the shared products in the search results.

Figure 2 illustrates the usage of the Levenshtein distance on search results. Formally, let R be the top-K search result returned from reference query translation and R' is from the MT query translation. Then we compute the edits (deletion, insertion and substitution) needed to make R' become R. Less edits indicates better search performance.[2]

3 Experimental Setup

Language pairs and locales: We select 4 language pairs from two e-commerce locales for our experiments, they are:

- Spanish-English (es-en) and Hebrew-English (he-en) in the US marketplace and
- English-German (en-de) and Polish-German (pl-de) in the German marketplace

Test data: The test data is created as described Step 1 and Step 2 from Section 2.1 as proposed in 2.1. The test set comprises 4000 queries per marketplace each translated into their respective

[2]The best possible score to achieve is when the $R' = R$ that results in a score of 0.0.

language pairs. To compare our proposed framework and metric with traditional relevance based evaluation, we also stored the purchased product IDs associated with the queries.

Machine Translation (MT) models: We trained two models per language pair to compare (i) a *generic MT* system trained on general news and internal crawled data with (ii) a domain-specific MT that is fined tuned on human translated search queries and synthetically generated query translations through back-translation. These in-house MT models are trained on proprietary data using vanilla transformer architecture (Vaswani et al., 2017) with Sockeye MT toolkit (Domhan et al., 2020).

Metric hyper-parameters: We set K to 16 for the top-k search results, using the top-16 products in the search results to compute nDCG@16 and Levenshtein edit-distance metric (Lev@16); the edit cost for Levenshtein is set uniformly at 1 for substitution, deletion, and insertion.

4 Results and Analysis

Language	Model	↑ Bleu	↑ nDCG@16	↓ Lev@16	Upper Bound (nDCG@16)
es-en	Generic	51.69	0.46	10.62	0.60
	Search	**54.04**	**0.53**	**10.23**	
he-en	Generic	48.25	0.43	11.49	0.60
	Search	**56.12**	**0.47**	**10.00**	
en-de	Generic	42.59	0.45	11.23	0.62
	Search	**63.08**	**0.54**	**7.91**	
pl-de	Generic	35.62	0.39	12.51	0.62
	Search	**56.24**	**0.48**	**9.49**	

Table 1: MT quality metrics, ranking metrics and distance-based metrics for all the MT models

For the purpose of this paper, we are less concerned with the accuracy of the MT models and more interested in the difference in the MT quality as per measured by traditional MT metrics and their evaluation based on our proposed framework. Thus the brevity in the model description. Table 1 presents the traditional BLEU [3] machine translation evaluation metric, normalized discounted cumulative gain with top-16 search results (nDCG@16) with behavioral signal-purchased product IDs as a proxy to relevance for computation, and the proposed Levenshtein edit-distance based CLIR metric proposed in this paper (Lev@16).

As an upper-bound reference, Spanish to English (*es-en*) and Hebrew to English (*he-en*) achieve an nDCG@16 score of 0.60 when using the reference translation that produces the R_{ref} search results. Likewise, English to German (*en-de*) and Polish to German models (*pl-de*), they achieve an nDCG@16 score of 0.62 for their respective R_{ref}.

We can use these upper-bounds to expect the possible improvements that can be made to the machine translation in the cross-lingual IR setting. For example, *es-en* language pair has an 0.53 nDCG score while *he-en* in the same marketplace scores at 0.47, we can expect that there is more room for improvement for the *he-en*, given that the reference translation R_{ref} achieved a score of 0.60.

Juxtaposing the generic and search MT models, we expect the search models to perform better given the domain-specific tuning. The difference in machine translation performance as

[3] Sacrebleu version 2.0.0 (Post, 2018)

measured by BLEU in Table 1 is correspondingly reflected in the relevance-based and edit-distance based search metrics. Most notably, the Polish to German model differs in BLEU score for generic and search variants by over 20 BLEU and nDCG@16 improved by +0.09 and Lev@16 improved from 12.5 to 9.5, (25% improvements for both nDCG and Lev).

4.1 Correlation between MT, relevance-based and Edit-distance metric

In order to understand the proposed edit-distance based metric with regard to the MT and search metrics, we further conduct a correlation study of the following three metrics: BLEU, nDCG and Levenstein Distance.

The Pearson's R correlation values between the traditional machine translation metric (BLEU), relevance-based search metric (nDCG@16) and edit-distance based search metric (Lev@16) of the Search MT and Generic MT models are presented in Table 2 and 3.[4], the nDCG is scaled to 0-100 for the computation convenience. As Levenshtein measures of the divergence between the search results from human query translation and MT query translation, we use the absolute value of ΔnDCG between MT and human query translations for this correlation study.

	Search MT		
Language	BLEU / nDCG	BLEU / Lev	ΔnDCG / Lev
en-de	0.32	0.89	0.61
pl-de	0.36	0.88	0.60
es-en	0.38	0.88	0.58
he-en	0.41	0.89	0.59

Table 2: Pearson Correlation between MT and Search Metrics for Search MT Models

	Generic MT		
Language	BLEU / nDCG	BLEU / Lev	Δ nDCG / Lev
en-de	0.33	0.86	0.56
pl-de	0.38	0.84	0.53
es-en	0.39	0.88	0.57
he-en	0.41	0.86	0.56

Table 3: Pearson Correlation between MT and Search Metrics for Generic MT Model

We can interpret the above correlation values as the mean cross-product of the standardized MT and search metrics (Lee Rodgers and Nicewander, 1988), values closer to 1.0 reflects correlation between the metrics and values closer to 0.0 indicates disassociation. Similar to Sloto et al. (2018), we find that BLEU does not correlate with nDCG improvements. However, we find it interesting that BLEU is strongly correlated to Levenshtein metric that demonstrates that higher BLEU values would correspond to lower Levenshtein distance and vice versa. Moreover, ΔnDCG has a moderate positive correlation to Levenshtein distance. Therefore, Levenstein distance can be an effective approximate metric for the search performance of query translation when it is impossible to compute the rank-based search metrics such as nDCG.

[4]As Levenshtein metric is inversely related to BLEU, i.e. lower Lev is better and higher BLEU is better, we multiply Lev with coefficient -1 before computing Pearson R.

4.2 Edit-distance metric with Varying K

Search engines adjust the number of top-K search results for different applications. Within e-commerce search, there are also varying K values implemented for practical reasons. For example, sponsored search results have limited real estate on the site, thus sponsored search has small values of K; normal product search has more allowance for larger k values. We investigate how edit-distance based search metrics differs with varying K search results.

k	es-en	he-en	en-de	pl-de
4	2.39	2.33	1.82	2.21
8	4.95	4.84	3.82	4.59
16	10.23	10.00	11.49	9.49
100	66.52	65.3	50.66	61.31

Table 4: Levenshtein Metric of Search MT models with different top-K search results

As the number of search candidates increases, we expect the distance between the R_{mt} to diverge from the R_{ref} and metric scores would linearly to the K value. Table 4 presents the Levenshtein metric results for the Search MT models with varying top-K search results.

	Generic MT			
Language	ΔnDCG@4 /Lev@4	ΔnDCG@8 /Lev@8	ΔnDCG@16 /Lev@16	ΔnDCG@100 /Lev@100
pl-de	0.56	0.55	0.53	0.49
en-de	0.59	0.58	0.56	0.52
he-en	0.60	0.59	0.56	0.52
es-en	0.61	0.59	0.57	0.53

Table 5: Pearson Correlation between Levenstein distance and ΔnDCG for Generic MT

	Search MT			
Language	ΔnDCG@4 /Lev@4	ΔnDCG@8 /Lev@8	ΔnDCG@16 /Lev@16	ΔnDCG@100 /Lev@100
pl-de	0.63	0.62	0.60	0.57
en-de	0.63	0.62	0.61	0.57
he-en	0.62	0.61	0.59	0.55
es-en	0.61	0.60	0.58	0.54

Table 6: Pearson Correlation between Levenstein distance and ΔnDCG for Search MT

As top-4, top-8, top-16 are commonly used for top-K search result evaluation for the cross-lingual E-commerce search, we also conduct a correlation study for the ΔnDCG and Levenstein distance with varying K as Table 5 and 6. The experiment setup is identical to the correlation study in section 4.1. As K increases, the correlation slightly decreases for both search and generic MT. We observe that there is subtle distinction in correlation in the range of $K \leq 16$; For search MT, there is moderate positive correlation between the ΔnDCG and Levenstein distance when $K \leq 16$. It further shows that Levenstein distance can be an effective approximate metric to evaluate the search performance of query translation in various cross-lingual E-commerce search scenarios when it is impossible to compute the rank-based search metrics.

5 Related Work

Machine Translation is necessary to bridge the gap between query translation and cross-lingual information retrieval Bi et al. (2020). Query translation a key component in large e-commerce stores, previous studies have demonstrated that better translation quality improves retrieval accuracy (Goldfarb et al., 2019; Brynjolfsson et al., 2019).

Queries are naturally short and search engines usually have preferred word choices and collocations based on users' query patterns (Lv and Zhai, 2009; Vechtomova and Wang, 2006). This complicates the evaluation of machine translation for cross-lingual information retrieval in the context of 'fitting in well to the search index'. While machine translation evaluation is well-studied, translation evaluation in downstream task requires more attention esp. in the e-commerce cross-lingual information retrieval.

Traditionally, information retrieval evaluation relies on behavioral signals as ground truth to measure relevance of search results; mean reciprocal ranking (MRR), mean average precision (MAP), normalized discounted cumulative gain (nDCG) (Järvelin and Kekäläinen, 2002; Wu et al., 2018; Nigam et al., 2019b).

Previous studies in cross-lingual information retrieval (CLIR) evaluation relies on pre-annotated datasets that are relatively small and specific to domains outside of e-commerce; for example, the CLEF eHealth test sets Saleh and Pecina (2018); Suominen et al. (2018); Zhang et al. (2013) and Wikipedia cross-lingual test set Sas et al. (2020).

6 Conclusion

In this study, we introduce a framework which provides a recipe to evaluate machine translation in the context of cross-lingual e-commerce search at scale. Additionally, we proposed an edit-distance based metric `Lev@K` to evaluate MT quality that bypasses the reliance on behavioral signals and/or expensive and slow relevance annotations from human.

The proposed metric has shown correlations with traditional relevance-based search metric and it is also strongly associated with the classic machine translation evaluation metric. The difference between a machine translation system as measured by BLEU can be demonstrated with the proposed edit-distance based metric in the context of cross-lingual search. We suggest the use of the `Lev@K` metric in future CLIR researches in addition to the traditional search metrics, especially when relevance information is unavailable.

References

Akiba, Y., Federico, M., Kando, N., Nakaiwa, H., Paul, M., and Tsujii, J. (2004). Overview of the iwslt04 evaluation campaign. In *IWSLT*, pages 1–12.

Amrhein, C. and Sennrich, R. (2022). Identifying weaknesses in machine translation metrics through minimum bayes risk decoding: A case study for comet.

Anastasopoulos, A., Bojar, O., Bremerman, J., Cattoni, R., Elbayad, M., Federico, M., Ma, X., Nakamura, S., Negri, M., Niehues, J., Pino, J., Salesky, E., Stüker, S., Sudoh, K., Turchi, M., Waibel, A., Wang, C., and Wiesner, M. (2021). FINDINGS OF THE IWSLT 2021 EVALUATION CAMPAIGN. In *Proceedings of the 18th International Conference on Spoken Language Translation (IWSLT 2021)*, pages 1–29, Bangkok, Thailand (online). Association for Computational Linguistics.

Banerjee, S. and Lavie, A. (2005). METEOR: An automatic metric for MT evaluation with improved correlation with human judgments. In *Proceedings of the ACL Workshop on Intrinsic and Extrinsic Evaluation Measures for Machine Translation and/or Summarization*, pages 65–72, Ann Arbor, Michigan. Association for Computational Linguistics.

Bi, T., Yao, L., Yang, B., Zhang, H., Luo, W., and Chen, B. (2020). Constraint translation candidates: A bridge between neural query translation and cross-lingual information retrieval.

Brynjolfsson, E., Hui, X., and Liu, M. (2019). Does machine translation affect international trade? evidence from a large digital platform. *Management Science*, 65(12):5449–5460.

Callison-Burch, C., Fordyce, C., Koehn, P., Monz, C., and Schroeder, J. (2007). (meta-) evaluation of machine translation. In *Proceedings of the Second Workshop on Statistical Machine Translation*, pages 136–158, Prague, Czech Republic. Association for Computational Linguistics.

Chatterjee, R., Gebremelak, G., Negri, M., and Turchi, M. (2017). Online automatic post-editing for MT in a multi-domain translation environment. In *Proceedings of the 15th Conference of the European Chapter of the Association for Computational Linguistics: Volume 1, Long Papers*, pages 525–535, Valencia, Spain. Association for Computational Linguistics.

Chatterjee, R., Weller, M., Negri, M., and Turchi, M. (2015). Exploring the planet of the APEs: a comparative study of state-of-the-art methods for MT automatic post-editing. In *Proceedings of the 53rd Annual Meeting of the Association for Computational Linguistics and the 7th International Joint Conference on Natural Language Processing (Volume 2: Short Papers)*, pages 156–161, Beijing, China. Association for Computational Linguistics.

Cuong, H., Frank, S., and Sima'an, K. (2016). ILLC-UvA adaptation system (scorpio) at WMT'16 IT-DOMAIN task. In *Proceedings of the First Conference on Machine Translation: Volume 2, Shared Task Papers*, pages 423–427, Berlin, Germany. Association for Computational Linguistics.

Daniel, W. (1990). *Applied Nonparametric Statistics*. Duxbury advanced series in statistics and decision sciences. PWS-KENT Pub.

Doddington, G. (2002). Automatic evaluation of machine translation quality using n-gram co-occurrence statistics. In *Proceedings of the Second International Conference on Human Language Technology Research*, HLT '02, page 138–145, San Francisco, CA, USA. Morgan Kaufmann Publishers Inc.

Domhan, T., Denkowski, M., Vilar, D., Niu, X., Hieber, F., and Heafield, K. (2020). The sockeye 2 neural machine translation toolkit at AMTA 2020. In *Proceedings of the 14th Conference of the Association for Machine Translation in the Americas (Volume 1: Research Track)*, pages 110–115, Virtual. Association for Machine Translation in the Americas.

Freitag, M., Foster, G., Grangier, D., Ratnakar, V., Tan, Q., and Macherey, W. (2021). Experts, errors, and context: A large-scale study of human evaluation for machine translation. *Transactions of the Association for Computational Linguistics*, 9:1460–1474.

Goldfarb, A., Trefler, D., et al. (2019). Artificial intelligence and international trade. *The economics of artificial intelligence: an agenda*, pages 463–492.

Graham, Y., Baldwin, T., Moffat, A., and Zobel, J. (2013). Continuous measurement scales in human evaluation of machine translation. In *Proceedings of the 7th Linguistic Annotation Workshop and Interoperability with Discourse*, pages 33–41, Sofia, Bulgaria. Association for Computational Linguistics.

Hui, K., Yates, A., Berberich, K., and de Melo, G. (2017). PACRR: A position-aware neural IR model for relevance matching. In *Proceedings of the 2017 Conference on Empirical Methods in Natural Language Processing*, pages 1049–1058, Copenhagen, Denmark. Association for Computational Linguistics.

Jaccard, P. (1912). The distribution of the flora in the alpine zone.1. *New Phytologist*, 11(2):37–50.

Järvelin, K. and Kekäläinen, J. (2002). Cumulated gain-based evaluation of ir techniques. *ACM Transactions on Information Systems (TOIS)*, 20(4):422–446.

Jiang, Z., El-Jaroudi, A., Hartmann, W., Karakos, D., and Zhao, L. (2020). Cross-lingual information retrieval with BERT. In *Proceedings of the workshop on Cross-Language Search and Summarization of Text and Speech (CLSSTS2020)*, pages 26–31, Marseille, France. European Language Resources Association.

Kendall, M. G. (1938). A NEW MEASURE OF RANK CORRELATION. *Biometrika*, 30(1-2):81–93.

Laoudi, J., Tate, C. R., and Voss, C. R. (2006). Task-based MT evaluation: From who/when/where extraction to event understanding. In *Proceedings of the Fifth International Conference on Language Resources and Evaluation (LREC'06)*, Genoa, Italy. European Language Resources Association (ELRA).

Lee Rodgers, J. and Nicewander, W. A. (1988). Thirteen ways to look at the correlation coefficient. *The American Statistician*, 42(1):59–66.

Levenshtein, V. I. et al. (1966). Binary codes capable of correcting deletions, insertions, and reversals. In *Soviet physics doklady*, volume 10, pages 707–710. Soviet Union.

Li, J., Liu, C., Bing, L., Liu, X., Li, H., Wang, J., Zhao, D., and Yan, R. (2020). Cross-lingual low-resource set-to-description retrieval for global e-commerce. *ArXiv*, abs/2005.08188.

Li, S., Lv, F., Jin, T., Lin, G., Yang, K., Zeng, X., Wu, X.-M., and Ma, Q. (2021). Embedding-based product retrieval in taobao search. In *Proceedings of the 27th ACM SIGKDD Conference on Knowledge Discovery & Data Mining*, pages 3181–3189.

Lowndes, M. and Vasudevan, A. (2021). Market guide for digital commerce search.

Lu, H., Hu, Y., Zhao, T., Wu, T., Song, Y., and Yin, B. (2021). Graph-based multilingual product retrieval in E-commerce search. In *Proceedings of the 2021 Conference of the North American Chapter of the Association for Computational Linguistics: Human Language Technologies: Industry Papers*, pages 146–153, Online. Association for Computational Linguistics.

Lv, Y. and Zhai, C. (2009). Adaptive relevance feedback in information retrieval. In *Proceedings of the 18th ACM conference on Information and knowledge management*, pages 255–264.

McDonald, R., Brokos, G., and Androutsopoulos, I. (2018). Deep relevance ranking using enhanced document-query interactions. In *Proceedings of the 2018 Conference on Empirical Methods in Natural Language Processing*, pages 1849–1860, Brussels, Belgium. Association for Computational Linguistics.

Navarro, G. (2001). A guided tour to approximate string matching. *ACM computing surveys (CSUR)*, 33(1):31–88.

Nie, J.-Y. (2010). Cross-language information retrieval. *Synthesis Lectures on Human Language Technologies*, 3(1):1–125.

Nigam, P., Song, Y., Mohan, V., Lakshman, V., Ding, W. A., Shingavi, A., Teo, C. H., Gu, H., and Yin, B. (2019a). Semantic product search. In *Proceedings of the 25th ACM SIGKDD International Conference on Knowledge Discovery Data Mining*, KDD '19, page 2876–2885, New York, NY, USA. Association for Computing Machinery.

Nigam, P., Song, Y., Mohan, V., Lakshman, V., Weitian, Ding, Shingavi, A., Teo, C. H., Gu, H., and Yin, B. (2019b). Semantic product search.

Papineni, K., Roukos, S., Ward, T., and Zhu, W.-J. (2002). Bleu: a method for automatic evaluation of machine translation. In *Proceedings of the 40th Annual Meeting of the Association for Computational Linguistics*, pages 311–318, Philadelphia, Pennsylvania, USA. Association for Computational Linguistics.

Pierce, J. R. and Carroll, J. B. (1966). Language and machines: Computers in translation and linguistics. In *A report by the Automatic Language Processing Advisory Committee, Division of Behavioral Sciences, National Academy of Sciences, National Research Council. Washington, D.C.*, page 124. National Research Council.

Popović, M. (2015). chrF: character n-gram F-score for automatic MT evaluation. In *Proceedings of the Tenth Workshop on Statistical Machine Translation*, pages 392–395, Lisbon, Portugal. Association for Computational Linguistics.

Post, M. (2018). A call for clarity in reporting BLEU scores. In *Proceedings of the Third Conference on Machine Translation: Research Papers*, pages 186–191, Brussels, Belgium. Association for Computational Linguistics.

Rei, R., Stewart, C., Farinha, A. C., and Lavie, A. (2020). COMET: A neural framework for MT evaluation. In *Proceedings of the 2020 Conference on Empirical Methods in Natural Language Processing (EMNLP)*, pages 2685–2702, Online. Association for Computational Linguistics.

Roy, S., Brunk, C., Kim, K.-Y., Zhao, J., Freitag, M., Kale, M., Bansal, G., Mudgal, S., and Varano, C. (2021). Using machine translation to localize task oriented nlg output. *arXiv preprint arXiv:2107.04512*.

Rücklé, A., Swarnkar, K., and Gurevych, I. (2019). Improved cross-lingual question retrieval for community question answering. In *The World Wide Web Conference*, WWW '19, page 3179–3186, New York, NY, USA. Association for Computing Machinery.

Saleh, S. and Pecina, P. (2018). Cuni team: Clef ehealth consumer health search task 2018. In *CLEF (Working Notes)*.

Saleh, S. and Pecina, P. (2020). Document translation vs. query translation for cross-lingual information retrieval in the medical domain. In *Proceedings of the 58th Annual Meeting of the Association for Computational Linguistics*, pages 6849–6860, Online. Association for Computational Linguistics.

Sas, C., Beloucif, M., and Søgaard, A. (2020). WikiBank: Using Wikidata to improve multilingual frame-semantic parsing. In *Proceedings of the 12th Language Resources and Evaluation Conference*, pages 4183–4189, Marseille, France. European Language Resources Association.

Scarton, C. and Specia, L. (2016). A reading comprehension corpus for machine translation evaluation. In *Proceedings of the Tenth International Conference on Language Resources and Evaluation (LREC'16)*, pages 3652–3658, Portorož, Slovenia. European Language Resources Association (ELRA).

Schneider, A. H., van der Sluis, I., and Luz, S. (2010). Comparing intrinsic and extrinsic evaluation of MT output in a dialogue system. In *Proceedings of the 7th International Workshop on Spoken Language Translation: Papers*, pages 329–336, Paris, France.

Sellam, T., Das, D., and Parikh, A. (2020). BLEURT: Learning robust metrics for text generation. In *Proceedings of the 58th Annual Meeting of the Association for Computational Linguistics*, pages 7881–7892, Online. Association for Computational Linguistics.

Sloto, S., Clifton, A., Hanneman, G., Porter, P., Gates, D., Hildebrand, A. S., and Kumar, A. (2018). Leveraging data resources for cross-linguistic information retrieval using statistical machine translation. In *Proceedings of the 13th Conference of the Association for Machine Translation in the Americas (Volume 2: User Track)*, pages 223–233.

Song, K., Zhang, Y., Yu, H., Luo, W., Wang, K., and Zhang, M. (2019). Code-switching for enhancing NMT with pre-specified translation. In *Proceedings of the 2019 Conference of the North American Chapter of the Association for Computational Linguistics: Human Language Technologies, Volume 1 (Long and Short Papers)*, pages 449–459, Minneapolis, Minnesota. Association for Computational Linguistics.

Sudo, K., Sekine, S., and Grishman, R. (2004). Cross-lingual information extraction system evaluation. In *COLING 2004: Proceedings of the 20th International Conference on Computational Linguistics*, pages 882–888, Geneva, Switzerland. COLING.

Suominen, H., Kelly, L., Goeuriot, L., Névéol, A., Ramadier, L., Robert, A., Kanoulas, E., Spijker, R., Azzopardi, L., Li, D., et al. (2018). Overview of the clef ehealth evaluation lab 2018. In *International Conference of the Cross-Language Evaluation Forum for European Languages*, pages 286–301. Springer.

Tan, L., Dehdari, J., and van Genabith, J. (2015). An awkward disparity between BLEU / RIBES scores and human judgements in machine translation. In *Proceedings of the 2nd Workshop on Asian Translation (WAT2015)*, pages 74–81, Kyoto, Japan. Workshop on Asian Translation.

Thomas, K. (1999). Designing a task-based evaluation methodology for a spoken machine translation system. In *Proceedings of the 37th Annual Meeting of the Association for Computational Linguistics*, pages 569–572, College Park, Maryland, USA. Association for Computational Linguistics.

Thompson, B. and Post, M. (2020). Automatic machine translation evaluation in many languages via zero-shot paraphrasing. In *Proceedings of the 2020 Conference on Empirical Methods in Natural Language Processing (EMNLP)*, pages 90–121, Online. Association for Computational Linguistics.

Tillmann, C., Vogel, S., Ney, H., Zubiaga, A., and Sawaf, H. (1997). Accelerated dp based search for statistical translation. In *In European Conf. on Speech Communication and Technology*, pages 2667–2670.

Vaswani, A., Shazeer, N., Parmar, N., Uszkoreit, J., Jones, L., Gomez, A. N., Kaiser, Ł., and Polosukhin, I. (2017). Attention is all you need. *Advances in neural information processing systems*, 30.

Vechtomova, O. and Wang, Y. (2006). A study of the effect of term proximity on query expansion. *Journal of Information Science*, 32(4):324–333.

Vela, M. and Tan, L. (2015). Predicting machine translation adequacy with document embeddings. In *Proceedings of the Tenth Workshop on Statistical Machine Translation*, pages 402–410, Lisbon, Portugal. Association for Computational Linguistics.

Wu, L., Hu, D., Hong, L., and Liu, H. (2018). Turning clicks into purchases: Revenue optimization for product search in e-commerce. SIGIR '18, page 365–374, New York, NY, USA. Association for Computing Machinery.

Zhang, L., Rettinger, A., Färber, M., and Tadić, M. (2013). A comparative evaluation of cross-lingual text annotation techniques. In *International Conference of the Cross-Language Evaluation Forum for European Languages*, pages 124–135. Springer.

Association for Computational Linguistics
209 N. Eighth Street
Stroudsburg, Pennsylvania 18360

ISBN 978-1-7138-6757-9

CURRAN ASSOCIATES INC.
proceedings.com